NEW PERSPECTIVES ON

HTML and CSS

6th Edition

INTRODUCTORY

NEW PERSPECTIVES ON

HTML and CSS
6th Edition

INTRODUCTORY

Patrick Carey

COURSE TECHNOLOGY
CENGAGE Learning™

Australia • Brazil • Japan • Korea • Mexico • Singapore • Spain • United Kingdom • United States

New Perspectives on HTML and CSS, 6th Edition, Introductory

Vice President, Publisher: Nicole Jones Pinard

Executive Editor: Marie L. Lee

Associate Acquisitions Editor: Amanda Lyons

Senior Product Manager: Kathy Finnegan

Product Manager: Leigh Hefferon

Associate Product Manager: Julia Leroux-Lindsey

Editorial Assistant: Jacqueline Lacaire

Director of Marketing: Elisa Roberts

Senior Marketing Manager: Ryan DeGrote

Developmental Editor: Sasha Vodnik

Content Project Manager: Jennifer Goguen McGrail

Composition: GEX Publishing Services

Art Director: Marissa Falco

Text Designer: Althea Chen

Cover Designer: Roycroft Design

Cover Art: © Veer Incorporated

Copyeditor: Suzanne Huizenga

Proofreader: Kathy Orrino

Indexer: Alexandra Nickerson

For product information and technology assistance, contact us at
Cengage Learning Customer & Sales Support, 1-800-354-9706
For permission to use material from this text or product, submit all requests online at **www.cengage.com/permissions**
Further permissions questions can be emailed to
permissionrequest@cengage.com

Some of the product names and company names used in this book have been used for identification purposes only and may be trademarks or registered trademarks of their respective manufacturers and sellers.

Microsoft and the Office logo are either registered trademarks or trademarks of Microsoft Corporation in the United States and/or other countries. Course Technology, Cengage Learning is an independent entity from the Microsoft Corporation, and not affiliated with Microsoft in any manner.

Disclaimer: Any fictional data related to persons or companies or URLs used throughout this book is intended for instructional purposes only. At the time this book was printed, any such data was fictional and not belonging to any real persons or companies.

Library of Congress Control Number: 2011927664

ISBN-13: 978-1-111-52648-1

ISBN-10: 1-111-52648-6

Course Technology
20 Channel Center Street
Boston, MA 02210
USA

Cengage Learning is a leading provider of customized learning solutions with office locations around the globe, including Singapore, the United Kingdom, Australia, Mexico, Brazil, and Japan. Locate your local office at:
international.cengage.com/global

Cengage Learning products are represented in Canada by Nelson Education, Ltd.

To learn more about Course Technology, visit **www.cengage.com/course technology**

To learn more about Cengage Learning, visit **www.cengage.com**

Purchase any of our products at your local college store or at our preferred online store
www.cengagebrain.com

Printed in the United States of America
2 3 4 5 6 7 8 9 15 14 13 12

Preface

The New Perspectives Series' critical-thinking, problem-solving approach is the ideal way to prepare students to transcend point-and-click skills and take advantage of all that HTML and CSS have to offer.

In developing the New Perspectives Series, our goal was to create books that give students the software concepts and practical skills they need to succeed beyond the classroom. We've updated our proven case-based pedagogy with more practical content to make learning skills more meaningful to students. With the New Perspectives Series, students understand *why* they are learning *what* they are learning, and are fully prepared to apply their skills to real-life situations.

About This Book

This book provides thorough coverage of HTML and CSS, and includes the following:
- Up-to-date coverage of using HTML5 and CSS3 to create Web sites
- Instruction on using CSS3 styles and pseudo-classes, storyboarding complete Web sites, and creating and applying client-side image maps
- Coverage of integrating Web tables into page design

New for this edition!
- Each session begins with a Visual Overview, which includes colorful, enlarged figures with numerous callouts and key term definitions, giving students a comprehensive preview of the topics covered in the session, as well as a handy study guide.
- New ProSkills boxes provide guidance for how to use the software in real-world, professional situations, and related ProSkills exercises integrate the technology skills students learn with one or more of the following soft skills: decision making, problem solving, teamwork, verbal communication, and written communication.
- Important steps are highlighted in yellow with attached margin notes to help students pay close attention to completing the steps correctly and avoid time-consuming rework.

System Requirements

This book assumes that students have an Internet connection, a text editor, and a current browser that supports HTML5 and CSS3. The following is a list of the most recent versions of the major browsers at the time this text was published: Internet Explorer 9 (public beta), Firefox 4.0.2 (public beta), Safari 5.0.2, Opera 10.6, and Google Chrome (6.04). More recent versions may have come out since the publication of this book. Students should go to the Web browser home page to download the most current version. All browsers interpret HTML and CSS code in slightly different ways. It is highly recommended that students have several different browsers installed on their systems for comparison. Students might also want to run older versions of these browsers to highlight compatibility issues. The screenshots in this book were produced using Internet Explorer 9.0 running on Windows 7 Professional (64-bit), unless otherwise noted. If students are using different browsers or operating systems, their screens will vary slightly from those shown in the book; this should not present any problems in completing the tutorials.

www.cengage.com/ct/newperspectives

v

The New Perspectives Approach

> "New Perspectives texts provide up-to-date, real-world application of content, making book selection easy. The step-by-step, hands-on approach teaches students concepts they can apply immediately."
>
> —John Taylor
> Southeastern Technical College

Context

Each tutorial begins with a problem presented in a "real-world" case that is meaningful to students. The case sets the scene to help students understand what they will do in the tutorial.

Hands-on Approach

Each tutorial is divided into manageable sessions that combine reading and hands-on, step-by-step work. Colorful screenshots help guide students through the steps. **Trouble?** tips anticipate common mistakes or problems to help students stay on track and continue with the tutorial.

VISUAL OVERVIEW

Visual Overviews

New for this edition! Each session begins with a Visual Overview, a new two-page spread that includes colorful, enlarged figures with numerous callouts and key term definitions, giving students a comprehensive preview of the topics covered in the session, as well as a handy study guide.

PROSKILLS

ProSkills Boxes and Exercises

New for this edition! ProSkills boxes provide guidance for how to use the software in real-world, professional situations, and related ProSkills exercises integrate the technology skills students learn with one or more of the following soft skills: decision making, problem solving, teamwork, verbal communication, and written communication.

KEY STEP

Key Steps

New for this edition! Important steps are highlighted in yellow with attached margin notes to help students pay close attention to completing the steps correctly and avoid time-consuming rework.

INSIGHT

InSight Boxes

InSight boxes offer expert advice and best practices to help students achieve a deeper understanding of the concepts behind the software features and skills.

TIP

Margin Tips

Margin Tips provide helpful hints and shortcuts for more efficient use of the software. The Tips appear in the margin at key points throughout each tutorial, giving students extra information when and where they need it.

REVIEW
APPLY

Assessment

Retention is a key component to learning. At the end of each session, a series of Quick Check questions helps students test their understanding of the material before moving on. Engaging end-of-tutorial Review Assignments and Case Problems have always been a hallmark feature of the New Perspectives Series. Colorful bars and brief descriptions accompany the exercises, making it easy to understand both the goal and level of challenge a particular assignment holds.

REFERENCE
GLOSSARY/INDEX

Reference

Within each tutorial, Reference boxes appear before a set of steps to provide a succinct summary and preview of how to perform a task. In addition, each book includes a combination Glossary/Index to promote easy reference of material.

www.cengage.com/ct/newperspectives

Our Complete System of Instruction

Coverage To Meet Your Needs

Whether you're looking for just a small amount of coverage or enough to fill a semester-long class, we can provide you with a textbook that meets your needs.

- Brief books typically cover the essential skills in just 2 to 4 tutorials.
- Introductory books build and expand on those skills and contain an average of 5 to 8 tutorials.
- Comprehensive books are great for a full-semester class, and contain 9 to 12+ tutorials.

So if the book you're holding does not provide the right amount of coverage for you, there's probably another offering available. Go to our Web site or contact your Course Technology sales representative to find out what else we offer.

CourseCasts – Learning on the Go. Always available…always relevant.

Want to keep up with the latest technology trends relevant to you? Visit our site to find a library of podcasts, CourseCasts, featuring a "CourseCast of the Week," and download them to your mp3 player at http://coursecasts.course.com.

Our fast-paced world is driven by technology. You know because you're an active participant—always on the go, always keeping up with technological trends, and always learning new ways to embrace technology to power your life.

Ken Baldauf, host of CourseCasts, is a faculty member of the Florida State University Computer Science Department where he is responsible for teaching technology classes to thousands of FSU students each year. Ken is an expert in the latest technology trends; he gathers and sorts through the most pertinent news and information for CourseCasts so your students can spend their time enjoying technology, rather than trying to figure it out. Open or close your lecture with a discussion based on the latest CourseCast.

Visit us at http://coursecasts.course.com to learn on the go!

Instructor Resources

We offer more than just a book. We have all the tools you need to enhance your lectures, check students' work, and generate exams in a new, easier-to-use and completely revised package. This book's Instructor's Manual, ExamView testbank, PowerPoint presentations, data files, solution files, figure files, and a sample syllabus are all available on a single CD-ROM or for downloading at http://www.cengage.com/coursetechnology.

Content for Online Learning

Course Technology has partnered with the leading distance learning solution providers and class-management platforms today. To access this material, visit www.cengage.com/webtutor and search for your title. Instructor resources include the following: additional case projects, sample syllabi, PowerPoint presentations, and more. For students to access this material, they must have purchased a WebTutor PIN-code specific to this title and your campus platform. The resources for students might include (based on instructor preferences): topic reviews, review questions, practice tests, and more. For additional information, please contact your sales representative.

www.cengage.com/ct/newperspectives

SAM: Skills Assessment Manager

SAM is designed to help bring students from the classroom to the real world. It allows students to train and test on important computer skills in an active, hands-on environment.

SAM's easy-to-use system includes powerful interactive exams, training, and projects on the most commonly used Microsoft Office applications. SAM simulates the Office application environment, allowing students to demonstrate their knowledge and think through the skills by performing real-world tasks, such as bolding text or setting up slide transitions. Add in live-in-the-application projects, and students are on their way to truly learning and applying skills to business-centric documents.

Designed to be used with the New Perspectives Series, SAM includes handy page references, so students can print helpful study guides that match the New Perspectives textbooks used in class. For instructors, SAM also includes robust scheduling and reporting features.

Acknowledgments

I would like to thank the people who worked so hard to make this book possible. Special thanks to my developmental editor, Sasha Vodnik, for his hard work and valuable insights, and to my Product Manager, Kathy Finnegan, who has worked tirelessly in overseeing this project and made my task so much easier with her enthusiasm and good humor. Other people at Course Technology who deserve credit are Marie Lee, Executive Editor; Julia Leroux-Lindsey, Associate Product Manager; Jacqueline Lacaire, Editorial Assistant; Jennifer Goguen McGrail, Senior Content Project Manager; Christian Kunciw, Manuscript Quality Assurance (MQA) Supervisor; and John Freitas, Serge Palladino, Susan Pedicini, Danielle Shaw, and Susan Whalen, MQA testers.

Feedback is an important part of writing any book, and thanks go to the following reviewers for their helpful ideas and comments: Bernice Howard, St. Johns River Community College; Lisa Macon, Valencia Community College; Sharon Scollard, Mohawk College; Luke Sui, Daytona State College; and John Taylor, Southeastern Technical College.

I want to thank my wife Joan and my six children for their love, encouragement and patience in putting up with a sometimes distracted husband and father. This book is dedicated to the memory of Mac Mendelsohn, who generously gave me my chance in this business and whose constant encouragement in the early years inspired me and taught me so much.
– Patrick Carey

BRIEF CONTENTS

HTML

Level I Tutorials

Level II Tutorials

TABLE OF CONTENTS

TUTORIAL 1

Getting Started with HTML5

Creating a Product Page for a Small Business

Case | *The J-Prop Shop*

Dave Vinet owns a small business called the J-Prop Shop that builds and sells circus props and equipment. Dave is looking to expand his business and his visibility by upgrading his Web site. Dave has already written the text for the Web site's home page and has generated some of the graphic images for it. He has come to you for help in designing a Web page and writing the code. Dave hopes to build on his Web page in the future as his business expands, so he would like you to write code that takes advantage of the latest Web standards, including HTML5. Your job will be to create a sample home page that Dave can use as a foundation for his new Web site.

STARTING DATA FILES

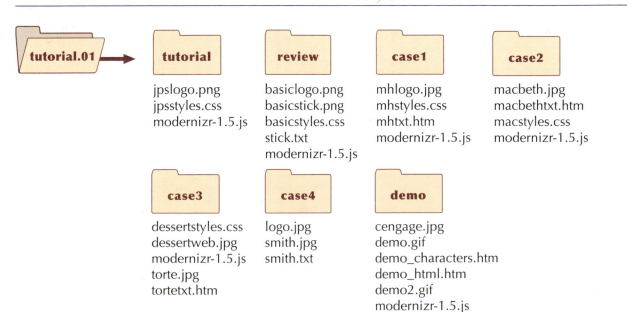

tutorial.01 →

tutorial
jpslogo.png
jpsstyles.css
modernizr-1.5.js

review
basiclogo.png
basicstick.png
basicstyles.css
stick.txt
modernizr-1.5.js

case1
mhlogo.jpg
mhstyles.css
mhtxt.htm
modernizr-1.5.js

case2
macbeth.jpg
macbethtxt.htm
macstyles.css
modernizr-1.5.js

case3
dessertstyles.css
dessertweb.jpg
modernizr-1.5.js
torte.jpg
tortetxt.htm

case4
logo.jpg
smith.jpg
smith.txt

demo
cengage.jpg
demo.gif
demo_characters.htm
demo_html.htm
demo2.gif
modernizr-1.5.js

SESSION 1.1 VISUAL OVERVIEW

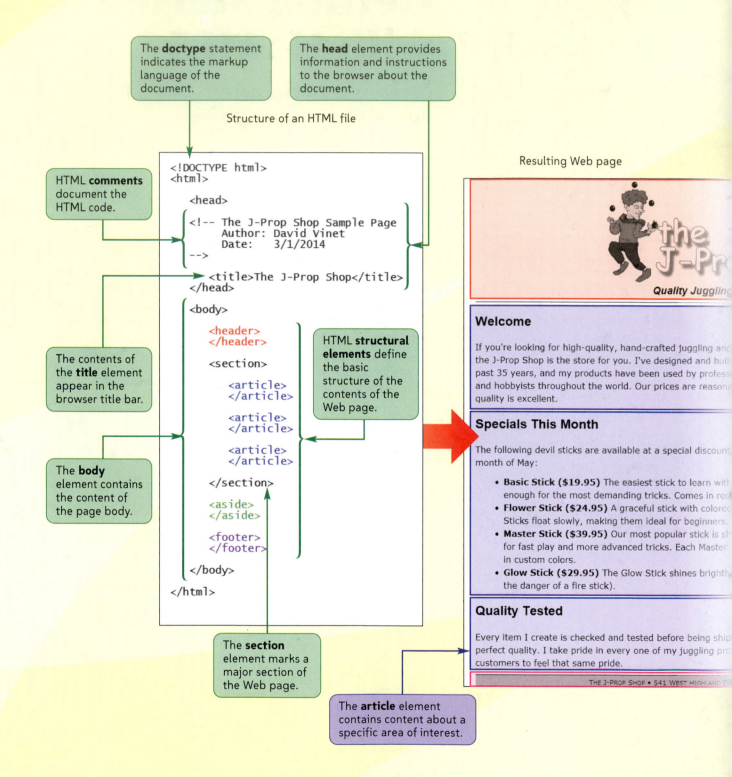

The **doctype** statement indicates the markup language of the document.

The **head** element provides information and instructions to the browser about the document.

Structure of an HTML file

Resulting Web page

HTML **comments** document the HTML code.

The contents of the **title** element appear in the browser title bar.

The **body** element contains the content of the page body.

HTML **structural elements** define the basic structure of the contents of the Web page.

```
<!DOCTYPE html>
<html>

  <head>

  <!-- The J-Prop Shop Sample Page
       Author: David Vinet
       Date:   3/1/2014
  -->

    <title>The J-Prop Shop</title>
  </head>

  <body>

    <header>
    </header>

    <section>

      <article>
      </article>

      <article>
      </article>

      <article>
      </article>

    </section>

    <aside>
    </aside>

    <footer>
    </footer>

  </body>

</html>
```

The **section** element marks a major section of the Web page.

The **article** element contains content about a specific area of interest.

Quality Juggling

Welcome

If you're looking for high-quality, hand-crafted juggling and the J-Prop Shop is the store for you. I've designed and buil past 35 years, and my products have been used by profess and hobbyists throughout the world. Our prices are reasona quality is excellent.

Specials This Month

The following devil sticks are available at a special discount month of May:

- **Basic Stick ($19.95)** The easiest stick to learn with enough for the most demanding tricks. Comes in red
- **Flower Stick ($24.95)** A graceful stick with colore Sticks float slowly, making them ideal for beginners
- **Master Stick ($39.95)** Our most popular stick is sh for fast play and more advanced tricks. Each Master in custom colors.
- **Glow Stick ($29.95)** The Glow Stick shines brightly the danger of a fire stick).

Quality Tested

Every item I create is checked and tested before being ship perfect quality. I take pride in every one of my juggling pro customers to feel that same pride.

THE J-PROP SHOP • 541 WEST HIGHLAND

THE STRUCTURE OF AN HTML5 DOCUMENT

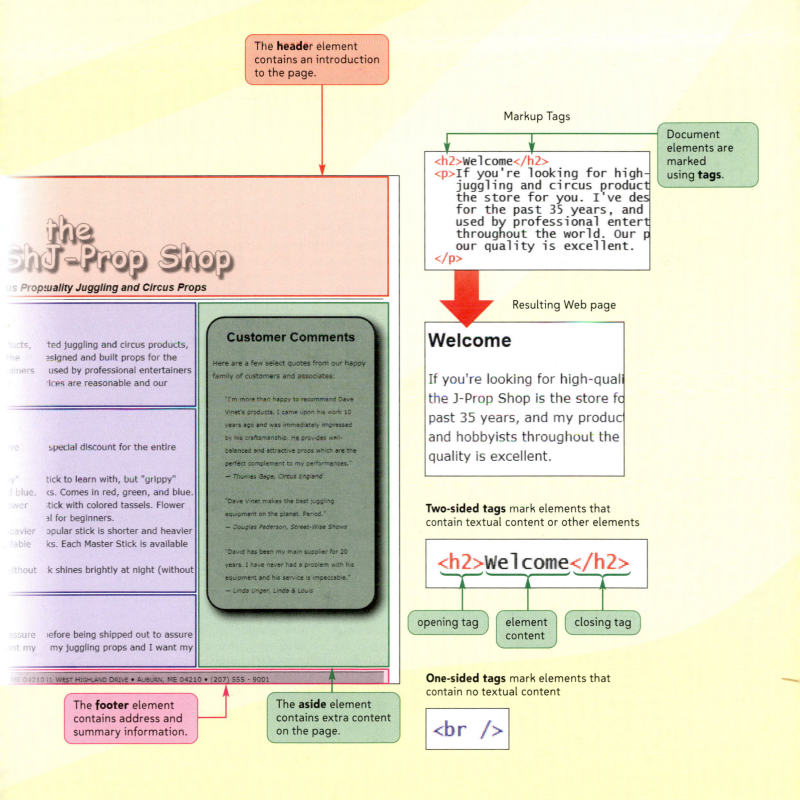

The **header** element contains an introduction to the page.

Markup Tags

Document elements are marked using **tags**.

```
<h2>Welcome</h2>
<p>If you're looking for high-
  juggling and circus product
  the store for you. I've des
  for the past 35 years, and
  used by professional entert
  throughout the world. Our p
  our quality is excellent.
</p>
```

Resulting Web page

Welcome

If you're looking for high-quali
the J-Prop Shop is the store fo
past 35 years, and my produc
and hobbyists throughout the
quality is excellent.

Two-sided tags mark elements that contain textual content or other elements

```
<h2>Welcome</h2>
```

opening tag   element content   closing tag

One-sided tags mark elements that contain no textual content

```
<br />
```

the
ShJ-Prop Shop

us Propsuality Juggling and Circus Props

tucts, ted juggling and circus products,
the esigned and built props for the
ainers used by professional entertainers
ices are reasonable and our

re special discount for the entire

y" tick to learn with, but "grippy"
d blue. ks. Comes in red, green, and blue.
ower tick with colored tassels. Flower
al for beginners.

eavier opular stick is shorter and heavier
lable ks. Each Master Stick is available

ithout k shines brightly at night (without

assure efore being shipped out to assure
nt my my juggling props and I want my

Customer Comments

Here are a few select quotes from our happy family of customers and associates:

"I'm more than happy to recommend Dave Vinet's products. I came upon his work 10 years ago and was immediately impressed by his craftsmanship. He provides well-balanced and attractive props which are the perfect complement to my performances."
— *Thomas Gage, Circus England*

"Dave Vinet makes the best juggling equipment on the planet. Period."
— *Douglas Pederson, Street-Wise Shows*

"David has been my main supplier for 20 years. I have never had a problem with his equipment and his service is impeccable."
— *Linda Unger, Linda & Louis*

ME 04210 1 WEST HIGHLAND DRIVE • AUBURN, ME 04210 • (207) 555 - 9001

The **footer** element contains address and summary information.

The **aside** element contains extra content on the page.

Exploring the History of the World Wide Web

Before you start creating a Web page for Dave, it will be helpful to first look at the history of the Web and the development of HTML. You'll start by reviewing networks and learn how they led to the creation of the World Wide Web.

Networks

A **network** is a structure that allows devices known as **nodes** or **hosts** to be linked together to share information and services. Hosts can include devices such as computers, printers, and scanners because they are all capable of sending and receiving data electronically over a network.

A host that provides information or a service is called a **server**. For example, a **print server** is a network host that provides printing services to the network; a **file server** is a host that provides storage space for saving and retrieving files. A computer or other device that receives a service is called a **client**. Networks can follow several different designs based on the relationship between the servers and the clients. One of the most commonly used designs is the **client-server network** in which several clients access information provided by one or more servers. You might be using such a network to access your data files for this tutorial.

Networks can also be classified based on the range they cover. A network confined to a small geographic area, such as within a building or department, is referred to as a **local area network** or **LAN**. A network that covers a wider area, such as several buildings or cities, is called a **wide area network** or **WAN**. Wide area networks typically consist of two or more interconnected local area networks.

The largest WAN in existence is the **Internet**, which incorporates an almost uncountable number of networks and hosts involving computers, mobile phones, PDAs, MP3 players, gaming systems, and television stations. Like many business owners, Dave uses the Internet to advertise his business to potential customers.

Locating Information on a Network

One of the biggest obstacles to effectively using the Internet is the network's sheer scope and size. Most of the early Internet tools required users to master a bewildering array of terms, acronyms, and commands. Because network users had to be well versed in computers and network technology, Internet use was limited to universities and the government. To make the Internet accessible to the general public, it needed to be easier to use. The solution turned out to be the World Wide Web.

The foundations for the **World Wide Web**, or the **Web** for short, were laid in 1989 by Timothy Berners-Lee and other researchers at the CERN nuclear research facility near Geneva, Switzerland. They needed an information system that would make it easy for their researchers to locate and share data on the CERN network with minimal training and support. To meet this need, they developed a system of hypertext documents that enabled users to easily navigate from one topic to another. **Hypertext** is a method of organization in which data sources are interconnected through a series of **links** or hyperlinks that users can activate to jump from one piece of information to another. Hypertext is ideally suited for the Internet because end users do not need to know where a particular document, information source, or service is located—they need to know only how to activate the link. The fact that the Internet and the World Wide Web are synonymous in many users' minds is a testament to the success of the hypertext approach.

Web Pages and Web Servers

Each document on the World Wide Web is referred to as a **Web page** and is stored on a **Web server**. When you access a Web page, a **Web browser** retrieves the page from its Web server and renders it on your computer or other device.

The earliest browsers, known as **text-based browsers**, were limited to displaying only text. Today's browsers are capable of handling text, images, audio, video, and interactive programs. In the early days of the Internet, Web browsing was limited to computers. Now browsers are installed on devices such as mobile phones, cars, handheld media devices, and gaming systems, to name only a few. How does a Web page work with so many combinations of browsers and devices? To understand, you need to look at how Web pages are created.

Introducing HTML

Web pages are text files written in **Hypertext Markup Language** (**HTML**). We've already discussed hypertext, but what is a markup language? A **markup language** is a language that describes the content and structure of a document by identifying, or **tagging**, different elements in the document. For example, this tutorial contains paragraphs, figure captions, page headings, and so forth; each of these items could be tagged as a distinct element using a markup language. Thus, HTML is a markup language that supports both hypertext and the tagging of distinct document elements.

The History of HTML

HTML evolved as the Web itself evolved. Thus, in order to fully appreciate the nuances of HTML, it's a good idea to review the language's history. The first popular markup language was the **Standard Generalized Markup Language** (**SGML**). Introduced in the 1980s, SGML is device- and system-independent, meaning that it can be applied to almost any type of document stored in almost any format. While powerful, SGML is also quite complex; for this reason, SGML is limited to those organizations that can afford the cost and overhead of maintaining complex SGML environments. However, SGML can also be used to create other markup languages that are tailored to specific tasks and are simpler to use and maintain. HTML is one of the languages created with SGML.

In the early years after HTML was created, no single organization was responsible for the language. Web developers were free to define and modify HTML in whatever ways they thought best. This led to incompatibilities between the various browsers and, as a result, Web page authors faced the challenge of writing HTML code that would satisfy different browsers and browser versions.

Ultimately, a group of Web designers and programmers called the **World Wide Web Consortium**, or the **W3C**, created a set of standards or specifications for all browser manufacturers to follow. The W3C has no enforcement power; but because using a uniform language is in everyone's best interest, the W3C's recommendations are usually followed, though not always immediately. For more information on the W3C and the services it offers, see its Web site at *www.w3.org*.

As HTML evolves, earlier features of the language are often **deprecated**, or phased out. While deprecated features might not be part of the current specification for HTML, that doesn't mean that you won't encounter them in your work—indeed, if you are maintaining older Web sites, you will often need to be able to interpret code from earlier versions of HTML.

XHTML and the Development of HTML5

Near the end of the 1990s, the W3C released the final specifications for the 4th version of HTML, called HTML 4, and began charting a course for the next version. The path chosen by the W3C was to reformulate HTML in terms of XML. **XML** (**Extensible Markup Language**) is a compact offshoot of SGML and is used to define new markup languages, known as **XML vocabularies**. A document based on an XML vocabulary is forced to obey specific rules for content and structure to avoid being rejected as invalid. By contrast, HTML allows for a wide variety in syntax between one HTML document and another. Another important aspect of XML is that several XML vocabularies can be combined within a single document, making it easier to extend XML into different areas of application.

The W3C developed an XML vocabulary that was a stricter version of HTML4, known as **XHTML** (**Extensible Hypertext Markup Language**). XHTML was designed to confront some of the problems associated with the various competing versions of HTML and to better integrate HTML with other markup languages. Because XHTML was an XML version of HTML, most of what Web designers used with HTML could be applied to XHTML with only a few modifications, and many tools and features associated with XML could be easily applied to XHTML.

By 2002, the W3C had released the specifications for XHTML 1.1. This version was intended to be only a minor upgrade on the way to **XHTML 2.0**, which would contain a set of XML vocabularies moving HTML into the future with robust support for multimedia, social networking, interactive Web forms, and other features needed by Web designers. One problem was that XHTML 2.0 would not be backward compatible with earlier versions of HTML and thus older Web sites could not be easily integrated with the proposed new standard.

Web designers rebelled at this development. In 2004, Ian Hickson, who was working for Opera Software at the time, proposed a different path. Hickson's proposal would have allowed for the creation of new Web applications while still maintaining backward compatibility with HTML 4. He argued that HTML was whatever the browser market determined it to be, and that trying to enforce a new specification that did not accommodate the needs and limitations of the market was a fruitless exercise.

Hickson's proposal was rejected by the W3C and, in response, a new group of Web designers and browser manufacturers formed the **Web Hypertext Application Technology Working Group (WHATWG)** with the mission to develop a rival version to XHTML 2.0, called **HTML5**. For several years, it was unclear which specification would represent the future of the Web; but by 2006, work on XHTML 2.0 had completely stalled. The W3C issued a new charter for an HTML Working Group to develop HTML5 as the next HTML specification. Work on XHTML 2.0 was halted in 2009, leaving HTML5 as the de facto standard for the next generation of HTML.

Figure 1-1 **Versions of HTML**

Version	Date	Description
HTML 1.0	1989	The first public version of HTML.
HTML 2.0	1995	Added interactive elements including Web forms.
HTML 3.0	1996	A proposed replacement for HTML 2.0 that was never widely adopted.
HTML 3.2	1997	Included additional support for Web tables and expanded the options for interactive form elements and a scripting language.
HTML 4.01	1999	Added support for style sheets to give Web designers greater control over page layout and appearance, and provided support for multimedia elements such as audio and video. Current browsers support almost all of HTML 4.01.
XHTML 1.0	2001	A reformulation of HTML 4.01 in the XML language in order to provide enforceable standards for HTML content and to allow HTML to interact with other XML languages.
XHTML 1.1	2002	A minor update to XHTML 1.0 that allows for modularity and simplifies writing extensions to the language.
XHTML 2.0	discontinued	The follow-up version to XHTML 1.1 designed to fix some of the problems inherent in HTML 4.01 syntax. Work on this version was discontinued in 2009 due to lack of browser support.
HTML 5.0	In development	An update to HTML 4.01 that provides support for a variety of new features including semantic page elements, column layout, form validation, offline storage, and enhanced multimedia.
XHTML 5.0	In development	A version of HTML 5.0 written under the XML language; unlike XHTML 2.0, XHTML 5.0 will be backward compatible with XHTML 1.1.

Figure 1-1 summarizes the various versions of HTML that have been developed over the past 20 years. You may be wondering how on Earth anything can be written with so many versions of HTML to consider. At the time of this writing, you can write your code following the standards of HTML 4.01 or XHTML 1.1 and be assured that it will be supported by all major browsers. Many features of HTML5 are also being rapidly adopted by the market even as work continues on developing the language. HTML5 is the future, but the challenges for Web designers today lie in knowing which parts of HTML5 are supported by which browsers, and in developing strategies for supporting older browsers even as HTML5 is being implemented.

In this book you'll use HTML5 code for those features that have already achieved support among current browsers, but you'll also learn the standards used for HTML 4.01 and XHTML 1.1 and practice writing code that will support both current and older browsers.

HTML and Style Sheets

HTML marks the different parts of a document, but it does not indicate how document content should be displayed by browsers. This is a necessary facet of HTML because a Web page author has no control over what device will actually view his or her document. An end user might be using a large-screen television monitor, a mobile phone, or even a device that renders Web pages in Braille or in aural speech.

For this reason, the exact appearance of each page element is described in a separate document known as a **style sheet**. Each browser has its own **internal style sheet** that specifies the appearance of different HTML elements. For example, content that is marked as containing the text of an address is rendered by most Web browsers in italic, while major headings usually appear in large bold-faced fonts.

A Web page author can also create a style sheet that takes precedence over the internal style sheets of browsers. In addition, an author can create multiple style sheets for different output devices: one for rendering a page on a computer screen, another for printed output, and another for rendering the page aurally. In each case, the markup of the document content is the same, but the presentation is determined by the style sheet.

Tools for Creating HTML Documents

Because HTML documents are simple text files, you can create them using nothing more than a basic text editor such as Windows Notepad. Other software programs that enable you to create documents in different formats, such as Microsoft Word or Adobe Acrobat, include tools to convert their documents into HTML for quick and easy publishing on the Web.

If you intend to create a large Web site incorporating dozens of Web pages, you should invest in specialized Web publishing software to manage all of the code and extended features of your site. Programs such as Adobe Dreamweaver and Microsoft Expression Web are among the leaders in this field.

Since this book is focused on the HTML language itself and not how to work with different software programs, you'll need nothing more than a text editor and a Web browser to complete the assignments that follow.

Entering Elements and Attributes

Now that you've had a chance to review a brief history of the Web and the role of HTML in its development, you are ready to write your first HTML document for the J-Prop Shop. You'll start by studying the rules for entering HTML code.

Introducing HTML Tags

An HTML document is composed of **elements** that represent distinct items in the Web page, such as a paragraph, the page heading, or even the entire body of the page itself. Each element is marked within the HTML file by one or more **tags**. If an element contains text or another element, it is marked using a **two-sided tag set** in which an **opening tag** and a **closing tag** enclose the element content. The syntax of a two-sided tag set is

```
<element>content</element>
```

where *element* is the name of the element and *content* is the content of the element. For example, the following code marks a paragraph using a two-sided tag set:

```
<p>Welcome to the J-Prop Shop.</p>
```

In this example, the `<p>` tag marks the beginning of the paragraph, the text *Welcome to the J-Prop Shop.* is the content of the paragraph element, and the `</p>` tag marks the end of the paragraph. Elements can also contain other elements. For example, in the code

```
<p>Welcome to <em>Dave's Devil Sticks</em>.</p>
```

the paragraph tags enclose both the text of the paragraph and the tag set `<em> ... </em>`, which is used to mark content that should be treated by the browser as emphasized text. Note that the `<em>` tag set must be completely enclosed, or **nested**, within the `<p>` tags. It's improper to have tags overlap as in the following code sample:

```
<p>Welcome to <em>Dave's Devil Sticks.</p></em>
```

In this example, the closing `</em>` tag is placed *after* the closing `</p>` tag, which is improper because one element must be completely contained within another.

An element that does not enclose content is an **empty element** and it is marked with a **one-sided tag** using the syntax

```
<element />
```

where element is the name of the element. For example, you can mark a line break using the br element, which has the following syntax:

```
<br />
```

Since empty elements don't contain content, they're often employed to send directives to browsers regarding how a page should be rendered. A browser encountering the br element would insert a line break, causing the text of the next element in the document to be placed on a new line.

Specifying an Element Attribute

In addition to content, elements also support **attributes** that specify the use, the behavior, and in some cases the appearance of an element. Attribute values don't appear in the rendered Web page; rather, they provide information to the browser about the properties of the element.

To add an attribute to an element, you insert the attribute within the element's opening tag. For a two-sided tag, the syntax is:

```
<element attribute1="value1" attribute2="value2" ...>
    content
</element>
```

Attributes are added to one-sided tags in the same way:

```
<element attribute1="value1" attribute2="value2" ... />
```

In these examples, attribute1, attribute2, etc. are the names of attributes associated with the element, and value1, value2, etc. are the values of those attributes. For instance, the following code adds the id attribute to a paragraph marked with the p element:

```
<p id="opening">Welcome to the J-Prop Shop.</p>
```

A browser interpreting this code would recognize that the text *Welcome to the J-Prop Shop.* should be treated as a paragraph and given the id value *opening*.

> **TIP**
>
> Attributes can be listed in any order, but they must be separated from one another by a blank space and enclosed within single or double quotation marks.

REFERENCE

Adding an Attribute to an Element

- To add an element attribute, use the format

```
<element attribute1="value1"
         attribute2="value2" ...>content</element>
```

where attribute1, attribute2, etc. are the names of attributes associated with the element, and value1, value2, etc. are the values of those attributes.

White Space and HTML

Since an HTML file is a text file, it's composed of text characters and white space. **White space** includes the blank spaces, tabs, and line breaks found within the file. As far as a browser is concerned, there is no difference between a blank space, a tab, or a line break. Browsers also ignore consecutive occurrences of white space, collapsing extra white space characters into a single blank space. Thus, browsers treat the following paragraph elements in the same way:

```
<p>Welcome to the J-Prop Shop.</p>


<p>
    Welcome to the J-Prop Shop.
</p>


<p>Welcome
to the J-Prop Shop.</p>


<p>Welcome   to   the   J-Prop   Shop.</p>
```

Because HTML handles white space in this way, you can make your code easier for others to read by indenting lines and adding extra blank lines to separate one tag from another in the file.

INSIGHT

HTML5 and XHTML Syntax

The rules that govern how code should be entered are called **syntax**. The way that HTML has been implemented by most browsers through the Web's history has allowed for minor variations in syntax. One reason for the success of the Web is that HTML has made it easy for non-programmers to write and edit code without being ensnarled by syntax violations.

On the other hand, XHTML forces strict syntax on page authors. If an author's code does not follow the rules, browsers do not render the page. One advantage of this approach is that it forces authors to write clear and more concise code; indeed, one of the driving forces behind the development of XHTML was the desire to clean up some of the messy and inconsistent code found on the Web.

For example, XHTML requires that all tag names be placed in lowercase letters and that all attribute values be enclosed within quotation marks. HTML allows either uppercase or lowercase tag names and does not require attribute values to be quoted. In addition, XHTML requires that every one-sided tag be entered with a closing slash: for instance, the br element must be entered as `<br />` for XHTML compatibility. Most browsers, however, accept HTML code in which one-sided tags are entered without closing slashes; thus, the br element could be entered either as `<br>` or as `<br />`.

HTML5 supports the informal standards accepted by most browsers and will continue to allow for minor variations in syntax. However, it is still good practice to write all code to be XHTML compliant whenever possible, since it will allow that code to be easily transferred to XHTML environments if necessary.

Exploring the Structure of an HTML Document

The structure of an HTML document consists of different elements nested within each other in a hierarchy of elements. The top element in that hierarchy is the **html element**, which contains all of the other elements within an HTML file. Directly below the **html** element in the hierarchy are the **head** and **body** elements. The **head element** contains general information about the document—for example, the document's title, or a list of keywords that would aid search engines in directing interested users to the page. The **body element** contains all of the content that appears in the rendered Web page. Thus, the general structure of an HTML file is

```
<html>
    <head>
        head content
    </head>
    <body>
        body content
    </body>
</html>
```

where *head content* and *body content* are the content you want to place within the document's head and body. Note that the body element is always placed after the head element.

The Document Type Declaration

Prior to the opening `<html>` tag, many HTML files also include a **Document Type Declaration**, or **doctype**, to indicate the type of markup language used in the document. The doctype is used by **validators**, which are programs that examine document code to ensure that it meets all the syntax requirements of the specified language. All XHTML files require a doctype because those documents must be validated against a set of standards.

Most current browsers also use the presence or absence of a doctype to decide which mode they should use to render a document in a process known as **doctype switching**. If a doctype is included, such browsers render the Web page in **standards mode**, in accordance with the most current specifications of the language. If no doctype is provided, these browsers render the document in **quirks mode** based on practices followed in the 1990s. The differences can be striking. Figure 1-2 shows an example of two documents rendered by Internet Explorer under standards mode and quirks mode. The only difference in the code between these two documents is the presence or absence of a doctype, but the browser renders the two documents very differently.

Figure 1-2   **A Web page rendered in standards mode and quirks mode**

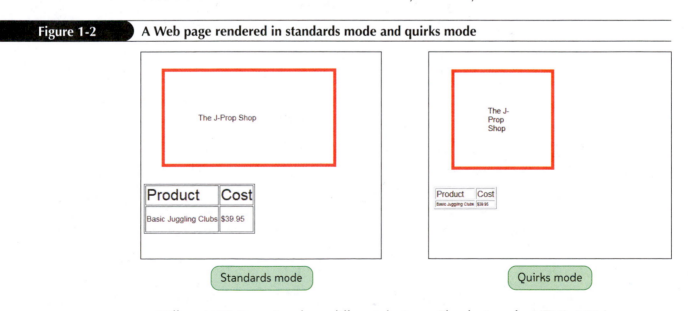

Different HTML versions have different doctypes. The doctype for HTML 4.01 is:

```
<!DOCTYPE HTML PUBLIC "-//W3C//DTD HTML 4.01/EN"
    "http://www.w3.org/TR/html4/strict.dtd">
```

The doctype for XHTML is:

```
<!DOCTYPE html PUBLIC "-//W3C//DTD XHTML 1.0 Strict//EN"
    "http://www.w3.org/TR/xhtml1/DTD/xhtml1-strict.dtd">
```

Finally, the doctype for HTML5 is much simpler than what was required for HTML 4.01 or XHTML:

```
<!DOCTYPE html>
```

HTML5 documents should always be opened in standards mode because they are based on the latest specifications for the HTML language.

You can learn more about standards mode and quirks mode by searching the Web for examples of the differences between the two modes.

Creating the Initial Document

Now that you've seen the basic structure of an HTML document, you are ready to begin creating the sample Web page for Dave's Web site.

REFERENCE

Creating the Basic Structure of an HTML Document

Enter the HTML tags

```
doctype
<html>
    <head>
        head content
    </head>
    <body>
        body content
    </body>
</html>
```

where *doctype* is the Document Type Declaration, and *head content* and *body content* are the content of the document's head and body.

You can start creating Dave's Web page using a basic editor such as Windows Notepad. Since Dave wants his document to be based on HTML5, you'll use the HTML5 doctype in your file.

To create the basic structure of an HTML document:

1. Start your text editor, opening a blank text document.

    Trouble? If you don't know how to start or use your text editor, ask your instructor or technical support person for help. Note that some editors do not save files in text file format by default, so check your editor's documentation to ensure that you are creating a basic text document.

> **Make sure you include the exclamation point (!) within the doctype; otherwise, browsers will not recognize the doctype.**

2. Type the following lines of code in your document. Press the **Enter** key after each line. Press the **Enter** key twice for a blank line between lines of code. See Figure 1-3.

```
<!DOCTYPE html>
<html>

   <head>
   </head>

   <body>
   </body>

</html>
```

Figure 1-3   **Basic structure of an HTML file**

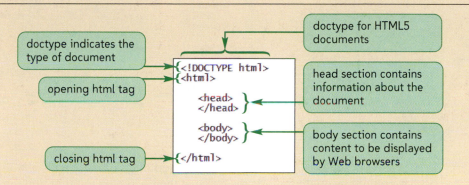

3. Save the file as **jprop.htm** in the tutorial.01\tutorial folder included with your Data Files.

Trouble? If you are using the Windows Notepad text editor to create your HTML file, make sure you don't save the file with the extension *.txt*, which is the default file extension for Notepad. Instead, save the file with the file extension *.htm* or *.html*. Using the incorrect file extension might make the file unreadable to Web browsers, which require file extensions of *.htm* or *.html*.

> **TIP**
>
> To make it easier to link to your Web pages, follow the Internet convention of naming HTML files and folders using only lowercase letters with no spaces.

Now that you've entered the basic structure of your HTML file, you can start entering the content of the `head` element.

Marking the Head Element

In general, the `head` element is where you provide browsers with information about your document. This can include the page's title, the location of any style sheets used with the document, the location of any programs that browsers should run when they load the page, and information for use by search engines to aid users in locating the Web site.

Defining the Page Title

The first element you'll add to the head of Dave's document is the `title` element, which has the syntax

```
<title>document title</title>
```

where *document title* is the text of the document title. The document title is not displayed within the page, but is usually displayed in a browser's title bar or on a browser tab. The document title is also used by search engines like Google or Yahoo! when compiling an index of search results.

TIP

Indent your markup tags and insert extra blank spaces as shown in this book to make your code easier to read. These indentations and spaces do not affect how the page is rendered by browsers.

To add a title to your Web page:

1. Click at the end of the opening `<head>` tag, and then press the **Enter** key to insert a new line in your text editor.

2. Press the **Spacebar** several times to indent the new line of code, and then type `<title>The J-Prop Shop</title>` as shown in Figure 1-4.

Figure 1-4   **Specifying the page title**

```
<!DOCTYPE html>
<html>

    <head>
        <title>The J-Prop Shop</title>
    </head>

    <body>
    </body>

</html>
```

text will appear in browser title bar or on browser tab

Adding Comments

As you write your HTML file, you can add notes or comments about your code. These comments might include the name of the document's author and the date the document was created. Such notes are not intended to be displayed by browsers, but are instead used to help explain your code to yourself and others. To add notes or comments, insert a **comment tag** using the syntax

```
<!-- comment -->
```

where *comment* is the text of the comment or note. For example, the following code inserts a comment describing the page you'll create for Dave's business:

```
<!-- Sample page for the J-Prop Shop -->
```

A comment can also be spread out over several lines as follows:

```
<!-- Sample page for the J-Prop Shop.
     Created by Dave Vinet -->
```

Because they are ignored by the browser, comments can be added anywhere within the `html` element.

REFERENCE

Adding an HTML Comment

To insert an HTML comment anywhere within your document, enter

```
<!-- comment -->
```

where *comment* is the text of the HTML comment.

You'll add a comment to the *jprop.htm* file, identifying the author and purpose of this document.

To add a comment to the document head:

1. Click at the end of the opening `<head>` tag, and then press the **Enter** key to insert a new line in your text editor directly above the opening `<title>` tag,

2. Type the following lines of code as shown in Figure 1-5:

```
<!-- The J-Prop Shop Sample Page
     Author: your name
     Date:   the date
-->
```

where *your name* is your name and *the date* is the current date.

Figure 1-5 **Adding comments to the HTML file**

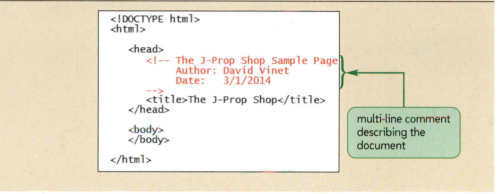

```
<!DOCTYPE html>
<html>

    <head>
        <!-- The J-Prop Shop Sample Page
             Author: David Vinet
             Date:   3/1/2014
        -->
        <title>The J-Prop Shop</title>
    </head>

    <body>
    </body>

</html>
```

multi-line comment describing the document

Displaying an HTML File

As you continue modifying the HTML code, you should occasionally view the page with your Web browser to verify that you have not introduced any errors. You might even want to view the results using different browsers to check for compatibility. In this book, Web pages are displayed using the Windows Internet Explorer 9 browser. Be aware that if you are using a different browser or a different operating system, you might see slight differences in the layout and appearance of the page.

To view Dave's Web page:

1. Save your changes to the **jprop.htm** file.

2. Start your Web browser. You do not need to be connected to the Internet to view local files stored on your computer.

    Trouble? If you start your browser and are not connected to the Internet, you might get a warning message. Click the OK button to ignore the message and continue.

3. After your browser loads its home page, open the **jprop.htm** file from the tutorial.01\tutorial folder.

    Trouble? If you're not sure how to open a local file with your browser, check for an Open or Open File command under the browser's File menu. If you are still having problems accessing the *jprop.htm* file, talk to your instructor or technical resource person.

Your browser displays the Web page shown in Figure 1-6. Note that in this case, the page title appears in the browser tab; in other cases, it will appear in the browser's title bar. The page itself is empty because you have not yet added any content to the body element.

| Figure 1-6 | Viewing the initial HTML file in a Web browser |

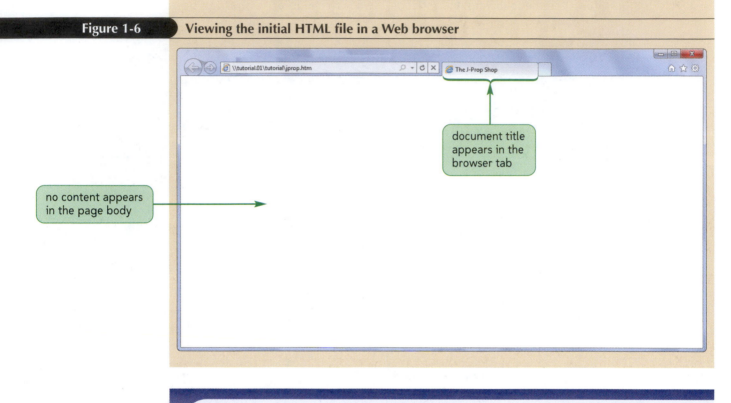

document title appears in the browser tab

no content appears in the page body

INSIGHT

Converting an HTML Document into XHTML

There is considerable overlap between HTML and XHTML. You can quickly change an HTML document into an XHTML document just by altering the first three lines of code. To convert an HTML file into an XHTML file, replace the doctype and the opening `<html>` tag with the following:

```
<?xml version="1.0" encoding="UTF-8" standalone="no" ?>
<!DOCTYPE html PUBLIC "-//W3C//DTD XHTML 1.0 Strict//EN"
   "http://www.w3.org/TR/xhtml1/DTD/xhtml1-strict.dtd">
<html xmlns="http://www.w3.org/1999/xhtml">
```

Since XHTML is an XML vocabulary, the first line notifies browsers that the document is an XML file. The version number—1.0—tells the browser that the file is written in XML 1.0. The second line provides the doctype for an XHTML document written under a strict interpretation of XHTML syntax. The third line of the file contains the opening `<html>` tag. In XHTML, the `<html>` tag must include what is known as a **namespace declaration** indicating that any markup tags in the document should, by default, be considered part of the XHTML language. Because XML documents can contain a mixture of several different vocabularies, the namespace declaration is necessary to specify the default language of the document. With these three lines in place, browsers will recognize the file as an XHTML document.

Defining the Structure of the Page Body

Now that you've marked the document head and inserted a page title, you'll turn to the contents of the body of the Web page. It's always a good idea to plan your Web page before you start coding it. You can do this by drawing a sketch or by creating a sample document within a word processor. Your preparatory work can weed out textual errors or point to potential problems in your page layout. In this case, Dave has already drawn up a flyer that he's passed out at juggling and circus conventions. Figure 1-7 shows the handout, which provides information about Dave's company and his products.

Figure 1-7	Dave's flyer

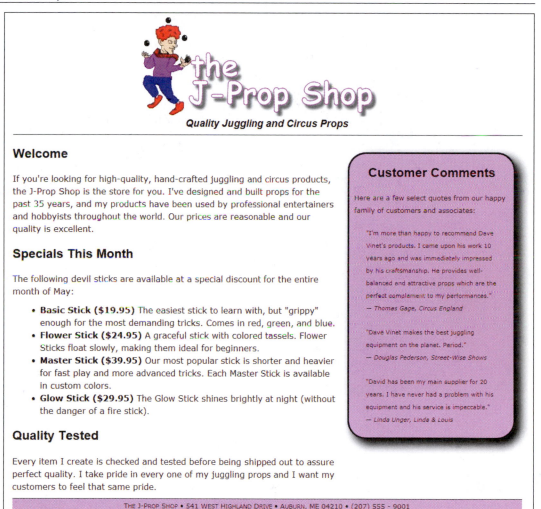

Dave's flyer contains several elements that are common to many Web pages, as shown in Figure 1-8. A header displays the company's logo and a footer displays contact information for the J-Prop Shop. The main section, which describes Dave's business, includes several subsections, also known as articles. A second section that appears as a sidebar displays quotes from some J-Prop customers.

Figure 1-8   Structure of Dave's Web page

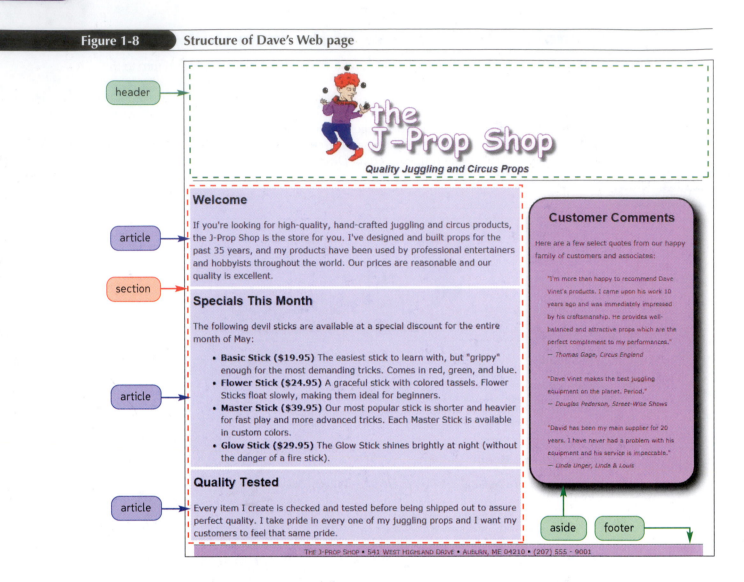

Working with HTML5 Structural Elements

Each of these parts of Dave's document can be marked using HTML5 **structural elements**, which are the elements that define the major sections of a Web page. Figure 1-9 describes some of these elements.

Figure 1-9   HTML5 structural elements

Structural Element	Description
article	A subsection covering a single topic
aside	Content containing tangential or side issues to the main topic of the page
footer	Content placed at the bottom of the page
header	Content placed at the top of the page
nav	A navigation list of hypertext links
section	A major topical area in the page

For example, to mark the header of your Web page, you would enter a `header` element within the page body, using the syntax

```
<header>
    header content
</header>
```

where *header content* is the page content that you want displayed within the page header. One of the reasons we want to define these structural elements is that we can write styles for them and define the layout of the Web page content.

Marking Structural Elements in HTML5

- To mark the page header, use the `header` element.
- To mark the page footer, use the `footer` element.
- To mark a main section of page content, use the `section` element.
- To mark a sidebar, use the `aside` element.
- To mark an article, use the `article` element.

Based on Dave's sample document shown in Figure 1-8, you'll add the `header`, `section`, `aside`, and `footer` structural elements to your HTML file.

To insert the HTML5 structural elements:

1. Return to the **jprop.htm** file in your text editor.

2. Within the `body` element, insert the following tags as shown in Figure 1-10:

```
<header>
</header>

<section>
</section>

<aside>
</aside>

<footer>
</footer>
```

Figure 1-10 **Inserting structural elements**

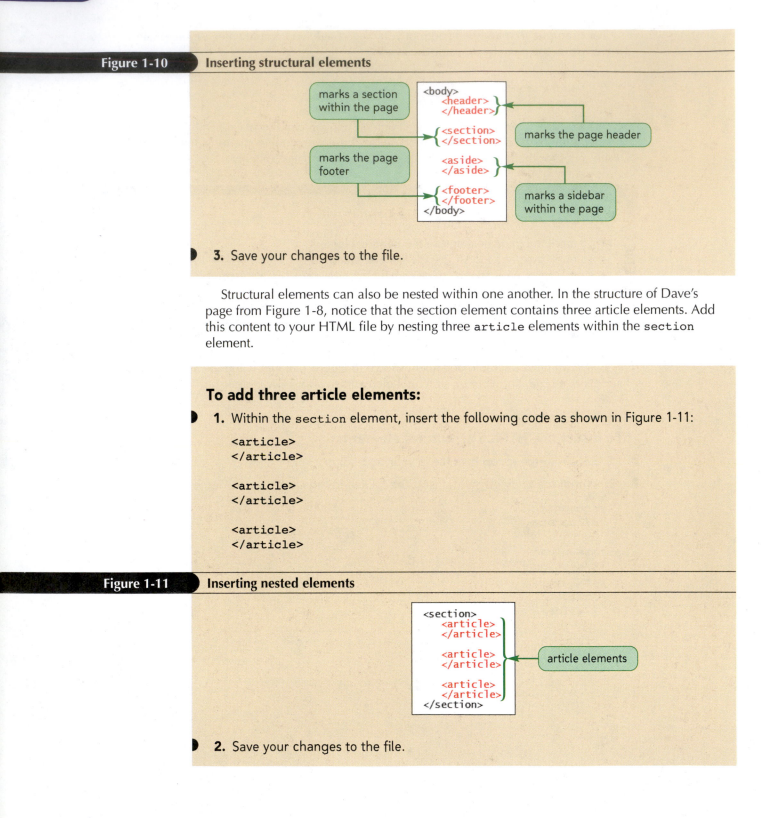

3. Save your changes to the file.

Structural elements can also be nested within one another. In the structure of Dave's page from Figure 1-8, notice that the section element contains three article elements. Add this content to your HTML file by nesting three `article` elements within the `section` element.

To add three article elements:

1. Within the `section` element, insert the following code as shown in Figure 1-11:

```
<article>
</article>

<article>
</article>

<article>
</article>
```

Figure 1-11 **Inserting nested elements**

2. Save your changes to the file.

Marking a Section with the `div` Element

The structural elements are part of the current specifications for HTML5, but they are not part of HTML 4.01 or XHTML. Pages written to those languages instead use the **div element** to identify different page divisions. The syntax of the div element is

```
<div id="id">
   content
</div>
```

where *id* is a unique name assigned to the division and *content* is page content contained within the division. While not required, the **id** attribute is useful to distinguish one **div** element from another. This becomes particularly important if you apply different styles to different page divisions.

Figure 1-12 shows how the same page layout marked up using structural elements under HTML5 would be marked up in HTML 4.01 using the **div** element.

Figure 1-12   **Structural elements in HTML5 and HTML 4.01**

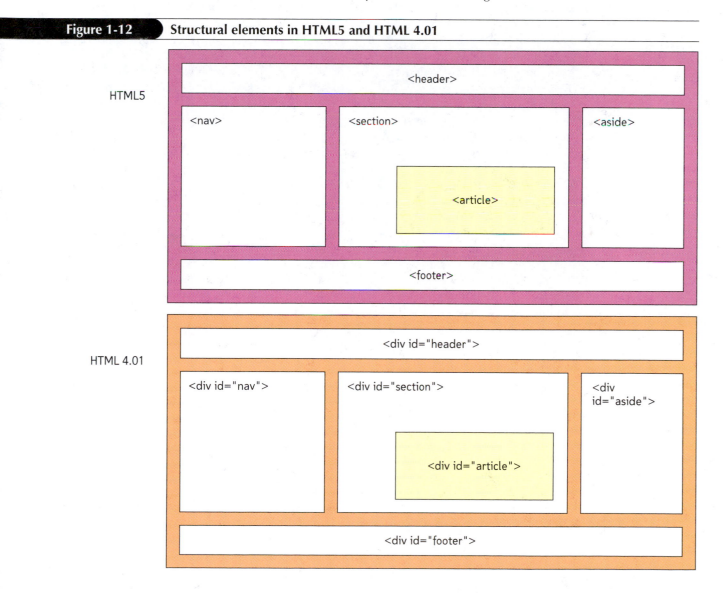

You can use either HTML5's structural elements or HTML 4.01's `div` elements to identify the major sections of your document. The HTML5 approach is preferred because it represents the future standard of the Web, and structural elements are more descriptive than the generic `div` element. One problem with the `div` element is that there are no rules for id names. One Web designer might identify the page heading with the id name *header* while another designer might use *heading* or *top*. This makes it harder for Web search engines to identify the main topics of interest in each Web page.

PROSKILLS

Written Communication: Writing Effective HTML Code

Part of writing good HTML code is being aware of the requirements of various browsers and devices, as well as understanding the different versions of the language. Here are a few guidelines for writing good HTML code:

- *Become well versed in the history of HTML and the various versions of HTML and XHTML.* Unlike other languages, HTML's history does impact how you write your code.
- *Know your market.* Do you have to support older browsers, or have your clients standardized on one particular browser or browser version? Will your Web pages be viewed on a single device such as a computer, or do you have to support a variety of devices?
- *Test your code on several different browsers and browser versions.* Don't assume that if your page works in one browser it will work in other browsers, or even in earlier versions of the same browser. Also check on the speed of the connection. A large file that performs well with a high-speed connection might be unusable with a dial-up connection.
- *Read the documentation on the different versions of HTML and XHTML at the W3C Web site and keep up to date with the latest developments in the language.*

In general, any HTML code that you write should be compatible with the current versions of the following browsers: Internet Explorer (Windows), Firefox (Windows and Macintosh), Safari (Windows and Macintosh), Chrome (Windows and Macintosh), and Opera (Windows and Macintosh). In addition, you should also view your pages on a variety of devices including laptops, mobile phones, and tablets. To effectively communicate with customers and users, you need to make sure your Web site is always readable.

At this point, you've created the basic framework of Dave's Web page. In the next session, you'll insert the page content and learn how to apply a visual style to that content to create a nicely formatted Web page. If you want to take a break before starting the next session, you can close any open files or applications.

REVIEW

Session 1.1 Quick Check

1. What is a markup language?
2. What is XHTML? How does XHTML differ from HTML?
3. What is the W3C? What is the WHATWG?
4. What is a doctype? What are two uses of the doctype?
5. What is incorrect about the syntax of the following code?

   ```
   <p>Welcome to the <em>J-Prop Shop</p></em>
   ```

6. What is white space? How does HTML treat consecutive occurrences of white space?
7. What structural element would you use to mark a sidebar?
8. What structural element would you use to mark the page footer?

SESSION 1.2 VISUAL OVERVIEW

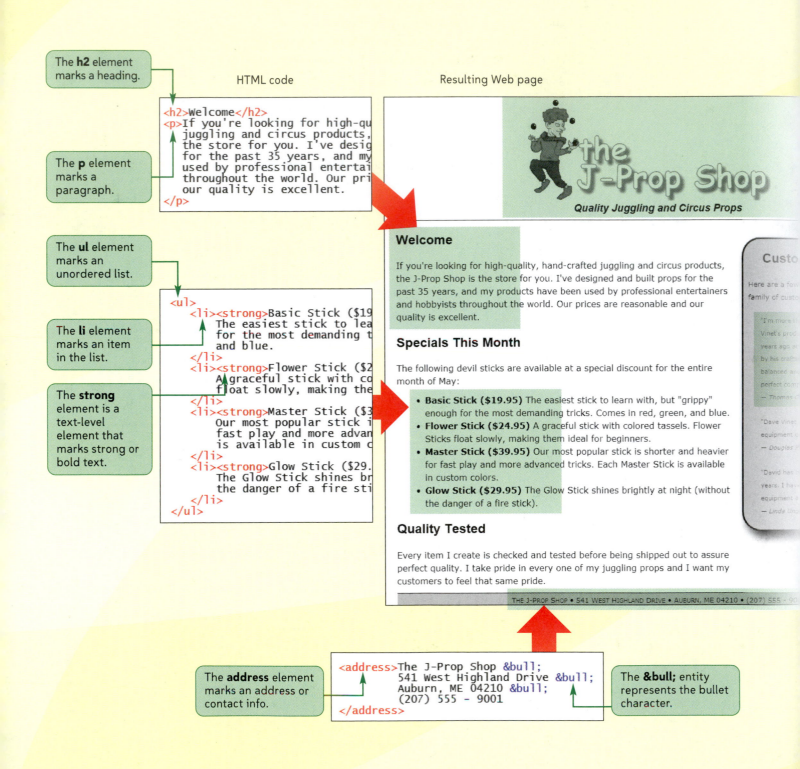

The **h2** element marks a heading.

The **p** element marks a paragraph.

The **ul** element marks an unordered list.

The **li** element marks an item in the list.

The **strong** element is a text-level element that marks strong or bold text.

HTML code

```
<h2>Welcome</h2>
<p>If you're looking for high-qu
   juggling and circus products,
   the store for you. I've desig
   for the past 35 years, and my
   used by professional entertai
   throughout the world. Our pri
   our quality is excellent.
</p>
```

```
<ul>
   <li><strong>Basic Stick ($19
      The easiest stick to lea
      for the most demanding t
      and blue.
   </li>
   <li><strong>Flower Stick ($2
      A graceful stick with co
      float slowly, making the
   </li>
   <li><strong>Master Stick ($3
      Our most popular stick i
      fast play and more advan
      is available in custom c
   </li>
   <li><strong>Glow Stick ($29.
      The Glow Stick shines br
      the danger of a fire sti
   </li>
</ul>
```

Resulting Web page

the J-Prop Shop
Quality Juggling and Circus Props

Welcome

If you're looking for high-quality, hand-crafted juggling and circus products, the J-Prop Shop is the store for you. I've designed and built props for the past 35 years, and my products have been used by professional entertainers and hobbyists throughout the world. Our prices are reasonable and our quality is excellent.

Specials This Month

The following devil sticks are available at a special discount for the entire month of May:

- **Basic Stick ($19.95)** The easiest stick to learn with, but "grippy" enough for the most demanding tricks. Comes in red, green, and blue.
- **Flower Stick ($24.95)** A graceful stick with colored tassels. Flower Sticks float slowly, making them ideal for beginners.
- **Master Stick ($39.95)** Our most popular stick is shorter and heavier for fast play and more advanced tricks. Each Master Stick is available in custom colors.
- **Glow Stick ($29.95)** The Glow Stick shines brightly at night (without the danger of a fire stick).

Quality Tested

Every item I create is checked and tested before being shipped out to assure perfect quality. I take pride in every one of my juggling props and I want my customers to feel that same pride.

THE J-PROP SHOP • 541 WEST HIGHLAND DRIVE • AUBURN, ME 04210 • (207) 555 - 90

Custo

Here are a few
family of custo

"I'm more th
Vinet's prod
years ago a
by his craftsr
balanced an
perfect com
— Thomas

"Dave Vines
equipment
— Douglas

"David has
years. I ha
equipment
— Linda Unu

The **address** element marks an address or contact info.

```
<address>The J-Prop Shop &bull;
         541 West Highland Drive &bull;
         Auburn, ME 04210 &bull;
         (207) 555 - 9001
</address>
```

The **•** entity represents the bullet character.

PAGE CONTENT ELEMENTS

HTML code

The **hgroup** element groups main headings and subheadings.

The **img** element is used to insert images into the Web page.

```
<hgroup>
    <h1>
        <img src="jpslogo.png" alt="The J-Prop Shop" />
    </h1>
    <h2>
        Quality Juggling and Circus Props
    </h2>
</hgroup>
```

```
<blockquote>
    <p>"I'm more than happy to reco
    products. I came upon his wo
    was immediately impressed by
    He provides well-balanced an
    props which are the perfect
    performances."
    <br />
    &#8212; <cite>Thomas Gage, C
    </p>
```

The **blockquote** element marks large blocks of quoted material.

The **cite** element marks a citation.

The **—** entity represents the em-dash character.

A page rendered with the default browser style sheet

The same page rendered with a user-defined style sheet

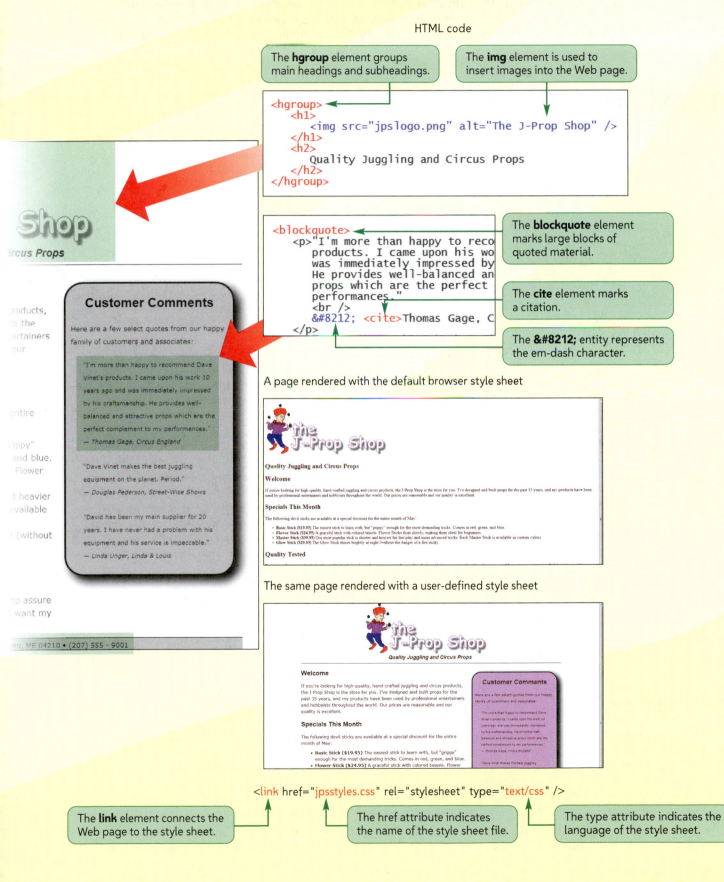

```
<link href="jpsstyles.css" rel="stylesheet" type="text/css" />
```

The **link** element connects the Web page to the style sheet.

The href attribute indicates the name of the style sheet file.

The type attribute indicates the language of the style sheet.

Working with Grouping Elements

You're now ready to begin entering content into the body of Dave's Web page. The first elements you'll add are **grouping elements**, which are elements that contain content that is viewed as a distinct block within the Web page. Paragraphs, which were presented in the last session, are one example of a grouping element, as are page divisions marked using the `div` element. Figure 1-13 lists some of the commonly used grouping elements.

Figure 1-13   Grouping elements

Grouping Element	Description
address	Contact information (usually rendered as *italicized* text)
blockquote	An extended quotation (usually indented from the left and right margins)
dd	A definition from a description list
div	A generic grouping element
dl	A description list
dt	A definition term from a description list
figure	A figure or illustration (HTML5 only)
figcaption	The caption of a figure, which must be nested within the figure element (HTML5 only)
hn	A heading, where n is a value from 1 to 6, with h1 as the most prominent heading and h6 the least prominent (usually displayed in **bold** text)
li	A list item from an ordered or unordered list
ol	An ordered list
p	A paragraph
pre	Preformatted text, retaining all white space and special characters (usually displayed in a `fixed width` font)
ul	An unordered list

To explore how grouping elements are typically rendered by your Web browser, a demo page has been prepared for you.

To open the HTML Tags demo page:

1. Use your browser to open the **demo_html.htm** file from the tutorial.01\demo folder.

2. If your browser prompts you to allow code from the Web page to be run, click the **Allow blocked content** button.

Marking Content Headings

The first grouping elements you'll explore are **heading elements**, which contain the text of main headings on a Web page. They're often used for introducing new topics or for dividing the page into topical sections. The syntax to mark a heading element is

```
<hn>content</hn>
```

where n is an integer from 1 to 6. Content marked with `<h1>` tags is considered a major heading, and is usually displayed in large bold text. Content marked with `<h2>` through `<h6>` tags is used for subheadings, and is usually displayed in progressively smaller bold text.

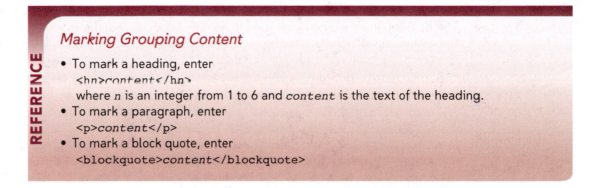

Marking Grouping Content

- To mark a heading, enter
  `<hn>content</hn>`
  where *n* is an integer from 1 to 6 and *content* is the text of the heading.
- To mark a paragraph, enter
  `<p>content</p>`
- To mark a block quote, enter
  `<blockquote>content</blockquote>`

To see how these headings appear on your computer, use the demo page.

To view heading elements:

1. Click in the blue box in the lower-left corner of the demo page, type `<h1>The J-Prop Shop</h1>` and then press the **Enter** key to go to a new line.

2. Type `<h2>Quality Juggling and Circus Props</h2>`.

3. Click the **Preview Code** button located below the blue code window. Your browser displays a preview of how this code would appear in your Web browser (see Figure 1-14).

Figure 1-14   **Previewing h1 and h2 headings**

Trouble? If you are using a browser other than Internet Explorer 9 running on Windows 7, your screen might look slightly different from that shown in Figure 1-14.

4. To see how an `h3` heading would look, change the opening tag for the store description from `<h2>` to `<h3>` and change the closing tag from `</h2>` to `</h3>`. Click the **Preview Code** button again.

Your browser renders the code again, this time with the store information displayed in a smaller font. If you continued to change the heading element from `h3` to each of the elements down to `h6`, you would see the second line in the Preview box get progressively smaller.

It's important not to treat markup tags as simply a way of formatting the Web page. The h1 through h6 elements are used to identify headings, but the exact appearance of these headings depends on the browser and the device being used. While most browsers display an h1 heading in a larger font than an h2 heading, remember that the headings might not even be displayed at all. A screen reader, for example, doesn't display text, but rather conveys the presence of an h1 heading with increased volume or with special emphasis preceded by an extended pause.

Now that you've seen how to mark page headings, you can add them to Dave's Web page. The first heading Dave wants to add is an h1 heading containing the company's name. He also wants you to insert h2 headings in several places—as titles for the three articles on the page, as a title for the sidebar containing the customer comments, and as a subheading to the main heading on the page.

To add headings to Dave's document:

1. Return to the **jprop.htm** file in your text editor.

   Trouble? If you are using the Macintosh TextEdit program, you must select the *Ignore rich text commands* check box when reopening the file.

2. Within the header element, insert the following tags:

   ```
   <h1>The J-Prop Shop</h1>
   <h2>Quality Juggling and Circus Props</h2>
   ```

3. Within the first article element, insert the following h2 heading:

   ```
   <h2>Welcome</h2>
   ```

4. Within the second article element, insert

   ```
   <h2>Specials This Month</h2>
   ```

5. Within the third and final article element, insert

   ```
   <h2>Quality Tested</h2>
   ```

6. Finally, within the aside element, insert

   ```
   <h2>Customer Comments</h2>
   ```

   Figure 1-15 highlights the revised code in the file.

Figure 1-15	Inserting h1 and h2 headings

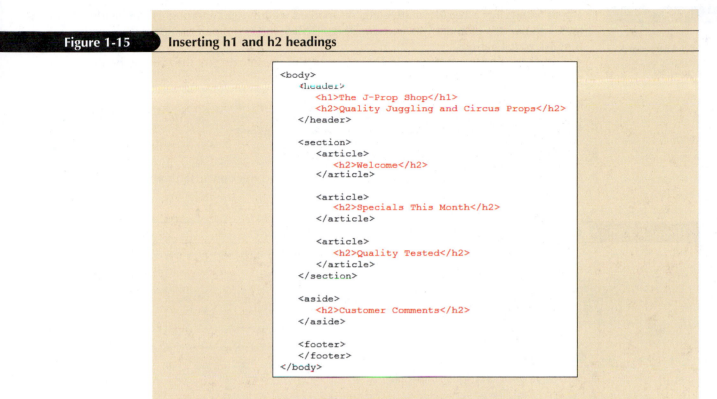

```
<body>
   <header>
      <h1>The J-Prop Shop</h1>
      <h2>Quality Juggling and Circus Props</h2>
   </header>

   <section>
      <article>
         <h2>Welcome</h2>
      </article>

      <article>
         <h2>Specials This Month</h2>
      </article>

      <article>
         <h2>Quality Tested</h2>
      </article>
   </section>

   <aside>
      <h2>Customer Comments</h2>
   </aside>

   <footer>
   </footer>
</body>
```

7. Save your changes to the file and then reload or refresh the **jprop.htm** file in your Web browser. Figure 1-16 shows the initial view of the page body content.

Figure 1-16	Viewing h1 and h2 headings in Dave's document

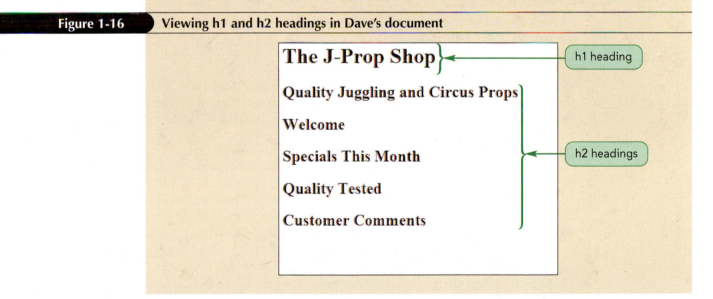

Grouping Headings

The interpretation of a particular heading depends on how it's used. For example, the h2 headings you just entered were used either to provide a title for articles or sections in the Web page or as a subtitle to the main title of the page. You can indicate that an h2 heading acts as a subtitle by grouping it with a main title heading using the **hgroup element**. The hgroup element uses the syntax

```
<hgroup>
   heading elements
</hgroup>
```

TIP

The hgroup element can contain only h1 through h6 elements or other hgroup elements.

where *heading elements* are elements marked with the `<h1>` through `<h6>` heading tags. The `hgroup` element was introduced in HTML5 and is not part of older HTML or XHTML specifications.

Group the first two headings in Dave's document to indicate that they should be interpreted as a main title and a subtitle.

To group the first two headings in the document:

1. Return to the **jprop.htm** file in your text editor.

2. Indent the first two headings in the document and then enclose them within `<hgroup>` tags as shown in Figure 1-17.

Figure 1-17   **Grouping the h1 and h2 headings**

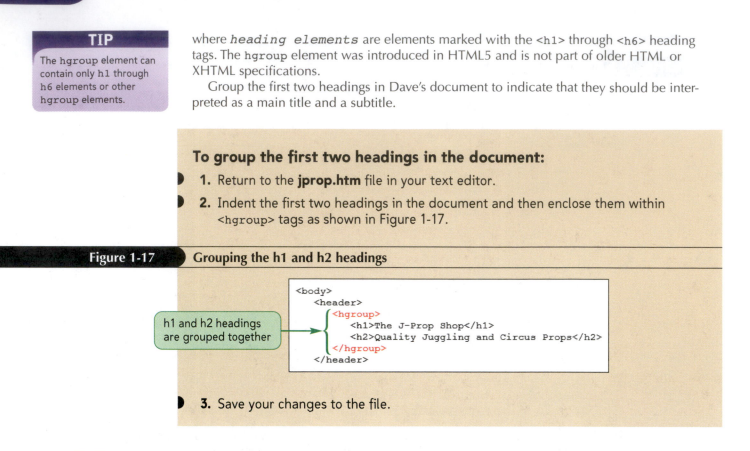

```
<body>
    <header>
        <hgroup>
            <h1>The J-Prop Shop</h1>
            <h2>Quality Juggling and Circus Props</h2>
        </hgroup>
    </header>
```

h1 and h2 headings are grouped together

3. Save your changes to the file.

Marking Paragraph Elements

As you saw earlier, you can mark a paragraph element using the `<p>` tag, which has the syntax

```
<p>content</p>
```

where `content` is the content of the paragraph. In older HTML code, you might occasionally see paragraphs marked with only the opening `<p>` tags, omitting closing tags. In those situations, a `<p>` tag marks the start of each new paragraph. While this convention is still accepted by many browsers, it violates HTML's syntax rules. In addition, if you want XHTML-compliant code, you must always include closing tags.

Many articles on the J-Prop Shop page are enclosed within paragraphs. You'll add these paragraphs now.

To add four paragraphs to Dave's Web page:

1. Return to the **jprop.htm** file in your text editor.

2. Directly below the h2 heading *Welcome*, insert the following paragraph code, indented as shown in Figure 1-18:

```
<p>If you're looking for high-quality, hand-crafted
    juggling and circus products, the J-Prop Shop is
    the store for you. I've designed and built props
    for the past 35 years, and my products have been
    used by professional entertainers and hobbyists
    throughout the world. Our prices are reasonable and
    our quality is excellent.
</p>
```

3. Directly below the h2 heading *Specials This Month*, insert the following:

```
<p>The following devil sticks are available at a
    special discount for the entire month of May:
</p>
```

4. Directly below the h2 heading *Quality Tested*, insert the following:

```
<p>Every item I create is checked and tested before
    being shipped out to assure perfect quality. I take
    pride in every one of my juggling props and I want
    my customers to feel that same pride.
</p>
```

5. Finally, below the h2 heading *Customer Comments*, insert the following:

```
<p>Here are a few select quotes from our happy family
    of customers and associates:
</p>
```

Figure 1-18 highlights the newly added paragraphs in the document.

Figure 1-18	Adding paragraph elements

```
<section>
    <article>
        <h2>Welcome</h2>
        <p>If you're looking for high-quality, hand-crafted
            juggling and circus products, the J-Prop Shop is
            the store for you. I've designed and built props
            for the past 35 years, and my products have been
            used by professional entertainers and hobbyists
            throughout the world. Our prices are reasonable and
            our quality is excellent.
        </p>
    </article>

    <article>
        <h2>Specials This Month</h2>
        <p>The following devil sticks are available at a
            special discount for the entire month of May:
        </p>
    </article>

    <article>
        <h2>Quality Tested</h2>
        <p>Every item I create is checked and tested before
            being shipped out to assure perfect quality. I take
            pride in every one of my juggling props and I want
            my customers to feel that same pride.
        </p>
    </article>
</section>

<aside>
    <h2>Customer Comments</h2>
    <p>Here are a few select quotes from our happy family
        of customers and associates:
    </p>
</aside>
```

Trouble? Don't worry if your lines do not wrap at the same locations shown in Figure 1-18. Where the line wraps in the HTML code does not affect how the page is rendered by the browser.

6. Save your changes to the file and then refresh the **jprop.htm** file in your Web browser. Figure 1-19 shows the new paragraphs added to the Web page.

Figure 1-19   Paragraphs in the Web page

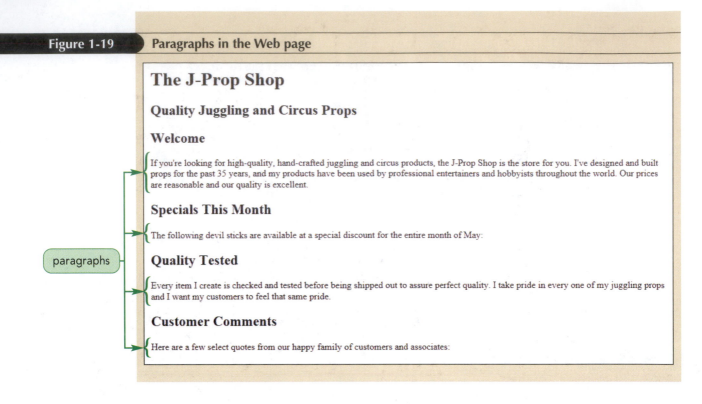

Marking a Block Quote

Next, Dave wants you to enter a few select quotes from his satisfied customers. You mark extended quotes with the HTML `blockquote` element, which uses the syntax

```
<blockquote>content</blockquote>
```

where `content` is the text of the quote. Most browsers render block quotes by indenting them to make it easier for readers to separate quoted material from the author's own words. You'll add the customer comments as block quotes.

To create the customer comment block quotes:

1. Return to the **jprop.htm** file in your text editor.

2. Scroll down to the `aside` element, and after the paragraph within that element, insert the following block quote, as shown in Figure 1-20:

```
<blockquote>
    <p>"I'm more than happy to recommend Dave Vinet's
        products. I came upon his work 10 years ago and
        was immediately impressed by his craftsmanship.
        He provides well-balanced and attractive
        props which are the perfect complement to my
        performances."
    </p>
    <p>"Dave Vinet makes the best juggling equipment on
        the planet. Period."
    </p>
    <p>"David has been my main supplier for 20 years. I
        have never had a problem with his equipment and
        his service is impeccable."
    </p>
</blockquote>
```

Figure 1-20	Adding a block quote

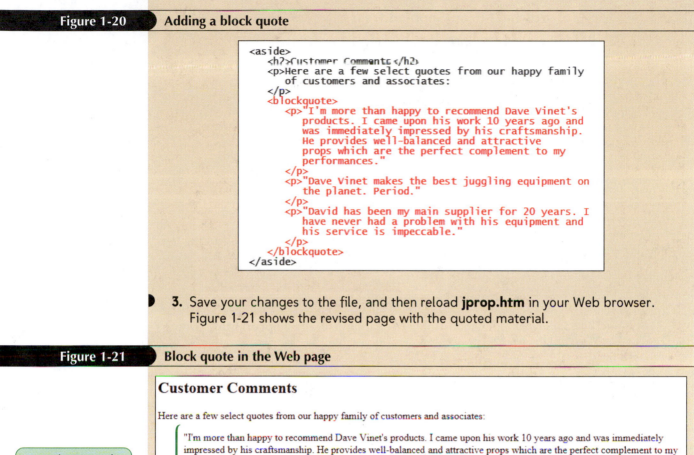

```
<aside>
    <h2>Customer Comments </h2>
    <p>Here are a few select quotes from our happy family
        of customers and associates:
    </p>
    <blockquote>
        <p>"I'm more than happy to recommend Dave Vinet's
            products. I came upon his work 10 years ago and
            was immediately impressed by his craftsmanship.
            He provides well-balanced and attractive
            props which are the perfect complement to my
            performances."
        </p>
        <p>"Dave Vinet makes the best juggling equipment on
            the planet. Period."
        </p>
        <p>"David has been my main supplier for 20 years. I
            have never had a problem with his equipment and
            his service is impeccable."
        </p>
    </blockquote>
</aside>
```

3. Save your changes to the file, and then reload **jprop.htm** in your Web browser. Figure 1-21 shows the revised page with the quoted material.

Figure 1-21	Block quote in the Web page

Customer Comments

Here are a few select quotes from our happy family of customers and associates:

> quoted paragraphs are indented in the page

> "I'm more than happy to recommend Dave Vinet's products. I came upon his work 10 years ago and was immediately impressed by his craftsmanship. He provides well-balanced and attractive props which are the perfect complement to my performances."
>
> "Dave Vinet makes the best juggling equipment on the planet. Period."
>
> "David has been my main supplier for 20 years. I have never had a problem with his equipment and his service is impeccable."

Note that the customer quote also included three paragraph elements nested within the blockquote element. The indentation applied by the browser to the block quote was also applied to any content within that element, so those paragraphs were indented even though browsers do not indent paragraphs by default.

Marking an Address

Dave wants to display the company's address at the bottom of the body of his page. Contact information such as addresses can be marked using the address element, which uses the syntax

```
<address>content</address>
```

where *content* is the contact information. Most browsers render addresses in italic. You'll use the address element to display the address of the J-Prop Shop.

To add the J-Prop Shop address:

1. Return to the **jprop.htm** file in your text editor.

2. Scroll down to the bottom of the file, and then within the `footer` element insert the following code, as shown in Figure 1-22:

```
<address>The J-Prop Shop
         541 West Highland Drive
         Auburn, ME 04210
         (207) 555 - 9001
</address>
```

Figure 1-22	Adding an address

```
<footer>
    <address>The J-Prop Shop
             541 West Highland Drive
             Auburn, ME 04210
             (207) 555 - 9001
    </address>
</footer>
</body>
```

3. Save your changes to the file, and then refresh **jprop.htm** in your Web browser. Figure 1-23 shows the revised page with the address text.

Figure 1-23	Address as rendered in the Web page

Customer Comments

Here are a few select quotes from our happy family of customers and associates:

"I'm more than happy to recommend Dave Vinet's products. I came upon his work 10 years ago and was immediately impressed by his craftsmanship. He provides well-balanced and attractive props which are the perfect complement to my performances."

"Dave Vinet makes the best juggling equipment on the planet. Period."

"David has been my main supplier for 20 years. I have never had a problem with his equipment and his service is impeccable."

address text is displayed in italic by default → *The J-Prop Shop 541 West Highland Drive Auburn, ME 04210 (207) 555 - 9001*

The address text appears in italic at the bottom of the page. Note that even though you entered the company name, street address, city, state, and phone number on multiple lines, in the browser they all appear to run together on a single line. Remember that the browser ignores the occurrence of line breaks, tabs, and other white space in your text document. Shortly, you'll learn how to make this text more readable by adding a character symbol to separate the different parts of the address. For now, you'll leave the address text as it is.

Marking a List

Dave wants to display a list of products on this sample page. This information is presented on his flyer as a bulleted list. He wants something similar on the Web site. HTML supports three kinds of lists: ordered, unordered, and description.

REFERENCE

Marking Lists

- To mark an ordered list, enter

```
<ol>
    <li>item1</li>
    <li>item2</li>
...
</ol>
```

where *item1*, *item2*, and so forth are the items in the list.
- To mark an unordered list, enter

```
<ul>
    <li>item1</li>
    <li>item2</li>
...
</ul>
```

- To mark a description list, enter

```
<dl>
    <dt>term1</dt>
    <dd>description1</dd>
    <dt>term2</dt>
    <dd>description2a</dd>
    <dd>description2b</dd>
...
</dl>
```

where *term1*, *term2*, etc. are the terms in the list and *description1*, *description2a*, *description2b*, etc. are descriptions associated with the preceding terms.

Ordered Lists

Ordered lists are used for items that follow some defined sequential order, such as lists ordered from smallest to greatest or from oldest to youngest. The beginning of an ordered list is marked by the `<ol>` (ordered list) tag. Each item within an ordered list is marked using the `<li>` (list item) tag. The structure of an ordered list is therefore

```
<ol>
    <li>item1</li>
    <li>item2</li>
...
</ol>
```

where *item1*, *item2*, and so forth are the items in the list. To explore creating an ordered list, you'll return to the HTML demo page.

To create an ordered list:

1. Return to the **demo_html.htm** file in your Web browser.

2. Delete the HTML code in the left box and replace it with the following:

```
<ol>
    <li>First Item</li>
    <li>Second Item</li>
    <li>Third Item</li>
</ol>
```

3. Click the **Preview Code** button. Figure 1-24 shows how the browser renders the ordered list contents.

Figure 1-24 **Viewing an ordered list**

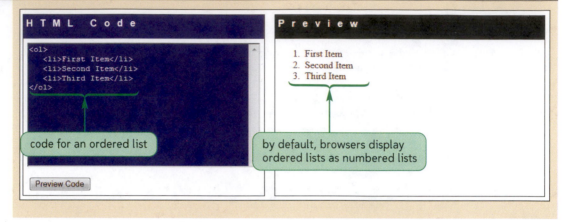

By default, entries in an ordered list are numbered, with the numbers added automatically by the browser.

Unordered Lists

To mark a list in which the items are not expected to occur in any specific order, you create an **unordered list**. The structure of ordered and unordered lists is the same, except that the list items for an unordered list are nested within the ul element, as follows:

```
<ul>
    <li>item1</li>
    <li>item2</li>
...
</ul>
```

You'll practice creating an unordered list with the demo page.

To create an unordered list:

1. Delete the HTML code in the left box and replace it with the following:

```
<ul>
    <li>Basic Stick</li>
    <li>Flower Stick</li>
    <li>Master Stick</li>
    <li>Glow Stick</li>
</ul>
```

2. Click the **Preview Code** button. Figure 1-25 shows how the browser renders the unordered list.

Figure 1-25   **Viewing an unordered list**

code for an unordered list

by default, browsers display unordered lists as bulleted lists

Trouble? In some browsers, the list appears with diamond shapes rather than circular bullets.

By default, most browsers display unordered lists using a bullet symbol. The exact bullet symbol depends on the browser, but most browsers use a filled-in circle.

Nesting Lists

You can place one list inside of another to create several levels of list items. The top level of a nested list contains the major items, with each sublevel containing items of lesser importance. Most browsers differentiate the various levels by increasing the indentation and using a different list symbol at each level. You'll use the demo page to see how this works with unordered lists.

To create a nested list:

1. Click after the word *Stick* in the `<li>Basic Stick</li>` line, and then press the **Enter** key to insert a new blank line.

2. Indent the following code between the code `<li>Basic Stick` and the closing `</li>` tag:

   ```
   <ul>
       <li>Red</li>
       <li>Blue</li>
       <li>Green</li>
   </ul>
   ```

3. Click the **Preview Code** button. Figure 1-26 shows the resulting nested list in the browser.

Figure 1-26   Viewing a nested list

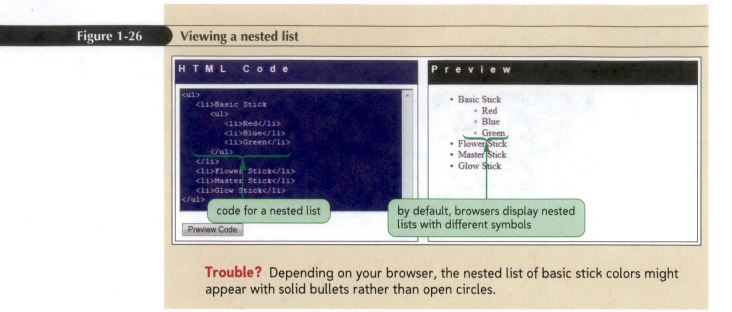

Trouble? Depending on your browser, the nested list of basic stick colors might appear with solid bullets rather than open circles.

The lower level of items is displayed using an open circle as the list bullet and additional indentation on the page. Once again, the exact format applied to these lists is determined by each browser's internal style sheet.

Description Lists

A third type of list is the **description list**, which contains a list of terms, each followed by its description. The structure of a description list is

```
<dl>
    <dt>term1</dt>
    <dd>description1</dd>
    <dt>term2</dt>
    <dd>description2a</dd>
    <dd>description2b</dd>
...
</dl>
```

where *term1*, *term2*, etc. are the terms in the list and *description1*, *description2a*, *description2b*, etc. are the descriptions associated with the terms. Note that description lists must follow a specified order, with each dt (definition term) element followed by one or more dd (definition description) elements.

You'll study how to work with description lists by returning to the demo page.

To create a description list:

1. Replace the code in the left box of the HTML demo page with

```
<dl>
    <dt>Basic Stick</dt>
    <dd>Easiest stick to learn</dd>
    <dt>Flower Stick</dt>
    <dd>A graceful stick with tassels</dd>
    <dt>Master Stick</dt>
    <dd>Our most popular stick</dd>
</dl>
```

> **2.** Click the **Preview Code** button. Figure 1-27 shows the appearance of the description list in the browser.

Figure 1-27 **Viewing a description list**

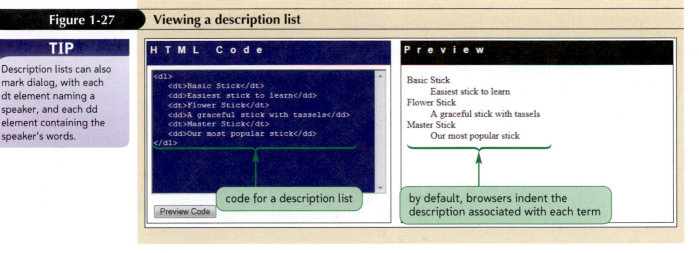

The demo page shows each term followed by its description, which is placed in a new block below the term and indented on the page. If you had included multiple dd elements for a single dt element, each description would have been contained within its own block and indented.

Now that you've experimented with the three types of HTML lists, you'll add an unordered list of products to Dave's Web page. By default, the product names will appear as a bulleted list.

To add an unordered list to Dave's Web page:

> **1.** Return to the **jprop.htm** file in your text editor.

> **2.** Within the Specials This Month article, directly below the p element, insert the following code, as shown in Figure 1-28:

```
<ul>
   <li>Basic Stick ($19.95)
        The easiest stick to learn with, but "grippy" enough
        for the most demanding tricks. Comes in red, green,
        and blue.
   </li>
   <li>Flower Stick ($24.95)
        A graceful stick with colored tassels. Flower Sticks
        float slowly, making them ideal for beginners.
   </li>
   <li>Master Stick ($39.95)
        Our most popular stick is shorter and heavier for
        fast play and more advanced tricks. Each Master Stick
        is available in custom colors.
   </li>
   <li>Glow Stick ($29.95)
        The Glow Stick shines brightly at night (without
        the danger of a fire stick).
   </li>
   </ul>
```

Figure 1-28   **Adding an unordered list**

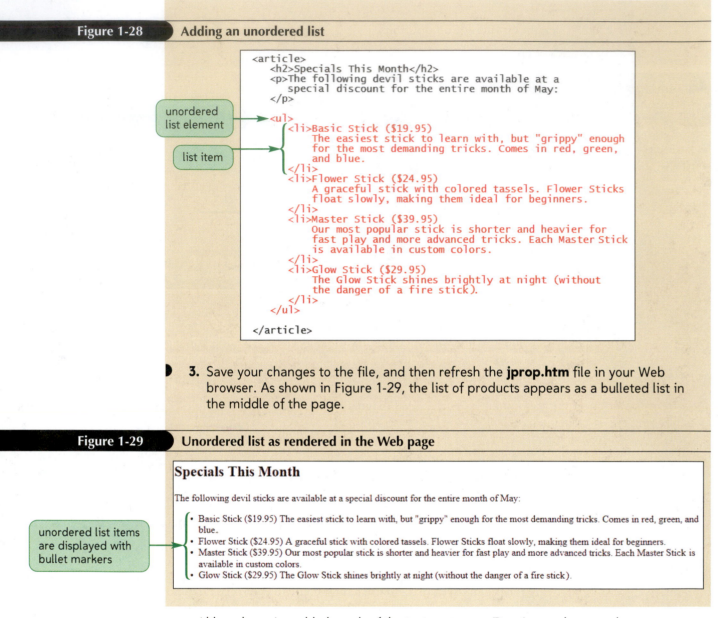

unordered list element

list item

```
<article>
   <h2>Specials This Month</h2>
   <p>The following devil sticks are available at a
      special discount for the entire month of May:
   </p>

   <ul>
      <li>Basic Stick ($19.95)
         The easiest stick to learn with, but "grippy" enough
         for the most demanding tricks. Comes in red, green,
         and blue.
      </li>
      <li>Flower Stick ($24.95)
         A graceful stick with colored tassels. Flower Sticks
         float slowly, making them ideal for beginners.
      </li>
      <li>Master Stick ($39.95)
         Our most popular stick is shorter and heavier for
         fast play and more advanced tricks. Each Master Stick
         is available in custom colors.
      </li>
      <li>Glow Stick ($29.95)
         The Glow Stick shines brightly at night (without
         the danger of a fire stick).
      </li>
   </ul>

</article>
```

3. Save your changes to the file, and then refresh the **jprop.htm** file in your Web browser. As shown in Figure 1-29, the list of products appears as a bulleted list in the middle of the page.

Figure 1-29   **Unordered list as rendered in the Web page**

Specials This Month

The following devil sticks are available at a special discount for the entire month of May:

unordered list items are displayed with bullet markers

- Basic Stick ($19.95) The easiest stick to learn with, but "grippy" enough for the most demanding tricks. Comes in red, green, and blue.
- Flower Stick ($24.95) A graceful stick with colored tassels. Flower Sticks float slowly, making them ideal for beginners.
- Master Stick ($39.95) Our most popular stick is shorter and heavier for fast play and more advanced tricks. Each Master Stick is available in custom colors.
- Glow Stick ($29.95) The Glow Stick shines brightly at night (without the danger of a fire stick).

Although you've added much of the text content to Dave's sample page, the page as rendered by the browser still looks nothing like the flyer shown in Figure 1-7. That's because all of the page elements have been rendered using your browser's internal style sheet. To change the page's appearance, you need to substitute your own style sheet for the browser's internal one.

Applying an External Style Sheet

Style sheets are written in the **Cascading Style Sheet (CSS)** language. Like HTML files, CSS files are text files and can be created and edited using a simple text editor. A style sheet file has the file extension .css, which distinguishes it from an HTML file. Dave already has a style sheet for his Web page stored in the file *jpsstyles.css*.

Linking to an External Style Sheet

To apply an external style sheet to a Web page, you create a link within the document head to the style sheet file using the `link` element

```
<link href="file" rel="stylesheet" type="text/css" />
```

where `file` is the filename and location of the style sheet file. When a browser loads the page, it substitutes the style from the external style sheet file for its own internal style sheet.

   See how the format and layout of Dave's sample page change when the page is linked to the *jpsstyles.css* file.

To apply Dave's external style sheet:

 1. Return to the **jprop.htm** file in your text editor.

 2. Within the head element at the top of the file, insert the following link element, as shown in Figure 1-30:

```
<link href="jpsstyles.css" rel="stylesheet" type="text/css" />
```

Figure 1-30   **Linking to the jpsstyles.css style sheet**

```
<!DOCTYPE html>
<html>

    <head>
    <!-- The J-Prop Shop Sample Page
         Author: David Vinet
         Date:   3/1/2014
    -->
        <title>The J-Prop Shop</title>
        <link href="jpsstyles.css" rel="stylesheet" type="text/css" />
    </head>
```

link element →

filename of style sheet

style sheet language

 3. Save your changes to the file.

 4. Reload the **jprop.htm** file in your Web browser. As shown in Figure 1-31, the format and the layout change to reflect the styles in Dave's style sheet.

Figure 1-31 **Web page rendered with the jpsstyles.css style sheet**

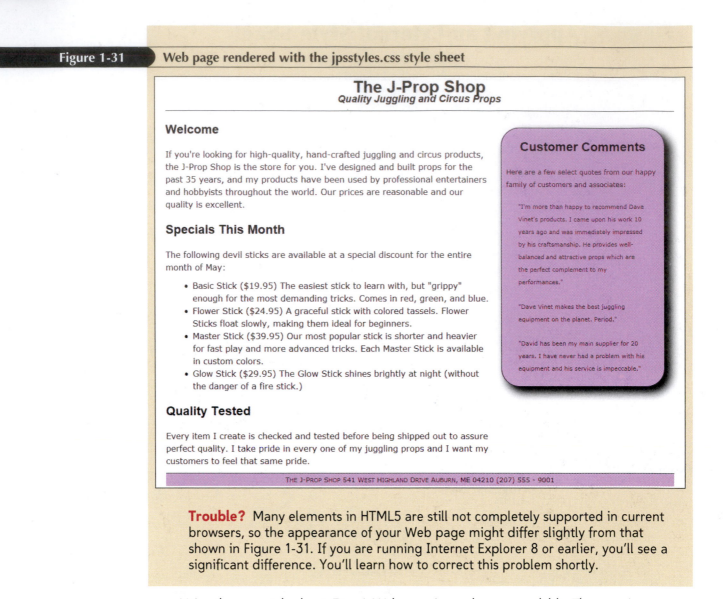

Trouble? Many elements in HTML5 are still not completely supported in current browsers, so the appearance of your Web page might differ slightly from that shown in Figure 1-31. If you are running Internet Explorer 8 or earlier, you'll see a significant difference. You'll learn how to correct this problem shortly.

Using the new style sheet, Dave's Web page is much more readable. The page is displayed in a two-column layout with the main content of the `section` element displayed in the left column. The content of the `aside` element is shown as a sidebar in the right column with a light purple background, rounded corners, and a drop shadow. The content of the `footer` element is styled with a smaller font, a top border line, and a light purple background.

Styles for HTML5 Elements

The `section`, `aside`, and `footer` elements used in the code of the *jprop.htm* file are new HTML5 elements that were not part of earlier HTML specifications. For most browsers this is not a problem, and the Web page should be rendered with a format and layout close to what Dave requested. An important exception, though, is the Internet Explorer browser. Internet Explorer version 8 and earlier versions provide almost no support for HTML5 and do not recognize styles applied to HTML5 elements. For example, as Figure 1-32 shows, even with the new style sheet, Internet Explorer 8 displays Dave's Web page with a few of the styles shown in Figure 1-31.

Figure 1-32   **Web page as it appears in Internet Explorer 8**

The J-Prop Shop

Quality Juggling and Circus Props

Welcome

If you're looking for high-quality, hand-crafted juggling and circus products, the J-Prop Shop is the store for you. I've designed and built props for the past 35 years, and my products have been used by professional entertainers and hobbyists throughout the world. Our prices are reasonable and our quality is excellent.

Specials This Month

The following devil sticks are available at a special discount for the entire month of May:

- Basic Stick ($19.95) The easiest stick to learn with, but "grippy" enough for the most demanding tricks. Comes in red, green, and blue.
- Flower Stick ($24.95) A graceful stick with colored tassels. Flower Sticks float slowly, making them ideal for beginners.
- Master Stick ($39.95) Our most popular stick is shorter and heavier for fast play and more advanced tricks. Each Master Stick is available in custom colors.
- Glow Stick ($29.95) The Glow Stick shines brightly at night (without the danger of a fire stick).

Quality Tested

Every item I create is checked and tested before being shipped out to assure perfect quality. I take pride in every one of my juggling props and I want my customers to feel that same pride.

Customer Comments

Here are a few select quotes from our happy family of customers and associates:

"I'm more than happy to recommend Dave Vinet's products. I came upon his work 10 years ago and was immediately impressed by his craftsmanship. He provides well-balanced and attractive props which are the perfect complement to my performances."

"Dave Vinet makes the best juggling equipment on the planet. Period."

"David has been my main supplier for 20 years. I have never had a problem with his equipment and his service is impeccable."

The J-Prop Shop 541 West Highland Drive Auburn, ME 04210 (207) 555 - 9001

Dave needs this problem fixed because he can't assume that users will always be running the latest version of Internet Explorer. Workarounds for this problem involve running an external program known as a **script**. The most often used program language for the Web is **JavaScript**. Like HTML and CSS files, JavaScript files are text files that require no special software other than a Web browser to run. At this point, you don't need to know how to write a JavaScript program to correct Internet Explorer's problem with HTML5 elements; someone else has already done that. You just need to know how to access and run their program.

One of the most useful programs to enable HTML5 support in older browsers is Modernizr. **Modernizr** is a free, open-source, MIT-licensed JavaScript library of functions that provides support for many HTML5 elements and for the newest CSS styles. One of the many uses of Modernizr is to enable support for HTML5 in older browsers. Modernizr is distributed in a single JavaScript file that you can download from *www.modernizr.com* and add to your Web site. To link a Web page to a JavaScript file, you add the `script` element

```
<script src="file"></script>
```

to the document head, where *file* is the name of the JavaScript file. The current version of Modernizr at the time of this writing is stored in the file *modernizr-1.5.js*. To link to this file, you add the following to the document head:

```
<script src="modernizr-1.5.js"></script>
```

The *modernizr-1.5.js* file has already been added to your data folder. Link to this file now to apply it to Dave's Web page.

To link to the Modernizr file:

1. Return to the **jprop.htm** file in your text editor.

2. Scroll to the top of the file and add the following tag pair above the `link` element, as shown in Figure 1-33:

```
<script src="modernizr-1.5.js"></script>
```

Figure 1-33	Linking to the Modernizr script

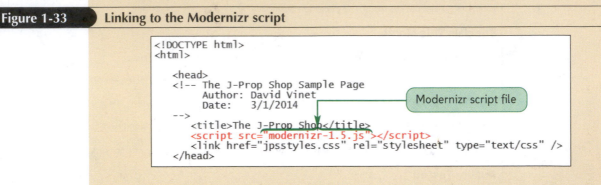

```
<!DOCTYPE html>
<html>

    <head>
    <!-- The J-Prop Shop Sample Page
        Author: David Vinet
        Date:    3/1/2014
    -->
        <title>The J-Prop Shop</title>
        <script src="modernizr-1.5.js"></script>
        <link href="jpsstyles.css" rel="stylesheet" type="text/css" />
    </head>
```

Modernizr script file

3. Save your changes to the file.

4. If you have access to Internet Explorer 8, use that browser to open the **jprop.htm** file. As shown in Figure 1-34, the browser renders the Web page employing the page layout and many of the formats shown earlier in Figure 1-29.

Figure 1-34	Web page as it appears in Internet Explorer 8 with Modernizr

The J-Prop Shop
Quality Juggling and Circus Props

Welcome

If you're looking for high-quality, hand-crafted juggling and circus products, the J-Prop Shop is the store for you. I've designed and built props for the past 35 years, and my products have been used by professional entertainers and hobbyists throughout the world. Our prices are reasonable and our quality is excellent.

Specials This Month

The following devil sticks are available at a special discount for the entire month of May:

- Basic Stick ($19.95) The easiest stick to learn with, but "grippy" enough for the most demanding tricks. Comes in red, green, and blue.
- Flower Stick ($24.95) A graceful stick with colored tassels. Flower Sticks float slowly, making them ideal for beginners.
- Master Stick ($39.95) Our most popular stick is shorter and heavier for fast play and more advanced tricks. Each Master Stick is available in custom colors.
- Glow Stick ($29.95) The Glow Stick shines brightly at night (without the danger of a fire stick).

Quality Tested

Every item I create is checked and tested before being shipped out to assure perfect quality. I take pride in every one of my juggling props and I want my customers to feel that same pride.

Customer Comments

Here are a few select quotes from our happy family of customers and associates:

"I'm more than happy to recommend Dave Vinet's products. I came upon his work 10 years ago and was immediately impressed by his craftsmanship. He provides well-balanced and attractive props which are the perfect complement to my performances."

"Dave Vinet makes the best juggling equipment on the planet. Period."

"David has been my main supplier for 20 years. I have never had a problem with his equipment and his service is impeccable."

rounded corners and drop shadows are not supported in IE8

The J-Prop Shop 541 West Highland Drive Auburn, ME 04210 (207) 555 - 9001

The rendering done by Internet Explorer 8 does not completely match what was shown under Internet Explorer 9 or many of the other competing browsers such as Firefox, Safari, or Google Chrome. For example, Internet Explorer 8 doesn't support styles for rounded corners and drop shadows. All of this underscores an important point: You may find variations between one browser and another in how your page is rendered, especially when using the newest HTML5 elements and CSS styles. This means you have to test your page under multiple browsers and devices, and make sure that any differences in format or layout do not impact your users' ability to read and understand your page.

Marking Text-Level Elements

Grouping elements like paragraphs and headings start their content on a new line. Another type of element is a **text-level element**, which marks content within a grouping element. A text-level element is like a phrase or a collection of characters within a paragraph or heading. Text-level elements do not start out on a new line, but instead flow alongside of, or **inline** with, the rest of the characters in the grouping element. Figure 1-35 lists some of the text-level elements in HTML.

| Figure 1-35 | Text-level elements |

Text-Level Element	Description
a	A hypertext link
abbr	An abbreviation
b	Text offset from the surrounding content (usually displayed in **boldface** text)
cite	A citation (usually displayed in *italics*)
code	Program code (usually displayed in a `fixed width` font)
del	Deleted text (usually displayed with a ~~strikethrough~~ line)
dfn	A definition term (usually displayed in *italics*)
em	Emphasized content (usually displayed in *italics*)
i	Text representing an alternate voice or mood (usually displayed in *italics*)
ins	Inserted text (usually displayed with an underline)
kbd	Keyboard text (usually displayed in a `fixed width` font)
mark	Highlighted or marked text (usually displayed with a highlight. HTML5 only)
q	Quoted text (occasionally enclosed in "quotes")
samp	Sample computer code (usually displayed in a `fixed width` font)
small	Text displayed in a smaller font than surrounding content
span	A span of generic text
strong	Strongly emphasized content (usually displayed in **boldface** text)
sub	Subscripted text
sup	Superscripted text
time	A date and time value (HTML5 only)
var	Programming variables (usually displayed in *italic*)

TIP

Text-level elements should always be nested within grouping elements such as paragraphs or headings.

To practice using text-level elements in conjunction with grouping elements, you'll return to the HTML demo page.

To explore the use of inline elements:

1. Return to the **demo_html.htm** file in your Web browser.

2. Replace the code in the HTML Code box with the following:

```
<p>Welcome to the J-Prop Shop, owned and operated by David
Vinet</p>
```

3. Click the **Preview Code** button to display this paragraph in the Preview box.

   To mark *J-Prop Shop* as strongly emphasized text, you can enclose that phrase within a set of `<strong>` tags.

4. Insert the `<strong>` opening tag directly before the word *J-Prop* in the box on the left. Insert the closing `</strong>` tag directly after the word *Shop*. Click the **Preview Code** button to confirm that *J-Prop Shop* is now displayed in a bold-faced font.

   Another text-level element is the `cite` element used to make citations. Explore how citations are rendered by your browser by enclosing *David Vinet* within a set of `<cite>` tags.

5. Insert an opening `<cite>` tag directly before the word *David* and insert the closing `</cite>` tag directly after *Vinet*. Click the **Preview Code** button to view the revised code. Figure 1-36 shows the result of applying the `<strong>` and `<cite>` tags to the paragraph text.

Figure 1-36	Applying the strong and cite text-level elements

6. Continue exploring other HTML elements listed in Figure 1-35 to see their effects on the rendered text. Close the demo file when you're done.

You can nest text-level tags to mark a single text string with more than one element. For example, the HTML code

```
<p>Welcome to the <strong><em>J-Prop Shop</em></strong>.</p>
```

marks the text string *J-Prop Shop* as both strong and emphasized text. In most browsers it appears in a ***bold italic*** font.

Dave wants the names of all of the items in his product list to be marked as strong text. Revise the code for the product names now.

To mark strong text:

1. Return to the **jprop.htm** file in your text editor.

2. Scroll down to the unordered list and enclose the name and price of each product within a set of `<strong>` tags as shown in Figure 1-37.

Figure 1-37   **Marking product names using the strong element**

```
<article>
    <h2>Specials This Month</h2>
    <p>The following devil sticks are available at a
        special discount for the entire month of May:
    </p>

    <ul>
        <li><strong>Basic Stick ($19.95)</strong>
            The easiest stick to learn with, but "grippy" enough
            for the most demanding tricks. Comes in red, green,
            and blue.
        </li>
        <li><strong>Flower Stick ($24.95)</strong>
            A graceful stick with colored tassels. Flower Sticks
            float slowly, making them ideal for beginners.
        </li>
        <li><strong>Master Stick ($39.95)</strong>
            Our most popular stick is shorter and heavier for
            fast play and more advanced tricks. Each Master Stick
            is available in custom colors.
        </li>
        <li><strong>Glow Stick ($29.95)</strong>
            The Glow Stick shines brightly at night (without
            the danger of a fire stick).
        </li>
    </ul>

</article>
```

3. Save your changes to the file and then reload the **jprop.htm** file in your Web browser. Figure 1-38 shows the revised appearance of the bulleted list of products.

Figure 1-38   **Product names rendered in a boldfaced font**

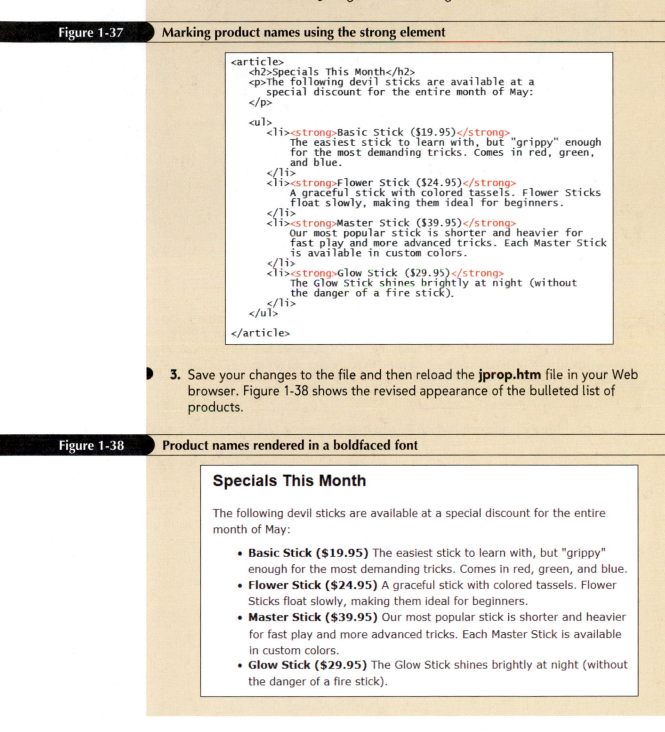

Specials This Month

The following devil sticks are available at a special discount for the entire month of May:

- **Basic Stick ($19.95)** The easiest stick to learn with, but "grippy" enough for the most demanding tricks. Comes in red, green, and blue.
- **Flower Stick ($24.95)** A graceful stick with colored tassels. Flower Sticks float slowly, making them ideal for beginners.
- **Master Stick ($39.95)** Our most popular stick is shorter and heavier for fast play and more advanced tricks. Each Master Stick is available in custom colors.
- **Glow Stick ($29.95)** The Glow Stick shines brightly at night (without the danger of a fire stick).

Written Communication: Logical and Physical Interpretation of Elements

As you learn more HTML, you'll notice some overlap in how browsers display certain elements. To display italicized text, you could use the `<dfn>`, `<em>`, `<i>`, or `<var>` tags; or if you wanted to italicize an entire block of text, you could use the `<address>` tag. However, browsers differ in how they display elements, so you should not rely on the way any browser or group of browsers commonly displays an element.

In addition, it's important to distinguish between the way a browser displays an element, and the purpose of the element in the document. Although it can be tempting to ignore this difference, your HTML code benefits when you respect that distinction because search engines often look within specific elements for information. For example, a search engine may look for the `address` element to find contact information for a particular Web site. It would be confusing to end users if you used the `address` element to simply italicize a block of text. Web programmers can also use elements to extract information from a page. For example, a JavaScript program could automatically generate a bibliography from all of the citations listed within a Web site by looking for occurrences of the `cite` element.

The best practice for communicating the purpose of your document is to use HTML to mark content but not to rely on HTML to format that content. Formatting should be done solely through style sheets, using either the internal style sheets built into browsers or through your own customized styles.

Using the Generic Elements **div** and **span**

Most of the page elements you've examined have a specific meaning. However, sometimes you want to add an element that represents a text block or a string of inline text without it having any other meaning. HTML supports two such generic elements: `div` and `span`. The `div` element is used to mark general grouping content and has the following syntax:

```
<div>content</div>
```

The `span` element, which is used to mark general text-level content, has the following syntax:

```
<span>content</span>
```

Browsers recognize both elements but do not assign any default format to content marked with these elements. This frees Web authors to develop styles for these elements without worrying about overriding any styles imposed by browsers. Note that the main use of the `div` element to mark sections of the page has been superseded in HTML5 by the sectional elements such as `header` and `article`; however, you will still encounter the `div` element in many current and older Web sites.

Presentational Attributes

Early versions of HTML were used mostly by scientists and researchers who, for the most part, didn't need flashy graphics, decorative text fonts, or even much color on a page. The earliest Web pages weren't fancy and didn't require much from the browsers that displayed them. This changed as the Web became more popular and attracted the attention of commercial businesses, graphic designers, and artists.

One way that HTML changed to accommodate this new class of users was to introduce **presentational elements** and **presentational attributes** designed to describe how each element should be rendered by Web browsers. For example, to align text on a page, Web authors would use the `align` attribute

```
<element align="alignment">content</element>
```

where *alignment* is either *left*, *right*, *center*, or *justify*. Thus, to center an `h1` heading on a page, you could apply the following `align` attribute to the `<h1>` tag:

```
<h1 align="center">The J-Prop Shop</h1>
```

Almost all presentational elements and attributes are now deprecated in favor of style sheets, but you may still see them used in older Web sites. Using a deprecated attribute like `align` would probably not cause a Web page to fail, but it's still best to focus your HTML code on describing the content of a document and not its appearance.

Marking a Line Break

After examining your work, Dave notices that the list of customer comments lacks the names of the customers who made them. He asks you to add this information to the Web page, marking the customer information as citations.

To append customer names to the Customer Comments section:

1. Return to the **jprop.htm** file in your text editor.

2. Locate the first customer comment and then add the following code at the end of the paragraph, directly before the closing `</p>` tag:

   ```
   <cite>Thomas Gage, Circus England</cite>
   ```

3. At the end of the paragraph for the second customer comment, insert

   ```
   <cite>Douglas Pederson, Street-Wise Shows</cite>
   ```

4. Finally, at the end of the paragraph for the third customer comment, insert

   ```
   <cite>Linda Unger, Linda & Louis</cite>
   ```

   Figure 1-39 shows the revised code in the file.

Figure 1-39 **Providing citations for the customer quotes**

```
<aside>
   <h2>Customer Comments</h2>
   <p>Here are a few select quotes from our happy family
      of customers and associates:
   </p>
   <blockquote>
      <p>"I'm more than happy to recommend Dave Vinet's
         products. I came upon his work 10 years ago and
         was immediately impressed by his craftsmanship.
         He provides well-balanced and attractive
         props which are the perfect complement to my
         performances."
         <cite>Thomas Gage, Circus England</cite>
      </p>
      <p>"Dave Vinet makes the best juggling equipment on
         the planet. Period."
         <cite>Douglas Pederson, Street-Wise Shows</cite>
      </p>
      <p>"David has been my main supplier for 20 years. I
         have never had a problem with his equipment and
         his service is impeccable."
         <cite>Linda Unger, Linda & Louis</cite>
      </p>
   </blockquote>
</aside>
```

5. Save your changes to the file and then refresh the **jprop.htm** file in your Web browser. Figure 1-40 shows the revised text of the Customer Comments sidebar.

Figure 1-40 **Revised Customer Comments sidebar**

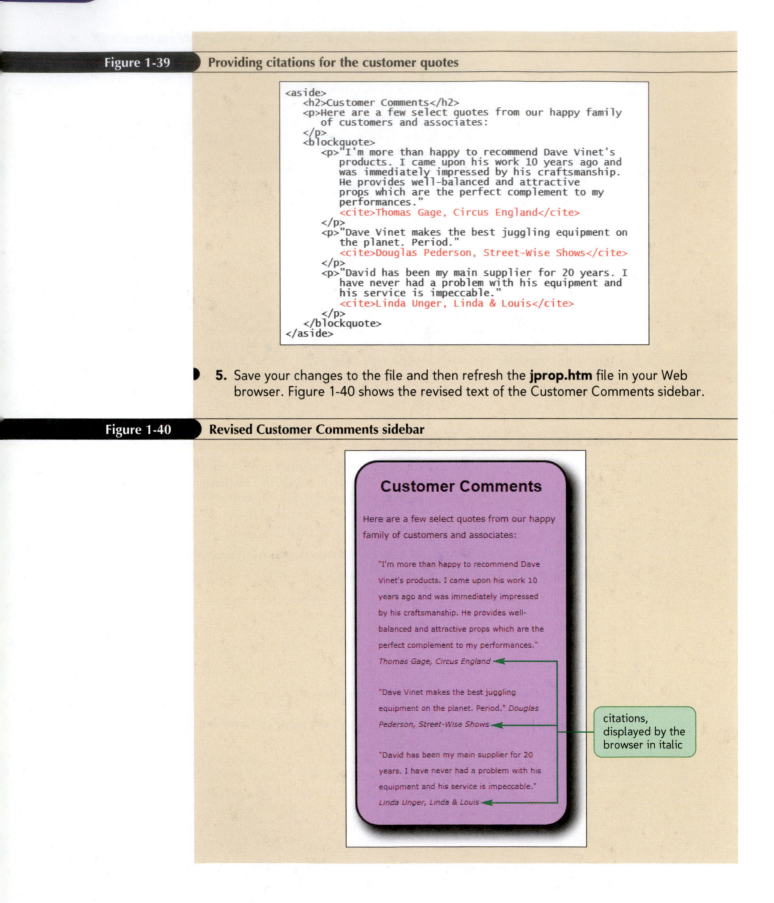

citations, displayed by the browser in italic

Dave thinks the comments are difficult to read when the text of a comment runs into the citation. He suggests that you start each citation on a new line. To do this, you can insert a line break into the Web page using the following empty element tag:

```
<br />
```

Line breaks must be placed within grouping elements such as paragraphs or headings. Some browsers accept line breaks placed anywhere within the body of a Web page; however, this is not good coding technique. A browser displaying an XHTML document will reject code in which a text-level element such as `br` is placed outside of any grouping element.

You'll use the `br` element to mark a line break between each customer comment and its associated citation in Dave's Web page.

To insert line breaks in the comments:

1. Return to the **jprop.htm** file in your text editor.

2. Insert the tag **
** between the comment and the citation for each of the three customer comments in the file. See Figure 1-41.

Figure 1-41	Inserting line breaks

```
<blockquote>
  <p>"I'm more than happy to recommend Dave Vinet's
     products. I came upon his work 10 years ago and
     was immediately impressed by his craftsmanship.
     He provides well-balanced and attractive
     props which are the perfect complement to my
     performances."
     <br />                    ← line break element
     <cite>Thomas Gage, Circus England</cite>
  </p>
  <p>"Dave Vinet makes the best juggling equipment on
     the planet. Period."
     <br />
     <cite>Douglas Pederson, Street-Wise Shows</cite>
  </p>
  <p>"David has been my main supplier for 20 years. I
     have never had a problem with his equipment and
     his service is impeccable."
     <br />
     <cite>Linda Unger, Linda & Louis</cite>
  </p>
</blockquote>
```

3. Save your changes to the file and then refresh the **jprop.htm** file in your Web browser. Verify that each citation starts on a new line below the associated customer comment.

INSIGHT

Marking a Horizontal Rule

Another empty element is `hr`, the horizontal rule element, which marks a major topic change within a section. The syntax of the `hr` element is as follows:

```
<hr />
```

The exact appearance of the `hr` element is left to the browser. Most browsers display a gray-shaded horizontal line a few pixels in height. The `hr` element was originally used as a quick way of inserting horizontal lines within a Web page. Although that task now should be left to style sheets, you will still see the `hr` element in older Web pages.

Inserting an Inline Image

Dave wants you to replace the name of the company at the top of his Web page with an image of the company logo. Because HTML files are simple text files, non-textual content such as graphics must be stored in separate files, which are then loaded by browsers as they render pages. To add a graphic image to a Web page, you have to insert an inline image into your code.

The img Element

Inline images are inserted into a Web page using the one-sided img element with the syntax

```
<img src="file" alt="text" />
```

where *file* is the name of the graphic image file and *text* is text displayed by browsers in place of the graphic image. In this tutorial, you'll assume that the graphic image file is located in the same folder as the Web page, so you don't have to specify the location of the file. In the next tutorial, you'll learn how to reference files placed in other folders or locations on the Web.

Browsers retrieve the specified image file and display the image alongside the rest of the Web page content. The size of the image is based on the dimensions of the image itself; however, you can specify a different size using the width and height attributes

```
width="value" height="value"
```

where the width and height values are expressed in pixels. If you specify only the width, browsers automatically set the height to maintain the proportions of the image; similarly, if you define the height, browsers automatically set the width to maintain the image proportions. Thus, by setting the width and height values yourself, you can enlarge or reduce the size of the rendered image.

Inline images are considered text-level elements and thus must be placed within a grouping element such as a heading or a paragraph. An inline image is most commonly stored in one of three formats: GIF (Graphics Interchange Format), JPEG (Joint Photographic Experts Group), or PNG (Portable Network Graphics). Dave has already created his graphic image in PNG format and stored it with his other files using the filename *jpslogo.png*. You'll replace the text of the h1 heading with this inline image.

To insert the company logo at the top of the page:

1. Return to the **jprop.htm** file in your text editor.

2. Go to the h1 heading element at the top of the body section, delete the text *The J-Prop Shop* from between the opening and closing <h1> tags, and then replace it with

```
<img src="jpslogo.png" alt="The J-Prop Shop" />
```

Figure 1-42 highlights the revised code in the **jprop.htm** file.

Figure 1-42   Adding an inline image

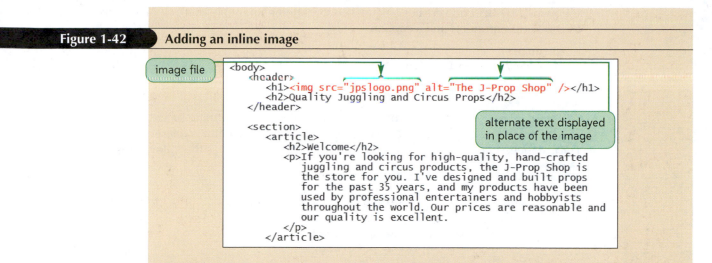

image file

```
<body>
    <header>
        <h1><img src="jpslogo.png" alt="The J-Prop Shop" /></h1>
        <h2>Quality Juggling and Circus Props</h2>
    </header>

    <section>
        <article>
            <h2>Welcome</h2>
            <p>If you're looking for high-quality, hand-crafted
            juggling and circus products, the J-Prop Shop is
            the store for you. I've designed and built props
            for the past 35 years, and my products have been
            used by professional entertainers and hobbyists
            throughout the world. Our prices are reasonable and
            our quality is excellent.
            </p>
        </article>
```

alternate text displayed in place of the image

3. Save your changes to the file, and then refresh the Web page in your browser. Figure 1-43 shows the new heading with the logo centered across the page.

Figure 1-43   Viewing the company logo

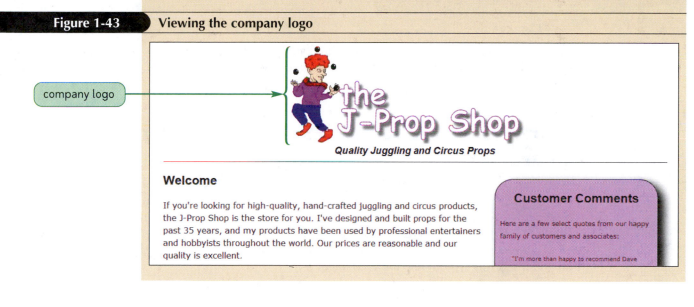

company logo

Figures and Figure Captions

In books and magazines, figures and figure captions are often placed within boxes that stand aside from the main content of an article. HTML5 introduced this type of object to Web page markup with the `figure` and `figcaption` elements

```
<figure>
    content
    <figcaption>caption</figcaption>
</figure>
```

where *content* is the content that will appear in the figure box and *caption* is the text of the figure caption. The `figcaption` element is optional; but if the `figcaption` element is used, it must be nested within a set of <figure> tags either directly after the opening <figure> tag or directly before the closing </figure> tag. For example, the following HTML5 code creates a figure box containing an inline image of one of the J-Prop Shop's products and a caption:

```
<figure>
   <img src="stick03.png" alt="Master Stick" />
   <figcaption>Master Stick ($39.95)</figcaption>
</figure>
```

The figure element doesn't necessarily need to contain an inline image. It can be used to mark any content that stands aside from a main article but is referenced by it. For instance, it could be used to contain an excerpt of a poem, as the following code demonstrates:

```
<figure>
   <p>'Twas brillig, and the slithy toves<br />
      Did gyre and gimble in the wabe;<br />
      All mimsy were the borogoves,<br />
      And the mome raths outgrabe.
   </p>
   <figcaption>
      <cite>Jabberwocky,
      Lewis Carroll, 1832-98</cite>
   </figcaption>
</figure>
```

As with other HTML elements, the exact appearance of a figure box is determined by a style sheet. At this time, Dave does not need to create a figure box for his company's home page.

Working with Character Sets and Special Characters

Dave likes the work you've done so far on the Web page. He has only one remaining concern: The company's address in the page footer is difficult to read because the street address, city name, zip code, and phone number all run together on one line. Dave would like to have the different parts of the address separated by a solid circular marker (•). However, this marker is not represented by any keys on your keyboard. How, then, do you insert this symbol into the Web page?

Character Sets

Every character that your browser is capable of rendering belongs to a collection of characters and symbols called a **character set**. Character sets come in a wide variety of sizes. For English, no more than about 127 characters are needed to represent all of the upper- and lowercase letters, numbers, punctuation marks, spaces, and special typing symbols in the language. Other languages, such as Japanese or Chinese, require character sets containing thousands of symbols. Beyond the basic characters used by a language are special characters such as ©, ½, π, and ®. Thus, a complete character set that includes all possible printable characters is made up of hundreds of symbols.

The character set used for the alphabet of English characters is called **ASCII** (**American Standard Code for Information Interchange**). A more extended character set, called **Latin-1** or the **ISO 8859-1** character set, supports 255 characters and can be used by most languages that employ the Latin alphabet, including English, French, Spanish, and Italian. **Unicode**, the most extended character set, supports up to 65,536 symbols and can be used for any of the world's languages. The most commonly used character set on the Web is **UTF-8**, which is a compressed version of Unicode and is probably the default character set assumed by your browser. You can learn more about character sets by visiting the W3C Web site and the Web site for the Internet Assigned Numbers Authority at *www.iana.org*.

Character Encoding

Character encoding associates each symbol from a character set with a numeric value called the **numeric character reference**. For example, the copyright symbol © from the UTF-8 character set is encoded with the number 169. If you know the character encoding number, you can insert the corresponding character directly into your Web page using the entity

        &#code;

where *code* is the encoding number. Thus, to display the © symbol in your Web page, you would enter

        ©

into your HTML file.

Character Entity References

Another way to insert a special symbol is to use a **character entity reference**, which is a short memorable name used in place of the encoding number. Character entity references are inserted using the syntax

        &char;

where *char* is the character's entity reference. The character entity reference for the copyright symbol is *copy*. So to display the © symbol in your Web page, you could insert

        ©

into your HTML code.

REFERENCE

Inserting Symbols from a Character Set

- To insert a symbol based on the encoding number, use the entity
    &#code;
    where *code* is the encoding number.
- To insert a symbol based on a character entity reference, use the entity
    &char;
    where *char* is the name assigned to the character.
- To insert a nonbreaking space, use the following entity:

- To insert the < symbol, use the following entity:
    <
- To insert the > symbol, use the following entity:
    >

You can explore various encoding numbers and character entity references by opening the demo page supplied with your Data Files.

To view the demo page:

1. Use your Web browser to open the **demo_characters.htm** file from the tutorial.01\demo data folder.

2. Type £ in the input box and then click the **Show** button. The Web browser displays the £ symbol in the ivory-colored box below.

3. Replace the value in the input box with ® and then click the **Show** button. The browser now displays the ® symbol, the symbol for registered trademarks, which you specified using a character entity reference.

   You can also view a collection of numeric character references and character entity references by selecting a table from the list box on the page.

4. Verify that General Symbols is displayed in the selection list box, and then click the **Show Table** button. As shown in Figure 1-44, the browser displays a list of 35 symbols with the character entity reference and the numeric character reference displayed beneath each symbol.

Figure 1-44 HTML characters demo page

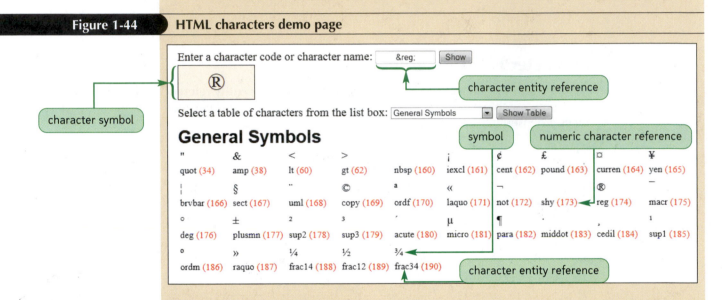

5. Take some time to explore the variety of numeric character references and character entity references supported by your browser. Close the demo page when you're finished, but leave your browser open.

INSIGHT

Special Characters

One use of character codes is to insert text about HTML itself. For example, if you want your Web page to describe the use of the `<h1>` tag, you cannot simply type

    The <h1> tag is used to mark h1 headings.

because browsers would interpret the `<h1>` text as marking the beginning of an h1 heading! Instead, you have to use the `&lt;` and `&gt;` entity references to insert the < and > symbols. The text would then be:

    The <h1> tag is used to mark h1 headings.

Another use of character codes is to add extra spaces to your Web page. Remember that browsers ignore extra blank spaces in an HTML file. To insert an additional space, use the ` ` entity reference (*nbsp* stands for *nonbreaking space*), which forces browsers to insert an extra space.

On Dave's Web page, you decide to use the bullet symbol (•) to break up the address text into sections. The symbol has a character encoding number of 8226 and the character entity reference name *bull*. Dave suggests that you also add a long horizontal line known as an em-dash (—) to mark the customer names in the customer comments section. The character encoding number for an em-dash is 0212 and the entity reference is *mdash*.

To add bullets and an em-dash to Dave's Web page:

1. Return to the **jprop.htm** file in your text editor.

2. Locate the customer comment from Thomas Gage, and then directly before the opening <cite> tag insert the character code `&#8212;` followed by a space.

3. Repeat Step 2 for the two remaining customer comments.

4. Scroll down to the `address` element within the page footer. At the end of each line within the address (except the last line), insert a space followed by the `&bull;` character entity. Figure 1-45 highlights the revised code in the Web page.

> Always include a semi-colon so that browsers recognize the entry as a character code.

Figure 1-45   Adding symbols from a character set

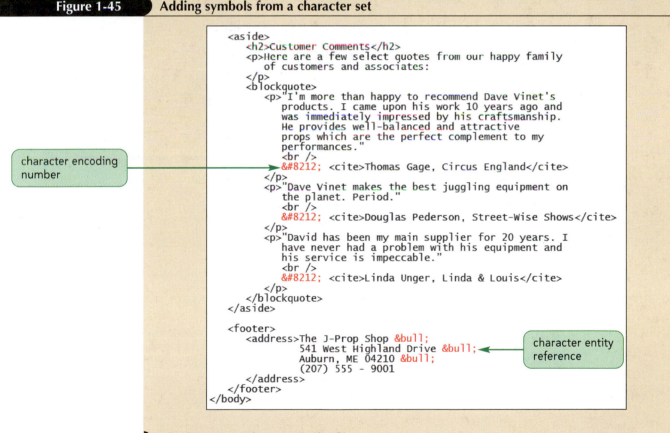

character encoding number

character entity reference

```
<aside>
  <h2>Customer Comments</h2>
  <p>Here are a few select quotes from our happy family
     of customers and associates:
  </p>
  <blockquote>
     <p>"I'm more than happy to recommend Dave Vinet's
        products. I came upon his work 10 years ago and
        was immediately impressed by his craftsmanship.
        He provides well-balanced and attractive
        props which are the perfect complement to my
        performances."
        <br />
        &#8212; <cite>Thomas Gage, Circus England</cite>
     </p>
     <p>"Dave Vinet makes the best juggling equipment on
        the planet. Period."
        <br />
        &#8212; <cite>Douglas Pederson, Street-Wise Shows</cite>
     </p>
     <p>"David has been my main supplier for 20 years. I
        have never had a problem with his equipment and
        his service is impeccable."
        <br />
        &#8212; <cite>Linda Unger, Linda & Louis</cite>
     </p>
  </blockquote>
</aside>

<footer>
  <address>The J-Prop Shop &bull;
           541 West Highland Drive &bull;
           Auburn, ME 04210 &bull;
           (207) 555 - 9001
  </address>
</footer>
</body>
```

5. Save your changes to the file.

6. Refresh the **jprop.htm** file in your Web browser. Figure 1-46 shows the final content of Dave's Web page.

Figure 1-46   Completed Web page

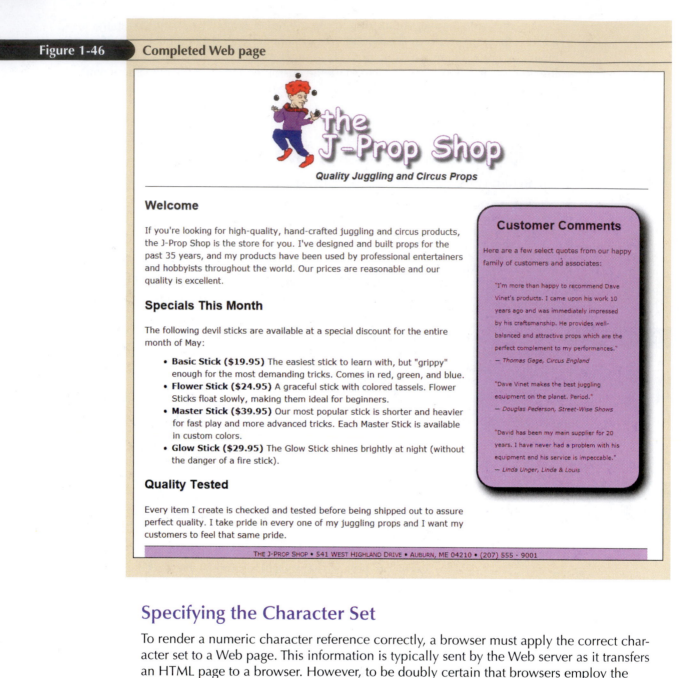

Specifying the Character Set

To render a numeric character reference correctly, a browser must apply the correct character set to a Web page. This information is typically sent by the Web server as it transfers an HTML page to a browser. However, to be doubly certain that browsers employ the correct character set, you can specify the character set within the `head` element of your HTML document. For HTML 4.01 and XHTML, you add the `meta` element

```
<meta http-equiv="Content-Type"
      content="text/html; charset=character_set" />
```

to the document head, where *character_set* is the name of the character set you want the browser to employ when interpreting your HTML code. Under HTML5, the `meta` element is simply:

```
<meta charset="character_set" />
```

HTML5 also supports the syntax of the HTML 4.01 and XHTML `meta` element. You should always specify the character encoding in your document, even if you are not using any special symbols. It relieves the browser from having to guess about the correct encoding; and in certain situations, not specifying the encoding can lead to a security hole in the transfer of a page from the Web server to the client.

You'll add the `meta` element to Dave's document to specify that his file has been encoded using the UTF-8 character set.

To specify the character encoding for Dave's document:

1. Return to the **jprop.htm** file in your text editor.

2. Scroll to the top of the file. Directly below the comment in the head section, insert the following `meta` element as shown in Figure 1-47:

   ```
   <meta charset="UTF-8" />
   ```

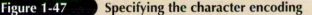

Figure 1-47   Specifying the character encoding

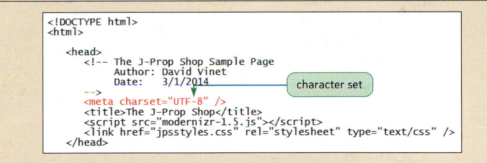

```
<!DOCTYPE html>
<html>

   <head>
      <!-- The J-Prop Shop Sample Page
           Author: David Vinet
           Date:   3/1/2014                          character set
      -->
      <meta charset="UTF-8" />
      <title>The J-Prop Shop</title>
      <script src="modernizr-1.5.js"></script>
      <link href="jpsstyles.css" rel="stylesheet" type="text/css" />
   </head>
```

3. Close the **jprop.htm** file, saving your changes.

4. Refresh the **jprop.htm** file in your browser and verify that the browser renders the page with no errors.

Written Communication: Publishing Your Web Page

Once you've completed your Web page, your next step is to get it on the Web. You first need to find a Web server to host the page. In choosing a Web server, you'll need to consider how much you want to pay, how much space you need, and how much traffic you expect at your Web site. If you'd prefer a free or low-cost option and don't need much space, you might first look toward the company that provides your Internet access. Most **Internet service providers** (ISPs) offer space on their Web servers as part of their regular service or for a small fee. However, they usually limit the amount of space available to you, unless you pay an extra fee to host a larger site. There are also free Web hosts, which provide space on servers for personal or noncommercial use. Once again, the amount of space you get is limited. Free Web hosting services make their money from selling advertising space on your site, so you should be prepared to act as a billboard in return for space on their servers. Finally, you can pay a monthly fee to an ISP to host your Web site to get more space and bandwidth.

Once you identify a Web host, you next need to consider the domain name that identifies your site. If you're planning to create a commercial site to advertise a product or service, you'll want the domain name to reflect your business. Free Web hosts usually include their names in your Web address. Thus, instead of having a Web address like

   thejpropshop.com

you might have something like

   freewebhosting.net/members/thejpropshop.html

If you're running a site for personal use, this might not be a problem—but it would look unprofessional on a commercial site. If you are planning a commercial site and simply want to advertise your product by publishing an online brochure, you can usually find an inexpensive host and pay a nominal yearly fee to reserve a Web address that reflects your company's name.

Session 1.2 Quick Check

1. Specify the code you would enter to mark the text *The J-Prop Shop* as an `h1` heading and the text *Product List* as an `h2` heading. Add code to group these two headings so browsers recognize them as a heading and subheading, respectively.

2. Specify the code you would enter to mark the text *Hamlet by William Shakespeare* as an `h1` heading, with a line break after the word *Hamlet*.

3. Create an ordered list of the following items: Packers, Bears, Lions, Vikings.

4. Specify the code to access the CSS style sheet file *uwstyles.css*. Where should you place this code within an HTML file?

5. Mark the graphic file *portrait.gif* as an inline image, setting the dimensions to 250 pixels wide by 300 pixels high. Specify the text *David Vinet* as alternate text to be displayed in place of the image for non-graphical browsers.

6. Specify the code to place the *portrait.gif* image from the previous question within a figure box with the caption *David Vinet, owner of the J-Prop Shop*.

7. The trademark symbol (™) has the character encoding number 8482. Provide the HTML code to enter this symbol into your Web page.

8. The Greek letter ß has the character entity name *beta*. How would you enter this symbol into your Web page?

PRACTICE

Review Assignments

Data Files needed for the Review Assignments: basiclogo.png, basicstick.png, basicstyles.css, modernizr-1.5.js, stick.txt

Dave has found a host for his Web page and has published the document you helped him create on the Internet. Now he wants to start adding more pages to his Web site. He's come to you for help in creating a page describing his basic stick. He's already written the text for the Web page; he needs you to mark up that text with HTML code. Figure 1-48 shows a preview of the page you'll create for Dave.

Figure 1-48   **The Basic Stick product page**

Specials This Month

The Basic Stick

The Basic Stick is the perfect stick for beginners. The stick rotates slowly to provide extra time for performing stick tricks, but is flashy enough to impress your friends. Enjoy the following:

Patented Dura-Coat® finish ensures sticks can withstand all weather conditions. More durable than other sticks, these props will keep looking like new for as long as you own them.

Enhanced stick flexibility provides more bounce, allowing for better tricks. A soft rubber core adds a whole new element to the sticking experience that you have to feel to believe!

Full customization will give you the chance to own a pair of sticks unlike any others out there. I make exactly what you want, with your colors and your designs.

A personal touch through both my customization options and hand-crafted designs.

Our Basic Stick

Specifications

- Main Stick
  - Weight: 7 oz.
  - Length: 24 inches
  - Tape: Dura-Coat® finish with laser-style color choices
- Handle Sticks (one pair)
  - Weight: 2 oz.
  - Length: 18 inches
  - Tape: Soft ivory tape with rubber core

THE J-PROP SHOP ♦ 541 WEST HIGHLAND DRIVE ♦ AUBURN, ME 04210 ♦ (207) 555 - 9001

Complete the following:

1. Use your text editor to create a new file named **basic.htm**, and then save it in the tutorial.01\review folder included with your Data Files.
2. Add the doctype for an HTML5 document.
3. Create the root `html` element and nest the `head` and `body` elements within it.

4. Within the `head` element, insert the comment

   ```
   The J-Prop Shop
   Sample Page for the Basic Stick
   Author: your name
   Date:   the date
   ```

   where *your name* is your name and *the date* is the current date.

5. Add code to specify that the page uses the UTF-8 character set.

6. Set the page title as **Basic Sticks**.

7. Link the file to the **modernizr-1.5.js** script file to enable HTML5 support for older browsers.

8. Link the file to the **basicstyles.css** style sheet file.

9. Within the `body` element, create structural elements for the page header, main section, and footer.

10. Within the page header, insert an `h1` heading containing the inline image file **basiclogo.png**. Specify the following alternate text for the image: **The J-Prop Shop**. Below the `h1` heading, insert an `h2` heading containing the text **Specials This Month**. Group the `h1` and `h2` headings using the `hgroup` element.

11. Within the `section` element, insert an `aside` element. The `aside` element should contain an inline image pointing to the *basicstick.png* file and having the text string **photo** as the alternate text. Below the inline image within the `aside` element, insert a paragraph containing the text string **Our Basic Stick**.

12. Add two `article` elements to the `section` element.

13. Within the first article, insert an `h2` heading containing the text **The Basic Stick**. Add a paragraph containing the following text:

    The Basic Stick is the perfect stick for beginners. The stick rotates slowly to provide extra time for performing stick tricks, but is flashy enough to impress your friends. Enjoy the following:

14. Add a block quote containing the following four paragraphs (you can copy this text from the *stick.txt* file):

    Patented Dura-Coat finish ensures sticks can withstand all weather conditions. More durable than other sticks, these props will keep looking like new for as long as you own them.

    Enhanced stick flexibility provides more bounce, allowing for better tricks. A soft rubber core adds a whole new element to the sticking experience that you have to feel to believe!

    Full customization will give you the chance to own a pair of sticks unlike any others out there. I make exactly what you want, with your colors and your designs.

    A personal touch through both my customization options and hand-crafted designs.

15. Mark the first few words of each of the four paragraphs as strong text, as shown in Figure 1-48.

16. Within the second article element, insert an `h2` heading with the title **Specifications**.

17. Directly below the `h2` heading, insert an unordered list. The list should contain two items: **Main Stick** and **Handle Sticks (one pair)**.

18. Within the *Main Stick* list item, insert a nested unordered list containing the following items:
    - **Weight: 7 oz.**
    - **Length: 24 inches**
    - **Tape: Dura-Coat finish with laser-style color choices**

19. Within the *Handle Sticks (one pair)* list item, insert a nested unordered list containing the following items:
    - **Weight: 2 oz.**
    - **Length: 18 inches**
    - **Tape: Soft ivory tape with rubber core**

20. Locate the two occurrences of *Dura-Coat* in the document. Directly after the word *Dura-Coat*, insert the registered trademark symbol ®. The character entity name of the ® symbol is *reg*. Display the ® symbol as a superscript by placing the character within the sup element.

21. Within the page footer, insert the company's address:
    The J-Prop Shop
    541 West Highland Drive
    Auburn, ME 04210
    (207) 555 - 9001

22. Separate the different sections of the address using a solid diamond (character code 9830).

23. Save your changes to the file, open it in your Web browser, and then compare your Web page to Figure 1-48 to verify that it was rendered correctly. Older browsers may display some slight differences in the design.

24. Submit your completed files to your instructor, in either printed or electronic form, as requested.

Apply your knowledge of HTML5 to create a Web page for a mathematics Web site.

APPLY

Case Problem 1

Data Files needed for the Case Problem: mhlogo.jpg, mhstyles.css, mhtxt.htm, modernizr-1.5.js

Math High   Professor Lauren Coe of the Mathematics Department of Coastal University in Anderson, South Carolina, is one of the founders of *Math High*, a Web site containing articles and course materials for high school and college math instructors. She has written a series of biographies of famous mathematicians for the Web site and would like you to transfer content she's already written to an HTML5 file. You'll create the first one in this exercise. Figure 1-49 shows a preview of the page you'll create, which profiles the mathematician Leonhard Euler.

Figure 1-49   Math High Web page

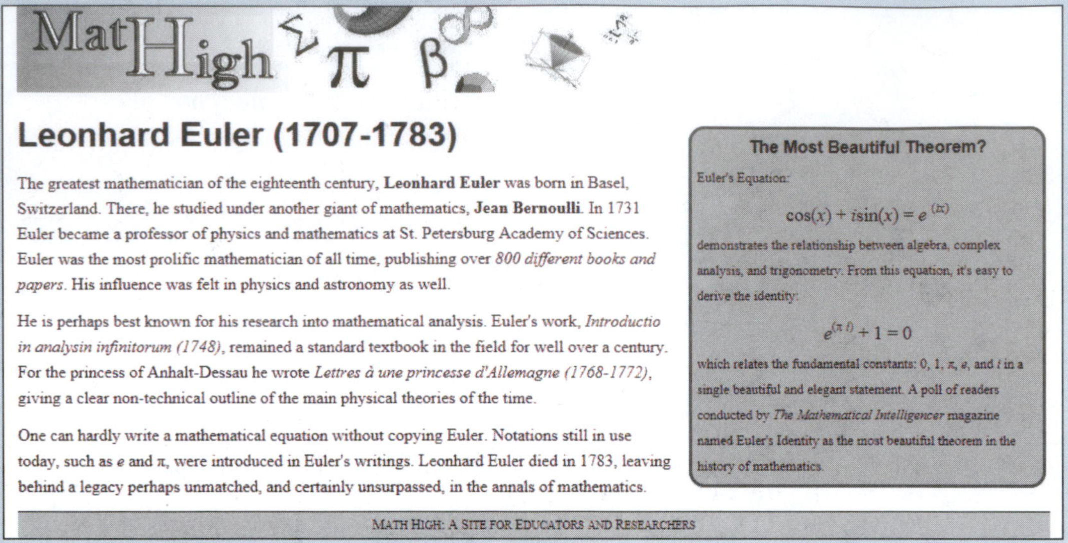

Complete the following:

1. In your text editor, open the **mhtxt.htm** file from the tutorial.01\case1 folder included with your Data Files. Save the file as **mathhigh.htm** in the same folder.

2. Enclose the contents of the file within a set of opening and closing `<html>` tags. Set the doctype of the file to indicate that this is an HTML5 document.

3. Add `head` and `body` elements to the file, enclosing the page contents within the body element.

4. Within the document head, insert the comment

   Math High: Leonhard Euler

   Author: *your name*

   Date: *the date*

   where *your name* is your name and *the date* is the current date.

5. Set the character set of the document to **UTF-8**.

6. Add the page title **Math High: Leonhard Euler** to the document head.

7. Link to the **modernizr-1.5.js** script file.

8. Link to the **mhstyles.css** style sheet.

9. Within the page body, create a `header` element. Within this element, insert an inline image using the **mhlogo.jpg** file as the source and **Math High** as the alternate text.

10. Mark the page text from the line *Leonhard Euler (1707 - 1783)* up to (but not including) the line *The Most Beautiful Theorem?* as an article.

11. Mark the first line in the article element, containing *Leonhard Euler (1707 - 1783)*, as an `h1` heading.

12. Mark the next three blocks of text describing Euler's life as paragraphs.

13. Within the first paragraph, mark the names *Leonhard Euler* and *Jean Bernoulli* using the `strong` element. Mark the phrase *800 different books and papers* as emphasized text using the `em` element.

14. In the second paragraph, mark the phrase *Introductio in analysin infinitorum (1748)* as a citation.

15. In the phrase *Lettres a une princesse d'Allemagne*, replace the one-letter word *a* with *à* (the character entity name is *agrave*). Mark the entire publication name as a citation.

16. In the third paragraph, mark the notation for *e* as a `var` element and replace *pi* with the character π (the character reference name is *pi*).

17. Enclose the next section of text from the line *The Most Beautiful Theorem?* up to (but not including) the line *Math High: A Site for Educators and Researchers* as an aside.

18. Mark the text *The Most Beautiful Theorem?* as an `h1` heading.

19. Mark the next five blocks of text as individual paragraphs.

20. In the first equation, mark the letters *e*, *i*, and *x* using the `var` element (but do not italicize the *i* in *sin*). Mark the term (ix) as a superscript.

21. In the second equation, replace *pi* with the character π. Mark the letters *e* and *i* using the `var` element. Mark (πi) as a superscript.

22. In the last paragraph, mark the notations for *e* and *i* with the `var` element and replace *pi* with π.

23. Mark the journal name *The Mathematical Intelligencer* as a citation.

24. Mark the final line in the file as a footer.

25. Save your changes to the file, and then verify that the page appears correctly in your Web browser.

26. Submit your completed files to your instructor, in either printed or electronic form, as requested.

Apply your knowledge of HTML to create a page showing text from a scene of a Shakespeare play.

APPLY

Case Problem 2

Data Files needed for the Case Problem: macbeth.jpg, macbethtxt.htm, macstyles.css, modernizr-1.5.js

Mansfield Classical Theatre Steve Karls is the director of Mansfield Classical Theatre, a theatre company for young people located in Mansfield, Ohio. This summer the company is planning to perform the Shakespeare play *Macbeth*. Steve wants to put the text of the play on the company's Web site and has asked for your help in designing and completing the Web page. Steve wants a separate page for each scene from the play. A preview of the page you'll create for Act I, Scene 1 is shown in Figure 1-50. Steve has already typed the text of the scene. He needs you to supply the HTML code.

Figure 1-50   **Macbeth Act I, Scene 1 Web page**

Presented by: Mansfield Classical Theatre

ACT I

SCENE 1

Summary A thunderstorm approaches and three witches convene. They agree to confront the great Scot general Macbeth upon his victorious return from a war between Scotland and Norway. Soon, heroic Macbeth will receive the title of Thane of Cawdor from King Duncan. However, Macbeth learns from the witches that he is fated for greater things and he will be led down the path of destruction by his unquenchable ambition.

A desert place.

Thunder and lightning. Enter three Witches.

First Witch

    When shall we three meet again

    In thunder, lightning, or in rain?

Second Witch

    When the hurlyburly's done,

    When the battle's lost and won.

Third Witch

    That will be ere the set of sun.

First Witch

    Where the place?

Second Witch

    Upon the heath.

Third Witch

    There to meet with Macbeth.

First Witch

    I come, Graymalkin!

Second Witch

    Paddock calls.

Third Witch

    Anon.

ALL

    Fair is foul, and foul is fair:

    Hover through the fog and filthy air.

Exeunt

Go to Scene 2 ⇒

TEXT PROVIDED BY ONLINE SHAKESPEARE

Complete the following:

1. Open the **macbethtxt.htm** file from the tutorial.01\case2 folder included with your Data Files. Save the file as **macbeth.htm** in the same folder.

2. Enclose the entire Macbeth text within the structure of an HTML document including the `html`, `head`, and `body` elements. Add a doctype to the document head to indicate that the page is written in HTML5.

3. Within the head section, insert a comment containing the following text:

   Macbeth: Act I, Scene 1
   Author: *your name*
   Date: *the date*

4. Add the page title **Macbeth: Act I, Scene 1**.

5. Link the file to the **modernizr-1.5.js** script file and to the **macstyles.css** style sheet. Set the character set to **UTF-8**.

6. Within the `body` element, insert a heading group consisting of an `h1` heading and an `h2` heading. Within the `h1` heading, insert an inline image containing the *macbeth.jpg* image file. Specify **Macbeth** as the alternate text. Within the `h2` heading, enter the text **Presented by: Mansfield Classical Theatre**.

7. Enclose the text of the play within a `section` element.

8. Mark the text *ACT I* as an `h2` heading. Mark *SCENE 1* as an `h3` heading. Group the two headings within an `hgroup` element.

9. Mark the summary of the scene as a paragraph. Mark the word *Summary* using the strong element.

10. In the text of the play, mark the descriptions of setting, scene, and exits as separate paragraphs and italicize the text using the `i` element, as shown in Figure 1-50.

⊕ **EXPLORE** 11. Mark the dialog as a description list, with each character's name marked as a description term and each speech marked as a description. When a speech includes two lines, add a line break at the end of the first line to keep the speech on separate lines, as shown in the figure.

⊕ **EXPLORE** 12. Directly below the paragraph containing the text *Exeunt*, insert the line **Go to Scene 2**. Mark this line as a `div` element with the id value *direction*. At the end of this line, insert a **right arrow character** using the 8658 character number. Add horizontal rules directly above and below this statement.

13. Mark the line *Text provided by Online Shakespeare* as a footer. Make sure the `footer` element is below the `section` element.

14. Save your changes to the file, and then confirm the layout and content of the page in your Web browser.

15. Submit the completed files to your instructor, in either printed or electronic form, as requested.

Explore how to use HTML to create a recipe page.

CHALLENGE

Case Problem 3

Data Files needed for the Case Problem: dessertstyles.css, dessertweb.jpg, modernizr-1.5.js, torte.jpg, tortetxt.htm

dessertWEB   Amy Wu wants to take her enjoyment of cooking and her love of sharing recipes to the World Wide Web. She's interested in creating a new Web site called *dessertWEB* where other cooks can submit and review dessert recipes. Each page within her site will contain a photo and description of a dessert, along with a list of ingredients, cooking directions, and a list of reviews. Each recipe will be rated on a five-star scale. She already has information on one recipe: Apple Bavarian Torte. She's asked for your help in creating a Web page from the data she's collected. A preview of the completed page is shown in Figure 1-51.

Figure 1-51   dessertWeb menu page

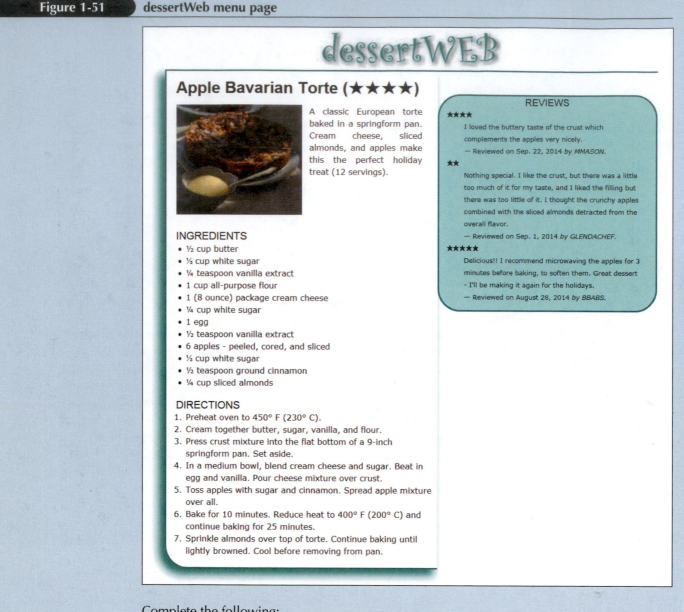

Complete the following:

1. Open the **tortetxt.htm** file from the tutorial.01\case3 folder included with your Data Files. Save the file as **torte.htm** in the same folder.

2. Add the structure of an HTML5 document around the recipe text. Within the `head` element, insert a comment containing the following text:

   Apple Bavarian Torte
   Author: *your name*
   Date: *the date*

3. Set the character set of the document to **ISO-8859-1**.

4. Link the document to the **modernizr-1.5.js** script file and the **dessertstyles.css** style sheet file.

5. Specify **Apple Bavarian Torte Recipe** as the page title.

6. Within the `body` element, add a `header` element. Within the `header` element, insert an `h1` heading containing the inline image **dessertweb.jpg** with the alternate text **dessertWEB**.

7. Enclose the recipe description, ingredients list, and directions within a `section` element. Enclose the recipe reviews within an `aside` element.

8. Mark the text *Apple Bavarian Torte* as an `h1` heading.

EXPLORE 9. Replace the text *(4 stars)* in the `h1` heading with a set of four **star symbols** (character number 9733).

EXPLORE 10. Directly below the `h1` heading, insert the inline image **torte.jpg**. Specify the alternate text **Torte image**. Set the width of the image to **250** pixels.

11. Mark the description of the dessert as a paragraph.

12. Mark *INGREDIENTS* and *DIRECTIONS* as `h2` headings.

13. Mark the list of ingredients as an unordered list. Mark the list of directions as an ordered list.

EXPLORE 14. Within the ingredients, replace the occurrences of 1/2 with the character symbol ½ (reference number 189), the occurrences of 1/4 with the symbol ¼ (reference number 188), and the occurrences of 1/3 with the symbol ⅓ (reference number 8531.)

EXPLORE 15. Replace each occurrence of the word *degrees* in the directions with the degree symbol (°) (character name *deg*).

16. Mark *REVIEWS* within the `aside` element as an `h1` heading.

17. Change the text of each customer star rating to a set of **star symbols** using character number 9733 placed within a paragraph.

EXPLORE 18. Enclose the text of each customer review in a paragraph nested within a `blockquote` element. Place the name of the reviewer and the date on a new line within that paragraph. Insert an **em-dash** (character name *mdash*) before the word *Reviewed* in each of the reviews. Enclose the date of each review within a `time` element and enclose by *reviewer* within a `cite` element where *reviewer* is the name of the reviewer.

19. Save your changes to the file, and then verify the layout and content of the page in your Web browser.

20. Submit the completed files to your instructor, in either printed or electronic form, as requested.

Test your knowledge of HTML and use your creativity to design a Web page for an exercise equipment company.

RESEARCH

Case Problem 4

Data Files needed for the Case Problem: logo.jpg, smith.jpg, and smith.txt

Body Systems Body Systems is a leading manufacturer of home gyms. The company recently hired you to assist in developing its Web site. Your first task is to create a Web page for the LSM400, a popular weight machine sold by the company. You've been given a text file describing the features of the LSM400. You've also received two image files: one of the company's logo and one of the LSM400. You are free to supplement these files with any other resources available to you. You are responsible for the page's content and appearance.

Complete the following:

1. Create a new HTML5 file named **smith.htm** and save it in the tutorial.01\case4 folder included with your Data Files.

2. Add the appropriate doctype for HTML5 to the beginning of the file.

3. Add a comment to the document head describing the document's content and containing your name and the date.

4. Add an appropriate page title to the document head.

5. Set the character set of the file to **UTF-8**.

6. Use the contents of the **smith.txt** document (located in the tutorial.01\case4 folder) as the basis of the document body. Include at least one example of each of the following:

- structural elements such as the `header`, `footer`, `section`, and `aside` elements
- grouping elements including a heading and a paragraph
- an ordered or unordered list
- a text-level element
- an inline image
- a character entity reference or a character encoding number

7. Structure your HTML5 code so that it's easy for others to read and understand.

8. Save your changes to the file, and then open it in your Web browser to verify that it is readable.

9. Submit your completed files to your instructor, in either printed or electronic form, as requested.

ENDING SOLUTION FILES

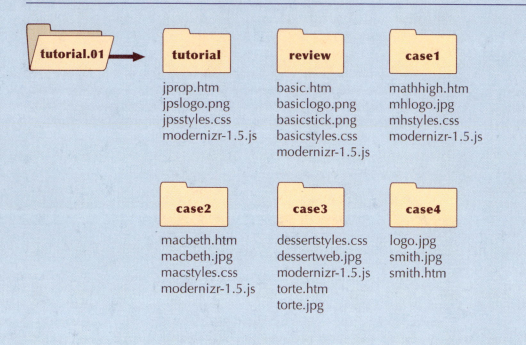

tutorial.01 → **tutorial**

jprop.htm
jpslogo.png
jpsstyles.css
modernizr-1.5.js

review

basic.htm
basiclogo.png
basicstick.png
basicstyles.css
modernizr-1.5.js

case1

mathhigh.htm
mhlogo.jpg
mhstyles.css
modernizr-1.5.js

case2

macbeth.htm
macbeth.jpg
macstyles.css
modernizr-1.5.js

case3

dessertstyles.css
dessertweb.jpg
modernizr-1.5.js
torte.htm
torte.jpg

case4

logo.jpg
smith.jpg
smith.htm

TUTORIAL 2

Developing a Web Site

Creating a Web Site for Amateur Photographers

OBJECTIVES

Session 2.1
- Explore how to storyboard a Web site
- Create navigation lists
- Create links between documents in a Web site
- Understand absolute and relative folder paths
- Set a base path
- Mark a location with the id attribute
- Create a link to an id

Session 2.2
- Mark an image as a link
- Create an image map
- Understand URLs
- Link to a resource on the Web
- Link to an e-mail address
- Work with hypertext attributes
- Work with metadata

Case | *CAMshots*

Gerry Hayward is an amateur photographer and digital camera enthusiast. He's creating a Web site named *CAMshots*, where he can offer advice and information to people who are just getting started with digital photography, or who are long-time hobbyists like himself and are looking to share tips and ideas. Gerry's Web site will contain several pages, with each page dedicated to a particular topic. He has created a few sample pages for the Web site, but he hasn't linked them together. He has asked for your help in designing his site and creating links between the pages.

STARTING DATA FILES

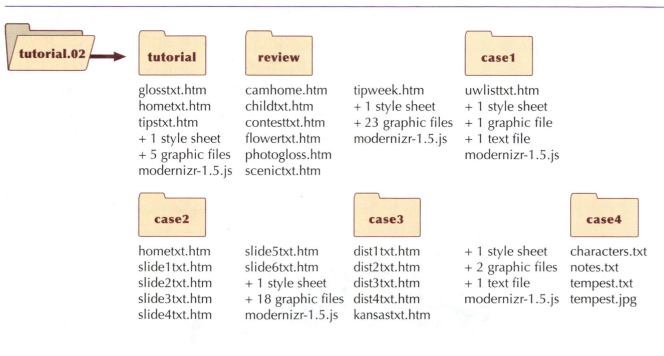

tutorial.02 → **tutorial**
glosstxt.htm
hometxt.htm
tipstxt.htm
+ 1 style sheet
+ 5 graphic files
modernizr-1.5.js

review
camhome.htm
childtxt.htm
contesttxt.htm
flowertxt.htm
photogloss.htm
scenictxt.htm

case1
uwlisttxt.htm
+ 1 style sheet
+ 1 graphic file
+ 1 text file
modernizr-1.5.js

tipweek.htm
+ 1 style sheet
+ 23 graphic files
modernizr-1.5.js

case2
hometxt.htm
slide1txt.htm
slide2txt.htm
slide3txt.htm
slide4txt.htm

slide5txt.htm
slide6txt.htm
+ 1 style sheet
+ 18 graphic files
modernizr-1.5.js

case3
dist1txt.htm
dist2txt.htm
dist3txt.htm
dist4txt.htm
kansastxt.htm

case4
+ 1 style sheet
+ 2 graphic files
+ 1 text file
modernizr-1.5.js

characters.txt
notes.txt
tempest.txt
tempest.jpg

SESSION 2.1 VISUAL OVERVIEW

The nav element marks a list of hypertext links used to navigate through the pages in the Web site.

```
<nav>
    <ul>
        <li><a href="home.htm">Home</a></li>
        <li><a href="tips.htm">Tips</a></li>
        <li><a href="glossary.htm"> Glossary</a></li>
    </ul>
</nav>
```

The **<a> tag** is used to mark hyperlinks to external documents or to locations within the current document. The **href** attribute indicates the reference or address of the linked resource.

CAMshots

Tips   Photo Glo

| Home | Tips | Glossary |

Welcome to CAMshots, a site for people passionat about digital photography. This site has grown ou decades of photographic experience. I offer advice for both beginners and advanced users. I hope yo enjoy what you find, but please be considerate of work it took to do all this. The entire site content including all images and articles are copyrighted. Please honor my work and do not copy anything without permission. If you are interested in publishing any of my images or articles or using t in other ways, please contact me and we can disc your needs. Happy Shooting!

— Gerry

By default, browsers underline hypertext links.

CAMSHOTS >>> ADVICE AND NEWS FROM THE W

```
<a href="glossary.htm#flash_mode">Flash Mode</a>
```

Links to locations within a document are referenced using the form *file#id*, where file is the name of the file and id is the id marking the location within the file.

CREATING HYPERLINKS

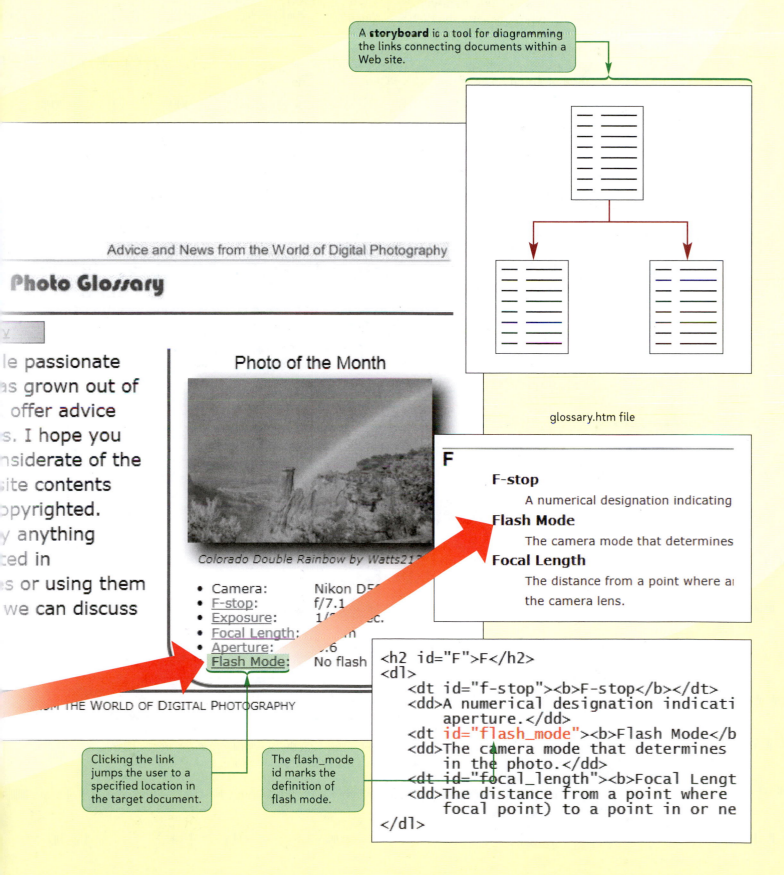

A **storyboard** is a tool for diagramming the links connecting documents within a Web site.

glossary.htm file

Advice and News from the World of Digital Photography

Photo Glossary

le passionate
as grown out of
offer advice
s. I hope you
nsiderate of the
site contents
opyrighted.
y anything
ted in
s or using them
we can discuss

Photo of the Month

Colorado Double Rainbow by Watts21

- Camera: Nikon D5
- F-stop: f/7.1
- Exposure: 1/   ec.
- Focal Length:
- Aperture: .6
- Flash Mode: No flash

OM THE WORLD OF DIGITAL PHOTOGRAPHY

F

F-stop
    A numerical designation indicating

Flash Mode
    The camera mode that determines

Focal Length
    The distance from a point where a
    the camera lens.

```
<h2 id="F">F</h2>
<dl>
    <dt id="f-stop"><b>F-stop</b></dt>
    <dd>A numerical designation indicati
        aperture.</dd>
    <dt id="flash_mode"><b>Flash Mode</b
    <dd>The camera mode that determines
        in the photo.</dd>
    <dt id="focal_length"><b>Focal Lengt
    <dd>The distance from a point where
        focal point) to a point in or ne
</dl>
```

Clicking the link jumps the user to a specified location in the target document.

The flash_mode id marks the definition of flash mode.

Exploring Web Site Structures

You meet with Gerry to discuss his plans for the CAMshots Web site. Gerry has already created a prototype for the Web site containing three pages written in HTML5: One page is the site's home page and contains general information about CAMshots; the second page contains tips about digital photography; and the third page contains a partial glossary of photographic terms. The pages are not complete, nor are they linked to one another. You'll begin your work for Gerry by viewing these files in your text editor and browser.

To view Gerry's Web pages:

1. Start your text editor, and then open the **hometxt.htm**, **tipstxt.htm**, and **glosstxt.htm** files, located in the tutorial.02\tutorial folder included with your Data Files.

2. Within each file, go to the comment section at the top of the file and add **your name** and **the date** in the space provided.

3. Save the files as **home.htm**, **tips.htm**, and **glossary.htm**, respectively, in the tutorial.02\tutorial folder.

4. Take some time to review the HTML code within each document so that you understand the structure and content of the files.

5. Start your Web browser and open the **home.htm**, **tips.htm**, and **glossary.htm** files. Figure 2-1 shows the current layout and appearance of Gerry's three Web pages.

Figure 2-1 Versions of HTML

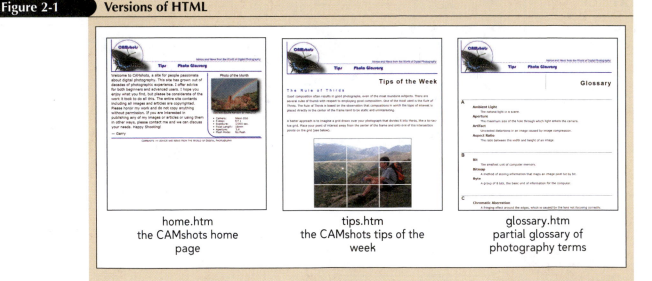

home.htm
the CAMshots home page

tips.htm
the CAMshots tips of the week

glossary.htm
partial glossary of photography terms

Gerry wants to create links among the three pages so that users can easily navigate from one page to another. Before you write code for the links, it's worthwhile to use a technique known as storyboarding to map out exactly how you want the pages to relate to each other. A storyboard is a diagram of a Web site's structure, showing all the pages in the site and indicating how they are linked together. Because Web sites use a variety of structures, it's important to storyboard your Web site before you start creating your pages. This helps you determine which structure works best for the type of information your site contains. A well-designed structure ensures that users will be able to navigate the site without getting lost or missing important information.

Every Web site should begin with a single **home page** that acts as a focal point for the Web site. It is usually the first page that users see. From that home page, you add links to other pages in the site, defining the site's overall structure. The Web sites you commonly encounter as you navigate the Web employ several different Web structures. You'll examine some of these structures to help you decide how to design your own sites.

Linear Structures

If you wanted to create an online version of a famous play, like Shakespeare's *Hamlet*, one method would be to link the individual scenes of the play in a long chain. Figure 2-2 shows the storyboard for this **linear structure**, in which each page is linked with the pages that follow and precede it. Readers navigate this structure by moving forward and backward through the pages, much as they might move forward and backward through the pages of a book.

Figure 2-2   **A linear structure**

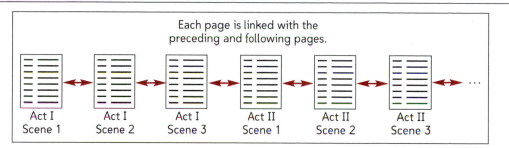

Linear structures work for Web sites that are small in size and have a clearly defined order of pages. However, they can be difficult to work with as the chain of pages increases in length. An additional problem is that in a linear structure, you move farther and farther away from the home page as you progress through the site. Because home pages often contain important general information about a site and its author, this is usually not the best design technique.

You can modify this structure to make it easier for users to return immediately to the home page or other main pages. Figure 2-3 shows this online play with an **augmented linear structure**, in which each page contains an additional link back to the opening page of each act.

Figure 2-3   **An augmented linear structure**

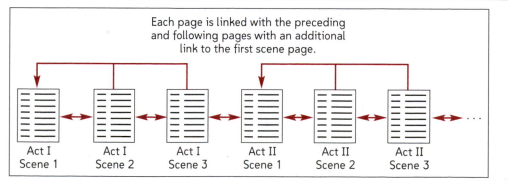

Hierarchical Structures

Another popular structure is the **hierarchical structure**, in which the home page links to pages dedicated to specific topics. Those pages, in turn, can be linked to even more specific topics. A hierarchical structure allows users to easily move from general to specific and back again. In the case of the online play, you could link an introductory page containing general information about the play to pages that describe each of the play's acts, and within each act you could include links to individual scenes. See Figure 2-4. Within this structure, a user could move quickly to a specific scene within the play, bypassing the need to move through each scene that precedes it.

Figure 2-4 **A hierarchical structure**

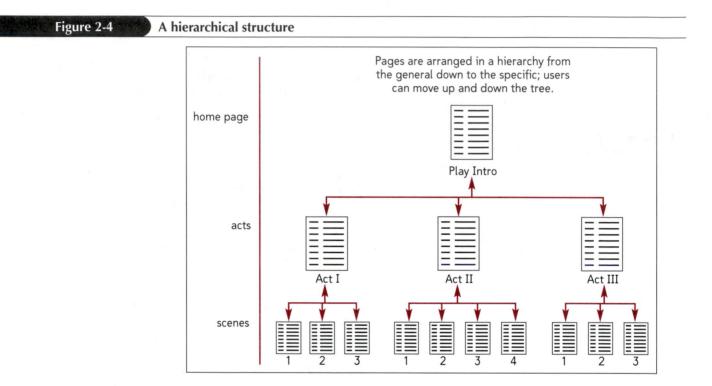

Pages are arranged in a hierarchy from the general down to the specific; users can move up and down the tree.

home page — Play Intro

acts — Act I, Act II, Act III

scenes — 1 2 3 / 1 2 3 4 / 1 2 3

Mixed Structures

With larger and more complex Web sites, you often need to use a combination of structures. Figure 2-5 shows the online play using a mixture of hierarchical and linear structures. The overall form is hierarchical, as users can move from a general introduction down to individual scenes; however, users can also move through the site in a linear fashion, going from act to act and scene to scene. Finally, each individual scene contains a link to the home page, allowing users to jump to the top of the hierarchy without moving through the different levels.

Figure 2-5   **A mixed structure**

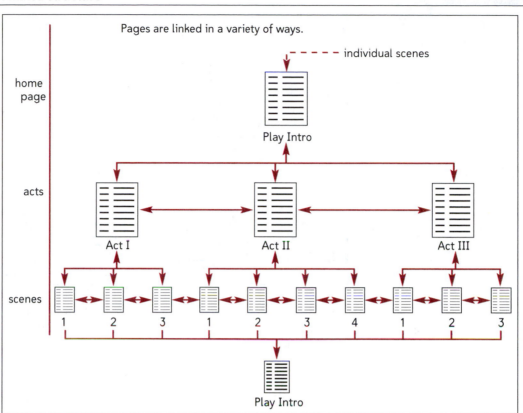

As these examples show, a little foresight can go a long way toward making your Web site easier to use. Also keep in mind that search results from a Web search engine such as Google or Yahoo! can point users to any page in your Web site—not just your home page—so they will need to be able to quickly understand what your site contains and how to navigate it. At a minimum, each page should contain a link to the site's home page or to the relevant main topic page. In some cases, you might want to supply your users with a **site index**, which is a page containing an outline of the entire site and its contents. Unstructured Web sites can be difficult and frustrating to use. Consider the storyboard of the site displayed in Figure 2-6.

Figure 2-6   Web site with no coherent structure

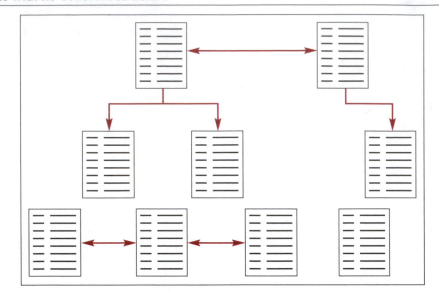

This confusing structure makes it difficult for users to grasp the site's contents and scope. The user might not even be aware of the presence of some pages because there are no connecting links, and some of the links point in only one direction. The Web is a competitive place; studies have shown that users who don't see how to get what they want within the first few seconds often leave a Web site. How long would a user spend on a site like the one shown in Figure 2-6?

Protected Structures

Sections of most commercial Web sites are off-limits except to subscribers and registered customers. As shown in Figure 2-7, these sites have a password-protected Web page that users must go through to get to the off-limits areas. The same Web site design principles apply to the protected section as the regular, open section of the site.

Figure 2-7   A protected structure

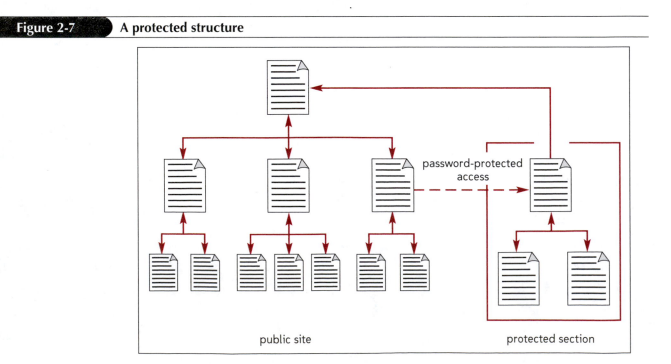

Storyboarding a protected structure is particularly important to ensure that no unauthorized access to the protected area is allowed in the site design.

Creating a Navigation List

Every Web site should include a **navigation list**, which is a list containing links to the main topic areas of the site. Ideally, this same list should appear prominently on every page, usually near the top of the page as part of the header or as a sidebar to the main content.

HTML5 introduced the `nav` structural element to make it easier to mark up navigation lists. The syntax of the element is

```
<nav>
    list of navigation links
</nav>
```

where `list of navigation links` is a list of elements that are linked to other pages on the Web site. Prior to HTML5, such lists would often be inserted within the generic `div` element as

```
<div id="id">
    list of navigation links
</div>
```

where `id` is whatever id the page author would supply to identify the navigation list.

Gerry suggests you add the topics for his three sample pages as an unordered list within the `nav` element as follows:

```
<nav>
    <ul>
        <li>Home</li>
        <li>Tips</li>
        <li>Glossary</li>
    </ul>
</nav>
```

Gerry has already designed styles for these new elements and placed them within the camstyles.css style sheet. The style sheet will format the elements so that the list appears as a horizontally aligned set of boxes. As Gerry adds more sample pages, he can easily extend this list to include the new topics, but for now he needs only these three.

Add this navigation list to each of the three sample pages that Gerry has given you.

To create the navigation list:

1. Return to the **home.htm** file in your text editor.

2. At the top of the file directly below the header element, insert the following code as shown in Figure 2-8:

```
<nav>
    <ul>
        <li>Home</li>
        <li>Tips</li>
        <li>Glossary</li>
    </ul>
</nav>
```

Figure 2-8   **Marking a navigation list**

navigation list marked
with the nav element

```
<body>

    <header>
        <img src="camshots.jpg" alt="CAMshots" />
    </header>

    <nav>
        <ul>
            <li>Home</li>
            <li>Tips</li>
            <li>Glossary</li>
        </ul>
    </nav>
```

3. Save your changes to the file.

4. Go to the **tips.htm** file in your text editor and then repeat Steps 2 and 3, placing the navigation list in the same place as you did in the home.htm file and saving your changes.

5. Go to the **glossary.htm** file in your text editor and then repeat Steps 2 and 3 to add a navigation list to that file.

6. Open or refresh the **home.htm** file in your Web browser. Verify that the navigation list appears directly below the page header as shown in Figure 2-9.

Figure 2-9   **Navigation list in the CAMshots home page**

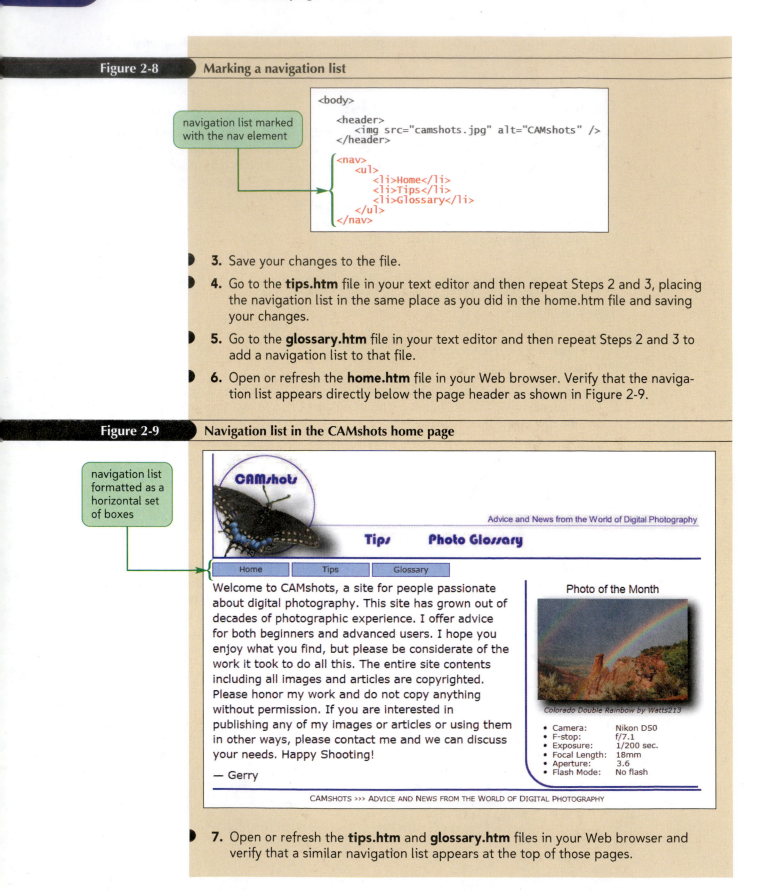

navigation list
formatted as a
horizontal set
of boxes

7. Open or refresh the **tips.htm** and **glossary.htm** files in your Web browser and verify that a similar navigation list appears at the top of those pages.

INSIGHT

Navigation Lists and Web Accessibility

One challenge of Web design is creating Web documents that are accessible to users with disabilities. Studies indicate that about 20% of the population has some type of disability. Many of these disabilities don't affect users' capacity to interact with the Web. But in some cases, users may need specialized Web browsers, such as screen readers that provide Web content aurally for visually impaired users.

To accommodate these users, Web page authors can take advantage of the structural elements provided by HTML5. For example, the nav element can allow users to either quickly jump to a list of links or bypass such a list if they are more interested in the content of the current document. Prior to HTML5 and the nav element, there was no way of differentiating one list from another, and thus disabled users would be forced to wait through a rendering of the same navigation list for each page they visited.

Because support for HTML5 is still in its infancy at the time of this writing, most specialized browsers have not incorporated features that enable users to quickly access the structural elements of most interest to them. However, as the specifications for HTML5 are finalized and fully supported by the browser market, this ability will become more commonly supported. Thus you should use the nav element and other structural elements from HTML5 to provide more information to browsers about the content and structure of your Web documents.

Working with Hypertext Links

Now that you've added a navigation list to each of the three sample pages, you will change each item in those lists into a hypertext link so that users can easily move between the three sample pages. Figure 2-10 shows the storyboard for the simple structure you have in mind.

Figure 2-10   **Storyboard for the CAMshots sample Web site**

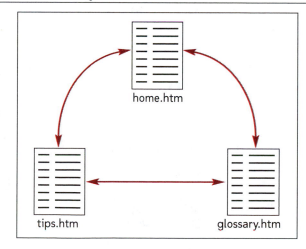

Hypertext links are created by enclosing some document content within a set of opening and closing <a> tags. The general syntax to create a hypertext link is

```
<a href="reference">content</a>
```

where *reference* is the location being linked to and *content* is the document content that is being marked as a link. The *reference* value can be a page on the World Wide

Web, a local file, an e-mail address, or a network server. For example, to create a hypertext link to the tips.htm file, you could enter the following code:

```
<a href="tips.htm">Photography Tips</a>
```

This code marks the text *Photography Tips* as a hypertext link. If a user clicks the text, the browser will load the linked resource (tips.htm). Note that filenames are case sensitive on some operating systems, such as the UNIX operating system. Web servers running on those systems differentiate between files named tips.htm and Tips.htm. For this reason, you might find that links you create on your computer do not work when you transfer your files to a Web server. To avoid this problem, the current standard is to always use lowercase filenames for all Web site files and to avoid using special characters and blank spaces.

Most browsers underline hypertext links unless a different style is specified in a user-defined style sheet. The font color of a link also changes based on whether or not the user has also visited the linked resource. By default, most browsers display hypertext links as follows:

- An unvisited link is underlined and blue.
- A previously visited link is underlined and purple.
- A link currently being clicked or activated is underlined and red.

However, Web page authors can use CSS to override these default settings.

TIP

Keep your filenames short and descriptive so that users are less apt to make a typing error when accessing your Web site.

REFERENCE

Marking a Hypertext Link

- To mark content as a hypertext link, use

  ```
  <a href="reference">content</a>
  ```

  where *reference* is the location being linked to and *content* is the document content that is being marked as a link.

You'll mark the names of the three sample pages in the navigation list you just created as hypertext links.

To create a hypertext link to a document:

1. Return to the **home.htm** file in your text editor and go to the navigation list at the top of the page.

2. Mark the text *Home* as a hypertext link using a set of <a> tags as follows:

   ```
   <a href="home.htm">Home</a>
   ```

3. Mark the text *Tips* as a hypertext link using the following code:

   ```
   <a href="tips.htm">Tips</a>
   ```

4. Mark the text *Glossary* as a hypertext link as follows:

   ```
   <a href="glossary.htm">Glossary</a>
   ```

   Figure 2-11 highlights the revised text in the home.htm file.

Figure 2-11   Marking hypertext links in the navigation list

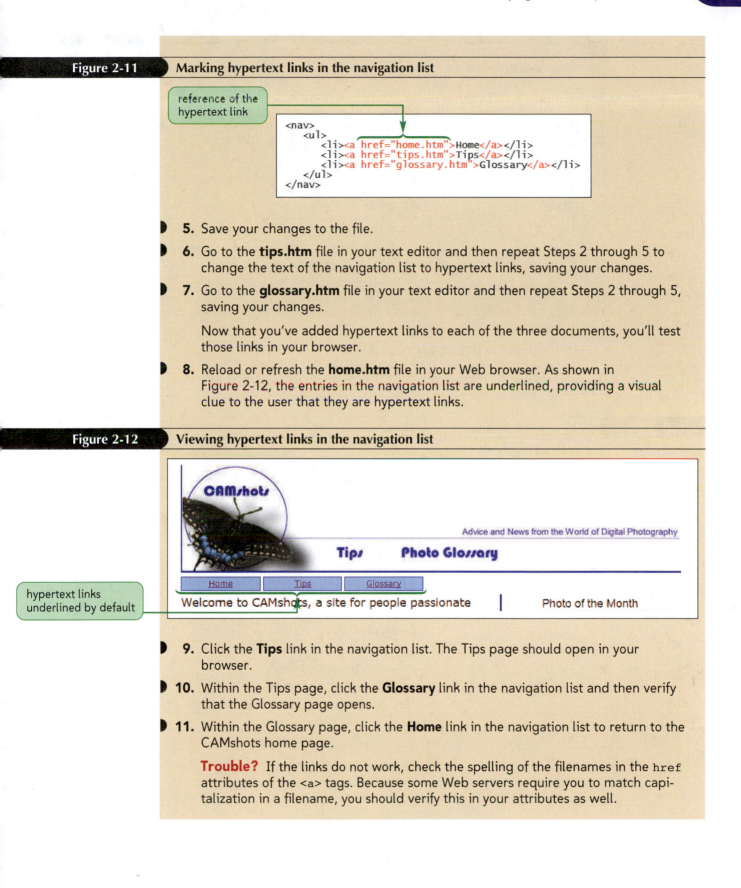

reference of the hypertext link

```
<nav>
    <ul>
        <li><a href="home.htm">Home</a></li>
        <li><a href="tips.htm">Tips</a></li>
        <li><a href="glossary.htm">Glossary</a></li>
    </ul>
</nav>
```

5. Save your changes to the file.

6. Go to the **tips.htm** file in your text editor and then repeat Steps 2 through 5 to change the text of the navigation list to hypertext links, saving your changes.

7. Go to the **glossary.htm** file in your text editor and then repeat Steps 2 through 5, saving your changes.

   Now that you've added hypertext links to each of the three documents, you'll test those links in your browser.

8. Reload or refresh the **home.htm** file in your Web browser. As shown in Figure 2-12, the entries in the navigation list are underlined, providing a visual clue to the user that they are hypertext links.

Figure 2-12   Viewing hypertext links in the navigation list

CAMshots

Advice and News from the World of Digital Photography

Tips   Photo Glossary

| Home | Tips | Glossary |

hypertext links underlined by default

Welcome to CAMshots, a site for people passionate | Photo of the Month

9. Click the **Tips** link in the navigation list. The Tips page should open in your browser.

10. Within the Tips page, click the **Glossary** link in the navigation list and then verify that the Glossary page opens.

11. Within the Glossary page, click the **Home** link in the navigation list to return to the CAMshots home page.

    Trouble? If the links do not work, check the spelling of the filenames in the href attributes of the <a> tags. Because some Web servers require you to match capitalization in a filename, you should verify this in your attributes as well.

Interpreting the <a> Tag in Different Versions of HTML

The <a> tag is treated slightly differently in versions of HTML prior to HTML5. In HTML 4.01 and XHTML, the <a> tag can be used to enclose only text-level elements and should not be used to group content or structural elements. This means that the code

```
<a href="home.htm">
    <p>Go to the home page</p>
</a>
```

would not be allowed because the hyperlink is applied to an entire paragraph. HTML5 does not make this distinction, allowing the <a> tag to enclose text-level, grouping, and structural elements.

A second important difference is that in HTML 4.01 and XHTML, the <a> tag can also be used as an anchor to mark specific locations within the document. For that reason, the <a> tag is commonly referred to as the tag for the anchor element. HTML5 does not support this interpretation; the <a> tag can be used only to mark hypertext links.

Attributes of the a Element

The a element supports several attributes in addition to the href attribute. Some of these attributes are listed in Figure 2-13.

Figure 2-13 Attributes of the anchor (a) element

Attribute	Description
charset="encoding"	Specifies the character encoding used in the linked resource (not supported in HTML5)
href="url"	Indicates the resource targeted by the hypertext link
media="media type"	Indicates the media device in which the linked resource should be viewed (HTML5)
name="name"	Assigns a name for the section anchored by the <a> tag (not supported in HTML5)
rel="relationship"	Specifies the relationship between the current document and the linked resource
ping="url"	A space-separated list of resources that get notified when the user follows the hyperlink (HTML5)
target="target_type"	Specifies where to open the linked resource
type="mime-type"	Specifies the content (the mime-type) of the linked resource

For example, the following code uses the `media` attribute to indicate to browsers that the linked resource is suitable for printing:

```
<a href="orderform.htm" media="print">
   View an Order Form
</a>
```

The `media` attribute doesn't instruct the browser to print the linked file; it just tells the browser for what kind of output media the file has been designed. On the other hand, the following code uses the `type` attribute to indicate the file format of the linked file:

```
<a href="photo.png" mime-type="image/png">
   View the photo of the month
</a>
```

In this case, the browser is forewarned that the linked file is a graphic image file in the PNG format. Some browsers can use the `mime-type` attribute to load applications and programs to view the linked document. But in most cases, the browser determines the file format as it receives the document from the Web server, and thus no `mime-type` attribute is required.

Specifying a Folder Path

In the links you just created, you specified the filename but not the location of the file. When you specify only the filename, the browser assumes that the file is in the same folder as the document containing the hypertext link. However, large Web sites containing hundreds of documents often place documents in separate folders to make them easier to manage.

As Gerry adds more files to his Web site, he will probably want to use folders to organize the files. Figure 2-14 shows a preview of how Gerry might employ those folders. In this case, the top folder containing all of the content of the Web site is named *camshots*. Gerry might place some of his HTML files within the *pages* folder, which he would then divide into three subfolders, named *tips*, *glossary*, and *articles*. He could also create separate folders for the images and video clips used on his Web site.

Figure 2-14   **A sample folder structure**

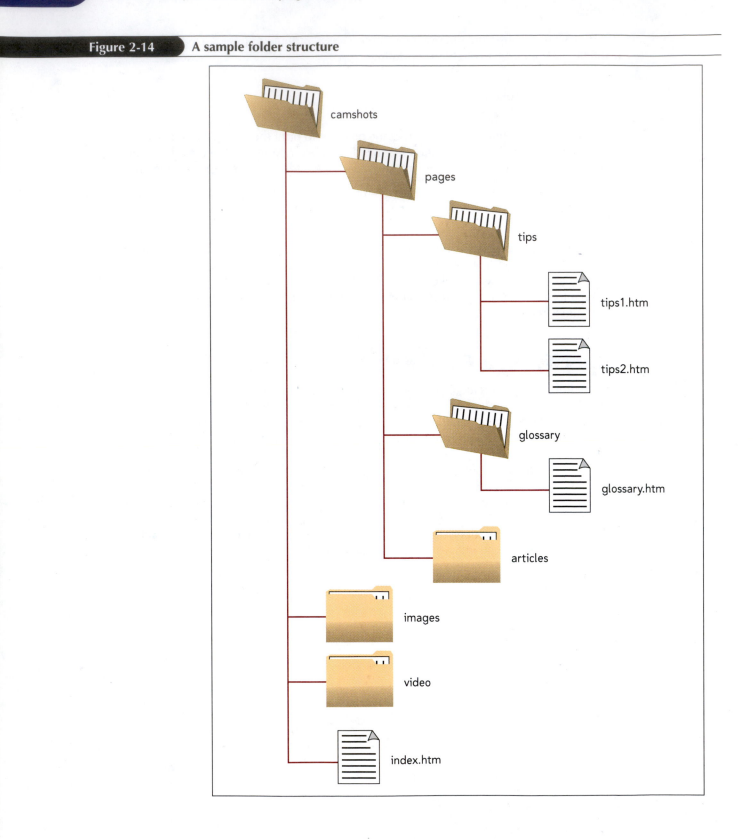

TIP

To make your Web site easier to maintain, organize your folders to match the organization of the pages on the Web site, and group images and other media files within folders separate from your HTML files.

To create a link to a file located in a folder other than the current document's folder, you must specify that file's location, or **path**. HTML supports two kinds of paths: absolute and relative.

Absolute Paths

An **absolute path** specifies a file's precise location within the entire folder structure of a computer. Absolute paths employ the syntax

```
/folder1/folder2/folder3/file
```

where *folder1* is the top folder in the hierarchy, followed by *folder2*, *folder3*, and so forth, down to the file you want to link to. Figure 2-15 shows how you would express absolute paths to the four files listed in Figure 2-14.

| Figure 2-15 | Absolute paths |

Absolute Path	Interpretation
/camshots/pages/tips/tips1.htm	The tips1.htm file located in the pages/tips subfolder
/camshots/pages/tips/tips2.htm	The tips2.htm file located in the pages/tips subfolder
/camshots/pages/glossary/glossary.htm	The glossary.htm file located in the pages/glossary subfolder
/camshots/index.htm	The index.htm file located in the camshots folder

If files are located on different drives as well as in different folders, you must include the drive letter in the path

```
/drive|/folder1/folder2/folder3/file
```

where *drive* is the letter assigned to the drive. For example, the tips1.htm file located on drive C in the */camshots/pages/tips* folder would have the absolute path

```
/C|/camshots/pages/tips/tips1.htm
```

Note that you don't have to include a drive letter if the linked document is located on the same drive as the current file.

TIP

Because hypertext links cannot contain blank spaces, avoid blank spaces in the names you give to your Web site folders and files.

Relative Paths

When many folders and subfolders are involved, absolute paths can be cumbersome and confusing to use. For this reason, most Web designers prefer to use relative paths. A **relative path** specifies a file's location in relation to the location of the current document. If the file is in the same location as the current document, the relative path is simply the filename. If the file is in a subfolder of the current document, include the name of the subfolder without the forward slash, as follows

```
folder/file
```

where *folder* is the name of the subfolder, which is also known as a **child folder**. Note that folders used in relative paths are often referenced using relative names, such as parent, child, sibling, and so forth. For example, to go farther down the folder tree to other sub-folders, include those folder names in the relative path separated by forward slashes, as in

```
folder1/folder2/folder3/file
```

where *folder1*, *folder2*, *folder3*, and so forth are subfolders, or **descendent folders**, of the current folder. Going in the opposite direction, a relative path moving up the folder tree to a **parent folder** is indicated by starting the path with a double period (..) followed by a forward slash and the name of the file. Thus, the relative path

    ../file

TIP

You can reference the current folder using a single period (.) character.

references the *file* document located in the parent folder. Finally, to reference a different folder on the same level as the current folder, known as a **sibling folder**, you move up the folder tree using the double period (..) to the parent and then back down to a different folder. The general syntax is

    ../folder/file

where *folder* is the name of the sibling folder. Figure 2-16 shows the relative paths to the six files in the tree from Figure 2-14, starting from the *camshots/pages/tips* subfolder.

Figure 2-16	Relative paths

Relative Path from the /camshots/pages/tips Subfolder	Interpretation
tips1.htm	The tips1.htm file located in the current folder
tips2.htm	The tips2.htm file located in the current folder
../glossary/glossary.htm	The glossary.htm file located in the sibling glossary folder
../../index.htm	The index.htm file located in the parent camshots folder

You should almost always use relative paths in your links. If you have to move your files to a different computer or server, you can move the entire folder structure without having to edit the relative paths you've created. If you use absolute paths, you will probably have to revise each link to reflect the new location of the folder tree on the computer.

Setting the Base Path

As you've just seen, a browser resolves relative paths based on the location of the current document. You can change this behavior by using the `base` element to specify a different starting location for all relative paths. The `base` element has the syntax

    <base href="path" />

where *path* is the folder location that you want the browser to use when resolving relative paths in the current document. The `base` element must be nested within the `head` element of the HTML file so it can be applied to all hypertext links found within the document.

REFERENCE

Using the base *Element*

• To set the default location for a relative path, add the element

    <base href="path" />

to the document head, where *path* is the folder location that you want browsers to use when resolving relative paths in the current document.

The base element is useful when a single document is moved to a new folder. Rather than rewriting all of the relative paths to reflect the document's new location, the base element redirects browsers to the document's old location, allowing any relative paths to be resolved as they were before.

PROSKILLS

Problem Solving: Managing Your Web Site

Web sites can quickly grow from a couple of pages to dozens or hundreds of pages. As the size of a site increases, it becomes more difficult to get a clear picture of the site's structure and content. Imagine deleting or moving a file in a Web site that contains dozens of folders and hundreds of files. Could you easily project the effect of this change? Would all of your hypertext links still work after you moved or deleted the file?

To effectively manage a Web site, you should follow a few important rules. The first is to be consistent in how you structure the site. If you decide to collect all image files in one folder, you should continue that practice as you add more pages and images. Web sites are more likely to break down if files and folders are scattered throughout the server without a consistent rule or pattern. Decide on a structure early and stick with it.

The second rule is to create a folder structure that matches the structure of the Web site itself. If the pages can be easily categorized into different groups, those groupings should also be reflected in the groupings of the subfolders. The names you assign to your files and folders should also reflect their uses on the Web site. This makes it easier for you to predict how modifying a file or folder might impact other pages on the site.

Finally, you should document your work by adding comments to each new Web page. Comments are useful not only for colleagues who may be working on the site, but also for the author who must revisit those files months or even years after creating them. The comments should include:

- The page's filename and location
- The page's author and the date the page was initially created
- A list of any supporting files used in the document, such as image and audio files
- A list of the files that link to the page, and their locations
- A list of the files that the page links to, and their locations

By following these rules, you can reduce a lot of the headaches associated with maintaining a large and complicated Web site.

Linking to Locations within a Document

Gerry has studied the navigation lists you created and would like you to add another navigation list to the Glossary page. Recall that the Glossary page contains a list of digital photography terms. The page is very long, requiring users to scroll through the document to find a term of interest. Gerry would like you to create a navigation list containing the letters A through Z. From this list, Gerry wants to give users the ability to jump to a specific section in the glossary matching the clicked letter.

See Figure 2-17.

Figure 2-17 ▶ **Jumping to a location within a document**

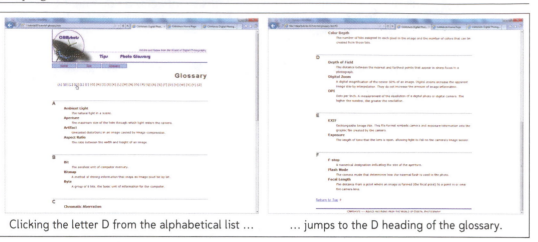

Clicking the letter D from the alphabetical list ...   ... jumps to the D heading of the glossary.

Add the navigation list to the glossary page now.

To create the navigation list:

1. Return to the **glossary.htm** file in your text editor.

2. Scroll down to the section element. Directly below the h1 *Glossary* heading, insert the following navigation list (see Figure 2-18):

```
<nav>
    [A] [B] [C]
    [D] [E] [F]
    [G] [H] [I]
    [J] [K] [L]
    [M] [N] [O]
    [P] [Q] [R]
    [S] [T] [U]
    [V] [W] [X]
    [Y] [Z]
</nav>
```

Figure 2-18 ▶ **Adding a navigation element to the glossary**

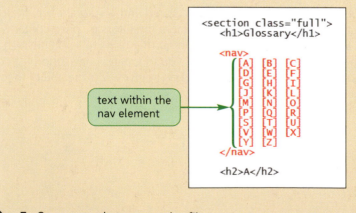

```
<section class="full">
    <h1>Glossary</h1>

    <nav>
        [A]  [B]  [C]
        [D]  [E]  [F]
        [G]  [H]  [I]
        [J]  [K]  [L]
        [M]  [N]  [O]
        [P]  [Q]  [R]
        [S]  [T]  [U]
        [V]  [W]  [X]
        [Y]  [Z]
    </nav>

    <h2>A</h2>
```

text within the nav element

3. Save your changes to the file.

Marking Locations with the `id` Attribute

To enable users to jump to a specific location within a document, you first need to mark that location. One way of doing this is to add the `id` attribute to an element at that location in the document. Recall that the syntax of the `id` attribute is

```
id="text"
```

where `text` is the name you want to assign to the id. For example, the following code marks an `h2` element with an id of `H`:

```
<h2 id="H">H</h2>
```

Note that id names must be unique. If you assign the same id name to more than one element on a Web page, browsers use the first occurrence of the id name. XHTML documents are rejected if they contain elements with duplicate ids. Id names are also case sensitive and most browsers other than Internet Explorer differentiate between ids named, for example, *top* and *TOP*.

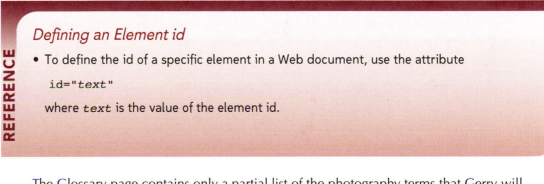

REFERENCE

Defining an Element id

• To define the id of a specific element in a Web document, use the attribute

```
id="text"
```

where *text* is the value of the element id.

The Glossary page contains only a partial list of the photography terms that Gerry will eventually add to his Web site. For now, you'll mark only sections in the glossary corresponding to the letters A through F.

To add the `id` attribute to `h2` headings:

1. Scroll down the file and locate the `h2` heading for the letter A. Within the opening `<h2>` tag, insert the following attribute:

   ```
   id="A"
   ```

2. Locate the `h2` heading for the letter B and insert the following attribute in the opening `<h2>` tag:

   ```
   id="B"
   ```

   Figure 2-19 highlights the revised code.

Figure 2-19   Adding the id attribute to h2 headings

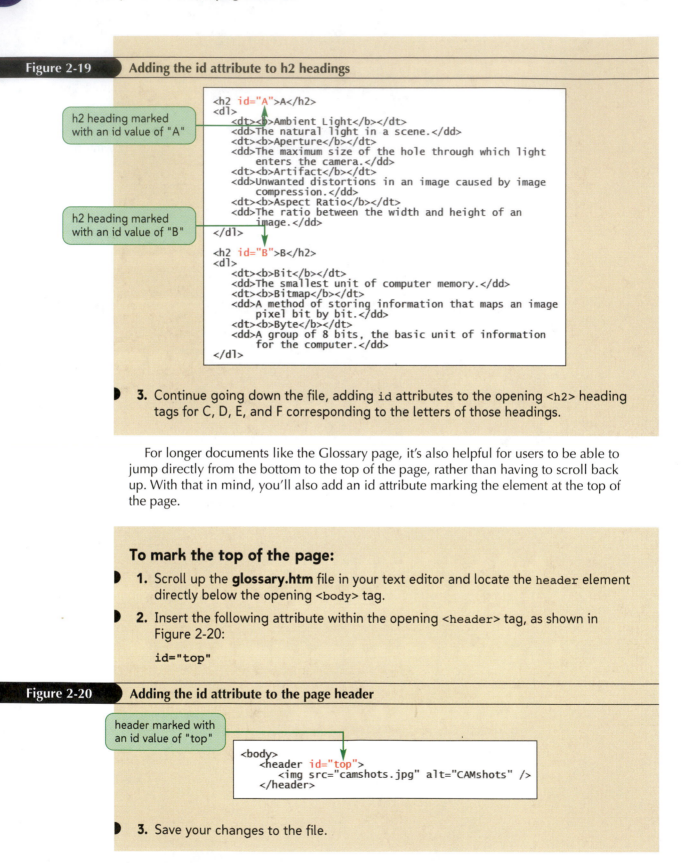

h2 heading marked
with an id value of "A"

h2 heading marked
with an id value of "B"

```
<h2 id="A">A</h2>
<dl>
    <dt><b>Ambient Light</b></dt>
    <dd>The natural light in a scene.</dd>
    <dt><b>Aperture</b></dt>
    <dd>The maximum size of the hole through which light
        enters the camera.</dd>
    <dt><b>Artifact</b></dt>
    <dd>Unwanted distortions in an image caused by image
        compression.</dd>
    <dt><b>Aspect Ratio</b></dt>
    <dd>The ratio between the width and height of an
        image.</dd>
</dl>

<h2 id="B">B</h2>
<dl>
    <dt><b>Bit</b></dt>
    <dd>The smallest unit of computer memory.</dd>
    <dt><b>Bitmap</b></dt>
    <dd>A method of storing information that maps an image
        pixel bit by bit.</dd>
    <dt><b>Byte</b></dt>
    <dd>A group of 8 bits, the basic unit of information
        for the computer.</dd>
</dl>
```

3. Continue going down the file, adding `id` attributes to the opening `<h2>` heading tags for C, D, E, and F corresponding to the letters of those headings.

For longer documents like the Glossary page, it's also helpful for users to be able to jump directly from the bottom to the top of the page, rather than having to scroll back up. With that in mind, you'll also add an id attribute marking the element at the top of the page.

To mark the top of the page:

1. Scroll up the **glossary.htm** file in your text editor and locate the `header` element directly below the opening `<body>` tag.

2. Insert the following attribute within the opening `<header>` tag, as shown in Figure 2-20:

   `id="top"`

Figure 2-20   Adding the id attribute to the page header

header marked with
an id value of "top"

```
<body>
    <header id="top">
        <img src="camshots.jpg" alt="CAMshots" />
    </header>
```

3. Save your changes to the file.

Linking to an id

Once you've marked an element using the `id` attribute, you can create a hypertext link to that element using the `a` element

```
<a href="#id">content</a>
```

where `id` is the value of the `id` attribute of the element. For example, to create a link to the `h2` heading for the letter A in the glossary document, you would enter the following code:

```
<a href="#A">A</a>
```

You'll change each entry on the Glossary page to a hypertext link pointing to the section of the glossary corresponding to the selected letter.

To change the list of letters to hypertext links:

1. Locate the letter A in the list of letters at the top of the **glossary.htm** file.

2. After the [character, insert the following opening tag:

```
<a href="#A">
```

3. Between the letter A and the] character, insert the closing `</a>` tag. Figure 2-21 shows the revised code.

Figure 2-21   **Marking a hypertext link for "A"**

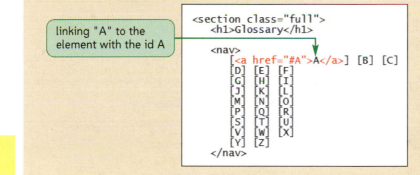

linking "A" to the element with the id A

```
<section class="full">
    <h1>Glossary</h1>

    <nav>
        [<a href="#A">A</a>] [B] [C]
        [D] [E] [F]
        [G] [H] [I]
        [J] [K] [L]
        [M] [N] [O]
        [P] [Q] [R]
        [S] [T] [U]
        [V] [W] [X]
        [Y] [Z]
    </nav>
```

Make sure you include the pound symbol (#) in the hypertext link, and ensure that the id text matches both upper- and lowercase letters in the linked id.

4. Mark the letters B through F in the list as hypertext links pointing to the appropriate `h2` headings in the document. Figure 2-22 shows the revised code for the list of letters.

Figure 2-22   **Hypertext links for the list of letters**

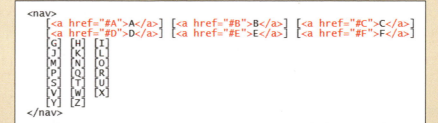

```
<nav>
    [<a href="#A">A</a>] [<a href="#B">B</a>] [<a href="#C">C</a>]
    [<a href="#D">D</a>] [<a href="#E">E</a>] [<a href="#F">F</a>]
    [G] [H] [I]
    [J] [K] [L]
    [M] [N] [O]
    [P] [Q] [R]
    [S] [T] [U]
    [V] [W] [X]
    [Y] [Z]
</nav>
```

Gerry also wants you to create a hypertext link at the bottom of the file that points to the top. You'll use the `id` attribute you created in the last set of steps.

5. Scroll to the bottom of the file and locate the text *Return to Top*.

6. Mark the text as a hyperlink, pointing to the element with an id value of *top*. See Figure 2-23.

Figure 2-23 ▶ **Hypertext link to jump to the top**

link to the element with the id *top*

```
     <div><a href="#top">Return to Top</a> &#8657;</div>
</section>

<footer>
   <address>
      CAMshots &#8250;&#8250;&#8250; Advice and News from
      the World of Digital Photography
   </address>
</foooter>
```

7. Save your changes to the file and then reload or refresh the **glossary.htm** file in your Web browser. As shown in Figure 2-24, the letters A through F in the alphabetical list are displayed as hypertext links.

8. Click the link for **F** and verify that you jump down to the end of the document, where the photographic terms starting with the letter F are listed.

Figure 2-24 ▶ **Hypertext links in the glossary page**

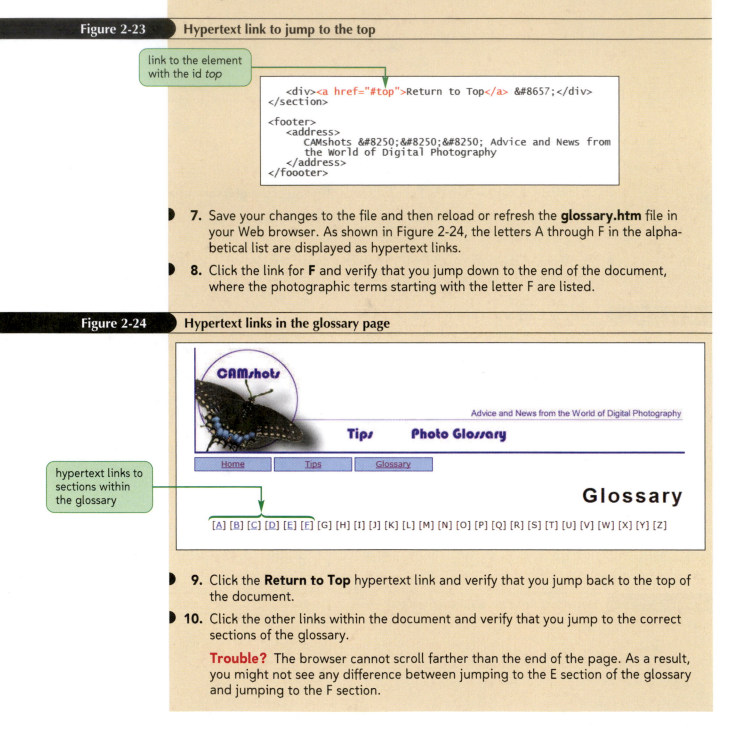

hypertext links to sections within the glossary

9. Click the **Return to Top** hypertext link and verify that you jump back to the top of the document.

10. Click the other links within the document and verify that you jump to the correct sections of the glossary.

   Trouble? The browser cannot scroll farther than the end of the page. As a result, you might not see any difference between jumping to the E section of the glossary and jumping to the F section.

INSIGHT

Anchors and the name Attribute

Early Web pages did not support the use of the id attribute as a way of marking locations within a document. Instead, they used the <a> tag as an **anchor** or bookmark using the name attribute

```
<a name="anchor">content</a>
```

where *anchor* is the name of the anchor that marks the location of the document content. For example, to add an anchor to an h2 heading, you would enter the following code:

```
<h2><a name="A">A</a></h2>
```

Marking a location with an anchor does not change your document's appearance in any way; it merely creates a destination within your document. You use the same syntax to link to locations marked with an anchor as you would with locations marked with id attributes. To link to the above anchor, you could use the following code:

```
<a href="#A">A</a>
```

The use of anchors is a deprecated feature of HTML and is not supported in strict applications of XHTML. The name attribute is not part of HTML5, but you will still see anchors used in older code and in code generated by HTML editors and converters.

Creating Links to ids in Other Documents

Gerry knows that the glossary will be one of the most useful parts of his Web site, especially for novice photographers. However, he's also aware that most people do not read through glossaries. He would like to create links from the words he uses in his articles to glossary entries so that readers of his articles can quickly access definitions for terms they don't understand. His articles are not on the same page as his Glossary page, so he'll have to create a link between those pages and specific glossary entries.

To create a link to a specific location within a document, mark the hypertext link as follows

```
<a href="reference#id">content</a>
```

where *reference* is a reference to an HTML or XHTML file and *id* is the id of an element marked with the *id* attribute within that file. For example, the HTML code

```
<a href="glossary.htm#D">"D" terms in the Glossary</a>
```

creates a hypertext link to the D entries in the glossary.htm file. Note that this assumes that the glossary.htm file is located in the same folder as the document containing the hypertext link. If not, you have to include either the absolute or relative path information along with the filename, as described earlier.

Linking to an id

- To link to a specific location within the current file, use

  `<a href="#id">content</a>`

  where *id* is the id value of an element within the document.
- To link to a specific location in another file, use

  `<a href="reference#id">content</a>`

  where *reference* is a reference to an external file and *id* is the id value of an element in that file.

On Gerry's home page, he wants to showcase a Photo of the Month, displaying a photo that his readers might find interesting or useful in their own work. Along with the photo, he has included the digital camera settings used in taking the photo. Many of the camera settings are described on the Glossary page. Gerry suggests that you create a link between the setting name and the glossary entry. The five entries he wants to link to are F-stop, Exposure, Focal Length, Aperture, and Flash Mode. Your first step is to mark these entries in the glossary using the id attribute.

To mark the glossary entries:

1. Return to the **glossary.htm** file in your text editor.

2. Scroll through the file and locate the *Aperture* definition term.

3. As shown in Figure 2-25, within the opening `<dt>` tag, insert the following attribute:

   `id="aperture"`

Figure 2-25   **Adding the id attribute to the aperture definition**

```
<h2 id="A">A</h2>
<dl>
    <dt><b>Ambient Light</b></dt>
    <dd>The natural light in a scene.</dd>
    <dt id="aperture"><b>Aperture</b></dt>
    <dd>The maximum size of the hole through which light
        enters the camera.</dd>
    <dt><b>Artifact</b></dt>
    <dd>Unwanted distortions in an image caused by image
        compression.</dd>
    <dt><b>Aspect Ratio</b></dt>
    <dd>The ratio between the width and height of an
        image.</dd>
</dl>
```

4. Scroll down the file and locate the *Exposure* definition term.

5. Within the opening `<dt>` tag, insert the following attribute:

   `id="exposure"`

6. Go to the F section of the glossary and mark the terms with the following ids (see Figure 2-26):

   F-stop with the id `f-stop`

   Flash Mode with the id `flash_mode`

   Focal Length with the id `focal_length`

Figure 2-26   **Adding ids to the other photographic definitions**

```
<h2 id="C">C</h2>
<dl>
    <dt><b>EXIF</b></dt>
    <dd>Exchangeable Image File. This file format embeds camera
        and exposure information into the graphic file created
        by the camera.</dd>
    <dt id="exposure"><b>Exposure</b></dt>
    <dd>The length of time that the lens is open, allowing light
        to fall on the camera's image sensor.</dd>
</dl>

<h2 id="F">F</h2>
<dl>
    <dt id="f-stop"><b>F-stop</b></dt>
    <dd>A numerical designation indicating the size of the
        aperture.</dd>
    <dt id="flash_mode"><b>Flash Mode</b></dt>
    <dd>The camera mode that determines how the internal flash is used
        in the photo.</dd>
    <dt id="focal_length"><b>Focal Length</b></dt>
    <dd>The distance from a point where an image is formed (the
        focal point) to a point in or near the camera lens.</dd>
</dl>
```

> **7.** Save your changes to the **glossary.htm** file.

Next you'll go to the Home page and create links from these terms in the Photo of the Month description to their entries on the Glossary page.

To create links to the glossary entries:

> **1.** Open the **home.htm** file in your text editor.

> **2.** Scroll down the file and locate the *F-stop* term in the unordered list.

> **3.** Mark *F-stop* as a hypertext link using the following code:

```
<a href="glossary.htm#f-stop">F-stop</a>
```

> **4.** Mark *Exposure* as a hypertext link using the following code:

```
<a href="glossary.htm#exposure">Exposure</a>
```

> **5.** Mark the remaining three entries in the unordered list as hypertext pointing to their corresponding entries on the Glossary page. Figure 2-27 highlights the revised code in the file.

Figure 2-27   **Linking to a location within another document**

```html
<aside>
    <h1>Photo of the Month</h1>

    <figure>
        <img src="rainbow.png" alt="Photo" />
        <figcaption>Colorado Double Rainbow by Watts213</i></figcaption>
    </figure>

    <ul>
        <li>Camera:
                    
            Nikon D50
        </li>
        <li><a href="glossary.htm#f-stop">F-stop</a>:
                      
            f/7.1
        </li>
        <li><a href="glossary.htm#exposure">Exposure</a>:
                  
            1/200 sec.
        </li>
        <li><a href="glossary.htm#focal_length">Focal Length</a>:
             
            18mm
        </li>
        <li><a href="glossary.htm#aperture">Aperture</a>:
                   
            3.6
        </li>
        <li><a href="glossary.htm#flash_mode">Flash Mode</a>:
               
            No flash
        </li>
    </ul>
</aside>
```

document   element id

6. Save your changes to the file.

7. Refresh the **home.htm** file in your Web browser. As shown in Figure 2-28, the settings from the Photo of the Month description are now displayed as hypertext links.

Figure 2-28   **Linked photography terms**

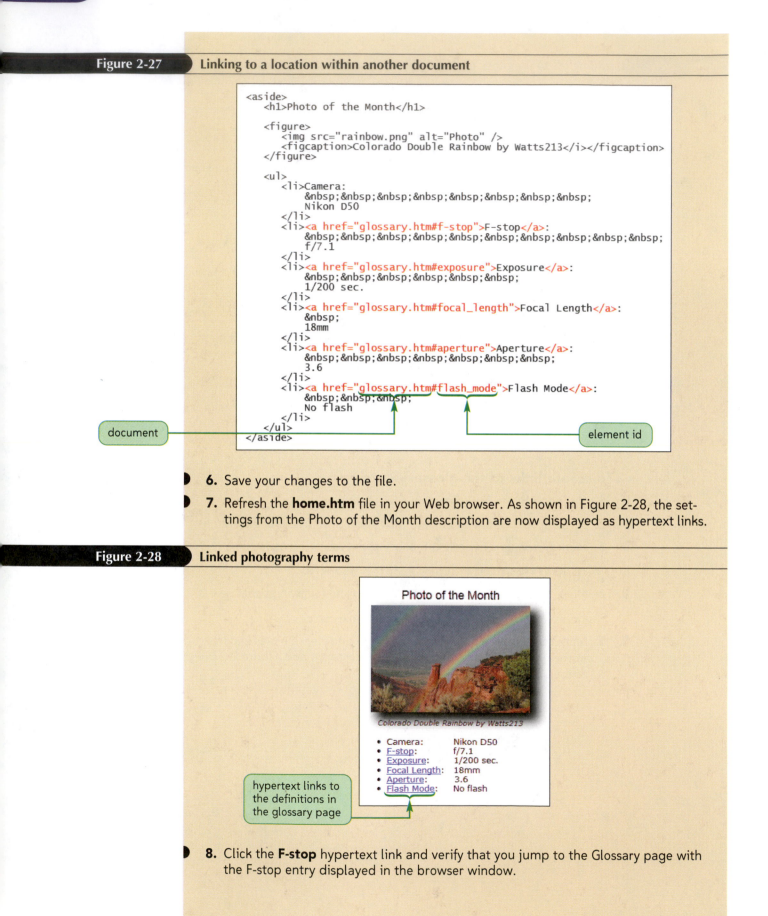

Photo of the Month

Colorado Double Rainbow by Watts213

- Camera: Nikon D50
- F-stop: f/7.1
- Exposure: 1/200 sec.
- Focal Length: 18mm
- Aperture: 3.6
- Flash Mode: No flash

hypertext links to the definitions in the glossary page

8. Click the **F-stop** hypertext link and verify that you jump to the Glossary page with the F-stop entry displayed in the browser window.

9. Return to the CAMshots home page and click the hypertext links for the other terms in the list of photo settings, verifying that you jump to the section of the glossary that displays each term's definition.

PROSKILLS

Written Communication: Creating Effective Hypertext Links

To make it easier for users to navigate your Web site, the text of your hypertext links should tell readers exactly what type of document the link points to. For example, the link text

Click here for more information.

doesn't tell the user what type of document will appear when *here* is clicked. In place of phrases like *click here*, use descriptive link text such as

For more information, view our list of frequently asked questions.

If the link points to a non-HTML file, such as a PDF document, include that information in the link text. If the linked document is extremely large and will take a while to download to the user's computer, include that information in your link text so that users can decide whether or not to initiate the transfer. For example, the following link text informs users of both the type of document and its size before they initiate the link:

Download our complete manual (PDF 2 MB).

Finally, when designing the style of your Web site, make your links easy to recognize. Because most browsers underline hypertext links, don't use underlining for other text elements; use italic or boldface fonts instead. Users should never be confused about what is a link and what is not. Also, if you apply a color to your text, do not choose colors that make your hyperlinks harder to pick out against the Web page background.

You've completed your initial work linking the three files in Gerry's Web site. In the next session, you'll learn how to work with linked images and how to create links to external Web sites and Internet resources. If you want to take a break before starting the next session, you can close your files and your Web browser now.

REVIEW

Session 2.1 Quick Check

1. What is a navigation list? How would you mark up a navigation list in HTML5? How would you mark up a navigation list prior to HTML5?
2. What is a linear structure? What is a hierarchical structure?
3. What code would you enter to link the text *Sports Info* to the sports.htm file? Assume that the current document and sports.htm are in the same folder.
4. What's the difference between an absolute path and a relative path?
5. What is the purpose of the `base` element?
6. Specify the code for marking the text *CAMshots FAQ* as an `h2` heading with the id *faq*.
7. Specify the code for marking the text *Read our FAQ* as a hypertext link to an element in the current document with the id *faq*.
8. Specify the code for marking the text *Read our FAQ* as a hypertext link pointing to an element with the id *faq* in the help.htm file. Assume that help.htm lies in the same folder as the current document.

SESSION 2.2 VISUAL OVERVIEW

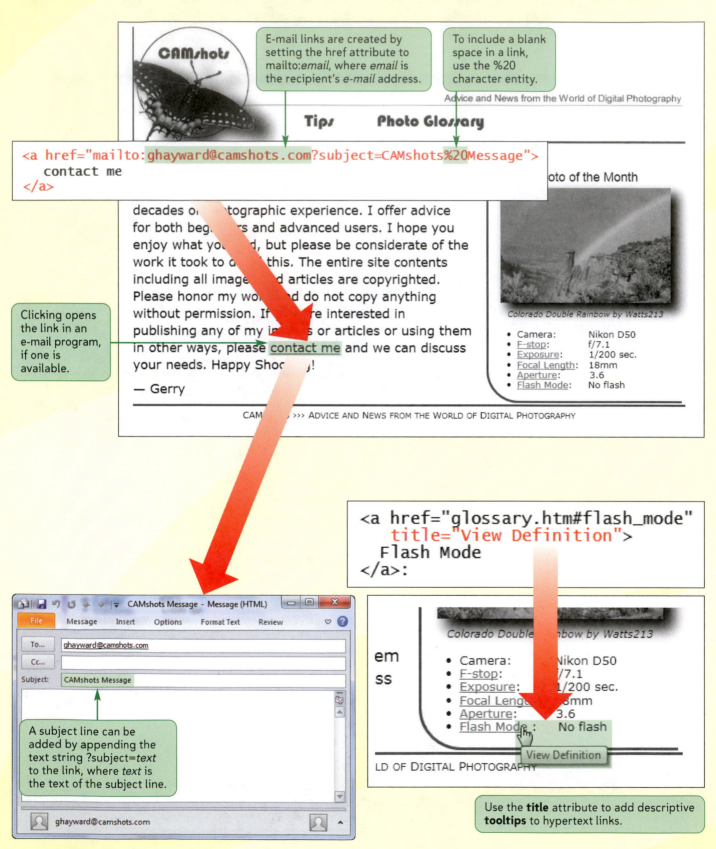

E-mail links are created by setting the href attribute to mailto:*email*, where *email* is the recipient's *e-mail* address.

To include a blank space in a link, use the %20 character entity.

Advice and News from the World of Digital Photography

Tips   Photo Glossary

```
<a href="mailto:ghayward@camshots.com?subject=CAMshots%20Message">
   contact me
</a>
```

oto of the Month

decades o ... tographic experience. I offer advice for both beg... rs and advanced users. I hope you enjoy what yo... d, but please be considerate of the work it took to d... this. The entire site contents including all image... d articles are copyrighted. Please honor my wo... d do not copy anything without permission. If ... re interested in publishing any of my im... s or articles or using them in other ways, please contact me and we can discuss your needs. Happy Shoo... g!

— Gerry

Clicking opens the link in an e-mail program, if one is available.

Colorado Double Rainbow by Watts213

- Camera: Nikon D50
- F-stop: f/7.1
- Exposure: 1/200 sec.
- Focal Length: 18mm
- Aperture: 3.6
- Flash Mode: No flash

CAM... >>> ADVICE AND NEWS FROM THE WORLD OF DIGITAL PHOTOGRAPHY

```
<a href="glossary.htm#flash_mode"
   title="View Definition">
   Flash Mode
</a>:
```

CAMshots Message - Message (HTML)

File Message Insert Options Format Text Review

To...   ghayward@camshots.com
Cc...
Subject: CAMshots Message

A subject line can be added by appending the text string ?subject=*text* to the link, where *text* is the text of the subject line.

ghayward@camshots.com

Colorado Double ... bow by Watts213

em
ss

- Camera: Nikon D50
- F-stop: /7.1
- Exposure: 1/200 sec.
- Focal Leng... 8mm
- Aperture: 3.6
- Flash Mode :   No flash

View Definition

LD OF DIGITAL PHOTOGRAPHY

Use the **title** attribute to add descriptive **tooltips** to hypertext links.

IMAGE MAPS AND EXTERNAL LINKS

```
<img src="camshots.jpg" alt="CAMshots" usemap="#logomap" />

<map name="logomap">
    <area shape="circle" coords="82, 78,80"
    href="home.htm" alt="Home Page" />
    <area shape="rect" coords="235, 120, 310, 150"
    href="tips.htm" alt="Tips" />
    <area shape="rect" coords="340, 120, 510, 150"
    href="glossary.htm" alt="Glossary" />
</map>
```

An inline image is attached to an image map with the usemap attribute.

An **image map** maps areas called **hotspots** within an image to different linked documents.

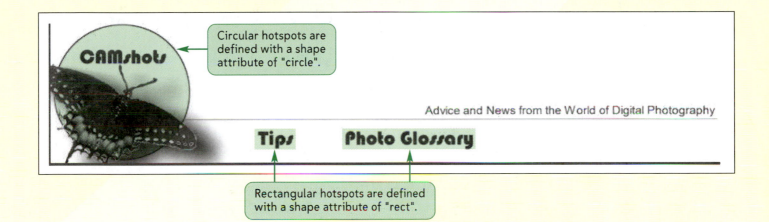

Circular hotspots are defined with a shape attribute of "circle".

Advice and News from the World of Digital Photography

Tips   Photo Glossary

Rectangular hotspots are defined with a shape attribute of "rect".

Sample URLs to link to Internet resources

URL	Description
file:///C\server\camshots.htm	Links to the camshots.htm file in the server folder on the C drive
ftp://ftp.microsoft.com	Links to the FTP server at ftp.microsoft.com
http://www.camshots.com	Links to the Web site www.camshots.com
https://www.camshots.com	Links to the Web site www.camshots.com over a secure connection

Working with Linked Images and Image Maps

Inline images can be marked as hyperlinks using the same techniques you employed in the last session. For example, a standard practice on the Web is to turn a Web site's logo into a hyperlink pointing to the home page. This gives users quick access to the home page rather than spending time searching for a link. To mark an inline image as a hyperlink, you enclose the `<img>` tag within a set of `<a>` tags as follows:

```
<a href="reference"><img src="file" alt="text" /></a>
```

Once the image has been marked as hypertext, clicking anywhere within the image jumps the user to the linked file.

The target of the link need not be a Web page; it can also be another image file. This is commonly done for **thumbnail images** that are small representations of larger image files. Gerry has done this for his image of the photo of the month. The image on the site's home page is a thumbnail of the larger photo. Gerry wants users to be able to view the larger image file by clicking the thumbnail.

You'll turn the Photo of the Month image into a hyperlink pointing to the larger image file.

TIP

Always include alternate text for your linked images to allow non-graphical browsers to display a text link in place of the linked image.

To link the Photo of the Month image:

1. Return to the **home.htm** file in your text editor.

2. Scroll down to the `img` element for the Photo of the Month and then enclose the inline image within a set of `<a>` tags as follows (see Figure 2-29):

   ```
   <a href="rainbow_lg.png">
      <img src="rainbow.png" alt="Photo" />
   </a>
   ```

Figure 2-29   **Linking an inline image**

```
<aside>
   <h1>Photo of the Month</h1>

   <figure>
      <a href="rainbow_lg.png">
         <img src="rainbow.png" alt="Photo" />
      </a>
      <figcaption>Colorado Double Rainbow by Watts213</i></figcaption>
   </figure>
```

link to a large image of the photo

3. Save your changes to the file.

4. Reload the **home.htm** file in your Web browser. Click the Photo of the Month image and verify that the browser displays a larger, more detailed version of the image.

INSIGHT

Removing Image Borders

By default, Web browsers underline hypertext links. If an image is linked, browsers usually display the image with a colored border. To remove the border, you can add the following `style` attribute to the img element:

```
<img src="file" alt="text" style="border-width: 0px" />
```

This attribute sets the width of the border to 0 pixels, effectively removing it from the rendered Web page. You can also set the border width to 0 by using the following `border` attribute:

```
<img src="file" alt="text" border="0" />
```

Note that the `border` attribute is not supported in HTML5 but you will still see it used in many Web sites. Despite the fact that many browsers still support the use of the `border` attribute, you should not use it, relying instead on either the style attribute or styles set within an external style sheet.

Introducing Image Maps

When you mark an inline image as a hyperlink, the entire image is linked to the same destination file. However, HTML also allows you to divide an image into different zones, or **hotspots,** each linked to a different destination. Gerry is interested in doing this with the current image in the CAMshots header. He would like you to create hotspots for the logo so that if a user clicks anywhere within the CAMshots circle on the left side of the logo, the user jumps to the Home page; and if the user clicks either Tips or Photo Glossary in the logo, the user jumps to the Tips page or to the Glossary page, respectively. See Figure 2-30.

Figure 2-30   **Hotspots within the CAMshots header image**

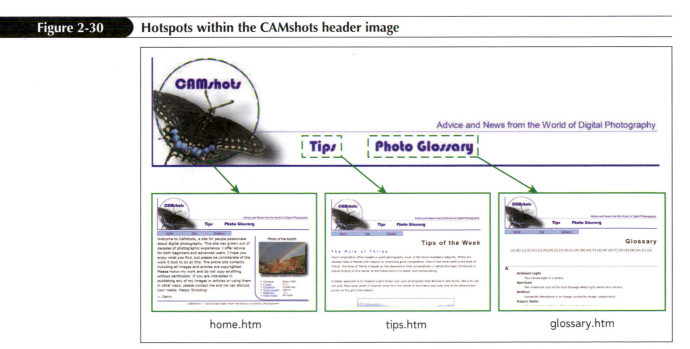

home.htm   tips.htm   glossary.htm

To define these hotspots, you create an **image map** that links a specified region of the inline image to a specific document. HTML supports two kinds of image maps: client-side image maps and server-side image maps. A **client-side image map** is an image map that is defined within the Web page and handled entirely by the Web browser running on a user's computer, while a **server-side image map** relies on a program running on the Web server to create and administer the map. For the CAMshots Web site, you'll create a client-side image map.

Client-Side Image Maps

Client-side image maps are defined with the `map` element

```
<map name="text">
    hotspots
</map>
```

where `text` is the name of the image map and `hotspots` are the locations of the hotspots within the image. For example, the following `map` element creates a client-side image map named *logomap*:

```
<map name="logomap">
    ...
</map>
```

TIP

For XHTML documents, use the `id` attribute in place of the `name` attribute to identify an image map.

Client-side image maps can be placed anywhere within the body of a Web page because they are not actually displayed by browsers, but simply used as references for mapping hotspots to inline images. The most common practice is to place a `map` element below the corresponding inline image.

Defining Hotspots

An individual hotspot is defined using the `area` element

```
<area shape="shape" coords="coordinates" href="reference"
  alt="text" />
```

where `shape` is the shape of the hotspot region, `coordinates` are the list of points that define the boundaries of the region, `reference` is the file or location that the hotspot is linked to, and `text` is alternate text displayed for non-graphical browsers. Hotspots can be created in the shapes of rectangles, circles, or polygons (multisided figures). You use a shape value of `rect` for rectangular hotspots, `circle` for circular hotspots, and `poly` for polygonal or multisided hotspots. A fourth possible value for the `shape` attribute, `default`, represents the remaining area of the inline image not covered by any hotspots. There is no limit to the number of hotspots you can add to an image map. Hotspots can also overlap. If they do and the user clicks an overlapping area, the browser opens the link of the first hotspot listed in the map.

Hotspot coordinates are measured in **pixels**, which are the smallest unit or dot in a digital image or display. Your computer monitor might have a size of 1024 x 768 pixels, which means that the display is 1024 dots wide by 768 dots tall. For example, the header image that Gerry uses in his Web site has dimensions of 780 pixels wide by 167 pixels tall. When used with the `coords` attribute of the `area` element, pixel values exactly define the location and size of a hotspot region.

Each hotspot shape has a different set of coordinates that define it. To define a rectangular hotspot, apply the `area` element

```
<area shape="rect" coords="x1, y1, x2, y2" ... />
```

where `x1, y1` are the coordinates of the upper-left corner of the rectangle and `x2, y2` are the coordinates of the rectangle's lower-right corner. Figure 2-31 shows the coordinates of the rectangular region surrounding the Photo Glossary hotspot.

Figure 2-31   Defining a rectangular hotspot

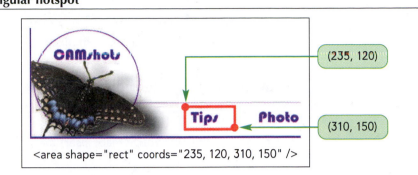

The upper-left corner of the rectangle has the image coordinates (235, 120), indicating that it is 235 pixels to the right and 120 pixels down from the upper-left corner of the image. The lower-right corner is found at the image coordinates (310, 150), placing it 310 pixels to the right and 150 pixels down from the upper-left corner of the image. Note that coordinates are always expressed relative to the upper-left corner of the image, regardless of the position of the image on the page.

Circular hotspots are defined using the coordinates

```
<area shape="circle" coords="x, y, r" ... />
```

where x and y are the coordinates of the center of the circle and r is the circle's radius. Figure 2-32 shows the coordinates for a circular hotspot around the CAMshots image from the Web site logo. The center of the circle is located at the coordinates (92, 82) and the circle has a radius of 80 pixels.

Figure 2-32   Defining a circular hotspot

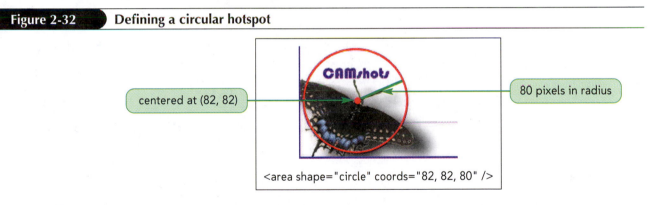

Polygonal hotspots are defined with

```
<area shape="poly" coords="x1, y1, x2, y2, x3, y3, ..." ... />
```

where ($x1$, $y1$), ($x2$, $y2$), ($x3$, $y3$) and so forth define the coordinates of each corner in the multisided shape. Figure 2-33 shows the coordinates for a polygonal region that covers the CAMshots logo, including the butterfly wings.

Figure 2-33   Defining a polygonal hotspot

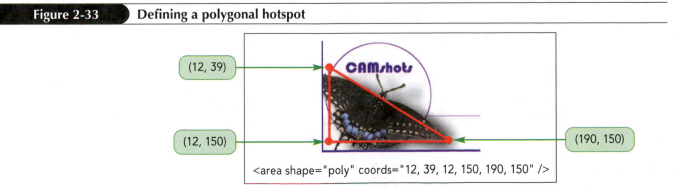

Finally, to define the default hotspot for an image, use

```
<area shape="default" coords="0, 0, x, y" ... />
```

where x is the width of the inline image in pixels and y is the height of the image. Any spot in an inline image that is not covered by another hotspot activates the default hotspot link.

Creating a Client-Side Image Map

- To create a client-side image map, insert the map element

```
<map name="text">
    hotspots
</map>
```

anywhere within the Web page body, where *text* is the name of the image map and *hotspots* is a list of hotspot areas defined within the image map. (Note: For XHTML, use the `id` attribute in place of the `name` attribute.)

- To add a hotspot to the image map, place the `area` element

```
<area shape="shape" coords="coordinates" href="reference"
 alt="text" />
```

within the map element, where *shape* is the shape of the hotspot region, *coordinates* is the list of points that defines the boundaries of the region, *reference* is the file or location that the hotspot is linked to, and *text* is alternate text displayed for non-graphical browsers.

- To define a rectangular-shaped hotspot, use

```
<area shape="rect" coords="x1, y1, x2, y2" ... />
```

where $x1, y1$ are the coordinates of the upper-left corner of the rectangle and $x2, y2$ are the coordinates of the lower-right corner of the rectangle.

- To define a circular hotspot, use

```
<area shape="circle" coords="x, y, r" ... />
```

where x and y are the coordinates of the center of the circle and r is the radius of the circle.

- To define a polygonal hotspot, use

```
<area shape="poly" coords="x1, y1, x2, y2, x3, y3, ..." ... />
```

where $(x1, y1)$, $(x2, y2)$, $(x3, y3)$, and so forth define the coordinates of each corner in the multisided shape.

- To define the default hotspot, use

```
<area shape="default" coords="0, 0, x, y" ... />
```

where x is the width of the inline image in pixels and y is the height in pixels.

- To apply an image map to an inline image, add the `usemap` attribute

```
<img src="file" alt="text" usemap="#map" />
```

to the inline image, where *map* is the name assigned to the image map.

To determine the coordinates of a hotspot, you can use either a graphics program such as Adobe Photoshop or image map software that automatically generates the HTML code for the hotspots you define.

In this case, assume that Gerry has already determined the coordinates for the hotspots in his image map and provided them for you. He wants you to create three hotspots, which are shown earlier in Figure 2-30. The first is a circular hotspot linked to the home.htm file, centered at the point (92, 82) and with a radius of 80 pixels. The second is a rectangular hotspot linked to the tips.htm file, with corners at (235, 120) and (310, 150). The third is also rectangular, linked to the glossary.htm file, with corners at (340, 120) and (510, 150). You do not have to create a polygonal hotspot.

You'll name the image map containing these hotspots *logomap*.

To create an image map:

1. Return to the **home.htm** file in your text editor.

2. Directly below the `<img>` tag for the CAMshots header image, insert the following map element:

   ```
   <map name="logomap">
   </map>
   ```

3. Within the `map` element, insert a circular hotspot that points to the home.htm file using the following `area` element:

   ```
   <area shape="circle" coords="82, 82, 80"
    href="home.htm" alt="Home Page" />
   ```

4. Directly below the `<area>` tag for the circular hotspot, insert the following two rectangular hotspots pointing to the tips.htm and glossary.htm files:

   ```
   <area shape="rect" coords="235, 120, 310, 150"
    href="tips.htm" alt="Tips" />
   ```

   ```
   <area shape="rect" coords="340, 120, 510, 150"
    href="glossary.htm" alt="Glossary" />
   ```

   Figure 2-34 highlights the new code in the file.

Figure 2-34	Creating the logomap image map

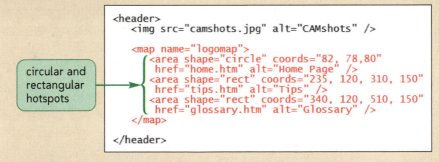

```
<header>
    <img src="camshots.jpg" alt="CAMshots" />

    <map name="logomap">
      <area shape="circle" coords="82, 78,80"
       href="home.htm" alt="Home Page" />
      <area shape="rect" coords="235, 120, 310, 150"
       href="tips.htm" alt="Tips" />
      <area shape="rect" coords="340, 120, 510, 150"
       href="glossary.htm" alt="Glossary" />
    </map>

</header>
```

circular and rectangular hotspots

5. Save your changes to the file.

With the image map defined, your next task is to apply that map to the CAMshots header.

Applying an Image Map

To apply an image map to an image, you add the `usemap` attribute

```
<img src="file" alt="text" usemap="#map" />
```

to the inline image, where *map* is the name assigned to the image map.

Apply the *logomap* image map to the CAMshots logo and then test it in your Web browser.

To apply the *logomap* image map:

1. Add the following attribute to the `<img>` tag for the CAMshots logo, as shown in Figure 2-35:

   ```
   usemap="#logomap"
   ```

 Figure 2-35 **Applying the logomap image map**

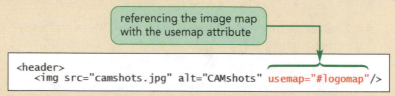

2. Save your changes to the file and then reload or refresh the **home.htm** file in your Web browser.

3. Click anywhere within the word **Tips** in the header image and verify that the browser opens the Tips page.

4. Return to the home page and click anywhere within the words **Photo Glossary** in the header image to verify that the browser opens the Glossary page.

Now that you've created an image map for the logo on the home page, you can create similar image maps for the logos on the Tips and Glossary pages.

To add image maps to the other Web pages:

1. Return to the **tips.htm** file in your text editor.

2. Replace the code within the header element with the code shown earlier in Figure 2-34. (Hint: You can use the copy and paste feature of your text editor to copy the code from the home.htm file into the tips.htm file.)

3. Save your changes to the file.

4. Go to the **glossary.htm** file in your text editor.

5. As you did for the tips.htm file, replace the code within the header element for the inline image with the code from the home.htm file. Save your changes to the file.

6. Reload the **home.htm** file in your Web browser and verify that you can switch among the three Web pages by clicking the hotspots in the CAMshots header image.

INSIGHT

Server-Side Image Maps

The other type of image map you might encounter on the Web is a server-side image map, in which information about the hotspots is stored on the Web server rather than entered into the HTML code of a Web page. When you click a hotspot on a server-side image map, the coordinates of the mouse click are sent to the server, which activates the corresponding link, sending the linked page to your Web browser.

The server-side image map was the original HTML standard and is still supported on the Web. However, server-side maps have some limitations compared to client-side image maps. Because the map is located on the server, you need server access to test your image map code. Also, server-side image maps might be slower because information must be sent to the server with each mouse click. Finally, unlike client-side image maps, server-side image maps require the use of a mouse to send the information to the server. This makes them unsuitable for users with disabilities or users running non-graphical browsers.

To create a server-side image map, you enclose an inline image within a hypertext link such as

```
<a href="map">
    <img src="file" alt="text" ismap="ismap" />
</a>
```

where *map* is the name of a program or file running on the Web server that handles the image map. The `ismap` attribute tells the Web browser to treat the inline image as an image map.

Linking to Resources on the Internet

In the tips.htm file, Gerry has listed some of the Web sites he finds useful in his study of photography. He would like to change the entries in this list to hypertext links that his readers can click to quickly access the sites.

Introducing URLs

To create a link to a resource on the Internet, you need to know its URL. A **Uniform Resource Locator** (**URL**) specifies the location and type of a resource on the Internet. Examples of URLs include *www.whitehouse.gov*, the home page of the President of the United States, and *www.w3.org*, the home page of the World Wide Web consortium. All URLs share the general structure

scheme:location

where *scheme* indicates the type of resource referenced by the URL and *location* is the location of that resource. For Web pages, the location refers to the location of the HTML file; but for other resources, the location might simply be the name of the resource. For example, a link to an e-mail account has the recipient's e-mail address as the location.

The name of the scheme is taken from the network protocol used to access the resource. A **protocol** is a set of rules defining how information is passed between two devices. Your Web browser communicates with Web servers using the **Hypertext Transfer Protocol** (**HTTP**). Therefore, the URLs for all Web pages must start with the http scheme. Other Internet resources, described in Figure 2-36, use different communication protocols and thus have different scheme names.

Figure 2-36   **Internet protocols**

Protocol	Used To
file	Access documents stored locally on a user's computer
ftp	Access documents stored on an FTP server
http	Access Web pages
https	Access Web pages over a secure encrypted connection
mailto	Open a user's e-mail client and address a new message

Linking to a Web Site

The URL for a Web page has the general form

```
http://server/path/filename#id
```

where *server* is the name of the Web server, *path* is the path to the file on that server, *filename* is the name of the file, and if necessary, *id* is the name of an id or anchor within the file. A Web page URL can also contain specific programming instructions for a browser to send to the Web server (a topic beyond the scope of this tutorial). Figure 2-37 identifies the different parts of a sample URL for a sample Web page.

Figure 2-37   **Parts of a URL**

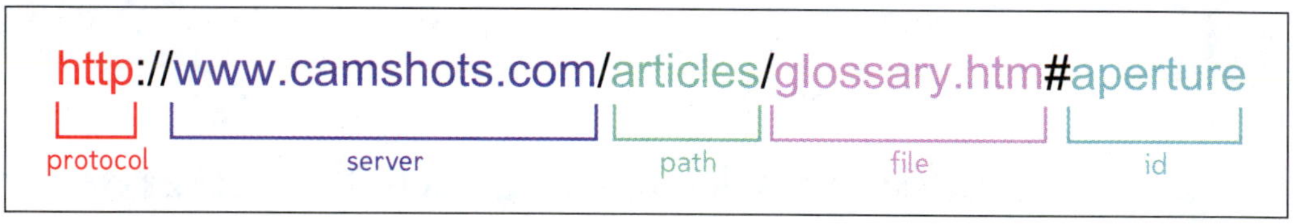

You might have noticed that a URL like *http://www.camshots.com* doesn't include any pathname or filename. If a URL doesn't specify a path, then it indicates the top folder in the server's directory tree. If a URL doesn't specify a filename, the server returns the default home page. Many servers use index.html as the filename for the default home page, so the URL *http://www.camshots.com/index.html* would be equivalent to *http://www.camshots.com*.

INSIGHT

Understanding Domain Names

The server name portion of a URL is also called the **domain name**. By studying a domain name, you learn about the server hosting the Web site. Each domain name contains a hierarchy of names separated by periods (.), with the top level appearing at the end. The top level, called an **extension**, indicates the general audience supported by the Web server. For example, *.edu* is the extension reserved for educational institutions, *.gov* is used for agencies of the United States government, and *.com* is used for commercial sites or general-use sites.

The next lower level appearing before the extension displays the name of the individual or organization hosting the site. The domain name *camshots.com* indicates a commercial or general-use site owned by CAMshots. To avoid duplicating domain names, the top two levels of the domain must be registered with the IANA (Internet Assigned Numbers Authority) before they can be used. You can usually register your domain name through your Web host. Be aware that you must pay an annual fee to keep a domain name.

The lowest levels of the domain, which appear farthest to the left in the domain name, are assigned by the individual or company hosting the site. Large Web sites involving hundreds of pages typically divide their domain names into several levels. For example, a large company like Microsoft might have one domain name for file downloads—*downloads.microsoft.com*—and another for customer service—*service.microsoft.com*. Finally, the first part of the domain name displays the name of the hard drive or resource storing the Web site files. Many companies have standardized on *www* as the initial part of their domain names.

Gerry has listed four Web pages that he wants his readers to be able to access. He's also provided you with the URLs for these pages, which are shown in Figure 2-38.

Figure 2-38 **Photography URLs**

Web Site	URL
Apogee Photo	http://www.apogeephoto.com
Outdoor Photographer	http://www.outdoorphotographer.com
Digital Photo	http://www.dpmag.com
Popular Photography and Imaging	http://www.popphoto.com

You'll link the names of the Web sites that Gerry has listed in the Tips page to the URLs listed in Figure 2-38. For example, to link the text *Apogee Photo* to the Apogee Photo Web site, you would use the following <a> tag:

```
<a href="http://www.apogeephoto.com">Apogee Photo</a>
```

REFERENCE

Linking to Internet Resources

- The URL for a Web page is

  ```
  http://server/path/filename#id
  ```

  where *server* is the name of the Web server, *path* is the path to a file on that server, *filename* is the name of the file, and if necessary, *id* is the name of an id or anchor within the file.
- The URL for an FTP site is

  ```
  ftp://server/path/filename
  ```

  where *server* is the name of the FTP server, *path* is the folder path, and *filename* is the name of the file.
- The URL for an e-mail address is

  ```
  mailto:address?header1=value1&header2=value2&...
  ```

  where *address* is the e-mail address; *header1*, *header2*, etc. are different e-mail headers; and *value1*, *value2*, and so on are the values of the headers.
- The URL to reference a local file is

  ```
  file://server/path/filename
  ```

  where *server* is the name of the local server or computer, *path* is the path to the file on that server, and *filename* is the name of the file. If you are accessing a file on your own computer, the server name is replaced by a third slash (/).

You'll use the information that Gerry has given you to create links to all four of the Web sites listed on his Tips page.

To create links to sites on the Web:

1. Return to the **tips.htm** file in your text editor.

2. Scroll to the bottom of the file and locate the definition list containing the list of Web sites.

3. Mark the entry for Apogee Photo as a hypertext link using the following code:

   ```
   <a href="http://www.apogeephoto.com">Apogee Photo</a>
   ```

4. Mark the remaining three entries in the list as hypertext links pointing to each company's Web site. Figure 2-39 highlights the revised code in the file.

Figure 2-39 Linking to sites on the Web

```
<article>
    <h1>Photography Sites on the Web</h1>
    <p>The Web is an excellent resource for articles on photography and
        digital cameras. Here are a few of my favorites.
    </p>

    <dl>
        <dt>&#9758; <a href="http://www.apogeephoto.com">Apogee Photo</a></dt>
        <dd>An established online photography magazine with articles by
            top pros, discussion forums, workshops, and more.
        </dd>
        <dt>&#9758; <a href="http://www.outdoorphotographer.com">Outdoor Photographer</a></dt>
        <dd>The premier magazine for outdoor photography. The site
            includes extensive tips on photographing wildlife, action
            sports, scenic vistas, and travel sites.
        </dd>
        <dt>&#9758; <a href="http://www.dpmag.com">Digital Photo</a></dt>
        <dd>An excellent site for novices and professionals with
            informative reviews and buying guides for the latest equipment
            and software.
        </dd>
        <dt>&#9758; <a href="http://www.popphoto.com">Popular Photography and Imaging</a></dt>
        <dd>A useful and informative site with articles from the
            long-established magazine of professional and amateur
            photographers.
        </dd>
    </dl>
</article>
```

5. Save your changes to the file.

6. Reload or refresh the **tips.htm** file in your Web browser. Figure 2-40 shows the revised list with each entry appearing as a hypertext link.

Figure 2-40 Links on the Tips page

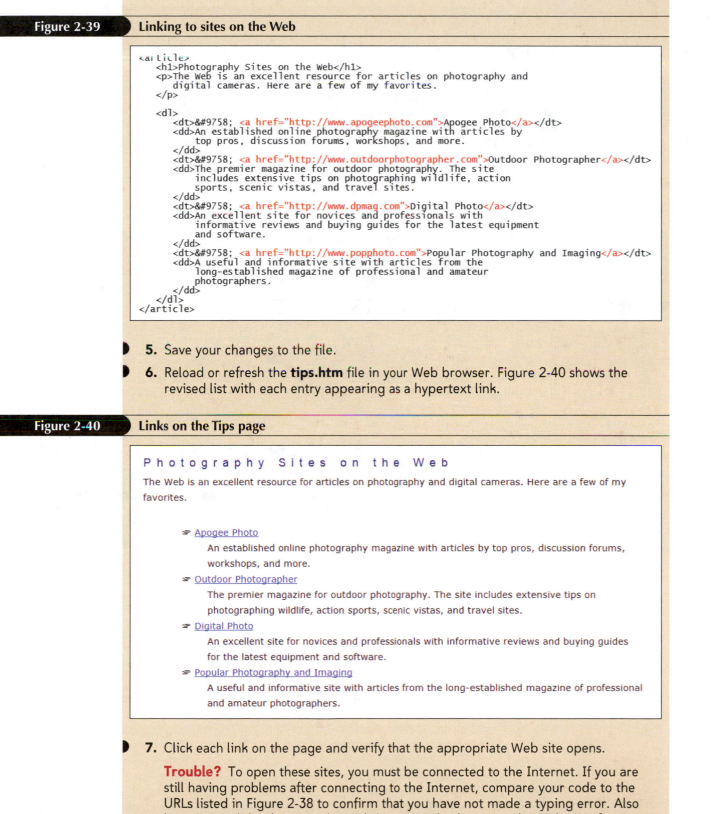

P h o t o g r a p h y   S i t e s   o n   t h e   W e b

The Web is an excellent resource for articles on photography and digital cameras. Here are a few of my favorites.

☞ Apogee Photo
  An established online photography magazine with articles by top pros, discussion forums, workshops, and more.
☞ Outdoor Photographer
  The premier magazine for outdoor photography. The site includes extensive tips on photographing wildlife, action sports, scenic vistas, and travel sites.
☞ Digital Photo
  An excellent site for novices and professionals with informative reviews and buying guides for the latest equipment and software.
☞ Popular Photography and Imaging
  A useful and informative site with articles from the long-established magazine of professional and amateur photographers.

7. Click each link on the page and verify that the appropriate Web site opens.

Trouble? To open these sites, you must be connected to the Internet. If you are still having problems after connecting to the Internet, compare your code to the URLs listed in Figure 2-38 to confirm that you have not made a typing error. Also keep in mind that because the Web is constantly changing, the Web sites for some of these links might have changed, or a site might have been removed since this book was published.

Web pages are only one type of resource that you can link to. Before continuing work on the CAMshots Web site, you'll explore how to access some of these other resources.

Linking to FTP Servers

Another method of storing and sharing files on the Internet is through FTP servers. **FTP servers** are file servers that act like virtual file cabinets in which users can store and retrieve data files, much as they store files on and retrieve files from their own computers. FTP servers transfer information using a communication protocol called **File Transfer Protocol** (**FTP**). The URL to access an FTP server follows the general format

```
ftp://server/path/
```

where *server* is the name of the FTP server and *path* is the folder path on the server that contains the files you want to access. When you access an FTP site, you can navigate through its folder tree as you would navigate the folders on your own hard disk. Figure 2-41 shows an example of an FTP site viewed as a directory listing within the Internet Explorer browser, and viewed as a collection of folders that can be navigated as if they were on the user's local machine.

Figure 2-41	Accessing an FTP site over the Web

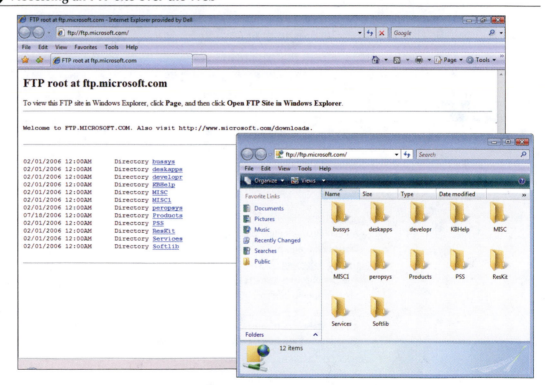

FTP servers require each user to enter a password and a username to gain access to the server's files. The standard username is *anonymous* and requires no password. Your browser supplies this information automatically, so in most situations you don't have to worry about passwords and usernames. However, some FTP servers do not allow anonymous access. In these cases, either your browser prompts you for the username and password, or you can supply a username and password within the URL using the format

```
ftp://username:password@server/path
```

where *username* and *password* are a username and password that the FTP server recognizes. It is generally *not* a good idea, however, to include usernames and passwords in URLs, as it can allow others to view your sensitive login information. It's better to let the browser send this information or to use a special program called an **FTP client**, which can encrypt or hide this information during transmission.

Linking to a Local File

HTML is a very useful language for creating collections of linked documents. Many software developers have chosen to distribute their online help in the form of HTML files. The Web sites for these help files then exist locally on a user's computer or network. If a Web site needs to reference local files (as opposed to files on the Internet or another wide area network), the URLs need to reflect this fact. The URL for a local file has the general form

```
file://server/path/filename
```

where *server* is the name of the local network server, *path* is the path on that server to the file, and *filename* is the name of the file. If you're accessing a file from your own computer, the server name can be omitted and replaced by an extra slash (/). Thus, a file from the *documents/articles* folder might have the following URL:

```
file:///documents/articles/tips.htm
```

If the file is on a different disk within your computer, the hard drive letter would be included in the URL as follows:

```
file://D:/documents/articles/tips.htm
```

Unlike the other URLs you've examined, the `file` scheme in this URL does not imply any particular communication protocol; instead, browsers retrieve the document using whatever method is the local standard for the type of file specified in the URL.

Linking to an E-Mail Address

Many Web sites use e-mail to allow users to communicate with a site's owner, sales representative, or technical support staff. You can turn an e-mail address into a hypertext link; when a user clicks the link, the user's e-mail program opens and automatically inserts the e-mail address into the *To* field of a new outgoing message. The URL for an e-mail address follows the form

```
mailto:address
```

where *address* is the e-mail address. To create a hypertext link to the e-mail address *ghayward@camshots.com*, you could use the following URL:

```
mailto:ghayward@camshots.com
```

The mailto protocol also allows you to add information to the e-mail, including the subject line and the text of the message body. To add this information to the link, you use the form

```
mailto:address?header1=value1&header2=value2&...
```

where *header1*, *header2*, etc. are different e-mail headers and *value1*, *value2*, and so on are the values of the headers. Thus, to create a link containing the e-mail message

```
TO: ghayward@camshots.com
SUBJECT: Test
BODY: This is a test message
```

you would use the following URL:

```
mailto:ghayward@camshots.com?subject=Test&Body=This%20is%20a%
20test%20message
```

Notice that the spaces in the message body *This is a test message* have been replaced with the %20 character code. This is necessary because URLs cannot contain blank spaces.

Although the mailto protocol is not technically an approved communication protocol, it is supported by almost every Web browser. However, note that a user's browser may not automatically access Web-based mail clients, such as Hotmail or Gmail, when the user clicks an e-mail link. End users accessing their mail from a Web-based mail client must configure their browsers to automatically open those Web sites in response to a mailto link.

Gerry wants you to add a link to his e-mail address on the CAMshots home page. This will give people who view his site the ability to contact him with additional questions or ideas.

To link to an e-mail address on Gerry's home page:

1. Return to the **home.htm** file in your text editor.

2. Go to the first paragraph and locate the text *contact me*.

3. Mark *contact me* as a hypertext link using the following code, as shown in Figure 2-42:

   ```
   <a href="mailto:ghayward@camshots.com?subject=CAMshots%20Message">
      contact me
   </a>
   ```

Figure 2-42 Linking to an e-mail address

```
<p>Welcome to CAMshots, a site for people passionate about
   digital photography. This site has grown out of decades
   of photographic experience. I offer advice for both
   beginners and advanced users. I hope you enjoy what you find,
   but please be considerate of the work it took to do all this.
   The entire site contents including all images and articles
   are copyrighted. Please honor my work and do not copy anything
   without permission. If you are interested in publishing any
   of my images or articles or using them in other ways,
   please <a href="mailto:ghayward@camshots.com?subject=CAMshots%20Message">contact me</a>
   and we can discuss your needs. Happy Shooting!</p>
<p>&mdash; Gerry</p>
```

e-mail address   e-mail subject heading

4. Save your changes to the file.

5. Refresh the **home.htm** file in your browser. Verify that the text *contact me* in the opening paragraph now appears as a hypertext link.

6. Click **contact me** and verify that your e-mail program displays a message with *ghayward@camshots.com* as the recipient and *CAMshots Message* as the subject.

   Trouble? If you are using a Web-based e-mail client such as Gmail or Hotmail, the browser will not open your e-mail client. You can view online documentation for your browser to determine whether it supports linking to Web-based e-mail clients.

7. Close your message window without saving the message.

PROSKILLS

Problem Solving: E-Mail Links and Spam

Use caution when adding e-mail links to your Web site. While it may make it more convenient for users to contact you, it also might make you more vulnerable to spam. **Spam** is unsolicited e-mail sent to large numbers of people, promoting products, services, and in some cases inappropriate Web sites. Spammers create their e-mail lists by scanning discussion groups, stealing Internet mailing lists, and using programs called **e-mail harvesters** to scan HTML code for the e-mail addresses contained in mailto URLs. Many Web developers have removed e-mail links from their Web sites in order to foil these harvesters, replacing the links with Web forms that submit e-mail requests to a secure server. If you need to include an e-mail address as a link on your Web page, you can take a few steps to reduce your exposure to spammers:

- Replace the text of the e-mail addresses with inline images that are more difficult for e-mail harvesters to read.
- Write a program to scramble any e-mail addresses in the HTML code, unscrambling the e-mail address only when a user clicks it.
- Replace the characters of the e-mail address with escape characters. For example, you can replace the @ symbol with the escape sequence %40.

There is no quick and easy solution to this problem. Fighting spammers is an ongoing battle, and they have proved very resourceful in overcoming some of the defenses people have created. As you develop your Web site, you should carefully consider how to handle e-mail addresses and review the most current methods for safeguarding that information.

Working with Hypertext Attributes

TIP

All of the hypertext attributes associated with the `<a>` tag can also be applied to the `<area>` tags within your image maps.

HTML provides several attributes to control the behavior and appearance of your links. Gerry suggests that you study a few of these to see whether they would be effective in his Web site.

Opening a Secondary Window or Tab

By default, each page you open replaces the contents of the current page in the browser window. This means that when Gerry's readers click on one of the four external links listed on the Tips page, they leave the CAMshots Web site. To return to the Web site, a user would have to click the browser's Back button.

Gerry wants his Web site to stay open when a user clicks one of the links to the external Web sites. Most browsers allow users to open multiple browser windows or multiple tabs within the same browser window. Gerry suggests that links to external sites be opened in a second browser window or tab. This arrangement allows continual access to his Web site, even as users are browsing other sites.

To force a document to appear in a new window or tab, you add the `target` attribute to the `<a>` tag. The general syntax is

```
<a href="url" target="window">content</a>
```

where *window* is a name assigned to the new browser window or browser tab. The value you use for the `target` attribute doesn't affect the appearance or content of the page being opened; the target simply identifies the different windows or tabs that are currently open. You can choose any name you wish for the target. If several links have the same target name, they all open in the same location, replacing the previous content in the browser window or tab. HTML also supports the special target names described in Figure 2-43.

Figure 2-43 Target names for browser windows and tabs

Target Name	Description
target	Opens the link in a new window or tab named *target*
_blank	Opens the link in a new, unnamed window or tab
_self	Opens the link in the current browser window or tab

Whether the new page is opened in a tab or in a browser window is determined by the browser settings. It cannot be set by the HTML code.

REFERENCE

Opening a Link in a New Window or Tab

- To open a link in a new browser window or browser tab, add the attribute

  `target="window"`

  to the <a> tag, where `window` is a name assigned to the new browser window or tab. The target attribute can also be set to `_blank` for a new, unnamed browser window or tab, or to `_self` for the current browser window or tab.

Gerry suggests that all of the external links from his page be opened in a browser window or tab identified with the target name *new*.

To specify a link target:

1. Return to the **tips.htm** file in your text editor.

2. Scroll to the bottom of the file and locate the four links to the external Web sites.

3. Within each of the opening <a> tags, insert the following attribute, as shown in Figure 2-44:

   `target="new"`

Figure 2-44 Setting a target for hyperlinks

```
<dl>
    <dt>&#9758; <a href="http://www.apogeephoto.com" target="new">Apogee Photo</a></dt>
    <dd>An established online photography magazine with articles by
        top pros, discussion forums, workshops, and more.
    </dd>
    <dt>&#9758; <a href="http://www.outdoorphotographer.com" target="new">Outdoor Photographer</a></dt>
    <dd>The premier magazine for outdoor photography. The site
        includes extensive tips on photographing wildlife, action
        sports, scenic vistas, and travel sites.
    </dd>
    <dt>&#9758; <a href="http://www.dpmag.com" target="new">Digital Photo</a></dt>
    <dd>An excellent site for novices and professionals with
        informative reviews and buying guides for the latest equipment
        and software.
    </dd>
    <dt>&#9758; <a href="http://www.popphoto.com" target="new">Popular Photography and Imaging</a></dt>
    <dd>A useful and informative site with articles from the
        long-established magazine of professional and amateur
        photographers.
    </dd>
</dl>
</article>
```

4. Save your changes to the file.

5. Refresh the **tips.htm** file in your browser. Click each of the four links to external Web sites and verify that each opens in the same new browser window or tab.

6. Close the secondary browser window or tab.

You should use the `target` attribute sparingly in your Web site. Creating secondary windows can clutter up a user's desktop. Also, because the page is placed in a new window, users cannot use the Back button to return to the previous page in that window; they must click the browser's program button or the tab for the original Web site. This confuses some users and annoys others. Many Web designers now advocate not using the target attribute at all, leaving the choice of opening a link in a new tab or window to users. Note that the target attribute is not supported in strict XHTML-compliant code.

Creating a Tooltip

If you want to provide additional information about a link on your Web page, you can add a tooltip to the link. A **tooltip** is descriptive text that appears when a user positions the mouse pointer over a link. Figure 2-45 shows an example of a tooltip applied to one of Gerry's links.

Figure 2-45   **Viewing a tooltip**

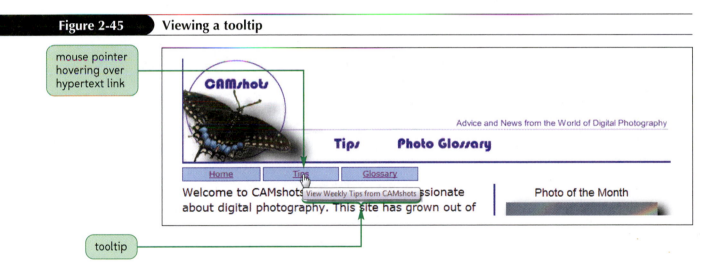

To create the tooltip, add the title attribute to the opening <a> tag in the form

```
<a href="url" title="text">content</a>
```

where *text* is the text that appears in the tooltip. To create the tooltip shown in Figure 2-45, you would enter the following HTML code:

```
<a href="tips.htm"
   title="View Weekly Tips from CAMshots">
   Tips
</a>
```

Tooltips can also be added to image map hotspots to provide more useful feedback to the user.

Creating a Semantic Link

The text of a hypertext link should always describe to users the type of document that the link opens. You can also use the `rel` attribute to indicate the type of document that a link calls. For example, in the links to the site's home page, Gerry could insert the following `rel` attribute, setting its value to *first* to indicate that the home page is the first document in the CAMshots Web site:

```
<a href="home.htm" rel="first">Home Page</a>
```

A hypertext link containing the `rel` attribute is called a **semantic link** because the tag contains information about the relationship between the link and its destination. This information is not intended for the user, but for the browser. For example, a browser could be set up to mark the first Web page in a site with a special icon or to provide scripts that allow quick access to a site's first page.

Although the `rel` attribute is not limited to a fixed set of values, the specifications for HTML and XHTML include a proposed list of special values. Figure 2-46 shows some of these proposed relationship values.

Figure 2-46   **Proposed values for the rel attribute**

rel Attribute	Link To ...
alternate	An alternate version of the document
archives	A collection of historical documents
author	Information about the author of the document
external	An external document
first	The first document in a selection
help	A help document
index	An index for the document
last	The last document in a selection
license	Copyright information for the document
next	The next document in a selection
prev	The previous document in a selection
search	A search tool for the selection
sidebar	A document that should be shown in the browser's sidebar
stylesheet	An external style sheet

HTML 4.01 and XHTML also support the `rev` attribute to describe the reverse relationship: how a linked document views the current document. For example, if you're linking to the Glossary page from the home page, the reverse relation is *first* (because that is how the Glossary page views the home page). The HTML code would be

```
<a href="glossary.htm" rel="glossary" rev="first">Glossary</a>
```

The `rev` attribute is not supported in HTML5.

At this point, Gerry decides against using the `rel` and `rev` attributes on his Web site. However, he'll keep them in mind as an option as his Web site expands in size and complexity.

Using the `link` Element

Another way to add a hypertext link to your document is to add a `link` element to the document's head with the syntax

```
<link href="url" rel="text" rev="text" target="window" />
```

where the *href*, *rel*, *rev*, and *target* attributes serve the same purpose as in the `<a>` tag. You've already used the `link` element to link your Web pages to external style sheets, but you can use it to link to other types of documents as well. For example, to use the `link` element to create semantic links to the three pages of Gerry's Web site, you could add the following link elements to the `head` element of each document:

```
<link rel="first" href="home.htm" />
<link rel="help" href="tips.htm" />
<link rel="index" href="glossary.htm" />
```

Because they are placed within a document's head, `link` elements do not appear as part of the Web page. Instead, if a browser supports it, the links can be displayed in a browser toolbar. The advantage of the `link` element used in this way is that it places the list of links outside of the Web page, freeing up page space for other content. Also, because the links appear in a browser toolbar, they are always easily accessible to users. Currently, Opera is one of the few browsers with built-in support for the `link` element. Third-party software exists to provide this support for Internet Explorer and Firefox. Because no single list of relationship names is widely accepted, you must check with each browser's documentation to find out what relationship names it supports. Until semantic links are embraced by more browsers, you should use them only if you duplicate that information elsewhere on the page.

Working with Metadata

Gerry is happy with the work you've done on the design for his CAMshots Web site. Now he wants to start working on getting the site noticed. When someone searches for "digital photography tips" or "camera buying guide," will they find Gerry's Web site? There are thousands of photography sites on the Web. Gerry knows he needs to add a few extra touches to his home page to make it more likely that the site will be picked up by major search engines such as Yahoo! and Google.

Optimizing a Web site for search engines can be a long and involved process. For the best results, Web authors often turn to **search engine optimization** (**SEO**) tools to make their sites appear more prominently in search engines. Because CAMshots is a hobby site, Gerry does not want to invest any money in improving the site's visibility; but he would like to do a few simple things that would help.

Using the `meta` Element

To be noticed on the Web, a site needs to include information about itself for search engines to read and add to their search indices. Information about a site is called **metadata**. You can add metadata to your Web pages by adding a `meta` element to the document head. In the last tutorial, you saw how to use the `meta` element to store information about the character set used by the page; but you can also use it to store other information about the document. The syntax of the `meta` element is

```
<meta name="text" content="text" scheme="text" http-equiv="text" />
```

where the `name` attribute specifies the type of metadata, the `content` attribute stores the metadata value, the `scheme` attribute defines the metadata format, and the `http-equiv` attribute is used to attach metadata or commands to the communication stream between the Web server and the browser. Note that the scheme attribute is not supported under HTML5, while the charset attribute (not listed above) is supported only under HTML5.

There are three uses of the meta element:

- To store information about a document that can be read by the author, other users, and Web browsers
- To control how browsers handle a document, including forcing browsers to automatically refresh the page at timed intervals
- To assist Web search engines in adding a document to their search index

For example, the following meta element stores the name of the Web page's author:

```
<meta name="author" content="Gerry Hayward" />
```

For search engines, you should include metadata describing the site and the topics it covers. This is done by adding a meta element containing the site description and another meta element with a list of keywords. The following two elements would summarize the CAMshots Web site for search engines:

```
<meta name="description" content="CAMshots provides advice on
digital cameras and photography" />

<meta name="keywords" content="photography, cameras, digital
imaging" />
```

Figure 2-47 lists some other examples of metadata that you can use to describe your documents.

Figure 2-47 **Examples of the uses of the meta element**

Meta Name	Example	Description
author	`<meta name="author" content="Gerry Hayward" />`	Supplies the name of the document author
classification	`<meta name="classification" content="photography" />`	Classifies the document category
copyright	`<meta name="copyright" content="&copy; 2014 CAMshots" />`	Provides a copyright statement
description	`<meta name="description" content="Digital photography and advice" />`	Provides a description of the document
generator	`<meta name="generator" content="Dreamweaver" />`	Indicates the name of the program that created the HTML code for the document
keywords	`<meta name="keywords" content="photography, cameras, digital imaging" />`	Provides a list of keywords describing the document
owner	`<meta name="owner" content="CAMshots" />`	Indicates the owner of the document
rating	`<meta name="rating" content="general" />`	Provides a rating of the document in terms of its suitability for minors
reply-to	`<meta name="reply-to" content="ghayward@camshots.com (G. Hayward)" />`	Supplies a contact e-mail address and name for the document

In recent years, search engines have become more sophisticated in evaluating Web sites. In the process, the meta element has decreased in importance. However, it is still used by search engines when adding a site to their indices. Because adding metadata requires very little effort, you should still include meta elements in your Web documents.

Working with Metadata

- To document the contents of a Web page, use the meta element

  ```
  <meta name="text" content="text" />
  ```

  where the name attribute specifies the type of metadata and the content attribute stores the metadata value.
- To add metadata or a command to the communication stream between the Web server and Web browsers, use

  ```
  <meta http-equiv="text" content="text" />
  ```

  where the http-equiv attribute specifies the type of data or command attached to the communication stream and the content attribute specifies the data value or command.

Having discussed metadata issues with you, Gerry asks that you include a few meta elements to describe his new site.

To add metadata to Gerry's document:

1. Return to the **home.htm** file in your text editor.
2. Directly below the meta element that defines the document's character set, insert the following meta elements, as shown in Figure 2-48:

   ```
   <meta name="author" content="your name" />
   <meta name="description" content="A site for sharing information on
   digital photography and cameras" />
   <meta name="keywords" content="photography, cameras, digital
   imaging" />
   ```

Figure 2-48	Adding meta elements to the CAMshots home page

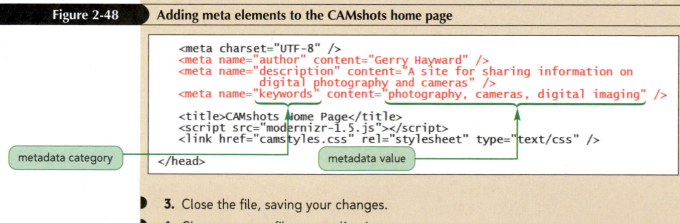

```
<meta charset="UTF-8" />
<meta name="author" content="Gerry Hayward" />
<meta name="description" content="A site for sharing information on
        digital photography and cameras" />
<meta name="keywords" content="photography, cameras, digital imaging" />

<title>CAMshots Home Page</title>
<script src="modernizr-1.5.js"></script>
<link href="camstyles.css" rel="stylesheet" type="text/css" />
</head>
```

metadata category

metadata value

3. Close the file, saving your changes.
4. Close any open files or applications.

Using the meta Element to Reload a Web Page

Describing your document is not the only use of the meta element. As you learned earlier, servers transmit Web pages using a communication protocol called HTTP. You can add information and commands to this communication stream with the http-equiv attribute of the meta element. One common use of the http-equiv attribute is to force browsers to refresh a Web page at timed intervals, which is useful for Web sites that publish scoreboards or stock tickers. For example, to automatically refresh a Web page every 60 seconds, you would apply the following meta element:

```
<meta http-equiv="refresh" content="60" />
```

Another use of the meta element is to redirect the browser from the current document to a new document. This might prove useful to Gerry someday if he changes the URL of his site's home page. As his readers get accustomed to the new Web address, he can keep the old address online, automatically redirecting readers to the new site. The meta element to perform an automatic redirect has the general form

```
<meta http-equiv="refresh" content="sec;url=url" />
```

where *sec* is the time in seconds before the browser redirects the user and *url* is the URL of the new site. To redirect users after five seconds to the Web page at *http://www. camshots.com*, you could enter the following meta element:

```
<meta http-equiv="refresh" content="5;url=http://www.camshots.com" />
```

At this point, Gerry does not need to use the meta element to send data or commands through the HTTP communication protocol. However, he will keep this option in mind if he moves the site to a new address.

Gerry is happy with the Web site you've started. He'll continue to work on the site and will come back to you for more assistance as he adds new pages and elements.

TIP

When redirecting a Web site to a new URL, avoid confusion by always including text notifying users that the page is being redirected, and provide users several seconds to read the text.

Session 2.2 Quick Check

REVIEW

1. The CAMmap image map has a circular hotspot centered at the point (50, 75) with a radius of 40 pixels pointing to the faq.htm file. Specify the code to create a map element containing this circular hotspot.

2. An inline image based on the logo.jpg file with the alternate text *CAMshots* needs to use the CAMmap image map. Specify the code to apply the image map to the image.

3. What are the five parts of a URL?

4. Specify the code to link the text *White House* to the URL *http://www. whitehouse.gov*, with the destination document displayed in a new unnamed browser window.

5. Specify the code to link the text *University of Washington* to the FTP server at *ftp.uwash.edu*.

6. Specify the code to link the text *President of the United States* to the e-mail address *president@whitehouse.gov*.

7. What attribute would you add to a hypertext link to display the tooltip *Tour the White House*?

8. Specify the code to add the description *United States Office of the President* as metadata to a document.

9. Specify the code to automatically refresh your Web document every 5 minutes.

Practice the skills you learned in the tutorial using the same case scenario.

PRACTICE

Review Assignments

Data Files needed for the Review Assignments: camhome.htm, child1.jpg–child3.jpg, childtxt.htm, conlogo.jpg, constyles.css, contest1.png–contest3.png, contesttxt.htm, flower1.jpg–flower3.jpg, flowertxt.htm, modernizr-1.5.js, photogloss.htm, scenic1.jpg–scenic3.jpg, scenictxt.htm, thirdstip.jpg, thumb1.jpg–thumb9.jpg, tipweek.htm

Gerry has been working on the CAMshots Web site for a while. During that time, the site has grown in popularity with amateur photographers. Now he wants to host a monthly photo contest to highlight the work of his colleagues. Each month Gerry will pick the three best photos from different photo categories. He's asked for your help in creating the collection of Web pages highlighting the winning entries. Gerry has already created four pages. The first page contains information about the photo contest; the remaining three pages contain the winning entries for child photos, scenic photos, and flower photos. Although Gerry has already entered much of the page content, he needs you to work on creating the links between and within each page. Figure 2-49 shows a preview of the photo contest's home page.

Figure 2-49   CAMshots Contest Winners page

Complete the following:

1. Use your text editor to open the **contesttxt.htm**, **childtxt.htm**, **scenictxt.htm**, and **flowertxt.htm** files from the tutorial.02\review folder included with your Data Files. Enter *your name* and *the date* within each file, and then save them as **contest.htm**, **child.htm**, **scenic.htm**, and **flower.htm**, respectively, in the same folder.

2. Go to the **child.htm** file in your text editor. Directly below the `header` element, create a navigation list containing an unordered list with the following list items as hyperlinks:
   a. **Home** linked to the camhome.htm file
   b. **Tips** linked to the tipweek.htm file
   c. **Contest** linked to the contest.htm file
   d. **Glossary** linked to the photogloss.htm file

3. Go to the `section` element and locate the contest1.png inline image. Directly below the inline image, insert an image map with the following properties:
   a. Set the name of the image map as **contestmap**.
   b. Add a polygonal hotspot pointing to the child.htm file containing the points (427, 5), (535, 20), (530, 59), and (421, 43). Enter **Child Photos** as the alternate text for the hotspot.
   c. Add a polygonal hotspot pointing to the flower.htm file containing the points (539, 57), (641, 84), (651, 46), and (547, 26). Enter **Flower Photos** as the alternate text for the hotspot.
   d. Add a polygonal hotspot pointing to the scenic.htm file containing the points (650, 86), (753, 125), (766, 78), and (662, 49). Enter **Scenic Photos** as the alternate text for the hotspot.

4. Apply the contestmap image map to the contest1 inline image.

5. Locate the three `h2` elements naming the three child photo winners. Assign the `h2` elements the ids **photo1**, **photo2**, and **photo3**, respectively.

6. Save your changes to the file.

7. Go to the **flower.htm** file in your text editor. Repeat Steps 2 through 6, applying the image map to the contest2.png image at the top of the `section` element.

8. Go to the **scenic.htm** file in your text editor. Repeat Steps 2 through 6 applying the image map to the contest3.png image at the top of the `section` element.

9. Go to the **contest.htm** file in your text editor. Repeat Step 2 to insert a navigation list at the top of the page.

10. Scroll down to the second article. Link the text *Child Photos* to the child.htm file. Link *Flower Photos* to the flower.htm file. Link *Scenic Photos* to the scenic.htm file.

11. Scroll down to the nine thumbnail images (named *thumb1.jpg* through *thumb9.jpg*). Link each inline image to the corresponding `h2` heading in the child.htm, flower.htm, or scenic.htm file you identified in Step 5.

12. Scroll down to the aside element. Mark the text *Gerry Hayward* as a hypertext link to an e-mail address with **ghayward@camshots.com** as the e-mail address and **Photo Contest** as the subject line.

13. Mark the text *BetterPhoto.com* as a hypertext link pointing to the URL **http://www.betterphoto.com**. Set the attribute of the link so that it opens in a new browser window or tab.

14. Save your changes to the file.

15. Open **contest.htm** in your Web browser. Verify that the e-mail link opens a new mail message window with the subject line *Photo Contest*. Verify that the link to BetterPhoto.com opens that Web site in a new browser window or tab. Verify that you can navigate through the Web site using the hypertext links in the navigation list. Finally, click each of the nine thumbnail images at the bottom of the page and verify that each connects to the larger image of the photo on the appropriate photo contest page.

16. Go to the **child.htm** file in your Web browser. Verify that you can navigate forward and backward through the three photo contest pages by clicking the hotspots in the image map.

17. Submit your completed files to your instructor, in either printed or electronic form, as requested.

Apply your knowledge of hypertext links to create a directory of universities and colleges.

APPLY

Case Problem 1

Data Files needed for this Case Problem: colleges.txt, hestyles.css, highered.jpg, modernizr-1.5.js, uwlisttxt.htm

HigherEd   Adella Coronel is a guidance counselor for Eagle High School in Waunakee, Wisconsin. She wants to take her interest in helping students choose colleges to the Web by starting a Web site called HigherEd. She's come to you for help in creating the site. The first page she wants to create is a simple directory of Wisconsin colleges and universities. She's created the list of schools, but has not yet marked the entries in the list as hypertext links. The list is very long, so she has broken it down into three categories: private colleges and universities, technical colleges, and public universities. Because of the length of the page, she wants to include hypertext links that allow students to jump down to a specific college category. Figure 2-50 shows a preview of the page you'll create for Adella.

Figure 2-50   HigherEd Web site

Complete the following:

1. In your text editor, open the **uwlisttxt.htm** file from the tutorial.02\case1 folder included with your Data Files. Enter *your name* and *the date* in the file comments. Save the file as **uwlist.htm** in the same folder.

2. Directly below the h1 heading, insert a navigation list containing an unordered list with following list items: **Private Colleges and Universities**, **Technical College System**, and **University of Wisconsin System**.

3. Add the ids **private**, **technical**, and **public** to the three h2 headings that categorize the list of schools.

4. Mark each of the school entries on the page as a hypertext link. Use the URLs provided in the colleges.txt file. (Hint: Use the copy and paste feature of your text editor to efficiently copy and paste the URL text.)

✦ EXPLORE 5. Adella wants the links to the school Web sites to appear in a new tab or window. Because there are so many links on the page, add a base element to the document head specifying that all links open by default in a new browser window or tab named **collegeWin**.

6. Link the three items in your navigation list to the corresponding h2 headings.

✦ EXPLORE 7. For each of the hypertext links you marked in Step 6, set the link to open in the current browser window and not in a new browser window or tab.

8. Save your changes to the file.

9. Open **uwlist.htm** in your Web browser and verify that the school links all open in the same browser window or tab, and that the links within the document to the different school categories bring the user to those locations on the page but not in a new window or tab.

10. Submit your completed files to your instructor, in either printed or electronic form, as requested.

Apply your knowledge of HTML to create a slide show Web site.

APPLY

Case Problem 2

Data Files needed for this Case Problem: fiddler.jpg, fidstyles.css, first.png, home.png, hometxt.htm, last.png, modernizr-1.5.js, next.png, prev.png, slide1.jpg–slide6.jpg, slide1txt.htm–slide6txt.htm, thumb1.jpg–thumb6.jpg

Lakewood School   Tasha Juroszek is a forensics teacher at Lakewood School, a small private school in Moultrie, Georgia. Tasha has just finished directing her students in *Fiddler on the Roof, Jr.* and wants to place a slide show of the performances on the Web. She has already designed the layout and content of the pages, but needs help to finish the slide show. She has asked you to add hypertext links between the slide pages and the site's home page. Figure 2-51 shows a preview of one of the slide pages on the Web site.

Figure 2-51 Fiddler on the Roof, Jr. slide page

If I Were a Rich Man sung by T. Gates

Complete the following:

1. Use your text editor to open the **hometxt.htm** file and the **slide1txt.htm** through **slide6txt.htm** files from the tutorial.02\case2 folder included with your Data Files. Enter *your name* and *the date* in the comment section of each file. Save the files as **home.htm** and **slide1.htm** through **slide6.htm**, respectively.

2. Return to the **slide1.htm** file in your text editor. At the top of the page are five buttons used to navigate through the slide show. Locate the inline image for the home button (home.png) and mark it as a hypertext link pointing to the home.htm file. Add the tooltip **Home Page** to the hyperlink.

3. There are six slides in Tasha's slide show. Mark the First Slide button as a hypertext link pointing to the slide1.htm file. Mark the Last Slide button as a link to the slide6.htm file. Link the Previous Slide button to slide1.htm, the first slide in the show. Link the Next Slide button to the slide2.htm file. Add an appropriate tooltip to each hyperlink.

4. Directly below the slide show buttons are thumbnail images of the six slides. Link each thumbnail image to its slide page.

5. Save your changes to the file.

6. Repeat Steps 2 through 5 for the five remaining slide pages. Within each page, set the navigation buttons to go back and forth through the slide show. For the slide6.htm file, the Next Slide button should point to the slide6.htm file because it is the last slide in the show.

7. Go to the **home.htm** file in your text editor. Go to the first paragraph in the article and mark the text string *slide show* as a hypertext link pointing to the slide1.htm file.

8. Go to the end of the second paragraph and mark the phrase *contact me* as a hypertext link pointing to the e-mail address **tashajur@lakewood.edu**, with the subject heading **Digital Photo**.

9. Save your changes to the file.

10. Load the **home.htm** file in your Web browser. Test the links in the Web site and verify that they allow the user to easily move back and forth through the slide show.

11. Submit your completed files to your instructor, in either printed or electronic form, as requested.

Explore how to use HTML to create an election results Web site.

CHALLENGE

Case Problem 3

Data Files needed for this Case Problem: dcoords.txt, dist1txt.htm–dist4txt.htm, ewlogo.png, ewstyles.css, kansasmap.png, kansastxt.htm, modernizr-1.5.js

ElectionWeb Allison Hawks is a political science student at the University of Kansas. As part of a project for one of her courses, she is setting up a Web site to report results from the upcoming elections. She's asked for your help in designing and writing the hypertext links and image maps to be used throughout her site. She has created a set of sample files detailing hypothetical results for the races for governor, senator, and the four Kansas congressional districts. A preview of the site's home page is shown in Figure 2-52.

Figure 2-52   Kansas results from ElectionWeb

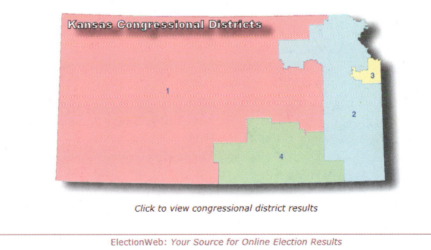

Click to view congressional district results

ElectionWeb: Your Source for Online Election Results

Complete the following:

1. Use your text editor to open the **kansastxt.htm** file and the **dist1txt.htm** through **dist4txt.htm** files from the tutorial.02\case3 folder included with your Data Files. Enter *your name* and *the date* in the comment section of each file. Save the files as **kansas.htm** and **district1.htm** through **district4.htm,** respectively.

 EXPLORE

2. Go to the **kansas.htm** file in your text editor. Use the `meta` element to specify *your name* as the document author, and **Kansas** and **elections** as keywords for Web search engines.

EXPLORE

3. Create a semantic link in the document head linking this document to the Office of the Kansas Secretary of State at the following address:
http://www.kssos.org/elections/elections_statistics.html
Use a `rel` attribute value of **external** for the link.

4. Set the base target of the Web page to **new** so that links on the page open, by default, in a new browser window or tab.

5. Go to the page body, and then directly below the header element insert a navigation list with the following content:

   a. An h2 heading with the text **News Sources**

   b. An unordered list containing the following entries: **Yahoo! News**, **FOX News**, **CNN**, **MSNBC**, **Google News**, **New York Times**, **digg**, **Washington Post**, **LATimes**, **Reuters**, **ABCNews**, and **USA Today**.

   c. Look up the Web addresses of the 12 news sources and link your list entries to the appropriate Web sites. Set the rel attribute of each link to **external**.

6. Scroll down to the last paragraph before the figure box and link the text *Secretary of State* to the Office of the Kansas Secretary of State Web site.

7. Directly below the figure box, create an image map named **kansasdistricts** containing four polygonal hotspots for each of the four Kansas congressional districts. Use the coordinates found in the dcoords.txt file as the coordinates of the hotspots.

✛ EXPLORE

8. Set the hotspots in your image map to access the district1.htm, district2.htm, district3.htm, and district4.htm files, using the target attribute value of **_self** so that those Web pages open within the current browser window or tab.

9. Apply the kansasdistricts image map to the kansasmap.png inline image.

10. Save your changes to the file.

11. Go to the **district1.htm** file in your text editor.

12. Directly below the opening <section> tag, insert a navigation list containing an unordered list with the items **District 1**, **District 2**, **District 3**, and **District 4**. Link each entry to its corresponding Web page in the ElectionWeb Web site.

13. Scroll down to the last paragraph before the figure box and link the text *statewide races* to the kansas.htm file.

14. Apply the same image map you created in Step 7 for the kansas.htm file to the kansasmap.png inline image.

15. Save your changes to the file.

16. Open the **district2.htm**, **district3.htm**, and **district4.htm** files in your text editor and repeat Steps 12 through 15 for each file.

17. Open the **kansas.htm** file in your Web browser and verify that you can navigate through Allison's sample pages by clicking the hypertext links within the page body and within the image maps. Verify that you can access the external Web sites listed in the news sources and the Office of the Kansas Secretary of State.

18. Submit your completed project to your instructor, in either printed or electronic form, as requested.

Test your knowledge of HTML and use your creativity to design a Web site documenting a Shakespeare play.

RESEARCH

Case Problem 4

Data Files needed for this Case Problem: characters.txt, notes.txt, tempest.jpg, tempest.txt

Mansfield Classical Theatre   Steve Karls continues to work as the director of Mansfield Classical Theatre in Mansfield, Ohio. The next production he plans to direct is *The Tempest*. Steve wants to put the text of this play on the Web, but he also wants to augment the dialog of the play with notes and commentary. However, he doesn't want his commentary to get in the way of a straight-through reading of the text, so he has hit on the idea of linking his commentary to key phrases in the dialog. Steve has created text files containing an excerpt from *The Tempest* as well as his commentary and other supporting documents. He would like you to take his raw material and create a collection of linked pages.

Complete the following:

1. Create HTML files named **tempest.htm**, **commentary.htm**, and **cast.htm**, saving them in the tutorial.02\case4 folder included with your Data Files. Add comment tags to the head section of each document containing your name and the date. Add an appropriate page title to each document.

2. Using the contents of the tempest.txt, notes.txt, and characters.txt text files, create the body of the three Web pages in Steve's Web site. You can supplement the material on the page with appropriate material you find on your own.

3. Use the tempest.jpg file as a logo for the page. Create an image map from the logo pointing to the tempest.htm, commentary.htm, and cast.htm files. The three rectangular boxes on the logo have the following coordinates for their upper-left and lower-right corners:
   The Play: (228, 139) (345, 173)
   Commentary: (359, 139) (508, 173)
   The Cast: (520, 139) (638, 173)

4. Use this image map in all three of the Web pages for this Web site.

5. Create links between the dialog on the play page and the notes on the commentary page. The notes contain line numbers to aid you in linking each line of dialog to the appropriate note.

6. Create a link between the first appearance of each character's name in the tempest.htm page and the character's description on the cast.htm page.

7. Include a link to Steve Karls' e-mail address on the tempest.htm page. Steve's e-mail address is **stevekarls@mansfieldct.com**. E-mail sent to Steve's account from this Web page should have the subject line **Comments on the Tempest**.

8. Add appropriate `meta` elements to each of the three pages documenting the page's contents and purpose.

9. Search the Web for sites that would provide additional material about the play. Add links to these pages on the tempest.htm page. The links should open in a new browser window or tab.

10. Submit your completed files to your instructor, in either printed or electronic form, as requested.

ENDING DATA FILES

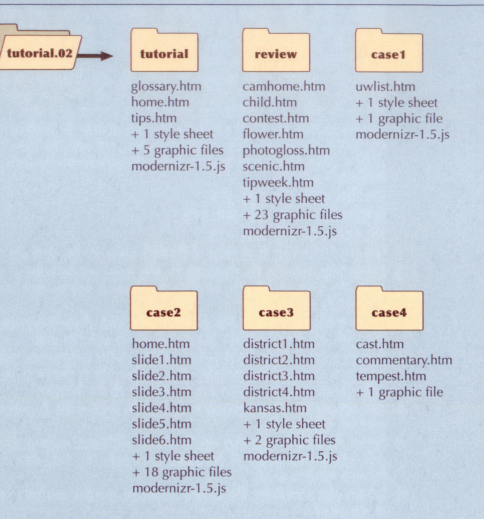

tutorial.02 →

tutorial

glossary.htm
home.htm
tips.htm
+ 1 style sheet
+ 5 graphic files
modernizr-1.5.js

review

camhome.htm
child.htm
contest.htm
flower.htm
photogloss.htm
scenic.htm
tipweek.htm
+ 1 style sheet
+ 23 graphic files
modernizr-1.5.js

case1

uwlist.htm
+ 1 style sheet
+ 1 graphic file
modernizr-1.5.js

case2

home.htm
slide1.htm
slide2.htm
slide3.htm
slide4.htm
slide5.htm
slide6.htm
+ 1 style sheet
+ 18 graphic files
modernizr-1.5.js

case3

district1.htm
district2.htm
district3.htm
district4.htm
kansas.htm
+ 1 style sheet
+ 2 graphic files
modernizr-1.5.js

case4

cast.htm
commentary.htm
tempest.htm
+ 1 graphic file

Written Communication

Avoiding Common Mistakes in Written Communication

Most written communication errors can be easily avoided, yet are often overlooked. It's particularly important to catch writing errors on a personal Web site or online resume, which often help determing the first impression that a colleague or potential employer forms of you. Whether you are pressed for time, don't pay attention to detail, or have never learned the basics of good writing in the first place, these guidelines should help turn your writing into works you can be proud to claim.

Plan and Focus Your Writing

- Think about your audience. Who will read what you write? What knowledge do they already possess, and what attitudes might they have about your subject? Who will be viewing your Web documents, and what will they expect to see?
- Be clear about why you are writing in the first place. Are you writing to inform, or do you want action to be taken? Do you hope to change a belief or simply state your position? For a personal Web site or resume, make sure you understand what information potential employers and professional contacts will mostly likely be looking for.
- Research your topic. Provide all the necessary information the reader will need to make a decision or take action, if needed. If facts are included, be sure you can substantiate them. For a resume, ensure all your dates are accurate, and look up the exact names of organizations, institutions, and endorsements.
- Don't be afraid to rewrite or revise. If it's an important document, consider having someone else read it so you can determine whether your meaning is clear. At a minimum, read what you have written out loud to determine whether the message and impact come across as you intended. For online documents, continue the revision process on a regular basis so your documents do not become inaccurate or outdated.

Check Grammar and Spelling

Text editing programs remove all excuses for not checking your spelling and grammar in written communications. Keep in mind that spellchecking doesn't catch every error, so be sure to review your work carefully. Hiring managers are often inundated with resumes for a job opening, and an error in spelling or grammar is sometimes all it takes for an otherwise promising application to be rejected.

Set the Right Tone

When you write informal communications, you may use abbreviated or incomplete sentences and phrases or slang. In the workplace, however, you must carefully consider the tone of your written communication so you don't unintentionally offend your readers. Using contractions is considered friendly and is usually all right, but it is never acceptable to use offensive language. Anything you post about yourself online may be viewed by colleagues or a prospective employer, no matter how informal the context, so be sure that anything you write reflects well on you.

ProSkills

Write Clearly and Accessibly

When you write, your language should be free of buzzwords and jargon that will weaken your message, or make it difficult for your reader to understand your meaning.

PROSKILLS

Create Your Own Web Site

The Web has become an important medium for advertising yourself. By making your resume available online, you can quickly get prospective employers the information they need to make a hiring decision. There are many sites that will assist you in writing and posting your resume. They will also, for a fee, present your online resume to employers in your chosen field. Assuming you don't want to pay to use such a site, you can also create your own Web site containing your employment history and talents. In this exercise, you'll use the skills you learned in Tutorials 1 and 2 to design your own Web site and create an online resume.

Note: Please be sure *not* to include any personal information of a sensitive nature in the documents you create to be submitted to your instructor for this exercise. Later on, you can update the documents with such information for your own personal use.

1. Collect material about yourself that would be useful in an online resume. You should include material for a page on your employment history, talents and special interests, a general biography, and a summary of the main points of your resume.

2. Create a storyboard outlining the pages on your Web site. Clearly indicate the links between the pages. Make sure that your site is easy to navigate no matter which page users start on.

3. Collect or create graphical image files to make your site interesting to viewers. If you obtain graphics from the Web, be sure to follow all copyright restrictions on the material.

4. Start designing your site's home page. It should include an interesting and helpful logo. The home page should be brief and to the point, summarizing the main features of your resume. Its height should not be greater than two screens.

5. Add other pages containing more detailed information. Each page should have a basic theme and topic. The pages should follow a unified theme and design.

6. Use the `em` and `strong` elements to highlight important ideas. Do not overuse these page elements; doing so can detract from your page's readability rather than enhancing it.

7. Use numbered and bulleted lists to list the main points in your resume.

8. Use block quotes to highlight recommendations from colleagues and former employers.

9. Use the `hr` element to divide longer pages into topical sections.

10. If sites on the Web would be relevant to your online resume (such as the Web sites of former or current employers), include links to those sites.

11. Include a link to your e-mail address. Write the e-mail address link so that it automatically adds an appropriate subject line to the e-mail message it creates.

12. Save your completed Web site and present it to your instructor.

TUTORIAL 3

OBJECTIVES

Session 3.1
- Explore the history and theory of CSS
- Define a style rule
- Study style precedence and inheritance
- Apply color using CSS
- Explore CSS3 color extensions

Session 3.2
- Use contextual selectors
- Work with attribute selectors
- Apply text and font styles
- Install a Web font

Session 3.3
- Define list styles
- Use pseudo-classes and pseudo-elements
- Create a rollover effect

Designing a Web Page with CSS

Creating a Web Site for a Rural Farm

Case | *Sunny Acres*

Tammy Nielsen and her husband, Brent, live and work at Sunny Acres, a 200-acre farm near Council Bluffs, Iowa. Over the past 25 years, the Nielsen family has expanded the farm's operations to include a farm shop, which sells fresh produce, baked goods, jams, jellies, and gifts; a pick-your-own garden, which operates from May through October and offers great produce at discounted prices; a petting barn with over 100 animals and the opportunity to bottle-feed the baby animals; a corn maze with over 4 miles of twisting trails through harvested corn fields; and a Halloween Festival featuring the corn maze haunted with dozens of spooky effects and tricks. The farm also hosts special holiday events during the winter.

Tammy created a Web site for Sunny Acres several years ago to make information about the farm easily accessible to her customers. The Web site has become outdated, so Tammy would like to enliven it with a new design based on the latest elements and styles from HTML and CSS. Tammy's knowledge of HTML and Web styles is limited, so she's come to you for help in creating a new look for the Sunny Acres Web site.

STARTING DATA FILES

tutorial.03 →

tutorial

haunttxt.htm
hometxt.htm
mazetxt.htm
pettingtxt.htm
producetxt.htm
sa_stylestxt.css

+ 1 style sheet
+ 7 graphic files
+ 4 Web fonts
+ 1 text file
modernizr-1.5.js

review

holidaytxt.htm
hs_stylestxt.css
+ 1 style sheet
+ 3 graphic files
+ 4 Web fonts
+ 1 text file
modernizr-1.5.js

case1

crypttxt.htm
c_stylestxt.css
+ 5 HTML files
+ 1 style sheet
+ 3 graphic files
modernizr-1.5.js

case2

bmtourtxt.htm
mw_stylestxt.css
+ 1 style sheet
+ 2 graphic files
modernizr-1.5.js

case3

civilwartxt.htm
cw_stylestxt.css
+ 1 style sheet
+ 3 graphic files
modernizr-1.5.js

case4

choirtxt.htm
gcc_stylestxt.css
+ 1 style sheet
+ 2 graphic files
+ 4 Web fonts
+ 1 text file
modernizr-1.5.js

demo

demo_color_names.htm
demo_css.htm
+ 3 graphic files

SESSION 3.1 VISUAL OVERVIEW

Style comments provide information about the style sheet.

```
/*
    Sunny Acres Style Sheet

    Author: Tammy Nielsen
    Date:   3/1/2014
*/

/* Body styles */

body {
    background-color: white;
    font-family: Verdana, Geneva, sans-serif;
    line-height: 1.4em;
}
```

The appearance of the Web page is determined by the styles in a style sheet.

```
h2 {
    background-color: rgb(0, 165, 0);
    color: rgba(255, 255, 255, 0.8);
}
```

The color is 80% opaque.

Color values using the rgba or hsla properties can include opacity to create semi-transparent colors.

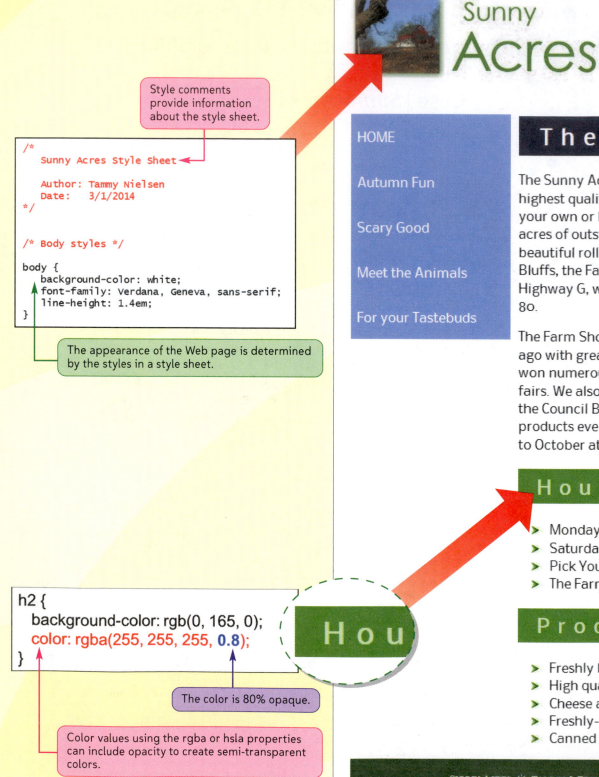

Sunny
Acres

HOME

Autumn Fun

Scary Good

Meet the Animals

For your Tastebuds

The Farm Sh

The Sunny Acres Farm Shop aims to of highest quality fresh produce. You can your own or buy it in our shop. Set am acres of outstanding natural beauty or beautiful rolling hills northeast of Cou Bluffs, the Farm Shop is easily reached Highway G, with easy access from Inte 80.

The Farm Shop was established over 25 ago with great success. Our products h won numerous awards at local festiva fairs. We also cater to local supermarke the Council Bluffs/Omaha area. Look f products every Saturday morning from to October at the Council Bluffs Farme

Hours

Hou

- > Monday - Friday: 9 am - 5 pm
- > Saturday: 9 am - 3 pm
- > Pick Your Own Produce is availab
- > The Farm Shop is open year-roun

Products

- > Freshly baked breads and quiches
- > High quality meats
- > Cheese and other dairy products
- > Freshly-picked fruits and vegetab
- > Canned goods and preserves

SUNNY ACRES ✳ TAMMY & BRENT NIELSEN ✳ 1977 HIGHWAY G ✳

STYLE SHEETS AND COLOR

Tammy and Brent Nielsen
1973 Hwy G
Council Bluffs, IA 51503

rm Shop

h o p

n Shop aims to offer the
produce. You can pick
our shop. Set amidst
natural beauty on the
northeast of Council
is easily reached on
access from Interstate

stablished over 25 years
ss. Our products have
s at local festivals and
local supermarkets in
aha area. Look for our
day morning from May
ncil Bluffs Farmers' Market.

: 9 am - 5 pm
- 3 pm
Produce is available from May 15 - October 22
s open year-round

ts

eads and quiches
ats
r dairy products
ruits and vegetables (in season)
nd preserves

Every style rule needs to be enclosed in curly braces, with the style property values separated by semicolons.

The **selector** defines what element or elements are affected by a rule.

```
h1 {
    color: white;
    background-color: rgb(50, 69, 99);
}
```

The background-color style property sets the background color.

The color style property sets the text color.

CSS supports **color names** for a select group of commonly used colors.

The **HSL model** selects color from a color wheel at varying levels of saturation and lightness.

CSS Color Models

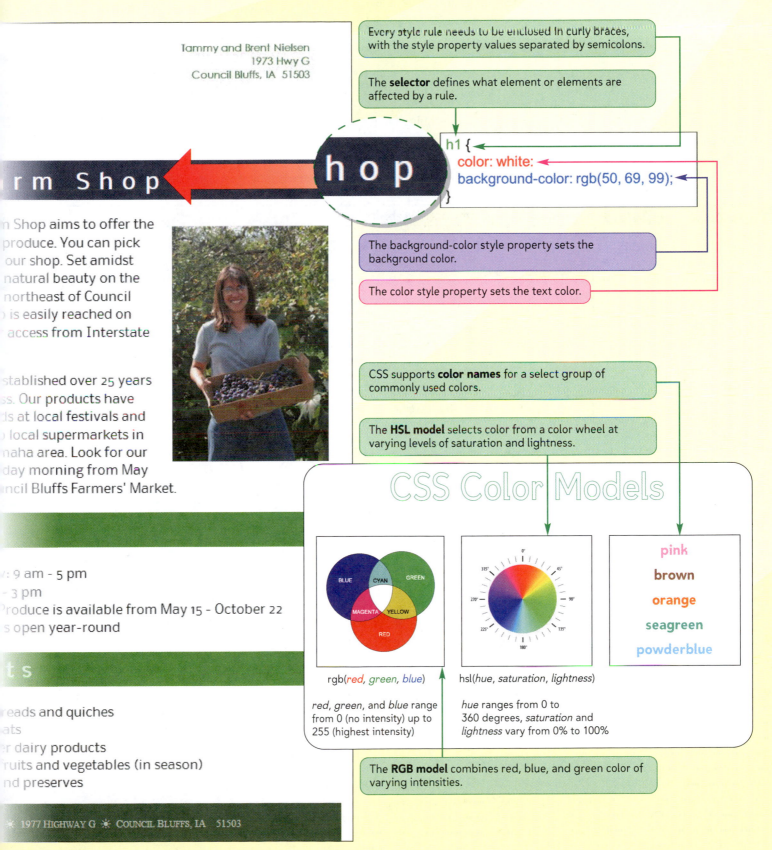

rgb(*red*, *green*, *blue*)

red, *green*, and *blue* range from 0 (no intensity) up to 255 (highest intensity)

hsl(*hue*, *saturation*, *lightness*)

hue ranges from 0 to 360 degrees, *saturation* and *lightness* vary from 0% to 100%

pink
brown
orange
seagreen
powderblue

The **RGB model** combines red, blue, and green color of varying intensities.

Introducing CSS

You and Tammy met to discuss her ideas for upgrading the design of the Sunny Acres Web site. She's created a few sample pages that she wants you to work with:

- *home.htm*—the home page, describing the operations and events sponsored by the farm
- *maze.htm*—a page describing the farm's corn maze
- *haunted.htm*—a page describing the farm's annual Halloween Festival and haunted maze
- *petting.htm*—a page describing the farm's petting barn
- *produce.htm*—a page describing the Sunny Acres farm shop and the pick-your-own produce garden

Figure 3-1 shows the links among these sites in the Sunny Acres storyboard.

Figure 3-1   **Storyboard of the Sunny Acres Web site**

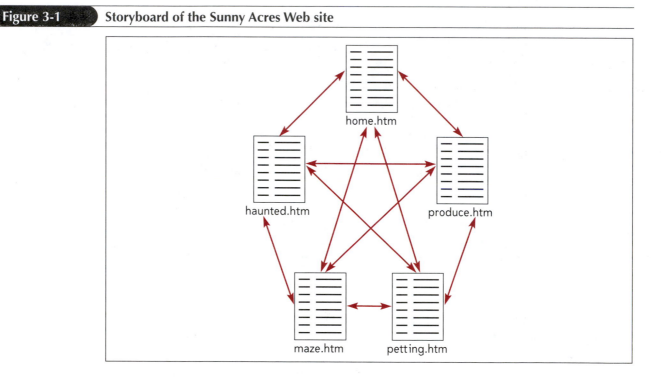

You'll start by opening these files in your text editor and browser.

To view the Sunny Acres Web pages:

1. Use your text editor to open the **haunttxt.htm**, **hometxt.htm**, **mazetxt.htm**, **pettingtxt.htm**, and **producetxt.htm** files, located in the tutorial.03\tutorial folder included with your Data Files. Within each file, go to the comment section at the top of the file and add **your name** and **the date** in the space provided. Save the files as **haunted.htm**, **home.htm**, **maze.htm**, **petting.htm**, and **produce.htm**, respectively, in the same folder.

2. Take some time to review the HTML code within each document so that you understand the structure and content of the files.

3. Open the **home.htm** file in your Web browser, and then click the links at the top of the page to view the current appearance of the *haunted.htm*, *maze.htm*, *petting.htm*, and *produce.htm* files. Figure 3-2 shows the current layout and appearance of the Sunny Acres home page.

Figure 3-2 **Initial Sunny Acres home page**

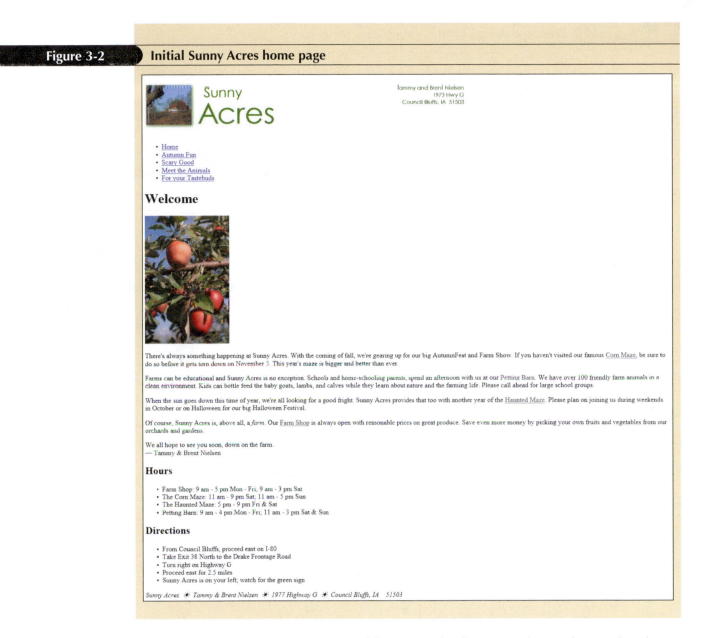

Tammy already has created most of the content for the new and revised pages, but she has not upgraded the Web site design. She needs your help with that. In Figure 3-3, she sketches the basic design she has in mind for her pages.

Figure 3-3 Proposed design for the Sunny Acres home page

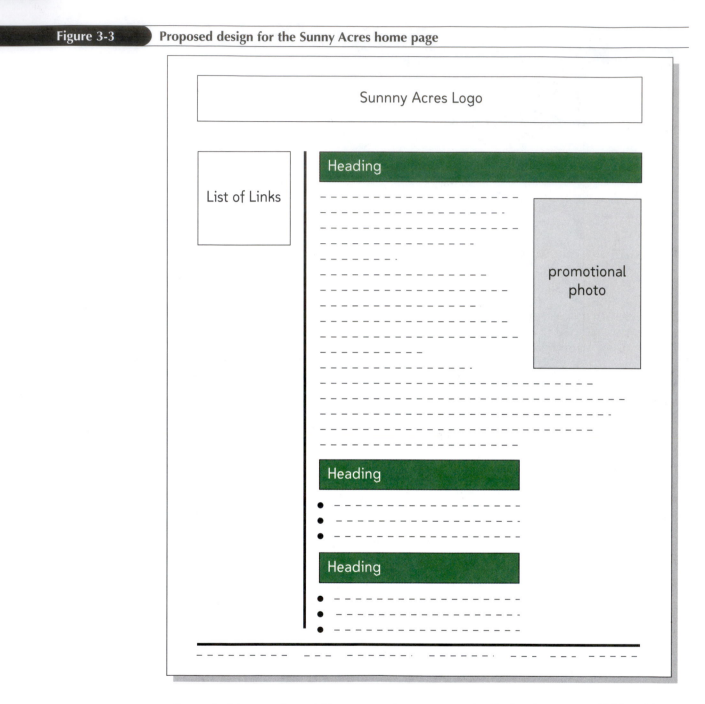

To apply this page format, Tammy wants you to use the design features available with CSS. Before starting, you'll review the history and concepts behind CSS.

The History of CSS

You learned in Tutorial 1 that HTML specifies a document's content and structure, but not how that document should be rendered. To render a document, the device displaying the page needs a style sheet that specifies the appearance of each page element. The style sheet language used on the Web is the Cascading Style Sheets language, also known as CSS.

The specifications for CSS are maintained by the World Wide Web Consortium (W3C); and as with HTML and XHTML, several versions of CSS exist with varying levels of browser support. The first version of CSS, called **CSS1**, was introduced in 1996 and enabled Web designers to create styles to:

- Set the font size, type, and other properties of Web page text
- Control text alignment and apply decorative elements such as underlining, italic, and capitalization
- Specify background and foreground colors of different page elements
- Apply a background image to any element
- Set the margins, internal space, and borders of grouping elements such as paragraphs and headings

CSS1 made it possible to create Web pages that had visually interesting and attractive designs and layouts. The second version of CSS, **CSS2**, was introduced in 1998, expanding the language to provide styles to:

- Position elements at specific locations on a page
- Clip and hide element content
- Design styles for different output devices, including printed media and aural devices
- Control the appearance and behavior of browser features such as scroll bars and mouse cursors

An update to CSS2, **CSS 2.1**, was introduced by the W3C in April 2002. Although the update did not add any new features to the language, it cleaned up minor errors that were introduced in the original specification. At the time of this writing, almost all aspects of CSS2 are supported by current browsers.

As browsers were implementing all of the features of CSS2, in December 2005 the W3C pressed forward to the next version, **CSS3**, which further expanded the design tools available to Web page authors. Currently still in a working draft, CSS3 adds styles for:

- Enhanced text effects, including drop shadows and Web fonts
- Semi-transparent colors and overlays
- Column-based layout
- Rounded borders, drop shadows, and box outlines
- Transformations of page elements, including scaling, skewing, and rotation

With CSS, as with HTML, Web page designers need to be aware of compatibility issues that arise not just among different versions of the language, but also among different versions of the same browser. Although it's tempting to always apply the latest and most exciting features of CSS, you should not create a situation where users of older browsers will not be able to view your Web pages.

Browser Extensions

Not content to wait for the W3C's final specifications, several browser manufacturers are creating their own extensions to the CSS language. Many of these extensions have been incorporated in the CSS3 specification. By putting forward their own extensions, these vendors are able to test and debug new styles that are still in the development stage with CSS3. You can use these browser extensions as long as you realize that they might not be supported by other browsers and you do not make their use crucial to your page's readability.

Defining a Style Rule

In every version of CSS, you apply a **style rule** containing a list of style properties to an element or a group of elements known as a selector. The general syntax of a CSS style rule is

```
selector {
    property1: value1;
    property2: value2;
    property3: value3;
    ...
}
```

where `selector` identifies an element or a group of elements within the document and the `property: value` pairs specify the style properties and their values. For example, to display the text of all `h1` headings in blue and centered horizontally on the page, you could use the following style rule:

```
h1 {
    color: blue;
    text-align: center;
}
```

To apply these style properties to more than one element, you specify the elements in a comma-separated list. The following style rule causes all `h1` through `h6` headings to be displayed in blue and centered on the page:

```
h1, h2, h3, h4, h5, h6 {
    color: blue;
    text-align: center;
}
```

Like HTML, CSS ignores the use of white space, so you can also enter your styles on a single line, as in the following example:

```
h1 {color: blue; text-align: center;}
```

Writing a style rule on a single line saves space, but entering each style property on a separate line often makes your code easier to read and edit. You will see both approaches used in the CSS files you encounter on the Web.

Applying a Style Sheet

TIP

You can make your style sheets easier to manage by entering the style names in alphabetical order.

The design you apply to a Web site is usually a combination of several style sheets. In general, the style sheet that is loaded last has precedence over style sheets loaded earlier. Figure 3-4 summarizes the different types of style sheets in the order they are usually installed and processed by browsers.

Figure 3-4 **Order in which style sheets are interpreted**

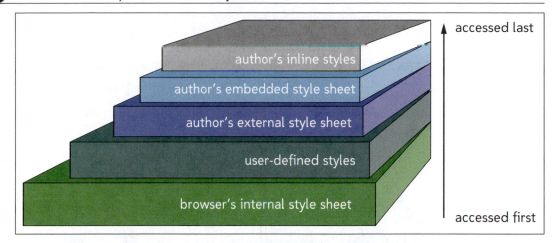

The first style sheet interpreted by the browser is the one built into the browser itself. The current appearance of the Sunny Acres Web page displayed in Figure 3-2 is based on styles applied by the browser itself that are contained within its own style rules about how headings, paragraphs, inline images and so forth, should be rendered. Browsers use similar default styles. So if you rely only on the browser's internal style sheet, your Web sites should appear alike across most browsers.

User-Defined Styles

Almost all browsers allow users to modify the default settings of the internal style sheet. For example, a user could change the font size assigned to paragraph and heading text, set foreground and background colors, and specify whether or not to display inline images. Browsers such as Internet Explorer and Safari also allow users to substitute their own style sheets for the browser's internal sheet, providing more control over how the browser renders the pages it encounters. One advantage of user-defined style sheets is that they make the Web more accessible to visually impaired users who may require larger fonts or the absence of clashing color schemes. Figure 3-5 shows the Advanced dialog box from Safari, in which users can replace the browser's internal style sheet with their own.

Figure 3-5 **Choosing a user-defined style sheet in Safari**

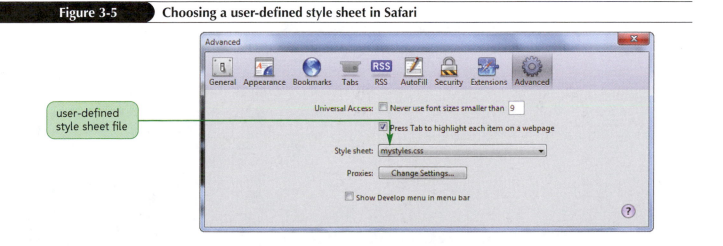

External Style Sheets

Styles set by the author of a Web page and stored in an external style sheet are loaded after internal and user-defined style sheets. You've already worked with external style sheets in the first two tutorials using CSS files created for you. Recall that an external style sheet is included by adding the `link` element

```
<link href="url" rel="stylesheet" type="text/css" />
```

to the document head, where `url` is the URL of the external style sheet file. The style sheet rules in an external style sheet take precedence over any rules set in the browser's internal style sheet or in a user-defined style sheet.

Tammy already has created a style sheet for her sample pages to define how the elements should be laid out on the page. You'll apply the style rules from her *sa_layout.css* file to the Sunny Acres home page now.

To link to the layout style sheet:

1. Return to the **home.htm** file in your text editor.

2. Directly above the closing `</head>` tag, insert the following `link` element (see Figure 3-6):

```
<link href="sa_layout.css" rel="stylesheet" type="text/css" />
```

| Figure 3-6 | Linking to an external style sheet |

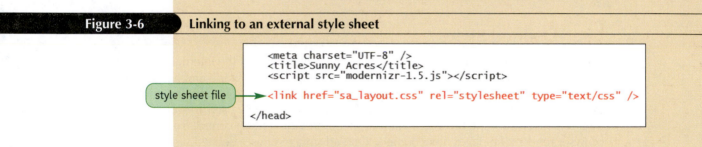

```
<meta charset="UTF-8" />
<title>Sunny Acres</title>
<script src="modernizr-1.5.js"></script>
```
style sheet file → `<link href="sa_layout.css" rel="stylesheet" type="text/css" />`
```
</head>
```

3. Save your changes to the file.

4. Reopen the **home.htm** file in your browser. As shown in Figure 3-7, the layout of the page has been altered using the design styles present in the *sa_layout.css* file.

Figure 3-7   **Sunny Acres home page using the sa_layout.css style sheet**

Sunny
Acres

Tammy and Brent Nielsen
1973 Hwy G
Council Bluffs, IA 51503

- Home
- Autumn Fun
- Scary Good
- Meet the Animals
- For your Tastebuds

Welcome

There's always something happening at Sunny Acres. With the coming of fall, we're gearing up for our big AutumnFest and Farm Show. If you haven't visited our famous Corn Maze, be sure to do so before it gets torn down on November 5. This year's maze is bigger and better than ever.

Farms can be educational and Sunny Acres is no exception. Schools and home-schooling parents, spend an afternoon with us at our Petting Barn. We have over 100 friendly farm animals in a clean environment. Kids can bottle feed the baby goats, lambs, and calves while they learn about nature and the farming life. Please call ahead for large school groups.

When the sun goes down this time of year, we're all looking for a good fright. Sunny Acres provides that too with another year of the Haunted Maze. Please plan on joining us during weekends in October or on Halloween for our big Halloween Festival.

Of course, Sunny Acres is, above all, a *farm*. Our Farm Shop is always open with reasonable prices on great produce. Save even more money by picking your own fruits and vegetables from our orchards and gardens.

We all hope to see you soon, down on the farm.
— Tammy & Brent Nielsen

Hours

- Farm Shop: 9 am - 5 pm Mon - Fri; 9 am - 3 pm Sat
- The Corn Maze: 11 am - 9 pm Sat; 11 am - 5 pm Sun
- The Haunted Maze: 5 pm - 9 pm Fri & Sat
- Petting Barn: 9 am - 4 pm Mon - Fri; 11 am - 3 pm Sat & Sun

Directions

- From Council Bluffs, proceed east on I-80
- Take Exit 38 North to the Drake Frontage Road
- Turn right on Highway G
- Proceed east for 2.5 miles
- Sunny Acres is on your left; watch for the green sign

Sunny Acres ☀ Tammy & Brent Nielsen ☀ 1977 Highway G ☀ Council Bluffs, IA   51503

The *sa_layout.css* style sheet changes the layout of the page, displaying the navigation links in a column on the left and the main page content in a column on the right. The width of the page also has been reduced to make the content easier to read.

Importing Style Sheets

On large Web sites that involve hundreds of pages, you might decide to use different styles for different groups of pages to give a visual cue to users about where they are on the site. One way of organizing these different styles is to break them into smaller, more manageable units. The different style sheets then can be imported into a single sheet. To import a style sheet, add the command

```
@import url(url);
```

to the style sheet file, where *url* is the URL of an external style sheet file. For example, a company might have one style sheet named *company.css* that contains basic styles used in all Web pages, and another style sheet named *support.css* that only applies to Web pages containing technical support information. The following code added to a style sheet imports both files:

```
@import url(company.css);
@import url(support.css);
```

The `@import` statement must always come before any other style rules in the style sheet. When a browser encounters the `@import` statement, it imports the content of the style sheet file directly into the current style sheet, much as if you had typed the style declarations yourself.

The `@import` rule has the same impact as adding multiple `link` elements to the HTML file. An advantage of the `@import` rule is that it simplifies your HTML file (since you only need to access one style sheet file), and it places all style rules and decisions about which style sheets to include and exclude in an external file. This is an important distinction if you want to put all of your design choices in the external style sheet file, which you can then easily edit and modify without having to touch the HTML document.

Embedded Style Sheets

Another type of style sheet created by a Web page author is an embedded style sheet, in which the styles are inserted directly within the `head` element of an HTML document using the `style` element

```
<style type="text/css">
   styles
</style>
```

where *styles* are the rules of the style sheet. For example, the following embedded style sheet applies a rule to display the text of all `h1` headings from the current document centered horizontally and in red:

```
<style type="text/css">
   h1 {
   color: red;
   text-align: center;
   }
</style>
```

The exact order in which external style sheets and embedded style sheets are processed by the browser depends on the order in which they are listed within the HTML file. The HTML code

```
<link href="sa_layout.css" rel="stylesheet" type="text/css" />
<style type="text/css">
   h1 {color: red; }
</style>
```

loads the external style sheet first and then the embedded sheet. However, if that order is switched as in the code

```
<style type="text/css">
   h1 {color: red; }
</style>
<link href="sa_layout.css" rel="stylesheet" type="text/css" />
```

then the external style sheet is processed after the embedded sheet.

Unlike an external style sheet, an embedded style sheet is applied only to the Web page in which it is placed. Thus, if you want to apply the same style to all of the headings on your Web site, it is more efficient and easier to manage if you define your styles only once within an external style sheet and link all of the pages to that file. If you later need to change the site design, you'll have to edit only one file, rather than dozens.

TIP

Always place embedded styles after external style sheets to avoid confusion about which style sheet is loaded last.

Inline Styles

The very last styles to be interpreted by the browser are inline styles, which are styles applied directly to specific elements using the `style` attribute

```
<element style="style rules"> … </element>
```

where `element` is the HTML element and `style rules` are CSS styles applied to that element. For example, the following `style` attribute is used to display the text of a specific `h1` heading in green and centered on the page:

```
<h1 style="color: green; text-align: center;">
   Sunny Acres
</h1>
```

The advantage in using inline styles is that it is clear exactly what page element is being formatted; however, inline styles are not recommended in most cases because they make changing styles tedious and inefficient. For example, if you wanted to use inline styles to format all of your headings, you would have to locate all of the `h1` through `h6` elements in all of the Web pages within the entire Web site and add `style` attributes to each tag. This would be no small task on a large Web site containing hundreds of headings spread out among dozens of Web pages, and it would be a nightmare if you had to modify the design of a large Web site that was created using inline styles.

However, the primary reason to not use inline styles is that you want to, as much as possible, separate document content from document design. Ideally, the HTML code and CSS styles should be so separate that one group of employees could define the page content using HTML and another group could define the page design using CSS. This isn't possible with inline styles because the code for the page design is intermingled with the code for the page content.

TIP

View your Web site with and without your style sheet. It should be readable even if a user is limited to the default styles supplied by a Web browser.

Exploring the Style Cascade

With the potential for many different style sheets to be applied to the same Web page, there has to be an orderly method by which conflicts between those different style sheets are resolved. CSS does this by assigning a level of importance to each style, with the most important style rule taking precedence over other competing rules.

Style Precedence and Specificity

Many factors determine how the importance of each style is calculated. But as a general rule of thumb, *all other things being equal, the more specific style is applied instead of the more general*. Thus, a style applied to a specific paragraph is given more importance than a general style applied to an entire Web page, and a style applied to a section of text within that paragraph has more importance than the style for the entire paragraph. For example, the following set of style rules would set the text color of the Web page to black, except for text within the `header` element:

```
body {color: black;}
header {color: red;}
```

Specificity is only a concern when two or more styles conflict. If the style rules involve different properties, there is no conflict and both rules are applied. If two style rules have equal specificity, and thus equal importance, then the one that is defined last in the style sheet is the one used.

Style Inheritance

An additional factor in applying a style sheet is that properties are passed from a parent element to its children in a process known as **style inheritance**. For example, to set the text color of a page to blue, you could apply the style

```
body {color: blue;}
```

and every element nested within the `body` element (which is every element on the Web page) would inherit this style. This means that the text of every heading, every paragraph, every numbered list, and so forth would be displayed in blue unless a different text color were defined for those specific elements. Thus, the style rules

```
body {color: blue;}
h1 {text-align: center;}
```

would result in the `h1` heading text appearing in blue and centered even though only the text alignment is specifically set within the style rule for the `h1` element.

Not all properties are inherited. For example, the style property above that defines the text color for the page body has no meaning if applied to an inline image.

The final rendering of any page element thus becomes the result of multiple style sheets and multiple style rules. You may have to track a set of styles as they are passed from one style sheet to another. For example, browsers typically display all `h1` headings in a large bold black font and left-aligned on the page. The following rule applied within an external style sheet modifies the color of `h1` headings on the Web site, but does nothing to change the default settings for size, weight, or alignment:

```
h1 {color: red;}
```

The combination of the internal and external style sheets results in all `h1` headings being displayed in a large bold red font and left-aligned on the page. However, if a particular heading is formatted with the inline style

```
<h1 style="text-align: center;">Sunny Acres</h1>
```

then that `h1` heading will be centered, displayed in red (defined in the external style sheet), and rendered in a large bold font (defined in the browser's default style sheet). The final appearance is thus a result of a combination of several styles drawn from multiple sources. Many Web browsers now include developer tools to allow page designers to track each style back to its source.

Defining Important Styles

If you need browsers to enforce a style, you can append the `!important` keyword to the style property, using the syntax

```
property: value !important;
```

where *property* is the style property and *value* is the property value. The following style rule sets the color of all `h1` headings to orange; and because this property is marked as important, it takes precedence over any other style that may be defined in the style sheet:

```
h1 {color: orange !important;}
```

The `!important` keyword is often necessary for visually impaired users who require their pages rendered with large, clear text and highly contrasting colors. Such a user could set the text size in a user-defined style sheet and override any styles specified by the page author through the use of the `!important` keyword. In general, Web page authors should not use the `!important` keyword and should instead write style sheets that are based on the content of the Web documents. This practice makes the style sheets easier to edit and maintain if the content or design of the Web site changes.

Writing Style Comments

Now that you've reviewed some principles of style sheet design and application, you can begin creating your own style sheets. You'll start by creating an external style sheet that will be used to format the appearance of text on the Sunny Acres Web site. Because style sheets are text files, you can create your style sheets with the same text editor you used for creating and editing your HTML files.

To start creating the sa_styles.css style sheet:

1. Use your text editor to open the blank text file **sa_stylestxt.css** from the tutorial.03/tutorial folder.

2. Save the file as **sa_styles.css**.

Style sheets can be as long and complicated as HTML files. To help others read your style sheet code, you should document the content and purpose of the style sheet using style sheet comments. Style sheet comments are entered as follows

```
/* comment */
```

where *comment* is the text of the comment. Like HTML, CSS ignores the presence of white space, so you can place style comments on several lines to make them easier to read. For example, the following style comment extends over four lines in the style sheet:

```
/*
   Sunny Acres
   Style Sheet
*/
```

Add style comments to the *sa_styles.css* file now to document the purpose and authorship of the style sheet.

To document the style sheet:

1. At the top of the file, insert the following style comments, as shown in Figure 3-8:

```
/*
    Sunny Acres Style Sheet

    Author: your name
    Date:   the date
*/
```

Figure 3-8   **Entering style sheet comments**

```
/*
    Sunny Acres Style Sheet

    Author: Tammy Nielsen
    Date:   3/1/2014
*/
```

2. Save your changes to the file.

Next, you'll link the Sunny Acres home page to this new style sheet.

To link to the sa_styles.css file:

1. Return to the **home.htm** file in your text editor.

2. Directly below the link element for the *sa_layout.css* file, insert the following:

```
<link href="sa_styles.css" rel="stylesheet" type="text/css" />
```

3. Save your changes to the file.

Defining Color in CSS

The first part of your style sheet will focus on color. If you've worked with graphics software, you've probably made your color selections using a graphical interface where you can see your color options. Specifying color with CSS is somewhat less intuitive because CSS is a text-based language and requires colors to be defined in textual terms. This is done through either a color value or a color name.

RGB Color Values

A **color value** is a numerical expression that describes the properties of a color. To better understand how numbers can represent colors, it can help to review some of the basic principles of color theory and how they relate to the way colors are rendered in a browser.

In classical color theory, all colors are based on adding three primary colors—red, green, and blue—at different levels of intensity. For example, adding all three primary colors at maximum intensity produces the color white, while adding any two of the three primary colors at maximum intensity produces the trio of complementary colors—yellow, magenta, and cyan (see Figure 3-9).

Figure 3-9   **Color addition in the RGB color model**

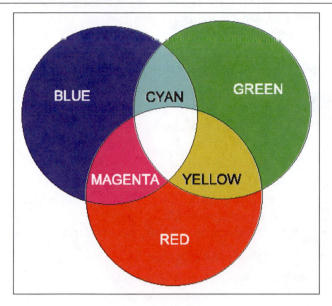

Varying the intensity of the three primary colors creates other colors. Orange, for example, is created from a high intensity of red, a moderate intensity of green, and a total absence of blue. CSS represents these intensities mathematically as a set of numbers called an **RGB triplet**, which has the format

```
rgb(red, green, blue)
```

where *red*, *green*, and *blue* are the intensities of the red, green, and blue components of the color. Intensity values range from 0 (absence of color) to 255 (maximum intensity); thus, the color white has the color value `rgb(255, 255, 255)`, indicating that red, green, and blue are mixed equally at the highest intensity, and orange is represented by `rgb(255, 165, 0)`. RGB triplets can describe 256^3 (16.7 million) possible colors, which is a greater number of colors than the human eye can distinguish. You can also enter each component value as a percentage, with 100% representing the highest intensity. In this form, you would specify the color orange with the following values:

```
rgb(100%, 65%, 0%)
```

The percentage form is less commonly used than RGB values, but many page designers find it easier to work with.

CSS also allows RGB values to be entered as hexadecimal numbers. A **hexadecimal** number is a number expressed in the base 16 numbering system rather than in the commonly used base 10 system. In base 10 counting, numeric values are expressed using combinations of 10 characters (0 through 9); hexadecimal numbering includes six extra characters: A (for 10), B (for 11), C (for 12), D (for 13), E (for 14), and F (for 15). For values above 15, you use a combination of those 16 characters. For example, 16 has a hexadecimal representation of 10, and a value of 255 is represented as FF in hexadecimal numbering. The style value for color represented as a hexadecimal number has the form

```
#redgreenblue
```

where *red*, *green*, and *blue* are the hexadecimal values of the red, green, and blue components. Therefore, the color yellow could be represented either by the RGB triplet

```
rgb(255,255,0)
```

or by the hexadecimal

```
#FFFF00
```

One advantage of using the compact hexadecimal format is that it results in smaller style sheet files; the disadvantage is that hexadecimals are more difficult to read and interpret. Most graphics programs provide color values in either a decimal or a hexadecimal format that you can easily copy into a style sheet. So a common practice is to use graphics software to choose your colors, and then copy the color values from your graphics package.

REFERENCE

Defining Color Values

- To define a color value using the RGB color model, use the property value

  `rgb(red, green, blue)`

  where *red*, *green*, and *blue* are the intensities of red, green, and blue ranging in value from 0 up to 255.
- To define a color value using the HSL color mode, use

  `hsl(hue, saturation, lightness)`

  where *hue* is the tint of the color on the color wheel measured in degrees, *saturation* is the intensity of the color in percent, and *lightness* is the brightness of the color in percent.
- To create a semi-transparent color, use either

  `rgba(red, green, blue, opacity)`

  or

  `hsla(hue, saturation, lightness, opacity)`

  where *opacity* ranges from 0 (transparent) up to 1 (opaque).

Using Color Names

If you don't want to use color values, you can also specify colors by name. CSS supports the 16 basic color names shown in Figure 3-10.

Figure 3-10   **The 16 basic CSS2 color names**

Color Name	RGB Triplet	Hexadecimal	Color Name	RGB Triplet	Hexadecimal
Aqua	(0, 255, 255)	00FFFF	Navy	(0, 0, 128)	000080
Black	(0, 0, 0)	000000	Olive	(128, 128, 0)	808000
Blue	(0, 0, 255)	0000FF	Purple	(128, 0, 128)	FF0000
Fuchsia	(255, 0, 255)	FF00FF	Red	(255, 0, 0)	C0C0C0
Gray	(128, 128, 128)	808080	Silver	(192, 192, 192)	008080
Green	(0, 128, 0)	008000	Teal	(0, 128, 128)	FFFFFF
Lime	(0, 255, 0)	00FF00	White	(255, 255, 255)	FFFF00
Maroon	(128, 0, 0)	800000	Yellow	(255, 255, 0)	

Sixteen colors are not a lot, so most browsers support an extended list of 140 color names, including such colors as orange, crimson, khaki, and brown. Although this extended color list was not part of the CSS specification until CSS3, most browsers support it. You can view these color names in the appendix and in a demo page.

To view the extended list of color names:

1. Use your browser to open the **demo_color_names.htm** file from the tutorial.03\demo folder included with your Data Files.

2. As shown in Figure 3-11, the demo page displays the list of 140 color names along with their color values expressed both as RGB triplets and in hexadecimal form.

Figure 3-11   A partial list of extended color names

Sample	Name	RGB	Hexadecimal
	aliceblue	(240,248,255)	#F0F8FF
	antiquewhite	(250,235,215)	#FAEBD7
	aqua	(0,255,255)	#00FFFF
	aquamarine	(127,255,212)	#7FFFD4
	azure	(240,255,255)	#F0FFFF
	beige	(245,245,220)	#F5F5DC
	bisque	(255,228,196)	#FFE4C4
	black	(0,0,0)	#000000
	blanchedalmond	(255,235,205)	#FFEBCD
	blue	(0,0,255)	#0000FF
	blueviolet	(138,43,226)	#8A2BE2
	brown	(165,42,42)	#A52A2A
	burlywood	(222,184,135)	#DEB887

3. Close the page when you are finished reviewing the extended color names list.

PROSKILLS

Written Communication: Communicating in Color

Humans are born to respond to color. Studies have shown that infants as young as two months prefer colorful objects to non-colored objects, and that memory is often associated with color. While marketing products such as clothes, companies rely on knowing what colors are "in" and what colors are passé. Your color choices can also impact the way your Web pages are received. You want to choose a color scheme that is tailored to the personality and interests of your target audience.

Color also evokes an emotional response, in which certain colors are associated with particular feelings or concepts, such as:

- *red*—assertive, powerful, sexy, dangerous
- *pink*—innocent, romantic, feminine
- *black*—strong, classic, stylish
- *gray*—business-like, detached
- *yellow*—warm, cheerful, optimistic
- *blue*—consoling, serene, quiet
- *orange*—friendly, vigorous, inviting
- *white*—clean, pure, straightforward, innocent

International businesses need to understand how cultural differences can affect people's responses to color. For instance, white, which is associated with innocence in Western cultures, is the color of mourning in China; yellow is considered a bright, cheerful color in the West, while in Buddhist countries it represents spirituality.

When you develop a Web site design, you should test it out before a group of potential customers. In addition to evaluating responses to the content of your Web site, pay attention to reactions to its presentation and appearance, including your color choices.

Defining Text and Background Colors

Now that you've studied how CSS works with colors, you can start applying color to some of the elements of the Sunny Acres Web site. CSS supports styles to define both the text and background color for each element on your page. You've already seen examples of how to set the text color of a page element using the `color` property, which has the form

```
color: color;
```

where *color* is either a color value or a color name. Background colors are defined using the property

```
background-color: color;
```

where once again *color* is either a color name or value. Tammy wants the body of each page on her Web site to have a white background. Although most browsers by default will apply a white background, it's a good idea to make this explicit. Also, she wants the text of the `h2` headings to be displayed in white on a green background. The style rules to apply these two design choices are:

```
body {
    background-color: white;
}

h2 {
    background-color: rgb(0, 154, 0);
    color: white;
}
```

Whether to use a color value in place of a color name is often a matter of personal preference. This code does both, with the RGB triplet (0, 154, 0) representing the color green, and the color name *white* used for the text color of the `h2` headings and the background color of the page body. You'll add these style rules to the *sa_styles.css* style sheet.

To format the text and background colors:

1. Return to the **sa_styles.css** file in your text editor.

2. Directly below the style comments, insert the following style rules, as shown in Figure 3-12:

```
/* Body styles */

body {
    background-color: white;
}


/* Heading styles */

h2 {
    background-color: rgb(0, 165, 0);
    color: white;
}
```

Make sure you end every style property value with a semicolon to separate it from other style properties.

TIP

About 8% of all men and 0.5% of all women have some form of color blindness. Because red-green color blindness is the most common form of color impairment, you should avoid using red text on a green background or vice versa.

Figure 3-12   Setting the foreground and background colors

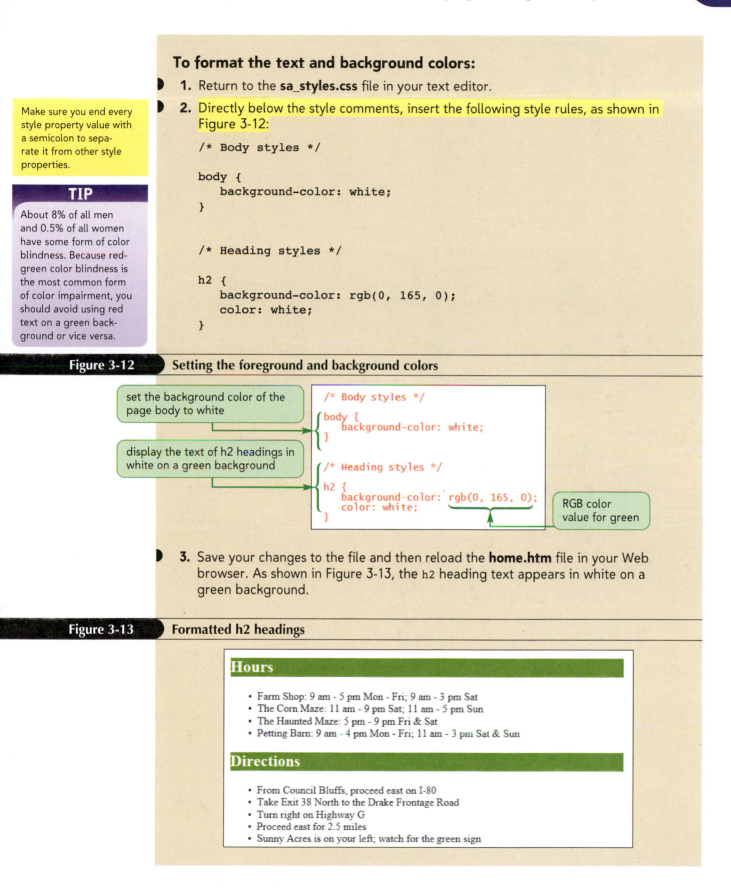

set the background color of the page body to white

display the text of h2 headings in white on a green background

RGB color value for green

3. Save your changes to the file and then reload the **home.htm** file in your Web browser. As shown in Figure 3-13, the h2 heading text appears in white on a green background.

Figure 3-13   Formatted h2 headings

Hours

- Farm Shop: 9 am - 5 pm Mon - Fri; 9 am - 3 pm Sat
- The Corn Maze: 11 am - 9 pm Sat; 11 am - 5 pm Sun
- The Haunted Maze: 5 pm - 9 pm Fri & Sat
- Petting Barn: 9 am - 4 pm Mon - Fri; 11 am - 3 pm Sat & Sun

Directions

- From Council Bluffs, proceed east on I-80
- Take Exit 38 North to the Drake Frontage Road
- Turn right on Highway G
- Proceed east for 2.5 miles
- Sunny Acres is on your left; watch for the green sign

INSIGHT

Deprecated Approaches to Color

Because CSS was not part of the original HTML specifications, older HTML code used HTML attributes to define page colors. If you work with older Web pages, you may encounter some of these deprecated attributes. For example, the `bgcolor` attribute in the `<body>` tag was used to define the background color for an entire page. To define the text color for the entire page, the `text` attribute was used. Both attributes required the page author to enter either a hexadecimal color value or a recognized color name. Thus, the following code set the page background to yellow and the page text color to sky blue with the hexadecimal color value 99CCFF:

```
<body bgcolor="yellow" text="#99CCFF">
```

To color a section of text, page authors enclosed the text within a two-sided `<font>` tag, which supported several design attributes. One of these, `color`, defined the font color of the enclosed text. For example, the following deprecated code sets the text color of an `h1` heading to green:

```
<h1><font color="green">Sunny Acres</font></h1>
```

These attributes, as well as the `<font>` tag, have been deprecated due to the desire to completely separate page content from page design. Although you may still encounter them and browsers still support them, you should always use style sheets to set your page design.

Enhancements to Color in CSS3

RGB color values and color names have been part of Web page design since the introduction of CSS. However, graphic designers have long wanted additional options for creating and working with colors in CSS. For this reason, CSS3 introduced additional tools to allow Web page designers to create more interesting and flexible designs based on color.

HSL Color Values

The RGB color model is only one way of describing colors. CSS3 also supports the Hue Saturation Lightness (HSL) model that describes colors based on hue, saturation, and lightness. **Hue** is the tint of the color and is based on the color's location on the color wheel. Hue values range from 0° up to 360°, where 0° matches the location of red on the color wheel, 120° matches green, and 240° matches blue. **Saturation** measures the intensity of the chosen color and ranges from 0% (no color) up to 100% (full color). Finally, **lightness** measures the brightness of the color and ranges from 0% (black) up to 100% (white). Color values using the HSL model are described in CSS3 using

```
hsl(hue, saturation, lightness)
```

where *hue* is the tint of the color in degrees, *saturation* is the intensity of the color in percent, and *lightness* is the brightness of the color in percent. Figure 3-14 shows how setting the hue to 38°, the saturation to 90%, and the lightness to 60% results in a medium shade of orange.

Figure 3-14   HSL color saturation model

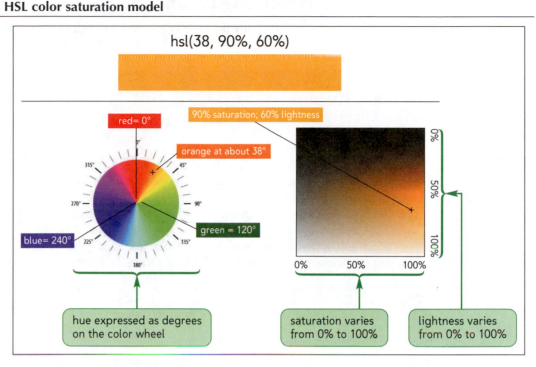

Graphic designers consider HSL easier to use because it allows you to guess at an initial color based on hue and then tweak the saturation and lightness values to fine-tune the final color. This is more difficult in the RGB model because you have to balance three completely different colors to achieve the right mix. For example, the RGB equivalent to the color in Figure 3-14 would be the color value rgb(245, 177, 61); however, it's not immediately apparent why that mixture of red, green, and blue would result in that particular shade of orange.

Opacity Values in CSS3

CSS3 also allows page designers to augment RGB and HSL color values by specifying a color's opacity. Opacity defines how much of the colors below the surface of the current object show through to affect its appearance. The opacity of a color can be specified using either of the following `rgba` and `hsla` color values

```
rgba(red, green, blue, opacity)
hsla(hue, saturation, lightness, opacity)
```

where *opacity* sets the transparency of the color as a decimal ranging from 0 (completely transparent) up to 1.0 (completely opaque). For example, the following style displays the text of `h1` headings in a medium shade of orange at 70% opacity:

```
hsla(38, 90%, 60%, 0.7)
```

TIP

The *a* in rgba and hsla stands for *alpha* and refers to the alpha channel, a color concept developed in the 1970s to add transparency to the color model.

With semi-transparent colors, the final color rendered by a browser depends on the background color of the parent element. Displayed against a white background, this medium orange color would appear in a lighter shade of orange, while displayed against a black background it would appear as very dark orange. The advantage of using semi-transparent colors is that it makes it easier to create a color theme in which similarly tinted colors are used throughout the page.

Styles Using Progressive Enhancement

Tammy suggests that you modify the style of the `h2` headings to make the text appear as a semi-transparent white against a green background. To create this effect, you can employ the following style rule:

```
h2 {
    background-color: rgb(0, 154, 0);
    color: white;
    color: rgba(255, 255, 255, 0.8);
}
```

Notice that this code doesn't remove the initial `color` property that set the text color to white, but simply adds another `color` property to the style rule. This is an example of a technique known as **progressive enhancement**, which places code conforming to older standards before newer properties. Older browsers that do not support CSS3 will ignore the RGBA color value and display the text in white, while newer browsers that do support CSS3 will apply the RGBA color value because that color value, being declared last, has precedence. Thus, both older and newer browsers are served by this style rule.

To make the heading text semi-transparent:

1. Return to the **sa_styles.css** file in your text editor.

2. Within the style rule for the `h2` selector, insert the following `color` property, as shown in Figure 3-15:

   ```
   color: rgba(255, 255, 255, 0.8);
   ```

Figure 3-15	Setting a semi-transparent color

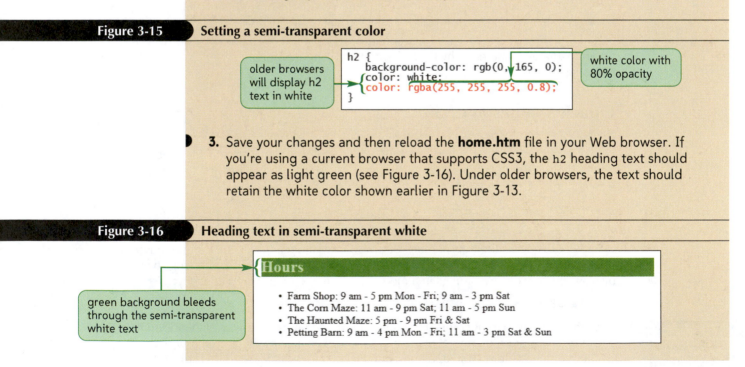

3. Save your changes and then reload the **home.htm** file in your Web browser. If you're using a current browser that supports CSS3, the `h2` heading text should appear as light green (see Figure 3-16). Under older browsers, the text should retain the white color shown earlier in Figure 3-13.

Figure 3-16	Heading text in semi-transparent white

PROSKILLS

Problem Solving: Choosing a Color Scheme

One of the worst things you can do to your Web site is to associate interesting and useful content with jarring and disagreeable color. Many designers prefer the HSL color system because it makes it easier to select visually pleasing color schemes. The following are some basic color schemes you may want to apply to your own Web sites:

- *monochrome*—a single hue with varying values for saturation and lightness; this color scheme is easy to manage but is not as vibrant as other designs
- *complementary*—two hues separated by 180° on the color wheel; this color scheme is the most vibrant and offers the highest contrast and visual interest, but can be misused and might distract users from the page content
- *triad*—three hues separated by 120° on the color wheel; this color scheme provides the same opportunity for pleasing color contrasts as a complementary design, but might not be visibly striking
- *tetrad*—four hues separated by 90° on the color wheel; perhaps the richest of all color schemes, it is also the hardest one in which to achieve color balance
- *analogic*—two hues close to one another on the color wheel in which one color is the dominant color and the other is a supporting color used only for highlights and nuance; this scheme lacks color contrasts and is not as vibrant as other color schemes

Once you have selected a color design and the main hues, you then vary those colors by altering the saturation and lightness. One of the great advantages of style sheets is that you can quickly modify your color design choices and view the impact of those changes on your Web page content.

You show Tammy the work you've done on colors. She's pleased with the ease of using CSS to modify the design and appearance of elements on the Sunny Acres Web site. In the next session, you'll continue to explore CSS styles, focusing on text and image styles.

REVIEW

Session 3.1 Quick Check

1. What are inline styles, embedded styles, and external style sheets? Which would you use to define a design for an entire Web site?
2. What keyword do you add to a style property to override style precedence and style inheritance?
3. Specify the code to enter the comment *Sunny Acres Color Styles* in a style sheet.
4. Provide the style rule to display blockquote text in red using an RGB triplet.
5. The color chartreuse is located at 90° on the color wheel with 100% saturation and 50% lightness. Provide a style rule to display address text with chartreuse as the background color.
6. What is progressive enhancement?
7. Based on the following style rule for paragraph text, which style property will be used by an older browser that supports only CSS2?

```
p {
   color: rgb(232, 121, 50);
   color: hsla(23, 80%, 55%, 0.75);
}
```

8. Provide a style rule to display h1 and h2 headings with a background color of yellow (an equal mixture of red and green at highest intensity with no blue) at 70% opacity.

SESSION 3.2 VISUAL OVERVIEW

The font-family property sets the typeface of the font.

```
h1 {
    font-family: Geneva, sans-serif;
}
```

A **generic font** describes the general appearance of a font.

A **specific font** references a font installed on users' computers.

The text-indent property shifts the text from the margin.

```
h2 {
    text-indent: 10px;
    font-weight: bold;
}
```

The font-weight property sets the weight or bolding of the font.

The font-style property sets the appearance of the font as either italic, oblique, or normal.

```
address {
    font-style: normal;
    font-variant: small-caps;
}
```

The font-variant property provides a variation of the font such as small capital letters.

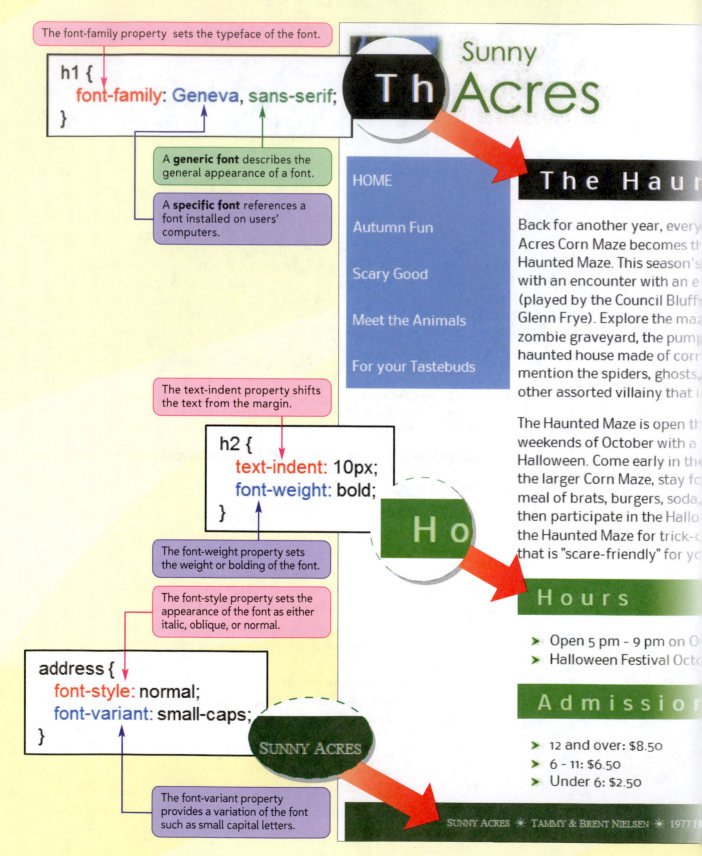

Sunny Acres

HOME

Autumn Fun

Scary Good

Meet the Animals

For your Tastebuds

The Haun

Back for another year, every
Acres Corn Maze becomes th
Haunted Maze. This season's
with an encounter with an e
(played by the Council Bluff
Glenn Frye). Explore the ma
zombie graveyard, the pump
haunted house made of corn
mention the spiders, ghosts,
other assorted villainy that

The Haunted Maze is open th
weekends of October with a
Halloween. Come early in the
the larger Corn Maze, stay fo
meal of brats, burgers, soda,
then participate in the Hallo
the Haunted Maze for trick-o
that is "scare-friendly" for yo

Hours

> Open 5 pm - 9 pm on O
> Halloween Festival Oct

Admission

> 12 and over: $8.50
> 6 - 11: $6.50
> Under 6: $2.50

SUNNY ACRES ✳ TAMMY & BRENT NIELSEN ✳ 1977 H

SELECTORS AND TEXT STYLES

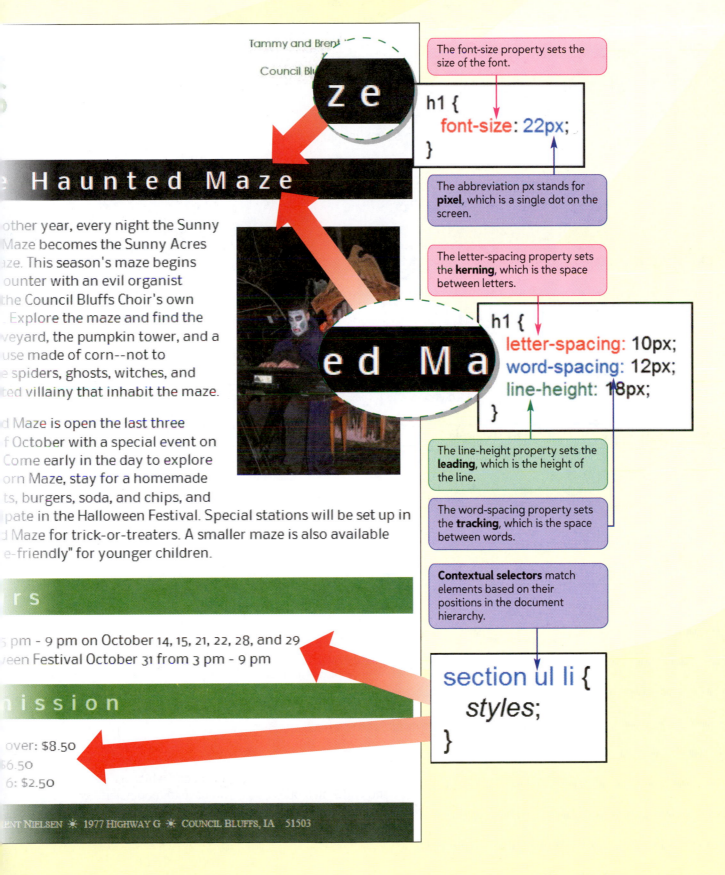

Tammy and Bren[...]

Council Blu[...]

e H a u n t e d   M a z e

other year, every night the Sunny
Maze becomes the Sunny Acres
ze. This season's maze begins
ounter with an evil organist
the Council Bluffs Choir's own
. Explore the maze and find the
veyard, the pumpkin tower, and a
use made of corn--not to
e spiders, ghosts, witches, and
ted villainy that inhabit the maze.

d Maze is open the last three
f October with a special event on
Come early in the day to explore
orn Maze, stay for a homemade
ts, burgers, soda, and chips, and
pate in the Halloween Festival. Special stations will be set up in
d Maze for trick-or-treaters. A smaller maze is also available
e-friendly" for younger children.

rs

pm - 9 pm on October 14, 15, 21, 22, 28, and 29
een Festival October 31 from 3 pm - 9 pm

nission

over: $8.50
$6.50
6: $2.50

ENT NIELSEN ✷ 1977 HIGHWAY G ✷ COUNCIL BLUFFS, IA   51503

The font-size property sets the size of the font.

```
h1 {
    font-size: 22px;
}
```

The abbreviation px stands for **pixel**, which is a single dot on the screen.

The letter-spacing property sets the **kerning**, which is the space between letters.

```
h1 {
    letter-spacing: 10px;
    word-spacing: 12px;
    line-height: 18px;
}
```

The line-height property sets the **leading**, which is the height of the line.

The word-spacing property sets the **tracking**, which is the space between words.

Contextual selectors match elements based on their positions in the document hierarchy.

```
section ul li {
    styles;
}
```

Exploring Selector Patterns

Tammy has examined your work on color styles from the last session and asks that you create another color style for h1 headings. She suggests that you display the text of your h1 headings in white on a sky blue background.

To format h1 headings:

▶ 1. Return to the **sa_styles.css** file in your text editor.

▶ 2. Directly above the style rule for h2 headings, insert the following style rule, as shown in Figure 3-17:

```
h1 {
    background-color: rgb(125, 186, 240);
    color: white;
}
```

Figure 3-17   **Creating a style for h1 headings**

display h1 headings in white on a sky blue background

```
/* Heading styles */

h1 {
    background-color: rgb(125, 186, 240);
    color: white;
}
```

▶ 3. Save your changes to the file and then reload the **home.htm** file in your Web browser. Figure 3-18 shows the revised appearance of the page.

Figure 3-18   **Effect of the h1 style rule**

sky blue background added to the company logo

formatted h1 heading

Tammy notices that the sky blue background has been added to the Welcome text in the h1 heading, but it also has been added to the company logo. A quick investigation of the HTML code reveals that the logo itself is also within an h1 heading:

```
<header>
    <h1>
        <img src="salogo.png" alt="Sunny Acres" />
    </h1>
</header>
```

Tammy doesn't want all h1 headings formatted the same way. To specify which h1 headings receive a sky blue background and which ones don't, you have to modify the selector in the style rule you just entered.

Contextual Selectors

So far, the only selectors you've studied involve either single elements or groups of elements in a comma-separated list. However, this approach doesn't take into account that Web pages are structured documents in which elements are nested within other elements, forming a hierarchy of elements. Figure 3-19 shows an example of such a tree structure for a Web page consisting of a few headings, a couple of paragraphs, and a few text-level elements, all descending from the `body` element.

Figure 3-19   **A sample hierarchy of page elements**

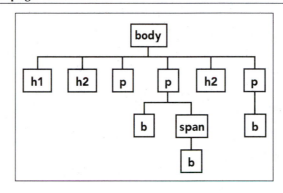

To create styles that take advantage of this tree structure, CSS allows you to create contextual selectors whose values represent the locations of elements within the hierarchy. As with the folder structure discussed in Tutorial 2, elements in a Web page are often referenced using their familial relationships. A **parent element** is an element that contains one or more other elements, which are **child elements** of the parent. Two child elements that share the same parent are referred to as **sibling elements**. Each child element may contain children of its own and so forth down the hierarchy, creating a set of **descendant elements** that are all descended from a common parent. The ultimate parent element for the HTML file is the `html` element itself, and the parent element for all elements within the page body is the `body` element.

One commonly used selector that takes advantage of these familial relationships has the form

```
parent descendant {styles}
```

where *parent* is the parent element, *descendant* is a descendant of the parent, and *styles* are the style properties applied to the descendant element. For example, to display the text of all `h1` headings found within a page header in blue, you could apply the following style rule:

```
header h1 {color: blue;}
```

In this case, `header` is the parent element and `h1` is the descendant element (because it is contained within the `header` element). Any `h1` heading that is not placed within a page header is not affected by this style. Note that the descendant element does not have to be a direct child of the parent; it can appear several levels below the parent in the hierarchy. This style applies equally to the following HTML code:

```
<header>
   <hgroup>
      <h1>Sunny Acres</h1>
   </hgroup>
</header>
```

Here, the `h1` element is a direct child only of the `hgroup` element; but because it is still a descendant of the `header` element, it would still appear in blue.

Contextual selectors take advantage of the general rule that the more specific style is applied in preference to the more general. For instance, the styles

```
section h1 {color: red;}
h1          {color: blue;}
```

would result in any h1 heading text nested within a section element appearing in red, even though the last style sets the text color to blue. The more specific style using the contextual selector takes precedence over the general style in which no context has been given.

Contextual selectors also can be listed with other selectors. The following style rule is applied both to strong elements nested within list items and to h2 headings:

```
li strong, h2 {color: blue;}
```

The parent/descendant form is only one example of a contextual selector. Figure 3-20 describes some of the other contextual forms supported by CSS.

Figure 3-20   **Contextual selectors**

Selector	Description
*	Matches any element in the hierarchy
e	Matches any element, e, in the hierarchy
e1, e2, e3, ...	Matches the group of elements e1, e2, e3, ...
e f	Matches any element, f, that is a descendant of an element, e
e>f	Matches any element, f, that is a direct child of an element, e
e+f	Matches any element, f, that is immediately preceded by a sibling element, e
e~f	Matches any element, f, that is a sibling to an element, e

For example, the style rule

```
* {color: blue;}
```

uses the asterisk (*) selector—also known as the **wildcard selector**—to select all elements in the document. The result is that the text of all elements in the document appears in blue. On the other hand, the rule

```
p > em {color: blue;}
```

applies the blue text color only to emphasized text placed as a direct child of a paragraph. Figure 3-21 provides additional examples of selectors applied to a document tree. Selected elements are highlighted in red for each pattern. Remember that because of style inheritance, any style applied to an element is passed down the document tree. Thus, a style applied to a paragraph element is automatically passed down to elements contained within that paragraph unless that style conflicts with a more specific style.

Figure 3-21   Examples of contextual selectors

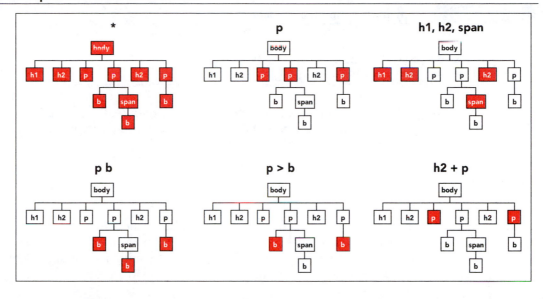

Using Contextual Selectors

- To apply a style to all elements in a document, use the * selector.
- To apply a style to a single element, use the *e* selector, where *e* is the name of the element.
- To apply a selector to a descendant element, *f*, use the *e* *f* selector, where *e* is the name of the parent element and *f* is an element nested within the parent.
- To apply a selector to a child element, *f*, use the *e* > *f* selector, where *e* is the name of a parent element and *f* is an element that is a direct child of the parent.
- To apply a selector to a sibling element, use the *e* + *f* selector, where *e* and *f* are siblings and *f* immediately follows *e* in the document tree.
- To apply a selector to any sibling element, use the *e* ~ *f* selector, where *e* and *f* are siblings.

Now that you've seen how to create contextual selectors, you can fix the style rule you created earlier. Rather than applying white text and a sky blue background to every h1 heading, you'll apply those properties only to h1 headings that are descendants of the section element. The style rule thus becomes

```
section h1 {
    background-color: rgb(125, 186, 240);
    color: white;
}
```

with the section h1 selector replacing simply h1. You'll revise the style sheet accordingly.

To revise the style sheet:

1. Return to the **sa_styles.css** file in your text editor.

2. Change the selector for the h1 heading rule to **section h1** (see Figure 3-22).

Figure 3-22   **Applying a contextual selector**

style rule applied only to h1 headings
nested within section elements

```
section h1 {
    background-color: rgb(125, 186, 240);
    color: white;
}
```

3. Save your changes to the style sheet and then reload the **home.htm** file in your Web browser. Verify that the sky blue background is applied only to the Welcome heading.

Attribute Selectors

Selectors also can be defined based on attributes and attribute values associated with elements. Two attributes, `id` and `class`, are often key in targeting styles to a specific element or group of elements. Recall that the `id` attribute is used to identify specific elements within the Web document. To apply a style to an element based on its id, you use the selector

   `#id`

where `id` is the value of the `id` attribute. Thus, to format the text of the `h1` heading

   `<h1 id="main">Sunny Acres</h1>`

to appear in red, you could apply the following style rule:

   `#main {color: red;}`

> **TIP**
>
> A style rule involving an `id` selector has precedence over any rule except those defined within an inline style.

Because no two elements can share the same id value, HTML uses the `class` attribute to identify groups of elements that share a similar characteristic or property. The attribute has the syntax

   `<elem class="className"> … </elem>`

where `className` is the name of the element class. For example, the following `h1` heading and paragraph both belong to the *intro* class of elements.

```
<h1 class="intro">Sunny Acres</h1>
<p class="intro">
   Welcome to Sunny Acres, where there's always
   something happening on the farm.
</p>
```

> **TIP**
>
> You can associate a single element with several classes by listing each class name, separated by a space, as part of the `class` attribute value.

One reason to use the `class` attribute is to assign the same style to multiple elements that belong to the same class. A selector based on a class has the form

   `.class {styles}`

where `class` is the name of the class and `styles` are styles associated with that class of element. Thus, to display the text of all elements belonging to the *intro* class in blue, you could apply the following style:

   `.intro {color: blue;}`

Because different types of elements can belong to the same class, you can also specify exactly which kinds of elements within that class receive the style rule by using the selector

   `elem.class {styles}`

where *elem* is the name of the element. Thus, the style rule

```
h1.intro {color: blue;}
```

causes the text of all `h1` headings that belong to the intro class to appear in blue.

While `id` and `class` are the most common attributes to use with selectors, any attribute or attribute value can be the basis for a selector. Figure 3-23 lists the selector patterns that are based on attributes and their values.

Figure 3-23   **Attribute selectors**

Selector	Description	Example	Matches
`#id`	The element with the id value, *id*	`#intro`	The element with the id *intro*
`.class`	All elements with the class value, *class*	`.main`	All elements belonging to the *main* class
`elem.class`	All *elem* elements with the class value *class*	`p.main`	All paragraphs belonging to the *main* class
`elem[att]`	All *elem* elements containing the *att* attribute	`a[href]`	All hypertext elements containing the `href` attribute
`elem[att="text"]`	All *elem* elements whose *att* attribute equals *text*	`a[href="gloss.htm"]`	All hypertext elements whose `href` attribute equals *gloss.htm*
`elem[att~="text"]`	All *elem* elements whose *att* attribute contains the word *text*	`a[rel~="glossary"]`	All hypertext elements whose `rel` attribute contains the word *glossary*
`elem[att|="text"]`	All *elem* elements whose *att* attribute value is a hyphen-separated list of words beginning with *text*	`p[id|="first"]`	All paragraphs whose `id` attribute starts with the word *first* in a hyphen-separated list of words
`elem[att^="text"]`	All *elem* elements whose *att* attribute begins with *text* (CSS3)	`a[rel^="prev"]`	All hypertext elements whose `rel` attribute begins with *prev*
`elem[att$="text"]`	All *elem* elements whose *att* attribute ends with *text* (CSS3)	`a[href$="org"]`	All hypertext elements whose `href` attribute ends with *org*
`elem[att*="text"]`	All *elem* elements whose *att* attribute contains the value *text* (CSS3)	`a[href*="faq"]`	All hypertext elements whose `href` attribute contains the text string *faq*

All current browsers support the attribute selector patterns listed in Figure 3-23; be aware, however, that some older browsers—primarily IE6—may not support these selectors in your style sheets.

Using Attribute Selectors

- To apply a style based on the id value of an element, use the #*id* selector, where *id* is the value of the id attribute.
- To apply a style based on the class value of elements, use either the .*class* or the *elem*.*class* selectors, where *class* is the value of the class attribute and *elem* is the element name.
- To apply a style based on whether an element contains an attribute, use the *elem*[*att*] selector, where *class* is the class name and *att* is the attribute name.
- To apply a style based on whether the attribute value for elements equals a specified value, use the *elem*[*att*="*val*"] where *val* is the specified value.

In the Sunny Acres home page, Tammy has added the following class attribute to the last paragraph that introduces the Web site:

```
<p class="closing">We all hope to see you soon,
    down on the farm.<br />
    &mdash; <span>Tammy &amp; Brent Nielsen</span>
</p>
```

She suggests that you format this paragraph so that it appears in green and is right-aligned on the page. To do this, you'll add the following style to the *sa_styles.css* style sheet:

```
section p.closing {
    color: rgb(0, 165, 0);
    text-align: right;
}
```

Note that this style rule applies to paragraphs belonging to the closing class and nested within the section element. You could have simply used the .closing selector, but then the style rule would apply to any element belonging to the *closing* class. Usually, you want to be as specific as possible in your style sheet so that you are always targeting exactly the elements that you want to target.

To create a style based on the class attribute:

1. Return to the **sa_styles.css** file in your text editor.

2. Add the following style rule at the bottom of style sheet (see Figure 3-24):

```
/* Section styles */

section p.closing {
    color: rgb(0, 165, 0);
    text-align: right;
}
```

Figure 3-24   Applying a selector based on class

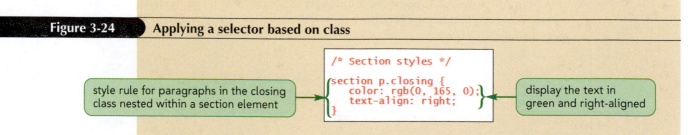

style rule for paragraphs in the closing class nested within a section element

```
/* Section styles */

section p.closing {
    color: rgb(0, 165, 0);
    text-align: right;
}
```

display the text in green and right-aligned

3. Save your changes to the style sheet and then reload the **home.htm** file in your Web browser. Verify that the text of the last paragraph appears in green and is right aligned on the page (see Figure 3-25).

Figure 3-25   **Closing paragraph of the home page**

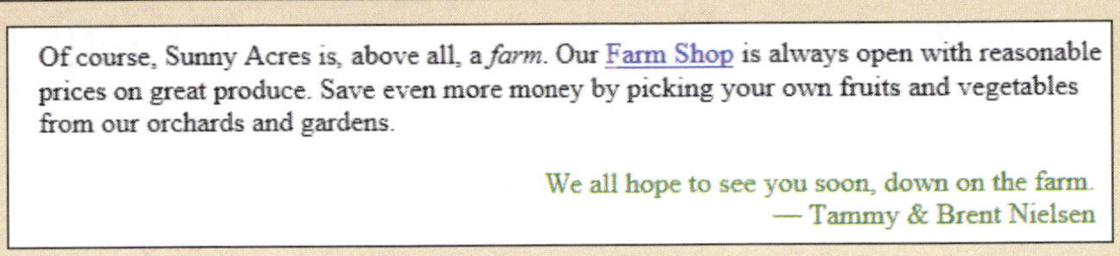

> Of course, Sunny Acres is, above all, a *farm*. Our Farm Shop is always open with reasonable prices on great produce. Save even more money by picking your own fruits and vegetables from our orchards and gardens.
>
> We all hope to see you soon, down on the farm.
> — Tammy & Brent Nielsen

Styling Web Page Text

The `text-align` property you used in your style rule to right-align the contents of the closing paragraph is an example of a text style. In this section, you'll explore other CSS styles used to format the appearance of Web page text.

Choosing the Text Font

Tammy has noticed that all of the text in her sample pages is displayed in the same typeface, or **font**. She'd like to see more variety in how the Web page text is rendered. The default font used by most browsers is Times New Roman, but you can specify a different font for any page element using the property

```
font-family: fonts;
```

where *fonts* is a comma-separated list of specific or generic font names. A specific font is a font that is identified by name, such as Times New Roman or Helvetica. When referenced by the `font-family` property, a specific font refers to a font definition that is stored on a user's computer. A generic font describes the general appearance of a typeface, but does not rely on a specific font definition. CSS supports the following generic font groups:

- *serif*—a typeface in which a small ornamentation appears at the tail end of each character
- *sans-serif*—a non-serif font without any ornamentation
- *monospace*—a typeface in which each character has the same width; often used to display programming code
- *cursive*—a typeface that mimics handwriting with highly stylized elements and flourishes; best used in small doses for decorative page elements
- *fantasy*—a highly ornamental typeface used for page decoration; should never be used with body text

When you use generic fonts, you have no control over which font a user's browser will choose for your Web page. Therefore, the common practice is to list specific fonts first, in order of preference, and end the list with a generic font. If a user's browser cannot find any of the specific fonts listed, it uses a generic font of its own choosing. For example, the style

```
font-family: 'Arial Black', Gadget, sans-serif;
```

tells a browser to use the Arial Black font if available; if not, to look for the Gadget font; and if neither are available, to use a generic sans-serif font of its own selection. Note that font names containing one or more blank spaces (such as Arial Black) must be enclosed within single or double quotes.

Because the available fonts vary with each user's operating system, the challenge is to choose a list of fonts known as **Web safe fonts**, which will be displayed in mostly the same way in all browsers and on all devices. Figure 3-26 shows several commonly used fonts.

Figure 3-26   Web safe fonts

Arial
abcdefghijklmnopqrstuvwxyz/1234567890
font-family: Arial, Helvetica, sans-serif;

Arial Black
abcdefghijklmnopqrstuvwxyz/1234567890
font-family: 'Arial Black', Gadget, sans-serif;

Century Gothic
abcdefghijklmnopqrstuvwxyz/1234567890
font-family: 'Century Gothic', sans-serif;

Comic Sans MS
abcdefghijklmnopqrstuvwxyz/1234567890
font-family: 'Comic Sans MS', cursive;

Courier New
abcdefghijklmnopqrstuvwxyz/1234567890
font-family: 'Courier New', Courier, monospace;

Georgia
abcdefghijklmnopqrstuvwxyz/1234567890
font-family: Georgia, serif;

Impact
abcdefghijklmnopqrstuvwxyz/1234567890
font-family: Impact, Charcoal, sans-serif;

Lucida Console
abcdefghijklmnopqrstuvwxyz/1234567890
font-family: 'Lucida Console', Monaco, monospace;

Lucida Sans Unicode
abcdefghijklmnopqrstuvwxyz/1234567890
font-family: 'Lucida Sans Unicode', 'Lucida Grande', sans-serif;

Palatino Linotype
abcdefghijklmnopqrstuvwxyz/1234567890
font-family: 'Palatino Linotype', 'Book Antiqua', Palatino, serif;

Tahoma
abcdefghijklmnopqrstuvwxyz/1234567890
font-family: Tahoma, Geneva, sans-serif;

Times New Roman
abcdefghijklmnopqrstuvwxyz/1234567890
font-family: 'Times New Roman', Times, serif;

Trebuchet MS
abcdefghijklmnopqrstuvwxyz/1234567890
font-family: 'Trebuchet MS', Helvetica, sans-serif;

Verdana
abcdefghijklmnopqrstuvwxyz/1234567890
font-family: Verdana, Geneva, sans-serif;

A general rule for printing is to use sans-serif fonts for headlines and serif fonts for body text. For computer monitors, which have lower resolutions than printed material, the general rule is to use sans-serif fonts for headlines and body text, leaving serif fonts for special effects and large text.

REFERENCE

Setting Font Face and Sizes

- To define a font face, use the style property

  font-family: *fonts*;

  where *fonts* is a comma-separated list of fonts that the browser can use with the element. List specific fonts first and complete the list with a generic font.
- To set a font size, use the style property

  font-size: *size*;

  where *size* is a CSS unit of length in either relative or absolute units.
- To set kerning (the space between letters), use the following style property:

  letter-spacing: *size*;

- To set tracking (the space between words), use the following style property:

  word-spacing: *size*;

Tammy expects that her Web page will be viewed only on computer monitors, so you'll use a sans-serif font for all of the body text by adding the style

```
font-family: Verdana, Geneva, sans-serif;
```

to the body selector. Browsers will first try to load the Verdana font, followed by the Geneva font. If both are unavailable, browsers will load a generic sans-serif font.

To apply a sans-serif font to the body text:

1. Return to the **sa_styles.css** file in your text editor.

2. Add the following style to the body style rule at the top of the style sheet, as shown in Figure 3-27:

```
font-family: Verdana, Geneva, sans-serif;
```

Figure 3-27	Specify the default font for the Web page body

```
body {
    background-color: white;
    font-family: Verdana, Geneva, sans-serif;
}
```

3. Save your changes to the style sheet and then reload the **home.htm** file in your Web browser. As shown in Figure 3-28, the text of the entire page is displayed in a sans-serif font.

Figure 3-28	Displaying the page text in a sans-serif font

Sunny **Acres**

Tammy and Brent Nielsen
1973 Hwy G
Council Bluffs, IA 51503

- Home
- Autumn Fun
- Scary Good
- Meet the Animals
- For your Tastebuds

Welcome

There's always something happening at Sunny Acres. With the coming of fall, we're gearing up for our big AutumnFest and Farm Show. If you haven't visited our famous Corn Maze, be sure to do so before it gets torn down on November 5. This year's maze is bigger and better than ever.

Farms can be educational and Sunny Acres is no exception. Schools and home-schooling parents, take an afternoon with us at our Petting Barn. We have over 100 friendly farm animals in a clean environment. Kids can bottle feed the baby goats, lambs, and calves while they learn about nature and the farming life. Please call ahead for large school groups.

Setting the Font Size

Tammy would like the Welcome heading on her home page to be displayed in slightly smaller text than is generally set by a browser's internal style sheet. The style to change the font size is

```
font-size: size;
```

where *size* is a length measurement. Lengths can be specified in four different ways:

- with a unit of measurement
- as a percentage of the size of the containing element
- with a keyword description
- with a keyword expressing the size relative to the size of the containing element

If you choose to specify lengths using measurement units, you can use absolute units or relative units. **Absolute units** are units that are fixed in size regardless of the device rendering the Web page. They are specified in one of five standard units of measurement: mm (millimeters), cm (centimeters), in (inches), pt (points), and pc (picas). Points and picas might not be as familiar to you as inches, millimeters, and centimeters. For comparison, there are 72 points in an inch, 12 points in a pica, and 6 picas in an inch. Size values for any of these measurements can be whole numbers (0, 1, 2 ...) or decimals (0.5, 1.6, 3.9 ...). For example, if you want your text to be 1/2 inch in size, you can use any of the following styles:

```
font-size: 0.5in
font-size: 36pt
font-size: 3pc
```

Note that you should not insert a space between the size value and the unit abbreviation.

Absolute measurements are appropriate when you know the physical properties of an output device and want to fix a size to a specific value. Of course, this is not often the case with Web pages that can be displayed on a variety of devices and under several possible screen or page resolutions. To cope with the uncertainty about how their pages will be viewed, many Web page designers opt to use **relative units**, which are expressed relative to the size of other objects within the Web page. One commonly used relative unit is the **em unit**. The exact meaning of the em unit depends on its use in the style sheet. If the em unit is used for setting font size, it expresses the size relative to the font size of the parent element. For an `h1` heading, the parent element is the Web page body. Thus, the style rule

```
h1 {font-size: 2em;}
```

sets the font size of `h1` headings to twice the font size of body text. If body text is displayed in a 12-point font, this style will cause `h1` headings to be displayed in a 24-point font. On the other hand, if the `h1` heading is nested within another element, such as a `section` element, the size of the `h1` heading will be twice the size of text in that parent element. Context is important when interpreting the effect of the em unit.

One of the great advantages of relative units like the em unit is that they can make your page **scalable**, allowing the page to be rendered the same way no matter what font size is used by the browser. Setting the font size of `h1` headings to 1.5em ensures the heading will be 50% larger than the body text for all users.

Another way to create relative font sizes is to express the font size as a percentage. Like the em unit, percentages are based on the font size of the parent element. The style

```
h1 {font-size: 200%;}
```

sets the font size of `h1` headings to 200%, or twice the font size of body text.

Another unit of measurement widely used on the Web is the **pixel**, which represents a single dot on the output device. The size or **resolution** of most output devices is typically expressed in terms of pixels. Thus a 1280 × 720 screen resolution on a computer monitor is 1280 pixels wide by 720 pixels tall, for a total of 921,600 pixels or 0.92 mega-pixels. A pixel is a relative unit because the actual rendered size depends on the **density** of the output device. A Windows PC, for example, has a density of 96 dpi (dots per inch), while a Macintosh computer has a density of 72 dpi. Some mobile phones have densities as high as 200 or 300 dpi. The pixel measure is the most precise unit of measure and gives designers the most control over the appearance of a page; however, pixels are not scalable. This can pose a problem for visually impaired users who need larger fonts, or for users of mobile devices with very dense screens.

Finally, you also can express font sizes using one of the following keywords: `xx-small`, `x-small`, `small`, `medium`, `large`, `x-large`, `xx-large`, `larger`, or `smaller`. The size corresponding to each of these keywords is determined by the browser. Note that the `larger` and `smaller` keywords are relative sizes, making the font size of the element one size larger or smaller than the surrounding text. For example, the following set of styles causes the `body` text to be displayed in a small font, while `h2` text is displayed in a font one size larger (medium):

```
body {font-size: small;}
h2   {font-size: larger;}
```

Tammy suggests that you set the size of the `h1` headings to 1.7em, making the headings 70% larger than the default size of the body text in the document.

To set the font size of the `h1` headings:

1. Return to the **sa_styles.css** file in your text editor.

2. Add the following style to the style rule for `h1` headings in the `section` element (see Figure 3-29):

   ```
   font-size: 1.7em;
   ```

Figure 3-29   **Setting the font size of h1 headings**

```
section h1 {
    background-color: rgb(125, 186, 240);
    color: white;
    font-size: 1.7em;
}
```

3. Save your changes to the file and then reload the **home.htm** file in your Web browser. Verify that the font size of the `h1` heading appears slightly smaller under the revised style sheet.

Decision Making: Selecting a Text Font

The challenge with designing Web text is that you don't have the same control over the output device as you do when choosing a font style for printed output. A user may not have that beautiful font you selected, and may have installed a font that will render your page unreadable. If you absolutely must have a section of text rendered in a specific font at a specific size, then your best choice may be to use an inline image in place of text.

Of course, you can't make your entire page an inline image, so you *always* should provide options for your customers in the form of extensive font lists. Other important things to consider when designing your text include the following:

- *Keep it plain*—Avoid large blocks of italicized text and boldfaced text. Those styles are designed for emphasis, not readability.
- *Sans-serif vs. serif*—Because they are more easily read on a computer monitor, use sans-serif fonts for your body text. Reserve the use of serif, cursive, and fantasy fonts for page headings and special decorative elements.
- *Relative vs. absolute*—Font sizes can be expressed in relative or absolute units. A relative unit like the em unit is more flexible and will be sized to match the screen resolution of the user's device; but you have more control over your page's appearance with an absolute unit. Generally, you want to use an absolute unit only when you know the configuration of the device the reader is using to view your page.
- *Size matters*—Almost all fonts are readable at a size of 14 pixels or greater; however, for smaller sizes you should choose fonts that were designed for screen display, such as Verdana and Georgia. On the other hand, Times and Arial often do not render well at smaller sizes. If you have to go really small (at a size of only a few pixels), you should either use a Web font that is specially designed for that purpose or replace the text with an inline image.
- *Avoid long lines*—With more users accessing the Web with widescreen monitors, you run the risk of presenting users with long lines of text. In general, try to keep the length of your lines to 60 characters or less. Anything longer is difficult to read.

When choosing any typeface and font style, the key is to test your selection on a variety of browsers, devices, screen resolutions, and densities. Don't assume that text that is readable and pleasing to the eye on your computer screen will work as well on another screen.

Controlling Spacing and Indentation

Tammy thinks that the text for the Welcome heading looks too crowded. She's wondering if you can further spread it out across the width of the page. She also would like to see more space between the first letter, W, and the left edge of the sky blue background.

CSS supports styles that allow you to control some basic typographic attributes, such as kerning and tracking. **Kerning** refers to the amount of space between characters, while **tracking** refers to the amount of space between words. The styles to control an element's kerning and tracking are

```
letter-spacing: value;
word-spacing:   value;
```

where *value* is the size of space between individual letters or words. You specify these sizes with the same units that you use for font sizing. The default value for both kerning and tracking is 0 pixels. A positive value increases the letter and word spacing, while a negative value reduces the space between letters and words. If you choose to make your pages scalable for a variety of devices and resolutions, you will want to express kerning and tracking values as percentages or in em units.

To see how modifying these values can affect the appearance of text, a demo page has been created for you.

To use the demo to explore kerning and tracking styles:

1. Open the **demo_css.htm** file from the tutorial.03/demo folder in your Web browser.

   The demo page contains a collection of CSS text styles. You can specify text style values using the boxes on the left side of the demo. In the top-right box, you can enter text to be displayed using the selected styles. The style as applied to the sample text appears in the middle box. The CSS code for the style appears in the bottom-right box. You press the Tab key to apply the style and view the results.

2. Click the top-right box, select and delete the text *Enter sample text here*, type **Sunny Acres**, press the **Enter** key, and then type **Corn Maze** on the second line. Press the **Tab** key to display this text in the Preview box.

3. Select **sans-serif** from the font-family box.

4. In the font-size box, replace the default text with **2**, and then select **em** in the corresponding unit box.

5. Enter **0.3** in the letter-spacing box, and then select **em** in the corresponding unit box. Press the **Tab** key.

6. Enter **0.8** in the word-spacing box and then select **em** in the corresponding unit box. Press the **Tab** key. Figure 3-30 shows the revised appearance of the text after applying the letter-spacing and word-spacing styles.

Figure 3-30   **Using the demo page to explore letter-spacing and word-spacing**

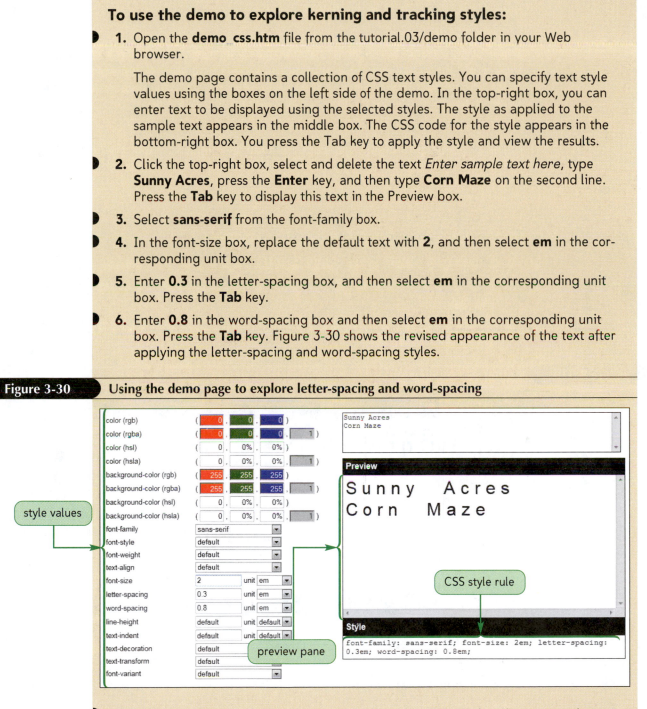

7. Experiment with other letter-spacing and word-spacing style values to see their effects on kerning and tracking.

Another typographic feature that you can set is **leading**, which is the space between lines of text. The style to set the leading value is

```
line-height: size;
```

where *size* is a specific length or a percentage of the font size of the text on the affected lines. If no unit is specified, most browsers interpret the number to represent the ratio of the line height to the font size. The standard ratio is 1.2:1, which means that the line height is usually 1.2 times the font size. By contrast, the style rule

```
p {line-height: 2em;}
```

makes all paragraphs double-spaced. A common technique for multi-line titles is to give title text more impact using large fonts and small line heights. Use the demo page to see how this works.

To use the demo to explore leading styles:

1. If necessary, return to the **demo_css.htm** page in your Web browser.

2. Enter **0.75** in the line-height box, and then select **em** from the corresponding unit box.

3. Press the **Tab** key to apply the line-height style. Figure 3-31 shows the revised appearance of the text.

Figure 3-31 **Setting the line height**

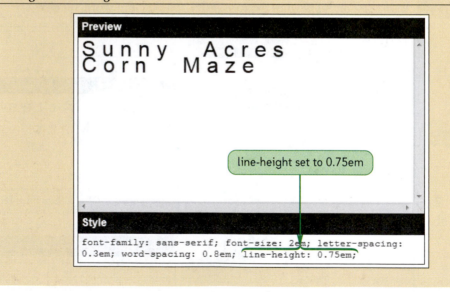

An additional way to control text spacing is to set the indentation for the first line of a block of text. The style is

```
text-indent: size;
```

where *size* is a length expressed in absolute or relative units, or as a percentage of the width of the text block. For example, an indentation value of 5% indents the first line by 5% of the width of the block. The indentation value also can be negative, extending the first line to the left of the text block to create a **hanging indent**.

Now you can use what you've learned about spacing to make the changes that Tammy has suggested. To spread out her heading text, you'll set the kerning of the `h1` heading to 0.4em. You'll also set the indentation to 1em, moving the text of both `h1` and `h2` headings to the left.

To change the spacing of the headings on the Web site:

1. Return to the **sa_styles.css** file in your text editor.

2. Within the style rules for the `section h1` selector and the `h2` selector, insert the following style values (see Figure 3-32):

   ```
   letter-spacing: 0.4em;
   text-indent: 1em;
   ```

Figure 3-32   Defining letter-spacing and text-indent

```
section h1 {
    background-color: rgb(125, 186, 240);
    color: white;
    font-size: 1.7em;
    letter-spacing: 0.4em;
    text-indent: 1em;
}

h2 {
    background-color: rgb(0, 165, 0);
    color: white;
    color: rgba(255, 255, 255, 0.8);
    letter-spacing: 0.4em;
    text-indent: 1em;
}
```

3. Save your changes to the file and then reload the **home.htm** file in your browser. As shown in Figure 3-33, the indent and the spacing between the letters have increased.

Figure 3-33   Revised spacing in h1 and h2 headings

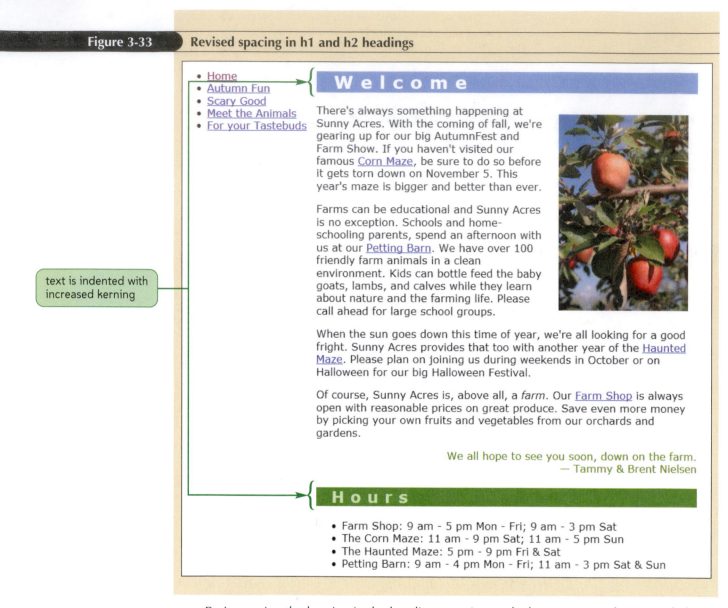

text is indented with increased kerning

By increasing the kerning in the headings, you've made the text appear less crowded, making it easier to read.

Working with Font Styles

Browsers often apply default font styles to particular types of elements; for instance, `address` elements are usually displayed in italic. You also can specify a different font style using the style

```
font-style: type;
```

where *type* is `normal`, `italic`, or `oblique`. The italic and oblique styles are similar in appearance, but might differ subtly depending on the font in use.

You also have seen that browsers render certain elements in heavier fonts. For example, most browsers render headings in a boldfaced font. You can specify the font weight for any page element using the style

```
font-weight: weight;
```

where *weight* is the level of bold formatting applied to the text. The *weight* value ranges from 100 to 900 in increments of 100. In practice, however, most browsers cannot

TIP

To prevent your browser from displaying address text in italic, you can set the `font-style` property to normal.

distinguish between nine different font weights. For practical purposes, you can assume that 400 represents normal (not bold) text, 700 is bold text, and 900 represents heavy bold text. You also can use the keywords `normal` or `bold` in place of a weight value, or you can express the font weight relative to the text of the containing element, using the keywords `bolder` or `lighter`.

Another style you can use to change the appearance of your text is

```
text-decoration: type;
```

where the `type` values include `none` (for no decoration), `underline`, `overline`, and `line-through`. You can apply several decorative features to the same element by listing them as part of the text-decoration style. For example, the style

```
text-decoration: underline overline;
```

places a line under and over the text in the element. Note that the text-decoration style has no effect on nontextual elements, such as inline images.

To control the case of the text within an element, use the style

```
text-transform: type;
```

where `type` is `capitalize`, `uppercase`, `lowercase`, or `none` (to make no changes to the text case). For example, if you want to capitalize the first letter of each word in an element, you could use the following style:

```
text-transform: capitalize;
```

Finally, you can display text in uppercase letters and a small font using the style

```
font-variant: type;
```

where `type` is `normal` (the default) or `small-caps` (small capital letters). Small caps are often used in legal documents, such as software agreements, in which the capital letters indicate the importance of a phrase or point, but the text is made small so as to not detract from other elements in the document.

REFERENCE

Setting Font and Text Appearance

- To specify the font style, use

  ```
  font-style: type;
  ```

  where `type` is normal, `italic`, or `oblique`.
- To specify the font weight, use

  ```
  font-weight: type;
  ```

  where `type` is normal, `bold`, `bolder`, `light`, `lighter`, or a font weight value.
- To specify a text decoration, use

  ```
  text-decoration: type;
  ```

  where `type` is none, `underline`, `overline`, or `line-through`.
- To transform text, use

  ```
  text-transform: type;
  ```

  where `type` is capitalize, `uppercase`, `lowercase`, or none.
- To display a font variant of text, use

  ```
  font-variant: type;
  ```

  where `type` is normal or `small-caps`.

To see the impact of these styles, you'll return to the demo page.

To use the demo to view the various font styles:

1. Return to the **demo_css.htm** page in your Web browser.

2. Select **bold** in the font-weight box.

3. Select **small-caps** in the font-variant box. Figure 3-34 shows the impact of applying the font-weight and font-variant styles.

Figure 3-34 Applying the font-weight and font-variant styles

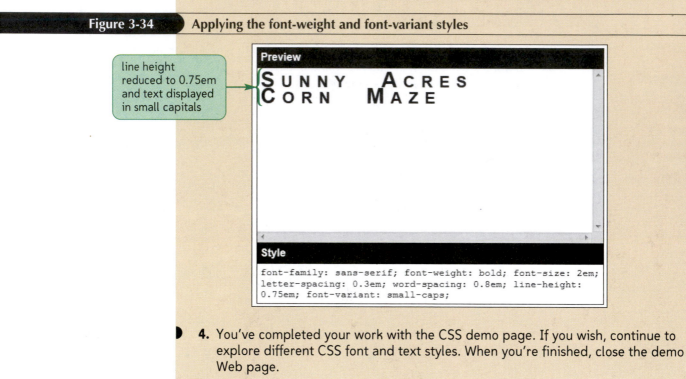

line height reduced to 0.75em and text displayed in small capitals

```
font-family: sans-serif; font-weight: bold; font-size: 2em;
letter-spacing: 0.3em; word-spacing: 0.8em; line-height:
0.75em; font-variant: small-caps;
```

4. You've completed your work with the CSS demo page. If you wish, continue to explore different CSS font and text styles. When you're finished, close the demo Web page.

Aligning Text Horizontally and Vertically

In earlier examples from this tutorial, you saw how the text-align style could be used to align text horizontally. The specific style is

```
text-align: alignment;
```

where *alignment* is left, right, center, or justify (align the text with both the left and the right margins). To vertically align the text, use the style

```
vertical-align: alignment;
```

where *alignment* is one of the keywords described in Figure 3-35.

Figure 3-35   Values of the vertical-align style

Value	Description
baseline	Aligns the element with the bottom of lowercase letters in surrounding text (the default)
bottom	Aligns the bottom of the element with the bottom of the lowest element in surrounding content
middle	Aligns the middle of the element with the middle of the surrounding content
sub	Subscripts the element
super	Superscripts the element
text-bottom	Aligns the bottom of the element with the bottom of the font of the surrounding content
text-top	Aligns the top of the element with the top of the font of the surrounding content
top	Aligns the top of the element with the top of the tallest object in the surrounding content

TIP

The subscript and super-script styles lower or raise text vertically, but do not resize it. To create true subscripts and super-scripts, you also must reduce the font size.

Instead of using keywords, you can specify a length or a percentage for an element to be aligned relative to the surrounding content. A positive value moves the element up and a negative value lowers the element. For example, the style

```
vertical-align: 50%;
```

raises the element by half of the line height of the surrounding content, while the style

```
vertical-align: -100%;
```

drops the element an entire line height below the baseline of the current line.

Combining All Text Formatting in a Single Style

You've seen a lot of different text and font styles. You can combine most of them into a single property using the shortcut `font` property

```
font: font-style font-variant font-weight font-size/line-height
      font-family;
```

where *font-style* is the font's style, *font-variant* is the font variant, *font-weight* is the weight of the font, *font-size* is the size of the font, *line-height* is the height of each line, and *font-family* is the font face. For example, the style

```
font: italic small-caps bold 18px/24px Arial, sans-serif;
```

displays the text of the element in italic, bold, and small capital letters in Arial or another sans-serif font, with a font size of 18 pixels and spacing between the lines of 24 pixels. You do not have to include all of the values in the `font` property; the only required values are *font-size* and *font-family*. A browser assumes the default value for any omitted property. However, you must place any properties that you do include in the order indicated above.

Tammy would like the address in the page footer formatted differently from the default style imposed by the browser's internal style sheet. She suggests that you display the text in a semi-transparent white Times New Roman font on a dark green background and centered on the page. She also suggests that you use the small-cap font variant to add visual interest, and increase the height of the address line to 4em. To make your CSS code more compact, you'll add all of the font values within a single line using the `font` property.

To change the style of the address element:

1. Return to the **sa_styles.css** file in your text editor.

2. At the bottom of the style sheet, add the following style rule for the address element nested within the footer element (see Figure 3-36):

```
/* Footer styles */

footer address {
    background-color: rgb(55, 102, 55);
    color: white;
    color: rgba(255, 255, 255, 0.8);
    font: normal small-caps 0.8em/4em 'Times New Roman', Times, serif;
    text-align: center;
}
```

Figure 3-36 Designing the footer address

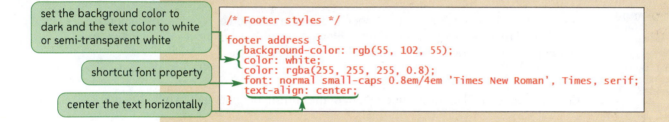

set the background color to dark and the text color to white or semi-transparent white

shortcut font property

center the text horizontally

```
/* Footer styles */

footer address {
    background-color: rgb(55, 102, 55);
    color: white;
    color: rgba(255, 255, 255, 0.8);
    font: normal small-caps 0.8em/4em 'Times New Roman', Times, serif;
    text-align: center;
}
```

3. Save your changes to the file and then reload the **home.htm** file in your Web browser. Scroll to the bottom of the page and verify that the style of the address element has been changed as shown in Figure 3-37.

Figure 3-37 Reformatted address text

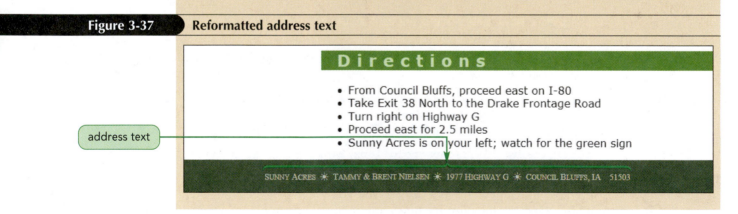

address text

Directions

- From Council Bluffs, proceed east on I-80
- Take Exit 38 North to the Drake Frontage Road
- Turn right on Highway G
- Proceed east for 2.5 miles
- Sunny Acres is on your left; watch for the green sign

SUNNY ACRES ✳ TAMMY & BRENT NIELSEN ✳ 1977 HIGHWAY G ✳ COUNCIL BLUFFS, IA 51503

Tammy likes the way the fonts appear on her Web site. She especially likes the fact that because these changes were made in a CSS style sheet, the styles automatically apply to the other Web pages on the site, as well as any Web page she adds to the site in the future.

Setting up Alternative Style Sheets

Many browsers recognize alternative style sheets. This is particularly useful in situations when you are supporting users who have special needs, such as a need for large text with highly contrasting colors. To support these users, you can make an alternative style sheet with the link element, using the code

```
<link href="url1" rel="alternate stylesheet"
      type="text/css" title="title1" />

<link href="url2" rel="alternate stylesheet"
      type="text/css" title="title2" />
```

where url1, url2, and so forth are the URLs of the style sheet files, and title1, title2, etc. are the titles of the alternate style sheets. For example, the following HTML code creates links to two style sheets, named *Large Text* and *Regular Text*:

```
<link href="large.css" rel="alternate stylesheet"
  type="text/css" title="Large Text" />

<link href="regular.css" rel="alternate stylesheet"
  type="text/css" title="Regular Text" />
```

Browsers that support alternative style sheets provide a menu option or toolbar that enables users to select which style sheet to apply. Among current browsers, Firefox, Opera, and Safari support alternative style sheets.

Working with Web Fonts

Text design on the Web largely has been limited to a few Web safe fonts that are supported by all major browsers. It would be better if a browser would automatically download whatever fonts are required for a Web page in the same way it downloads images. Specifications for downloadable fonts, or **Web fonts**, have been around for several years, but most browsers have begun to support this technology only in recent years. However, different browsers support different font file formats. Figure 3-38 describes these different formats and their current levels of browser support.

Figure 3-38   **Web font formats**

Format	Description	Browser
TrueType/OpenType	The most common font format, freely available on most computers; no support for licensing.	Chrome, Firefox, Opera, Safari
Embedded OpenType	Proprietary format developed by Microsoft for Internet Explorer; supports licensing and security against unauthorized use.	Internet Explorer
Scalable Vector Graphics	An XML vocabulary designed to describe resizable graphics and primarily supported by mobile browsers.	Chrome, Opera, Safari
Web Open Font Format	A new standard for Web fonts that is quickly gaining support; provides support for font licensing.	Firefox, other browsers in development

Web font files are available on several sites on the Web. In many cases, these are not free fonts and you must pay for their use. Other fonts are free but are licensed only for non-commercial use. You always should check the EULA (End User License Agreement) before downloading and using a Web font to make sure you are in compliance with the license. Finally, many Web fonts are available through **Web Font Service Bureaus**, which supply Web fonts on their servers that page designers can link to for a fee.

The great advantage of a Web font is that it gives a designer control over the typeface used in a document. The disadvantage is that it becomes another file for the browser to download and install, adding to the time required to render the page.

The @font-face Rule

To access and load a Web font, you add the rule

```
@font-face {
   font-family: name;
   src: url(url) format(text);
   descriptor:value;
   descriptor:value;
   ...
}
```

to the style sheet, where *name* is the name assigned to the Web font, *url* is the location of the font definition file, *text* is an optional text description of the font format, and the *descriptor:value* pairs are optional style properties that describe how and when the font should be used. For example, the following @font-face rule defines a font face named *GentiumBold*:

```
@font-face {
   font-family: GentiumBold;
   src: url(GentiumB.ttf) format('truetype');
   font-weight: bold;
}
```

The GentiumBold font in this code is a TrueType font based on a description stored in the *GentiumB.ttf* file. The font-weight properties tell browsers to apply this font only for bold text. Note that at the time of this writing, you should avoid including the font-weight and font-style properties in the @font-face rule because those features are not well supported by most browsers and can produce unexpected results.

Once you've defined a font using the @font-face rule, you can use the font elsewhere in your style sheets by including the font name in your font lists. For example, the style

```
font-family: GentiumBold, 'Arial Black', Gadget, sans-serif;
```

attempts to load the GentiumBold font defined above, followed by Arial Black, Gadget, and then a sans-serif font of the browser's choosing.

Installing a Cross-Browser Web Font

To support all of the font formats described in Figure 3-38, you can add additional source files to the `@font-face` rule. A browser then will go through the list, loading the last font file format from the list that it supports. Part of the challenge is that at the time of this writing, Internet Explorer does not support all of the features of the `@font-face` rule and returns an error if it attempts to load another font file. Thus, to define a font that works across different browsers, you should design the `@font-face` rule as follows

```
@font-face {
    font-family: name;
    src: url(eot);
    src: local('☺'),
        url(woff) format(text),
        url(ttf) format(text),
        url(svg) format(text);
    descriptor:value;
    …
}
```

where *eot* is the font defined in an Embedded OpenType file (the only format supported by Internet Explorer at the time of this writing), *woff* is the font defined in a Web Open Font file, *ttf* is the font defined in a TrueType or an OpenType file, and *svg* is the font defined in a Scalable Vector Graphics file. The `local('☺')` part of this code is a programming hack developed by Paul Irish (*www.paulirish.com*) to prevent Internet Explorer from attempting to load the other font files, causing an error. Note that to enter this symbol, your text must be stored using Unicode encoding rather than ASCII or ANSI. The sa_styles.css file already has been created for you using that text encoding.

Tammy is not completely pleased with the Verdana font you've used for the home page and would like a typeface with thinner lines. She has located a Web font named *NobileRegular* that she is free to use under the End User License Agreement and thinks would work better. In acquiring this font, she also obtained the following `@font-face` rule that can be used to load the font into a CSS style sheet:

```
@font-face {
    font-family: 'NobileRegular';
    src: url('nobile-webfont.eot');
    src: local('☺'),
        url('nobile-webfont.woff') format('woff'),
        url('nobile-webfont.ttf') format('truetype'),
        url('nobile-webfont.svg#webfontsKo9tqe9') format('svg');
}
```

Rather than retype this code, you'll copy it from her text file and paste it into your style sheet. Add this font definition now.

To insert and apply the NobileRegular font:

1. Using your text editor, open the **nobile.txt** text file located in the tutorial.03/tutorial folder.

2. Copy the `@font-face` rule located at the top of the file.

3. Return to the **sa_styles.css** file in your text editor.

4. Paste the copied text of the `@font-face` rule into your style sheet directly above the style rule for the `body` element.

   Next, you'll revise the style rule for the `body` element so that it uses the NobileRegular font as the first option, if available and supported by the browser. You'll also set the line height of body text to 1.4 em and the line height of the page headings to 1.8 em to accommodate the metrics of this new font.

5. Within the `font-family` property for the `body` element, insert **NobileRegular** followed by a comma and a space, at the beginning of the font list.

6. Add the property `line-height: 1.4em;` to the style rule for the `body` element and `line-height: 1.8em;` to the style rules for the `h1` and `h2` elements.

   Figure 3-39 highlights the newly inserted text in the style sheet.

Figure 3-39 Inserting a Web font

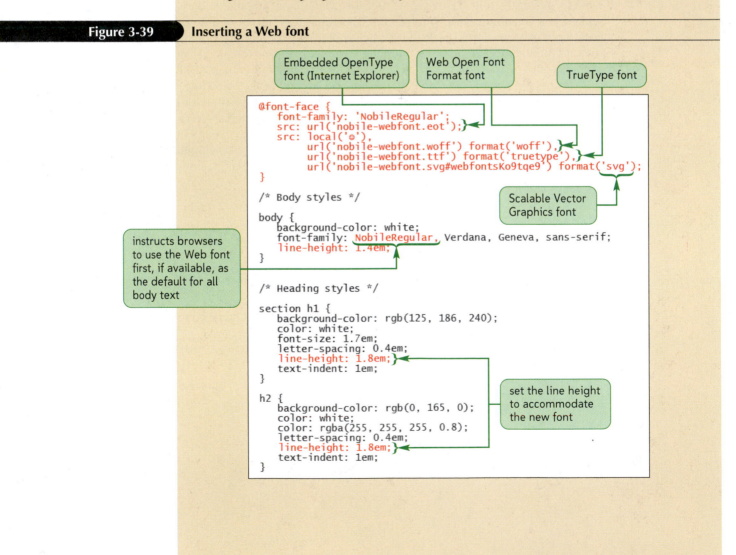

7. Save your changes to the file and then reload **home.htm** in your Web browser. As shown in Figure 3-40, the body text of the Web page has changed, using the NobileRegular font in place of the previous font.

Figure 3-40   **Text rendered in the NobileRegular font**

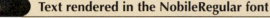

- Home
- Autumn Fun
- Scary Good
- Meet the Animals
- For your Tastebuds

Welcome

There's always something happening at Sunny Acres. With the coming of fall, we're gearing up for our big AutumnFest and Farm Show. If you haven't visited our famous Corn Maze, be sure to do so before it gets torn down on November 5. This year's maze is bigger and better than ever.

Understanding the CSS @rules

The @font-face rule is one example of a **CSS @rule**, which specifies a command or directive that controls how browsers interpret and run the contents of a CSS style sheet. Figure 3-41 lists the @rules and describes how they are used.

Figure 3-41   **CSS @rules**

@rule	Description
@charset "encoding";	Defines the character encoding used in an external style sheet where encoding is the name of the character set
@import url(url) media	Imports an external style sheet file located at url. The optional media attribute provides a comma-separated list of media devices to be used with the style sheet

@media media {
    styles
}
	Targets the style rules in styles to devices that match the media types specified in media

@page location {
    margins
}
	Defines the page margins for printed output where location is either left, right, or first for left page, right page, or first page, and margins set the margin widths

@font-face {
    font_description
}
	Defines the properties of a custom Web font where font_description indicates the source and features of the font

@namespace prefix uri	Defines an XML namespace where prefix is the namespace prefix and uri is the location of the namespace

In general, all of the CSS @rules should be placed at the top of the style sheet before the style properties that may use them.

Problem Solving: Finding and Fixing Style Sheet Errors

As a style sheet increases in size and complexity, you will likely encounter a major head-ache: a Web page whose appearance in a browser does not match the style you planned for it. Once you recognize that a syntax error in your style sheet likely caused the browser to ignore some of your style rules, you need to figure out where the error is. The following are some errors that can cause your style sheets to fail:

- *Missing semicolons*—All style properties need to be separated by a semicolon. If you omit a semicolon, all subsequent properties within the affected style rule will be ignored.
- *Missing curly braces*—Every style rule must be enclosed within a set of curly braces. Failure to close off the style rule will cause that style rule and all subsequent rules to be ignored.
- *Missing closing quotes*—If you use quotes within typeface names or other text strings, you need to enclose the entire text within either double or single quotation marks. Omitting a closing quotation mark will cause the rest of the style sheet to fail.
- *Typos*—All selector names, style properties, and style values need to be typed correctly.
- *Improper application of a style*—Some styles are associated with all elements, but some are not. For instance, you can't change the color of an inline image using the back-ground-color style, no matter how much you might want to.
- *Conflicting properties*—Remember the general principle that *the more specific style outweighs the less specific*. A style rule in one part of a style sheet might be superseded by a rule somewhere else in the file.
- *Inherited properties*—Properties are also inherited down the document tree. A style property applied to a `section` element affects all nested elements unless you override it with another rule.

If a problem persists after finding and fixing these common errors, try other techniques to locate the source of the trouble, such as removing style rules one by one until you locate the source of the trouble. Also consider using the `!important` keyword to temporar-ily force the browser to apply a rule regardless of specificity. Finally, many browsers now include debugging tools to assist you in writing your CSS code. Use these tools whenever you encounter an error that you can't easily find and fix.

You've completed your work on creating and editing the text styles used in the Sunny Acres home page. In the next session, you'll explore how to design styles for hypertext links and lists, and you'll learn how to use CSS to add special visual effects to your Web pages.

REVIEW

Session 3.2 Quick Check

1. Provide a style rule to display the text of all `address` elements nested within a `footer` element in red.

2. The initial `h1` heading in a document has the id *top*. Provide a style rule to display the text of this `h1` heading in Arial, Helvetica, or a sans-serif font.

3. Provide a style rule to display all `blockquote` elements belonging to the *reviews* class in italic and indented 3em.

4. Provide a style rule to center all `h1` through `h6` headings, and to display the text with normal weight.

5. What is the difference between an absolute unit and a relative unit?

6. Provide a style rule to double space the text of all paragraphs in the document.

7. Provide a style rule to remove underlining from the hypertext links for all elements marked with the <a> tag and nested within a navigation list.

8. If you want to use Web fonts with Internet Explorer, what font file format should you use?

9. Provide the `@font-face` rule to create a Web font named *Cantarell* based on the font file *cantarell.ttf*. Which browsers will be able to work with this font file?

SESSION 3.3 VISUAL OVERVIEW

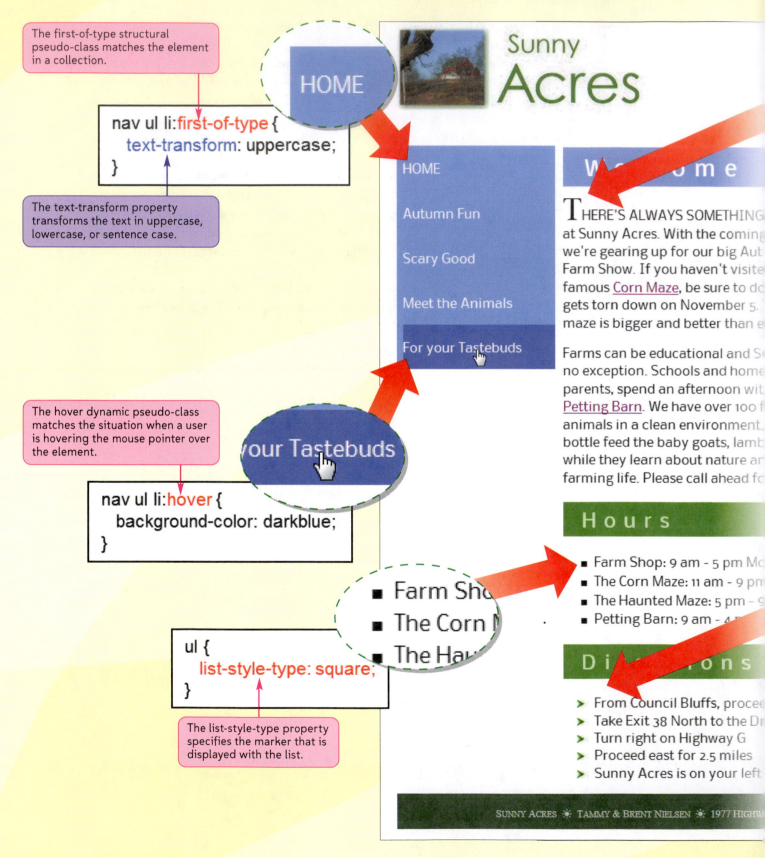

The first-of-type structural pseudo-class matches the element in a collection.

```
nav ul li:first-of-type {
    text-transform: uppercase;
}
```

The text-transform property transforms the text in uppercase, lowercase, or sentence case.

The hover dynamic pseudo-class matches the situation when a user is hovering the mouse pointer over the element.

```
nav ul li:hover {
    background-color: darkblue;
}
```

```
ul {
    list-style-type: square;
}
```

The list-style-type property specifies the marker that is displayed with the list.

LISTS AND PSEUDO-ITEMS

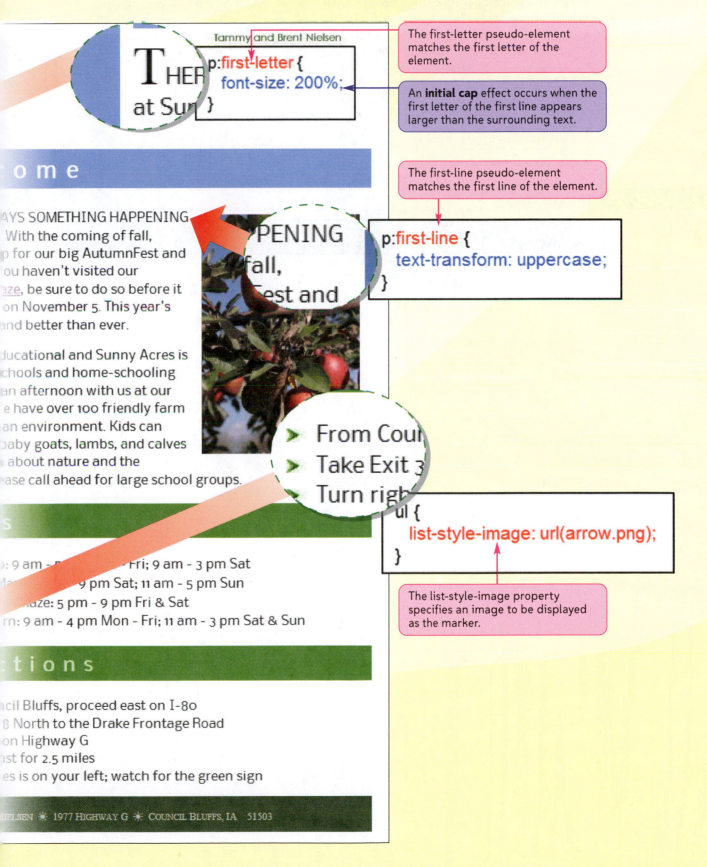

The first-letter pseudo-element matches the first letter of the element.

```
p:first-letter {
    font-size: 200%;
}
```

An **initial cap** effect occurs when the first letter of the first line appears larger than the surrounding text.

The first-line pseudo-element matches the first line of the element.

```
p:first-line {
    text-transform: uppercase;
}
```

```
ul {
    list-style-image: url(arrow.png);
}
```

The list-style-image property specifies an image to be displayed as the marker.

Designing Styles for Lists

Tammy has placed her navigation links in an unordered list set on the left page margin. As with all unordered lists, browsers display the list contents with bullet markers. Tammy would like the bullets removed. To alter the appearance of this navigation list, you change the default style applied by browsers.

Choosing a List Style Type

To change the marker displayed in ordered or unordered lists, you apply the style

```
list-style-type: type;
```

where `type` is one of the markers discussed in Figure 3-42.

Figure 3-42   **List style types**

list-style-type	Marker (s)
disc	●
circle	○
square	■
decimal	1, 2, 3, 4, …
decimal-leading-zero	01, 02, 03, 04, …
lower-roman	i, ii, iii, iv, …
upper-roman	I, II, III, IV, …
lower-alpha	a, b, c, d, …
upper-alpha	A, B, C, D, …
lower-greek	α, β, γ, δ, …
upper-greek	Α, Β, Γ, Δ, …
none	no marker displayed

For example, to display an ordered list with alphabetical markers such as

```
A. Home
B. Getting Started
C. Scrapbooking Tips
D. Supply List
```

you would apply the following list style to the `ol` element:

```
ol {list-style-type: upper-alpha;}
```

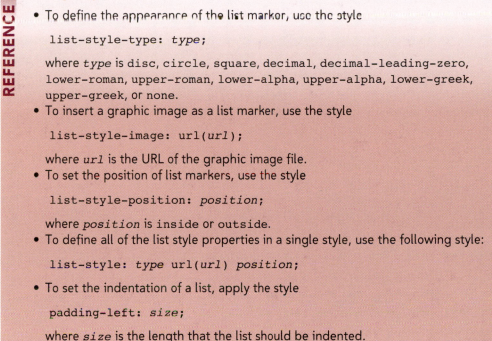

REFERENCE

Designing a List

- To define the appearance of the list marker, use the style

  ```
  list-style-type: type;
  ```

  where *type* is disc, circle, square, decimal, decimal-leading-zero, lower-roman, upper-roman, lower-alpha, upper-alpha, lower-greek, upper-greek, or none.
- To insert a graphic image as a list marker, use the style

  ```
  list-style-image: url(url);
  ```

  where *url* is the URL of the graphic image file.
- To set the position of list markers, use the style

  ```
  list-style-position: position;
  ```

  where *position* is inside or outside.
- To define all of the list style properties in a single style, use the following style:

  ```
  list-style: type url(url) position;
  ```

- To set the indentation of a list, apply the style

  ```
  padding-left: size;
  ```

  where *size* is the length that the list should be indented.

List style types can be used with contextual selectors to create an outline style based on nested lists. Figure 3-43 shows an example in which several levels of list style markers are used in formatting an outline. Note that each marker style is determined by the location of the ordered list within the outline hierarchy. The top level is displayed with uppercase Roman numerals; the bottom level, which is nested within three other ordered lists, uses lowercase letters for markers.

Figure 3-43   Creating an outline style

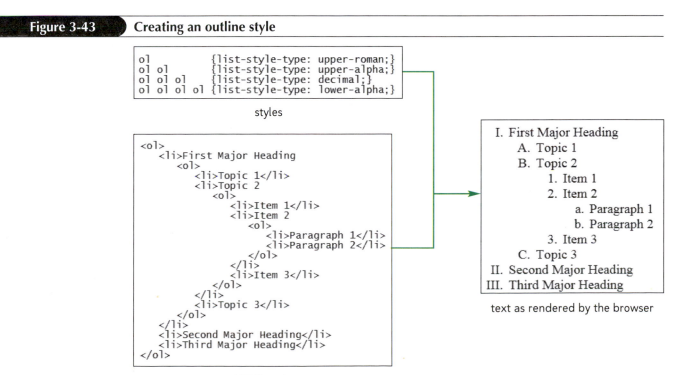

```
ol              {list-style-type: upper-roman;}
ol ol           {list-style-type: upper-alpha;}
ol ol ol        {list-style-type: decimal;}
ol ol ol ol     {list-style-type: lower-alpha;}
```

styles

```
<ol>
    <li>First Major Heading
        <ol>
            <li>Topic 1</li>
            <li>Topic 2
                <ol>
                    <li>Item 1</li>
                    <li>Item 2
                        <ol>
                            <li>Paragraph 1</li>
                            <li>Paragraph 2</li>
                        </ol>
                    </li>
                    <li>Item 3</li>
                </ol>
            </li>
            <li>Topic 3</li>
        </ol>
    </li>
    <li>Second Major Heading</li>
    <li>Third Major Heading</li>
</ol>
```

HTML code

> I. First Major Heading
>   A. Topic 1
>   B. Topic 2
>   1. Item 1
>   2. Item 2
>   a. Paragraph 1
>   b. Paragraph 2
>   3. Item 3
>   C. Topic 3
> II. Second Major Heading
> III. Third Major Heading

text as rendered by the browser

Because Tammy wants to remove the markers from the navigation list, you'll set the `list-style-type` value of that list to `none`. Because you don't want to remove the bullet markers from all lists on the Web site, you'll use a contextual selector that targets only unordered lists nested within a `nav` element.

To remove the bullets from the navigation links:

1. Return to the **sa_styles.css** file in your text editor.

2. Directly below the style rule for the `h2` element, insert the following (see Figure 3-44):

   ```
   /* Navigation list styles */

   nav ul {
       list-style-type: none;
   }
   ```

Figure 3-44   Removing bullet markers from navigation list items

```
        letter-spacing: 0.4em;
        line-height: 1.8em;
        text-indent: 1em;
    }

    /* Navigation list styles */
    nav ul {
        list-style-type: none;
    }
```

3. Save your changes to the file and then reload the **home.htm** file in your Web browser. Verify that the bullet markers have been removed from the items in the navigation list.

Using Images for List Markers

You can supply your own graphic image for the list marker using the style

```
list-style-image: url(url);
```

where `url` is the URL of a graphic file containing the marker image. This is only done for unordered lists, in which the marker is the same for every list item. For example, the style rule

```
ul {list-style-image: url(redball.gif);}
```

displays items from unordered lists marked with the graphic image in the *redball.gif* file. Tammy suggests that you display the list of hours and driving directions using a green arrow graphic she created. Both of these unordered lists are immediately preceded by an `h2` element and nested within a `section` element, so the style rule to change the list marker is:

```
section h2+ul {
    list-style-image: url(arrow.png);
}
```

You'll add this style rule to your style sheet.

To use an image for a list bullet:

1. Return to the **sa_styles.css** file in your text editor.

2. Directly below the style rule for the closing paragraph, insert the following as shown in Figure 3-45:

```
section h2+ul {
    list-style-image: url(arrow.png);
}
```

Figure 3-45   Displaying an image in place of a marker

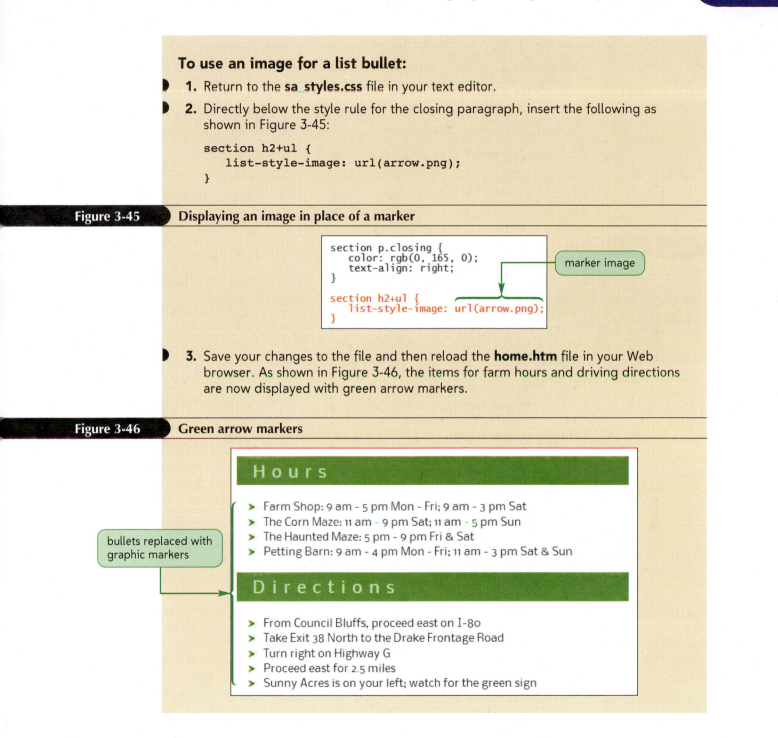

3. Save your changes to the file and then reload the **home.htm** file in your Web browser. As shown in Figure 3-46, the items for farm hours and driving directions are now displayed with green arrow markers.

Figure 3-46   Green arrow markers

Changing the List Layout

Tammy likes the revised markers, but she thinks there's too much empty space to the left of the entries in the navigation list. She would like you to modify the layout to remove the extra space. Each list item is treated as a group-level element and placed within its own box. By default, most browsers place the list marker to the left of this box, lining up each marker with its list item. You can change this default behavior using the property

```
list-style-position: position;
```

where *position* is either outside (the default) or inside. Placing the marker inside of the block causes the list text to flow around the marker. Figure 3-47 shows how the list-style-position property affects the appearance of a bulleted list.

Figure 3-47   **Marker positions**

• Farm Shop: 9 am - 5 pm Mon - Fri; 9 am - 3 pm Sat	• Farm Shop: 9 am - 5 pm Mon - Fri; 9 am - 3 pm Sat
• The Corn Maze: 11 am - 9 pm Sat; 11 am - 5 pm Sun	• The Corn Maze: 11 am - 9 pm Sat; 11 am - 5 pm Sun
• The Haunted Maze: 5 pm - 9 pm Fri & Sat	• The Haunted Maze: 5 pm - 9 pm Fri & Sat
• Petting Barn: 9 am - 4 pm Mon - Fri; 11 am - 3 pm Sat & Sun	• Petting Barn: 9 am - 4 pm Mon - Fri; 11 am - 3 pm Sat & Sun

list-style-position: outside;   list-style-position: inside;

All three of the list styles can be combined within the property

```
list-style: type image position;
```

where *type* is the marker type, *image* is an image to be displayed in place of the marker, and *position* is the location of the marker. For example, the style rule

```
ul {list-style: circle url(bullet.jpg) inside;}
```

displays all ordered lists with the marker found in the *bullet.jpg* image placed inside the containing block. If a browser is unable to display the bullet image, it uses a circle marker instead. You do not need to include all three style properties with the list style. Browsers will set any property you omit to the default value.

By default, browsers offset ordered and unordered lists from the surrounding text. Tammy has noticed this and worries that the entries in the navigation list are crowding the text in the Welcome paragraph by being shifted too far to the right. She would like you to move the navigation list to the left, aligning it more toward the left edge of the Sunny Acres logo. To reduce the space that the browser inserts, you use the style property

```
padding-left: size;
```

where *size* is the length that the list should be shifted to the right. The padding-left style is one of the styles you'll study in more detail in the next tutorial on page layout. For now, you'll limit your use of this style to reduce the extra space inserted by the browser in the navigation list. After some experimenting, you settle on the following value for the style:

```
padding-left: 0.5em;
```

You'll add this style to the style rule for the navigation list.

TIP

Any page element can be turned into a list item by applying the display: list-item style.

To move the navigation list to the left:

1. Return to the **sa_styles.css** file in your text editor.

2. Within the style rule for the navigation list, insert the following style value, as shown in Figure 3-48:

```
padding-left: 0.5em;
```

Figure 3-48   **Setting the padding space within a list**

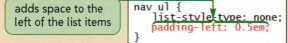

3. Save your changes to the file and then reload the **home.htm** file in your Web browser. Verify that the entries in the navigation list have been shifted to the left, aligned roughly with the left edge of the Sunny Acres logo.

To complete the design style for the navigation list, Tammy wants to change the background color of the list to sky blue, and to increase the space between the items by increasing the line height to 3.5em. Also, while browsers underline hypertext by default, the current Web design standard is to not underline the links in a navigation list; thus, Tammy also wants to change the text color of the navigation links to white and remove the underlining. You'll add these styles to the style sheet now.

To reformat the navigation list:

1. Return to the **sa_styles.css** file in your text editor.

2. Add the following style properties to the `nav ul` style rule

```
background-color: rgb(125, 186, 240);
line-height: 3.5em;
```

3. Directly below the `nav ul` style rule, add the following rule for navigation hypertext links (see Figure 3-49):

```
nav ul li a {
    color: white;
    text-decoration: none;
}
```

Figure 3-49   **Formatting the navigation list**

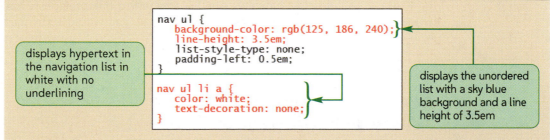

4. Save your changes to the file and then reload the **home.htm** file in your Web browser. Figure 3-50 shows the revised appearance of the navigation sidebar.

Figure 3-50   **Revised navigation list**

reformatted
navigation list

Using Pseudo-Classes and Pseudo-Elements

Without underlines, there is no visual clue that the links in the navigation list act as hypertext. Tammy has seen Web sites in which links are underlined or highlighted only when the mouse pointer hovers over the linked text. This type of effect is called a rollover effect because it is applied only when a user "rolls" the mouse pointer over an element. Tammy would like you to add a rollover effect to the navigation list.

Pseudo-Classes

Rollover effects can be created using pseudo-classes. A pseudo-class is a classification of an element based on its current status, position, or use in the document. Styles for pseudo-classes are created using the syntax

```
selector:pseudo-class {styles;}
```

where *selector* is an element or a group of elements within a document, *pseudo-class* is the name of a pseudo-class, and *styles* are the style properties applied to that selector pseudo-class. Pseudo-classes are organized into dynamic and structural classes. A dynamic pseudo-class changes with a user's actions. For example, the *visited* pseudo-class indicates whether a hypertext link previously has been visited by the user. To display the text of all such links in red, you would apply the following style rule to the a element:

```
a:visited {color: red;}
```

To change the text color to blue when users hover the mouse pointer over the link, you would add the following style rule:

```
a:hover {color: blue;}
```

Figure 3-51 lists the other dynamic pseudo-classes supported by CSS.

| Figure 3-51 | Dynamic pseudo-classes |

Pseudo-Class	Description	Example
link	The link has not yet been visited by the user.	`a:link {color: red;}`
visited	The link has been visited by the user.	`a:visited {color: green;}`
active	The element is in the process of being activiated or clicked by the user.	`a:active {color: yellow;}`
hover	The mouse pointer is hovering over the element.	`a:hover {color: blue;}`
focus	The element has received the focus of the keyboard or mouse pointer.	`input:focus {background-color: yellow;}`

In some cases, two or more pseudo-classes can apply to the same element. For example, a hypertext link can be both previously visited and hovered over. In such situations, the standard cascading rules apply—the pseudo-class that is listed last is applied to the element. You should enter the hypertext pseudo-classes in the following order in your style sheets—link, visited, hover, and active. The link pseudo-class comes first because it represents a hypertext link that has not yet been visited or even clicked by the user. The visited pseudo-class comes next, for links that previously have been visited or clicked. The hover pseudo-class follows, for the situation in which a user has once again moved the mouse pointer over a hypertext link before clicking the link. The active pseudo-class is last, representing the exact instant in which a link is clicked by a user. Any styles set with the link pseudo-class are inherited by the visited, hover, and active pseudo-classes.

REFERENCE

Creating a Hypertext Rollover

- To create a rollover for a hypertext link, apply the styles

```
a:link     {styles;}
a:visited  {styles;}
a:hover    {styles;}
a:active   {styles;}
```

to the a element, where *styles* are the CSS styles applied to hypertext links that have not been visited (link), have already been visited (visited), have the mouse pointer over them (hover), or are actively being clicked (active).

The hover, active, and focus dynamic pseudo-classes also can be applied to non-hypertext elements. For example, the following style rule causes the background color of each entry in a navigation list to change to medium blue whenever a user hovers the mouse pointer over it:

```
nav ul li:hover {
    background-color: rgb(83, 142, 213);
}
```

Tammy suggests that you add this style rule to provide users with the visual feedback that is missing from the navigation links as a result of removing the underlining.

To apply the `hover` **pseudo-class:**

1. Return to the **sa_styles.css** file in your text editor.

2. Add the following style rule, as shown in Figure 3-52:

```
nav ul li:hover {
    background-color: rgb(83, 142, 213);
}
```

Figure 3-52   Applying the hover pseudo-class

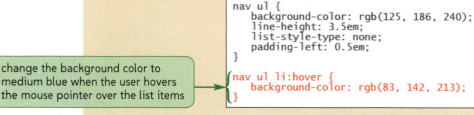

change the background color to medium blue when the user hovers the mouse pointer over the list items

```
nav ul {
    background-color: rgb(125, 186, 240);
    line-height: 3.5em;
    list-style-type: none;
    padding-left: 0.5em;
}
nav ul li:hover {
    background-color: rgb(83, 142, 213);
}
```

3. Save your changes to the file and then reload **home.htm** in your Web browser. Move your mouse pointer over the navigation list items. As shown in Figure 3-53, the background color of the navigation list items changes to medium blue in response to the hover event.

Figure 3-53   Viewing the rollover effect

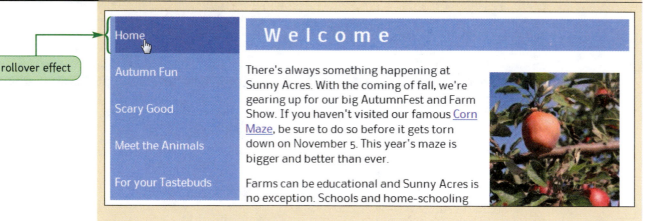

rollover effect

Home

Autumn Fun

Scary Good

Meet the Animals

For your Tastebuds

Welcome

There's always something happening at Sunny Acres. With the coming of fall, we're gearing up for our big AutumnFest and Farm Show. If you haven't visited our famous Corn Maze, be sure to do so before it gets torn down on November 5. This year's maze is bigger and better than ever.

Farms can be educational and Sunny Acres is no exception. Schools and home-schooling

---

INSIGHT

Deprecated Attributes for Hypertext Links

Earlier versions of HTML did not support CSS and the `link`, `visited`, `hover`, and `active` pseudo-classes. If a Web page author wanted to change the color of a hypertext link, he or she would have to add the attributes

```
<body link="color" vlink="color" alink="color">
```

to the `<body>` tag, where the `link` attribute specifies the color of unvisited links, the `vlink` attribute specifies the color of visited links, and the `alink` attribute specifies the color of active links. Colors had to be entered either as a supported color name or as a hexadecimal color value. The `link`, `vlink`, and `alink` attributes have been deprecated and their use is discouraged, but you still might see them in the code of older Web pages.

Structural pseudo-classes are used to classify items based on their locations within the hierarchy of page elements. For example, the style rule

```
body:first-child {background-color: yellow;}
```

changes the background color to yellow in the first child of the `body` element within the document. Notice that the selector does not specify the element. It could be an `h1` heading, a `section` element, or anything else, as long as it is the first child of the `body` element. Figure 3-54 describes the structural pseudo-classes.

| Figure 3-54 | Structural pseudo-classes |

Pseudo-Class	Matches
root	The top element in the document hierarchy (the `html` element)
empty	An element with no children
only-child	An element with no siblings
first-child	The first child of the parent element
last-child	The last child of the parent element
first-of-type	The first element of the parent that matches the specified type
last-of-type	The last element of the parent that matches the specified type
nth-of-type(n)	The nth element of the parent of the specified type
nth-last-of-type(n)	The nth from the last element of the parent of the specified type
only-of-type	An element that has no siblings of the same type
lang(code)	The element that has the specified language indicated by *code*
not(s)	An element not matching the specified selector, *s*

The first entry in a navigation list is often the most prominent or important. On the Sunny Acres Web site, the first entry is linked to the site's home page. Tammy would like this link to always be displayed in capital letters. Although you could edit the HTML code to make this happen, you decide to make this change to the style sheet using the following style rule because you want to separate content from design:

```
nav ul li:first-of-type {
    text-transform: uppercase;
}
```

The style rule uses the `first-of-type` pseudo-class to apply the uppercase transformation to the first `li` element found nested within the navigation list. You'll add this rule now to your style sheet.

TIP

For browsers that don't support the `first-of-type` pseudo-class, you can use the `id` attribute to mark the first list item and write the style based on that id.

To transform the text of the first navigation list element:

1. Return to the **sa_styles.css** file in your text editor.

2. Add the following style rule as shown in Figure 3-55:

```
nav ul li:first-of-type {
    text-transform: uppercase;
}
```

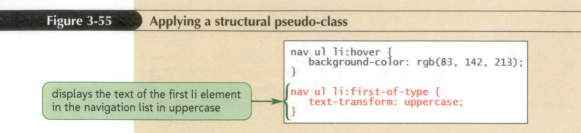

Figure 3-55   Applying a structural pseudo-class

```
nav ul li:hover {
    background-color: rgb(83, 142, 213);
}

nav ul li:first-of-type {
    text-transform: uppercase;
}
```

displays the text of the first li element in the navigation list in uppercase

3. Save your changes to the file and then reload **home.htm** in your Web browser. Verify that the first entry in the navigation list, Home, is displayed in uppercase letters.

   Trouble? If you are running a version of Internet Explorer earlier than 9, the first list item will not be displayed in uppercase letters.

Pseudo-Elements

Tammy has a few more changes she wants you to make to the Sunny Acres home page. In the first paragraph of the home page, she would like the following styling:

- The first line displayed in all uppercase letters
- The first letter increased in size and displayed as an initial cap

So far, all of your selectors have been based on elements that exist somewhere within the document hierarchy and are tagged in the HTML file. You also can define selectors based on pseudo-elements, which are not elements that exist in the document hierarchy but rather are based on objects that exist in the rendered Web page. For example, a paragraph is an element in the document hierarchy, but the first line of the paragraph is not. It only exists as an object once the paragraph has been rendered by the browser. Similarly, the first letter of that paragraph is also not a document element, but it certainly can be identified as an object in the Web page. Both the first line and the first letter are pseudo-elements, and you can create a style rule to format their appearance. A selector based on a pseudo-element is similar to one that is based on a pseudo-class, such as

```
selector:pseudo-element {styles;}
```

where *pseudo-element* is an abstract element from the rendered Web page. Figure 3-56 lists some of the pseudo-elements supported by CSS.

Figure 3-56   Pseudo-elements

Pseudo-Element	Description	Example
first-letter	The first letter of the element text	p:first-letter {font-size:200%}
first-line	The first line of the element text	p:first-line {text-transform: uppercase}
before	Content inserted directly before the element	p:before {content:"Special! "}
after	Content inserted directly after the element	p:after {content:"eof"}

In order to differentiate between pseudo-elements and pseudo-classes, CSS3 changes the syntax of pseudo-elements by adding an extra colon to the selector:

```
selector::pseudo-element {styles;}
```

To maintain backward compatibility with older browsers, however, you still should use the single colon syntax.

The style rules to format the first line and first letter of the opening paragraph are:

```
section > p:first-of-type:first-letter {
    font-size: 250%;
    font-family: 'Times New Roman', Times, serif;
}
section > p:first-of-type:first-line {
    text-transform: uppercase;
}
```

TIP

Only one pseudo-element may be used per selector.

Notice that the selector uses the `first-of-type` pseudo-class combined with the `first-letter` and `first-line` pseudo-elements so that the styles are applied only to the first paragraph of the `section` element and then to the first letter and first lines within that paragraph. After you apply the rule, the first letter will appear 250% larger than the surrounding text, and in a Times New Roman or other serif font. In addition, all of the text on the first line will appear in uppercase.

REFERENCE

Working with Pseudo-Elements

- To apply a style to the first line of an element, use the pseudo-element selector

  `selector:first-line`

  where `selector` is the name of the element or elements in the document.
- To apply a style to the first letter of an element, use the following pseudo-element selector:

  `selector:first-letter`

- To insert a text string before an element, use the style rule

  `selector:before {content: text;}`

  where `text` is the content of the text string.
- To insert a text string after an element, use the following style rule:

  `selector:after {content: text;}`

Since Tammy wants to apply this style rule only to the home page and not to every page on her Web site, you'll add the rule to an embedded style sheet placed within the *home.htm* file.

To create the initial cap and first line styles:

1. Go to the **home.htm** file in your text editor.

2. Directly above the closing `</head>` tag, insert the following code, as shown in Figure 3-57:

```
<style type="text/css">
    section > p:first-of-type:first-line {
        text-transform: uppercase;
    }

    section > p:first-of-type:first-letter {
        font-size: 250%;
        font-family: 'Times New Roman', Times, serif;
    }

</style>
```

Figure 3-57 Styling pseudo-elements

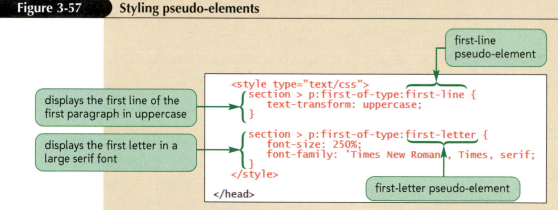

3. Save your changes to the file and then reload **home.htm** in your Web browser. As shown in Figure 3-58, the first line of the opening paragraph is displayed in uppercase letters, and the first letter of that line is larger than the surrounding text.

Figure 3-58 First letter and first line styles

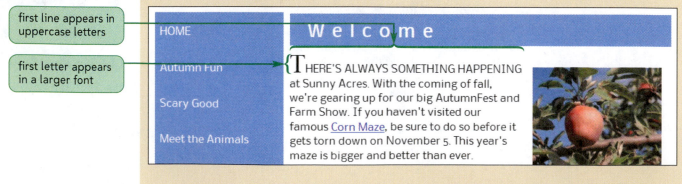

Trouble? At the time of this writing, neither Safari nor Chrome is able to apply the `text-transform` style property with the `first-line` pseudo-element.

Generating Content with CSS

You can generate page content using the following `before` and `after` pseudo-elements along with the `content` property

```
selector:before {content: text;}
selector:after {content: text;}
```

where *text* is the text you want to add to the element. For example, the style rule

```
em:after {content: " !";}
```

appends a space and an exclamation point to the end of every em element. You also can use the `before` and `after` pseudo-elements in conjunction with pseudo-classes. The style rules

```
a:hover:before {content: "<";}
a:hover:after {content: ">";}
```

create a rollover effect in which the < and > characters are placed around a hypertext link when a mouse pointer hovers over the link.

Another way to insert content using CSS is to retrieve information from an element attribute using the `attr` property, which has the syntax

```
content: attr(attribute)
```

where *attribute* is an attribute of the element. For example, the following style appends every hypertext link with the text of the link's URL as stored in the `href` attribute:

```
a:after {
    content: attr(" [" attr(href) "] ");
}
```

When applied to the hypertext link

```
<a href="home.htm">Sunny Acres</a>
```

this style will be rendered by the browser as follows:

Sunny Acres [home.htm]

Finally, you can insert an image by specifying the URL of the image file for the value of the `content` property, as the following code demonstrates:

```
a[href^="http"]:after {
    content: url(uparrow.png);
}
```

In this example, the *uparrow.png* file is appended to any hypertext link that contains the text string *http* within its `href` attribute. This technique is sometimes used to visually identify hypertext links that point to external Web sites.

By generating content through your CSS style sheets, you can create interesting dynamic effects for your Web site that are easy to develop and maintain. Note, however, that the `content` pseudo-class is not supported in older browsers, and so you should not rely on it to create text critical to the understanding of your Web site.

Tammy is pleased with your work on the style sheet for the Sunny Acres home page. Your only remaining task is to apply your style sheet to the other pages to confirm that your design choices work properly for every page. Tammy also would like a different background color for the `h1` headings on each page. You'll set the background colors using embedded style sheets in the other pages on the Web site.

To apply the style sheet to the other pages on the site:

1. Go to the **maze.htm** file in your text editor.

2. Directly above the closing `</head>` tag, insert the following `link` elements and embedded style sheet (see Figure 3-59):

```
<link href="sa_layout.css" rel="stylesheet" type="text/css" />
<link href="sa_styles.css" rel="stylesheet" type="text/css" />
<style type="text/css">
   section h1 {
      background-color: rgb(191, 141, 101);
   }
</style>
```

Figure 3-59   Style sheets for the maze.htm file

```
<link href="sa_layout.css" rel="stylesheet" type="text/css" />
<link href="sa_styles.css" rel="stylesheet" type="text/css" />
<style type="text/css">
   section h1 {
      background-color: rgb(191, 141, 101);
   }
</style>
</head>
```

3. Save your changes to the file.

4. Repeat Steps 2 and 3 for the **haunted.htm**, **petting.htm**, and **produce.htm** files. Set the `h1` background colors for these three files to **rgb(0, 0, 0)**, **rgb(133, 109, 85)**, and **rgb(50, 69, 99)**, respectively.

5. Reopen the **home.htm** file in your Web browser and navigate through Tammy's Web site. Verify that the layout and color scheme have been applied to every sample page that Tammy has developed. Figure 3-60 shows the completed Web page for the Farm Shop.

6. Submit your completed files to your instructor, in either printed or electronic form, as requested.

Figure 3-60   **Farm Shop Web page**

 Sunny
Acres

Tammy and Brent Nielsen
1973 Hwy G
Council Bluffs, IA 51503

HOME

Autumn Fun

Scary Good

Meet the Animals

For your Tastebuds

The Farm Shop

The Sunny Acres Farm Shop aims to offer the highest quality fresh produce. You can pick your own or buy it in our shop. Set amidst acres of outstanding natural beauty on the beautiful rolling hills northeast of Council Bluffs, the Farm Shop is easily reached on Highway G, with easy access from Interstate 80.

The Farm Shop was established over 25 years ago with great success. Our products have won numerous awards at local festivals and fairs. We also cater to local supermarkets in the Council Bluffs/Omaha area. Look for our products every Saturday morning from May to October at the Council Bluffs Farmers' Market.

Hours

- Monday - Friday: 9 am - 5 pm
- Saturday: 9 am - 3 pm
- Pick Your Own Produce is available from May 15 - October 22
- The Farm Shop is open year-round

Products

- Freshly baked breads and quiches
- High quality meats
- Cheese and other dairy products
- Freshly-picked fruits and vegetables (in season)
- Canned goods and preserves

SUNNY ACRES ✷ TAMMY & BRENT NIELSEN ✷ 1977 HIGHWAY G ✷ COUNCIL BLUFFS, IA 51503

PROSKILLS

Teamwork: Managing a Style Sheet

Your style sheets often will be as long and as complex as your Web site content. As the size of a style sheet increases, you might find yourself overwhelmed by multiple style rules and definitions. This can be an especially critical problem in a workplace where several people need to interpret and sometimes edit the same style sheet. Good management skills are as crucial to good Web design as a well-chosen color or typeface. As you create your own style sheets, here are some techniques to help you manage your creations:

- Use style comments throughout, especially at the top of the file. Clearly describe the purpose of the style sheet, where it's used, and who created it and when.
- Because color values are not always immediately obvious, include comments that describe your colors. For example, annotate a color value with a comment such as "body text is tan".
- Divide your style sheet into sections, with comments marking the section headings.
- Choose an organizing scheme and stick with it. You may want to organize style rules by the order in which they appear in your documents, or you may want to insert them alphabetically. Whichever you choose, be consistent and document the organizing scheme in your style comments.
- Keep your style sheets as small as possible, and break them into separate files if necessary. Use one style sheet for layout, another for text design, and perhaps another for color and graphics. Combine the style sheets using the @import rule, or combine them within each Web page. Also consider creating one style sheet for basic pages on your Web site, and another for pages that deal with special content. For example, an online store could use one style sheet (or set of sheets) for product information and another for customer information.

By following some of these basic techniques, you'll find your style sheets easier to manage and develop, and it will be easier for your colleagues to collaborate with you to create an eye-catching Web site.

You've completed your work on designing a style sheet to format the text and backgrounds on the Sunny Acres Web site. Tammy will continue to examine your work and get back to you with future projects or design changes.

REVIEW

Session 3.3 Quick Check

1. Provide a style rule to display all ordered lists with lowercase letters as the marker.
2. Provide a style rule to display all unordered lists using the *star.png* image file, placed inside of the containing box.
3. By default, most browsers indent lists from the surrounding text. Provide a style rule to remove the indentation from every unordered list nested within a section element.
4. Provide a style rule to display the text of all previously visited hypertext links in gray.
5. Describe the item selected by the following selector:

   `#top > p:first-of-type:first-line`

6. Describe the items selected by the following selector:

   `div.links img[usemap]`

7. Provide a style rule to insert the text string "*** " before every paragraph belonging to the *review* class.

*Practice the skills
you learned in
the tutorial using
the same case
scenario.*

PRACTICE

Review Assignments

Data Files needed for the Review Assignments: CloisterBlack.eot, CloisterBlack.svg, CloisterBlack.ttf, CloisterBlack.txt, CloisterBlack.woff, flake.png, holiday.jpg, holidaytxt.htm, hs_layout.css, hs_stylestxt.css, modernizr-1.5.js, salogo.png

Tammy has been working with the Web site you designed. She's returned to you for help with another Web page. The Sunny Acres farm is planning a festival called *Holidays on the Farm* to bring people to Sunny Acres during the months of November and December. The farm is planning to offer sleigh rides, sledding (weather permitting), and visits with Santa Claus. Tammy already has created the content for this page and located a few graphics she wants you to use. She needs you to complete the Web page by creating a style sheet for the text and colors in the page. A preview of the page you'll create for Tammy is shown in Figure 3-61.

Figure 3-61 Holidays on the Farm page

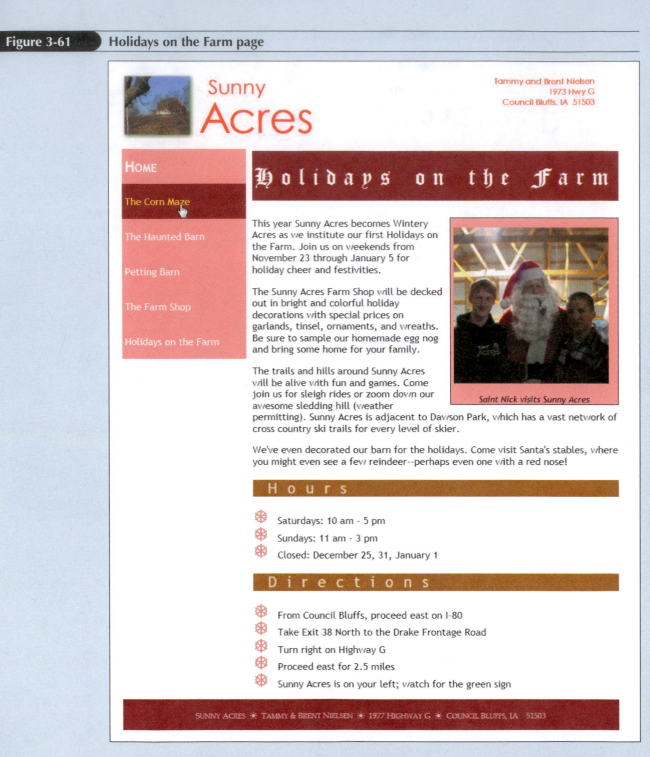

Complete the following:

1. Use your text editor to open the **holidaytxt.htm** and **hs_stylestxt.css** files from the tutorial.03\review folder included with your Data Files. Enter *your name* and *the date* within the comment section of each file, and then save them as **holiday.htm** and **hs_styles.css**, respectively.

2. Go to the **holiday.htm** file in your text editor and take some time to review the contents and structure of the document. Link the file to the **hs_layout.css** style sheet file. Open the Web page in your browser to study its current layout.

3. Tammy wants to use a Web font for the heading on the page. She has stored the CSS code for the font definition in the **CloisterBlack.txt** file. Open this file, copy the CSS code, and then go to the **hs_styles.css** style sheet file. Paste the copied CSS code into the file below the comment header.

4. Create a style rule for the page body, set the background color to **white**, and set the default font list to **Trebuchet MS**, **Helvetica**, and **sans-serif**.

5. Create a style rule for unordered lists within the `nav` element that: a) sets the background color to the value (**248, 175, 175**); b) sets the line height to **3.5em**; c) removes the bullet marker; d) sets the width of the `padding-left` property to **0** pixels; and e) indents the text **5** pixels. For the first list item, create a style rule to: a) increase the font size to **150%**; b) display the text in small caps; and c) display the text in **bold**. For every hypertext link within the navigation list, create a style that removes the underlining and sets the font color to **white**.

6. When the user hovers the mouse pointer over list items in the navigation list, change the background color to the value (**148, 51, 62**). When the user hovers the mouse pointer over a hypertext link in the navigation list, change the font color to **yellow**.

7. Tammy has placed a promotional photo in a figure box. Set the background color of figure boxes to the color value (**248, 175, 175**) and **center** the contents of figure boxes. For the caption within the figure box, add styles to: a) set the font size to **14** pixels; b) display the text in **italic**; and c) **center** the caption text.

8. For `h1` headings nested within the `section` element, create a style rule to: a) set the background color to the value (**148, 51, 62**); b) set the font color to **white**; c) use the font list containing the **CloisterBlack** and **fantasy** fonts; d) set the font size to **2.5em**; e) remove boldface from the text; f) set the kerning to **0.3em**; g) set the line height to **2em**; and h) indent the text **5** pixels.

9. For `h2` headings nested within the `section` element, create a style rule to: a) set the background color to the value (**182, 134, 52**); b) set the font color to **white** for older browsers and to the color value (**255, 255, 255**) with an opacity of **0.8** for newer browsers; c) set the font weight to **normal**; d) set the kerning to **0.7em**; and e) indent the text **1em**.

10. For unordered lists directly after `h2` headings nested within the `section` element, create a style rule that displays the image file **flake.png** as the bullet marker.

11. For `address` elements nested within the `footer` element, create a style rule to: a) set the background to the color (**148, 51, 62**); b) set the font color to **white** for older browsers and to the value (**255, 255, 255**) with 80% opacity for newer browsers; c) change the font style to **normal** weight in small caps, **0.8em** in size with a line height of **4em**, and use fonts from the list **Palatino Linotype**, **Book Antiqua**, **Palatino**, and **serif**; and d) **center** the address text.

12. Add comments to the style sheet to document what you've done.

13. Save your changes to the **hs_styles.css** style sheet.

14. Return to the **holiday.htm** file in your text editor and link to the **hs_styles.css** file.

15. Open the **holiday.htm** file in your Web browser and verify that the page matches the page shown in Figure 3-61.

16. Submit your completed files to your instructor, in either printed or electronic form, as requested.

Apply your knowledge of CSS text and color styles to format a Web page for a cryptographic institution.

APPLY

Case Problem 1

Data Files needed for this Case Problem: algo.htm, c_layout.css, c_stylestxt.css, crypttxt.htm, enigma.htm, history.htm, locks.jpg, logo.gif, modernizr-1.5.js, public.htm, scytale.gif, single.htm

International Cryptographic Institute   Sela Dawes is the media representative for the ICI, the International Cryptographic Institute. The ICI is an organization of cryptographers who study the science and mathematics of secret codes, encrypted messages, and code breaking. Part of the ICI's mission is to inform the public about cryptography and data security. Sela has asked you to work on a Web site containing information about cryptography for use by high school science and math teachers. She wants the design to be visually interesting in order to help draw students into the material. Figure 3-62 shows a preview of your design.

Figure 3-62   **Cryptography home page**

Complete the following:

1. In your text editor, open the **crypttxt.htm** and **c_stylestxt.css** files from the tutorial.03\case1 folder included with your Data Files. Enter *your name* and *the date* in the comment section of each file. Save the files as **crypt.htm** and **c_styles.css** respectively.

2. Go to the **crypt.htm** file in your text editor, and review the contents and structure of the document. Link the file to the **c_layout.css** style sheet.

3. Locate the three `strong` elements in the two paragraphs and add the `class` attribute to each element with the class value set to **keyword**.

4. Locate the *locks.jpg* inline image, and below the image create an image map with the name **locks**. Add the following hotspots to the image map:

   a. A circular hotspot linked to the **history.htm** file, centered at the coordinates (**52, 52**) with a radius of **43** pixels; the alternate text should be **History**.

   b. A circular hotspot with a radius of **43** pixels located at the coordinates (**155, 52**); link the hotspot to the **enigma.htm** file, and with the alternate text set to **Enigma**.

   c. A circular hotspot with a radius of **43** pixels located at the coordinates (**255, 52**); link the hotspot to the **algo.htm** file and set the alternate text to **Algorithms**.

   d. A circular hotspot with a radius of **43** pixels located at the coordinates (**355, 52**); link the hotspot to the **single.htm** file and set the alternate text to **Single Key**.

   e. A circular hotspot with a radius of **43** pixels located at the coordinates (**455, 52**); link the hotspot to the **public.htm** file and set the alternate text to **Public Key**.

5. Apply the **locks** image map to the *locks.jpg* inline image.

6. Save your changes to the **crypt.htm** file.

7. Go to the **c_styles.css** style sheet file in your text editor. Set the color of the page body background and text to **black** and **white**, respectively. Set the default font to a list consisting of **Century Gothic** followed by a generic **sans-serif** font.

8. Add a style rule for `h1` headings nested within a `header` element to: a) display the text in **yellow**; b) use **Courier New**, **Courier**, or another **monospace** font; c) set the font size to **28** pixels with a kerning of **20** pixels; and d) **center** the text.

9. Add a style rule for `h2` headings nested within an `article` element to: a) set the font size to **24** pixels; b) display the text without boldface; and c) set the kerning to **5** pixels.

10. Align paragraph text within the `article` element using full justification.

11. For `strong` elements belonging to the `keyword` class, create a style rule that displays the text in a **yellow**, non-bold font.

12. Center the contents of paragraphs nested within the `footer` element.

⊕ EXPLORE 13. You don't want image maps to appear with a colored border. To remove the border, create a style rule for inline images that contain the `usemap` attribute and set the border width to **0** pixels.

14. Document your work with style comments and then save your changes to the file.

15. Return to the **crypt.htm** file in your text editor and link the file to the **c_styles.css** style sheet.

16. Open **crypt.htm** in your Web browser and confirm that it matches the design shown in Figure 3-62.

17. Submit your completed files to your instructor, in either printed or electronic form, as requested.

Apply your knowledge of CSS to design a Web page for a bike touring company.

APPLY

Case Problem 2

Data Files needed for this Case Problem: bmtourtxt.htm, modernizr-1.5.js, mw_layout.css, mw_stylestxt.css, mwlogo.png, wheelmarker.png

Mountain Wheels   Adriana and Ivan Turchenko are the co-owners of Mountain Wheels, a bike shop and touring agency in Littleton, Colorado. One of their most popular tours is the Bike the Mountains Tour, a six-day excursion over some of the highest roads in Colorado. Adriana wants to update the company's Web site to provide more information about the Bike the Mountains Tour. She already has had a colleague design a three-column layout with a list of links in the first column and descriptive text in the second and third columns. She has asked for your help in completing the design by formatting the text and colors in the page. Figure 3-63 shows a preview of the Web page you'll create.

Figure 3-63   **Bike the Mountains page**

Mountain Wheels

Bike the Mountains Tour

Home

⊙ Learn More

Testimonials

Route Maps

Register

Lodging

Meals

Training

Equipment

Forums

FAQs

Contact Us

THE BIKE THE MOUNTAINS TOUR RISES from the town of Littleton, Colorado and explores the Colorado Front Range. Our tour crosses the Continental Divide twice, giving you the opportunity to bike the highest paved roads in the United States. This tour is a classic showcase of Colorado's Rocky Mountain scenery.

Not designed for the weekend cyclist, this tour is offered only for those fit enough to ride high mountain passes. We

"The Bike the Mountains Tour is *amazing.* I highly recommend it and would gladly return."

— *Steve H.*

provide sag wagons and support. Your lodging and meals are also part of the registration fee. We guarantee tough climbs, amazing sights, sweaty jerseys, and lots of fun.

This is the seventh year we've offered the Bike the Mountains Tour. It is our most popular tour and riders are returning again and again. Our experienced tour leaders will be there to guide, help, encourage, draft, and lead you every stroke of the way. Come join us!

Itinerary

Day 1
We start from the foothills above Littleton, Colorado, promptly at 9am. The first day is a chance to get your legs in shape, test your gearing, and prepare for what's to come.

Day 2
Day 2 starts with a climb up Bear Creek Canyon to Lookout Mountain, followed by a swift and winding descent into the town of Golden. Refresh yourself at the famous Coors Brewery.

Day 3
Day 3 takes you along the Peak to Peak Highway. This 55-mile route showcases the mountains of the Front Range, providing amazing vistas from Golden Gate Canyon State Park to Rocky Mountain National Park.

Day 4
Now for the supreme challenge: Day 4 brings some real high-altitude cycling through Rocky Mountain National Park and up Trail Ridge Road. It's an amazing ride, high above timberline, topping out at over 11,000 feet.

Day 5
We start Day 5 on the west side of the Continental Divide. From Grand Lake, you'll bike to Winter Park and then over Berthoud Pass, and back to the eastern side of the Continental Divide.

Day 6
On Day 6 we ride back to Littleton over Squaw Pass and Bear Creek and then enjoy a celebratory dinner as we share memories of a great tour.

Mountain Wheels • Littleton, CO 80123 • (303) 555 - 5499

Complete the following:

1. Open the **bmtourtxt.htm** and **mw_stylestxt.css** files from the tutorial.03\case2 folder. Enter *your name* and *the date* in the comment section of each file. Save the files as **bmtour.htm** and **mw_styles.css** in the same folder.

2. Return to the **bmtour.htm** file in your text editor. Link the file to the **mw_layout.css** style sheet. Take some time to review the contents and structure of the document.

3. You need to name different elements within the document using the `id` attribute. Add the following ids to the document: a) name the first `header` element **pageheader** and the second `header` element **articleheader**; and b) name the first `section` element **leftsection** and the second `section` element **rightsection**.

4. Save your changes to the file and then go to the **mw_styles.css** style sheet in your text editor.

5. Set the default font for the page body to a font list containing **Tahoma**, **Geneva**, and **sans-serif**.

6. For the `articleheader` id, apply a style rule that: a) sets the font size to **18** pixels and removes boldface; b) sets the kerning to **7** pixels; and c) centers the text.

7. Set the background color of the navigation list to the value (**125, 120, 89**) and set the line height to **3em**. Remove the bullet markers from the navigation list.

8. For hypertext links within the navigation list, create a style rule that: a) sets the font color to **white** for older browsers, and to **white** with 50% opacity for newer browsers; and b) removes the underlining from the link text.

⊕ EXPLORE

9. When a user hovers the mouse pointer over list items in the navigation list, change the background color to the value (**131, 121, 36**) and display the image file *wheelmarker.png* as the bullet image. When a user hovers the mouse pointer over a hypertext link in the navigation list, change the font color to **yellow** for older browsers, and to **white** with 100% opacity for newer browsers.

10. For paragraphs that are direct children of the `leftsection` id, set the font size to **22** pixels. Also, for the first paragraph that is also a direct child of the `leftsection` id, display the first line of the paragraph in uppercase.

11. For the `blockquote` element, create a style rule to set: a) the background color to (**131, 121, 36**); b) the font color to **white**; c) the font size to **16** pixels; and d) the font family to **Comic Sans MS**, **Times**, and cursive.

⊕ EXPLORE

12. For paragraphs within the `blockquote` element, create styles to insert a **double quotation mark** directly before and after the text of the paragraph.

13. For `h1` headings within the `rightsection` id, create a style rule to: a) set the font size to **22** pixels and the kerning to **3** pixels; b) remove the boldface from the text; and c) **center** the text. For `h2` headings within the `rightsection` id, create a style rule to: a) set the font size to **18** pixels; b) right-align the text; and c) remove the boldface from the text. Finally, for paragraphs within the `rightsection` id, create a style rule to: a) set the font color to **gray**; b) set the font size to **14** pixels; and c) **justify** the text.

14. For `address` elements within the page footer, create a style rule to: a) set the font size to **16** pixels; b) remove the italic style from the address; and c) **center** the text.

15. Add style comments to document your work and then save your changes to the file.

16. Return to the **bmtour.htm** file in your text editor and link that file to the **mw_styles.css** style sheet.

17. Open the **bmtour.htm** file in your Web browser and confirm that it matches the design and layout shown in Figure 3-63.

18. Submit your completed files to your instructor, in either printed or electronic form, as requested.

Explore how to use CSS to design a Web page for an online Civil War History course.

CHALLENGE

Case Problem 3

Data Files needed for this Case Problem: civilwartxt.htm, cw_layout.css, cw_stylestxt.css, cwphoto.png, modernizr-1.5.js, mwulogo.png, pcphoto.png

The Civil War and Reconstruction   Peter Craft is a professor of military history at Midwest University. The college is offering a series of online courses, one of which is *The Civil War and Reconstruction* taught by Professor Craft. He has developed the online content and has had a colleague help with the page layout. You've been asked to complete the project by creating text and color styles. A preview of the sample page is shown in Figure 3-64.

Figure 3-64   Civil War and Reconstruction page

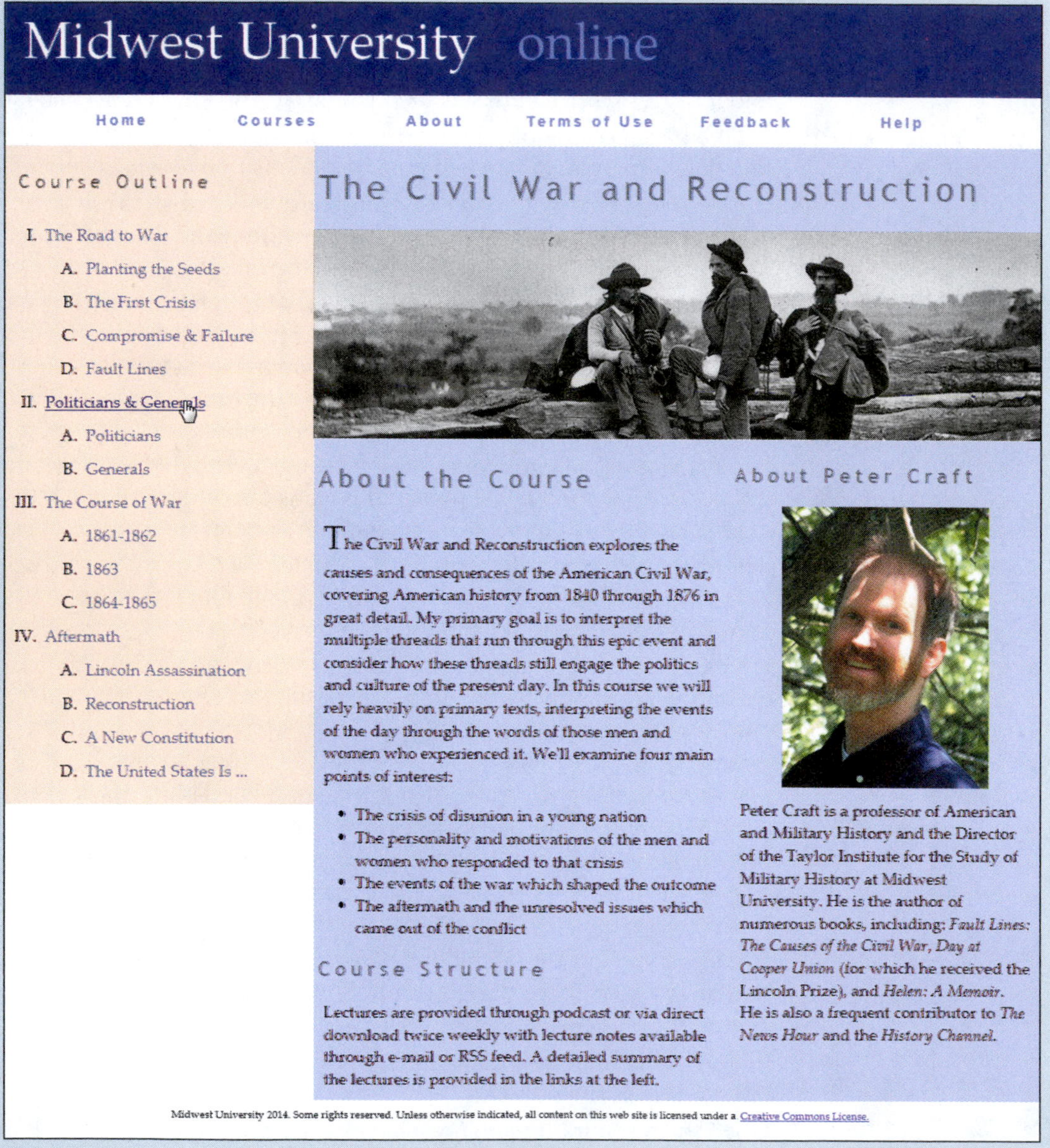

Complete the following:

1. Open the **civilwartxt.htm** and **cw_stylestxt.css** files in your text editor. Add *your name* and *the date* to the comment section of each file, and then save the files as **civilwar.htm** and **cw_styles.css**, respectively.

2. Go to the **civilwar.htm** file in your text editor. Take some time to review the content and structure of the Web page. There are two navigation lists in the document. Peter wants the first navigation list to be displayed horizontally and the second navigation list to be displayed vertically. Add the `class` attribute to each `nav` element, setting the class values to **horizontal** and **vertical** respectively.

3. Save your changes to the file, and then go to the **cw_styles.css** file in your text editor.

EXPLORE

4. Peter already has stored the layout styles in the *cw_layout.css* file. Directly after the opening comments, use the `@import` rule to import this style sheet. Add a comment describing the purpose of the `@import` rule.

5. Set the typeface of the page body to the font list **Palatino Linotype**, **Book Antiqua**, **Palatino**, and **serif**.

EXPLORE

6. For every `h1` through `h6` heading, apply styles to: a) set the color to the HSL value of (**212, 0%, 0%**) with an opacity of **0.4**; b) set the font family to **Trebuchet MS**, **Helvetica**, and **sans-serif**; c) remove the boldface; and d) set the kerning and text indent to **5** pixels.

7. For h1 headings that are direct children of a `header` element that is a direct child of the `body` element, set the background color to the HSL value (**212, 100%, 29%**).

8. For an unordered list within the horizontal navigation list, apply styles to: a) display the text in **Century Gothic MS** or another **sans-serif** font; b) set the font size to **14** pixels; c) display the text in **bold**; d) set the kerning to **3** pixels and the line height to **20** pixels; and e) remove the markers from the list.

9. For hypertext links within the horizontal navigation list, set the text to the HSL value (**212, 100%, 70%**) and remove the underlining. When the mouse hovers over a hypertext link in this list, change the font color to the HSL value (**212, 100%, 29%**).

10. Set the background color of the vertical navigation list to the HSL value (**32, 100%, 95%**).

11. For the `h4` element within the vertical navigation list, create a style rule to: a) set the color to the HSL value (**32, 0%, 0%**) with an opacity of **0.5**; and b) set the font size to **18** pixels and the text indent to **15** pixels.

12. Display the ordered list items in the vertical navigation list in an outline style with uppercase Roman numerals for the top level, and uppercase alphabetic letters for the second level. Set the line height of the lists to **2em**.

EXPLORE

13. Set the color of the hypertext links in the vertical navigation list to the HSL value (**212, 100%, 29%**) with an opacity of **0.6**. Remove the underlining from the hypertext links. If the user hovers the mouse pointer over a link in the list, increase the opacity to **1.0** and display the underline.

14. Set the background color of the `section` element to the HSL value (**212, 95%, 90%**).

15. For the first paragraph after the `h2` heading within the `article` element, create a style rule to display the first letter with a font size of **32** pixels.

16. For the paragraph within the page footer, create a style rule that sets the font size to **10** pixels and the line height to **30** pixels and centers the text.

17. Save your changes to the style sheet.

18. Return to the **civilwar.htm** file in your text editor and link the file to the **cw_styles.css** style sheet.

19. Add style comments to document your work and then save your changes to the style sheet.

20. Open the **civilwar.htm** file in your Web browser. Verify that the style layout and design match that of the Web page shown in Figure 3-64. Verify that when you hover the mouse pointer over the links in the horizontal navigation list, the text changes color. Verify that when you hover the mouse pointer over the links in the vertical navigation list, the text color changes and the text is underlined.

21. Submit your completed project to your instructor, in either printed or electronic form, as requested.

Test your knowledge of CSS to design text and color styles for a children's choir Web site.

APPLY

Case Problem 4

Data Files needed for this Case Problem: chen.png, choirtxt.htm, gcc_layout.css, gcc_stylestxt.css, gcclogo.png, modernizr-1.5.js, nobile.txt, nobile-webfont.eot, nobile-webfont.svg, nobile-webfont.ttf, nobile-webfont.woff

Gresham Children's Choir   Faye Dawson is the program director for Gresham Children's Choir in Mentor, Ohio. The choir offers a chance for talented youth to perform and to learn about music history. Faye is working on redesigning the choir's Web site and has asked for your help. She already has created a sample Web page for you to work on and has developed a page layout. She wants you to complete the design by creating styles for the text and colors in the page.

Complete the following:

1. Use your text editor to open the **choirtxt.htm** and **gcc_stylestxt.css** files from the tutorial.03\case4 folder. Add ***your name*** and ***the date*** in the comment section of each file. Save the files as **choir.htm** and **gcc_styles.css**, respectively.

2. Go to the **choir.htm** file in your text editor and link the file to the **gcc_layout.css** file. Take some time to study the content and structure of the document. Save your changes to the file and then view the current layout in your Web browser.

3. Go to the **gcc_styles.css** file and create a style sheet with style rules that:
   - modify the typeface, font weight, font size, kerning, and line height
   - employ a Web font
   - modify the appearance of list items
   - change the text and background color, including at least one example of a semi-transparent color
   - employ contextual selectors, pseudo-elements, and pseudo-classes
   - create rollover effects
   - employ progressive enhancement

   Document all of your work with informative style comments.

4. Add an embedded style sheet to the **choir.htm** file to apply a style rule of your own choosing to that page only.

5. Test your Web site in a variety of browsers to ensure your design works under different conditions.

6. Submit your completed files to your instructor, in either printed or electronic form, as requested.

ENDING DATA FILES

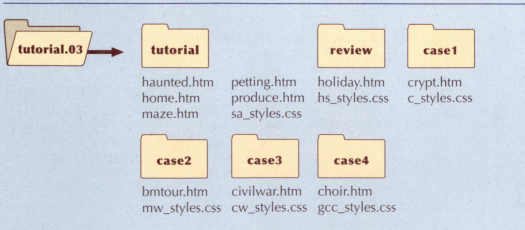

tutorial.03 →

tutorial
haunted.htm
home.htm
maze.htm

petting.htm
produce.htm
sa_styles.css

review
holiday.htm
hs_styles.css

case1
crypt.htm
c_styles.css

case2
bmtour.htm
mw_styles.css

case3
civilwar.htm
cw_styles.css

case4
choir.htm
gcc_styles.css

TUTORIAL **4**

Creating Page Layouts with CSS

Designing a Web Site for a Cycling Club

Case | *Cycle Pathology*

Dan Atwood is a cyclist who lives and works in Grand Junction, Colorado. About 30 years ago, he and a few friends started a cycling group called *Cycle Pathology*. At the beginning, the group's activities consisted of weekend rides through the western Colorado countryside. However, with the growth in the popularity of cycling, the group has expanded to several hundred active members and now organizes rides and tours for much of western Colorado.

To keep current and potential members informed about future rides and events, Dan created the Cycle Pathology Web site in the late 1990s. With the growth of the group, he has decided to redesign the site and has asked you for help in planning a new layout and design.

OBJECTIVES

Session 4.1
- Set display properties
- Create a reset style sheet
- Define a background image
- Set background image properties
- Use browser extension styles
- Explore fixed, fluid, and elastic layouts
- Float elements in a Web page

Session 4.2
- Set margin and padding spaces
- Format an element border
- Create rounded corners
- Display an element outline

Session 4.3
- Explore absolute and relative positioning
- Work with overflow content
- Explore clipped objects
- Stack objects in a page

STARTING DATA FILES

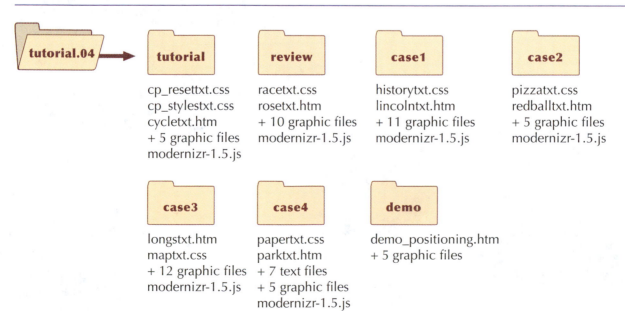

tutorial.04 →

tutorial
cp_resettxt.css
cp_stylestxt.css
cycletxt.htm
+ 5 graphic files
modernizr-1.5.js

review
racetxt.css
rosetxt.htm
+ 10 graphic files
modernizr-1.5.js

case1
historytxt.css
lincolntxt.htm
+ 11 graphic files
modernizr-1.5.js

case2
pizzatxt.css
redballtxt.htm
+ 5 graphic files
modernizr-1.5.js

case3
longstxt.htm
maptxt.css
+ 12 graphic files
modernizr-1.5.js

case4
papertxt.css
parktxt.htm
+ 7 text files
+ 5 graphic files
modernizr-1.5.js

demo
demo_positioning.htm
+ 5 graphic files

SESSION 4.1 VISUAL OVERVIEW

The **border box** contains the content and padding as well as the box border.

The **padding box** contains the space directly around the content but within the element box.

In the CSS box model, the **content box** contains the content of the element.

Home   Members Only   Market Place

From the President's Desk

— Dan Atwood

Hi fellow Cycle-Paths! The riding season is well underway and I'm recovering from the *Grand Mesa Century*, our first event of the summer tour schedule. Thanks to the volunteers who worked the relief and refreshment stations, and congratulations to all who finished.

Our next club meeting is Tuesday, July 8th at the DoubleTree Hotel in Grand Junction. Kaylee Frieze will talk about the upcoming *Gunnison Challenge* tour. Be sure to stay afterward for refreshments and fun.

A **margin** separates the box from other elements on the page.

background: url(back1.png)
    bottom left
    repeat-x;

The **background** property defines the element background by specifying the **source** of the image file, the **location** of the background image, and the **direction** in which the background image is repeated.

The **background-origin** property specifies where the background image originates; the default is border-box.

The **background-size** property specifies the size of the background image.

BACKGROUNDS AND FLOATING OBJECTS

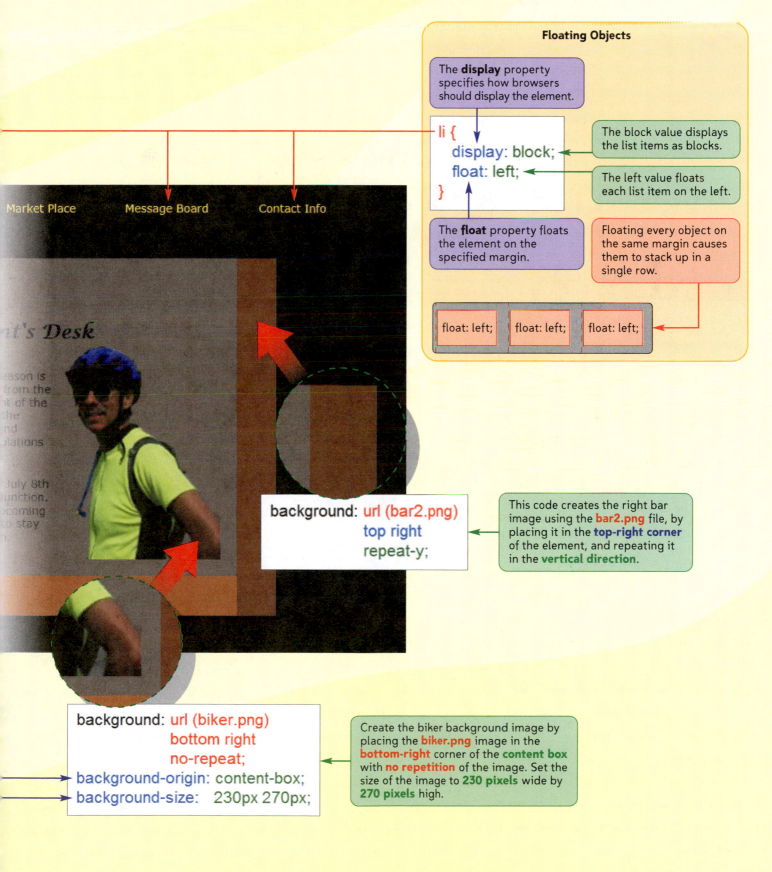

Floating Objects

The **display** property specifies how browsers should display the element.

```
li {
    display: block;
    float: left;
}
```

The block value displays the list items as blocks.

The left value floats each list item on the left.

The **float** property floats the element on the specified margin.

Floating every object on the same margin causes them to stack up in a single row.

| float: left; | float: left; | float: left; |

Market Place   Message Board   Contact Info

t's Desk

background: url (bar2.png)
top right
repeat-y;

This code creates the right bar image using the **bar2.png** file, by placing it in the **top-right corner** of the element, and repeating it in the **vertical direction**.

background: url (biker.png)
bottom right
no-repeat;
background-origin: content-box;
background-size: 230px 270px;

Create the biker background image by placing the **biker.png** image in the **bottom-right** corner of the **content box** with **no repetition** of the image. Set the size of the image to **230 pixels** wide by **270 pixels** high.

Exploring Display Styles

You and Dan meet to discuss the redesign of the Cycle Pathology Web site. Dan already has created a sample Web page for you to work on. He's written all of the content for the sample page but has not done any design work, so the current appearance of the page relies on the default styles of whatever Web browser opens it. View Dan's sample page now.

To open the Cycle Pathology Web page:

1. Use your text editor to open the **cycletxt.htm** file from the tutorial.04/tutorial folder. Enter *your name* and *the date* in the comment section of the file, and then save it as **cycle.htm**.

2. Take some time to review the content and structure of the *cycle.htm* file in your text editor.

3. Open the **cycle.htm** file in your Web browser. Figure 4-1 shows the current appearance of part of the page using one browser's internal style sheet.

Figure 4-1 | Part of the initial Cycle Pathology home page

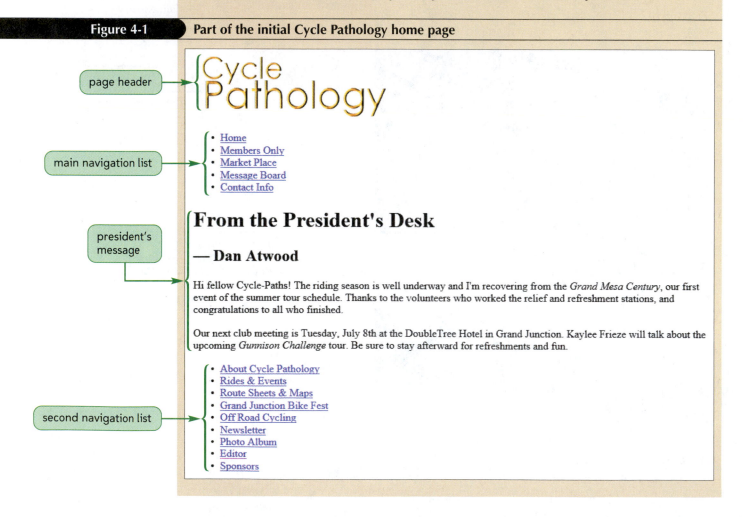

The Cycle Pathology Web page has the following main parts:

- the page header, including the Cycle Pathology logo
- a navigation list pointing to main topical areas on the site
- a section containing a message from the club president, Dan Atwood
- a second navigation list containing links to the club's newsletter, sponsored events, and other information
- a section containing an article by Kathy Rawlings about cycling in the Colorado National Monument and a figure box of a cyclist on Rim Rock Drive
- an aside describing upcoming tours and events
- a footer containing the Cycle Pathology address

Dan has sketched out how he would like each of these sections arranged in the page. His sketch is shown in Figure 4-2.

Figure 4-2 **Cycle Pathology layout design**

Dan wants the first navigation list placed in a horizontal bar at the top of the page, and the second list moved to a vertical column at the page's right margin. The president's message should appear in a rounded box at the top of the page, with Kathy Rawlings' article set below it and the image of Rim Rock Drive placed to the right. The sidebar describing upcoming club events should be moved to the page's lower-left corner, and the footer should be placed at the bottom of the page. Dan also wants to add images of himself, Kathy Rawlings, and another cyclist in the background of different sections of the page.

To create this type of layout, you'll need to work with the display properties of the different page elements. You'll start by learning how browsers arrange different types of elements, and how you can use CSS to change those default display styles.

The display style

Most page elements are displayed in one of two ways. **Blocks**, such as paragraphs or block quotes, occupy a defined rectangular area within a page. **Inline elements**, on the other hand, such as a sentence within a paragraph or a citation within a block quote, flow within a block. The browser market is pretty consistent in what is treated as a block and what is treated as an inline element. But if you need to, you can specify the display type using the style property

```
display: type;
```

where `type` is a display type like those shown in Figure 4-3.

Figure 4-3   **Values of the display property**

Display Value	Effect On Element
block	Displayed as a block
inline	Displayed in line within a block
inline-block	Treated as a block placed in line within another block
run-in	Displayed as a block unless its next sibling is also a block, in which it is displayed in line, essentially combining the two blocks into one
inherit	Inherits the display property of the parent element
list-item	Displayed as a list item along with a bullet marker
none	Prevented from displaying, removing it from the page structure

For example, most browsers display a citation in line within a block. But you can place a citation in its own block using the following style rule:

```
cite {
    display: block;
}
```

On the other hand, the style rule

```
blockquote {
    display: list-item;
}
```

would cause a browser to display all block quotes as items from a list, complete with bullet markers. You even can prevent browsers from displaying an element by setting its `display` property to `none`. In that case, the element is still part of the document structure but is not shown to users. This is useful for elements that include content that users shouldn't see or have no need to see.

The Box Model

Elements also are laid out in a Web page following the structure of the **box model**, shown in Figure 4-4, which is composed of the following series of concentric boxes:

- the content of the element itself
- the padding extending between the element's content and the border
- the border of the box surrounding the padding space
- the margin containing the space between the border and the next page element

Figure 4-4   The CSS box model

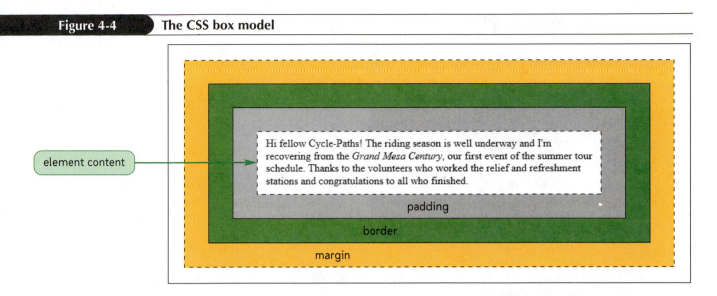

The size and appearance of these four sections control how an element is displayed by browsers and play an important role in determining page layout. Each browser's internal style sheet sets the size of the margin, border, and padding spaces, and those sizes differ between one page element and another. You already may have noticed that major headings, such as `h1` headings, often are offset from their surrounding content by a large external margin. As you'll learn later, CSS supports styles for modifying the margin, border, and padding space, allowing you to override the browser defaults.

Creating a Reset Style Sheet

Because the internal style sheets of various browsers have small—and sometimes not-so-small—differences, many designers create a **reset style sheet** to define their own default styles. Resetting the styles allows the designer to start from a known baseline, confident that no unwanted styles will creep in from any browser's internal style sheet.

You'll create a reset style sheet for the Cycle Pathology Web site. You'll start by adding a style rule that defines all HTML5 structural elements as block elements. This is necessary because currently Internet Explorer, unlike the other major browsers, does not define structural elements as block elements. Without a rule setting the `display` properties of all these elements to `block`, your choices for formatting those elements under Internet Explorer would be more limited.

To create the reset style sheet:

1. Use your text editor to open the **cp_resettxt.css** file from the tutorial.04/tutorial folder. Enter **your name** and **the date** in the comment section of the file and then save it as **cp_reset.css**.

2. Below the comment section, add the following comment and style rule:

```
/* Display HTML5 structural elements as blocks */

article, aside, figure, figcaption, footer, hgroup, header,
section, nav {
   display: block;
}
```

3. Save your changes to the file.

Next, you'll define some default styles for all of your page body elements. Your initial style rule will be as follows:

```
body * {
    font-family: Verdana, Geneva, sans-serif;
    font-size: 100%;
    font-weight: inherit;
    line-height: 1.2em;
    list-style: none;
    vertical-align: baseline;
}
```

Note that this style rule uses an asterisk selector (*) to apply the styles to every element nested within the `body` element. Thus, the text of every element will be displayed by default in a Verdana, Geneva, or sans-serif font at the default font size of 100%. The weight of each element will be inherited from its parent. Finally, the default line height will be set to 1.2 em units, there will be no bullet markers, and each element's text will be vertically aligned with the baseline. When you start formatting individual elements, you will override some of these default styles; but for now they'll establish a foundation for your future work.

To set the default styles for the Web site:

1. Below the style rule you just created in the **cp_reset.css** file, enter the following rule:

```
/* Set the default page element styles */

body * {
    font-family: Verdana, Geneva, sans-serif;
    font-size: 100%;
    font-weight: inherit;
    line-height: 1.2em;
    list-style: none;
    vertical-align: baseline;
}
```

2. Save your changes to the file.

Finally, as you lay out the Cycle Pathology home page, you'll format the main sections of the page one at a time. Rather than the page being cluttered with those sections that you haven't formatted yet, you'll temporarily hide each section. You'll do this by setting the initial `display` property for each section to `none`, and then re-displaying only the sections that you're ready to work on. Recall that the sections in the Cycle Pathology home page are the navigation lists (with class names of *horizontalNAV* and *verticalNAV*), the president's message (with an id value of *president*), another section containing an article and a figure about cycling on Rim Rock Drive (with the id value of *story*), a page header, a sidebar note about upcoming events, and finally the page footer. You'll add a style rule to the reset style sheet to initially hide all of these sections.

To hide the different sections of the page:

1. At the bottom of the **cp_reset.css** style sheet, enter the following style rule:

    ```
    /* Temporarily hide the page sections */

    nav.horizontalNAV, #president, nav.verticalNAV,
    #story, header, aside, footer {
        display: none;
    }
    ```

    Figure 4-5 shows the complete *cp_reset.css* style sheet.

Figure 4-5   **Initial reset style sheet**

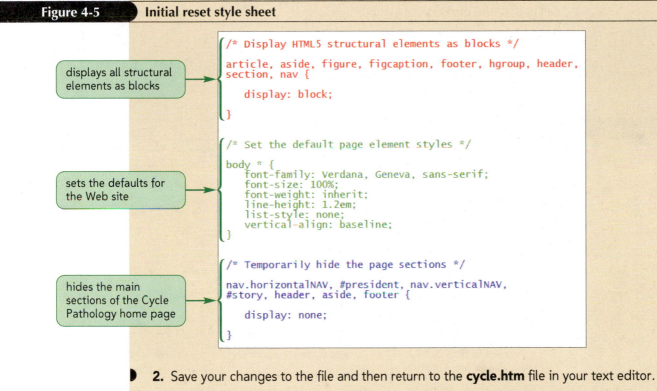

displays all structural elements as blocks

```
/* Display HTML5 structural elements as blocks */

article, aside, figure, figcaption, footer, hgroup, header,
section, nav {

    display: block;

}
```

sets the defaults for the Web site

```
/* Set the default page element styles */

body * {
    font-family: Verdana, Geneva, sans-serif;
    font-size: 100%;
    font-weight: inherit;
    line-height: 1.2em;
    list-style: none;
    vertical-align: baseline;
}
```

hides the main sections of the Cycle Pathology home page

```
/* Temporarily hide the page sections */

nav.horizontalNAV, #president, nav.verticalNAV,
#story, header, aside, footer {

    display: none;

}
```

2. Save your changes to the file and then return to the **cycle.htm** file in your text editor.

3. Directly above the closing `</head>` tag, insert the following link to the reset style sheet:

    ```
    <link href="cp_reset.css" rel="stylesheet" />
    ```

4. Save your changes to the file and then reload the **cycle.htm** file in your Web browser. Verify that no content is displayed in the browser window.

With the browser window now clear, you are ready to design. You'll start by working on the background for the page.

Designing the Background

In the last tutorial, you learned how to set the background color using the `background-color` property. CSS also supports background images using

```
background-image: url(url);
```

where *url* defines the name and location of the background image file. Background images can be added to almost any page element. For example, the style rule

```
body {
   background-image: url(cyclist.png);
}
```

displays the image file *cyclist.png* in the background of the Web page body.

Background Image Options

When a browser loads a background image, it repeats the image in both the vertical and horizontal directions until the entire background is filled. This process is known as **tiling** because of its similarity to the process of filling up a floor or other surface with tiles. You can specify the direction of tiling using the style

```
background-repeat: type;
```

where *type* is repeat (the default), repeat-x, repeat-y, no-repeat, round, or space. Figure 4-6 describes each of the repeat types. At the time of this writing, the round and space options are not well supported by current browsers.

Figure 4-6 **background-repeat property**

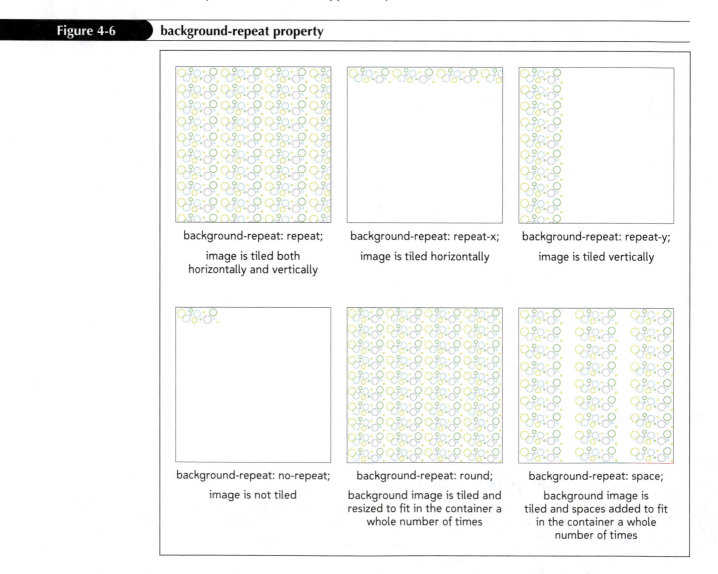

background-repeat: repeat;

image is tiled both horizontally and vertically

background-repeat: repeat-x;

image is tiled horizontally

background-repeat: repeat-y;

image is tiled vertically

background-repeat: no-repeat;

image is not tiled

background-repeat: round;

background image is tiled and resized to fit in the container a whole number of times

background-repeat: space;

background image is tiled and spaces added to fit in the container a whole number of times

TIP

You can use negative distances to move an image to the left or up from the top-left corner of an element.

By default, browsers place the background image in the element's upper-left corner; and then if the code specifies tiling, the image is repeated from there. You can change the initial position of a background image using the property

```
background-position: horizontal vertical;
```

where *horizontal* is the horizontal position of the image and *vertical* is its vertical position. The image's position is defined by: a) the distance from the top-left corner of the element using one of the CSS units of length, b) the distance from the top-left corner using a percentage of the element's width or height, or c) a keyword. Keyword options are top, center, or bottom for vertical position, and left, center, or right for horizontal placement. For example,

```
background-position: 10% 20%;
```

sets the initial position of the image 10% of the width to the right and 20% of the length down from the upper-left corner of the element, while

```
background-position: right bottom;
```

places the background image at the lower-right corner of the element. If you include only one position value, browsers apply that value to the horizontal position and vertically center the image. Thus, the style

```
background-position: 30px;
```

places the background image 30 pixels to the right of the element's left border and centers it vertically.

By default, a background image moves along with the element content as a user scrolls through the page. You can change this using the property

```
background-attachment: type;
```

where *type* is scroll, fixed, or local. The default, scroll, scrolls the background along with the document, while the fixed keyword fixes the background in the browser window, even as the user scrolls through the document. A fixed background image can be used to create a **watermark** effect, in which a subtle, often translucent graphic is displayed behind elements to mimic the watermarks found on some specialized stationery. Finally, the local keyword is similar to scroll but is used for elements such as scroll boxes to allow the element background to scroll along with the element content.

CSS3 Background Styles

CSS3 introduces several style properties for background images, most of which have now gained popular acceptance among current browsers. The first is the background-size property, which sets the size of an element's background image. This property has the syntax

```
background-size: width height;
```

where *width* and *height* are the width and height of the image in one of the CSS units of length or as a percentage of the element's width and height, or the keywords auto, cover, or contain. For example, the following style sets the size of the background image to 300 pixels wide by 200 pixels high:

```
background-size: 300px 200px;
```

The auto keyword allows the browser to set the background image automatically based on the size of the image in the image file. The style

```
background-size: auto 200px;
```

sets the height of the background image to 200 pixels and automatically sets the width to retain the image proportions.

The cover keyword tells browsers to scale the image in order to cover all of the background while still retaining the proportions of the image, even if that means cropping the image. The contain keyword, on the other hand, tells browsers to scale the image so that all of the image is completely contained within the element, even if that means that not all of the element is covered by the image. Figure 4-7 provides examples of a background image scaled to a specific size, and scaled using the cover and contain keywords.

Figure 4-7 **background-size property**

background-size: 300px 200px;

200px;

300px;

the image is displayed at a specific size

background-size: cover;

the image is scaled until it covers the entire element, but part of the image is cropped

background-size: contain;

the image is scaled so that the entire image is contained within the element, but part of the element remains uncovered

Vaclav Volrab/Shutterstock.com

Thus, to create a background image that is half the width and height of the containing element, centered vertically and horizontally, and not tiled, you could apply the following styles:

```
background-position: center center;
background-repeat: no-repeat;
background-size: 50% 50%;
```

In the box model discussed earlier, every element contains a content box, a padding box, and a border box. You can define the extent of a background image or color using the style

```
background-clip: box;
```

where *box* is content-box, padding-box, or border-box (the default). As shown in Figure 4-8, the keyword you choose controls whether the background image or color is clipped at the edge of the content or the edge of the padding, or runs all the way to the edge of the element border.

Figure 4-8   **background-clip property**

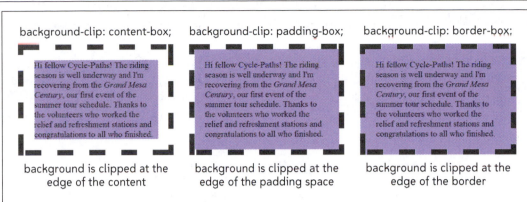

Finally, you can specify the context of the `background-position` property using

```
background-origin: box;
```

where *box* is once again `content-box`, `padding-box` (the default), or `border-box`. The `background-origin` property defines whether `background-position` values refer to the content box, the padding box, or the border box. Figure 4-9 shows the effect of different `background-origin` values on the location of the bottom-right position.

Figure 4-9   **background-origin property**

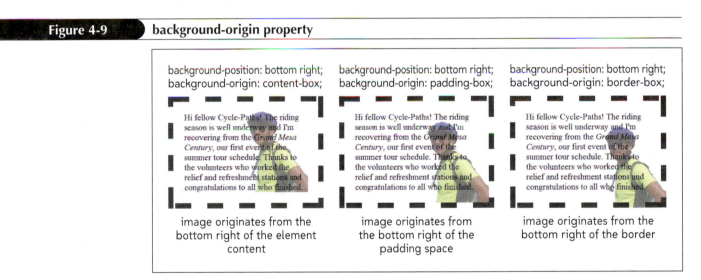

The `background` Shorthand Property

Like the `font` property discussed in the last tutorial, you can combine the various `background` properties into the shorthand property

```
background: color url(url) attachment position repeat;
```

where *color*, *url*, *attachment*, *position*, and *repeat* are values corresponding to the `background-color`, `background-image`, `background-attachment`, `background-position`, and `background-repeat` style properties, respectively. If you don't specify all of the values in the shorthand property, browsers assume default values for the missing properties. The style

```
background: yellow url(logo.png) fixed center center no-repeat;
```

creates a yellow background on which the image file *logo.png* is displayed. The image file is not tiled across the background, but is instead fixed in the horizontal and vertical center.

TIP

The different background properties can be listed in any order, but you should be consistent in your ordering to make your code easier to edit and easier for others to read.

CSS3 provides an expanded form of the `background` property that includes values for image size, origin, and the location of the clipping box

```
background: color url(url) position / size repeat attachment box box;
```

where *size* and *box box* are values corresponding to `background-size`, `background-origin`, and `background-clip` properties, respectively. If only one *box* value is present, browsers set both the `background-origin` and `background-clip` properties to that value. At the moment, few browsers support the expanded form; therefore, you only should use the brief form and set the size, origin, and clipping box values separately.

Multiple Image Backgrounds

There is no reason to limit your background to a single image. CSS allows you to specify multiple images and their properties in a comma-separated list. The general syntax is

```
background-property: value1, value2, … ;
```

where *background-property* is one of the CSS background image properties and *value1*, *value2*, etc. are values for each image associated with that property. For example, the following style rule creates two background images for the `header` element; one is located in the top-left corner, the other is located in the bottom-right corner, and both are superimposed on a yellow background:

```
header {
    background-color: yellow;
    background-image: url(logo.png), url(logo2.png);
    background-position: top left, bottom right;
    background-repeat: no-repeat;
}
```

Notice that if a value is listed just once, it is applied to all images in the list. Thus, neither the *logo.png* image nor the *logo2.png* image is tiled in the example above. Multiple backgrounds also can be applied using the `background` shorthand property as follows:

```
header {
    background: url(logo.png) top left no-repeat,
                url(logo2.png) bottom right no-repeat yellow;
}
```

TIP

With multiple backgrounds, specify the background color last so that your background images are loaded on top of it. You can specify only one background color.

When browsers render an element with multiple backgrounds, the images that are listed last are the first ones loaded. If images overlap, the first images listed appear on top of subsequent images.

REFERENCE

Formatting the Background

- To display a background image, use

```
background-image: url(url);
```

where `url` is the filename and location of the image file.
- To set how a background image repeats, use

```
background-repeat: type;
```

where `type` is repeat, no-repeat, repeat-x, repeat-y, round, or space.
- To set the position of a background image, use

```
background-position: horizontal vertical;
```

where `horizontal` is the horizontal position of the image and `vertical` is its vertical position.
- To set the attachment of an image to the background, use

```
background-attachment: type;
```

where `type` is scroll, fixed, or local.
- To set the size of a background image, use

```
background-size: width height;
```

where width and height are the width and height of the image in one of the CSS units of length or as a percentage of the element's width and height, or the keywords auto, cover, or contain.
- To clip a background, use

```
background-clip: box;
```

where `box` is content-box, padding-box, or border-box (the default).
- To specify the origin of a background image, use

```
background-origin: box;
```

where `box` is content-box, padding-box (the default), or border-box.

Adding a Page Background

You're now ready to create a background for the Cycle Pathology home page. Dan has a graphic image of a cyclist standing before a sunset. He wants you to place this image in the top-left corner of the page body against a black background. He does not want you to tile the image.

You'll place a style rule for the page background in a new style sheet file that you'll create now.

To format the page background:

1. Open the **cp_stylestxt.css** file in your text editor. Type *your name* and *the date* in the comment section at the top of the file, and then save the file as **cp_styles.css**.

2. Below the comment section, insert the following style rule (see Figure 4-10):

```
/* Styles for the Page Body */
body {
    background: black url(bike_bg.png) top left no-repeat;
}
```

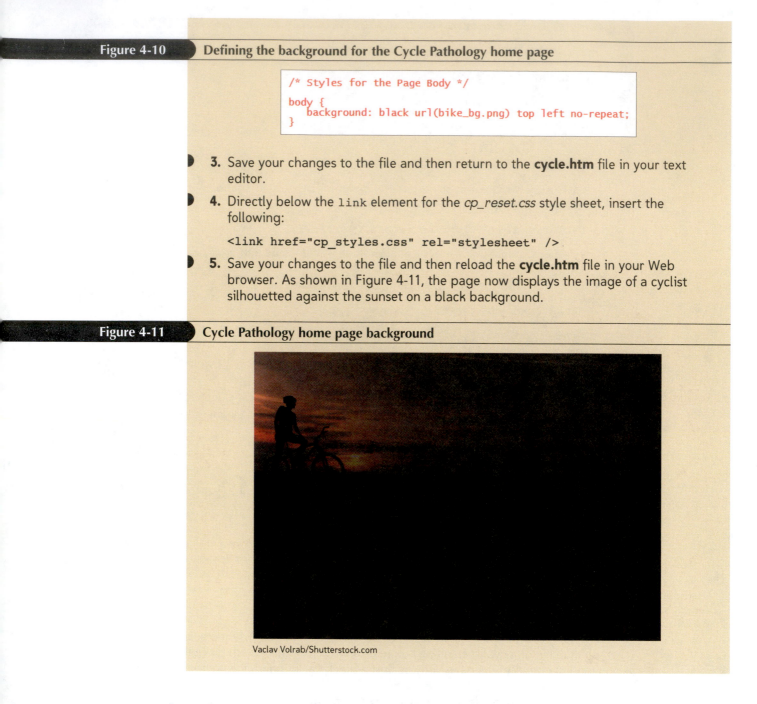

Figure 4-10   **Defining the background for the Cycle Pathology home page**

```
/* Styles for the Page Body */

body {
    background: black url(bike_bg.png) top left no-repeat;
}
```

3. Save your changes to the file and then return to the **cycle.htm** file in your text editor.

4. Directly below the link element for the *cp_reset.css* style sheet, insert the following:

   `<link href="cp_styles.css" rel="stylesheet" />`

5. Save your changes to the file and then reload the **cycle.htm** file in your Web browser. As shown in Figure 4-11, the page now displays the image of a cyclist silhouetted against the sunset on a black background.

Figure 4-11   **Cycle Pathology home page background**

Vaclav Volrab/Shutterstock.com

Exploring Browser Extensions

Some of the background styles you just examined were added to the CSS3 specifications in the last few years. Before that, many of them were extensions to CSS developed and supported by a few browser vendors. Browser extensions that are not part of the official CSS specifications can be identified through the use of a **vendor prefix** that indicates the browser vendor that created and supports the property. Figure 4-12 lists the browser extensions you'll encounter in your work on Web design.

| Figure 4-12 | Browser-specific extensions to CSS |

Vendor Prefix	Rendering Engine	Browsers
-khtml-	KHTML	Konqueror
-moz-	Mozilla	Firefox, Camino
-ms-	Trident	Internet Explorer
-o-	Presto	Opera, Nintendo Wii browser
-webkit-	WebKit	Android browser, Chrome, Safari

Older browser versions might not support the current CSS specifications, but might support one of the browser extensions. In order to support the widest range of browsers and browser versions, you should employ progressive enhancement with the most widely supported CSS2 property—if one exists—listed first, followed by the browser extensions, and then the latest CSS3 property. As you encounter this situation in this and future tutorials, you'll use the following structure:

```
selector {
    css2_property: value;
    -khtml-property: value;
    -o-property: value;
    -moz-property: value;
    -webkit-property: value;
    -ms-property: value;
    css3_property: value;
}
```

As always, the last property listed and recognized by the browser will be the one applied to the Web page; thus, you always should start with the oldest and most basic standard and finish with the most current. For example, several browsers have their own extensions to specify the origin of a background image and to ensure the widest possible support for this feature, you would apply the following style properties to the selector:

```
-o-background-origin: padding-box;
-moz-background-origin: padding;
-webkit-background-origin: padding-box;
background-origin: padding-box;
```

Notice that the background origin values differ among browser extensions. With the Mozilla rendering engine, you set the origin of the background image to the padding box by using the keyword `padding`; while the Presto and WebKit extensions employ the same `padding-box` keyword that was later adopted into the CSS3 specifications.

WebKit, Mozilla, and Presto support similar extensions that mirror the CSS3 `background-size` and `background-clip` properties. At this point you don't have a need for these browser extensions, but you will use them later in the tutorial.

Exploring Layout Designs

One challenge of Web page layout is that your document will be viewed on many different devices with different screen resolutions. As shown in Figure 4-13, the most common screen resolution at the time of this writing is 1024 × 768, though the majority of user devices are displaying the Web at even higher resolutions than that.

Figure 4-13 Screen resolutions on the Web

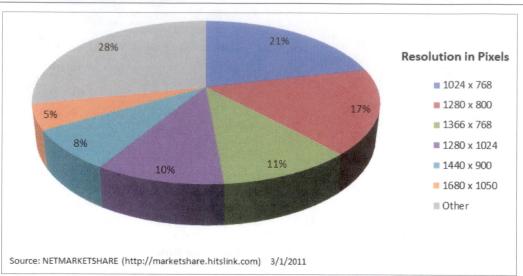

Source: NETMARKETSHARE (http://marketshare.hitslink.com)   3/1/2011

In page design, you're usually more concerned about the available page width than the total screen resolution. Users can scroll vertically down the length of a Web page, but it's considered bad design to make them scroll horizontally. Figure 4-14 breaks down current data on screen resolution in terms of page width.

Figure 4-14 Screen widths on the Web

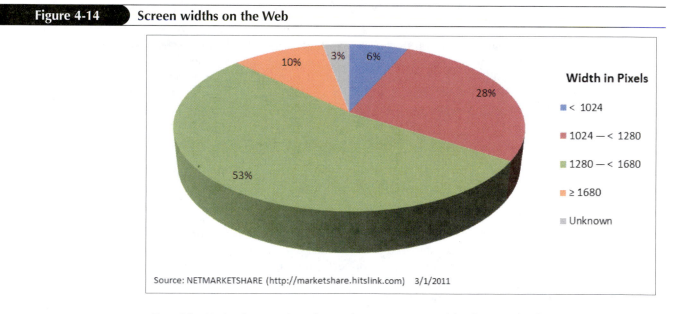

Source: NETMARKETSHARE (http://marketshare.hitslink.com)   3/1/2011

Roughly 63% of users view the Web at a screen width of 1280 pixels or more. On the other end of the scale, about 6% of users have their screens set at less than 1024 pixels. Complicating matters is that as more users access the Web through small mobile devices, some users will require page layouts that work with smaller screen widths. Finally, while screen widths represent the maximum space available to users, some space is also taken up with toolbars, sidebar panes, and other browser features. In addition, a user might not even have his or her browser window maximized to fill up the entire screen. Thus, you need a layout strategy to accommodate all of these possible screen and browser window configurations.

Fixed, Fluid, and Elastic Layouts

Web page layouts fall into three general categories: fixed, fluid, and elastic. A **fixed layout** is one in which the size of the Web page and the size of the elements within it are set without regard to the screen resolution. A **fluid** or **liquid layout** defines the size of the page and its elements as a percentage of the screen width, meaning that a Web page and its elements are wider on a wider screen (see Figure 4-15).

Figure 4-15   **Fixed and fluid layouts**

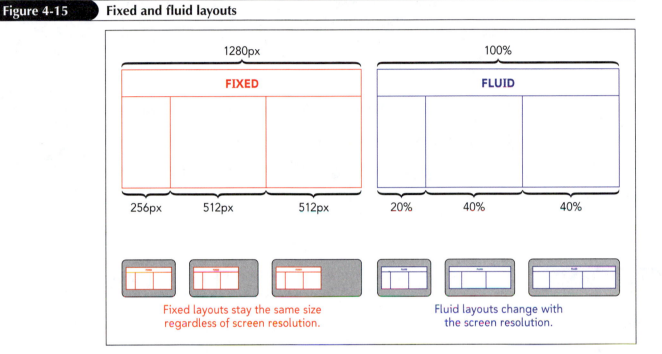

The advantages and disadvantages of the fixed and fluid approaches are laid out in Figure 4-16. In general, fixed layouts are easier to set up and maintain, but they're less pleasing to the eye when viewed on wider screens. A fluid layout may be more difficult to set up initially, but it's more adaptable to a market in which users access the Web from a variety of devices and screen resolutions.

Figure 4-16   **Comparing fixed and fluid layouts**

Fixed Layout	Fluid Layout
Pros	Pros
✓ Easier to use and maintain	✓ Easier for the user since it adapts to his or her screen resolution
✓ Works better with fixed-size objects such as images and embedded video clips	✓ All available screen space is used, allowing for more content on larger monitors
✓ Unless the user's screen is extremely wide, the page will still be readable	✓ Responds well to user-defined font sizes
✓ Can be used with more complicated page layouts	✓ Maintains a consistent look across different screen resolutions
Cons	Cons
✗ Can create excessive white space under higher resolutions	✗ Testing is more involved as the designer must confirm the layout works under a variety of resolutions
✗ Doesn't react well to user-defined font sizes	✗ May result in overly wide lines of text, making the page difficult to read
✗ Users with small screens may be forced to scroll horizontally to view all page content	✗ Less adaptable to more complicated page layouts
✗ Layout is less pleasing to the eye under higher screen resolutions	✗ Difficult to work with fixed-size objects such as images and video clips

TIP

If you're new to Web page design, try formatting the initial draft of your page using a fixed layout. Then, once you have a workable page design, you can change it to a fluid or an elastic design.

Many designers use a combination of fixed and fluid page elements, enabling them to have the best of both worlds. Another approach is to use a script that queries each browser about its screen resolution and then adapts the page to that resolution. Finally, some designers propose the use of **elastic layouts**, in which all measurements are expressed relative to the default font size using the em unit. If a user or the designer increases the font size, the width, height, and location of all of the other page elements, including images, change to match. Thus, images and text are always sized in proportion with each other. The disadvantage to this approach is that since sizing is based on the font size and not on the screen resolution, there is a danger that if a user sets the default font size large enough, the page will extend beyond the boundaries of the browser window.

Setting the Page Width and Height

Element widths and heights are set using the style properties

```
width: value;
height: value;
```

where *value* is the width or height using one of the CSS units of measurement or as a percentage of the width or height of the containing element. The width and height measures only apply to the element content, not to the padding space, borders, or margins around the element. Usually you do not set the height value because browsers automatically increase the height of an element to match its content.

Although you don't specify an exact width for fluid or elastic layouts, you might want to provide limits on how narrow or wide an element can extend. If an element is very wide, its lines of text might become too long to be easily readable; likewise, if it is too narrow, its text also can be difficult to read. Rather than allowing these problems to occur, you can specify a minimum or maximum height or width for an element using the style properties

```
min-width: value;
min-height: value;
max-width: value;
max-height: value;
```

where *value* is once again a length expressed in one of the CSS units of measure. For example, the style rule

```
body {
    width: 95%;
    min-width: 1000px;
    max-width: 1400px;
}
```

sets the width of the page body to 95% of the width of the browser window, and also limits the width to a range of 1000 to 1400 pixels. No matter the screen resolution, the page body width will never go below 1000 pixels or above 1400 pixels. After discussing the page layout issue with Dan, you both agree to develop the Cycle Pathology home page as a fluid layout starting with this particular style rule. You'll add it now to the *cp_styles.css* style sheet file.

To set the page width:

TIP

Keep your style sheets organized by placing style rules that relate to the same section near one another in the document.

1. Return to the **cp_styles.css** style sheet in your text editor.

2. Within the style rule for the body element, insert the following properties, as shown in Figure 4-17:

   ```
   width: 95%;
   min-width: 1000px;
   max-width: 1400px;
   ```

Figure 4-17   Setting the page width

width of Web page body is 95% of the width of the browser window

width is constrained to the range 1000 pixels to 1400 pixels

```
body {
    background: black url(bike_bg.png) top left no-repeat;
    width: 95%;
    min-width: 1000px;
    max-width: 1400px;
}
```

3. Save your changes to the file.

Written Communication: Getting to the Point with Layout

Page layout is one of the most important aspects of Web design. A well-constructed page layout naturally guides a reader's eyes to the most important information in the page. Use the following principles to help your readers quickly get to the point:

- *Guide the eye.* Usability studies have shown that a reader's eye first lands in the top center of the page, then scans to the left, and then to the right and down. Arrange your page content so that the most important items are the first items a user sees.
- *Avoid clutter.* If a graphic or an icon is not conveying information or making the content easier to read, remove it.
- *Avoid overcrowding.* Focus on a few key items that will be easy for readers to locate while scanning the page, and separate these key areas from one another with ample white space. Don't be afraid to move a topic to a different page if it makes the current page easier to scan.
- *Make your information manageable.* It's easier for the brain to process information when it's presented in smaller chunks. Break up long extended paragraphs into smaller paragraphs or bulleted lists.
- *Use a grid.* Users find it easier to scan content when page elements are aligned vertically and horizontally. Use a grid to help you line up your elements in a clear and consistent way.
- *Cut down on the noise.* If you're thinking about using blinking text or a cute animated icon, *don't.* The novelty of such features wears off very quickly and distracts users from the valuable content in your page.

Always remember that your goal is to convey information to readers, and that an important tool in achieving that is to make it as easy as possible for readers to find that information. A thoughtfully constructed layout is a great aid to effective communication.

Floating Elements

The first content you'll display in the Cycle Pathology home page is the navigation list for the main topical areas of the site. Lists are displayed vertically by default, but Dan wants this one displayed horizontally. One way to accomplish this is by floating each list item.

Setting a Float

Floating an element takes that element out of the normal flow of the document and positions it along the left or right edge of its containing element. Subsequent elements that are not floated are then moved up to occupy the position previously occupied by the floating element. Figure 4-18 shows a diagram of an element that is floated along the right margin of the page body.

Figure 4-18   **Floating an element**

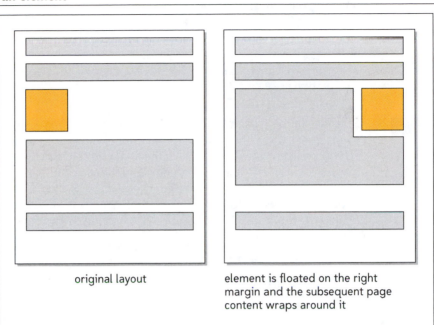

To float an element, you apply the style property

```
float: position;
```

where *position* is none (the default), left, or right. If sibling elements are floated in the same direction, they stack up, creating a row of elements each aligned with the margin of the previous element (see Figure 4-19).

Figure 4-19   **Floating multiple elements in a row**

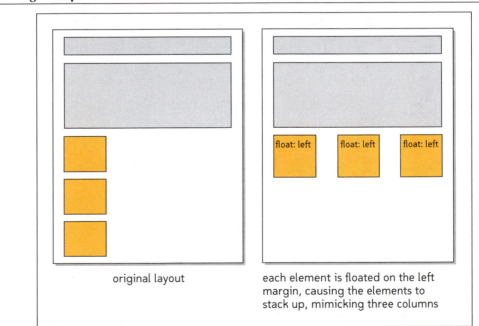

This is the effect you want for your navigation list. To float the items in that list, you'll apply the following style rule:

```
nav.horizontalNAV li {
    font-size: 87.5%;
    float: left;
    text-align: center;
    width: 20%;
}
```

TIP

If there is not enough room in a container for all of the floating elements, they automatically wrap to the next line in the page.

Besides floating each list item, this style rule also reduces the text to 87.5% of the default size, centers the text of the hyperlinks within each item, and sets the width of each of the five list items to 20% of the total width of the nav element. Because by default the width of the nav element is equal to the width of the page body, the five links will be equally spaced across the browser window.

You'll also need to format the text of the hypertext links so that they are visible against the black background. To do this, you'll use the following style rules:

```
nav a {
    text-decoration: none;
}
nav.horizontalNAV a {
    color: rgb(255, 255, 99);
}
nav.horizontalNAV a:hover {
    color: white;
}
```

The first rule removes underlining from all hypertext links within any navigation list. The next two rules set the color of the links in navigation lists that are part of the horizontalNAV class to yellow except when a user hovers the mouse pointer over a link, in which case the link color turns to white. You'll add these style rules to your style sheet with the appropriate comments.

To format the navigation list:

1. Return to the **cp_styles.css** style sheet in your text editor.

2. Below the style rule for the body selector, add the following code, as shown in Figure 4-20:

```
/* General Navigation List Style */

nav a {
    text-decoration: none;
}

/* Horizontal Navigation List */

nav.horizontalNAV li {
    font-size: 87.5%;
    float: left;
    text-align: center;
    width: 20%;
}
```

```
nav.horizontalNAV li a {
    color: rgb(255, 255, 99);
}

nav.horizontalNAV li a:hover {
    color: white;
}
```

Figure 4-20	Styling the horizontal navigation list

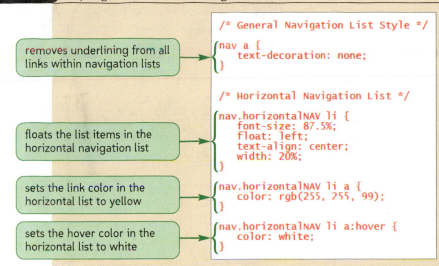

removes underlining from all links within navigation lists

```
/* General Navigation List Style */

nav a {
    text-decoration: none;
}


/* Horizontal Navigation List */

nav.horizontalNAV li {
    font-size: 87.5%;
    float: left;
    text-align: center;
    width: 20%;
}

nav.horizontalNAV li a {
    color: rgb(255, 255, 99);
}

nav.horizontalNAV li a:hover {
    color: white;
}
```

floats the list items in the horizontal navigation list

sets the link color in the horizontal list to yellow

sets the hover color in the horizontal list to white

3. Save your changes to the file.

   Next, you'll change the reset style sheet rules so that the horizontal navigation list is once again displayed.

4. Return to the **cp_reset.css** style sheet in your text editor and then scroll down to the style rule at the bottom of the page. Remove the selector *nav.horizontalNAV* along with the comma separator that follows it from the start of the selector list.

5. Save your changes to the reset style sheet and then reload **cycle.htm** in your Web browser. As shown in Figure 4-21, the hypertext links are now rendered in a single row across the top of the page.

6. Verify that the color of each link changes to white in response to the hover event.

Figure 4-21	Horizontal navigation list

each list item is floated left, creating a row of items

Vaclav Volrab/Shutterstock.com

Floating Elements and the Great Collapse

By default, elements are rendered in the page based on the element hierarchy in the HTML file. For example, a child element is positioned within its parent element in the Web page. However, this does not happen when you float an object; instead, the floated element is untethered from its parent element.

This can lead to some surprising results. For example, a parent element with all of its child elements floated has no content in the rendered page and collapses down to an empty element with zero height. If you're counting on using a parent element to set the background color for all of its floating children, you're out of luck unless you explicitly define a height for the parent that's large enough to provide a background for all of its child elements.

Clearing a Float

Sometimes you'll want to prevent an object from wrapping around a floating element; or in the case of a row of floats, you'll want to ensure that the following element appears after the row is completed. To place an element below a float, you use the style

    clear: *position*;

where *position* is none (the default), left, right, or both (to ensure that both margins are clear of floating elements). For example, the style

    clear: right;

causes an element not to be displayed until the right margin is clear of floating objects. See Figure 4-22.

Figure 4-22	Clearing a float

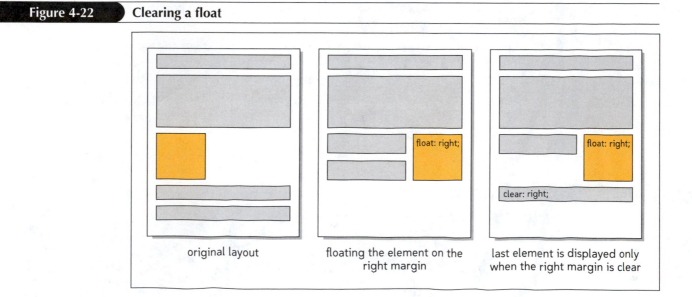

original layout   floating the element on the   last element is displayed only
                                  right margin   when the right margin is clear

REFERENCE

Floating an Element

- To float an element, use the style property

```
float: position;
```

where *position* is none (the default), `left`, or `right`.
- To display an element clear of floating elements, use

```
clear: position;
```

where *position* is none (the default), `left`, `right`, or `both`.

The next item you want to add to Dan's Web page is the president's message article. Because that article appears below the horizontal navigation list, you'll use the `clear` property to ensure that it's displayed only when the left margin is clear of floated objects. Dan also wants to stack this item alongside the second navigation list, so you'll float the president's message article on the left margin even as you clear it from the first navigation list. You'll add the following rule to your style sheet:

```
#president {
   background-color: rgb(105, 96, 87);
   background-color: rgba(255, 255, 255, 0.3);
   clear: left;
   float: left;
   width: 40%;
}
```

The style rule uses progressive enhancement to set the background color either to medium gray or to white with 30% opacity. The rule also sets the width of the article to 40% of the width of the page body.

To format the navigation list:

1. Return to the **cp_styles.css** style sheet in your text editor, and then at the bottom of the style sheet, insert the following rule (see Figure 4-23):

```
/* President's message */

#president {
   background-color: rgb(105, 96, 87);
   background-color: rgba(255, 255, 255, 0.3);
   clear: left;
   float: left;
   width: 40%;
}
```

Figure 4-23 Styling the president's message

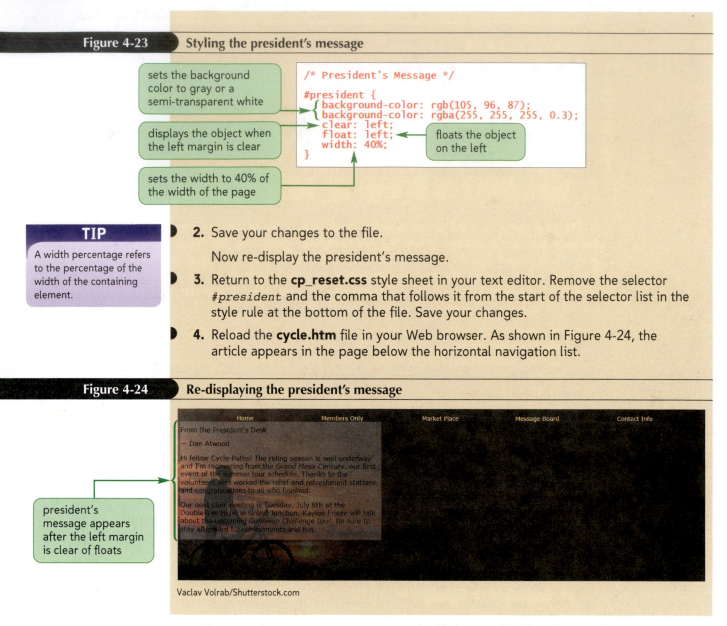

sets the background color to gray or a semi-transparent white

```
/* President's Message */

#president {
    background-color: rgb(105, 96, 87);
    background-color: rgba(255, 255, 255, 0.3);
    clear: left;
    float: left;
    width: 40%;
}
```

floats the object on the left

displays the object when the left margin is clear

sets the width to 40% of the width of the page

TIP

A width percentage refers to the percentage of the width of the containing element.

2. Save your changes to the file.

   Now re-display the president's message.

3. Return to the **cp_reset.css** style sheet in your text editor. Remove the selector *#president* and the comma that follows it from the start of the selector list in the style rule at the bottom of the file. Save your changes.

4. Reload the **cycle.htm** file in your Web browser. As shown in Figure 4-24, the article appears in the page below the horizontal navigation list.

Figure 4-24 Re-displaying the president's message

From the President's Desk

— Dan Atwood

Hi fellow Cycle-Paths! The riding season is well underway and I'm recovering from the *Grand Mesa Century*, our first event of the summer tour schedule. Thanks to the volunteers who worked the relief and refreshment stations, and congratulations to all who finished.

Our next club meeting is Tuesday, July 8th at the DoubleTree Hotel in Grand Junction. Kaylee Frieze will talk about the upcoming *Gunnison Challenge* tour. Be sure to stay afterward for refreshments and fun.

Home   Members Only   Market Place   Message Board   Contact Info

president's message appears after the left margin is clear of floats

Vaclav Volrab/Shutterstock.com

Dan stops by to see your progress on the Web page. He likes the page background and the navigation list. However, he wants you to move the president's message article farther to the right. You'll learn how to relocate page objects and work with margins, padding space, and borders in the next session.

REVIEW

Session 4.1 Quick Check

1. Provide a style rule to display all inline images as blocks.

2. Provide a style rule to add the file *author.jpg* as a background image to the `header` element, display the image on the bottom-right corner of the element without tiling, and set the background color to yellow.

3. What style rule would you use to tile the background image file *bar.png* horizontally in the background of the page body, starting from the top-left corner of the page?

4. Provide a style rule to display the *logo.png* and *side.png* image files in the page body background. Place *logo.png* in the top-left corner of the background and *side.png* in the top-right corner. Do not tile the *logo.png* image, and tile the *side.png* image only vertically. Set up your style so that *logo.png* is loaded last by the browser.

5. Provide a style rule for the first `section` element within the page body to set the size of the section's background image file, *author.png*, to 300 pixels wide by 200 pixels high. Use progressive enhancement to support the Presto, Mozilla, and WebKit rendering engines as well as browsers that support the CSS3 specifications.

6. What type of layout design should you use to set the width of the page to 1200 pixels, regardless of the rendering device?

7. Provide a style rule to float all figure boxes on the right margin when nested within an `article` element.

8. Provide a style rule to display the `footer` element only when both left and right margins are free of floating elements.

SESSION 4.2 VISUAL OVERVIEW

The **border** property creates a border around an element. These values create a **10-pixel-wide double line** with a color value of **(219, 152, 96)**.

border: 10px
      double;
      rgb(219, 152, 96) ;

The **outline** property creates an outline around an element. These values create a **1-pixel-wide**, **red single line**.

outline: 1px
      red
      single;

margin: 10px 5px 10px 20px;

The **margin** property sets the margin space around an element. These values create a margin that is **10 pixels** on top, **5 pixels** on the right, **10 pixels** on the bottom, and **20 pixels** on the left.

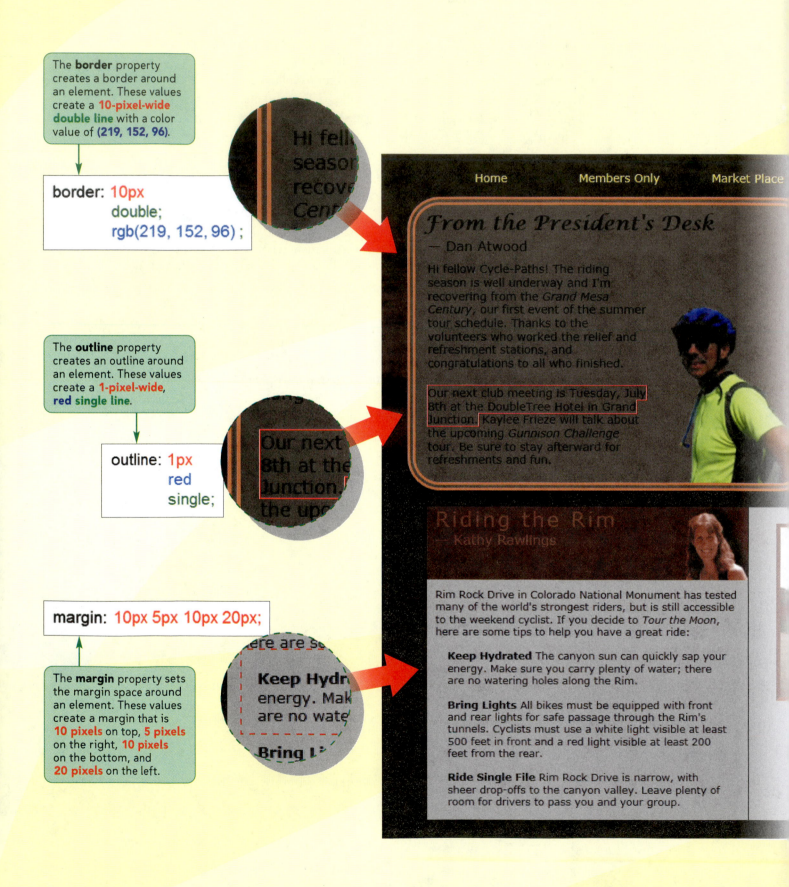

Home   Members Only   Market Place

From the President's Desk
— Dan Atwood

Hi fellow Cycle-Paths! The riding season is well underway and I'm recovering from the *Grand Mesa Century*, our first event of the summer tour schedule. Thanks to the volunteers who worked the relief and refreshment stations, and congratulations to all who finished.

Our next club meeting is Tuesday, July 8th at the DoubleTree Hotel in Grand Junction. Kaylee Frieze will talk about the upcoming *Gunnison Challenge* tour. Be sure to stay afterward for refreshments and fun.

Riding the Rim
— Kathy Rawlings

Rim Rock Drive in Colorado National Monument has tested many of the world's strongest riders, but is still accessible to the weekend cyclist. If you decide to *Tour the Moon*, here are some tips to help you have a great ride:

Keep Hydrated The canyon sun can quickly sap your energy. Make sure you carry plenty of water; there are no watering holes along the Rim.

Bring Lights All bikes must be equipped with front and rear lights for safe passage through the Rim's tunnels. Cyclists must use a white light visible at least 500 feet in front and a red light visible at least 200 feet from the rear.

Ride Single File Rim Rock Drive is narrow, with sheer drop-offs to the canyon valley. Leave plenty of room for drivers to pass you and your group.

MARGINS, PADDING, AND BORDERS

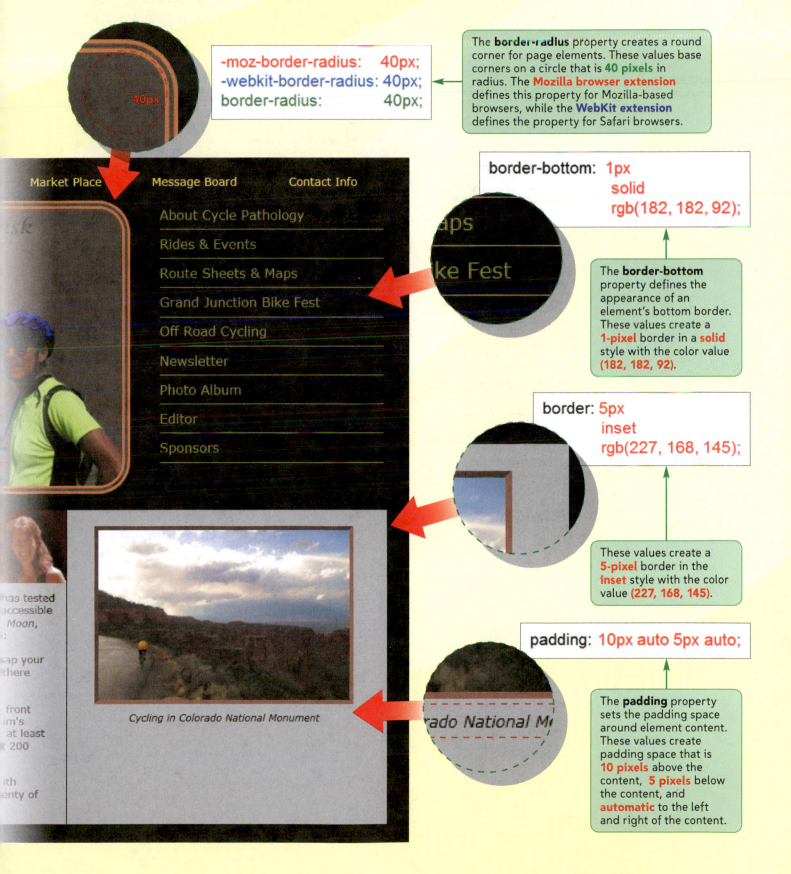

-moz-border-radius: 40px;
-webkit-border-radius: 40px;
border-radius: 40px;

The **border-radius** property creates a round corner for page elements. These values base corners on a circle that is **40 pixels** in radius. The **Mozilla browser extension** defines this property for Mozilla-based browsers, while the **WebKit extension** defines the property for Safari browsers.

border-bottom: 1px
               solid
               rgb(182, 182, 92);

The **border-bottom** property defines the appearance of an element's bottom border. These values create a **1-pixel** border in a **solid** style with the color value **(182, 182, 92)**.

border: 5px
        inset
        rgb(227, 168, 145);

These values create a **5-pixel** border in the **inset** style with the color value **(227, 168, 145)**.

padding: 10px auto 5px auto;

The **padding** property sets the padding space around element content. These values create padding space that is **10 pixels** above the content, **5 pixels** below the content, and **automatic** to the left and right of the content.

Market Place   Message Board   Contact Info

About Cycle Pathology

Rides & Events

Route Sheets & Maps

Grand Junction Bike Fest

Off Road Cycling

Newsletter

Photo Album

Editor

Sponsors

Cycling in Colorado National Monument

Setting Margins and Padding

You and Dan are continuing to work on the page layout for the Cycle Pathology home page. One layout principle suggests that the page should be divided into thirds with different page content placed in each of the three sections. You'll apply this general principle to the Cycle Pathology page (see Figure 4-25).

Figure 4-25   Page layout percentages

Based on the proposed layout for the page, you'll shift the horizontal navigation list and the president's message at the top of the page to the right, into the middle page section. One way to shift these two items is to change the margin space around those elements.

Margin Styles

Recall from Figure 4-4 in the last session that CSS uses the box model to format the space around element content. On the very outside of the box is the margin, separating one element from another. CSS supports several styles to set the size of this margin, including the properties

```
margin-top: length;
margin-right: length;
margin-bottom: length;
margin-left: length;
```

which set the sizes of the top, right, bottom, and left margins, respectively. Here, *length* is a length expressed in one of the CSS units of measure or a percentage of the containing element's width or height, or the keyword `auto` to allow browsers to automatically set the margin size for you. For example, the style rule

```
h1 {
    margin-top: 10px;
    margin-right: 20px;
    margin-bottom: 10px;
    margin-left: 20px;
}
```

creates margins of 10 pixels above and below every `h1` element, and margins of 20 pixels to the left and right of the heading.

These four margin styles can be combined into the single style

```
margin: top right bottom left;
```

where *top*, *right*, *bottom*, and *left* are the sizes of the top, right, bottom, and left margins, respectively. To help remember this order, think of moving clockwise around the element, starting with the top margin. The style rule

```
h1 {margin: 10px 20px 10px 20px;}
```

applies the same set of margins as in the previous code sample.

TIP

You can overlap page elements by specifying negative values for the margins.

You don't have to supply values for all of the margins. If you specify a single value, it's applied to all four sides equally. Likewise, two values set the top/bottom margins and the right/left margins, respectively. Finally, three values set the margins for the top, right/left, and bottom, respectively. For example, the style rule

```
h1 {margin: 10px 20px;}
```

applies a 10-pixel margin above and below every `h1` element, and a 20-pixel margin to the left and right. The style rule

```
h1 {margin: 10px;}
```

creates a 10-pixel margin around the entire heading.

REFERENCE

Setting Margin and Padding Space in the Box Model

- To set the margin space around an element, use

  `margin: length;`

  where *length* is the size of the margin using one of the CSS units of measure.
- To set the padding space within an element, use the following:

  `padding: length;`

- To set a margin or padding for one side of the box model only, specify the direction (top, right, bottom, or left). For example, use

  `margin-right: length;`

  to set the length of the right margin.
- To set multiple margin or padding spaces, specify the values in a space-separated list starting from the top and moving clockwise around the element. For example, the style

  `margin: top right bottom left;`

  sets margins for the top, right, bottom, and left sides of the element, respectively.
- To set matching top and bottom values and matching right and left values for margins and padding, enter only two values. For example, the style

  `margin: vertical horizontal;`

  sets margins for the top and bottom sides of the element to the value specified by *vertical*, and sets margins for the right and left sides of the element to the value specified by *horizontal*.

Each browser's internal style sheet sets the margins around block elements such as paragraphs and headings. One part of most reset style sheets is a style rule that sets the default margin size to 0 pixels so the page designer explicitly can define the margins for all elements.

To define the default margin size:

1. Return to the **cp_reset.css** style sheet file in your text editor.

2. Locate the style rule that defines the default page element styles and add the following style property (see Figure 4-26):

   `margin: 0px;`

Figure 4-26 Setting the default margin size for every element

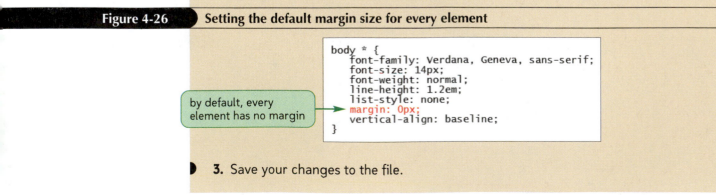

```
body * {
    font-family: Verdana, Geneva, sans-serif;
    font-size: 14px;
    font-weight: normal;
    line-height: 1.2em;
    list-style: none;
    margin: 0px;
    vertical-align: baseline;
}
```

by default, every element has no margin

3. Save your changes to the file.

Next, you'll change the left margins for the horizontal navigation list and the president's message so they are offset from the page's left edge by 33% of the page body width. You'll also resize the width of the navigation list to 66% of the total page width.

To change the margin spaces in the page:

1. Return to the **cp_styles.css** style sheet file in your text editor, and then directly below the comment *Horizontal Navigation List* add the following style rule:

```
nav.horizontalNAV {
    margin-left: 33%;
    width: 66%;
}
```

2. Scroll down to the style rule for the president's message and add the following style:

```
margin-left: 33%;
```

Figure 4-27 highlights the new and revised styles in the style sheet.

Figure 4-27   **Setting left margins**

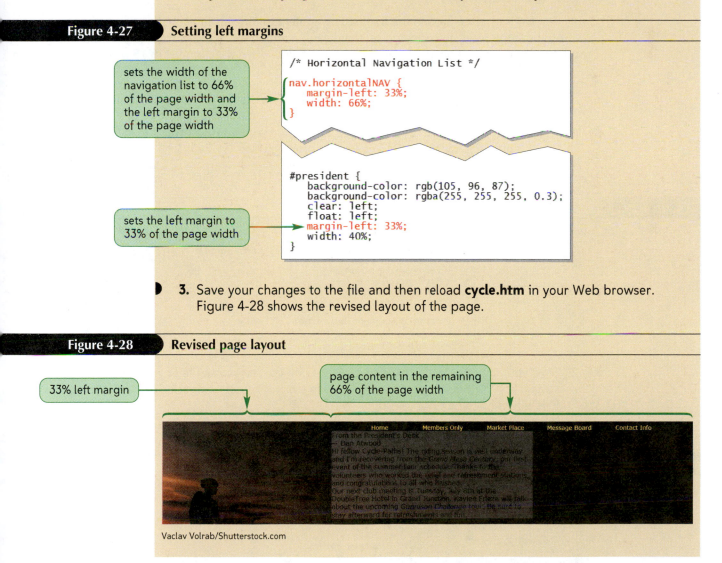

sets the width of the navigation list to 66% of the page width and the left margin to 33% of the page width

```
/* Horizontal Navigation List */

nav.horizontalNAV {
    margin-left: 33%;
    width: 66%;
}
```

```
#president {
    background-color: rgb(105, 96, 87);
    background-color: rgba(255, 255, 255, 0.3);
    clear: left;
    float: left;
    margin-left: 33%;
    width: 40%;
}
```

sets the left margin to 33% of the page width

3. Save your changes to the file and then reload **cycle.htm** in your Web browser. Figure 4-28 shows the revised layout of the page.

Figure 4-28   **Revised page layout**

33% left margin

page content in the remaining 66% of the page width

Home   Members Only   Market Place   Message Board   Contact Info

From the President's Desk
— Dan Atwood
Hi fellow Cycle-Paths! The riding season is well underway and I'm recovering from the Grand Mesa Century, our first event of the summer tour schedule. Thanks to the volunteers who worked the relief and refreshment stations, and congratulations to all who finished.
Our next club meeting is Tuesday, July 8th at the DoubleTree Hotel in Grand Junction. Kaylee Frieze will talk about the upcoming Gunnison Challenge tour. Be sure to stay afterward for refreshments and fun.

Vaclav Volrab/Shutterstock.com

Margin styles also can be applied to the body element. For example, by setting the margin around the page body to 0 pixels, you can remove the extra space many browsers insert by default between the page content and the edge of the browser window.

Padding Styles

While setting the default margin size to 0 pixels has made the appearance of page elements more predictable, it also has resulted in the navigation list crowding the president's message. You can increase the gap between them by increasing the padding around the text of the navigation links. Setting padding is similar to setting margins, with these separate styles available for specifying the padding space around element content

```
padding-top: length;
padding-right: length;
padding-bottom: length;
padding-left: length;
```

and the following style to set all of the padding spaces within one property:

```
padding: top right bottom left;
```

As with the `margin` property, you can specify any or all of the four padding values. When you specify a single value, it is applied to all four padding values. The style

```
h1 {padding: 5px;}
```

sets the padding space around the `h1` heading content to 5 pixels in each direction.

You'll use the reset style sheet to set the default padding for all elements to 0 pixels, and then you'll set the padding space above and below the navigation list to 15 pixels.

To modify the padding size:

1. Return to the **cp_reset.css** style sheet file in your text editor. Within the style rule for default page styles, add the following property (see Figure 4-29):

```
padding: 0px;
```

Figure 4-29 Setting the default padding size for every element

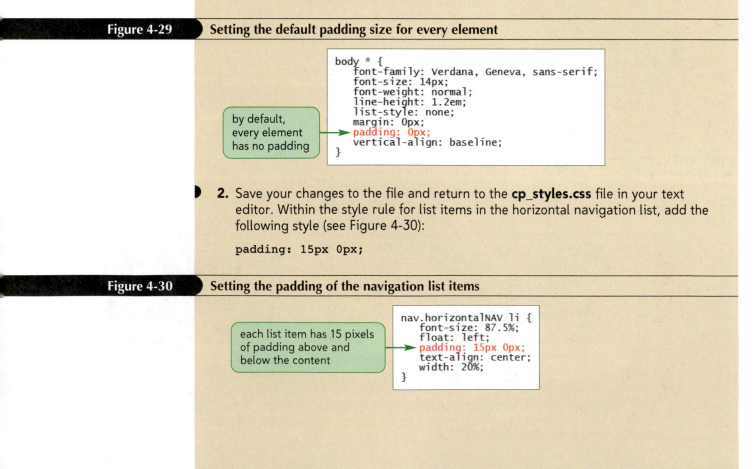

by default, every element has no padding

```
body * {
    font-family: Verdana, Geneva, sans-serif;
    font-size: 14px;
    font-weight: normal;
    line-height: 1.2em;
    list-style: none;
    margin: 0px;
    padding: 0px;
    vertical-align: baseline;
}
```

2. Save your changes to the file and return to the **cp_styles.css** file in your text editor. Within the style rule for list items in the horizontal navigation list, add the following style (see Figure 4-30):

```
padding: 15px 0px;
```

Figure 4-30 Setting the padding of the navigation list items

each list item has 15 pixels of padding above and below the content

```
nav.horizontalNAV li {
    font-size: 87.5%;
    float: left;
    padding: 15px 0px;
    text-align: center;
    width: 20%;
}
```

This style sets the top and bottom padding space to 15 pixels, and the right and left padding space to 0 pixels.

3. Save your changes to the file and then reload **cycle.htm** in your Web browser. Verify that additional space has been added above and below the horizontal navigation list.

Dan has several style rules he wants you to apply to the elements within the president's message. Complete the formatting of this page object by revising the *cp_styles.css* style sheet file.

To format the headings in the president's message:

1. Return to the **cp_styles.css** style sheet file in your text editor.

2. Add the following style rule at the bottom of the file to display the h1 heading in the president's message in a bold cursive-style font that is 158% of the size of the default text, with 10-pixel margins above and to the left of the text content:

```
#president h1 {
    font-family: 'Lucida Calligraphy', 'Apple Chancery', cursive;
    font-size: 158%;
    font-weight: bold;
    margin: 10px 0px 0px 10px;
}
```

3. Below that style rule, add the following style rule to display the h2 heading in the president's message in a font size that is 105% of the size of the default text, with a 10-pixel margin below the text and a 15-pixel margin to the left of the text:

```
#president h2 {
    font-size: 105%;
    margin: 0px 0px 10px 15px;
}
```

Figure 4-31 shows the new style rules.

Figure 4-31   Styling the h1 and h2 headings

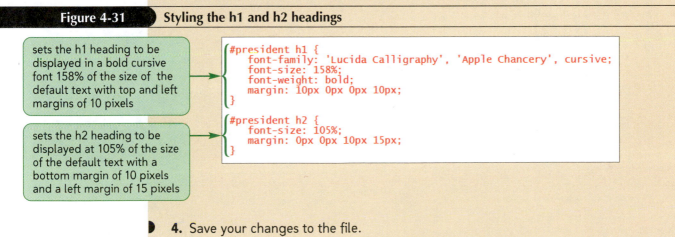

sets the h1 heading to be displayed in a bold cursive font 158% of the size of the default text with top and left margins of 10 pixels

```
#president h1 {
    font-family: 'Lucida Calligraphy', 'Apple Chancery', cursive;
    font-size: 158%;
    font-weight: bold;
    margin: 10px 0px 0px 10px;
}
```

sets the h2 heading to be displayed at 105% of the size of the default text with a bottom margin of 10 pixels and a left margin of 15 pixels

```
#president h2 {
    font-size: 105%;
    margin: 0px 0px 10px 15px;
}
```

4. Save your changes to the file.

Problem Solving: The Virtue of Being Negative

It's common to think of layout in terms of placing content, but good layout also must be concerned with placing emptiness. In art and page design, this is known as working with positive and negative space. Positive space is the part of the page occupied by text, graphics, borders, icons, and other page elements. Negative space, or white space, is the unoccupied area, and provides balance and contrast to elements contained in positive space.

A page that is packed with content leaves the eye with no place to rest; this also can mean that the eye has no place to focus and maybe even no clear indication about where to start reading. Instead, it's important to use negative space to direct users to resting stops before moving on to the next piece of page content. This can be done by providing a generous margin between page elements and by increasing the padding within an element. Even increasing the spacing between letters within an article heading can alleviate eye strain and make the text easier to read.

White space also has an emotional aspect. In the early days of print advertising, white space was seen as wasted space, and thus smaller magazines and direct mail advertisements would tend to crowd content together in order to reduce waste. By contrast, upscale magazines and papers could distinguish themselves from those publications with an excess of empty space. This difference carries over to the Web, where a page with less content and more white space often feels more classy and polished, while a page crammed with a lot of content feels more commercial. Both can be effective; you should decide which approach to use based on your customer profile.

The increase in screen sizes has reduced the need for designers to cram content into small spaces. The result has been a greater emphasis on designs that provide generous amounts of white space, which has improved the readability and visual appeal of Web pages.

Next, Dan wants to add a graphic image of himself in the background of the president's message box. He wants the image to be placed in the bottom-right corner of the box and sized to 40% of the width of the box. To make room for this image, you'll set the font size of the paragraph text to 87.5% of the default font size, and the right margins of the paragraphs to 40%. Note that in this context, a value of 40% refers not to the width of the page, but only to the width of the president's message box that contains the paragraphs.

To add the background image:

1. At the bottom of the **cp_styles.css** file, insert the following style rule to set the paragraph font size and margins (see Figure 4-32):

```
#president p {
    font-size: 87.5%;
    margin: 0px 40% 20px 15px;
}
```

Figure 4-32   **Setting the margin around the paragraph**

```
#president h2 {
    font-size: 105%;
    margin: 0px 0px 10px 15px;
}

#president p {
    font-size: 87.5%;
    margin: 0px 40% 20px 15px;
}
```

sets the paragraph margin to 20 pixels below, 15 pixels to the left, and 40% of the width of the president's message to the right

In this case, the margins are a mixture of absolute and relative lengths. The top, bottom, and left margins are set to 0 pixels, 20 pixels, and 15 pixels, respectively. The size of the right margin will depend on the size of the president's box, which in turn will vary depending on the width of the Web page.

Make sure you start every browser extension style with the - (hyphen) character.

2. Add the following properties to the `#president` selector style rule to define the source, position, tiling, and size of the background image (see Figure 4-33):

```
background-image: url(atwood.png);
background-position: bottom right;
background-repeat: no-repeat;

-o-background-size: 40%;
-moz-background-size: 40%;
-webkit-background-size: 40%;
background-size: 40%;
```

Figure 4-33   **Setting the padding of the navigation list items**

displays the atwood.png file as the background image in the bottom-right corner of the president's message

sets the width of the background image to 40% of the width of the president's message

```
#president {
    background-color: rgb(105, 96, 87);
    background-color: rgba(255, 255, 255, 0.3);
    background-image: url(atwood.png);
    background-position: bottom right;
    background-repeat: no-repeat;

    -o-background-size: 40%;
    -moz-background-size: 40%;
    -webkit-background-size: 40%;
    background-size: 40%;

    clear: left;
    float: left;
    margin-left: 33%;
    width: 40%;
}
```

progressive enhancement using browser extensions

Notice that the style rule uses progressive enhancement and vendor prefixes in order to provide support for the widest range of browsers and browser versions.

3. Save your changes to the file and then reload **cycle.htm** in your Web browser. Figure 4-34 shows the revised appearance of the president's message box.

Figure 4-34   **Formatted president's message**

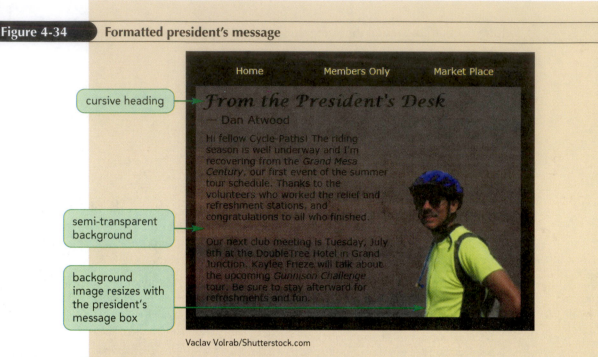

cursive heading

semi-transparent background

background image resizes with the president's message box

Vaclav Volrab/Shutterstock.com

▶ **4.** If you have a widescreen monitor in which you can change the width of the browser window from 1000 to 1400 pixels, resize the browser window and verify that the placement of the page elements and the size of the *atwood.png* background image change in response.

The next item on the Cycle Pathology home page is the vertical navigation list. Dan wants this list floated alongside the president's message. You'll redisplay that item and float it now.

To redisplay the vertical navigation list:

▶ **1.** Return to the **cp_reset.css** style sheet in your text editor and remove the selector `nav.verticalNAV` and the comma that follows it from the last style rule. Save your changes to the file.

▶ **2.** Go to the **cp_styles.css** style sheet in your text editor. At the bottom of the file, insert the following style rules to format the vertical navigation list (see Figure 4-35):

```
/* Vertical Navigation List */

nav.verticalNAV {
    float: left;
    margin-left: 3%;
    width: 23%;
}
nav.verticalNAV a {
    color: rgb(182, 182, 92);
    line-height: 2.2em;
}
```

Figure 4-35   **Redisplaying the vertical navigation list**

sets the width of the vertical navigation list to 23% of the page width, floated on the left, with a left margin of 3%

sets the color of the hyperlinks to a light yellow and the line height to 2.2 em units

```
/* Vertical Navigation List */

nav.verticalNAV {
    float: left;
    margin-left: 3%;
    width: 23%;
}

nav.verticalNAV a {
    color: rgb(182, 182, 92);
    line-height: 2.2em;
}
```

3. Save your changes to the file and then reload **cycle.htm** in your browser. Figure 4-36 shows the revised appearance of the page.

Figure 4-36   **Vertical navigation list**

33% left margin

president's message and navigation list are floated on the left of the margin

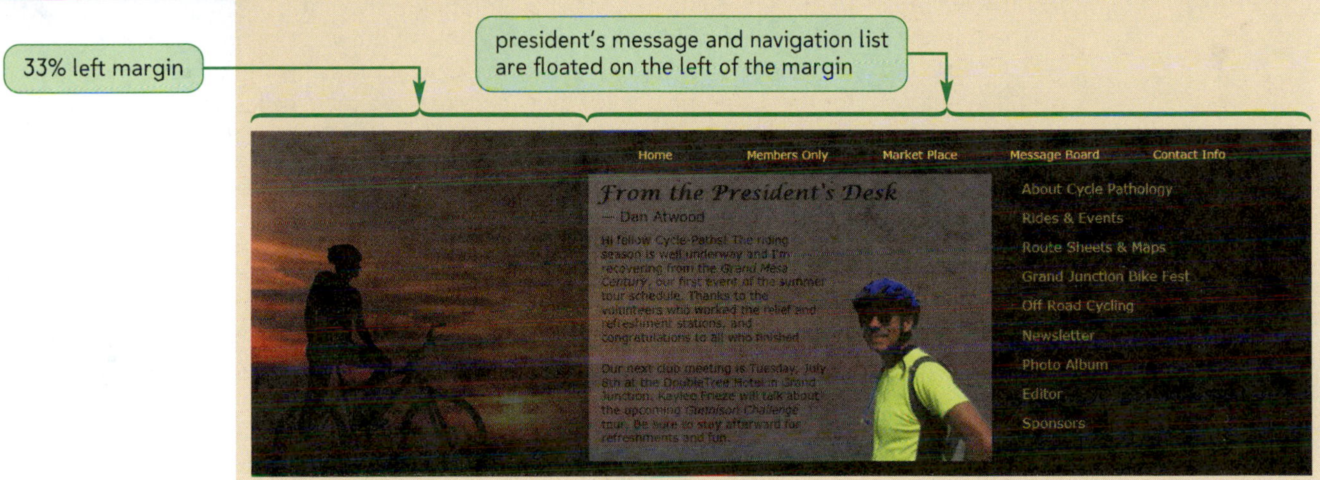

Vaclav Volrab/Shutterstock.com

Keeping It Centered

Many page layouts are based on centering objects either horizontally or vertically. You've already learned how to horizontally center inline elements using the following style:

```
text-align: center;
```

However, while this will center a block's contents, it won't center the entire block itself. To do that, you set the left and right margin values to `auto`. For example, the following style rule horizontally centers every paragraph in a Web page while also setting the top and bottom margins to 10 pixels:

```
p {
    margin: 10px auto;
    width: 600px;
}
```

Note that you must define the width of the block element or else the block will assume the entire width of its container, making centering irrelevant.

There is no CSS style to vertically center a block element, but you can find several workarounds on the Web to accomplish the trick. One approach is to create a container element for the block and display that container as a table cell with the `vertical-align` property set to `middle`. For example, to vertically center an h1 heading, you could place it within a `div` container, as in the code

```
<div>
    <h1>Cycle Pathology</h1>
</div>
```

and apply the style rule

```
div {
    display: table-cell;
    vertical-align: middle;
}
```

Note that this approach does not work with Internet Explorer versions before IE8 because those versions do not support the `table-cell` value for the `display` property. You'll learn more about tables and table cells in the next tutorial.

Another trick for vertically centering a block element is to use the `display` property to make the element into an inline element. You then can vertically center it by setting the line height equal to the height of the container box itself. This approach has the added benefit of enabling you to use the `text-align` property to horizontally center it at the same time. The disadvantage is that the element is no longer a block and thus may not be suitable as a container for other elements.

You'll examine one additional vertical centering technique in the next session on absolute and relative positioning.

Working with Borders

Dan wants you to format the vertical navigation list so that each list item has a bottom border; and when a user hovers the mouse pointer over the hypertext link, the background color of the entire length of the list item is highlighted (see Figure 4-37).

Figure 4-37   **Hover style for the vertical navigation list**

About Cycle Pathology

Rides & Events

Route Sheets & Maps

Grand Junction Bike Fest

Off Road Cycling

Newsletter

Photo Album

Editor

Sponsors

About Cycle Pathology

Rides & Events

Route Sheets & Maps

Grand Junction Bike Fest

Off Road Cycling

Newsletter

Photo Album

Editor

Sponsors

bottom border added to each hypertext link

hover effect changes the background color to a semi-transparent white

Vaclav Volrab/Shutterstock.com

To create this effect, you'll work with the CSS border styles.

Setting Border Width and Color

CSS supports several style properties to format the border around each element. As with the margin and padding styles, you can apply a style to the top, right, bottom, or left border, or to all borders at once. To define the thickness of a border, use the style properties

```
border-top-width: width;
border-right-width: width;
border-bottom-width: width;
border-left-width: width;
```

where `width` is defined as a percentage or as one of the CSS units of measure. Border widths also can be expressed using the keywords `thin`, `medium`, or `thick`; the exact application of these keywords depends on the browser. You also can define the border thickness using the following single style property:

```
border-width: top right bottom left;
```

As with the `margin` and `padding` properties, if you enter one value, it's applied to all four borders; two values set the width of the top/bottom and left/right borders, respectively; and three values are applied to the top, left/right, and bottom borders, in that order.

You set the border color with the style properties

```
border-top-color: color;
border-right-color: color;
border-bottom-color: color;
border-left-color: color;

border-color: top right bottom left;
```

where *color* is a color name, color value, or the keyword `transparent` to create an invisible border. For example, the following style rule adds a 4-pixel red border directly above the `address` element:

```
address {
    border-top-width: 4px;
    border-top-color: red;
}
```

Setting the Border Design

CSS allows you to further define the appearance of borders using the border styles

```
border-top-style: style;
border-right-style: style;
border-bottom-style: style;
border-left-style: style;


border-style: top right bottom left;
```

where *style* is one of the nine border styles displayed in Figure 4-38. The CSS3 specifications also include the `wavy`, `dot-dash`, and `dot-dot-dash` styles, but they have little browser support at the time of this writing.

| Figure 4-38 | Border style designs |

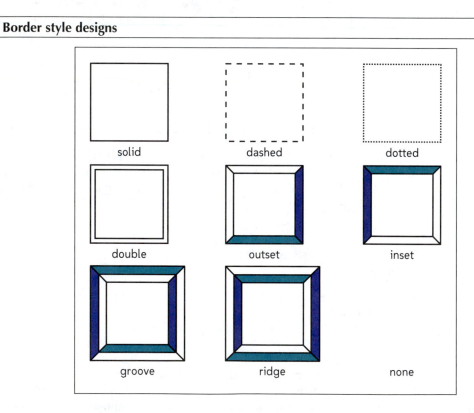

You specify styles for different sides in the same way you do for padding or margins. For example, the style

```
border-style-bottom: double single;
```

places a double border above and below the element, and a single border on the element's left and right edges.

TIP

Browsers will render a border correctly no matter the order in which you specify the *width*, *style*, and *color* values.

All of the border styles discussed above can be combined into a single style that defines each or all of the borders around the element. The syntax of these border styles is

```
border-top: width style color;
border-right: width style color;
border-bottom: width style color;
border-left: width style color;

border: width style color;
```

where *width* is the thickness of the border, *style* is the style of the border, and *color* is the border color. Thus, the style rule

```
h1 {border: 2px solid blue;}
```

adds a 2-pixel-wide solid blue border around every `h1` heading.

REFERENCE

Setting Border Styles in the Box Model

- To set the border width, use the property

  ```
  border-width: width;
  ```

  where *width* is the thickness of the border using one of the CSS units of measure.
- To set the border color, use

  ```
  border-color: color;
  ```

  where *color* is a color name or value.
- To set the border design, use

  ```
  border-style: style;
  ```

  where *style* is none, solid, dashed, dotted, double, outset, inset, groove, or ridge.
- To set all of the border options in one style, use the following:

  ```
  border: width color style;
  ```

You'll use the CSS border styles to add a bottom border to each hypertext link in the vertical navigation list. To extend the bottom border across the complete width of the list, you'll also change the `display` property of each hyperlink to block. By default, block-level elements have a width equal to the width of their containing element unless a different width is set by the page design.

To add a bottom border to the hypertext links:

1. Return to the **cp_styles.css** file in your text editor.

2. Within the style rule for the `nav.verticalNAV a` selector, add the following styles in alphabetical order within the curly braces as indicated in Figure 4-39:

```
border-bottom: 1px solid rgb(182, 182, 92);
display: block;
```

3. At the bottom of the file, add the following style rule to change the background color of the hyperlinks in the vertical navigation list in response to the hover event:

```
nav.verticalNAV a:hover {
    background-color: rgb(105, 96, 87);
    background-color: rgba(255, 255, 255, 0.3);
}
```

Figure 4-39 highlights the new code in the file.

Figure 4-39 **Adding a border to the hyperlinks**

displays each hyperlink as a block element with a light yellow bottom border

```
nav.verticalNAV a {
    border-bottom: 1px solid rgb(182, 182, 92);
    color: rgb(182, 182, 92);
    display: block;
    line-height: 2.2em;
}
```

changes the background color to medium gray or a semi-transparent white during the hover event

```
nav.verticalNAV a:hover {
    background-color: rgb(105, 96, 87);
    background-color: rgba(255, 255, 255, 0.3);
}
```

4. Save your changes to the file and reload **cycle.htm** in your Web browser. Verify that the hyperlinks now display a bottom border with the hover effect shown earlier in Figure 4-37.

Creating Rounded Corners

Dan thinks the current layout is too boxy and would like to soften the design by adding curves to some of the page elements. Specifically, he would like you to add rounded corners to the president's message box. Rounded corners can be applied to any of the four corners of a block element using the styles

```
border-top-left-radius: radius;
border-top-right-radius: radius;
border-bottom-right-radius: radius;
border-bottom-left-radius: radius;

border-radius: top-left top-right bottom-right bottom-left;
```

where *radius* is the radius of the rounded corner in one of the CSS units of measurement and *top-left*, *top-right*, *bottom-right*, and *bottom-left* are the radii of the individual corners. The radii are equal to the radii of hypothetical circles placed at the corners of the box with the arcs of the circles defining the rounded corners (see Figure 4-40).

Figure 4-40   **Setting the corner radii**

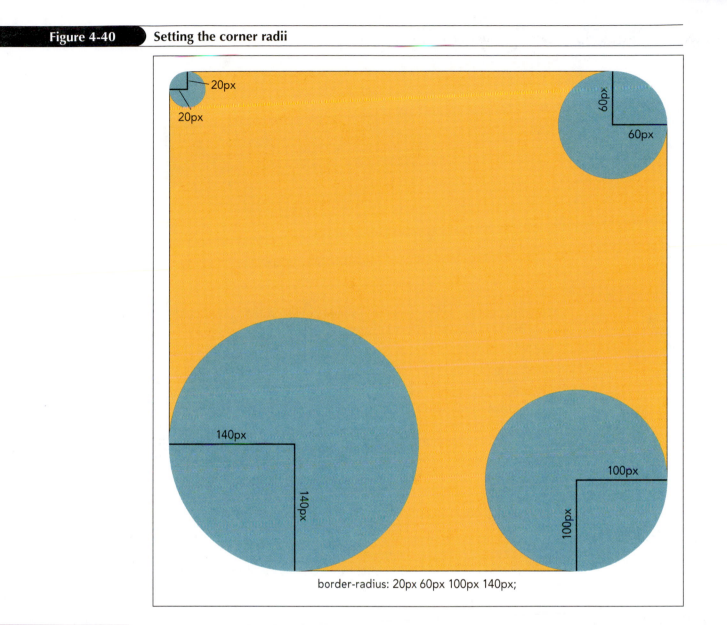

border-radius: 20px 60px 100px 140px;

If you enter only one value for the `border-radius` property, that radius is applied to all four corners; if you enter two values, the first is applied to the top-left and bottom-right corners, and the second is applied to the top-right and bottom-left corners. If you specify three radii, they are applied to the top-left, top-right/bottom-left, and bottom-right corners, in that order.

Elongated Corners

The CSS rounded-corner model also allows designers to create elongated or elliptical corners by specifying two values for the radius separated by a slash

    horizontal/vertical

where *horizontal* is the horizontal radius and *vertical* is the vertical radius (see Figure 4-41).

Figure 4-41 Creating an elongated corner

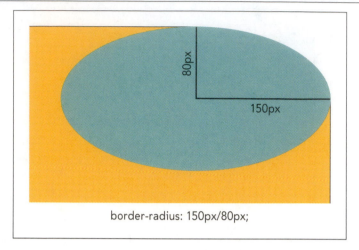

border-radius: 150px/80px;

To apply an elongated corner to a single corner, you do *not* include the slash between the horizontal and vertical radii. For example, to create an elongated bottom-left corner, you could apply the style

```
border-bottom-left-radius: 150px 80px;
```

which would set the horizontal radius of the bottom-left corner to 150 pixels and the vertical radius to 80 pixels.

Rounded and elongated corners do not clip element content. If the content of the element extends into the corner, it still will be displayed as part of the background. Because this is often unsightly, you should avoid heavily rounded or elongated corners unless you can be sure they will not obscure or distract from the element content.

Browser Extensions to Rounded Corners

Rounded corners were first introduced in both the WebKit and Mozilla browser extensions. The syntax is largely the same as that adopted by CSS3 except when applied to individual corners. Figure 4-42 compares the syntax of three versions of the rounded corner style.

Figure 4-42 Browser extensions to the rounded corner styles

CSS3	Mozilla	WebKit
border-radius	-moz-border-radius	-webkit-border-radius
border-top-right-radius	-moz-border-radius-topright	-webkit-border-top-right-radius
border-bottom-right-radius	-moz-border-radius-bottomright	-webkit-border-bottom-right-radius
border-bottom-left-radius	-moz-border-radius-bottomleft	-webkit-border-bottom-left-radius
border-top-left-radius	-moz-border-radius-topleft	-webkit-border-top-left-radius

For example, you would use progressive enhancement to set the radius of the top-right corner to 15 pixels with the following style values:

```
-moz-border-radius-topright: 15px;
-webkit-border-top-right-radius: 15px;
border-top-right-radius: 15px;
```

The other important difference is that the WebKit extension separates horizontal and vertical radii with a space rather than with a slash. Thus, to create elongated corners of 45 pixels wide and 15 pixels high, you would enter the following style values:

```
-moz-border-radius: 45px/15px;
-webkit-border-radius: 45px 15px;
border-radius: 45px/15px;
```

The current versions of both Firefox and Safari have adopted the CSS3 standard. You need to use the browser extension only if you have to support earlier versions of those browsers. Internet Explorer does not support rounded corners until IE9. There are work-arounds for Internet Explorer users involving nested `div` elements with background images displaying rounded corners, but they are difficult and cumbersome to create. As long as the rounded corners are used only to enhance your page's appearance and are not an essential part of understanding your page's content, you should feel free to use the CSS3 styles even with browsers that don't support them.

Modify your style sheet now to add 30-pixel rounded corners to the president's message box.

To create rounded corners:

1. Return to the **cp_styles.css** file in your text editor.

2. Within the style rule for the `#president` selector, add the following style properties as shown in Figure 4-43:

```
-moz-border-radius: 30px;
-webkit-border-radius: 30px;
border-radius: 30px;
```

Figure 4-43   Specifying the border radius

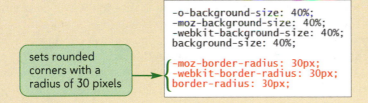

3. Save your changes to the file and then reload **cycle.htm** in your Web browser. As shown in Figure 4-44, the president's message should now display rounded corners.

Figure 4-44   **Rounded corners for the president's message**

Vaclav Volrab/Shutterstock.com

Creating an Irregular Line Wrap

Many desktop publishing and word-processing programs allow designers to create irregular line wraps in which the text appears to flow tightly around an image. This is not easily done in Web page design because all inline images appear as rectangles rather than as irregularly shaped objects. However, with the aid of a graphics package, you can simulate an irregularly shaped image.

The trick is to use your graphics package to slice the image horizontally into several pieces and then crop the individual slices to match the edge of the image you want to display. Once you've edited all of the slices, you can use CSS to stack the separate slices by floating them on the left or right margin, displaying each slice only after the previous slice has been cleared. For example, the following style rule stacks inline images on the right margin:

```
img {
    clear: right;
    float: right;
    margin-top: 0px;
    margin-bottom: 0px;
}
```

Always set the top and bottom margins to 0 pixels so that the slices join together seamlessly. You can see an example of this technique in Figure 4-78 as part of Case Problem 1 at the end of this tutorial.

Managing Your Layout

In layout design, you must be very aware of the width taken up by your page elements. If the total width allotted to an element extends beyond its container, the element will wrap to a new line, ruining your layout. The width taken up by an element is calculated as follows:

```
total width = content width + padding + border width
```

Thus, the style rule

```
div {
    border: 5px solid black;
    padding: 10px;
    width: 600px;
}
```

sets the total width allotted to the div element to 600 + 2(10) + 2(5) = 630 pixels. Note that this calculation must include the widths of both the left and right borders and padding space. In addition to knowing each element's total width, you also must keep track of the margin spaces around your elements if you want to ensure that your content will fit nicely within the width of your Web page.

Older versions of Internet Explorer calculated widths differently from the CSS standard. In those versions, the width property set the total width of an element including the content, padding, and border. Thus, a div element with the above style rule would measure 600 pixels wide, not 630, as Internet Explorer would assign only 570 pixels to the element content, leaving 20 pixels for the left and right padding and 10 pixels for the left and right borders. To avoid confusion—and to avoid ruining your layouts—always include a DOCTYPE declaration in your HTML file to put Internet Explorer and other browsers into Standards mode rather than Quirks mode. For a discussion of Standards vs. Quirks mode, see Tutorial 1.

Using the Outline Style

One way of simplifying your layout width calculations is to avoid using left and right padding. Instead, you can set the left and right padding to 0 pixels and separate your elements using only the left and right margins. In some cases, you also can replace your borders with outlines. An outline is a line drawn around an element; but unlike borders, an outline does not add to the total space allotted to an element, nor does it affect the position of the element in the page. Unlike borders, outlines also can be non-rectangular in shape (see Figure 4-45).

Figure 4-45   **Applying an irregularly shaped outline**

An outline covering a span of text within a paragraph

Our next club meeting is Tuesday, July 8th at the DoubleTree Hotel in Grand Junction. Kaylee Frieze will talk about the upcoming *Gunnison Challenge* tour. Be sure to stay afterwards for refreshments and fun.

An outline width is defined using the style property

```
outline-width: value;
```

where *value* is expressed in one of the CSS units of length, or with the keywords thin, medium, or thick. Outline colors are defined using the property

```
outline-color: color;
```

where *color* is a CSS color name or value. Finally, the outline design is defined using the style property

```
outline-style: style;
```

where *style* is one of the design styles listed in Figure 4-46.

Figure 4-46   **Outline design styles**

Value	Description
none	No outline is displayed
dotted	Outline is dotted
dashed	Outline is dashed
solid	Outline is a single solid line
groove	Creates the effect of an outline carved into the page
ridge	Creates the effect of an outline raised from the page
inset	Creates the effect of an outline embedded in the page
outset	Creates the effect of an outline coming out of the page
double	Outline is a double line

All of the outline styles can be combined into the shorthand property

```
outline: width color style;
```

just as you did with the margin, padding, and border styles. Note that there are no separate outline styles for left, right, top, or bottom. The outline always surrounds an entire element.

Outlines often are used to highlight interesting or important page content. Another use is to diagram your layout as an aid in page design. Because outlines take up no space, you can use them to mark the size and location of every page element by using the following style rule:

```
* {
    outline: 1px solid red;
}
```

REFERENCE

Adding an Outline

• To add an outline around an element, use the style property

```
outline: width color style;
```

where *width*, *color*, and *style* are the outline width, outline color, and outline style, respectively.

You'll try this now with the Cycle Pathology page to highlight the placement of each of the page elements you've displayed thus far.

To view the layout structure:

1. Return to the **cp_styles.css** file in your text editor.

2. At the bottom of the file, insert the following style rule:

```
* {
    outline: 1px solid red;
}
```

3. Save your changes to the file and then reload **cycle.htm** in your Web browser. As shown in Figure 4-47, each element in the page is outlined in red, showing its exact width, height, and location under your current design.

Figure 4-47	Outlining the page layout

Vaclav Volrab/Shutterstock.com

4. Return to the **cp_styles.css** file in your text editor and remove the style rule you created in Step 2. Save your changes to the file.

Putting It All Together

The next part of the Cycle Pathology page is the article written by Kathy Rawlings about cycling on Rim Rock Drive. The article is contained within a `section` element with the id *story* along with a figure box showing a cyclist on Rim Rock Drive. Dan wants the story section aligned with the president's message, with the article and the figure box placed side-by-side. To format these elements, you'll use all of the CSS tools you've learned about so far.

First, you'll edit the reset style sheet to re-display the story section and its contents; then you'll set the location of these elements in the Web page.

To display the story section:

1. Return to the **cp_reset.css** file in your text editor and then go to the style rule at the bottom of the file that hides page elements. Remove the selector *#story* and the comma that follows it from the style rule, and then save your changes to the file.

2. Return to the **cp_styles.css** file in your style sheet.

3. At the bottom of the file, add the following style rule to align the story section directly below the president's message, separated by a 20-pixel vertical margin:

```
/* Story section styles */

#story {
    background-color: gray;
    background-color: rgba(255, 255, 255, 0.8);
    clear: left;
    float: left;
    margin: 20px 0px 0px 33%;
    width: 66%;
}
```

4. Below the style rule you just added, add the following two style rules to float the article and figure box side-by-side, with each one taking up about half of the width of the story section:

```
/* Article styles */

#story article {
    border-right: 1px solid black;
    float: left;
    width: 50%;
}

/* Figure box styles */

#story figure {
    float: left;
    width: 49%;
}
```

Figure 4-48 highlights and further describes the new style rules you just entered into the style sheet.

Figure 4-48   **Styles for the story section**

displays the story section when the left margin is clear; floats the section on the left with a top margin of 20 pixels and a left margin of 33%; sets the background color to gray or semi-transparent white

floats the article on the left within the story section with a solid right border; sets the width of the article to half of the story section width

floats the figure box on the left with a width of about half that of the story section

```
/* Story section styles */

#story {
    background-color: gray;
    background-color: rgba(255, 255, 255, 0.8);
    clear: left;
    float: left;
    margin: 20px 0px 0px 33%;
    width: 66%;
}

/* Article styles */

#story article {
    border-right: 1px solid black;
    float: left;
    width: 50%;
}

/* Figure box styles */

#story figure {
    float: left;
    width: 49%;
}
```

5. Save your changes to the file and then reload **cycle.htm** in your Web browser. Figure 4-49 shows the placement of the story section as well as the Rim Rock Drive article and figure box within it.

Figure 4-49   **Placement of the story section**

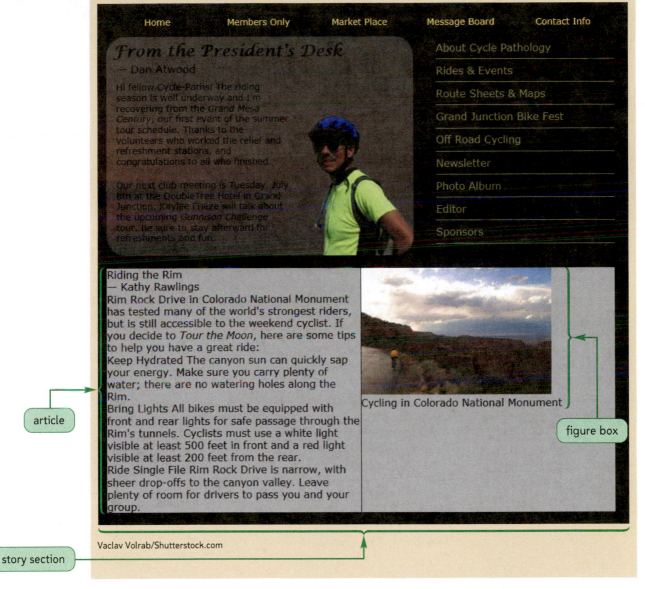

Vaclav Volrab/Shutterstock.com

The first part of the Rim Rock Drive article you'll format is the heading group. Dan wants the h1 and h2 headings displayed in a light brown font on a dark brown background. Furthermore, he wants the heading group resized to 90 pixels high with a background image of Kathy Rawlings displayed in the bottom-right corner of the box. You'll format the article heading now.

To format the article heading:

1. Return to the **cp_styles.css** file in your text editor. Directly below the style rule for the `story article` selector, insert the following rules to format the size, background, and text of the article heading group:

```
#story article hgroup {
    background: rgb(97, 30, 2) url(rawlings.png) bottom right
no-repeat;

    -o-background-size: contain;
    -moz-background-size: contain;
    -webkit-background-size: contain;
    background-size: contain;

    color: rgb(145, 98, 78);
    color: rgba(255, 255, 255, 0.3);

    height: 90px;
    text-indent: 10px;
}
```

2. Set the size of the `h1` heading in the article to 158% of the default font size, and set the kerning to 3 pixels by adding the following rule directly below the rule you created in Step 1:

```
#story article hgroup h1 {
    font-size: 158%;
    letter-spacing: 3px;
}
```

3. Finally, set the size of the `h2` headings to 105% of the default font size by adding the following style rule directly below the rule you created in Step 2:

```
#story article hgroup h2 {
    font-size: 105%;
}
```

Figure 4-50 shows the newly added style rules.

Figure 4-50   **Formatting the article heading**

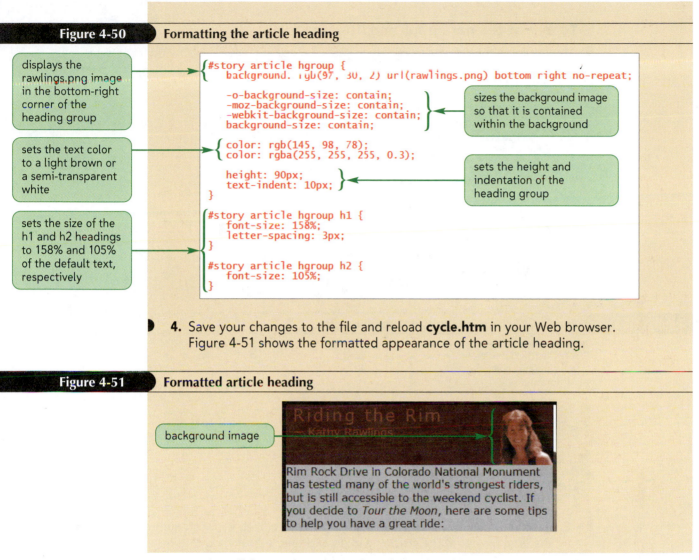

displays the rawlings.png image in the bottom-right corner of the heading group

sets the text color to a light brown or a semi-transparent white

sets the size of the h1 and h2 headings to 158% and 105% of the default text, respectively

```
#story article hgroup {
    background. rgb(97, 30, 2) url(rawlings.png) bottom right no-repeat;

    -o-background-size: contain;
    -moz-background-size: contain;
    -webkit-background-size: contain;
    background-size: contain;

    color: rgb(145, 98, 78);
    color: rgba(255, 255, 255, 0.3);

    height: 90px;
    text-indent: 10px;
}

#story article hgroup h1 {
    font-size: 158%;
    letter-spacing: 3px;
}

#story article hgroup h2 {
    font-size: 105%;
}
```

sizes the background image so that it is contained within the background

sets the height and indentation of the heading group

4. Save your changes to the file and reload **cycle.htm** in your Web browser. Figure 4-51 shows the formatted appearance of the article heading.

Figure 4-51   **Formatted article heading**

background image

Rim Rock Drive in Colorado National Monument has tested many of the world's strongest riders, but is still accessible to the weekend cyclist. If you decide to *Tour the Moon*, here are some tips to help you have a great ride:

Next, you'll format the paragraph and unordered list text. Dan wants the font size of both of these elements to be 80% of the default font size. He also wants you to increase the margin space around the paragraphs and list items.

To format the paragraph and list items:

1. Return to the **cp_styles.css** file in your text editor. Directly below the style rule for the h2 heading you created in the last set of steps, add the following rules (see Figure 4-52):

```
#story article p {
    font-size: 80%;
    margin: 10px;
}

#story article ul li {
    font-size: 80%;
    margin: 15px 25px;
}

#story article ul li strong {
    font-weight: bold;
}
```

Figure 4-52   **Formatting the paragraph and unordered list**

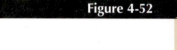

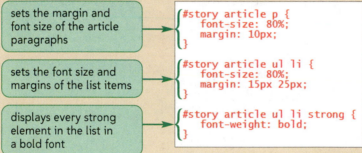

sets the margin and font size of the article paragraphs

```
#story article p {
    font-size: 80%;
    margin: 10px;
}
```

sets the font size and margins of the list items

```
#story article ul li {
    font-size: 80%;
    margin: 15px 25px;
}
```

displays every strong element in the list in a bold font

```
#story article ul li strong {
    font-weight: bold;
}
```

2. Save your changes and reload **cycle.htm** in your Web browser. Figure 4-53 shows the final format of the article heading and text.

Figure 4-53   **Formatted article heading and text**

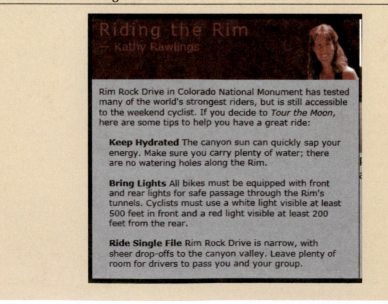

Riding the Rim
— Kathy Rawlings

Rim Rock Drive in Colorado National Monument has tested many of the world's strongest riders, but is still accessible to the weekend cyclist. If you decide to *Tour the Moon*, here are some tips to help you have a great ride:

Keep Hydrated The canyon sun can quickly sap your energy. Make sure you carry plenty of water; there are no watering holes along the Rim.

Bring Lights All bikes must be equipped with front and rear lights for safe passage through the Rim's tunnels. Cyclists must use a white light visible at least 500 feet in front and a red light visible at least 200 feet from the rear.

Ride Single File Rim Rock Drive is narrow, with sheer drop-offs to the canyon valley. Leave plenty of room for drivers to pass you and your group.

Finally, you'll format the contents of the figure box. One of these items is the inline image displaying the cyclist on Rim Rock Drive. You'll change the inline image into a block element and then center it horizontally within the figure box by setting its left and right margins to `auto` (see the Insight Box *Keeping It Centered* from earlier in this session for details on this setting). Dan also wants the size of the image to be based on the size of the figure box. Therefore, you'll set the image width to 80% of the figure box width so that browsers will determine the height automatically. You'll also add a 5-pixel-wide light brown inset border, and you'll center the figure caption, reduce its font size, and display the caption text in italic.

To format the figure box:

1. Return to the **cp_styles.css** file in your text editor. At the bottom of the style sheet, insert the following rules (see Figure 4-54):

```
#story figure img {
    border: 5px inset rgb(227, 168, 145);
    display: block;
    margin: 30px auto 10px;
    width: 80%;
}

#story figure figcaption {
    font-size: 75%;
    font-style: italic;
    text-align: center;
}
```

Figure 4-54 Style rules for the image and figure caption

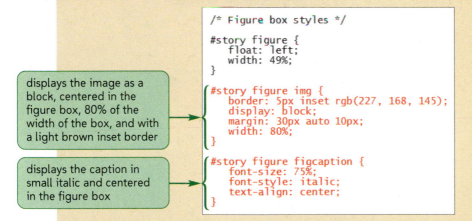

displays the image as a block, centered in the figure box, 80% of the width of the box, and with a light brown inset border

displays the caption in small italic and centered in the figure box

```
/* Figure box styles */

#story figure {
    float: left;
    width: 49%;
}

#story figure img {
    border: 5px inset rgb(227, 168, 145);
    display: block;
    margin: 30px auto 10px;
    width: 80%;
}

#story figure figcaption {
    font-size: 75%;
    font-style: italic;
    text-align: center;
}
```

2. Save your changes and then reload **cycle.htm** in your Web browser. Figure 4-55 shows the current state of the story section.

Figure 4-55   **Formatted figure box**

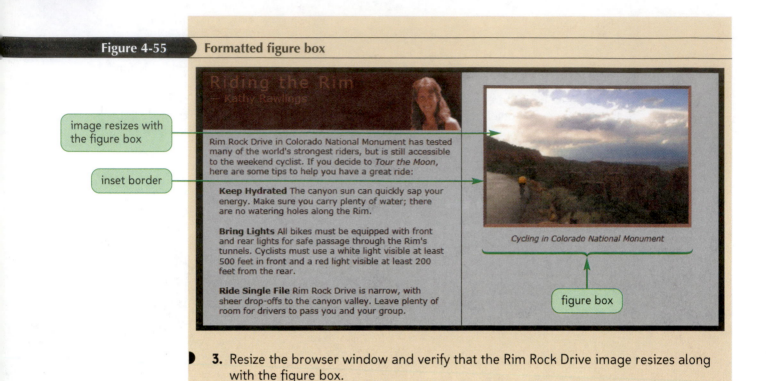

3. Resize the browser window and verify that the Rim Rock Drive image resizes along with the figure box.

You've completed your work on margins, padding space, and borders, and you've learned how to add special visual effects to your page elements through the use of rounded and elongated corners. The Cycle Pathology Web page is not finished yet, however; you still have to display the page header and the list of upcoming cycling events. You'll complete these tasks and others in the next session.

Session 4.2 Quick Check

1. Provide a style rule to set the margin space around the `header` element to 20 pixels above and below, and 30 pixels to the left and right.

2. Provide a style property that sets the padding space around every `article` element to 10 pixels on every side.

3. Provide a style rule to display every `footer` element with a 5-pixel solid red top border.

4. You want the `h1` heading with the id *mainHeading* to be displayed with a double green border 8 pixels wide. Provide the style rule.

5. Provide a style rule to display all hypertext links within a navigation list as block elements with a gray background, and with rounded corners 10 pixels in radius. Your rule should be accessible under CSS3 and all browser extensions.

6. Provide a style rule to display all `div` elements with elongated corners that have a 15-pixel horizontal radius and a 5-pixel vertical radius. Your code should work with all browser extensions and browsers that support CSS3.

7. What is the difference between a border and an outline?

8. Describe how the following style rule would differ in application between Internet Explorer running in Quirks mode and Internet Explorer running in Standards mode:

```
#mainHead {
    border: 10px solid blue;
    padding: 5px;
    width: 550px;
}
```

SESSION 4.3 VISUAL OVERVIEW

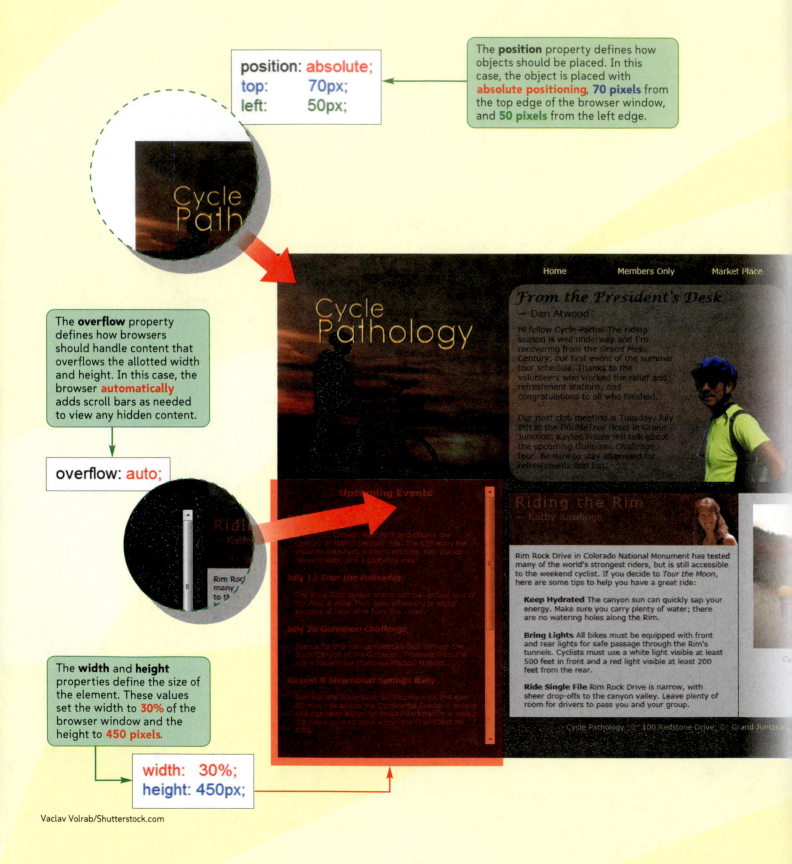

position: absolute;
top: 70px;
left: 50px;

The **position** property defines how objects should be placed. In this case, the object is placed with **absolute positioning**, **70 pixels** from the top edge of the browser window, and **50 pixels** from the left edge.

The **overflow** property defines how browsers should handle content that overflows the allotted width and height. In this case, the browser **automatically** adds scroll bars as needed to view any hidden content.

overflow: auto;

The **width** and **height** properties define the size of the element. These values set the width to **30%** of the browser window and the height to **450 pixels**.

width: 30%;
height: 450px;

Home   Members Only   Market Place

Cycle Pathology

From the President's Desk
— Dan Atwood

HI fellow Cycle-Paths! The riding season is well underway and I'm recovering from the *Grand Mesa Century*, our first event of the summer tour schedule. Thanks to the volunteers who worked the relief and refreshment stations, and congratulations to all who finished.

Our next club meeting is Tuesday, July 8th at the DoubleTree Hotel in Grand Junction. Kaylee Frieze will talk about the upcoming *Gunnison Challenge* tour. Be sure to stay afterward for refreshments and fun.

Upcoming Events

Riding the Rim
— Kathy Rawlings

Rim Rock Drive in Colorado National Monument has tested many of the world's strongest riders, but is still accessible to the weekend cyclist. If you decide to *Tour the Moon*, here are some tips to help you have a great ride:

Keep Hydrated The canyon sun can quickly sap your energy. Make sure you carry plenty of water; there are no watering holes along the Rim.

Bring Lights All bikes must be equipped with front and rear lights for safe passage through the Rim's tunnels. Cyclists must use a white light visible at least 500 feet in front and a red light visible at least 200 feet from the rear.

Ride Single File Rim Rock Drive is narrow, with sheer drop-offs to the canyon valley. Leave plenty of room for drivers to pass you and your group.

POSITIONING ELEMENTS

The **clip** property defines a clipping rectangle that crops the object's **top**, **right**, **bottom**, and **left** edges.

clip: rect(100px, 420px, 350px, 50px);

Market Place   Message Board   Contact Info

About Cycle Pathology

Rides & Events

Route Sheets & Maps

Grand Junction Bike Fest

Off Road Cycling

Newsletter

Photo Album

Editor

Sponsors

Cycling in Colorado National Monument

Drive ⊕ Grand Junction, CO 81501 ⊕ (970) 555 - 8944

z-index: 2;

ional Monument

The **z-index** property stacks overlapping objects with the highest z-index value placed on top of the others.

Positioning Objects

One page section you haven't added to the Cycle Pathology home page is the `header` element, which contains the group logo. Dan would like the header moved to the top-left corner of the page.

The ability to position an object was one of the first enhancements to the original CSS1 specifications. Collectively, the various positioning styles were known as **CSS-Positioning**, or more commonly, **CSS-P**. CSS-P became part of the specification for CSS2, and positioning styles were some of the first CSS2 styles to be adopted by browsers.

To place an element at a specific position, you use the style properties

```
position: type;
top: value;
right: value;
bottom: value;
left: value;
```

where `type` indicates the type of positioning applied to the element, and the `top`, `right`, `bottom`, and `left` properties indicate the coordinates of the top, right, bottom, and left edges of the element, respectively. In practice, usually only the left and top coordinates are specified because the right and bottom coordinates can be inferred given the element's height and width. Coordinates can be expressed in any of the CSS measuring units.

The `position` property has five possible values: `static` (the default), `absolute`, `relative`, `fixed`, and `inherit`. In static positioning, browsers place an element based on where it would naturally flow within the document. This is essentially the same as not using any CSS positioning at all. Browsers ignore any values specified for the `left` or `top` properties under static positioning.

REFERENCE

Positioning an Object with CSS

• To position an object at a specific coordinate, use the style properties

```
position: type;
top: value;
right: value;
bottom: value;
left: value;
```

where `type` indicates the type of positioning applied to the object (`absolute`, `relative`, `static`, `fixed`, or `inherit`), and the `top`, `right`, `bottom`, and `left` properties indicate the coordinates of the object.

Absolute Positioning

Absolute positioning places an element at specific coordinates either in the page or within a container element. For example, the style rule

```
header {
   position: absolute;
   left: 100px;
   top: 50px;
}
```

places the `header` element at the coordinates (100, 50), meaning 100 pixels to the right and 50 pixels down from upper-left corner of the page or the element that contains the header. Once an element has been moved using absolute positioning, it affects the placement of other objects in the Web page. To explore how absolute positioning affects page layout, you'll use a demo that explores the effect of different positioning options on page design.

To explore absolute positioning:

1. Use your Web browser to open the **demo_positioning.htm** file from the tutorial.04\demo folder.

   The demo page contains two colored boxes that you can move by changing the values in two sets of list boxes. The boxes are initially set to their default position, which is within the flow of the other elements in the page. To make it easier to place the boxes at specific positions, a grid marked in pixels has been added to the page background.

2. Select **absolute** from the list box for the outer box, and then press the **Tab** key.

3. Enter **275** in the left box, and then press the **Tab** key. Enter **350** in the top box, and then press the **Tab** key again. As shown in Figure 4-56, the red outer box is placed at the page coordinates (275, 350).

Figure 4-56   Viewing absolute positioning

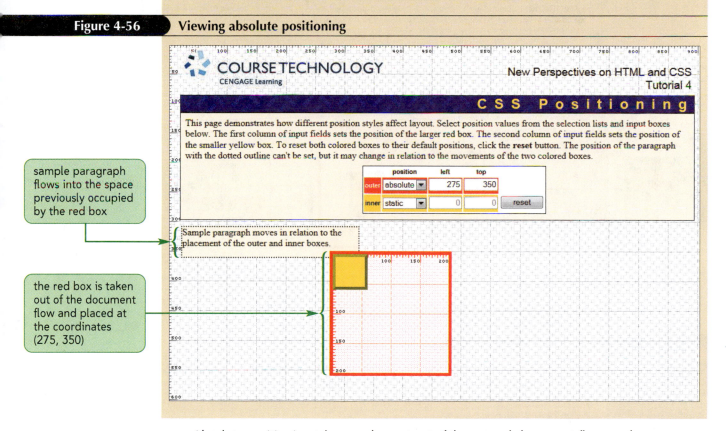

sample paragraph flows into the space previously occupied by the red box

the red box is taken out of the document flow and placed at the coordinates (275, 350)

Absolute positioning takes an element out of the normal document flow, so that any subsequent content flows into the space previously occupied by the element. Note that on the demo page, the sample paragraph moves up into the space that was previously occupied by the red outer box.

The location of the object depends on the context in which absolute positioning has been applied. If the object is contained within another object that has been placed using the position property, then those two objects are placed as a single unit and the nested object's coordinates are based on the position of the containing object. On the other hand, if the object is nested within containers that don't have a `position` property, then that object is placed relative to the browser window itself.

To see this effect in action, return to the demo page.

To view absolute positioning with a nested object:

1. Within the demo page, select **absolute** from the list box for the inner element.

2. Enter **90** in the left box for the inner object and **75** for the top box. As shown in Figure 4-57, the inner yellow box is placed at the coordinates (90, 75) within the outer box. It is *not* placed at the coordinates (90, 75) in the browser window.

| Figure 4-57 | Positioning a nested object |

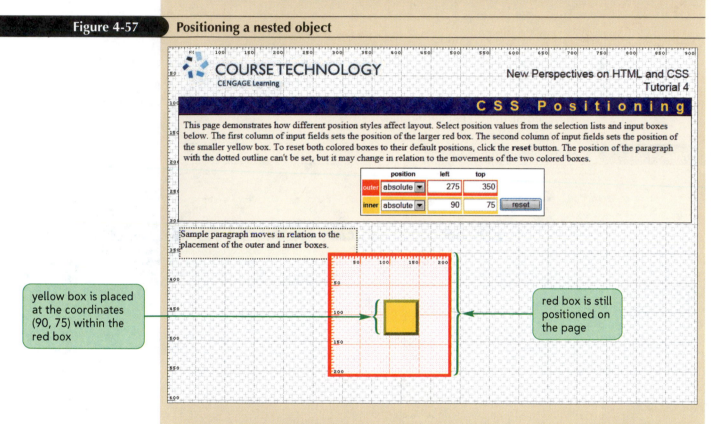

yellow box is placed at the coordinates (90, 75) within the red box

red box is still positioned on the page

Next, you'll examine what occurs when the outer box is no longer placed in the Web page using a positioning style.

TIP

You can enter negative values for the top and left styles to move page elements up and to the left from their default locations.

3. Select **static** from the list box for the outer element.

As shown in Figure 4-58, the red outer box is returned to its default position in the normal document flow, and the yellow inner box is placed at the coordinates (90, 75) in the browser window.

Figure 4-58 | **Absolute positioning for a nested object within a static container**

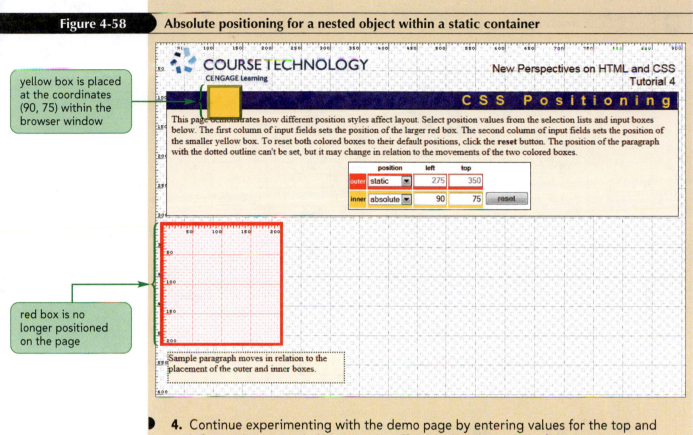

yellow box is placed at the coordinates (90, 75) within the browser window

red box is no longer positioned on the page

4. Continue experimenting with the demo page by entering values for the top and left coordinates and observing the effect on the placement of the boxes.

Next, you'll examine how to place objects using relative positioning.

Relative Positioning

Relative positioning is used to move an element relative to where the browser would have placed it if no positioning had been applied. For example, the style

```
position: relative;
left: 100px;
top: 50px
```

places an element 100 pixels to the right and 50 pixels down from its normal placement in a browser window. A relatively positioned object is still part of the normal document flow; its placement is simply adjusted from its default location. You'll return to the demo page to explore the impact and uses of relative positioning.

To explore relative positioning:

1. Click the **reset** button within the demo page to return both boxes to their default locations in the Web page.

2. Select **relative** from the list box for the outer element, and then enter **275** for the left value and **50** for the top value. As shown in Figure 4-59, the outer box moves 275 pixels to the right and 50 pixels down from its default location.

Figure 4-59 **Relative positioning**

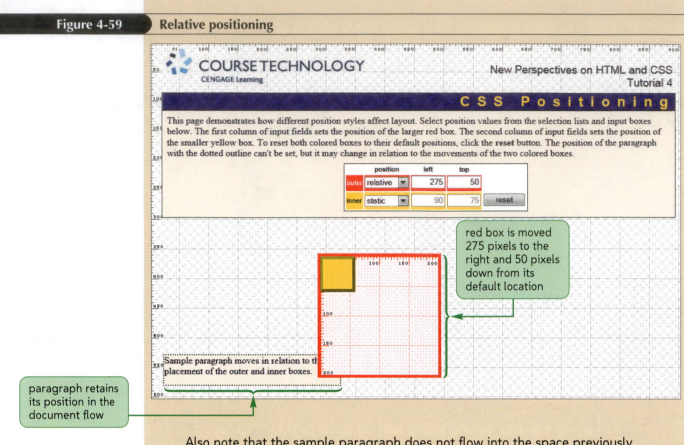

red box is moved 275 pixels to the right and 50 pixels down from its default location

paragraph retains its position in the document flow

Also note that the sample paragraph does not flow into the space previously occupied by the colored boxes. The layout of the rest of the page is unaffected because the red box and its contents are still part of the normal document flow.

3. Explore other combinations of absolute and relative positioning to see their effects on the layout of the demo page.

In many Web page layouts, you might want to absolutely position an object nested within a container element, but you don't want to move the container itself. In those cases, you simply can apply the style

```
position: relative;
```

to the container element without specifying the top and left coordinates. The browser assumes a default value of 0 for these missing coordinates and leaves the container in its default position in the normal document flow; however, any absolute positioning you apply to a nested element still will be applied relative to the top-left corner of the container element.

You can use this fact to center one object within another. If you know the total widths and heights of the nested object and its container, the center location of the nested object corresponds to the following coordinates:

$$\text{horizontal center} = \frac{\text{container object width}}{2} - \frac{\text{nested object width}}{2}$$

$$\text{vertical center} = \frac{\text{container object height}}{2} - \frac{\text{nested object height}}{2}$$

Note that the widths and heights are determined by calculating the sum of the widths and heights of the content, padding, and border space of each object. Try this by using positioning to center the yellow box within the red box.

To center an object within another object:

1. With the red box still relatively positioned, enter **0** for the left and top position to place the object at its default positioning in the normal document flow.

2. Select **absolute** for the yellow box.

   Because the yellow box is 60 pixels wide by 60 pixels high and the red box is 200 pixels wide by 200 pixels high, you can center it within the red box by placing it at the coordinates (70, 70).

3. Enter **70** for both the left and top coordinates (see Figure 4-60).

Figure 4-60   Centering one object within another

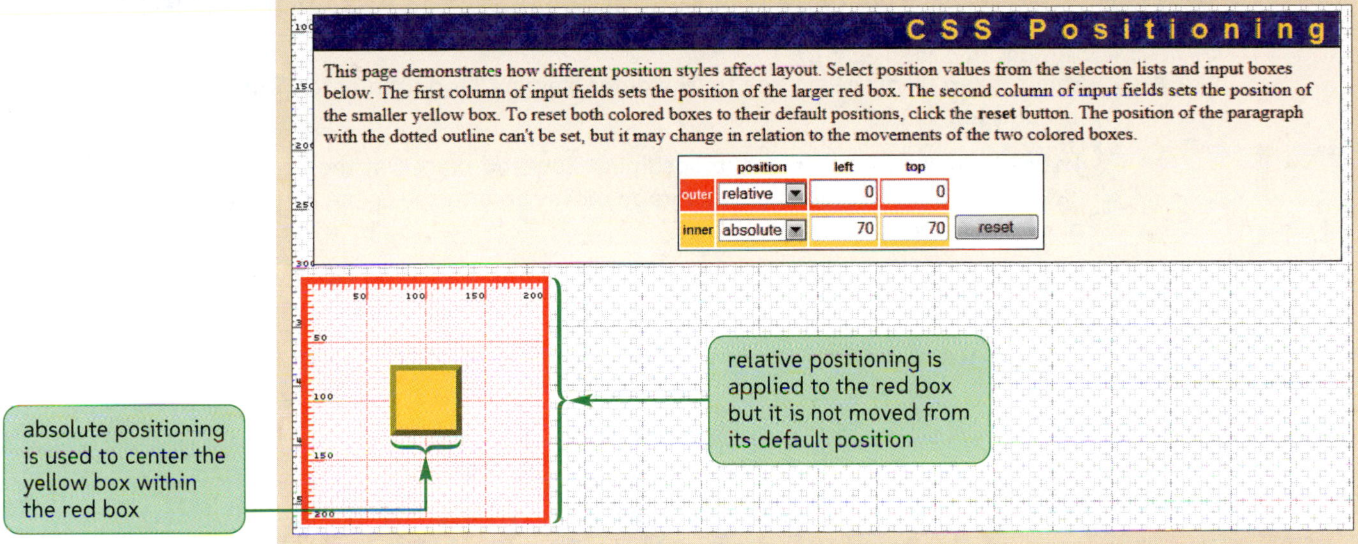

relative positioning is applied to the red box but it is not moved from its default position

absolute positioning is used to center the yellow box within the red box

---

Creating Drop Caps with CSS

INSIGHT

A popular design element is the **drop cap**, which consists of an enlarged initial letter in a body of text that drops down into the text body, like the first letter of this sentence. To create a drop cap, you increase the font size of an element's first letter and float it on the left margin. Drop caps also generally look better if you decrease the line height of the first letter, enabling the surrounding content to better wrap around the letter. Finding the best combination of font size and line height is a matter of trial and error; and unfortunately, what looks best in one browser might not look as good in another. The following style rule works well in applying a drop cap to the paragraph element:

```
p:first-letter {
    font-size: 400%;
    float: left;
    line-height: 0.8;
}
```

With older browsers that do not support the first-letter pseudo-element, you have to mark the first letter using a span element. For additional design effects, you can change the font face of the drop cap to a cursive or decorative font.

Fixed and Inherited Positioning

An element placed with absolute or relative positioning scrolls with the document content. Alternatively, you can fix an element at a specific spot in the browser window while the document scrolls by setting the value of the position property to fixed. Note that older browsers might not support fixed positioning, so you should use it with some caution if it is a crucial part of your Web page layout.

You also can assign the position property to inherit so that an element inherits the position value of its parent element. You'll explore both positioning styles on the demo page.

To explore fixed and inherited positioning:

1. Click the **reset** button within the demo page to return both boxes to their default locations in the Web page.

2. Select **fixed** from the list box for the outer element, and then enter **300** for the left and top values.

   The red box is moved out of the document flow and placed at the window coordinates (300, 300). The sample paragraph moves up into the space previously occupied by the red box.

   Trouble? If you are running an older browser, you might not see any change in the position of the red box.

3. Select **inherit** from the list box for the inner element, and then enter **600** for the left value and **300** for the top value.

   The yellow box inherits the position style of its parent. In this case, it uses fixed positioning and is placed to the right of the outer red box.

   Trouble? If your browser does not support the inherit position style, fix the position of the inner box by choosing fixed from the list box for the inner object.

4. Resize the browser window so it's small enough to force the browser to display vertical and horizontal scroll bars. Scroll through the document and verify that the two color boxes remain fixed at the same location within the window (see Figure 4-61).

| Figure 4-61 | **Fixed and inherited position** |

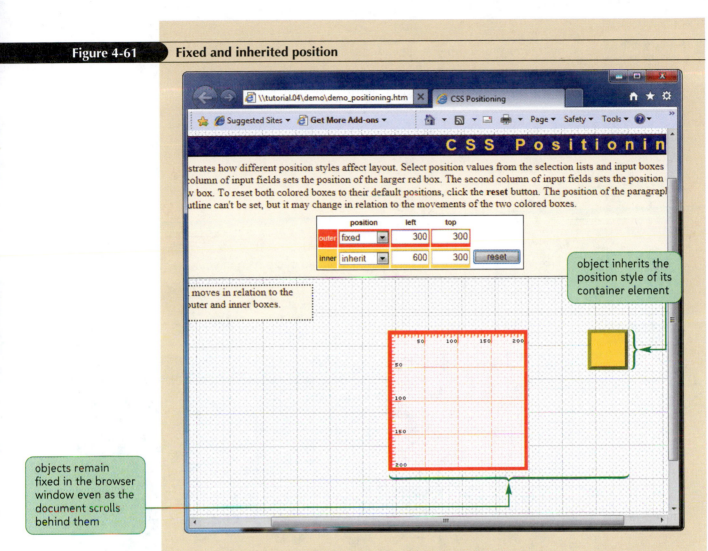

objects remain fixed in the browser window even as the document scrolls behind them

object inherits the position style of its container element

5. Continue to experiment with different positioning combinations. Close the demo page when you're finished.

Now that you've seen how to work with the positioning styles, you'll place the `header` element for the Cycle Pathology page at the coordinates (20, 20) using absolute positioning.

To place the page header:

1. Return to the **cp_reset.css** file in your text editor and remove the selector *header* and the comma that follows it from the style rule at the bottom of the file that hides the page elements. Save your changes to the file.

2. Go to the **cp_styles.css** file in your text editor. Directly below the style rule for the body selector near the top of the page, insert the following style rule (see Figure 4-62):

```
/* Styles for the Page Header */

header {
   position: absolute;
   top: 20px;
   left: 20px;
}
```

Figure 4-62	Setting the position of the page header

```css
body {
    background: black url(bike_bg.png) top left no-repeat;
    width: 95%;
    min-width: 1000px;
    max-width: 1400px;
}

/* Styles for the Page Header */

header {
    position: absolute;
    top: 20px;
    left: 20px;
}
```

header placed with absolute positioning

3. Save your changes to the file and then reload **cycle.htm** in your Web browser. As shown in Figure 4-63, the graphic image for the Cycle Pathology logo appears in the top-left corner of the browser window.

Figure 4-63	Page header positioned at the top-left corner of the page

logo placed at the coordinates (20, 20)

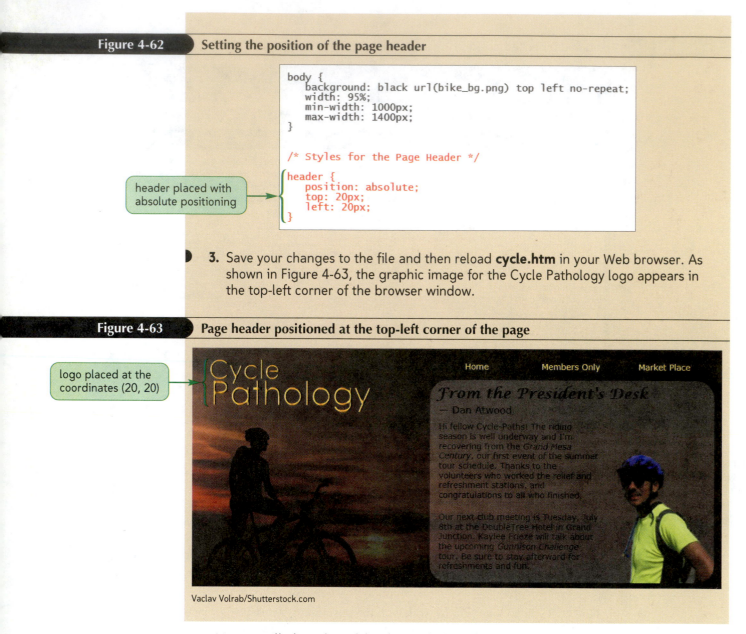

Vaclav Volrab/Shutterstock.com

Next, you'll place the sidebar listing the upcoming cycling events at the left edge of the browser window directly below the graphic image of the cyclist standing before the sunset.

To place the sidebar:

1. Go to the **cp_reset.css** file in your text editor and remove the selector *aside* and the comma that follows it from the style rule at the bottom of the file, leaving only the *footer* selector. Save your changes to the file.

2. Return to the **cp_styles.css** file in your text editor. At the bottom of the file, insert the following style rule to place the `aside` element halfway down the left edge of the page (see Figure 4-64):

```
/* Sidebar styles */

aside {
    color: rgb(145, 98, 78);

    position: absolute;
    top: 400px;
    left: 10px;

    width: 30%;
}
```

Figure 4-64   **Formatting the sidebar listing upcoming events**

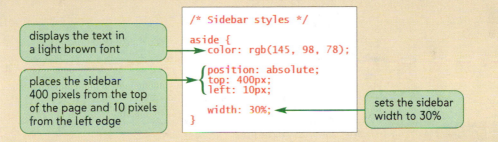

displays the text in a light brown font

places the sidebar 400 pixels from the top of the page and 10 pixels from the left edge

sets the sidebar width to 30%

```
/* Sidebar styles */

aside {
    color: rgb(145, 98, 78);

    position: absolute;
    top: 400px;
    left: 10px;

    width: 30%;
}
```

---

3. Save your changes to the file and then reload **cycle.htm** in your Web browser. As shown in Figure 4-65, the sidebar describing the upcoming rides starts halfway down the left edge of the page.

Figure 4-65   **Sidebar of upcoming events**

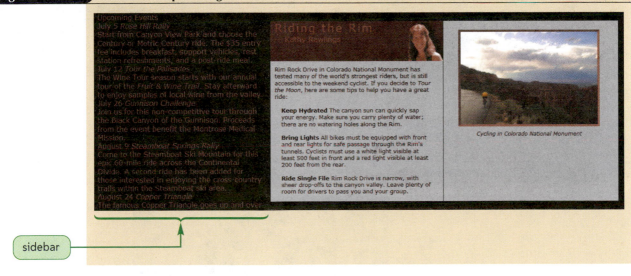

sidebar

The sidebar consists of `h1` and `h2` headings and paragraphs that describe each ride. You'll style these elements now.

To format the sidebar content:

1. Return to the **cp_styles.css** file in your text editor. At the bottom of the file, insert the following style rules for the `h1`, `h2`, and `p` elements in the `aside` element:

```
aside h1 {
    font-size: 105%;
    font-weight: bold;
    margin-bottom: 25px;
    text-align: center;
}

aside h2 {
    font-size: 85%;
    font-weight: bold;
}

aside p {
    font-size: 75%;
    margin: 15px;
}
```

   Figure 4-66 highlights and describes the new style rules.

Figure 4-66 Formatting the sidebar elements

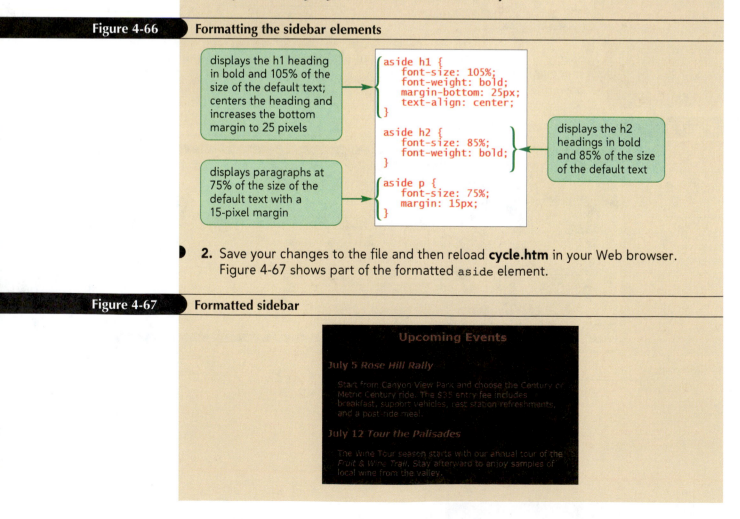

displays the h1 heading in bold and 105% of the size of the default text; centers the heading and increases the bottom margin to 25 pixels

```
aside h1 {
    font-size: 105%;
    font-weight: bold;
    margin-bottom: 25px;
    text-align: center;
}
```

displays the h2 headings in bold and 85% of the size of the default text

```
aside h2 {
    font-size: 85%;
    font-weight: bold;
}
```

displays paragraphs at 75% of the size of the default text with a 15-pixel margin

```
aside p {
    font-size: 75%;
    margin: 15px;
}
```

2. Save your changes to the file and then reload **cycle.htm** in your Web browser. Figure 4-67 shows part of the formatted `aside` element.

Figure 4-67 Formatted sidebar

Upcoming Events

July 5 Rose Hill Rally

Start from Canyon View Park and choose the Century or Metric Century ride. The $35 entry fee includes breakfast, support vehicles, rest station refreshments, and a post-ride meal.

July 12 Tour the Palisades

The Wine Tour season starts with our annual tour of the Fruit & Wine Trail. Stay afterward to enjoy samples of local wine from the valley.

Absolute Positioning and Element Widths

In Figure 4-64, you set the width of the `aside` element to 30%—but 30% of what? Percentages usually are based on the size of the container element. The 33% left margin you assigned to the president's message in Figure 4-27 represented a length that was 33% of the width of the Web page because the president's message was nested within the `body` element. The 50% width assigned to the `article` element in Figure 4-48 represented 50% of the width of the `section` element because the article was nested within the section.

However, the `aside` element, while nested within the `body` element in the HTML file, has been placed in the Web page using absolute positioning, and that takes it out of the normal document flow. The 30% width represents 30% of the width of the container element, but only if that container also has been placed using either absolute or relative positioning. If not, the percentage is based on the width of the browser window itself. This is the same effect you saw earlier in the demo when the position of the inner object depended on whether the outer object itself also had been placed using absolute or relative positioning.

In a fluid layout, you want the sizes of all the page sections to be based on the same thing so that they all are resized the same way. To fix this in the Cycle Pathology Web page, you'll place the entire page body using relative positioning. Recall that you simply can apply the style `position: relative` to any page element to place it at its default location; the key difference will be that the width of the `aside` element will be based on the width of the page body rather than the browser window.

To position the entire page body:

1. Return to the **cp_styles.css** file and locate the style rule for the body selector near the top of the page.

2. Add the following property to the style rule as shown in Figure 4-68:

   `position: relative;`

Figure 4-68   **Applying relative positioning to the page body**

```
body {
    background: black url(bike_bg.png) top left no-repeat;
    position: relative;
    width: 95%;
    min-width: 1000px;
    max-width: 1400px;
}
```

3. Save your changes to the file and then reload the **cycle.htm** file in your Web browser. Change the size of your browser window and verify that the width of the `aside` element changes proportionally along with the widths of the other page elements.

Dan likes the appearance of the Upcoming Events sidebar, but he feels it's too long and would like you to reduce the height of the object so that it appears within the boundaries of the browser window.

Problem Solving: Principles of Design

Good Web page design is based on the same common principles found in other areas of art, which include balance, unity, contrast, rhythm, and emphasis. A pleasing layout involves the application of most, if not all, of these principles, which are detailed below:

- **Balance** is the distribution of elements. It's common to think of balance in terms of **symmetrical balance**, in which similar objects offset each other like items on a balance scale; but you often can achieve more interesting layouts through **asymmetrical balance**, in which one large page object is balanced against two or more smaller objects.
- **Unity** is the ability to combine different design elements into a cohesive whole. This is accomplished by having different elements share common colors, font styles, and sizes. One way to achieve unity in a layout is to place different objects close to each other, forcing your viewers' eyes to see these items as belonging to a single unified object.
- **Contrast** consists of the differences among all of the page elements. To create an effective design, you need to vary the placement, size, color, and general appearance of the objects in the page so that your viewers' eyes aren't bored by the constant repetition of a single theme.
- **Rhythm** is the repetition or alternation of a design element in order to provide a sense of movement, flow, and progress. You can create rhythm by tiling the same image horizontally or vertically across the page, by repeating a series of elements that progressively increase or decrease in size or spacing, or by using elements with background colors of the same hue but that gradually vary in saturation or lightness.
- **Emphasis** involves working with the focal point of a design. Readers need a few key areas to focus on. It's a common design mistake to assign equal emphasis to all page elements. Without a focal point, there is nothing for your viewers' eyes to latch onto. You can give a page element emphasis by increasing its size, by giving it a contrasting color, or by assigning it a prominent position in the page.

 We usually have an intuitive sense of what works and what doesn't in page design, though often we can't say why. These design principles are important because they provide a context in which to discuss and compare designs. If your page design doesn't feel like it's working, evaluate it in light of these principles to identify where it might be lacking.

Working with Overflow and Clipping

The `aside` element is as long as it is because it must display several upcoming events. You can set a smaller height using the `height` property, but what would that do to the content that wouldn't fit under the reduced size?

   When you force an element into a specified height and width, you can define how browsers should handle content that overflows allotted space using the style

```
overflow: type;
```

TIP

CSS3 also includes the overflow-x and overflow-y properties to specify how to handle overflow content in the horizontal and vertical directions, respectively.

where *type* is `visible` (the default), `hidden`, `scroll`, or `auto`. A value of `visible` instructs browsers to increase the height of an element to fit the overflow content, which is what browsers normally do. The `hidden` value keeps the element at the specified height and width, but cuts off excess content. The `scroll` value keeps the element at the specified dimensions, but adds horizontal and vertical scroll bars to allow users to scroll through the overflow. Finally, the `auto` value keeps the element at the specified size, adding scroll bars only as they are needed. Figure 4-69 shows examples of the effects of each overflow value on content that is too large for its space.

| Figure 4-69 | Values of the overflow property |

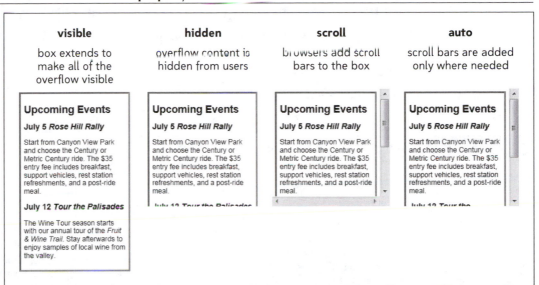

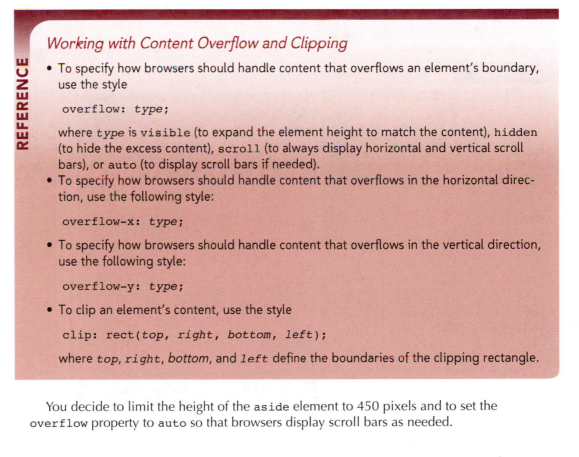

Working with Content Overflow and Clipping

REFERENCE

- To specify how browsers should handle content that overflows an element's boundary, use the style

  ```
  overflow: type;
  ```

  where `type` is `visible` (to expand the element height to match the content), `hidden` (to hide the excess content), `scroll` (to always display horizontal and vertical scroll bars), or `auto` (to display scroll bars if needed).

- To specify how browsers should handle content that overflows in the horizontal direction, use the following style:

  ```
  overflow-x: type;
  ```

- To specify how browsers should handle content that overflows in the vertical direction, use the following style:

  ```
  overflow-y: type;
  ```

- To clip an element's content, use the style

  ```
  clip: rect(top, right, bottom, left);
  ```

  where `top`, `right`, `bottom`, and `left` define the boundaries of the clipping rectangle.

You decide to limit the height of the `aside` element to 450 pixels and to set the `overflow` property to `auto` so that browsers display scroll bars as needed.

To define the overflow style for the `aside` element:

1. Return to **cp_styles.css** in your text editor and scroll down the style rule for the `aside` selector near the bottom of the file.

2. Add the following styles, as shown in Figure 4-70:

   ```
   height: 450px;
   overflow: auto;
   ```

Figure 4-70   **Setting the height and overflow properties**

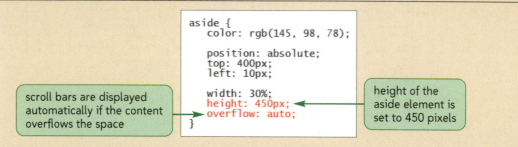

scroll bars are displayed automatically if the content overflows the space

```
aside {
    color: rgb(145, 98, 78);

    position: absolute;
    top: 400px;
    left: 10px;

    width: 30%;
    height: 450px;
    overflow: auto;
}
```

height of the aside element is set to 450 pixels

3. Save your changes to the file and then reload **cycle.htm** in your Web browser. As shown in Figure 4-71, a scroll bar is added to the `aside` element.

Figure 4-71   **aside element with scroll bar**

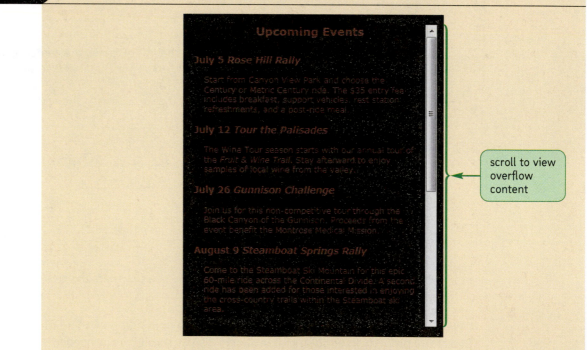

scroll to view overflow content

4. Verify that you can view the entire list of upcoming events by scrolling through the contents of the Upcoming Events sidebar.

   Trouble? To scroll through the `aside` element using a mobile device like an iPad, you must use the two-finger scroll gesture on the contents of the sidebar.

Horizontal Overflow and White Space

Scroll bars for overflow content are usually placed vertically so that you scroll down to view the extra content. In some page layouts, however, you may want to view content in a horizontal rather than a vertical direction. You can accomplish this by adding the following style properties to the element:

```
overflow: auto;
white-space: nowrap;
```

The white-space property defines how browsers should handle white space in the rendered document. The default is to collapse consecutive occurrences of white space into a single blank space, and to automatically wrap text to a new line if it extends beyond the width of the container. However, you can set the white-space property of the element to nowrap to keep inline content on a single line, preventing line wrapping. With the contents thus confined to a single line, browsers will display only horizontal scroll bars for the overflow content. Other values of the white-space property include normal (for default handling of white space), pre (to preserve all white space from the HTML file), and pre-wrap (to preserve white space but to wrap excess content to a new line).

Clipping an Element

Closely related to the overflow property is the clip property, which allows you to define a rectangular region through which an element's content can be viewed. Anything that lies outside the boundary of the rectangle is hidden. The syntax of the clip property is

```
clip: rect(top, right, bottom, left);
```

where top, right, bottom, and left define the coordinates of the clipping rectangle. For example, a clip value of rect(10, 175, 125, 75) defines a clip region whose top and bottom edges are 10 and 125 pixels from the top of the element, and whose right and left edges are 175 and 75 pixels from the left side of the element. See Figure 4-72.

Figure 4-72   Clipping an element

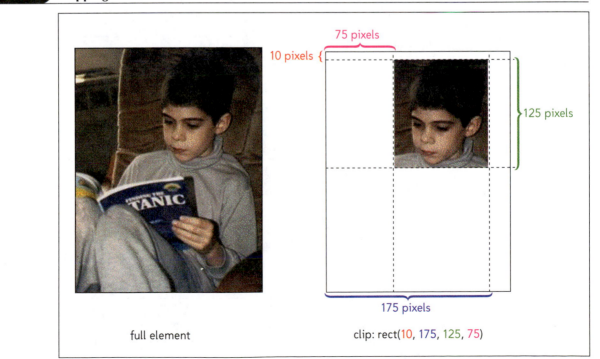

| 75 pixels |
| 10 pixels |
| 125 pixels |
| 175 pixels |

full element   clip: rect(10, 175, 125, 75)

The *top*, *right*, *bottom*, and *left* values also can be set to auto, which matches the specified edge of the clipping region to the edge of the parent element. For example, a clip value of rect(10, auto, 125, 75) creates a clipping rectangle whose right edge matches the right edge of the parent element. To remove clipping completely, apply the style clip: auto. Clipping can only be applied when the object is placed using absolute positioning.

Stacking Elements

Positioning elements can sometimes lead to objects that overlap each other. By default, elements that are loaded later by the browser are displayed on top of elements that are loaded earlier. In addition, elements placed using CSS positioning are stacked on top of elements that are not. To specify a different stacking order, use the style property

    z-index: *value*;

where *value* is a positive or negative integer, or the keyword auto. As shown in Figure 4-73, objects are stacked based on their z-index values, with the highest z-index values placed on top. A value of auto allows browsers to determine the stacking order using the default rules.

Figure 4-73   Using the z-index property to stack elements

The z-index property works only for elements that are placed with absolute positioning. Also, an element's z-index value determines its position relative only to other elements that share a common parent; the style has no impact when applied to elements

with different parents. Figure 4-74 shows a diagram in which the object with a high z-index value of 4 is still covered because it is nested within another object that has a low z-index value of 1.

Figure 4-74   **Nesting stacked elements**

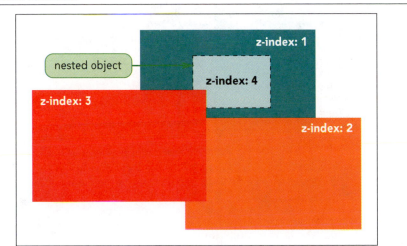

You do not need to include the `z-index` property in your style sheet as none of the page elements are stacked upon another.

The only remaining page section to include in the Cycle Pathology home page is the page footer and the Cycle Pathology address. You'll display the footer only after the left margin is clear of floating elements, and you'll apply a left margin of 33%. You'll also center the address text in the footer, remove any italic from the font style, and reduce the font size. Add these styles to the Cycle Pathology style sheet now.

To style the page footer and address:

1. Go to the **cp_reset.css** file in your text editor. Scroll to the bottom of the file and delete the entire style rule that hides page elements—which contains only the `footer` selector now—along with its style comment. No page elements should now be hidden in the page. Close the file, saving your changes.

2. Return to the **cp_styles.css** file in your text editor. At the bottom of the file, insert the following style rules for the page footer:

```
/* Page footer styles */

footer {
    clear: left;
    margin-left: 33%;
    width: 66%;
}
```

3. Directly below the `footer` style rule, add the following style rule for the `address` element:

```
footer address {
    color: rgb(182, 182, 92);
    font-size: 80%;
    font-style: normal;
    padding-top: 10px;
    text-align: center;
}
```

Figure 4-75 shows and describes the newly inserted style rules.

Figure 4-75 **Styles for the page footer and address**

floats the footer on the left margin after it clears the story section; sets the left margin to 33% of the page width

displays the address in a small normal style light yellow font; centers the text with a top padding of 10 pixels

```
/* Page footer styles */

footer {
    clear: left;
    margin-left: 33%;
    width: 66%;
}

footer address {
    color: rgb(182, 182, 92);
    font-size: 80%;
    font-style: normal;
    padding-top: 10px;
    text-align: center;
}
```

4. Close the file, saving your changes, and then reload **cycle.htm** in your Web browser. Figure 4-76 shows the final appearance of the Cycle Pathology home page.

Figure 4-76 **Final Cycle Pathology home page**

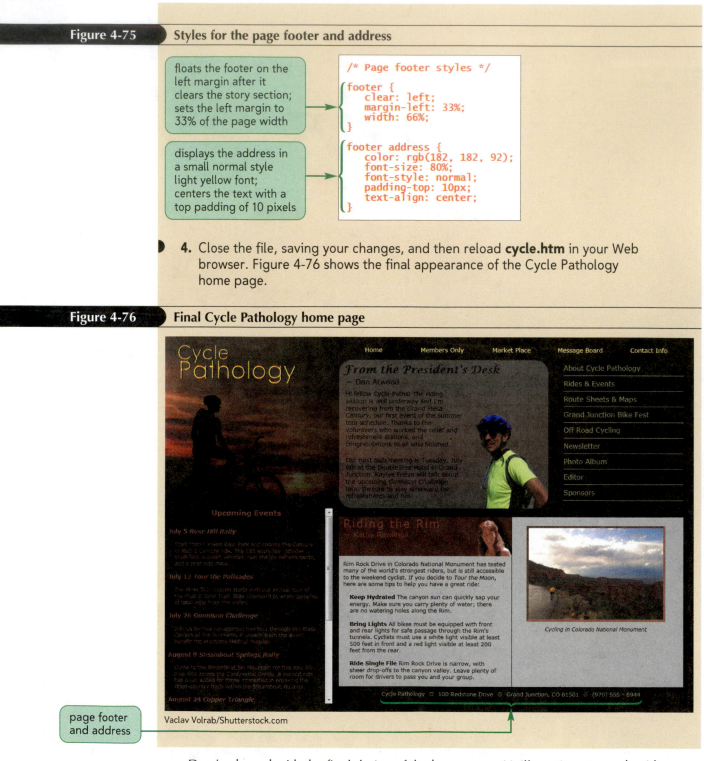

page footer and address

Vaclav Volrab/Shutterstock.com

Dan is pleased with the final design of the home page. He'll continue to work with the page and test it against different browsers and screen resolutions to verify that it's usable under different situations. He'll get back to you with future projects as he continues to overhaul the design of the entire Cycle Pathology Web site.

Session 4.3 Quick Check

1. Provide a style rule to place an element with the id *logo* at the coordinates (150, 75) using absolute positioning.

2. Provide a style rule to move the `header` element 5% down and 10% to the right of its default position.

3. Provide a style rule to fix a page element with the id *watermark* at the screen coordinates (400, 300).

4. Explain the difference between absolute and relative positioning in how they impact the placement of other elements in the Web page.

5. A navigation list has been set with a height of 300 pixels. Provide a style rule to show scroll bars only if there are too many entries in the navigation list to display within the space provided.

6. An inline image with the id *logo_img* is 400 pixels wide by 300 pixels high and needs to be clipped by 10 pixels on each edge. Provide a style rule to accomplish this.

7. One element has a z-index value of 1; a second element has a z-index value of 5. Will the second element always be displayed on top of the first? Explain why or why not.

Practice the skills you learned in the tutorial using the same case scenario.

PRACTICE

Review Assignments

Data Files needed for the Review Assignments: alisha.png, cp_logo2.png, modernizr-1.5.js, racetxt.css, rosetxt.htm, slide01.png-slide08.png

Dan wants your help in designing a layout for a Cycle Pathology Web page that describes one of the group's upcoming tours. He would like you to use a flexible layout with a list of navigation links displayed on the left 20% of the page, with the remaining 80% of the page width devoted to page content. He also wants the page to contain a slide show of images from previous events displayed with a horizontal scroll bar. Figure 4-77 shows a preview of the page you'll create for Dan.

Figure 4-77   Cycle Pathology tour page

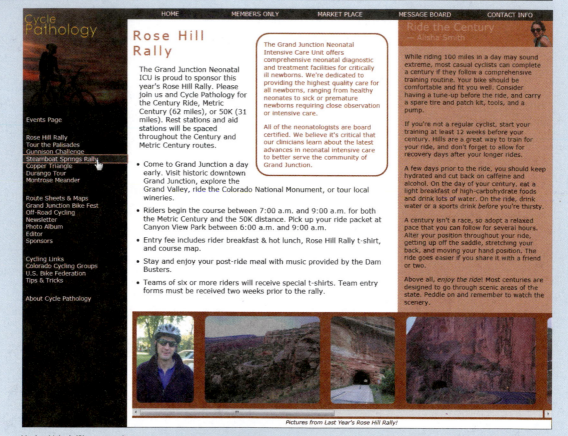

Vaclav Volrab/Shutterstock.com

Complete the following:

1. Use your text editor to open the **rosetxt.htm** and **racetxt.css** files from the tutorial.04\review folder. Enter *your name* and *the date* in the comment section of each file and then save them as **rose.htm** and **race.css**, respectively.

2. Go to the **rose.htm** file in your text editor and take some time to review the content and structure of the file. Link the file to the **race.css** style sheet and then save your changes to the file.

3. Return to the **race.css** file in your text editor. Add a style rule to display the `header`, `article`, `aside`, `figure`, `figcaption`, `hgroup`, `section`, and `nav` elements as blocks.

4. Create a style rule to set the default style for every element so that every element: a) is displayed in a Verdana, Geneva, or sans-serif font; b) has a font size of 100%; and c) has a padding and margin space of 0 pixels.

5. Remove the underlining from every hypertext link within a nav element.

6. Create a style rule for the page body that: a) positions the page using relative positioning; and b) sets the page width to 98% of the width of the browser window in a range from 1000 pixels up to 1400 pixels.

7. Create a style rule for the header element that: a) places the header at the coordinates (0, 0) using absolute positioning; b) sets the width to 20% of the page body; c) changes the background color to black; and d) adds a 500-pixel padding space to the bottom of the element.

8. For inline images within a header element, set the width to 100% of the width of the header.

9. Set the width of the horizontal navigation list to 80% with a left margin of 20%. For list items within the horizontal navigation list, add styles to: a) display each list item as a block floated on the left; b) set the width of each list item to 20%; c) set the background color to the value (49, 38, 31); d) set the upper and lower padding space to 5 pixels; e) horizontally center the list item text; and f) transform the text to uppercase letters, setting the font size to 85%.

10. Set the color of hypertext links in the horizontal navigation list to white. If the user hovers the mouse pointer over the link, change the color to the value (215, 181, 151).

11. For every list item in the vertical navigation list, set the font size to 85% and remove the list style marker. If the list item belongs to the *newgroup* class, add a top padding space of 25 pixels to add a bigger gap between that list item and the previous list item.

12. For every hypertext link within the vertical navigation list, set the font color to white, set the `display` property to block, and indent the text 10 pixels. If the user hovers the mouse pointer over the hypertext link, change the background color to the value (51, 51, 51) and add a 2-pixel solid outline with the color value (215, 181, 151).

13. Add the following styles to the main section of the page: a) float the main section on the left margin once the left margin has been clear of previously floated objects; b) set the size of the left margin to 21%; c) set the size of the top margin to 20 pixels; and d) set the width of the main section to 49% of the page body.

14. For `h1` headings that are direct children of the main section, add styles to: a) set the text color to the value (189, 131, 82); b) set the font size to 180% with normal weight; and c) set the letter spacing to 5 pixels.

15. Set the margins of paragraphs within the main section to 15 pixels. For the unordered list within the main section: a) display a disc marker; b) set the margin around the entire unordered list to 25 pixels; and c) set the bottom margin of each list item to 10 pixels.

16. For the `aside` element, create a style rule to: a) add a 3-pixel solid border with the color value (149, 91, 42) and set the text color to the value (149, 91, 42); b) float the `aside` element on the right with a margin of 10 pixels; c) set the width to 50% of the width of the main section; and d) add a rounded border with a radius of 30 pixels. For paragraphs within the `aside` element, set the font size to 90% and the margin to 20 pixels.

17. For the `article` element, create a style rule to: a) float the element on the left with a width of 29% and a left margin of 1%; and b) set the background color to the value (215, 181, 151).

18. For the header group within the `article` element, create a style rule to: a) display a background color with the value (189, 131, 82) with the background image *alisha. png* displayed in the bottom-right corner with no tiling; b) set the text color to the value (215, 181, 151); c) set the bottom margin to 10 pixels; d) set the height to 60 pixels; and e) indent the text 20 pixels. Set the size of `h1` headings within the header group to 150% with normal weight. Set the size of `h2` headings to 110% with normal weight.

19. For paragraphs within the `article` element, add styles to: a) set the font size to 90%; and b) set the margin to 15 pixels.

20. For the figure box, create a style rule to: a) float the figure box on the left once the left margin is clear; b) add a 21% left margin; c) set the width of the figure box to 79%; and d) set the background color to the value (149, 91, 42).

21. For the `div` element within the figure box, set the browser to display scroll bars automatically if the content overflows the assigned space, and use the `white-space` property to prevent the content from wrapping to a new line.

22. For inline images within the figure box: a) set the margin to 10 pixels; and b) add rounded corners with a radius of 10 pixels.

23. For the figure caption within the figure box, create a style rule to: a) set the background to white; b) set the font size to 80%, displayed in italic and centered; and c) set the top margin to 5 pixels.

24. Add descriptive comments to the style sheet to identify the style rules for the different sections of the Web page.

25. Save your changes to the file and then open **rose.htm** in your Web browser. Verify that the layout and design of the page resemble that shown in Figure 4-77. View your Web page under several different browser window widths to verify that the fluid layout correctly changes in response.

26. Submit your completed files to your instructor, in either printed or electronic form, as requested.

Apply your knowledge of CSS to create an elastic layout along with a drop cap and an irregular line wrap.

APPLY

Case Problem 1

Data Files needed for this Case Problem: arlogo.png, historytxt.css, lincoln01.png-lincoln10.png, lincolntxt.htm, modernizr-1.5.js

American Rhetoric   Professor Annie Chiu teaches rhetoric and history at White Sands College. She has asked for your help in designing a companion Web site for her course in American Rhetoric. She's given you the content and graphics for a sample page containing an excerpt from the second inaugural address by Abraham Lincoln. She wants you to create an elastic layout for the Web page so that it appears the same for different font sizes. Figure 4-78 shows a preview of the page you'll design for her.

Figure 4-78   Lincoln page

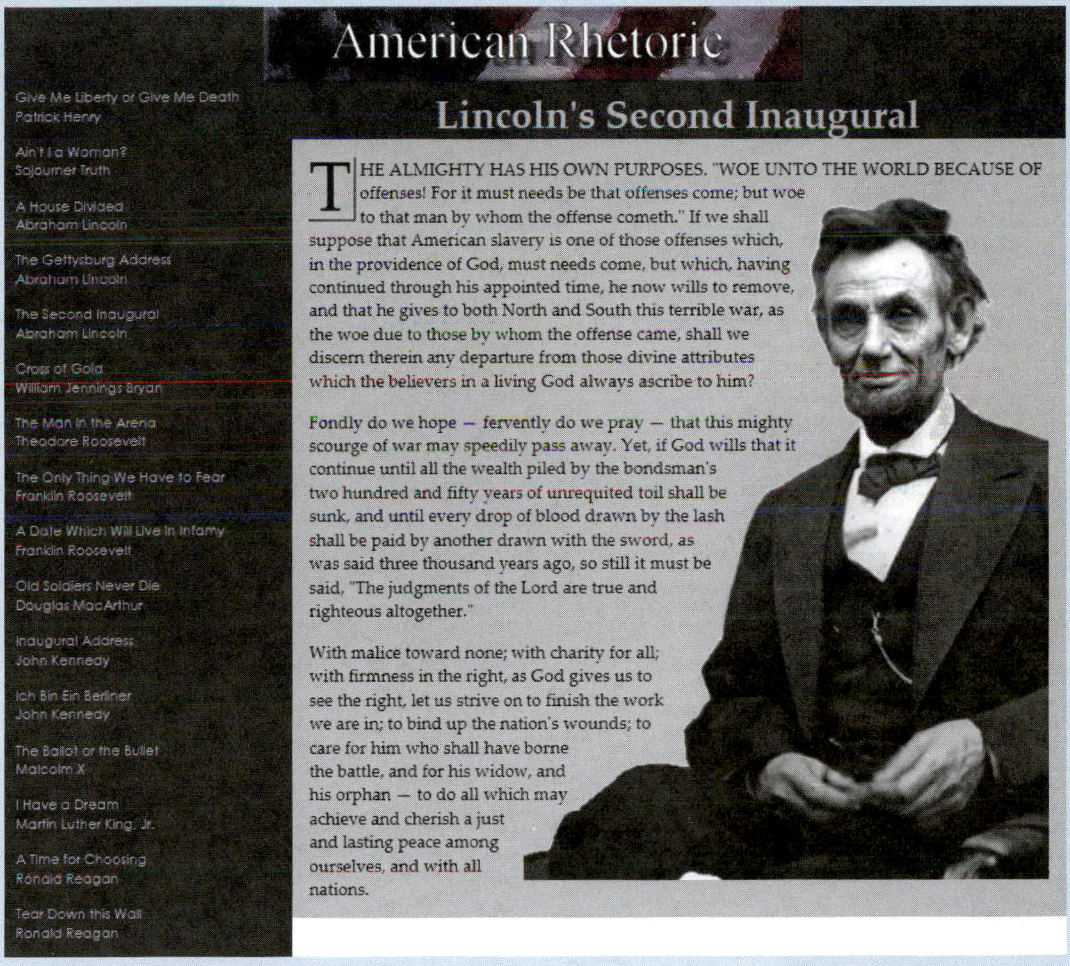

Complete the following:

1. In your text editor, open the **historytxt.css** and **lincolntxt.htm** files from the tutorial.04\case1 folder. Enter *your name* and *the date* in the comment section of each file. Save the files as **history.css** and **lincoln.htm**, respectively.

2. Return to the **lincoln.htm** file in your text editor and take some time to review the content and structure of the file. Link the document to the **history.css** style sheet. Close the file, saving your changes.

3. Go to the **history.css** file in your text editor. Create a style rule to display the `header`, `section`, and `nav` elements as blocks.

4. Set the default padding and margin space for every element to 0 pixels.

5. Define a style rule for the `header` element to: a) set the background color to the value (51, 51, 51); b) center the contents of the `header` element; and c) set the width to 55 em. Set the height of the inline image within the header to 4 em.

6. Float the navigation list on the left page margin, setting the width to 15 em and the background color to the value (51, 51, 51).

7. For list items within the navigation list, create a style rule to: a) set the typeface to Century Gothic or sans-serif; b) set the font size to 0.7 em; c) remove the list markers; d) set the line height to 1.4 em; and e) set the left and bottom margins to 1 em and 1.2 em, respectively.

8. For hypertext links within the navigation list, set the text color to the value (212, 212, 212) and remove the underlining. When the user hovers the mouse pointer over these links, change the text color to white.

9. For the speech section of the page, create a style rule to: a) set the background color to the value (212, 212, 212); b) set the width to 40 em and float the section on the left; and c) display the text in a Palatino Linotype, Book Antiqua, Palatino, or serif font.

10. For the `h1` heading within the speech section, create a style rule to: a) set the background color to the value (51, 51, 51); b) set the text color to the value (212, 212, 212) and the font size to 2 em; and c) center the text.

11. For the paragraphs within the speech section, set the font size to 0.9 em and the margin size to 1 em.

⊕ **EXPLORE**   12. Annie wants to create a drop-cap effect for the first letter in the first line of the first paragraph in the speech section. Using the `first-of-type` pseudo-class and the `first-letter` pseudo-element in your style rule selector, create this drop cap by: a) floating the first letter on the left; b) setting the font size and line height to 4 em and 0.8 em, respectively; c) setting the right margin to 0.3 em; d) setting the right and bottom padding to 0.2 em; and e) adding a solid black border 0.02 em in width to the right and bottom edge of the letter.

13. Display the text of the first line of the first paragraph in the speech section in uppercase letters.

⊕ **EXPLORE**   14. Next, you'll create the irregular line wrap shown in Figure 4-78. Stack the 10 slices of the Lincoln image by creating a style rule for the inline image elements within the speech section to: a) float each image on the right once the right margin is clear; and b) set the height of each image to 4 em.

15. Add appropriate style comments to your file to document your work and then save your changes.

16. Open the **lincoln.htm** file in your Web browser. Verify that the layout resembles that shown in Figure 4-78. (Note: Safari for the Macintosh does not at the time of this writing support the `first-line` pseudo-class with uppercase letters. Also, you might notice a slight difference in the layout with browsers running on the Macintosh, iPhone, or iPad.)

⊕ **EXPLORE**   17. Using the Options or Preferences dialog box of your browser, increase and decrease the browser's default font size. Verify that as the font size changes, the layout and size of the inline images in the page change in proportion.

18. Submit your completed files to your instructor, in either printed or electronic form, as requested.

Apply your knowledge of CSS to create a fixed layout design for a pizzeria Web site.

CHALLENGE

Case Problem 2

Data Files needed for this Case Problem: modernizr-1.5.js, notice.png, pizzatxt.css, rblogo.png, redballtxt.htm, redbar.png, slice.png, toppings.png

Red Ball Pizza   Alice Nichols is the owner of Red Ball Pizza, a well-established pizzeria in Ormond Beach, Florida. She's asked for your help in creating a design for the company's Web site. After discussing the issue with Alice, you settle on a fixed width layout. Alice has created a sample home page for you to work on. She's already created all of the content and the graphics. She needs your help with the design. Figure 4-79 shows a preview of the page you'll create for her.

Figure 4-79   Red Ball Pizza

Complete the following:

1. In your text editor, open the **pizzatxt.css** and **redballtxt.htm** files from the tutorial.04\case2 folder. Enter *your name* and *the date* in the comment section of each file. Save the files as **pizza.css** and **redball.htm**, respectively.

2. Return to the **redball.htm** file in your text editor. Take some time to review the content and structure of the document, and then link the file to the **pizza.css** style sheet. Close the file, saving your changes.

3. Go to the **pizza.css** file in your text editor. Create a style rule to display the `header`, `section`, `aside`, `footer`, and `nav` elements as blocks.

4. Set the default padding and margin size to 0 pixels.

5. Create a style for the `body` element to: a) set the background color to red; and b) set the font family to Verdana, Geneva, or sans-serif.

⊕ EXPLORE   6. The entire content of the page has been enclosed in a `div` container element with the id *container*. Create a style rule for this container to: a) set the width to 1000 pixels; b) center the container in the browser window by setting the top/bottom margins to 0 pixels and the left/right margins to `auto`; c) display a 1-pixel solid black border on the left and right edges; and d) set the background color to white and display the *redbar.png* image file as the background image, placing the image file in the top-left corner of the container and tiling it in the vertical direction only.

7. Change the background color of the `header` element to white and set its height to 100 pixels.

8. Create a style rule for the horizontal navigation list to: a) set the height to 70 pixels and the width to 100%; and b) set the background color to white.

9. For each list item within the horizontal navigation list, create a style rule to: a) set the background color to white; b) set the font size to 16 pixels, the height and the line height to 50 pixels, and the width to 180 pixels; c) display the item as a block and float it on the left; d) set the left and right margins to 5 pixels; and e) horizontally center the contents.

⊕ EXPLORE   10. For each hypertext link within a list item in the horizontal navigation list, create a style rule to: a) display the link as a block; b) set the background color to red and the text color to white; c) create elongated corners with a horizontal radius of 30 pixels and a vertical radius of 25 pixels (use progressive enhancement to support browser extensions); and d) remove the text underlining. If a user hovers a mouse pointer over these links, change the background color to the value (255, 101, 101) and the text color to black.

11. Create a style rule for the vertical navigation list to: a) float it on the left only when the left margin is clear; and b) set the width to 200 pixels.

12. For list items within the vertical navigation list, create a style rule to: a) remove the list item marker; b) indent the text 20 pixels; and c) set the top and bottom margins to 20 pixels.

13. For hypertext links within the vertical navigation list, set the text color to white and remove the text underlining. When a user hovers the mouse pointer over these links, change the text color to black.

14. The main content of the Web page is contained in a `section` element with the id *main*. Create a style rule for this element to: a) change the background color to the value (255, 211, 211); b) float the element on the left; and c) set the width to 600 pixels.

15. For paragraphs that are direct children of the main section, set the font size to 20 pixels and the margin to 15 pixels.

⊕ EXPLORE   16. For inline images within the main section, create a style rule to: a) float the image on the right; b) set the margin to 15 pixels; c) set the width to 350 pixels; and d) set the radius of the bottom-left corner to 350 pixels (use progressive enhancement to support the Mozilla and WebKit browser extensions).

17. Alice has included six coupons in the home page that have been nested within `div` elements belonging to the *coupon* class. For each *coupon* `div` element: a) add a 5-pixel dashed black border; b) float the coupons on the left; c) set the width to 170 pixels and the height to 150 pixels; and d) set the top and bottom margins to 20 pixels, and the left and right margins to 10 pixels.

⊕ EXPLORE   18. To the style rule for the coupons, add style properties to create the following two background images: a) place the *slice.png* image in the center of the coupon without tiling; and b) place the *notice.png* image in the bottom-right corner of the coupon without tiling. Set the background color of the coupon to white.

19. For `h1` headings within the coupons, add a style rule to: a) set the text color to white on a background with the color value (192, 0, 0); b) set the font size to 16 pixels and the kerning to 2 pixels; c) center the text; d) set the height to 25 pixels; and e) display the text in small caps.

20. For paragraphs within the coupons, create a style rule to: a) set the font size to 14 pixels; b) center the text; and c) set the margin to 5 pixels.

21. Alice has placed interesting tidbits about pizza in an `aside` element. Float the `aside` element on the left with a width of 200 pixels.

22. For `h1` headings within the `aside` element, create a style rule to: a) set the text color to the value (192, 0, 0); b) set the font size to 20 pixels and the kerning to 2 pixels; c) set the font weight to normal; and d) center the text of the headings.

23. For list items within the `aside` element, create a style rule to: a) set the background color to the value (255, 135, 135); b) add round corners with a 5-pixel radius; c) set the text color to black; d) remove the list style maker; and e) set the margin to 10 pixels and the padding to 5 pixels.

24. Display the `footer` element when the left margin is clear, and set the size of the left margin to 200 pixels.

25. For the `address` element within the `footer` element, create a style rule to: a) add a 1-pixel solid red border to the top of the element; b) change the text color to red; c) set the font size to 10 pixels, set the font style to normal, and center the address text; and d) set the top margin to 25 pixels and the bottom padding to 20 pixels.

26. Add style comments throughout your style sheet to document your work and then save your changes.

27. Open the **redball.htm** file in your Web browser and verify that the design and layout resemble that shown in Figure 4-79.

28. Submit your completed files to your instructor, in either printed or electronic form, as requested.

Explore how to use CSS to create an interactive map with popup boxes.

CHALLENGE

Case Problem 3

Data Files needed for this Case Problem: bluebar.png, image0.jpg–image9.jpg, longstxt.htm, lpmap.jpg, maptxt.css, modernizr-1.5.js

Longs Peak Interactive Map   Longs Peak is one of the most popular attractions of Rocky Mountain National Park (RMNP). Each year during the months of July, August, and September, thousands of people climb Longs Peak by the Keyhole Route to reach the 14,255-foot summit. Ron Bartlett, the head of the RMNP Web site team, has asked for your help in creating an interactive map of the Keyhole Route. The map will be installed at electronic kiosks in the park's visitor center. Ron envisions a map with 10 numbered waypoints along the Keyhole Route, displaying a popup photo and description when a mouse pointer hovers over one of the numbered points. Figure 4-80 shows a preview of the online map with the first waypoint highlighted by the user.

Figure 4-80 Longs Peak interactive map

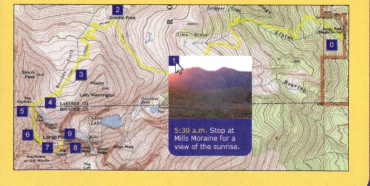

Complete the following:

1. Open the **longstxt.htm** and **maptxt.css** files in your text editor. Add *your name* and *the date* to the comment section of each file, and save the files as **longs.htm** and **map.css**, respectively.

2. Return to the **longs.htm** file in your text editor. Take some time to study the content and structure of the document. Link the file to the **map.css** style sheet and then close the file, saving your changes.

3. Go to the **map.css** style sheet.

4. Create a style rule to display the nav, section, figure, and figcaption elements as blocks.

EXPLORE

5. The estimated time that a hiker should arrive at each waypoint has been marked with the time element. Create another style rule to display the time element inline.

6. Set the margin and padding space of every element to 0 pixels.

7. Set the font family for the page body to Verdana, Geneva, or sans-serif.

8. The entire content of the page is nested within a div element with the id *page*. Create a style rule for this element to: a) set the background color to the value (255, 255, 128) and display the background image file, *bluebar.png*, tiled vertically along the left edge; b) add a ridged 15-pixel-wide border with a color value of (70, 76, 222); c) add rounded corners with a radius of 50 pixels; d) set the width and height to 900 pixels and 750 pixels, respectively; and e) horizontally center the div element within the browser window, setting its top margin to 10 pixels, setting its bottom margin to 200 pixels, and using auto for the left and right margins.

9. Float the vertical navigation list on the left margin with a width of 230 pixels. For each list item within the navigation list, remove the list markers, set the top and bottom margins to 25 pixels, and set the left and right margins to 20 pixels. Set the font color of hypertext links within the navigation list to white, and to yellow in response to the hover event. Remove the underlining from the hypertext links.

10. The description of the map is contained within the section element with the id *summary*. Float the summary section on the left with a left margin of 30 pixels and a width of 600 pixels.

11. Create a style rule for the h1 heading within the summary section to: a) set the text color to the value (70, 76, 222); b) set the font size to 24 pixels, with normal weight and kerning set to 5 pixels; and c) set the margin to 20 pixels.

12. For paragraphs within the summary section, set the margin to 10 pixels.

13. The interactive map has been enclosed in a section element with the id *map*. For the map section, create a style rule to: a) place it using relative positioning (do not specify the top or left coordinate); b) set the background color to white, with the *lpmap.jpg* image file as the background image placed in the top-left corner with no tiling; c) add a 1-pixel-wide solid black border; d) float the section on the left with a left margin of 30 pixels; and e) set the width and height to 600 pixels and 294 pixels, respectively.

⊕ EXPLORE 14. Each of the popup boxes has been placed within a figure box. Initially, these popup boxes should be clipped so that only the number is shown. Create a style rule for the `figure` element to: a) set the background color to the value (70, 76, 222); b) set the text color to white; c) set the width to 150 pixels; d) add rounded corners with a radius of 15 pixels; e) position the figure box using absolute positioning (but do not specify a top or left coordinate); f) set the z-index value to 1; and g) clip the content using a clipping rectangle that is 20 pixels wide by 20 pixels high and situated in the top-left corner of the figure box.

⊕ EXPLORE 15. If a user hovers the mouse pointer over a figure box, then remove the clipping rectangle and increase the z-index value to 2 (so that it appears on top of other objects).

16. For the figure caption within each figure box, set the font size to 12 pixels and the margin to 10 pixels.

17. Set the text color of each `time` element within each figure box to yellow.

18. Each of the 10 figure boxes has an id, ranging from point0 to point9. Set the (left, top) coordinates of the figure boxes as follows:

point0 at (560, 60)
point1 at (277, 90)
point2 at (175, 0)
point3 at (110, 115)
point4 at (55, 165)
point5 at (5, 180)
point6 at (15, 222)
point7 at (50, 245)
point8 at (100, 245)
point9 at (90, 220)

19. Save your changes to the file and then open **longs.htm** in your Web browser. Verify that the placement of the waypoints follows the locations shown in Figure 4-80. Confirm that when you hover your mouse over each of the 10 waypoints, a description of the waypoint appears on the top of the trail map.

20. Submit your completed files to your instructor, in either printed or electronic form, as requested.

Test your knowledge of CSS to design the layout for the front page of a local newspaper.

CREATE

Case Problem 4

Data Files needed for this Case Problem: address.txt, blake.jpg, cougar.jpg, links1.txt, links2.txt, modernizr-1.5.js, papertxt.css, parch.jpg, parch2.jpg, parktxt.htm, pcglogo.jpg, story1.txt–story4.txt

The Park City Gazette Park City, Colorado, is a rural mountain community noted for its ski slopes and fishing holes. Kevin Webber is the editor of the weekly *Park City Gazette*. The paper recently redesigned its printed layout, and Kevin wants you to do the same thing for the online version. He's prepared several files containing sample text from recent articles and a few lists of links that usually appear in the front page of the newspaper's Web site. He's also provided you with image files that can be used for the paper's logo and background. Your job will be to use all of these pieces to create a sample Web page for him to evaluate.

Complete the following:

1. Use your text editor to open the **parktxt.htm** and **papertxt.css** files from the tutorial.04\case4 folder. Add *your name* and *the date* in the comment section of each file. Save the files as **park.htm** and **paper.css**, respectively.
2. Using the content of the address, links, and story text files, create the content and structure of the *park.htm* file. You are free to supplement the material in these text files with additional content of your own if appropriate. Use the # symbol for the value of the href attribute in your hypertext links because you will be linking to pages that don't actually exist.
3. Link the *park.htm* file to the **paper.css** style sheet file and then save your changes.
4. Go to the **paper.css** style sheet file and create a layout for your *Park City Gazette* sample page. The layout should be based on a fluid design that will render well on page widths from 1000 up to 1400 pixels.
5. The specifics of the page design are up to your imagination and skill, but must include the following features:
   - use of the display property
   - application of width and height style properties
   - floated elements and cleared elements
   - defined margin and padding spaces as well as maximum and minimum widths
   - border styles
   - rounded or elongated corners
   - use of progressive enhancement along with one or more browser style extensions
   - a tiled or non-tiled background image
   - an example of relative or absolute positioning
6. Test your layout and design on a variety of devices, browsers, and screen resolutions to ensure that your sample page is readable under different conditions.
7. Submit your completed files to your instructor, in either printed or electronic form, as requested.

ENDING DATA FILES

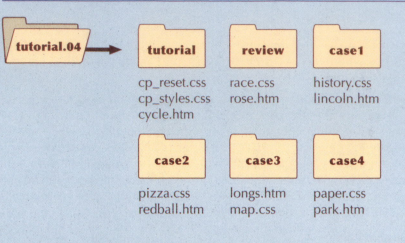

tutorial.04 →

tutorial
cp_reset.css
cp_styles.css
cycle.htm

review
race.css
rose.htm

case1
history.css
lincoln.htm

case2
pizza.css
redball.htm

case3
longs.htm
map.css

case4
paper.css
park.htm

TUTORIAL 5

OBJECTIVES

Session 5.1
- Explore the structure of a Web table
- Create headings and cells in a table
- Create cells that span multiple rows and columns
- Add a caption to a table
- Create row and column groups
- Add a summary to a table

Session 5.2
- Format a table using HTML attributes
- Format a table using CSS styles
- Collapse table borders
- Display page elements in tabular form
- Create a multi-column layout

Working with Tables and Columns

Creating a Radio Program Schedule

Case | *KPAF Radio*

Kyle Mitchell is the program director at KPAF, a public radio station broadcasting out of Bismarck, North Dakota. To remain viable, it's important for the station to continue to have a presence on the Web. With this in mind, Kyle has begun upgrading the KPAF Web site. He envisions a site in which listeners have quick and easy access to information about the station and its programs.

The Web site includes pages listing the KPAF morning, afternoon, and evening schedules. Kyle decides that this information is best conveyed to the listener in a table, with each column of the table displaying one day's program schedule and each row displaying the broadcast times for the various KPAF programs. Kyle has never created a Web table, so he's come to you for help in designing a Web page describing the KPAF evening schedule. Kyle wants the table you create to be easy to read and informative. He also wants you to add table styles that will enhance the appearance of the Web page.

STARTING DATA FILES

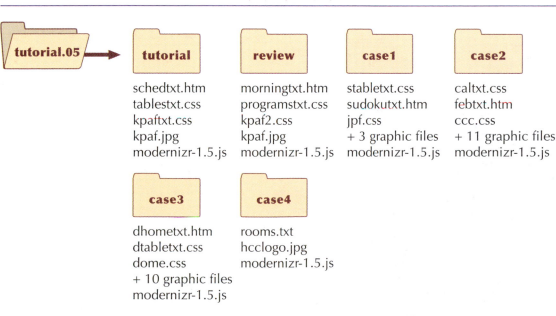

tutorial.05 →

tutorial
schedtxt.htm
tablestxt.css
kpaftxt.css
kpaf.jpg
modernizr-1.5.js

review
morningtxt.htm
programstxt.css
kpaf2.css
kpaf.jpg
modernizr-1.5.js

case1
stabletxt.css
sudokutxt.htm
jpf.css
+ 3 graphic files
modernizr-1.5.js

case2
caltxt.css
febtxt.htm
ccc.css
+ 11 graphic files
modernizr-1.5.js

case3
dhometxt.htm
dtabletxt.css
dome.css
+ 10 graphic files
modernizr-1.5.js

case4
rooms.txt
hcclogo.jpg
modernizr-1.5.js

SESSION 5.1 VISUAL OVERVIEW

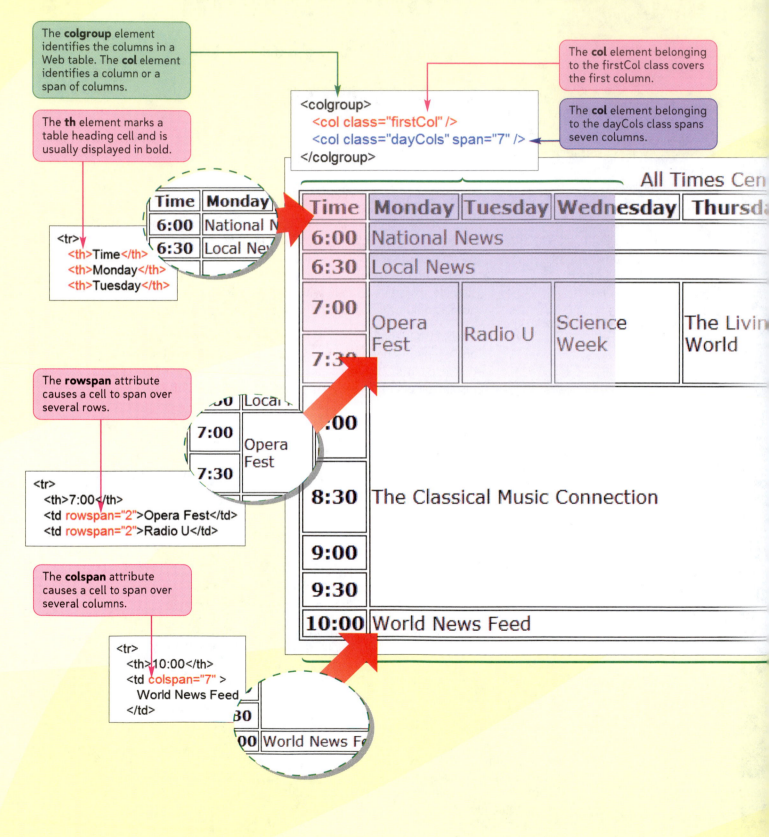

The **colgroup** element identifies the columns in a Web table. The **col** element identifies a column or a span of columns.

The **col** element belonging to the firstCol class covers the first column.

The **col** element belonging to the dayCols class spans seven columns.

The **th** element marks a table heading cell and is usually displayed in bold.

```
<colgroup>
  <col class="firstCol" />
  <col class="dayCols" span="7" />
</colgroup>
```

```
<tr>
  <th>Time</th>
  <th>Monday</th>
  <th>Tuesday</th>
```

The **rowspan** attribute causes a cell to span over several rows.

```
<tr>
  <th>7:00</th>
  <td rowspan="2">Opera Fest</td>
  <td rowspan="2">Radio U</td>
```

The **colspan** attribute causes a cell to span over several columns.

```
<tr>
  <th>10:00</th>
  <td colspan="7" >
    World News Feed
  </td>
```

STRUCTURE OF A WEB TABLE

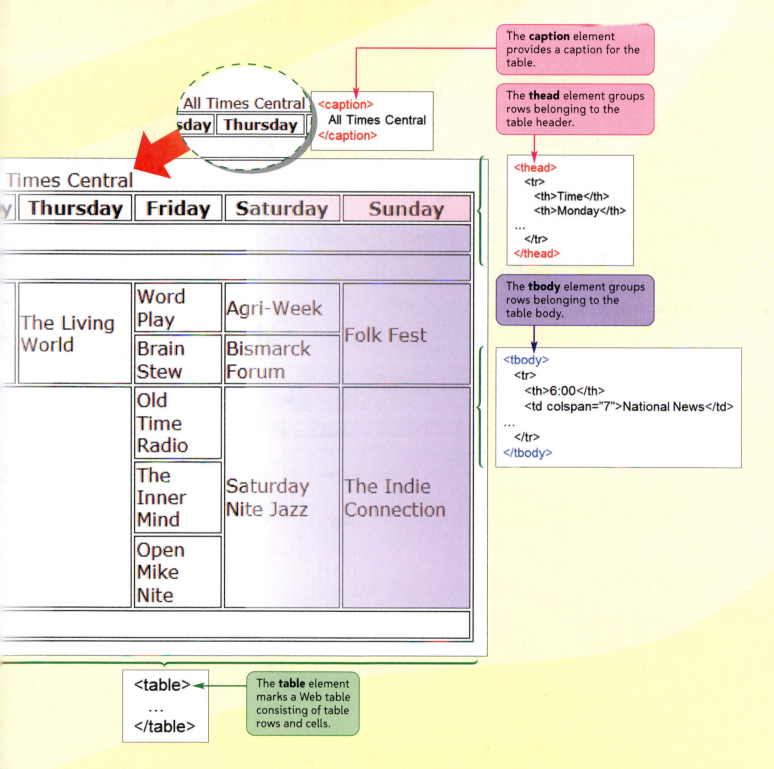

The **caption** element provides a caption for the table.

```
<caption>
   All Times Central
</caption>
```

The **thead** element groups rows belonging to the table header.

```
<thead>
   <tr>
      <th>Time</th>
      <th>Monday</th>
   ...
   </tr>
</thead>
```

The **tbody** element groups rows belonging to the table body.

```
<tbody>
   <tr>
      <th>6:00</th>
      <td colspan="7">National News</td>
   ...
   </tr>
</tbody>
```

```
<table>
   ...
</table>
```

The **table** element marks a Web table consisting of table rows and cells.

Introducing Web Tables

You meet with Kyle in his office at KPAF to discuss the design of the new Web site. Kyle already has created a basic Web page displaying the KPAF logo and a list of links to other pages and to upcoming shows. Open this file now.

To open the KPAF Web page:

1. In your text editor, open the **schedtxt.htm** and **kpaftxt.css** files, located in the tutorial.05\tutorial folder. Enter *your name* and *the date* in the comment section of each file. Save the files as **schedule.htm** and **kpaf.css**, respectively, in the same folder.

2. Review the **schedule.htm** file in your text editor to become familiar with its content and structure. Insert the following `link` element directly above the closing `</head>` tag:

   `<link href="kpaf.css" rel="stylesheet" type="text/css" />`

3. Save your changes to the file and then open the **schedule.htm** file in your Web browser. Figure 5-1 shows the current appearance of the Web page.

| Figure 5-1 | Initial nightly schedule page |

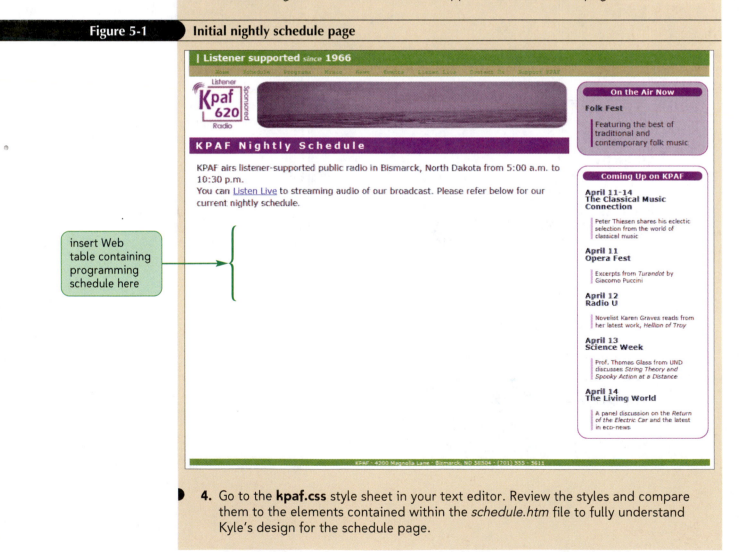

4. Go to the **kpaf.css** style sheet in your text editor. Review the styles and compare them to the elements contained within the *schedule.htm* file to fully understand Kyle's design for the schedule page.

Kyle wants you to add KPAF's nightly schedule, which runs from 6:00 p.m. to 10:30 p.m., to this Web page. The contents of the table are shown in Figure 5-2.

Figure 5-2   KPAF nightly schedule

Time	Monday	Tuesday	Wednesday	Thursday	Friday	Saturday	Sunday
6:00	National News	National News	National News	National News	National News	National News	National News
6:30	Local News	Local News	Local News	Local News	Local News	Local News	Local News
7:00	Opera Fest	Radio U	Science Week	The Living World	Word Play	Agri-Week	Folk Fest
7:30					Brain Stew	Bismarck Forum	
8:00	The Classical Music Connection				Old Time Radio	Saturday Nite Jazz	The Indie Connection
8:30					The Inner Mind		
9:00					Open Mike Nite		
9:30							
10:00	World News Feed	World News Feed	World News Feed	World News Feed	World News Feed	World News Feed	World News Feed

To create this program listing, you first have to understand the HTML table structure.

Marking Tables and Table Rows

Each Web table consists of a `table` element containing a collection of table rows. The general structure is

```
<table>
   <tr>
      table cells
   </tr>
   <tr>
      table cells
   </tr>
   ...
</table>
```

where `<table>` marks the `table` element, `<tr>` marks each row, and `table cells` are the cells within each row. Note that the dimension or size of the table is defined by the number of `tr` elements and the number of cells within those rows. Tables are considered block-level elements; so when rendered by a browser, they appear on a new line in the Web page. Like other block-level elements, you can float tables and resize them using the same styles you've already studied.

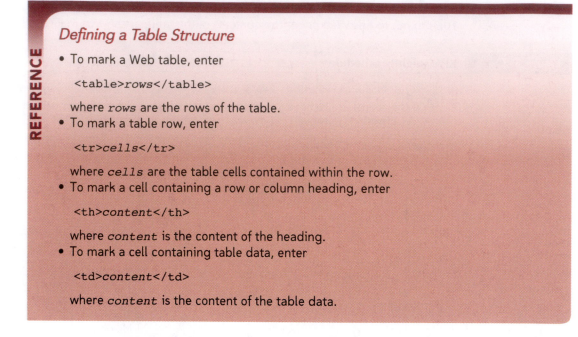

REFERENCE

Defining a Table Structure

- To mark a Web table, enter

  ```
  <table>rows</table>
  ```

  where *rows* are the rows of the table.
- To mark a table row, enter

  ```
  <tr>cells</tr>
  ```

  where *cells* are the table cells contained within the row.
- To mark a cell containing a row or column heading, enter

  ```
  <th>content</th>
  ```

  where *content* is the content of the heading.
- To mark a cell containing table data, enter

  ```
  <td>content</td>
  ```

  where *content* is the content of the table data.

Kyle's proposed Web table from Figure 5-2 contains 10 rows; the first row contains the days of the week, and the nine rows that follow list the KPAF shows from 6:00 p.m. to 10:30 p.m. in half-hour intervals. For now, you'll insert `tr` elements for just the first three rows of the table. You'll also include a class attribute, placing the table in the *schedule* class of elements to distinguish it from other tables on the KPAF Web site.

To insert the Web table:

▸ 1. Return to the **schedule.htm** file in your text editor.

▸ 2. Directly above the closing `</section>` tag, insert the following code, as shown in Figure 5-3:

```
<table class="schedule">
   <tr>
   </tr>
   <tr>
   </tr>
   <tr>
   </tr>
</table>
```

Figure 5-3 Marking a table and table rows

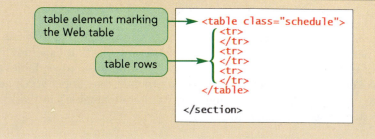

At this point, you have a table with three rows but no content. Your next task is to add table cells to each of those rows.

Marking Table Headings and Table Data

There are two types of table cells: those that contain headings and those that contain data. Table headings, the cells that identify the contents of a row or column, are marked using the `th` element. You can place a table heading anywhere in a table, but you'll most often place one at the top of a column or at the beginning of a row. Most browsers display table headings in a bold font, centered within the table cell.

Kyle wants you to mark the cells in the first row of the radio schedule as headings because the text identifies the contents of each column. He also wants the first cell in each of the remaining rows to be marked as a heading because these cells display the time. You'll start by adding heading cells to the first three rows of the schedule table.

To insert the table headings:

1. In the first table row of the Web table you just created in the *schedule.htm* file, insert the following `th` elements:

   ```
   <th>Time</th>
   <th>Monday</th>
   <th>Tuesday</th>
   <th>Wednesday</th>
   <th>Thursday</th>
   <th>Friday</th>
   <th>Saturday</th>
   <th>Sunday</th>
   ```

2. In the second row of the table, insert the following heading:

   ```
   <th>6:00</th>
   ```

3. In the third table row, insert the following heading:

   ```
   <th>6:30</th>
   ```

   Figure 5-4 shows the revised code in the schedule table.

Figure 5-4   Inserting table heading cells

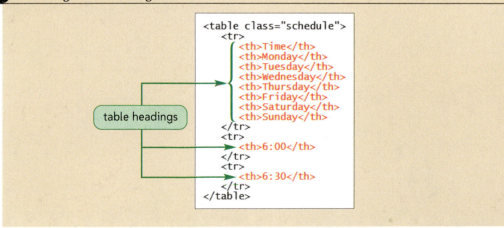

The other type of table cell is a data cell, which is marked using the `td` element and is used for any content that is not considered a heading. Most browsers display table data as unformatted text, left-aligned within the cell.

TIP

To place an empty table cell anywhere within a row, insert the `<td> </td>` tag into the row.

KPAF airs the national and local news at 6:00 and 6:30, respectively, every night of the week. You'll use table data cells to insert the names of the KPAF programs.

To insert table data for the next two rows of the table:

1. Within the second table row, add the following seven td elements after the initial th element:

```
<td>National News</td>
<td>National News</td>
<td>National News</td>
<td>National News</td>
<td>National News</td>
<td>National News</td>
<td>National News</td>
```

2. Within the third table row, insert another seven td elements after the initial th element:

```
<td>Local News</td>
<td>Local News</td>
<td>Local News</td>
<td>Local News</td>
<td>Local News</td>
<td>Local News</td>
<td>Local News</td>
```

Figure 5-5 shows the newly inserted HTML code.

Figure 5-5   Inserting table data

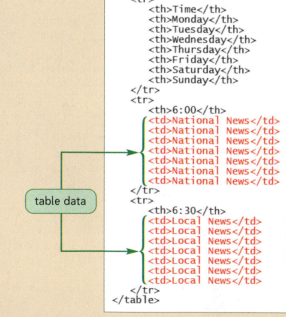

```
<table class="schedule">
    <tr>
        <th>Time</th>
        <th>Monday</th>
        <th>Tuesday</th>
        <th>Wednesday</th>
        <th>Thursday</th>
        <th>Friday</th>
        <th>Saturday</th>
        <th>Sunday</th>
    </tr>
    <tr>
        <th>6:00</th>
        <td>National News</td>
        <td>National News</td>
        <td>National News</td>
        <td>National News</td>
        <td>National News</td>
        <td>National News</td>
        <td>National News</td>
    </tr>
    <tr>
        <th>6:30</th>
        <td>Local News</td>
        <td>Local News</td>
        <td>Local News</td>
        <td>Local News</td>
        <td>Local News</td>
        <td>Local News</td>
        <td>Local News</td>
    </tr>
</table>
```

table data

3. Save your changes to the file, and then refresh the **schedule.htm** file in your Web browser. Figure 5-6 shows the current appearance of the program schedule. The headings are in bold and centered, and the table data is in a normal font and left-aligned.

Figure 5-6   **Viewing the Web table**

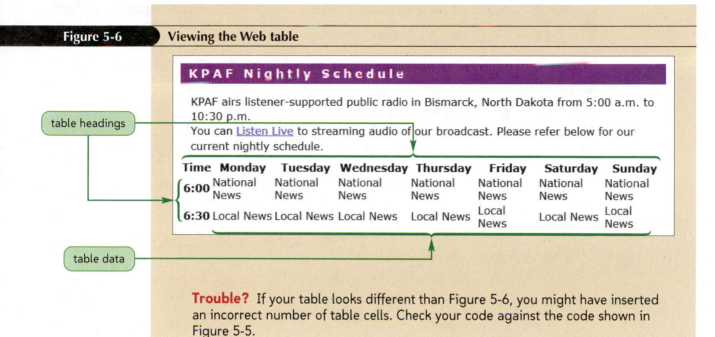

The table you created for Kyle has three rows and eight columns. Remember that the number of columns is determined by the maximum number of cells within each row. If one row has four cells and another row has five, the table will have five columns. The row with only four cells will have an empty space at the end, where the fifth cell should be.

Adding a Table Border

By default, no gridlines are displayed in a Web table, making it difficult to see the table structure. You decide the table would be easier to read with gridlines marking each cell in the table. In the next session, you'll learn how to do this using CSS. But for now, you'll use the HTML `border` attribute

```
<table border="value">
   ...
</table>
```

where `value` is the width of the table border in pixels. Figure 5-7 shows how different border values affect the appearance of a sample table.

Figure 5-7   **Tables with different border sizes**

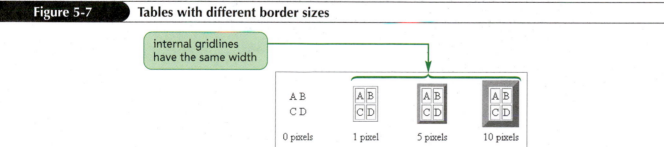

Note that the `border` attribute does not control the width of the internal gridlines that separate individual table cells. However, to display internal gridlines, you must add a border to the table. You can change the width of internal gridlines by changing the space between table cells, an issue you'll examine in the next session.

Adding a Table Border Using HTML

• To add a border to a Web table using HTML, use the `border` attribute

   `<table border="value"> ... </table>`

   where *value* is the size of the border in pixels.

You decide to add a 1-pixel border to the schedule table. As a result of the addition of the border, browsers also will insert gridlines around each of the table cells.

To add a border to the schedule:

1. Return to the **schedule.htm** file in your text editor and add the attribute

   `border="1"`

   to the `table` element as shown in Figure 5-8.

Figure 5-8	Adding a table border

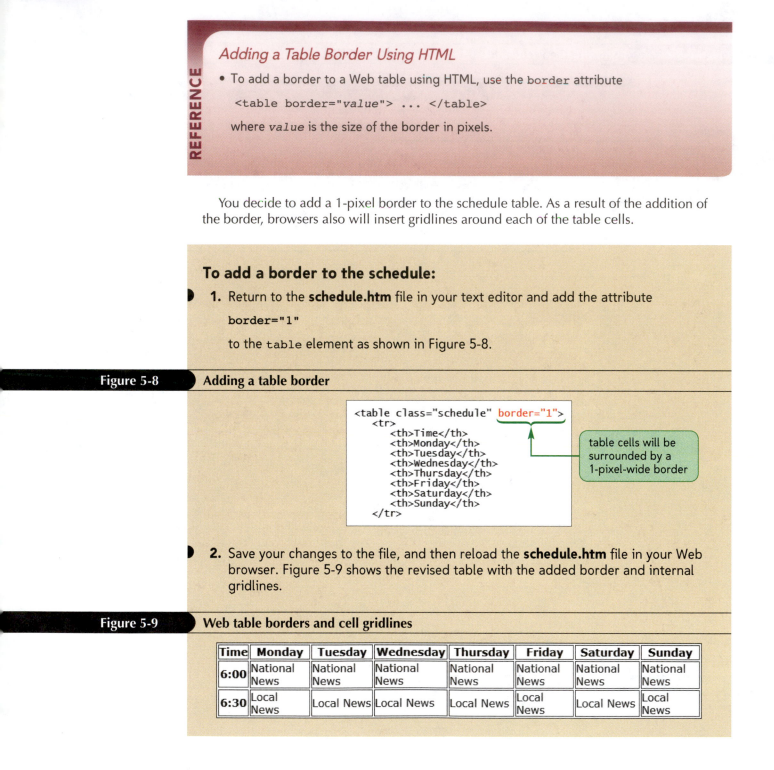

```
<table class="schedule" border="1">
    <tr>
        <th>Time</th>
        <th>Monday</th>
        <th>Tuesday</th>
        <th>Wednesday</th>
        <th>Thursday</th>
        <th>Friday</th>
        <th>Saturday</th>
        <th>Sunday</th>
    </tr>
```

table cells will be surrounded by a 1-pixel-wide border

2. Save your changes to the file, and then reload the **schedule.htm** file in your Web browser. Figure 5-9 shows the revised table with the added border and internal gridlines.

Figure 5-9	Web table borders and cell gridlines

Time	Monday	Tuesday	Wednesday	Thursday	Friday	Saturday	Sunday
6:00	National News	National News	National News	National News	National News	National News	National News
6:30	Local News	Local News	Local News	Local News	Local News	Local News	Local News

INSIGHT

Table Border Colors

Most browsers display a table border in gray, in a raised style that gives the border a 3D effect. There is no HTML attribute to change the border style, but many browsers allow you to change the color by adding the `bordercolor` attribute to the `table` element, using the syntax

```
<table border="value" bordercolor="color"> ... </table>
```

where *color* is either a recognized color name or a hexadecimal color value. For example, the following HTML code adds a 10-pixel blue border to a table:

```
<table border="10" bordercolor="blue"> ... </table>
```

The exact appearance of the table border differs among browsers. Internet Explorer, Google Chrome, and Safari display the border in a solid blue color; Firefox displays the border in a raised style using two shades of blue; and Opera does not support the `bordercolor` attribute at all. Thus, you should not rely on getting a consistent border color across all browsers with this attribute.

The `bordercolor` attribute has been deprecated by the World Wide Web Consortium (W3C) and is being gradually phased out. The recommended method is to use one of the CSS border styles discussed in Tutorial 4; however, you may still see this attribute used in many older Web pages.

Spanning Rows and Columns

Reviewing the schedule from Figure 5-2, you notice that several programs are longer than a half hour, and some are repeated across several days. For example, national news and local news air every day at 6:00 and 6:30, respectively. Likewise, from Monday through Thursday, the hour from 7:00 to 8:00 is needed for the shows Opera Fest, Radio U, Science Week, and The Living World, respectively. And finally, The Classical Music Connection airs Monday through Thursday for two hours from 8:00 to 10:00. Rather than repeat the names of programs in all of the half-hour slots, Kyle would prefer that the table cells stretch across those hours and days so that the text must be entered only once.

To do this, you create a spanning cell, which is a single cell that occupies more than one row or one column in the table. Spanning cells are created by adding either or both of the following rowspan and colspan attributes

```
rowspan="rows" colspan="columns"
```

to a th or td element, where *rows* is the number of rows that the cell should cover and *columns* is the number of columns. The spanning starts in the cell where you put the rowspan and colspan attributes, and goes downward and to the right from that cell. For example, to create a data cell that spans two columns and three rows, you'd enter the td element as follows:

```
<td colspan="2" rowspan="3"> ... </td>
```

It's important to remember that when a cell spans multiple rows or columns, it pushes other cells down or to the right. If you want to maintain the same number of rows and columns in your table, you must adjust the number of cells in a row or column that includes a spanning cell. To account for a column-spanning cell, you have to reduce the number of cells in the current row. For example, if a table is supposed to cover five columns, but one of the cells in the row spans three columns, you need only three cell elements in that row: two cells that occupy a single column each and one cell that spans the remaining three columns.

Creating a Spanning Cell

- To create a table cell that spans several columns, add the attribute

  `colspan="columns"`

  to the cell, where `columns` is the number of columns covered by the cell.
- To create a table cell that spans several rows, add the attribute

  `rowspan="rows"`

  to the cell, where `rows` is the number of rows covered by the cell.

To see how column-spanning cells work, you'll replace the cells for the National News and Local News programs that currently occupy seven cells each with a single cell spanning seven columns in each row.

To create cells that span several columns:

You must remove table cells from the table row when you add a cell that spans several columns or else the cell contents won't align properly within the columns.

1. Return to the **schedule.htm** file in your text editor and add the attribute

   `colspan="7"`

   to the second table cell in both the second and third rows of the table.

2. Delete the remaining six table cells in both the second and third table rows. Figure 5-10 shows the revised code for the schedule table.

Figure 5-10 **Marking cells to span several columns**

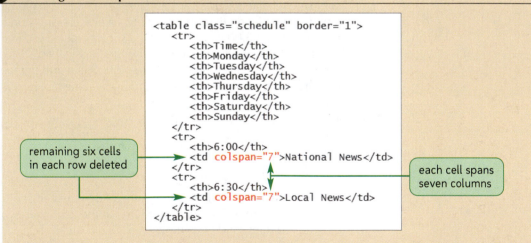

```
<table class="schedule" border="1">
    <tr>
        <th>Time</th>
        <th>Monday</th>
        <th>Tuesday</th>
        <th>Wednesday</th>
        <th>Thursday</th>
        <th>Friday</th>
        <th>Saturday</th>
        <th>Sunday</th>
    </tr>
    <tr>
        <th>6:00</th>
        <td colspan="7">National News</td>
    </tr>
    <tr>
        <th>6:30</th>
        <td colspan="7">Local News</td>
    </tr>
</table>
```

remaining six cells in each row deleted

each cell spans seven columns

3. Save your changes to the file, and then refresh the **schedule.htm** file in your Web browser. Figure 5-11 shows the revised appearance of the Web table.

Figure 5-11   **Column-spanning cells**

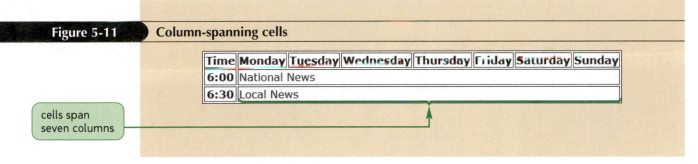

Time	Monday	Tuesday	Wednesday	Thursday	Friday	Saturday	Sunday
6:00	National News						
6:30	Local News						

cells span seven columns

To make the cells for the hour-long shows on Monday through Thursday, you'll need to span two rows, which lengthens the height of each cell. For row-spanning cells, you need to remove extra cells from the rows below the spanning cell. Consider the table shown in Figure 5-12, which contains three rows and four columns. The first cell spans three rows. You need four table cells in the first row, but only three in the second and third rows. This is because the spanning cell from row one occupies a position reserved for a cell that would normally appear in those rows.

Figure 5-12   **Row-spanning cell**

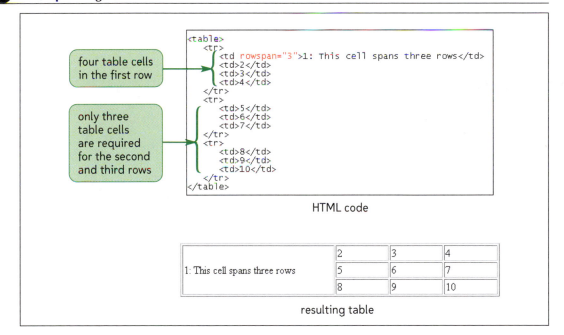

four table cells in the first row

only three table cells are required for the second and third rows

```
<table>
  <tr>
    <td rowspan="3">1: This cell spans three rows</td>
    <td>2</td>
    <td>3</td>
    <td>4</td>
  </tr>
  <tr>
    <td>5</td>
    <td>6</td>
    <td>7</td>
  </tr>
  <tr>
    <td>8</td>
    <td>9</td>
    <td>10</td>
  </tr>
</table>
```

HTML code

1: This cell spans three rows	2	3	4
	5	6	7
	8	9	10

resulting table

The 7:00 to 8:00 section of the KPAF schedule contains several programs that run for an hour. To insert these programs, you'll create row-spanning cells that span two rows in the schedule table. To keep the columns lined up, you must reduce the number of cells entered in the subsequent row.

To span several table rows:

1. Return to the **schedule.htm** file in your text editor and add the following row to the bottom of the schedule table:

```
<tr>
    <th>7:00</th>
    <td rowspan="2">Opera Fest</td>
    <td rowspan="2">Radio U</td>
    <td rowspan="2">Science Week</td>
    <td rowspan="2">The Living World</td>
    <td>Word Play</td>
    <td>Agri-Week</td>
    <td rowspan="2">Folk Fest</td>
</tr>
```

2. Add the following code for the next row, which adds table cells only for the two programs that start at 7:30:

```
<tr>
    <th>7:30</th>
    <td>Brain Stew</td>
    <td>Bismarck Forum</td>
</tr>
```

Figure 5-13 shows the code for the two new table rows.

Figure 5-13	Inserting cells that span two rows

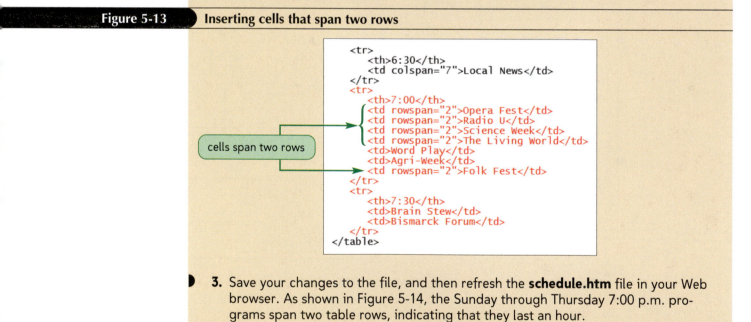

cells span two rows

3. Save your changes to the file, and then refresh the **schedule.htm** file in your Web browser. As shown in Figure 5-14, the Sunday through Thursday 7:00 p.m. programs span two table rows, indicating that they last an hour.

Figure 5-14   **Schedule table with several one-hour programs spanning two rows**

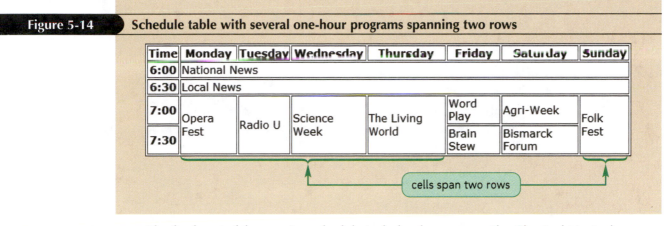

The final part of the evening schedule includes the program The Classical Musical Connection, which spans two hours on Monday through Thursday. Like the news programs, you don't want to repeat the name of the show each day; and like the five hour-long programs you just entered, you don't want to repeat the name of the show in each half-hour cell. Kyle suggests that you use both the `colspan` and `rowspan` attributes to create a table cell that spans four rows and four columns.

Other programs in the 8:00 to 10:00 time slots, such as Saturday Nite Jazz and The Indie Connection, also span four rows, but only one column. The last program aired before KPAF signs off is the World News Feed, which is played every night from 10:00 to 10:30. You'll add these and the other late evening programs to the schedule table now.

To add the remaining KPAF evening programs:

1. Return to the **schedule.htm** file in your text editor and enter the following table row for programs airing starting at 8:00:

```
<tr>
    <th>8:00</th>
    <td rowspan="4" colspan="4">The Classical Music Connection</td>
    <td>Old Time Radio</td>
    <td rowspan="4">Saturday Nite Jazz</td>
    <td rowspan="4">The Indie Connection</td>
</tr>
```

2. The Inner Mind is the only program that starts at 8:30 during the week. Add the 8:30 starting time and the program listing to the table using the following row:

```
<tr>
    <th>8:30</th>
    <td>The Inner Mind</td>
</tr>
```

3. The only program that starts at 9:00 is Open Mike Nite. Add the following row to the table to display this program in the schedule:

```
<tr>
    <th>9:00</th>
    <td rowspan="2">Open Mike Nite</td>
</tr>
```

4. There are no programs that start at 9:30, so you'll add the table row but without any programs listed. Add the following row:

```
<tr>
    <th>9:30</th>
</tr>
```

5. Complete the schedule table by adding the last table row for the World News Feed occurring every night from 10:00 to 10:30. This single program occupies a single row and spans seven columns. Add the following row:

```
<tr>
    <th>10:00</th>
    <td colspan="7">World News Feed</td>
</tr>
```

Figure 5-15 shows the code completing the structure of the schedule table.

Figure 5-15   **Adding the remaining KPAF evening programs**

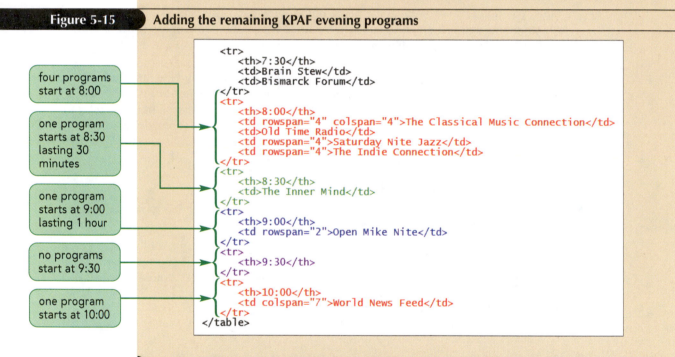

6. Save your changes to the file, and then reload the **schedule.htm** file in your Web browser. Figure 5-16 shows the complete evening schedule of programs offered by KPAF.

Figure 5-16   **The complete KPAF evening schedule**

Time	Monday	Tuesday	Wednesday	Thursday	Friday	Saturday	Sunday
6:00	National News						
6:30	Local News						
7:00	Opera Fest	Radio U	Science Week	The Living World	Word Play	Agri-Week	Folk Fest
7:30					Brain Stew	Bismarck Forum	
8:00	The Classical Music Connection				Old Time Radio	Saturday Nite Jazz	The Indie Connection
8:30					The Inner Mind		
9:00					Open Mike Nite		
9:30							
10:00	World News Feed						

The Web table you created matches the printout of KPAF's evening schedule. Kyle likes the clear structure of the table. He notes that many KPAF listeners tune into the station over the Internet, listening to KPAF's streaming audio feed. Because those listeners might be located in different time zones, Kyle suggests that you add a caption to the table indicating that all times in the schedule are based on the Central Time Zone.

Creating a Table Caption

Table captions are another part of the basic table structure and are marked using the `caption` element

```
<table>
   <caption>content</caption>
   ...
</table>
```

where *content* is the content contained within the caption. You can nest text-level elements within a `caption` element. For example, the following code marks the text *Program Schedule* using the em element:

```
<table>
   <caption><em>Program Schedule</em></caption>
   ...
</table>
```

Only one caption is allowed per Web table, and the `caption` element must be listed directly after the opening `<table>` tag.

Creating a Table Caption

- To create a table caption, add the `caption` element directly below the opening `<table>` tag using the syntax

  `<caption>`*content*`</caption>`

  where *content* is the content of the table caption.

Add Kyle's suggested caption to the program schedule.

To create a caption for the program schedule:

1. Return to the **schedule.htm** file in your text editor and insert the following `caption` element directly below the opening tag, as shown in Figure 5-17:

   `<caption>All Times Central</caption>`

Figure 5-17   Inserting a table caption

```
<table class="schedule" border="1">
    <caption>All Times Central</caption>
    <tr>
        <th>Time</th>
        <th>Monday</th>
        <th>Tuesday</th>
        <th>Wednesday</th>
        <th>Thursday</th>
        <th>Friday</th>
        <th>Saturday</th>
        <th>Sunday</th>
    </tr>
```

2. Save your changes to the file and refresh the **schedule.htm** file in your Web browser. As shown in Figure 5-18, Kyle's suggested caption appears centered above the Web table.

Figure 5-18   **Table caption for the KPAF programming schedule**

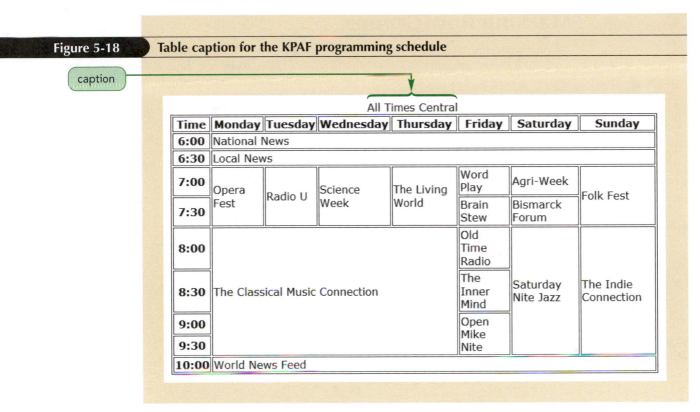

caption

Time	Monday	Tuesday	Wednesday	Thursday	Friday	Saturday	Sunday
6:00	National News						
6:30	Local News						
7:00	Opera Fest	Radio U	Science Week	The Living World	Word Play	Agri-Week	Folk Fest
7:30					Brain Stew	Bismarck Forum	
8:00	The Classical Music Connection				Old Time Radio	Saturday Nite Jazz	The Indie Connection
8:30					The Inner Mind		
9:00					Open Mike Nite		
9:30							
10:00	World News Feed						

All Times Central

Although table captions might lie outside of the borders of a Web table, they are still part of the Web table's structure. This means that they inherit any styles associated with the table. For example, if you create a style for the `table` element that sets the font color to red, the caption text also will be displayed in a red font. You'll explore how to apply styles to table captions in the next session.

INSIGHT

Aligning a Caption with HTML

A table caption is treated as a block element and by default placed directly above the table, but you can change the placement of the caption in HTML using the following `align` attribute:

```
<caption align="position">content</caption>
```

In this code, *position* can be either `top`, `bottom`, `left`, or `right`, to place the caption above, below, or to the left or right sides of the table, respectively.

The interpretation of the `left` and `right` values is not consistent among the major browsers. Firefox places the captions to the left or right of the Web table. Internet Explorer and Opera still place the caption above the table, but horizontally align the caption text to the left or right. Safari and Chrome ignore the `align` attribute altogether.

The `align` attribute is another example of a presentational attribute that has been deprecated in favor of style sheets, though you'll still often find it used on Web sites, both old and new. However, the best practice is to align the caption not in the HTML file, but in a style sheet using the `caption-side` property.

Marking Row Groups

You can combine sections of rows into row groups in which each row group represents a different collection of table data or information. HTML supports three row groups: one to mark the header rows, another for the body rows, and a third for the footer rows. The syntax to create these three row groups is

```
<table>
   <thead>
      table rows
   </thead>
   <tfoot>
      table rows
   </tfoot>
   <tbody>
      table rows
   </tbody>
</table>
```

where *table rows* are rows from the Web table. For example, the following code marks two rows as belonging to the table header row group:

```
<thead>
   <tr>
      <th colspan="2">KPAF Programs</th>
   </tr>
   <tr>
      <th>Time</th>
      <th>Program</th>
   </tr>
</thead>
```

Order is important. The `thead` element must appear first, and then the `tfoot` element, and finally the `tbody` element. A table can contain only one `thead` element and one `tfoot` element, but it can include any number of `tbody` elements. The reason the table body group appears last, rather than the footer group, is to allow the browser to render the footer before receiving what might be numerous groups of table body rows.

One purpose of row groups is to allow you to create different styles for groups of rows in your table. Any style that you apply to the `thead`, `tbody`, or `tfoot` element is inherited by the rows those elements contain. Row groups also are used for tables in which table body contents are made up of imported data from external data sources such as databases or XML documents. In those situations, a single table can span several Web pages, with different imported content displayed in the table body in each page but the same table header and table footer bracketing each page of content.

REFERENCE

Creating Row Groups

- Row groups must be entered in the following order: table header rows, table footer rows, and then table body rows.
- To create a row group consisting of header rows, add the element

```
<thead>
    rows
</thead>
```

within the table, where *rows* are the row elements within the table header.
- To create a row group consisting of footer rows, add the following element:

```
<tfoot>
    rows
</tfoot>
```

- To create a row group consisting of rows used in the body of the table, add the following element:

```
<tbody>
    rows
</tbody>
```

A table can contain multiple table body row groups.

To indicate the structure of the schedule table, you decide to use the `thead` element to mark the header row in the program schedule, and the `tbody` element to mark the rows that include the broadcast times of each program. You do not need to specify a footer for this table.

To mark the row groups:

1. Return to the **schedule.htm** file in your text editor and enclose the first row of the table within an opening and closing set of `<thead>` tags.

2. Enclose the remaining rows of the table within an opening and closing set of `<tbody>` tags. Figure 5-19 shows the markup tags for the two new row groups.

Figure 5-19   **Marking the table head and table body row groups**

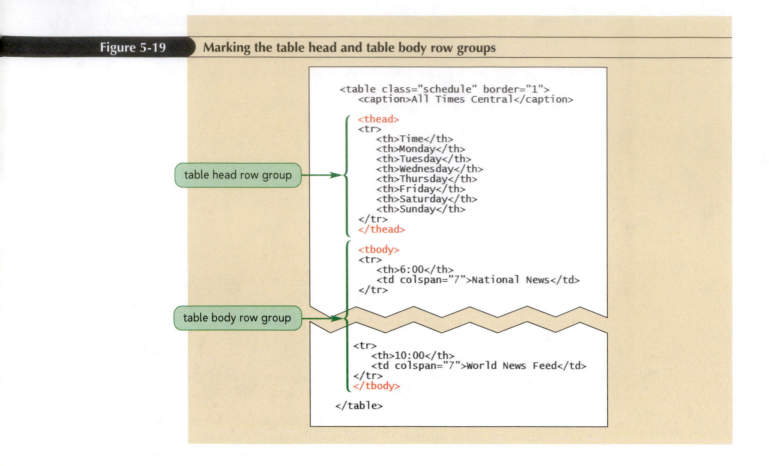

table head row group

table body row group

```
<table class="schedule" border="1">
    <caption>All Times Central</caption>
<thead>
<tr>
    <th>Time</th>
    <th>Monday</th>
    <th>Tuesday</th>
    <th>Wednesday</th>
    <th>Thursday</th>
    <th>Friday</th>
    <th>Saturday</th>
    <th>Sunday</th>
</tr>
</thead>

<tbody>
<tr>
    <th>6:00</th>
    <td colspan="7">National News</td>
</tr>


<tr>
    <th>10:00</th>
    <td colspan="7">World News Feed</td>
</tr>
</tbody>

</table>
```

Marking Column Groups

As you've seen, there is no HTML tag to mark table columns—the columns are created implicitly from the number of cells within each row. However, once browsers determine the columns, you can reference the columns through the use of column groups. Column groups give you the ability to assign a common format to all of the cells within a given column. Column groups are defined using the `colgroup` element

```
<colgroup>
   columns
</colgroup>
```

where `columns` are the individual columns with the group. The columns themselves are referenced using the following `col` element:

```
<col />
```

Once you create a column group, you can add `id` or `class` attributes to identify or classify individual columns. For example, the following code creates a column group consisting of three columns, each with a different class name:

```
<colgroup>
   <col class="column1" />
   <col class="column2" />
   <col class="column3" />
</colgroup>
```

The browser applies any style specified for the `col` element to cells within the corresponding column in the Web table. Thus, to style these three columns with different background colors, you could apply the following style rules:

```
col.column1 {background-color: red;}
col.column2 {background-color: blue;}
col.column3 {background-color: yellow;}
```

In this example, browsers would display the first table column with a background color of red, the second with blue, and the third with yellow. Note that not all CSS styles can be applied to table columns. You'll explore column styles in more detail in the next session.

The `col` element also supports the `span` attribute, allowing a column reference to cover several table columns. The syntax of the `span` attribute is

```
<col span="value" />
```

where `value` is the number of columns spanned by the `col` element. Thus, the column structure

```
<colgroup>
    <col class="column1" />
    <col class="nextColumns" span="2" />
</colgroup>
```

references a group of three columns; the first column belongs to the *column1* class and the next two columns belong to the *nextColumns* class. Note that you also can apply the span attribute to a column group itself. The following code uses two column groups to also reference three columns, the first belonging to the *column1* class and the last two belonging to the *nextColumns* class:

```
<colgroup class="column1"></colgroup>
<colgroup class="nextColumns" span="2"></colgroup>
```

Notice that in this case there are no `col` elements within the column group. Browsers will assume the number of columns indicated by the `span` attribute; if no `span` attribute is present, a column group is assumed to have only one column.

TIP

The total number of columns spanned by the `col` elements must match the total number of columns in the Web table.

REFERENCE

Creating Column Groups

- To create a column group, add the element

```
<colgroup>
    columns
</colgroup>
```

to the Web table, where *columns* are `col` elements representing individual columns within the group.
- To define a column or columns within a column group, use the `col` element

```
<col span="value" />
```

where *value* is the number of defined columns. The span attribute is not required if only one column is defined.

Now that you've seen how columns can be referenced through the use of column groups, you'll create a column group for the programming table. You'll mark the first column containing the broadcast times for the different KPAF programs using a `col` element with the class name *firstCol*, and mark the remaining seven columns containing the daily program listings with a `col` element spanning seven columns and identified with the class name *dayCols*. These groupings will allow you to format the two sets of columns in different ways later on in the next session.

To mark the column groups:

1. Return to the **schedule.htm** file in your text editor.

2. Directly below the `caption` element, insert the following `colgroup` element, as shown in Figure 5-20:

   ```
   <colgroup>
      <col class="firstCol" />
      <col class="dayCols" span="7" />
   </colgroup>
   ```

Figure 5-20   **Inserting a column group**

3. Save your changes to the file.

4. Creating row groups and column groups defines the table's structure but should not alter its appearance. To confirm that the row and column groups have not modified the table's appearance, refresh the **schedule.htm** file in your browser. Verify that the table layout is the same as that shown earlier in Figure 5-18.

PROSKILLS

Problem Solving: Using Tables for Page Layout

Table cells can contain any HTML elements including headings, lists, inline images, and even other tables. Because of the flexibility of tables in organizing content, before the widespread adoption of CSS for page layout, tables also were used to design the layout of entire pages. Using tables for page layout is strongly discouraged for several reasons:

- *Tabular layouts violate the purpose of HTML.* A basic philosophy of Web page design is that HTML code should indicate the structure of a document, but not how the document should be rendered by browsers. Tables take control of layout from style sheets, putting page design back into the HTML file.

- *Table layouts are difficult to revise.* Imagine a complex table layout consisting of two columns with several levels of additional tables nested within each column. Now imagine having to revise that table structure, changing it into a three-column layout. This would not be an easy task because the page content would be intertwined with the page layout. Further, imagine the difficulty of having to repeat that design change for dozens of pages across a large Web site. By contrast, a layout created with a properly designed style sheet is much easier to maintain and revise because it is separate from the page content.

- *Tables take longer to render.* Unless the size of every element in a table is specified, browsers need to first load the table content and then run algorithms to determine how to size each element of the table. This can be time-consuming for large, complex tables that involve many cells and nested elements.

- *Table layouts are code-heavy.* Creating a visually striking table layout often requires several levels of nested table cells, rows, and columns. The ratio of HTML code to actual page content thus becomes more heavily weighted toward the HTML code, resulting in a document that takes longer to load and that can be difficult to interpret by people who need to edit the underlying code.

- *Tables can be inaccessible to users with disabilities.* Aural or Braille browsers recite the Web page content line-by-line down through the file, but tables convey information both horizontally and vertically. The result is that information that is easily understood visually is unintelligible aurally. On the other hand, with style sheets an aural style could be designed that would better convey such information aurally.

Because CSS is so widely supported, there is little reason to use tables for page layout. However, Web table layouts will not disappear immediately. So as a Web page designer, you must be conversant with both approaches—especially if you are called upon to support older browser versions or have the task of maintaining the code of an older Web site that involves table layouts.

Adding a Table Summary

Nonvisual browsers, such as aural browsers that often are used by visually impaired people, can't display tables, and it's cumbersome for users to listen to each cell being read. For these situations, it is useful to include a summary of a table's contents. While a caption and the surrounding page text usually provide clues about a table and its contents, the summary attribute allows you to include a more detailed description. The syntax of the summary attribute is

```
<table summary="description"> ... </table>
```

where *description* is a text string that describes the table's content and structure. The summary attribute fulfills the same role that the alt attribute accomplishes for inline images: providing a textual (aural) alternative to essentially visual material. A user running a screen reader or other type of aural browser first will hear the summary of the table's contents, which can aid in interpreting the subsequent reading of the table's content.

Kyle definitely wants the KPAF Web page to be accessible to users with all types of disabilities, and he asks that you include a summary description of the program schedule.

To add a summary to the table:

1. Return to the **schedule.htm** file in your text editor.

TIP

In some browsers, you can view the summary description by right-clicking the table and selecting Properties from the shortcut menu.

2. Within the opening <table> tag, insert the following attribute, as shown in Figure 5-21:

```
summary="This table contains the nightly KPAF program schedule
aired from Bismarck, North Dakota. Program times are laid
out in thirty-minute increments from 6:00 p.m. to
10:00 p.m., Monday through Sunday night."
```

Figure 5-21   Inserting a table summary

```
<table class="schedule" border="1"
       summary="This table contains the nightly KPAF program schedule
                aired from Bismarck, North Dakota. Program times are laid
                out in thirty-minute increments from 6:00 p.m. to
                10:00 p.m., Monday through Sunday night.">
    <caption>All Times Central</caption>
```

table summary

3. Save your changes to the file and then reload the **schedule.htm** file in your Web browser. Verify that the summary description does not appear in the browser window.

Creating Tables with Preformatted Text

As you learned in Tutorial 1, browsers strip out white space from the HTML code when they render Web pages. You can force browsers to keep certain white space by marking your document text as preformatted text, in which browsers display the spacing and line breaks exactly as you enter them. Preformatted text is created using the `pre` element

```
<pre>content</pre>
```

where *content* is the text that will appear preformatted in browsers. One use of preformatted text is to quickly create tables that are neatly laid out in rows and columns. For example, the code

```
<pre>
Time    Friday      Saturday
====    ==========  ==============
7:30    Brain Stew  Bismarck Forum
</pre>
```

is displayed by browsers exactly as typed, with the spaces as shown:

```
Time    Friday      Saturday
====    ==========  ==============
7:30    Brain Stew  Bismarck Forum
```

Preformatted text is displayed by browsers in a monospace font in which each letter takes up the same amount of space. One of the advantages of monospace fonts that make them useful for entering tabular data is that the relative space between characters is unchanged as the font size increases or decreases. This means that if the font size of the above table were increased or decreased, the columns still would line up.

Although you probably should use the `table` element to display most of your data, you might consider using preformatted text for simple and quick text tables.

You've completed your work laying out the basic structure of the KPAF program schedule. The next thing Kyle wants you to focus on is formatting the table to look attractive and professional. In the next session, you'll explore how to apply design styles to make a Web table interesting and attractive.

Session 5.1 Quick Check

1. How is the number of columns in a Web table determined?
2. How does a browser usually render text marked with the `<th>` tag?
3. Specify the HTML attribute to add a 10-pixel-wide border to a Web table.
4. A table data cell contains the text *Monday* and should stretch across two rows and three columns. Provide the HTML code for the cell.
5. What adjustment do you have to make when a cell spans multiple columns?
6. Captions usually appear above or below their Web tables. Explain why a caption is still part of a table's structure.
7. What are the three table row groups, and in what order must they be specified in the code?
8. Specify the code to create a column group in which the first two columns belong to the *introCol* class and the next three columns belong to the *col1, col2,* and *col3* classes, respectively.
9. What is the purpose of the `table summary` attribute?

SESSION 5.2 VISUAL OVERVIEW

The **column-count** property sets the number of columns.

The **column-gap** property sets the space between columns.

The **column-rule** property adds a dividing line between columns.

```
p {
    column-count: 2;
    column-gap: 20px;
    column-rule: 2px solid purple;
}
```

```
table {
    border-collapse: collapse;
}
```

The **border-collapse** property merges adjacent borders into one border.

The thead selector applies to the table header row group.

```
table thead {
    background-color: rgb(203, 50, 203);
    color: white;
    color: rgba(255, 255, 255, 0.5);
}
```

The style rule displays the header row in semi-transparent white on a purple background.

The col.firstCol selector applies to the first column group.

The style rule displays the first column with a background color of yellow and a width 7% of the width of the table.

```
table col.firstCol {
    background-color: yellow;
    width: 7%;
}
```

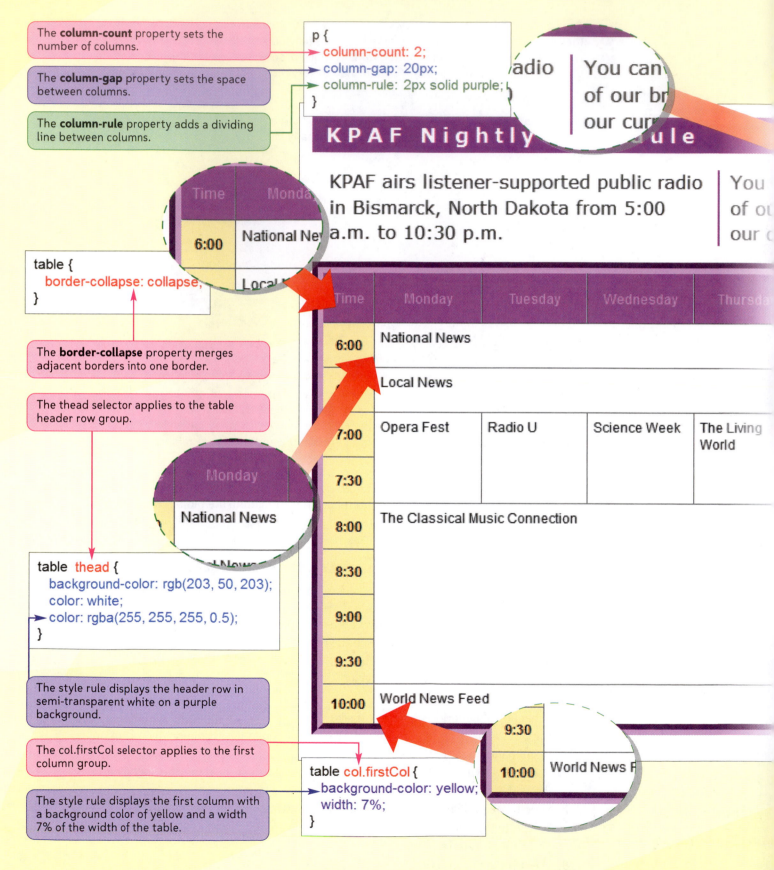

KPAF Nightly Schedule

KPAF airs listener-supported public radio in Bismarck, North Dakota from 5:00 a.m. to 10:30 p.m.

Time	Monday	Tuesday	Wednesday	Thursday
6:00	National News			
	Local News			
7:00	Opera Fest	Radio U	Science Week	The Living World
7:30				
8:00	The Classical Music Connection			
8:30				
9:00				
9:30				
10:00	World News Feed			

WEB TABLE STYLES

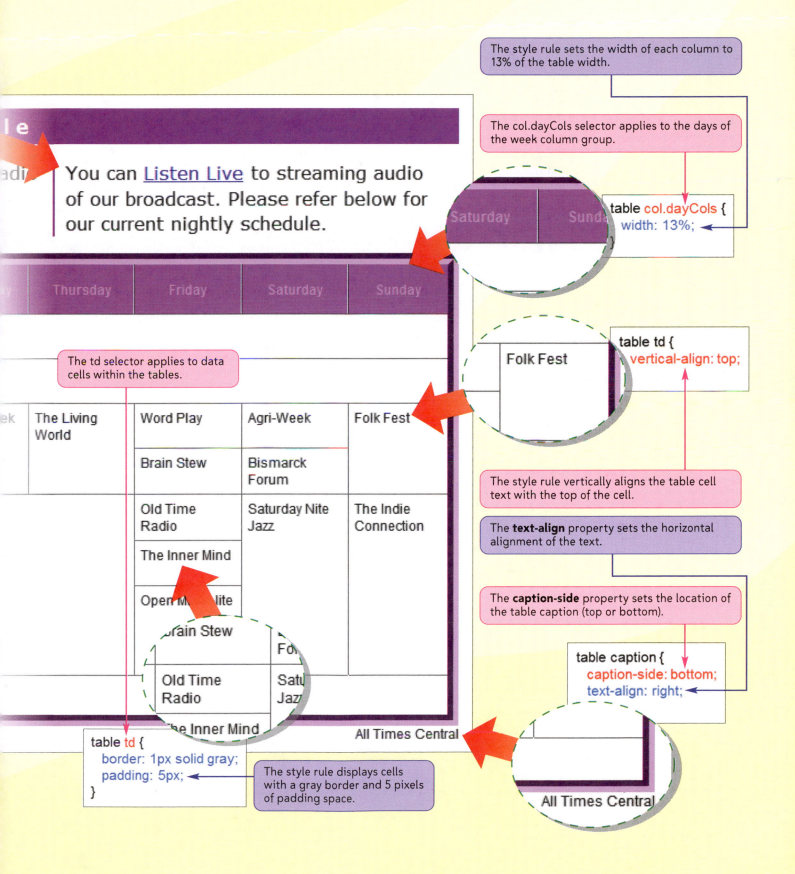

The style rule sets the width of each column to 13% of the table width.

The col.dayCols selector applies to the days of the week column group.

```
table col.dayCols {
    width: 13%;
}
```

The td selector applies to data cells within the tables.

```
table td {
    vertical-align: top;
}
```

The style rule vertically aligns the table cell text with the top of the cell.

The **text-align** property sets the horizontal alignment of the text.

The **caption-side** property sets the location of the table caption (top or bottom).

```
table caption {
    caption-side: bottom;
    text-align: right;
}
```

```
table td {
    border: 1px solid gray;
    padding: 5px;
}
```

The style rule displays cells with a gray border and 5 pixels of padding space.

Formatting Tables with HTML Attributes

After specifying the content and structure of the program schedule, you and Kyle are ready to format the table's appearance. There are two approaches to formatting Web tables: using HTML attributes, and using CSS styles. Because you'll see both approaches used on the Internet, you'll examine both techniques, starting with the HTML attribute approach.

Setting Cell Spacing with HTML

Web tables are one of the older HTML page elements, predating the introduction of Cascading Style Sheets. Because of this, HTML has long supported several attributes for controlling the layout and appearance of a table. In the last session, you used one of those attributes, the `border` attribute, to create a table border and display internal table gridlines. The next attribute you'll consider controls the amount of space between table cells. By default, most browsers separate cells by a 2-pixel space. To set a different spacing value, you add the `cellspacing` attribute

```
<table cellspacing="value"> ... </table>
```

to the `table` element, where `value` is the size of the cell spacing in pixels. If you have applied a border to your table, changing the cell spacing value also impacts the size of the internal gridlines. Figure 5-22 shows how different cell spacing values affect the appearance of the table border and internal gridlines. Note that if the cell spacing is set to 0 pixels, many browsers still display an internal gridline that results from the drop shadow that those browsers apply to cell and table borders.

Figure 5-22   **Cell spacing values**

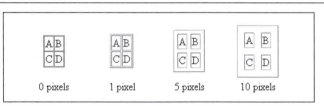

| 0 pixels | 1 pixel | 5 pixels | 10 pixels |

Cell spacing essentially sets the outside margins of table cells. Unlike the CSS `margin` style, you can specify cell spacing values only in pixels and not in other measuring units. You also can't set different cell spacing values for the different sides of a cell. In addition, the effect of setting the cell spacing value is limited by the width allotted to the entire table; browsers ignore cell spacing values that would push a table beyond its defined width.

Setting Cell Padding with HTML

Related to cell spacing is the padding between cell contents and the cell border. In HTML, you set the padding space using the `cellpadding` attribute

```
<table cellpadding="value"> ... </table>
```

where `value` is the size of the cell padding. Like the `cellspacing` attribute, the `cellpadding` attribute applies to every cell in a table. Figure 5-23 shows the impact of various cell padding values on a table's appearance. Cell padding is similar to the CSS `padding` style, though there is no option to define padding values for different sides of the cell. Also, as for the `cellspacing` attribute, values of the `cellpadding` attribute can be expressed only in pixels and not in other units of measure.

Figure 5-23   **Cell padding values**

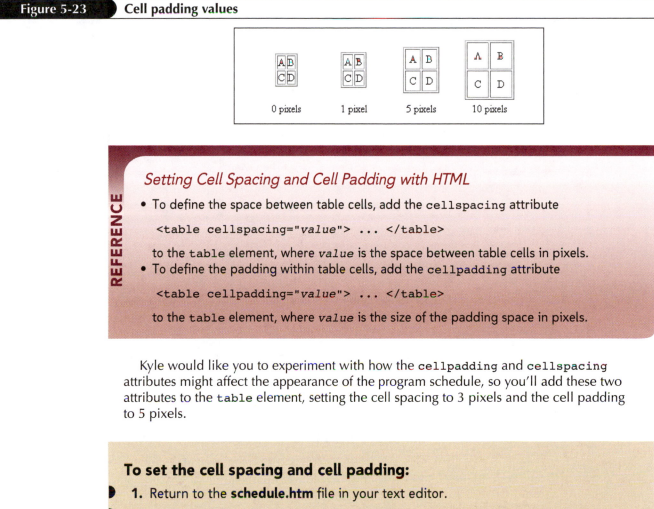

Setting Cell Spacing and Cell Padding with HTML

REFERENCE

- To define the space between table cells, add the `cellspacing` attribute

  `<table cellspacing="value"> ... </table>`

  to the `table` element, where *value* is the space between table cells in pixels.
- To define the padding within table cells, add the `cellpadding` attribute

  `<table cellpadding="value"> ... </table>`

  to the `table` element, where *value* is the size of the padding space in pixels.

Kyle would like you to experiment with how the `cellpadding` and `cellspacing` attributes might affect the appearance of the program schedule, so you'll add these two attributes to the `table` element, setting the cell spacing to 3 pixels and the cell padding to 5 pixels.

To set the cell spacing and cell padding:

1. Return to the **schedule.htm** file in your text editor.

2. Within the opening `<table>` tag, insert the following attributes, as shown in Figure 5-24:

   `cellspacing="3" cellpadding="5"`

Figure 5-24   **Setting the cell spacing and padding values**

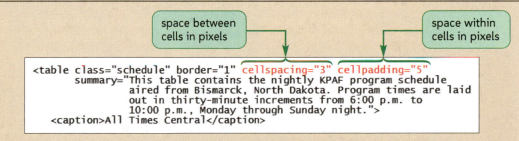

3. Save your changes to the file and then reopen **schedule.htm** in your Web browser. As shown in Figure 5-25, the spaces between and within the table cells have increased from their default values.

Figure 5-25   Increased padding and spacing within the Web table

Figure 5-25   **Increased padding and spacing within the Web table**

All Times Central

Time	Monday	Tuesday	Wednesday	Thursday	Friday	Saturday	Sunday
6:00	National News						
6:30	Local News						
7:00	Opera Fest	Radio U	Science Week	The Living World	Word Play	Agri-Week	Folk Fest
7:30					Brain Stew	Bismarck Forum	
8:00	The Classical Music Connection				Old Time Radio	Saturday Nite Jazz	The Indie Connection
8:30					The Inner Mind		
9:00					Open Mike Nite		
9:30							
10:00	World News Feed						

Setting Table Widths and Heights in HTML

You can use HTML to set the overall width and height of a table and of the individual cells within the table. By default, the width of a table ranges from the minimum necessary to display all the cell contents without line wrapping, up to the width of the container element. To set the width of a table to a specific value, you add the `width` attribute

```
<table width="value"> ... </table>
```

to the `table` element, where `value` is the width either in pixels or as a percentage of the width of the containing element. If the containing element is the page itself, you can set the table to fill the entire page width by specifying a width value of 100%. You still can never reduce a table to a width smaller than is required to display the content or larger than the width of its container. For example, if table content requires a width of 450 pixels, then browsers will ignore any `width` attribute that attempts to set a smaller table size.

Many browsers also support the `height` attribute, which has the syntax

```
<table height="value"> ... </table>
```

where `value` is the height of the table either in pixels or as a percentage of the height of the containing element. Even though the `height` attribute is widely supported for the `table` element, it is not part of the specifications for any version of HTML or XHTML. Like the `width` attribute, the `height` attribute indicates only the minimum height of the table. If table content cannot fit into the specified height, the table height increases to accommodate the content.

You also can set the widths of individual columns by applying the `width` attribute to either an individual column or a column group. For example, the HTML code

```
<colgroup width="100" span="7">
</colgroup>
```

sets the width of each of the seven columns in the column group to 100 pixels. To specify different column widths, you apply the width attribute to individual col elements as in the following code:

```
<colgroup>
   <col width="50" />
   <col width="100" span="5" />
   <col width="50" />
</colgroup>
```

This code sets the widths of the five middle columns to 100 pixels, but sets the widths of the first and seventh columns to 50 pixels each. Column widths also can be expressed as a percentage of the total width of a table. A column width of 50% causes a column to occupy half of the table width. Column widths always are limited by the total width of the table and by the content of each cell. For example, if you try to set the width of each column in a five-column table to 200 pixels, but only 800 pixels of space are available, browsers will reduce the column widths to fit the content.

In the code for many Web tables, you might see the width attribute applied to individual table cells. This is another way to set the width of an entire column because the remaining cells in a column where one cell has a width attribute also will adopt that width to keep the column cells aligned. Even so, the width value for a single cell might be overridden by browsers if other cells in the column require a larger width to display their content. With the introduction of column groups, there is little need to apply the width attribute to individual table cells. Also, the W3C has deprecated the use of the width attribute with the td and th elements. As you might expect, however, you still will see it supported by many of the current browsers.

Setting Row Heights with HTML

You can use HTML to set row heights by applying the height attribute

```
<tr height="value"> ... </tr>
```

to the tr element, where *value* is the height of the row in pixels. Internet Explorer also allows you to specify height values as a percentage of the height of the table. The height attribute is not part of the W3C specifications, but most browsers support it. Like setting the column width by setting the width of an individual cell, you also can set row height by applying the height attribute to an individual cell within a row. This approach also is supported by most browsers even though it has been deprecated by the W3C.

Formatting Table Borders with HTML

In the last session, you used the border attribute to add a border around the table and each of the table cells. You can modify the placement of the table borders using table frames and table rules. A **table frame** specifies which sides of the table (or which sides of the table cells) will have borders. To apply a frame to a table, you apply the frame attribute

```
<table border="value" frame="type"> ... </table>
```

to the table element, where *value* is the width of the table border and *type* is box (the default), above, border, below, hsides, vsides, lhs, rhs, or void. Figure 5-26 displays the impact of each of these frame options.

Figure 5-26   **Values of the frame attribute**

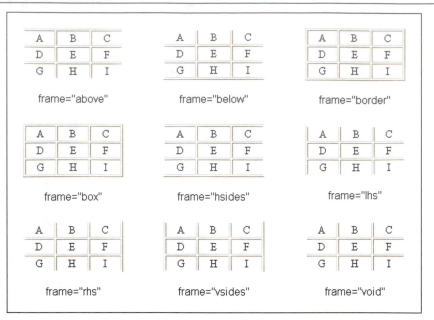

A **table rule** specifies how the internal gridlines are drawn within a table. To apply a table rule, you add the `rules` attribute to the `table` element using the syntax

```
<table border="value" rules="type"> ... </table>
```

where *type* is `all` (the default), `cols`, `groups`, `none`, or `rows`. Figure 5-27 displays the impact of each of these `rules` attribute values on the placement of the internal table gridlines.

Figure 5-27   Values of the rules attribute

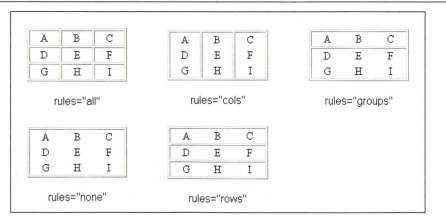

By combining `frame` and `rules` values, you can duplicate many of the same effects you could achieve using the CSS `border-style` property, which you'll explore shortly. Some Web page authors prefer to work with these HTML attributes because they enable them to set the appearance of the table borders from within the `<table>` tag rather than through an external style sheet.

Aligning Cell Contents with HTML

The final set of HTML table attributes you'll examine before looking at the CSS table styles are those attributes that control how content is aligned within each table cell. By default, browsers center the contents of table header cells horizontally and left-align the contents of table data cells. You can specify a different horizontal alignment using the `align` attribute, which has the syntax

```
align="position"
```

where *position* is `left`, `center`, `right`, `justify`, or `char`. The `align` attribute can be applied to table rows, row groups, columns, column groups, or individual table cells. For example, when applied to the column group

```
<colgroup>
   <col align="left" />
   <col span="6" align="right" />
</colgroup>
```

the `align` attribute left-aligns the first column of the Web table and right-aligns the remaining six columns.

When you apply the `align` attribute to the `table` element itself, it aligns the entire table with the surrounding page content but does not affect the alignment of the cells within the table. The `align` attribute has been deprecated for use with the `table` element, but not for the row, column, and cell elements within a table.

Vertical Alignment in HTML

You also can use HTML to vertically align the contents of each table cell. The default is to place the text in the middle of the cell. To choose a different placement, you apply the `valign` attribute using the syntax

```
valign="position"
```

where *position* is `top`, `middle`, `bottom`, or `baseline`. The `top`, `middle`, and `bottom` options align the content with the top, middle, and bottom borders of the cell, respectively. The `baseline` option places the text near the bottom of the cell, but aligns the bases of each letter. The `valign` attribute can be applied to table rows, row groups, columns, and column groups to set the vertical alignment of several cells at once.

Kyle feels that having the program names placed in the middle of each cell makes the program schedule more difficult to read. He prefers to have all of the program names lined up with the top of the cells. To change the cell alignment for all of the cells in the table body, you'll apply the `valign` attribute to the `tbody` row group.

To vertically align the text in the table:

1. Return to the **schedule.htm** file in your text editor.

2. Within the opening `<tbody>` tag, insert the following attribute, as shown in Figure 5-28:

   ```
   valign="top"
   ```

Figure 5-28 **Applying the valign attribute**

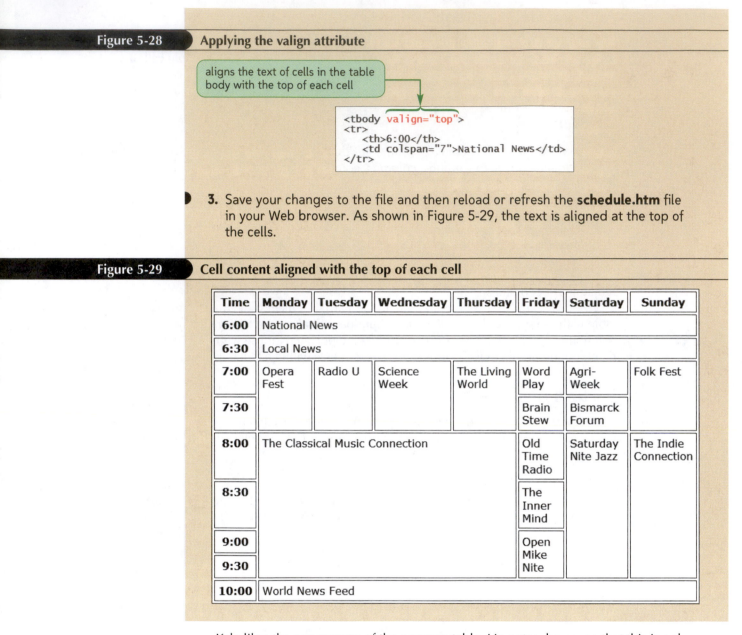

aligns the text of cells in the table body with the top of each cell

```
<tbody valign="top">
<tr>
    <th>6:00</th>
    <td colspan="7">National News</td>
</tr>
```

3. Save your changes to the file and then reload or refresh the **schedule.htm** file in your Web browser. As shown in Figure 5-29, the text is aligned at the top of the cells.

Figure 5-29 **Cell content aligned with the top of each cell**

Time	Monday	Tuesday	Wednesday	Thursday	Friday	Saturday	Sunday
6:00	National News						
6:30	Local News						
7:00	Opera Fest	Radio U	Science Week	The Living World	Word Play	Agri-Week	Folk Fest
7:30					Brain Stew	Bismarck Forum	
8:00	The Classical Music Connection				Old Time Radio	Saturday Nite Jazz	The Indie Connection
8:30					The Inner Mind		
9:00					Open Mike Nite		
9:30							
10:00	World News Feed						

Kyle likes the appearance of the program table. He notes, however, that this is only the evening schedule; he plans to create Web pages for the morning and afternoon schedules as well. To ensure that the tables match each other, you'll have to insert the various HTML attributes into each table's markup tags. Kyle would rather use CSS so he can easily apply the formatting he likes to all of the schedules at once using an external style sheet. He suggests that you explore the CSS table styles before continuing your design of the evening schedule.

Formatting Tables with CSS

Starting with CSS2, Cascading Style Sheets included support for Web tables. As browser support for these styles has grown, CSS gradually has replaced the HTML attributes you've just reviewed; although you will still frequently see those HTML attributes used on the Web. Kyle suggests that you replace the HTML table attributes with an external style sheet that he can apply to all of the program schedule tables on the KPAF Web site.

To create the style sheet:

1. Open the **tablestxt.css** file from the tutorial.05\tutorial folder. Enter *your name* and *the date* in the comment section of the file. Save the file as **tables.css** in the same folder.

2. Return to the **schedule.htm** file in your text editor and insert the following `link` element directly above the closing `</head>` tag:

   ```
   <link href="tables.css" rel="stylesheet" type="text/css" />
   ```

3. Because you'll be replacing the HTML attributes with CSS styles, delete the `border`, `cellpadding`, and `cellspacing` attributes from the opening `<table>` tag.

4. Delete the `valign` attribute from the opening `<tbody>` tag.

5. Save your changes to the file.

TIP

Don't combine HTML table attributes and CSS table styles in the same Web table design. Choose one or the other to avoid conflicts in the two approaches.

Now that you've linked the *schedule.htm* file to the *tables.css* style sheet and you've removed the old HTML table attributes, you're ready to begin creating the style sheet. You'll start with styles for the table border.

Table Border Styles

The first styles you'll apply to the program schedule are the border styles. Web tables use the same border styles you already used with other page elements in Tutorial 4. Unlike the HTML `border` attribute, you can apply one set of borders to a Web table itself and another set of borders to the individual cells within the table. You decide to add a 10-pixel purple border in the outset style around the entire schedule table. You'll also add a 1-pixel solid gray border around each cell within the table.

To add the table border styles:

1. Return to the **tables.css** file in your text editor. Add the following style to apply a border to the entire Web table:

   ```
   /* Styles for the schedule table */

   table.schedule {
       border: 10px outset rgb(153, 0, 153);
   }
   ```

2. Add the following style to apply borders to each table cell (see Figure 5-30):

   ```
   table.schedule th, table.schedule td {
       border: 1px solid gray;
   }
   ```

Figure 5-30   **Setting the table border styles**

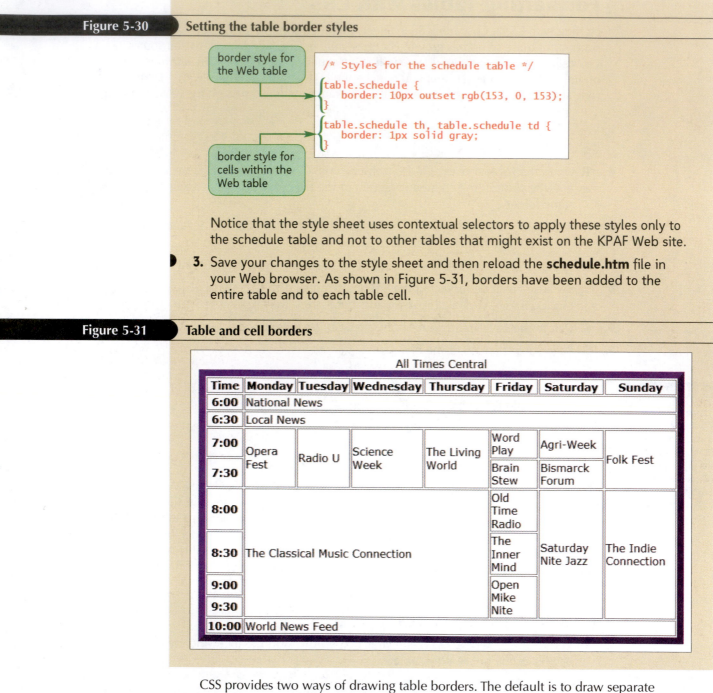

Notice that the style sheet uses contextual selectors to apply these styles only to the schedule table and not to other tables that might exist on the KPAF Web site.

3. Save your changes to the style sheet and then reload the **schedule.htm** file in your Web browser. As shown in Figure 5-31, borders have been added to the entire table and to each table cell.

Figure 5-31   **Table and cell borders**

Time	Monday	Tuesday	Wednesday	Thursday	Friday	Saturday	Sunday
6:00	National News						
6:30	Local News						
7:00	Opera Fest	Radio U	Science Week	The Living World	Word Play	Agri-Week	Folk Fest
7:30					Brain Stew	Bismarck Forum	
8:00	The Classical Music Connection				Old Time Radio	Saturday Nite Jazz	The Indie Connection
8:30					The Inner Mind		
9:00					Open Mike Nite		
9:30							
10:00	World News Feed						

All Times Central

CSS provides two ways of drawing table borders. The default is to draw separate borders around the table cells and the entire table. The other approach is to collapse the borders in upon each other. Figure 5-32 shows the impact of both style choices.

Figure 5-32 Separate and collapsed borders

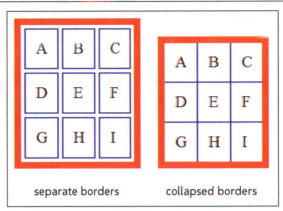

To determine whether to use the separate or collapsed borders model, you apply the style

```
border-collapse: type;
```

to the **table** element, where *type* is either **separate** (the default) or **collapse**. One of the key differences between the separate and collapsed borders models is that under the separate borders model, you can apply borders only to the table itself or to table cells. Under the collapsed borders model, any table object can have a border, including table rows, row groups, columns, and column groups. If the separate borders model is used, you can specify the distance between the borders by applying the style

```
border-spacing: value;
```

to the **table** element, where *value* is the space between the borders in one of the CSS units of measure. For example, the following style specifies that all borders within the table should be separated by a distance of 10 pixels:

```
table {
   border-collapse: separate;
   border-spacing: 10px;
}
```

The separate borders model, therefore, has the same effect as the HTML **cellspacing** attribute in providing additional space between table cells.

In the collapsed borders model, there is no space between borders; in fact, the adjacent borders are merged together to form a single line. It's important to understand that the borders are not simply moved together, but rather they are combined into a single border. For example, if two adjacent 1-pixel-wide borders are collapsed together, the resulting border is not 2 pixels wide, but only 1 pixel wide.

The situation is more complicated when adjacent borders have different widths, styles, or colors. How would you merge a double red border and a solid blue border into a single border of only one color and style? Those kinds of differences must be reconciled before the two borders can be merged. CSS employs the following five rules, listed in decreasing order of importance, to determine the style of a collapsed border:

1. If either border has a border style of **hidden**, the collapsed border is hidden.
2. A border style of **none** is overridden by any other border style.
3. If neither border is hidden, the style of the wider border takes priority over the narrower.

4. If the two borders have the same width but different styles, the border style with the highest priority is used. Double borders have the highest priority, followed by solid, dashed, dotted, ridge, outset, groove, and finally inset borders.

5. If the borders differ only in color, the color from the table object with the highest priority is used. The highest priority color belongs to the border surrounding individual table cells; followed by the borders for table rows, row groups, columns, and column groups; and finally the border around the entire table.

Any situation not covered by these rules is left to browsers to determine which border dominates when collapsing the two borders. Figure 5-33 provides an example of the first rule in action. In this example, the border around the entire table is hidden but a 1-pixel blue border is assigned to the cells within the table. When collapsed, any cell borders that are adjacent to the table border adopt the hidden border property.

Figure 5-33   **Reconciling hidden borders**

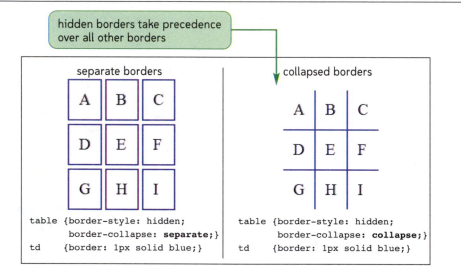

Figure 5-34 shows what happens when two borders of the same width but different styles meet. In this case, because of Rule 4, the table cell borders with the double blue lines take precedence over the solid red lines of the table border when the two borders are collapsed into one.

Figure 5-34   **Reconciling different border styles**

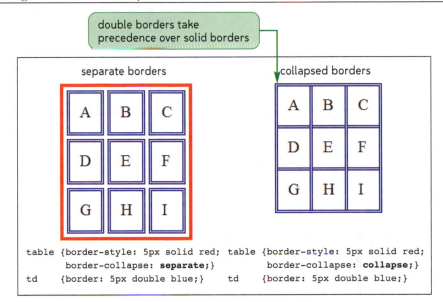

Although the collapsed borders model appears more complicated at first, the rules are reasonable and allow for a wide variety of border designs.

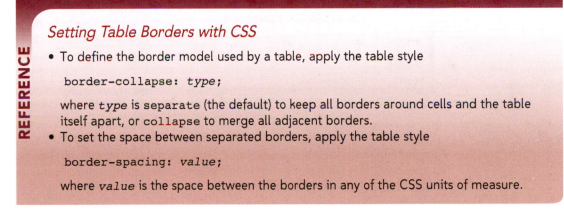

Setting Table Borders with CSS

- To define the border model used by a table, apply the table style

  `border-collapse: type;`

  where *type* is separate (the default) to keep all borders around cells and the table itself apart, or collapse to merge all adjacent borders.
- To set the space between separated borders, apply the table style

  `border-spacing: value;`

  where *value* is the space between the borders in any of the CSS units of measure.

For the KPAF program schedule, Kyle thinks the table would look better if there were no space between the table cells. He asks you to collapse the borders.

To collapse the cell borders:

1. Return to the **tables.css** file in your text editor. Add the following style to the `table` element, as shown in Figure 5-35:

   `border-collapse: collapse;`

Figure 5-35 **Adding the border-collapse style**

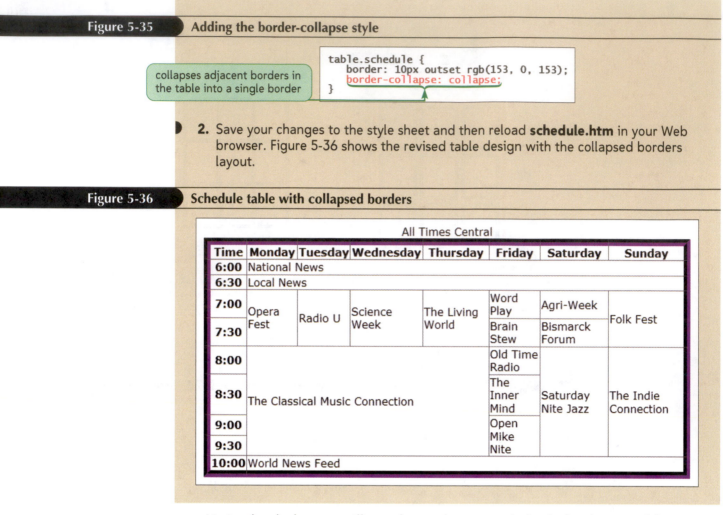

collapses adjacent borders in the table into a single border

```
table.schedule {
    border: 10px outset rgb(153, 0, 153);
    border-collapse: collapse;
}
```

2. Save your changes to the style sheet and then reload **schedule.htm** in your Web browser. Figure 5-36 shows the revised table design with the collapsed borders layout.

Figure 5-36 **Schedule table with collapsed borders**

All Times Central

Time	Monday	Tuesday	Wednesday	Thursday	Friday	Saturday	Sunday
6:00	National News						
6:30	Local News						
7:00	Opera Fest	Radio U	Science Week	The Living World	Word Play	Agri-Week	Folk Fest
7:30					Brain Stew	Bismarck Forum	
8:00	The Classical Music Connection				Old Time Radio	Saturday Nite Jazz	The Indie Connection
8:30					The Inner Mind		
9:00					Open Mike Nite		
9:30							
10:00	World News Feed						

Notice that the browser still uses the purple outset style for the border around the entire table. This is due to Rule 3 above. Because the border around the entire table is 10 pixels wide, it takes priority over the 1-pixel-wide borders around the individual table cells under the collapsed borders model.

Applying Styles to Rows and Columns

Kyle doesn't like the appearance of the table text. He suggests changing it to a sans-serif font that is 0.75 em units in size. He also suggests that the text in the header row be displayed in a semi-transparent white font on a purple background, and that the first column of the schedule, which contains the program times, appear on a light yellow background.

You can apply these styles to the row groups and column groups you created in the last session. Recall that the header row is part of the `thead` row group (see Figure 5-19), and that the first column of the table belongs to the *firstCol* class of columns (see Figure 5-20).

Thus, to apply Kyle's suggested styles, you could add the following declarations to the *tables.css* style sheet:

```
table.schedule {
    font-family: Arial, Helvetica, sans- serif;
    font-size: 0.75em;
}

table.schedule thead {
    background-color: rgb(203, 50, 203);
    color: white;
    color: rgba(255, 255, 255, 0.5);
}

table.schedule col.firstCol {
    background-color: rgb(255, 255, 192);
}
```

However, you notice a contradiction between these styles. The first cell in the schedule table belongs to both the header row and the first column. Will this cell have a purple background or a yellow background? Which style has precedence? Table objects, like other parts of CSS, have levels of precedence in which the more specific object takes priority over the more general. Figure 5-37 shows a diagram of the different levels of precedence in the Web table structure.

Figure 5-37   **Levels of precedence in Web table styles**

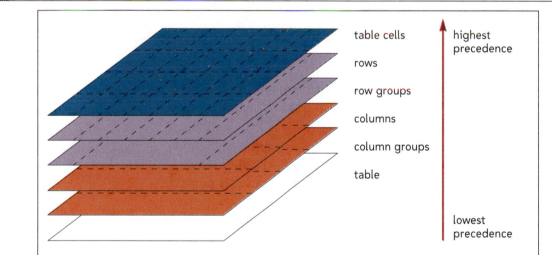

The most general styles are those applied to the entire table. Those styles are overruled by styles that are applied to column groups and then to columns. The next level up in precedence contains those styles applied to row groups and then to rows. The highest level of precedence is given to those styles applied to table cells. Be aware that not all style properties are supported by different layers of the table structure. In particular, columns and column groups accept only four CSS style properties: `border`, `background`, `width`, and `visibility`. If you want to apply a different CSS style property, you have to apply it to the cells within those columns.

Applying Styles to Cells within Rows

You can overcome the limits placed on the CSS styles available to columns and column groups by using pseudo-classes to identify specific cells within a row. For example, the selector

```
tbody tr td:first-of-type
```

matches all of the data cells listed first in any table body row. To match the cells listed last, you use the following selector:

```
tbody tr td:last-of-type
```

With pseudo-classes, you can apply the full range of CSS styles not available to columns and column groups. For example, the `text-align` property is not available for use with columns, but you can use the `last-of-type` pseudo-class to right-align the contents of the last cell in a row as follows:

```
tbody tr td:last-of-type {
    text-align: right;
}
```

For other cells, you can use the `nth-of-type` pseudo-class. Thus, the selector

```
tbody tr td:nth-of-type(7)
```

matches the seventh cell in the table rows. As long as you don't use spanning cells in these rows, this will also match the seventh column in the table.

Under Kyle's proposed style rules, the first cell should have a purple background because row groups take priority over columns or column groups. To verify that this is the case, add Kyle's proposed styles to the *tables.css* style sheet.

To set the text and background styles in the schedule table:

1. Return to the **tables.css** file in your text editor. Add the following styles to the style rule for the `table.schedule` selector:

   ```
   font-family: Arial, Helvetica, sans-serif;
   font-size: 0.75em;
   ```

2. At the bottom of the file, add the following style rule for the header of the schedule table:

   ```
   /* Table header styles */

   table.schedule thead {
       background-color: rgb(203, 50, 203);
       color: white;
       color: rgba(255, 255, 255, 0.5);
   }
   ```

3. Finally, add the following style for the first column of the schedule table:

   ```
   /* Styles for the first column */

   table.schedule col.firstCol {
       background-color: rgb(255, 255, 192);
   }
   ```

   Figure 5-38 highlights the new style rules in the style sheet.

Figure 5-38   **Adding font and color styles to the schedule table**

font styles for the table text

styles for the table header row group

styles for the first column of the table

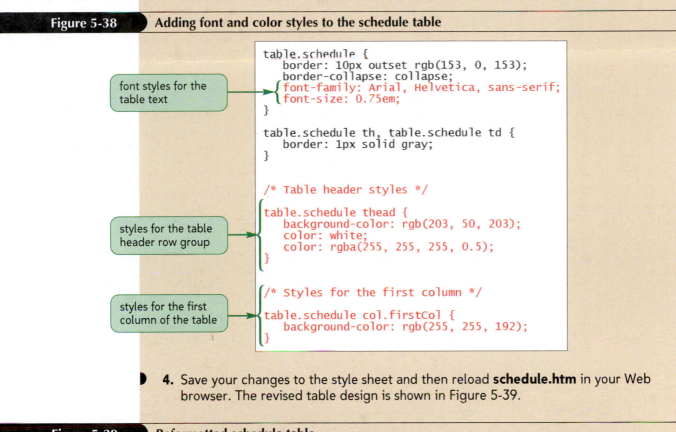

```
table.schedule {
    border: 10px outset rgb(153, 0, 153);
    border-collapse: collapse;
    font-family: Arial, Helvetica, sans-serif;
    font-size: 0.75em;
}

table.schedule th, table.schedule td {
    border: 1px solid gray;
}


/* Table header styles */

table.schedule thead {
    background-color: rgb(203, 50, 203);
    color: white;
    color: rgba(255, 255, 255, 0.5);
}


/* Styles for the first column */

table.schedule col.firstCol {
    background-color: rgb(255, 255, 192);
}
```

▶ **4.** Save your changes to the style sheet and then reload **schedule.htm** in your Web browser. The revised table design is shown in Figure 5-39.

Figure 5-39   **Reformatted schedule table**

table caption inherits the text styles from the table

As expected, the cell in the first column of the header row does indeed have a purple, rather than a light yellow, background. Also note that all of the cells in the table and the table caption have adopted the smaller sans-serif font. This is because the font style you entered for the schedule table is inherited by all table objects unless a different font style is specified.

Creating Banded Rows and Columns

A popular table design is to create table rows of alternating background colors to make it easier for users to read and locate information in a table. Before CSS3, this could be accomplished in CSS only by first assigning one class name to even-numbered rows and another class name to odd-numbered rows, and then applying different background styles to those classes.

However, with CSS3 you can create banded rows using the `nth-of-type` pseudo-class. For example, to create a table in which the background colors alternate between yellow on the odd-numbered rows and light green on the even-numbered rows, you could apply the following style rules to your table:

```
tr:nth-of-type(odd) {
    background-color: yellow;
}
tr:nth-of-type(even) {
    background-color: rgb(145, 255, 145);
}
```

The same technique can be used to create banded columns of different background colors. The style rules

```
colgroup col:nth-of-type(odd) {
    background-color: yellow;
}
colgroup col:nth-of-type(even) {
    background-color: rgb(145, 255, 145);
}
```

format a Web table so that the odd-numbered columns have a yellow background and the even-numbered columns are displayed against a light green background. Note that this technique assumes that none of the `col` elements span more than one column.

Like most CSS3 styles, these techniques might not be supported by older browsers, so you should design workarounds for those browsers.

Using the Width and Height Styles

Reducing the font size and changing the font family have resulted in a more compact table, but Kyle thinks it could be difficult to read and wonders if you could enlarge the table. Recall that browsers set table width to use the page space efficiently, never making tables wider than necessary to display the content. You can use the CSS `width` property to specify a different table size. Widths are expressed in one of the CSS units of measure or as a percentage of the containing element. Kyle suggests that you set the width of the table to 100% so that it covers the entire width of the `section` element that contains it.

To set the width of the table:

1. Return to the **tables.css** file in your text editor. Add the following style to the table element, as shown in Figure 5-40.

   ```
   width: 100%;
   ```

| Figure 5-40 | Setting the width of the schedule table |

```
table.schedule {
    border: 10px outset rgb(153, 0, 153);
    border-collapse: collapse;
    font-family: Arial, Helvetica, sans-serif;
    font-size: 0.75em;
    width: 100%;
}
```

2. Save your changes to the file and then reload **schedule.htm** in your Web browser. Figure 5-41 shows the layout of the enlarged table.

| Figure 5-41 | Table width set to 100% |

You notice that the column widths are inconsistent, with very little width given to the Time column and varying widths given to different days of the week. This results from browsers allotting space to each column as a function of the column's content. A Web browser will attempt to fit the most content possible within each column without having the text wrap to a new line. This means that columns with more text are wider than those with less text. When the width of the entire table is increased, the added space is divided evenly among the table columns.

You can set column widths using the same CSS width property you applied to the table itself. The column width is expressed either in a CSS unit of measure or as a percentage of the entire width of the table. You decide to set the width of the first column to 7% of the entire table width, while setting each of the seven remaining columns to 13% of the table width. Added together, 98% of the table width will be allotted to the eight table columns. The remaining table width is reserved for table and cell borders.

TIP

Always set the total width of table columns to be less than 100% of the table width to allow space for table borders and padding.

You'll set the column widths by applying the `width` property to the two column groups. The specified widths are then applied to the individual columns within those groups. The style rules are:

```
table.schedule col.firstCol {
    width: 7%;
}

table.schedule col.dayCols {
    width: 13%;
}
```

Add these styles to the *tables.css* style sheet.

To set the width of the table columns:

1. Return to the **tables.css** file in your text editor. Add the following style to the style rule for the *firstCol* selector:

   ```
   width: 7%;
   ```

2. Directly below the style rule for the *firstCol* selector, add the following style rule to set the widths of the columns in the *dayCols* class to 13%, as shown in Figure 5-42:

   ```
   /* Styles for the remaining columns */

   table.schedule col.dayCols {
       width: 13%;
   }
   ```

Figure 5-42   Setting the widths of the schedule table columns

the first column is 7% of the table width

each of the remaining seven columns is 13% of the table width

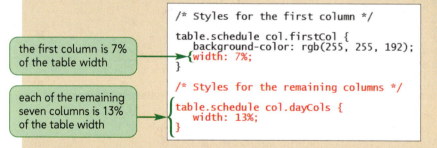

```
/* Styles for the first column */

table.schedule col.firstCol {
    background-color: rgb(255, 255, 192);
    width: 7%;
}

/* Styles for the remaining columns */

table.schedule col.dayCols {
    width: 13%;
}
```

3. Save your changes to the file and then reload **schedule.htm** in your Web browser. Figure 5-43 shows the revised layout of the table.

Figure 5-43   **Revised table column widths**

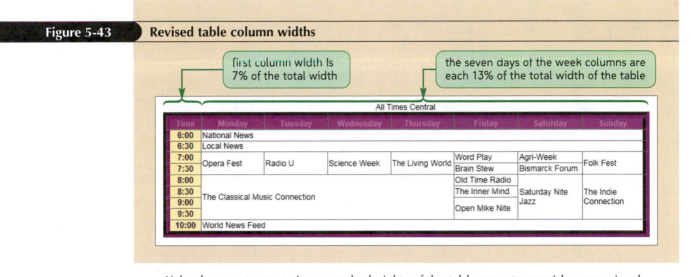

first column width is 7% of the total width

the seven days of the week columns are each 13% of the total width of the table

Kyle also wants you to increase the heights of the table rows to provide more visual space for the table contents. Heights are set using the CSS `height` property. You can apply heights to entire table rows or to individual table cells. You also can use the height style to set the height of an entire table. As with the `width` property, the `height` property should be interpreted as the minimum height for these table objects because the browser will enlarge the table, table row, or table cell if the content requires it.

You decide to set the height of the rows in the table header to 50 pixels and the height of the rows in the table body to 40 pixels. The styles to do this are as follows:

```
table.schedule thead tr {
    height: 50px;
}

table.schedule tbody tr {
    height: 40px;
}
```

Note that you don't apply the `height` property to the row groups themselves because that would set the width of the entire group and not the individual rows within the group.

To set the height of the table rows:

1. Return to the **tables.css** file in your text editor and add the following styles directly below the style rule for the `table.schedule thead` selector, as shown in Figure 5-44:

```
table.schedule thead tr {
    height: 50px;
}

/* Table body styles */

table.schedule tbody tr {
    height: 40px;
}
```

Figure 5-44   **Setting the height of the table rows**

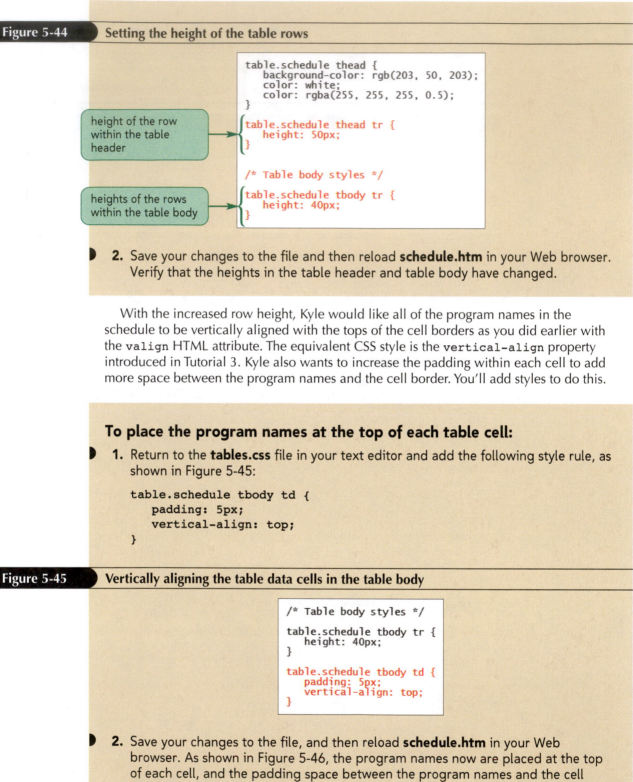

```
table.schedule thead {
    background-color: rgb(203, 50, 203);
    color: white;
    color: rgba(255, 255, 255, 0.5);
}
```

height of the row within the table header →

```
table.schedule thead tr {
    height: 50px;
}
```

```
/* Table body styles */
```

heights of the rows within the table body →

```
table.schedule tbody tr {
    height: 40px;
}
```

2. Save your changes to the file and then reload **schedule.htm** in your Web browser. Verify that the heights in the table header and table body have changed.

With the increased row height, Kyle would like all of the program names in the schedule to be vertically aligned with the tops of the cell borders as you did earlier with the `valign` HTML attribute. The equivalent CSS style is the `vertical-align` property introduced in Tutorial 3. Kyle also wants to increase the padding within each cell to add more space between the program names and the cell border. You'll add styles to do this.

To place the program names at the top of each table cell:

1. Return to the **tables.css** file in your text editor and add the following style rule, as shown in Figure 5-45:

```
table.schedule tbody td {
    padding: 5px;
    vertical-align: top;
}
```

Figure 5-45   **Vertically aligning the table data cells in the table body**

```
/* Table body styles */

table.schedule tbody tr {
    height: 40px;
}

table.schedule tbody td {
    padding: 5px;
    vertical-align: top;
}
```

2. Save your changes to the file, and then reload **schedule.htm** in your Web browser. As shown in Figure 5-46, the program names now are placed at the top of each cell, and the padding space between the program names and the cell borders has been increased.

Figure 5-46   **Revised table layout**

table header row is 50 pixels high

table body rows are each 40 pixels high

cell text is aligned with the top of each cell

Notice that only the data cells within the table body rows are placed at the top of the cell. The header cells still are centered vertically because they were not included in the contextual selector you specified in the style sheet.

Caption Styles

Kyle likes the new table design. His only remaining suggestion is that you align the table caption with the bottom-right corner of the table. Browsers usually place captions above the table, but you can specify the caption location using the `caption-side` property, which has the syntax

```
caption-side: position;
```

where *position* is either `top` (the default) or `bottom` to place the caption below the Web table. To align the caption text horizontally, you use the CSS `text-align` property. Thus, to place the schedule caption in the bottom-right corner of the table, you would enter the following CSS styles:

```
caption-side: bottom;
text-align: right;
```

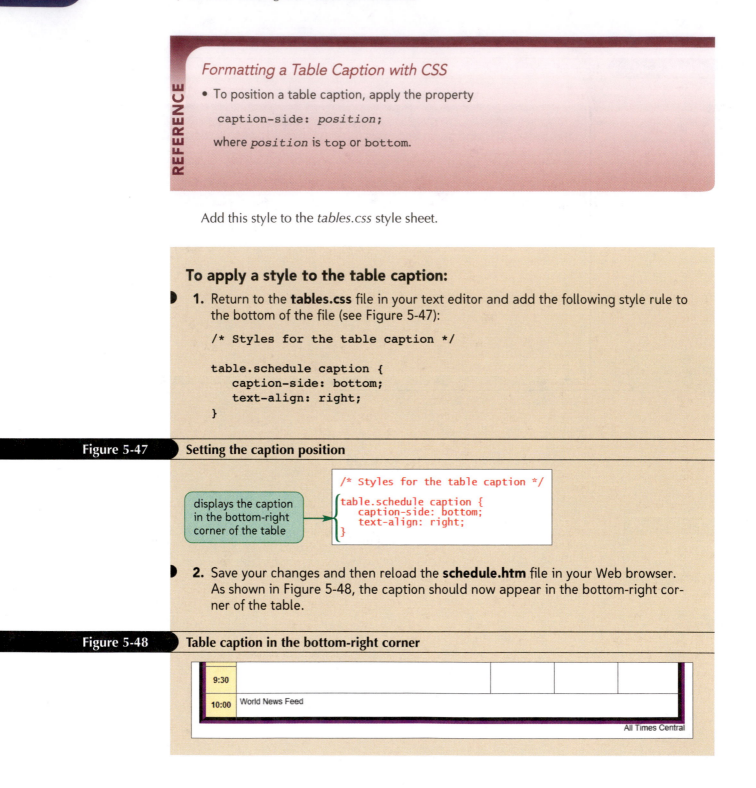

Formatting a Table Caption with CSS

• To position a table caption, apply the property

   `caption-side: position;`

where *position* is top or bottom.

Add this style to the *tables.css* style sheet.

To apply a style to the table caption:

1. Return to the **tables.css** file in your text editor and add the following style rule to the bottom of the file (see Figure 5-47):

   ```
   /* Styles for the table caption */

   table.schedule caption {
       caption-side: bottom;
       text-align: right;
   }
   ```

Figure 5-47 | **Setting the caption position**

displays the caption in the bottom-right corner of the table

```
/* Styles for the table caption */

table.schedule caption {
    caption-side: bottom;
    text-align: right;
}
```

2. Save your changes and then reload the **schedule.htm** file in your Web browser. As shown in Figure 5-48, the caption should now appear in the bottom-right corner of the table.

Figure 5-48 | **Table caption in the bottom-right corner**

| 9:30 | | | | | |
| 10:00 | World News Feed | | | | |

All Times Central

Applying Table Styles to Other Page Elements

As you can see, tables are useful for displaying information in an organized structure of rows and columns. Tables are so useful, in fact, that there's no reason to limit the table structure to Web tables. Using the CSS `display` property, you can apply a table layout to other HTML elements, such as paragraphs, block quotes, or lists. Figure 5-49 describes the various CSS table display styles and their HTML equivalents.

Figure 5-49	Table display styles

Display Style	Equivalent HTML Element
`display: table;`	table (treated as a block-level element)
`display: table-inline;`	table (treated as an inline element)
`display: table-row;`	tr
`display: table-row-group;`	tbody
`display: table-header-group;`	thead
`display: table-footer-group;`	tfoot
`display: table-column;`	col
`display: table-column-group;`	colgroup
`display: table-cell;`	td or th
`display: table-caption;`	caption

For example, the following definition list contains definitions of two networking terms:

```
<dl>
   <dt>bandwidth</dt>
   <dd>A measure of data transfer speed over a network</dd>
   <dt>HTTP</dt>
   <dd>The protocol used to communicate with Web servers</dd>
</dl>
```

Rather than accepting the default browser layout for this list, it might be useful to display the text in a table. However, you don't want to lose the meaning of the markup tags. After all, HTML is designed to mark content, but not indicate how browsers should render that content. To display this definition list as a table, you could enclose each set of terms and definitions within a `div` element as follows:

```
<dl>
   <div>
      <dt>bandwidth</dt>
      <dd>A measure of data transfer speed over a network</dd>
   </div>
   <div>
      <dt>HTTP</dt>
      <dd>The protocol used to communicate with Web servers</dd>
   </div>
</dl>
```

You then could apply the following style sheet to the list, treating the entire definition list as a table—the `div` elements as table rows, and the definition terms and descriptions as table cells within those rows:

```
dl     {display: table; border-collapse: collapse; width: 300px;}
dl div {display: table-row;}
dt, dd {display: table-cell; border: 1px solid black;
        vertical-align: top; padding: 5px;}
```

As Figure 5-50 shows, when viewed in a Web browser, the definition list looks exactly as if it were created using HTML table elements.

Figure 5-50	Applying table styles to a definition list

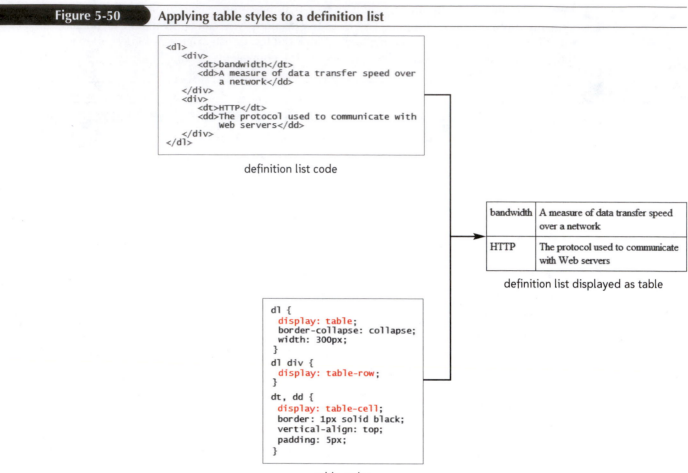

```
<dl>
    <div>
        <dt>bandwidth</dt>
        <dd>A measure of data transfer speed over
            a network</dd>
    </div>
    <div>
        <dt>HTTP</dt>
        <dd>The protocol used to communicate with
            Web servers</dd>
    </div>
</dl>
```

definition list code

bandwidth	A measure of data transfer speed over a network
HTTP	The protocol used to communicate with Web servers

definition list displayed as table

```
dl {
  display: table;
  border-collapse: collapse;
  width: 300px;
}
dl div {
  display: table-row;
}
dt, dd {
  display: table-cell;
  border: 1px solid black;
  vertical-align: top;
  padding: 5px;
}
```

table styles

In the same way, you can display other page elements in tabular form as long as the markup tags are nested in a way that mimics a table structure.

Written Communication: Designing Effective Web Tables

The primary purpose of a Web table is to convey data to the reader in a compact, easily understood way. You can apply several design principles to your Web tables to make them more effective at presenting data to interested readers:

- *Contrast the data cells from the header cells.* Make it easy for readers to understand your data by highlighting the header column or row in a different color or font size.
- *Avoid spanning rows and columns unless necessary.* Usability studies have shown that information can be gleaned quickly when presented in a simple grid layout. Unless data calls for it, don't break the grid by unnecessarily spanning a cell across the grid.
- *Break the monotony with icons.* If you are repeating the same phrase or word within a single row or column, consider replacing the text with an icon that conveys the same message. For example, in a table that describes the features of a product, use a check mark to indicate whether a particular feature is supported, rather than the words *yes* or *no*.
- *Alternate the row colors.* A large table with dozens of rows can be difficult for readers to scan and interpret. Consider using alternative background colors for the table rows to break the monotony and reduce eye strain.
- *Don't overwhelm the eye with borders.* Cell borders should be used only when they aid users by separating one cell from another. If they're not needed for this purpose, they actually can distract from the data. Rather than using borders, apply ample spacing to your cells to differentiate one data cell from another.
- *Keep it brief.* A table should not extend beyond what will fit compactly within the user's browser window. If your table is too extensive, consider breaking it into several tables that focus on different areas of information.

A Web table is judged not on its appearance but on its readability. This can best be accomplished by using a simple design whose features convey relevant information to readers. A good table gives users the data they want as quickly as possible and makes it easy to compare one value with another.

Creating Columnar Layouts

Kyle likes the design of the program schedule table. The only remaining change he wants you to make to the Web page is to break up the introductory paragraph into columns. Kyle feels that the lines of text in the paragraph are too long, making them difficult to quickly scan and read.

There are several ways to break page content into columns. You can separate the content into different block elements and float them as you did with the content in Tutorial 4. You also can nest the content in a two-column table with a single table row. Both of these options suffer from forcing the column layout to be static, as the content of each column is specified in the HTML markup tags. Ideally, in a column layout, the content should flow automatically from one column to the next as new text is inserted or old text is deleted. A third option that provides for a dynamic column layout is to use the column styles from CSS3. This is the approach you'll take.

TIP

Usability studies have shown that between 8 and 12 words is the ideal line length to enhance reading comprehension.

CSS3 Column Styles

Multi-column layouts are created with CSS3 by setting either the number of columns or the width of each column. To set the number of columns, you use the `column-count` property

```
column-count: number;
```

where `number` is the number of columns in the layout. Thus, the style rule

```
p {
   column-count: 3;
}
```

lays out the content from all paragraphs in three columns of equal width. Browsers calculate the width of each column so that the three columns extend across the paragraph. For example, a paragraph that is 600 pixels wide would be broken up into three columns of about 200 pixels each.

Alternately, you can set the width of each column by using the `column-width` property

```
column-width: width;
```

where `width` is the width of the column expressed in one of the CSS units of measure or as a percentage of the width of the element. The style rule

```
p {
   column-width: 200px;
}
```

creates a column layout in which each column is 200 pixels wide. The total number of columns will be based on how many 200-pixel-wide columns can fit into the space reserved for the paragraph. A paragraph that is 800 pixels wide could fit four columns. Because the columns must be whole columns, an 850-pixel-wide paragraph would still only fit four columns, with an extra 50 pixels of space left over.

By default, the gap between columns is 1 em in size, but you can specify a different gap using the `column-gap` property

```
column-gap: width;
```

where `width` is the width of the gap. You also can separate columns using a graphic border with the property

```
column-rule: border;
```

where `border` is the format of the border following the same syntax used with the CSS `border` property introduced in Tutorial 4. For example, the style

```
column-rule: 1px double red;
```

creates a 1-pixel-wide double red border. Column rules don't take up any space in the page layout; if they are wider than the specified gap, they will overlap the content of the columns. Like the `border` property, you can break up the `column-rule` property into the `column-rule-color`, `column-rule-width`, and `column-rule-style` properties to specify the color, width, and style of the dividing line, respectively.

Finally, you can extend content across columns using the `column-span` property

```
column-span: span;
```

where *span* is either 1 (to prevent spanning) or `all` (to enable spanning across all of the columns). In the following style rule, the contents of the `section` element are displayed in three columns but the `h1` heading within that section spans across the three columns:

```
section {
    column-count: 3;
}
section h1 {
    column-span: all;
}
```

Currently, the `column-span` property is not supported by any browser.

The `width` and `count` column styles can be combined into the shorthand property

```
columns: width count;
```

where *width* is the width of each column and *count* is the number of columns in the layout. For example, the style rule

```
section {
    columns: 250px 3;
}
```

creates a three-column layout for the `section` element with each column 250 pixels wide.

Browser Extensions to Columns

The column styles were first introduced in 2001 as part of the working draft of the proposed CSS3 specifications. However, they were not immediately adopted by the browser market. At the time of this writing, the only browsers that support column styles are Firefox, Google Chrome, and Safari, and all three do so through the use of browser extensions. Thus, to create a three-column layout for the paragraphs on your Web site that would be accepted by these browsers, you would use progressive enhancement with the following style rule:

```
p {
    -moz-column-count: 3;
    -webkit-column-count: 3;
    column-count: 3;
}
```

The browser extensions for the `column-width` and `column-rule` properties are expressed in the same way using the `-moz-` or `-webkit-` prefixes. Other column style properties have not been adopted by the market yet, and currently Internet Explorer and Opera do not support column styles at all. If you have to support those browsers, you should not design a layout that relies on multiple columns in order to be readable.

Designing Columnar Layouts with CSS3

- To specify the number of columns in the layout, use

```
column-count: number;
```

where *number* is the number of columns in the layout.
- To specify the width of the columns, use

```
column-width: width;
```

where *width* is the width of the columns expressed in one of the CSS units of measure or as a percentage of the width of the element.
- To set the size of the gap between columns, use

```
column-gap: width;
```

where *width* is the width of the gap.
- To add a border between the columns, use

```
column-rule: border;
```

where *border* is the format of the border.
- To specify the width and number of columns in a single style property, use

```
columns: width count;
```

where *width* is the width of each column and *count* is the total number of columns in the layout.
- For specific browsers, add the `-moz-` vendor prefix for Firefox and the `-webkit-` prefix for Safari and Chrome to these style properties.

Kyle suggests that you use browser extensions and the CSS3 column style properties to display the introductory paragraph in a two-column layout with a gap width of 20 pixels and a purple divider. Add this style rule to the *tables.css* style sheet.

To display the introductory paragraph in two columns:

1. Return to the **tables.css** file in your text editor and add the following style rule to the bottom of the file (see Figure 5-51):

```
/* Two column layout for the introductory paragraph */

section#main p {
   -moz-column-count: 2;
   -webkit-column-count: 2;
    column-count: 2;

   -moz-column-gap: 20px;
   -webkit-column-gap: 20px;
    column-gap: 20px;

   -moz-column-rule: 2px solid rgb(153, 0, 153);
   -webkit-column-rule: 2px solid rgb(153, 0, 153);
    column-rule: 2px solid rgb(153, 0, 153);
}
```

Figure 5-51   **Applying a two-column style**

creates a two-column layout

sets the gap between the columns to 20 pixels

adds a 2-pixel solid purple border between the columns

```
/* Two column layout for the introductory paragraph */

section#main p {
    -moz-column-count: 2;
    -webkit-column-count: 2;
    column-count: 2;

    -moz-column-gap: 20px;
    -webkit-column-gap: 20px;
    column-gap: 20px;

    -moz-column-rule: 2px solid rgb(153, 0, 153);
    -webkit-column-rule: 2px solid rgb(153, 0, 153);
    column-rule: 2px solid rgb(153, 0, 153);
}
```

2. Close the file, saving your changes, and then reload the **schedule.htm** file in your Web browser. Figure 5-52 shows the completed design of the nightly schedule page as it appears in Google Chrome.

Figure 5-52   **Final KPAF nightly schedule page**

two-column layout for the introductory paragraph

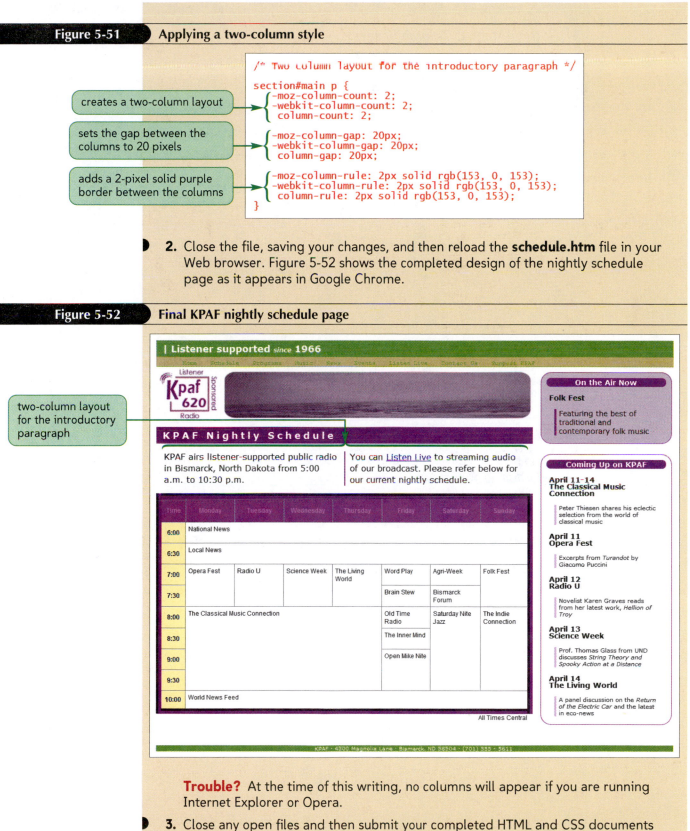

Trouble? At the time of this writing, no columns will appear if you are running Internet Explorer or Opera.

3. Close any open files and then submit your completed HTML and CSS documents to your instructor, in either printed or electronic form, as requested.

INSIGHT

Setting Manual Column Breaks

By default, browsers automatically break the content within a columnar layout in a way that keeps the columns roughly the same height. To create manual column breaks, CSS3 introduced the following style properties:

```
break-before: column;
break-after: column;
```

A column break created with one of these properties is placed directly before or after the element specified in the style rule selector, respectively. For example, the following style rule inserts a column break directly after any br element that appears within a paragraph:

```
p br {
    break-after: column;
}
```

CSS3 also provides styles to suppress column breaks with the following properties:

```
break-before: avoid-column;
break-after: avoid-column;
break-inside: avoid-column;
```

Thus, the following style rule prevents a column break from occurring within a blockquote element:

```
blockquote {
    break-inside: avoid-column;
}
```

No browser currently supports these manual column breaks. WebKit (used in Safari and Chrome) provides the column break properties

```
-webkit-column-break-before: type;
-webkit-column-break-after: type;
```

where *type* is always (to force a column break), avoid (to suppress a column break), inherit (to inherit the style of the container element), or auto (the default, which inserts a column break automatically when needed). Unfortunately, although they are part of the WebKit specifications, these styles to introduce manual column breaks are not currently implemented in any browser.

Kyle is pleased with the work you've done on the programming schedule page. He'll discuss your final design with other people at the station and get back to you with future projects.

Session 5.2 Quick Check

1. What HTML attribute do you add to the `table` element to set the space between cells to 10 pixels?

2. Specify the CSS style to collapse all adjacent borders within a Web table into single borders.

3. Two table cells have adjacent borders. One cell has a 5-pixel-wide double border and the other cell has a 6-pixel-wide solid border. If the table borders are collapsed, what type of border will the two cells share?

4. In the case of conflicting styles, which has highest precedence: the style of the row group or the style of the column group?

5. What style would you use to align the content of all table header cells with the bottoms of the cells?

6. What style would you use to display the table caption in the bottom-left corner of the table?

7. Provide a style rule to display the paragraphs within all `article` elements in three columns separated by a 1-pixel solid black border.

8. Provide a style rule to display the contents of all `div` elements belonging to the *columns* class in a columnar layout with the column widths set to 250 pixels and the space between the columns set to 10 pixels.

Practice the skills you learned in the tutorial using the same case scenario.

PRACTICE

Review Assignments

Data Files needed for the Review Assignments: kpaf.jpg, kpaf2.css, modernizr-1.5.js, morningtxt.htm, programstxt.css

Kyle has had a chance to work with the KPAF nightly schedule page. He wants you to make a few changes to the layout and apply the new design to a page that displays the KPAF morning schedule. Kyle already has entered much of the Web page content and style. He wants you to complete his work by creating and designing the Web table for the morning schedule. Figure 5-53 shows a preview of the morning schedule page.

Figure 5-53 **KPAF morning schedule**

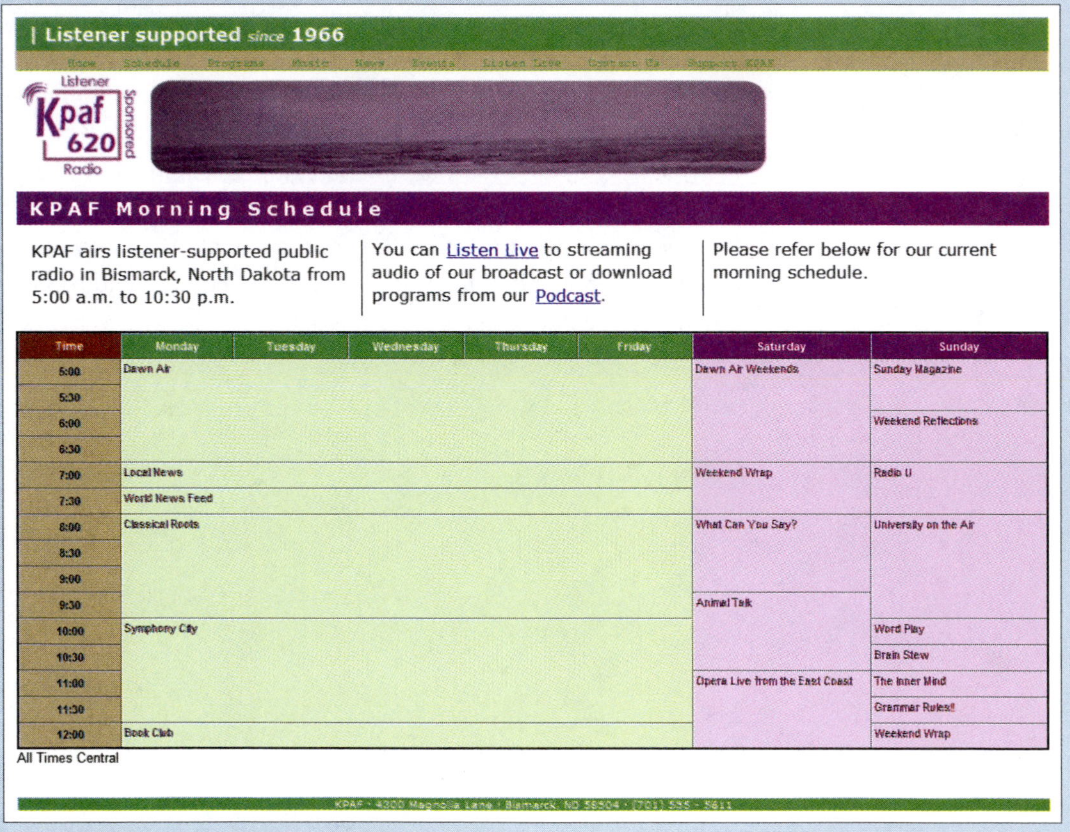

Complete the following:

1. Use your text editor to open the **morningtxt.htm** and **programstxt.css** files from the tutorial.05\review folder. Enter ***your name*** and ***the date*** in the comment section of each file. Save the files as **morning.htm** and **programs.css**, respectively, in the same folder.
2. Go to the **morning.htm** file in your text editor. Insert links to the **kpaf2.css** and **programs.css** style sheets.
3. Scroll down the file and directly below the paragraph element, insert a Web table with the class name **programs**.
4. Add a table caption containing the text **All Times Central**.
5. Below the caption, create a column group containing three columns. The first `col` element should have the class name **timeColumn**. The second `col` element should have the class name **wDayColumns** and span five columns in the table. The last `col` element should have the class name **wEndColumns** and span two columns.

6. Insert the following summary for the table: **Lists the morning programs aired by KPAF from 5:00 a.m. to 12:00 p.m. (central time)**.

7. Add the table header row group containing the headings shown in Figure 5-53.

8. Enter the table body row group containing the times and names of the different KPAF programs from 5:00 a.m. to 12:00 p.m., Monday through Sunday, in half-hour intervals. Create row- and column-spanning cells to match the layout of the days and times shown in Figure 5-53.

9. Close the morning.htm file, saving your changes.

10. Go to the **programs.css** file in your text editor. Create a style rule for the programs table to: a) set the width of the table to 100%; b) add a 2-pixel solid black border that is collapsed around the table; and c) set the font family to the following list of fonts: Arial, Verdana, and sans-serif.

11. Create a style rule to align the table caption with the bottom-left corner of the table. Set the caption font size to 0.8 em.

12. Create a style rule for all table data cells in the table body of the programs table to: a) set all table cells to a font size of 0.7 em; b) vertically align the text of all table data cells with the top of the cell; c) add a 1-pixel solid gray border around every cell, and d) setting the padding space to 2 pixels.

13. Set the height of all table rows to 25 pixels.

14. Display the header row group in white font with a background color of (105, 177, 60).

15. For table header cells within the header row group, set the font size to 0.7 em and add a 1-pixel solid gray border. For the first table header cell in the header row group, set the background color to the value (153, 86, 7). Use the `nth-of-type` pseudo-class to set the background color of the seventh and then the eighth table header cells in the header row group to the value (153, 0, 153).

16. Add the following style rules for the three column groups in the table: a) set the width of the timeColumn column group to 10% with a background color of (215, 205, 151); b) set the width of the wDayColumns column group to 11% with a background color of (236, 255, 211); and c) set the width of the wEndColumns column group to 17% with a background color of (255, 231, 255).

17. Create a three-column layout for the introductory paragraph within the intro section with three columns in the layout separated by a gap of 20 pixels with a 1-pixel solid black divider.

18. Add style comments throughout the style sheet to document your work, and then save your changes.

19. Open the **morning.htm** file in your Web browser and verify that the table layout and design resemble that shown in Figure 5-53. (Note: If you are using Internet Explorer or Opera, you will not see the three-column layout for the introductory paragraph.)

20. Submit your completed files to your instructor, in either printed or electronic form, as requested.

Apply your knowledge of Web tables and table styles to create a puzzle page with nested tables.

APPLY

Case Problem 1

Data Files needed for this Case Problem: gold.jpg, green.jpg, jpf.css, jpf.jpg, modernizr-1.5.js, stabletxt.css, sudokutxt.htm

The Japanese Puzzle Factory   Rebecca Peretz has a passion for riddles and puzzles. Her favorites are the Japanese logic puzzles that have become very popular in recent years. Rebecca and a few of her friends have begun work on a new Web site called *The Japanese Puzzle Factory (JPF)*, where they plan to create and distribute Japanese-style puzzles. Eventually, the JPF Web site will include interactive programs to enable users to solve the puzzles online, but for now Rebecca is interested only in the design and layout of the pages. You've been asked to help by creating a draft version of the Web page describing the Sudoku puzzle. Figure 5-54 shows a preview of the design and layout you'll create for Rebecca.

Figure 5-54   The Japanese Puzzle Factory Sudoku page

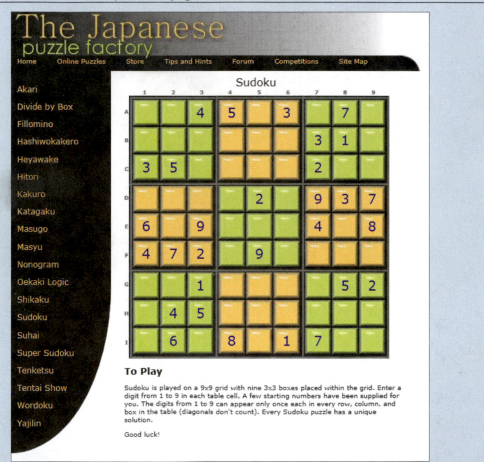

Rebecca has created some of the content and designs for this page. Your task is to complete the page by entering the code and styles for the Sudoku table, as well as adding some background images to other sections of the page layout.

Complete the following:

1. Use your text editor to open the files **stabletxt.css** and **sudokutxt.htm** from the tutorial.05\case1 folder. Enter *your name* and *the date* in the comment section of each file. Save the files as **stable.css** and **sudoku.htm**, respectively, in the same folder.

2. Return to the **sudoku.htm** file in your text editor. Add links to the **jpf.css** and **stable.css** style sheets.

3. Scroll down to the `section` element. Directly below the opening `<section>` tag, insert a `table` element that will be used to display the Sudoku puzzle. Give the `table` element the class name **spuzzle**.

4. Add a caption to the spuzzle table containing the text **Sudoku**.

5. Create a table head row group containing a single row. The row should display 10 heading cells. The first heading cell should be blank and the remaining nine cells should display the digits from 1 to 9.

6. Create the table body row group containing nine table rows with the first cell in each row containing a table heading cell displaying the letters A through I.

7. After the initial table heading cell in the first, fourth, and seventh rows, insert three table data cells spanning three rows and three columns each. Altogether, these nine data cells will store the nine 3×3 boxes that are part of the Sudoku puzzle.

8. In the first row of the table body, put the three table data cells in the greenBox, goldBox, and greenBox classes, respectively. In the fourth row, the three data cells belong to the goldBox, greenBox, and goldBox classes. In the seventh row, the three data cells belong to the greenBox, goldBox, and greenBox classes.

⊕ EXPLORE

9. Go to each of the nine table data cells you created in the last two steps. Within each data cell, insert a nested table belonging to the subTable class. Within each nested table, insert three rows and three columns of data cells. Enter the digits from Figure 5-54 in the appropriate table cells. Where there is no digit, leave the table cell empty.

10. Save your changes to the file, and then go to the **stable.css** style sheet in your text editor.

11. Create a style rule to collapse the borders of the spuzzle and subTable tables.

12. Add a 5-pixel outset gray border to the table data cells within the spuzzle table.

13. Set the font size of table header cells within the spuzzle table to 8 pixels and the font color to gray.

14. Set the height of table header cells within the table body row group of the spuzzle table to 40 pixels.

15. For table data cells within the subTable table, add the following styles: a) set the font size to 20 pixels and the font color to blue; b) set the width and height to 40 pixels and center the cell text both horizontally and vertically; and c) add a 1-pixel solid black border around the cell.

⊕ EXPLORE

16. For table data cells nested within the goldBox class of table data cells, display the background image file *gold.jpg* centered within the cell and not tiled. (Hint: Use background position values of 50% for both the horizontal and vertical directions.)

17. For table data cells nested within the greenBox class of data cells, set the background image to the *green.jpg* file, once again centered within the cell without tiling.

18. Add descriptive comments throughout your style sheet to document your work.

19. Save your changes to the file and then reload **sudoku.htm** in your Web browser. Verify that the layout and design of the Sudoku table resemble that shown in Figure 5-54.

20. Submit your completed files to your instructor, in either printed or electronic form, as requested.

Apply your knowledge of CSS and Web tables to create a calendar table for a community civic center.

APPLY

Case Problem 2

Data Files needed for this Case Problem: bottom.jpg, bottomleft.jpg, bottomright.jpg, caltxt.css, ccc.css, ccc.jpg, febtxt.htm, left.jpg, modernizr-1.5.js, right.jpg, tab.jpg, tabred.jpg, top.jpg, topleft.jpg, topright.jpg

The Chamberlain Civic Center   Lewis Kern is an events manager at the Chamberlain Civic Center in Chamberlain, South Dakota. The center is in the process of updating its Web site, and Lewis has asked you to work on the pages detailing events in the upcoming year. He's asked you to create a calendar page for the month of February. Lewis wants the page design to catch the reader's eye, so he suggests that you create a Web table with a background showing a spiral binding. The spiral binding graphic must be flexible enough to accommodate calendars of different sizes, so you'll build the borders by using eight different background images that are placed on the four corners and four sides of the table. The February calendar must list the following events:

- Every Sunday, the Carson Quartet plays at 1:00 p.m. ($8)
- February 1, 8:00 p.m.: Taiwan Acrobats ($16/$24/$36)
- February 5, 8:00 p.m.: Joey Gallway ($16/$24/$36)
- February 7-8, 7:00 p.m.: West Side Story ($24/$36/$64)
- February 10, 8:00 p.m.: Jazz Masters ($18/$24/$32)
- February 13, 8:00 p.m.: Harlem Choir ($18/$24/$32)
- February 14, 8:00 p.m.: Chamberlain Symphony ($18/$24/$32)
- February 15, 8:00 p.m.: Edwin Drood ($24/$36/$44)
- February 19, 7:00 p.m.: The Yearling ($8/$14/$18)
- February 21, 8:00 p.m.: An Ellington Tribute ($24/$32/$48)
- February 22, 8:00 p.m.: Othello ($18/$28/$42)
- February 25, 8:00 p.m.: Madtown Jugglers ($12/$16/$20)
- February 28, 8:00 p.m.: Ralph Williams ($32/$48/$64)
- March 1, 8:00 p.m.: Othello ($18/$28/$42)

Lewis wants the weekend events (Friday and Saturday night) to be displayed with a light red background. A preview of the page you'll create is shown in Figure 5-55.

Figure 5-55   The Chamberlain Civic Center February calendar

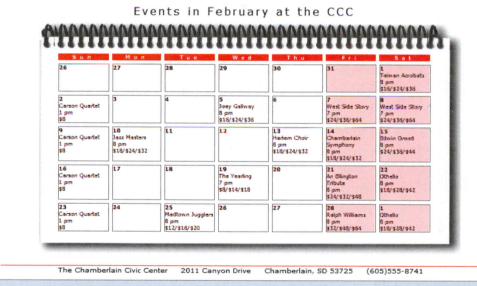

Complete the following:

1. In your text editor, open the **caltxt.css** and **febtxt.htm** files from the tutorial.05\case2 folder. Enter *your name* and *the date* in the comment section of each file. Save the files as **calendar.css** and **feb.htm**, respectively.

2. Go to the **feb.htm** file in your text editor. Create links to the **calendar.css** and **ccc.css** style sheets.

3. Scroll down to the events `section` element. Within the element, insert a table with the class name **calendar**. Add the table caption **Events in February at the CCC** to the calendar.

4. Create a column group for the calendar consisting of two `col` elements. The first `col` element should belong to the weekdays class and span five columns. The second `col` element should belong to the weekends class and span two columns.

5. Create a table header row group consisting of one row of table headings displaying the three-letter abbreviations for the days of the week, starting with *Sun* and ending with *Sat*.

6. Create a table body row group containing the days in the month of February. The row group should contain five rows and seven columns of table data cells. There are no spanning cells in any of the rows or columns.

7. Each table data cell should have the following content:
   - The day of the month should be marked as an `h3` heading (refer to Figure 5-55 for the starting and ending days in the calendar).
   - On the days when there is a CCC event, enter the event information as a definition list with the name of the event marked as a `dt` element, and the time and price of the event each marked with a `dd` element.

8. Save your changes to the file and then go to the **calendar.css** file in your text editor. Create a style rule for the calendar table to: a) create separate borders for the different parts of the table with a 5-pixel space between the borders; b) set the font size to 8 pixels; c) set the top margin to 20 pixels, the bottom margin to 5 pixels, and the left and right margins to `auto;` d) set the padding space to 40 pixels; and e) set the width to 650 pixels.

⊕ EXPLORE   9. In the style rule you created in the previous step, add a style that specifies multiple background images for the calendar table in the following order:
   - the *topleft.jpg* image in the top-left corner of the table with no tiling
   - the *topright.jpg* image in the top-right corner with no tiling
   - the *bottomleft.jpg* image in the bottom-left corner with no tiling
   - the *bottomright.jpg* image in the bottom-right corner with no tiling
   - the *top.jpg* image in the top-left corner, tiled only in the horizontal direction
   - the *left.jpg* image in the top-left corner, tiled only in the vertical direction
   - the *right.jpg* image in the top-right corner, tiled only in the vertical direction
   - the *bottom.jpg* image in the bottom-left corner, tiled only in the horizontal direction

10. Create a style rule to center the table caption along the top of the calendar table and do the following: a) set the bottom padding to 10 pixels; b) set the font size to 16 pixels; c) set the kerning to 3 pixels; and d) set the width to 650 pixels.

11. Set the width of the table columns to 14% of the width of the table. For columns belonging to the weekends class, change the background color to the value (255, 232, 232).

12. For table heading cells in the table header row group, set the background color to red, the font color to white, and the letter spacing to 5 pixels.

13. Set the height of the table row within the table header row group of the calendar table to 5%. Set the height of the table rows within the table body row group to 19% each.

14. Add a 1-pixel solid gray border to every table data cell within the calendar table. Set the vertical alignment of the cell content to the top of the cell.

15. Set the font size of h3 headings within the data table cells of the calendar table to 8 pixels.

16. The paragraphs in the summary section are enclosed within a div element. Create a style rule for this div element to: a) display the contents in a columnar layout with the column width set to 300 pixels; b) set the column gap to 20 pixels; and c) add a 1-pixel solid black divider rule between columns.

17. Save your changes to the file and then open **feb.htm** in your Web browser. Verify that the layout and design of the page resemble that shown in Figure 5-55. (Note: If you are running Internet Explorer or Opera, you might not see multiple columns in the description of the upcoming February events.)

18. Submit your completed files to your instructor, in either printed or electronic form, as requested.

Explore additional CSS table styles and pseudo-class techniques by designing a products table for a manufacturer of geodesic domes.

CHALLENGE

Case Problem 3

Data Files needed for this Case Problem: bottom.jpg, bottomleft.jpg, bottomright.jpg, dhomelogo.png, dhometxt.htm, dome.css, dtabletxt.css, left.jpg, modernizr-1.5.js, right.jpg, tableback.png, top.jpg, topleft.jpg, topright.jpg

dHome, Inc.   Olivia Moore is the director of advertising for dHome, one of the nation's newest manufacturers of geodesic dome houses. She's hired you to work on the company's Web site. Olivia has provided you with all of the text you need for the Web page, and your job is to design the page's layout. You'll start by designing a draft of the company's home page. Olivia wants the page to include information about dHome's pricing structure for various dome models. The page also contains links to other pages on the Web site.

Olivia also wants you to add some visual effects to the table's appearance. She would like a semi-transparent table background showing the pattern of a geodesic dome, and she would like banded rows colored with alternating bands of semi-transparent white and green. Finally, she'd like you to add rounded corners to the table using some graphic image files she's created.

A preview of the design you'll create for Olivia is shown in Figure 5-56.

Figure 5-56   dHome Web page

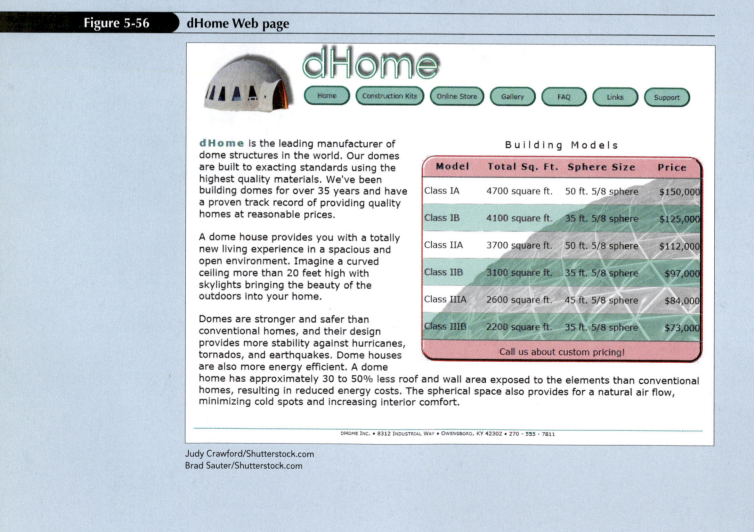

Judy Crawford/Shutterstock.com
Brad Sauter/Shutterstock.com

Complete the following:

1. Use your text editor to open the **dhometxt.htm** and **dtabletxt.css** files from the tutorial.05\case3 folder. Enter *your name* and *the date* in the comment section of each file. Save the files as **dhome.htm** and **dtable.css**, respectively.

2. Go to the **dhome.htm** file in your text editor. Create links to the **dome.css** and **dtable.css** style sheets.

3. Scroll down to the `section` element. Above the paragraphs within that element, insert a table with the class name *domeSpecs*. Add a table summary with the text **A table describing six dome models sold by dHome, Inc.** and add the table caption **Building Models**.

4. Create a column group containing three `col` elements with class names of *firstColumn*, *middleColumns*, and *lastColumn*. The *middleColumns* `col` element should span two columns in the table.

5. Create a table header row group containing a single table row with four table heading cells. The cells should contain the headings **Model**, **Total Sq. Ft.**, **Sphere Size**, and **Price**.

6. Insert a table footer row group containing a single row and three data cells. The first and third cells should be left blank. The middle cell should contain the text **Call us about custom pricing!** and should span two columns.

7. Create a table body row group consisting of six table rows with four cells each. Insert the model, square feet, sphere size, and price values from Figure 5-56.

8. Save your changes to the **dhome.htm** file and then go to the **dtable.css** file in your text editor.

9. Create a style for the `domeSpecs` table that: a) sets the font size to 16 pixels; b) sets the bottom and left margins to 20 pixels; c) floats the table on the right; and d) collapses the border.

EXPLORE 10. Add code to the style rule from the previous step to display the file *tableback.png* as the table background aligned with the bottom-right corner without tiling. Set the size of the background image to cover the table.

11. For every data cell in the `domeSpecs` table, set the top and bottom padding to 0 pixels and the left and right padding to 5 pixels.

12. Create a style rule for the table caption to: a) set the font size to 18 pixels and the kerning to 5 pixels; b) center the caption text above the table; and c) set the bottom margin to 10 pixels.

13. For the table header row group, create a style rule to: a) display a 2-pixel solid gray bottom border; and b) display the image file *top.jpg* tiled horizontally across the top of the row group.

14. Set the height of the table row in the header row group to 40 pixels.

15. For heading cells within the header row group: a) set the top/bottom padding to 0 pixels and the left/right padding to 5 pixels; and b) set the kerning to 2 pixels.

EXPLORE 16. Olivia wants a graphic image used for the top-left and top-right corners of the table header row group. Use the `first-of-type` pseudo-class to set the background image of the first heading cell in the header row group, placing the image file *topleft.jpg* in the top-left corner of the cell with no tiling. In the same way, use the `last-of-type` pseudo-class to place the image file *topright.jpg* as the background image for the last heading cell in the table header row group, positioning the image in the top-right corner of the cell with no tiling.

17. Create a style rule for the table footer row group that: a) adds a 2-pixel solid gray top border; b) centers the text of the row group; and c) adds the background image file *bottom.jpg* repeated horizontally along the bottom of the row group.

18. Set the height of the table rows within the table footer row group to 40 pixels.

19. As with the table header row group, add background graphic images to the corners of the footer. Use the `first-of-type` pseudo-class to add the image file *bottomleft.jpg* as the background image for the first data cell in the table footer row group, set along the bottom-left corner without tiling. Use the `last-of-type` pseudo-class to add the image file *bottomright.jpg* as the background image of the last data cell in the table footer row group, positioning it along the bottom-right corner of that cell without tiling.

20. Create a style rule for the table rows within the table body row group that: a) sets the height of each row to 50 pixels; and b) adds a 1-pixel dotted gray bottom border.

21. As with the table header and table footer row groups, create a graphic border for the first and last cells in each row of the table body row group. Use the `first-of-type` pseudo-class to display the image file *left.jpg* as the background image for the first data cell in each row, positioned at the top-left corner and tiled vertically. Use the `last-of-type` pseudo-class to display the image file *right.jpg* as the background image for the last data cell, positioned along the top-right corner of the cell and tiled vertically. In addition, for the last data cell in every row of the table body row group, right-align the cell contents.

EXPLORE 22. Olivia would like the table to display semi-transparent banded rows. Use the `nth-of-type` pseudo-class to display every even row in the body section with the background color (152, 228, 215) at 60% opacity. In the same way, display every odd row in the body section with the background color (255, 255, 255) at 60% opacity.

23. Set the width of the `firstColumn` column group to 22% of the table width. Set the width of the columns in the `middleColumns` column group to 28% of the table width. Finally, set the width of the `lastColumn` column group to 22% of the width of the table.

24. Add style comments to document your work.

25. Save your changes to the file and then open **dhome.htm** in your Web browser. Verify that the appearance of the product information table matches that shown in Figure 5-56. (Note: If you are using earlier versions of the major browsers, you will not see the semi-transparent effect in the rows and in the table background, nor will you see rounded graphic corners and edges.)

26. Submit your completed files to your instructor, in either printed or electronic form, as requested.

Test your knowledge of CSS to create a Web table listing room reservations at a popular conference center.

CREATE

Case Problem 4

Data Files needed for this Case Problem: hcclogo.jpg, modernizr-1.5.js, rooms.txt

Hamilton Conference Center   Yancy Inwe is the facilities manager at the Hamilton Conference Center in Hamilton, Ohio. The conference center, a general-use facility for the community, hosts several organizations and clubs as well as special events and shows by local vendors. The center recently upgraded its intranet capabilities, and Yancy would like to create a Web site where employees and guests can easily track which conference rooms are available and which are being used. She would like this information displayed in a Web table that lays out the room use for seven rooms and halls from 8:00 a.m. to 5:00 p.m. in half-hour increments. Eventually, this process will be automated by the conference's Web server; but for now, she has come to you for help in setting up a sample Web page layout and design.

Complete the following:

1. Use your text editor to create an HTML file named **conference.htm** and two style sheets named **hcc.css** and **schedule.css**. Enter *your name* and *the date* in a comment section of each file. Include any other comments you think aptly document the purpose and content of the files. Save the files in the tutorial.05\case4 folder.

2. Use the text files provided to create a Web page containing the reservation information. The design of the Web page is up to you, and you may supplement your Web page with any material you feel is appropriate. Place the styles for the page layout in the **hcc.css** style sheet.

3. Create a table containing the room reservation information. The table structure should contain the following elements:
   - a table caption and summary
   - table row and column groups
   - examples of row- and/or column-spanning cells
   - examples of both table heading and table data cells

4. Create a style for your table in the **schedule.css** style sheet. The layout and appearance of the table are up to you, but the table should include the following:
   - a border style applied to one or more table objects
   - a style that defines whether the table borders are separate or collapsed
   - styles applied to table rows and column groups
   - use of horizontal and vertical alignment of the table cell contents
   - different widths applied to different table columns
   - styles applied to the table caption

5. Document your style choices with appropriate comments.

6. Add a columnar layout to one section of your document. The number of columns and its appearance are up to you.

7. Submit your completed files to your instructor, in either printed or electronic form, as requested.

ENDING DATA FILES

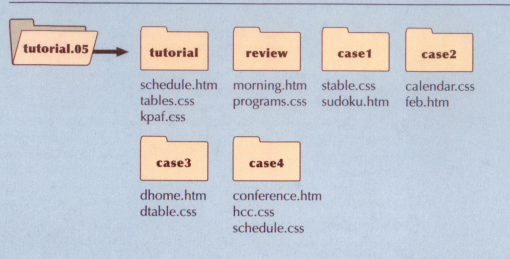

tutorial.05

tutorial
schedule.htm
tables.css
kpaf.css

review
morning.htm
programs.css

case1
stable.css
sudoku.htm

case2
calendar.css
feb.htm

case3
dhome.htm
dtable.css

case4
conference.htm
hcc.css
schedule.css

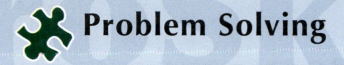

Problem Solving

Assessing Alternatives

At most any job, you'll regularly find yourself confronting questions or problems and needing to identify and choose among alternative solutions. Once you have a clear idea of the problem, a systematic approach can help you identify the path forward that best fits your needs.

Step #1: Determine Feasible Alternatives

In this step, document criteria by which you'll evaluate each course of action. Then, brainstorm on possible solutions by collecting as many ideas as possible about how to correct the problem. Write them all down. Don't discount any ideas as too radical, expensive, or impossible to achieve. In fact, don't even attempt to evaluate the ideas at all! Instead, encourage creative thinking. Ask "what if?"—What if we had unlimited resources? What if we had new skills? Be sure to include as many people or groups as necessary, since whatever solution is selected will need the buy-in of these same individuals and groups later on. Without their ownership, even the best alternative could end up failing.

Step #2: Collect Information Needed to Evaluate Alternatives

This step is where the pros and cons of each idea are evaluated. For each alternative developed in step #1, additional information will be needed to fill out the solution. Don't assume you know it all! Obtaining additional information will involve going back to people you spoke with at the outset to seek their input on the choices. It also may require securing financial information from other divisions in the organization, learning about operation schedules, documenting human resources constraints or training needs, or sourcing some market research intelligence to be able to verify observations or anecdotal evidence provided during initial data collection about the problem. You'll likely start to see relationships between the collected information that can provide insights into the feasibility of the possible solutions.

Step #3: Evaluate Each Alternative

Document both the benefits and costs of all alternatives, whether quantitative (cost savings) or qualitative (employee morale). Spreadsheet software often helps problem solvers track and quantify merits and drawbacks. Consider the resources required—financial, human, or other capital such as equipment. Are they affordable? Is there enough time to implement the different solutions? There may be risks involved with some alternatives; what are they? What would be the consequences if the chosen solution didn't work? The best choice is to go with the solution that offers the greatest reward for the least amount of risk. In some cases, the solution may require developing a "Plan B" to fall back on in case the chosen solution fails to solve the problem.

Step #4: Select an Alternative

Don't get stuck trying to select a solution that addresses every aspect of a problem, especially if it is complex. Rarely are solutions perfect. Instead, consider the effect each alternative course of action may have as the change ripples through the organization. Will the resulting change generate positive results and meet the criteria established at the

ProSkills

outset of the problem-solving process? Will the chosen alternative resolve the problem in the long term? What is realistic, given the merits and drawbacks identified in step #3? Make a choice and then develop the detailed plans to implement it. Also think about how to manage the transition or change from the old approach or process to the new one. Will employees require special training? Does a special newsletter with updates need to be distributed so people are well informed? Are there rumors that need to be dispelled, or undercurrents of unrest that may affect the alternative?

Research, Evaluate, and Implement Design Techniques

The Web is a valuable source of information, and it is particularly valuable for those who want to learn how to create and design Web sites. Each Web site presents an opportunity to study how other Web page designers solved problems involving layout and design. In addition, most Web designers are eager to share the methods, the techniques, and sometimes the tricks they've used to get the most out of HTML, CSS, and an occasional uncooperative browser. In this exercise, you'll use the skills and tasks you learned in Tutorials 3 through 5 to create a Web site on a hobby or personal interest of yours. First, you'll research and evaluate the techniques of published Web page designers.

Note: Please be sure *not* to include any personal information of a sensitive nature in the files you create to be submitted to your instructor for this exercise. Later on, you can update the files with such information for your personal use.

1. The W3C specifications for HTML5 and CSS3 represent a "gold standard" by which all browsers are rated. Conduct a Web search to determine the browsers that provide the best support for the W3C specifications. Which browsers provide the poorest level of support?

2. Deprecated elements and attributes are features of HTML that have been replaced, usually by CSS styles. Examine five different deprecated elements or attributes and explain what they were intended to accomplish and what has replaced them under the current specifications for HTML and CSS.

3. Web designers have come up with a variety of approaches to creating two-, three-, and four-column layouts. Search the Web for the pages of Web designers and report on the different techniques designers have used to create these classic layouts.

4. Many of the CSS3 styles are replacing coding techniques used in older browsers. Search the Web and explain how you would create rounded corners without using the `border-radius` property from CSS3.

5. Locate a Web page whose content and layout you enjoy. Take some time to download the underlying HTML and CSS code, and reconstruct exactly how the Web designer created the page. A few caveats: Be respectful about your use of copyrighted material, and avoid large and over-complicated Web sites. A site for a large company or organization would be difficult to interpret.

6. When you're finished studying the page's code, recreate the layout and design techniques in a page describing one of your hobbies or interests. As much as possible, try to duplicate the look and feel of the site that you studied.

7. Save your completed Web site and the answers from your research, and submit them to your instructor, in either printed or electronic form, as requested.

Color Names with Color Values, and HTML Character Entities

Both HTML and XHTML allow you to define colors using either color names or color values. HTML and XHTML support a list of 16 basic color names. Most browsers also support an extended list of color names, which are listed in Table A-1 in this appendix, along with their RGB and hexadecimal values. The 16 color names supported by HTML and XHTML appear highlighted in the table. Web-safe colors appear in a bold font.

If you want to use only Web-safe colors, limit your RGB values to 0, 51, 153, 204, and 255 (or limit your hexadecimal values to 00, 33, 66, 99, CC, and FF). For example, an RGB color value of (255, 51, 204) would be Web safe, while an RGB color value of (255, 192, 128) would not.

Table A-2 in this appendix lists the extended character set for HTML, also known as the ISO Latin-1 Character Set. You can specify characters by name or by numeric value. For example, you can use either ® or ® to specify the registered trademark symbol, ®. Not all browsers recognize all code names. Some older browsers that support only the HTML 2.0 standard do not recognize × as a code name, for instance. Code names that older browsers might not recognize are marked with an asterisk in Table A-2.

STARTING DATA FILES

There are no starting Data Files needed for this appendix.

Table A-1:
Color names and corresponding values

Color Name	RGB Value	Hexadecimal Value
aliceblue	(240,248,255)	#F0F8FF
antiquewhite	(250,235,215)	#FAEBD7
aqua	**(0,255,255)**	**#00FFFF**
aquamarine	(127,255,212)	#7FFFD4
azure	(240,255,255)	#F0FFFF
beige	(245,245,220)	#F5F5DC
bisque	(255,228,196)	#FFE4C4
black	**(0,0,0)**	**#000000**
blanchedalmond	(255,235,205)	#FFEBCD
blue	**(0,0,255)**	**#0000FF**
blueviolet	(138,43,226)	#8A2BE2
brown	(165,42,42)	#A52A2A
burlywood	(222,184,135)	#DEB887
cadetblue	(95,158,160)	#5F9EA0
chartreuse	(127,255,0)	#7FFF00
chocolate	(210,105,30)	#D2691E
coral	(255,127,80)	#FF7F50
cornflowerblue	(100,149,237)	#6495ED
cornsilk	(255,248,220)	#FFF8DC
crimson	(220,20,54)	#DC1436
cyan	**(0,255,255)**	**#00FFFF**
darkblue	(0,0,139)	#00008B
darkcyan	(0,139,139)	#008B8B
darkgoldenrod	(184,134,11)	#B8860B
darkgray	(169,169,169)	#A9A9A9
darkgreen	(0,100,0)	#006400
darkkhaki	(189,183,107)	#BDB76B
darkmagenta	(139,0,139)	#8B008B
darkolivegreen	(85,107,47)	#556B2F
darkorange	(255,140,0)	#FF8C00
darkorchid	(153,50,204)	#9932CC
darkred	(139,0,0)	#8B0000
darksalmon	(233,150,122)	#E9967A
darkseagreen	(143,188,143)	#8FBC8F
darkslateblue	(72,61,139)	#483D8B
darkslategray	(47,79,79)	#2F4F4F
darkturquoise	(0,206,209)	#00CED1
darkviolet	(148,0,211)	#9400D3
deeppink	(255,20,147)	#FF1493
deepskyblue	(0,191,255)	#00BFFF
dimgray	(105,105,105)	#696969
dodgerblue	(30,144,255)	#1E90FF
firebrick	(178,34,34)	#B22222
floralwhite	(255,250,240)	#FFFAF0
forestgreen	(34,139,34)	#228B22
fuchsia	**(255,0,255)**	**#FF00FF**

Color Name	RGB Value	Hexadecimal Value
gainsboro	(220,220,220)	#DCDCDC
ghostwhite	(248,248,255)	#F8F8FF
gold	(255,215,0)	#FFD700
goldenrod	(218,165,32)	#DAA520
gray	(128,128,128)	#808080
green	(0,128,0)	#008000
greenyellow	(173,255,47)	#ADFF2F
honeydew	(240,255,240)	#F0FFF0
hotpink	(255,105,180)	#FF69B4
indianred	(205,92,92)	#CD5C5C
indigo	(75,0,130)	#4B0082
ivory	(255,255,240)	#FFFFF0
khaki	(240,230,140)	#F0E68C
lavender	(230,230,250)	#E6E6FA
lavenderblush	(255,240,245)	#FFF0F5
lawngreen	(124,252,0)	#7CFC00
lemonchiffon	(255,250,205)	#FFFACD
lightblue	(173,216,230)	#ADD8E6
lightcoral	(240,128,128)	#F08080
lightcyan	(224,255,255)	#E0FFFF
lightgoldenrodyellow	(250,250,210)	#FAFAD2
lightgreen	(144,238,144)	#90EE90
lightgrey	(211,211,211)	#D3D3D3
lightpink	(255,182,193)	#FFB6C1
lightsalmon	(255,160,122)	#FFA07A
lightseagreen	(32,178,170)	#20B2AA
lightskyblue	(135,206,250)	#87CEFA
lightslategray	(119,136,153)	#778899
lightsteelblue	(176,196,222)	#B0C4DE
lightyellow	(255,255,224)	#FFFFE0
lime	**(0,255,0)**	**#00FF00**
limegreen	(50,205,50)	#32CD32
linen	(250,240,230)	#FAF0E6
magenta	**(255,0,255)**	**#FF00FF**
maroon	(128,0,0)	#800000
mediumaquamarine	(102,205,170)	#66CDAA
mediumblue	(0,0,205)	#0000CD
mediumorchid	(186,85,211)	#BA55D3
mediumpurple	(147,112,219)	#9370DB
mediumseagreen	(60,179,113)	#3CB371
mediumslateblue	(123,104,238)	#7B68EE
mediumspringgreen	(0,250,154)	#00FA9A
mediumturquoise	(72,209,204)	#48D1CC
mediumvioletred	(199,21,133)	#C71585
midnightblue	(25,25,112)	#191970
mintcream	(245,255,250)	#F5FFFA
mistyrose	(255,228,225)	#FFE4E1

Color Name	RGB Value	Hexadecimal Value
moccasin	(255,228,181)	#FFE4B5
navajowhite	(255,222,173)	#FFDEAD
navy	**(0,0,128)**	**#000080**
oldlace	(253,245,230)	#FDF5E6
olive	(128,128,0)	#808000
olivedrab	(107,142,35)	#6B8E23
orange	(255,165,0)	#FFA500
orangered	(255,69,0)	#FF4500
orchid	(218,112,214)	#DA70D6
palegoldenrod	(238,232,170)	#EEE8AA
palegreen	(152,251,152)	#98FB98
paleturquoise	(175,238,238)	#AFEEEE
palevioletred	(219,112,147)	#DB7093
papayawhip	(255,239,213)	#FFEFD5
peachpuff	(255,218,185)	#FFDAB9
peru	(205,133,63)	#CD853F
pink	(255,192,203)	#FFC0CB
plum	(221,160,221)	#DDA0DD
powderblue	(176,224,230)	#B0E0E6
purple	**(128,0,128)**	**#808080**
red	**(255,0,0)**	**#FF0000**
rosybrown	(188,143,143)	#BC8F8F
royalblue	(65,105,0)	#4169E1
saddlebrown	(139,69,19)	#8B4513
salmon	(250,128,114)	#FA8072
sandybrown	(244,164,96)	#F4A460
seagreen	(46,139,87)	#2E8B57
seashell	(255,245,238)	#FFF5EE
sienna	(160,82,45)	#A0522D
silver	(192,192,192)	#C0C0C0
skyblue	(135,206,235)	#87CEEB
slateblue	(106,90,205)	#6A5ACD
slategray	(112,128,144)	#708090
snow	(255,250,250)	#FFFAFA
springgreen	(0,255,127)	#00FF7F
steelblue	(70,130,180)	#4682B4
tan	(210,180,140)	#D2B48C
teal	(0,128,128)	#008080
thistle	(216,191,216)	#D8BFD8
tomato	(255,99,71)	#FF6347
turquoise	(64,224,208)	#40E0D0
violet	(238,130,238)	#EE82EE
wheat	(245,222,179)	#F5DEB3
white	**(255,255,255)**	**#FFFFFF**
whitesmoke	(245,245,245)	#F5F5F5
yellow	**(255,255,0)**	**#FFFF00**
yellowgreen	(154,205,50)	#9ACD32

Table A-2:
HTML character entities

Character	Code	Code Name	Description
	&#09;		Tab
	&#10;		Line feed
	&#32;		Space
!	&#33;		Exclamation mark
"	&#34;	&quot;	Double quotation mark
#	&#35;		Pound sign
$	&#36;		Dollar sign
%	&#37;		Percent sign
&	&#38;	&amp;	Ampersand
'	&#39;		Apostrophe
(	&#40;		Left parenthesis
)	&#41;		Right parenthesis
*	&#42;		Asterisk
+	&#43;		Plus sign
,	&#44;		Comma
-	&#45;		Hyphen
.	&#46;		Period
/	&#47;		Forward slash
0 - 9	0–9		Numbers 0–9
:	&#58;		Colon
;	&#59;		Semicolon
<	&#60;	&lt;	Less than sign
=	&#61;		Equal sign
>	&#62;	&gt;	Greater than sign
?	&#63;		Question mark
@	&#64;		Commercial at sign
A - Z	A–Z		Letters A–Z
[	&#91;		Left square bracket
\	&#92;		Back slash
]	&#93;		Right square bracket
^	&#94;		Caret
_	&#95;		Horizontal bar (underscore)
`	&#96;		Grave accent
a - z	a–z		Letters a–z
{	&#123;		Left curly brace
|	|		Vertical bar
}	&#125;		Right curly brace
~	&#126;		Tilde
‚	&#130;		Comma
ƒ	&#131;		Function sign (florin)
"	&#132;		Double quotation mark
…	&#133;		Ellipsis
†	&#134;		Dagger

Character	Code	Code Name	Description
‡	&#135;		Double dagger
ˆ	&#136;		Circumflex
‰	&#137;		Permil
Š	&#138;		Capital S with hacek
‹	&#139;		Left single angle
Œ	&#140;		Capital OE ligature
	–		Unused
'	&#145;		Single beginning quotation mark
'	&#146;		Single ending quotation mark
"	&#147;		Double beginning quotation mark
"	&#148;		Double ending quotation mark
•	&#149;		Bullet
–	&#150;		En dash
—	&#151;		Em dash
~	&#152;		Tilde
™	&#153;	™*	Trademark symbol
š	&#154;		Small s with hacek
›	&#155;		Right single angle
œ	&#156;		Lowercase oe ligature
Ÿ	&#159;		Capital Y with umlaut
		*	Non-breaking space
¡	&#161;	¡*	Inverted exclamation mark
¢	&#162;	¢*	Cent sign
£	&#163;	£*	Pound sterling
¤	&#164;	¤*	General currency symbol
¥	&#165;	¥*	Yen sign
¦	&#166;	¦*	Broken vertical bar
§	&#167;	§*	Section sign
¨	&#168;	¨*	Umlaut
©	&#169;	©*	Copyright symbol
ª	&#170;	ª*	Feminine ordinal
«	&#171;	«*	Left angle quotation mark
¬	&#172;	¬*	Not sign
	&#173;	­*	Soft hyphen
®	&#174;	®*	Registered trademark
¯	&#175;	¯*	Macron
°	&#176;	°*	Degree sign
±	&#177;	±*	Plus/minus symbol
²	&#178;	²*	Superscript 2
³	&#179;	³*	Superscript 3
´	&#180;	´*	Acute accent
µ	&#181;	µ*	Micro sign
¶	&#182;	¶*	Paragraph sign

Character	Code	Code Name	Description
·	&#183;	·*	Middle dot
ç	&#184;	¸*	Cedilla
1	&#185;	¹*	Superscript 1
º	&#186;	º*	Masculine ordinal
»	&#187;	»*	Right angle quotation mark
¼	&#188;	¼*	Fraction one-quarter
½	&#189;	½*	Fraction one-half
¾	&#190;	¾*	Fraction three-quarters
¿	&#191;	¿*	Inverted question mark
À	&#192;	&Agrave;	Capital A, grave accent
Á	&#193;	&Aacute;	Capital A, acute accent
Â	&#194;	&Acirc;	Capital A, circumflex accent
Ã	&#195;	&Atilde;	Capital A, tilde
Ä	&#196;	&Auml;	Capital A, umlaut
Å	&#197;	&Aring;	Capital A, ring
Æ	&#198;	&Aelig;	Capital AE ligature
Ç	&#199;	&Ccedil;	Capital C, cedilla
È	&#200;	&Egrave;	Capital E, grave accent
É	&#201;	&Eacute;	Capital E, acute accent
Ê	&#202;	&Ecirc;	Capital E, circumflex accent
Ë	&#203;	&Euml;	Capital E, umlaut
Ì	&#204;	&Igrave;	Capital I, grave accent
Í	&#205;	&Iacute;	Capital I, acute accent
Î	&#206;	&Icirc;	Capital I, circumflex accent
Ï	&#207;	&Iuml;	Capital I, umlaut
Ð	&#208;	Ð*	Capital ETH, Icelandic
Ñ	&#209;	&Ntilde;	Capital N, tilde
Ò	&#210;	&Ograve;	Capital O, grave accent
Ó	&#211;	&Oacute;	Capital O, acute accent
Ô	&#212;	&Ocirc;	Capital O, circumflex accent
Õ	&#213;	&Otilde;	Capital O, tilde
Ö	&#214;	&Ouml;	Capital O, umlaut
×	&#215;	×*	Multiplication sign
Ø	&#216;	&Oslash;	Capital O slash
Ù	&#217;	&Ugrave;	Capital U, grave accent
Ú	&#218;	&Uacute;	Capital U, acute accent
Û	&#219;	&Ucirc;	Capital U, circumflex accent
Ü	&#220;	&Uuml;	Capital U, umlaut
Ý	&#221;	&Yacute;	Capital Y, acute accent
Þ	&#222;	&THORN;	Capital THORN, Icelandic
ß	&#223;	&szlig;	Small sz ligature
à	&#224;	&agrave;	Small a, grave accent
á	&#225;	&aacute;	Small a, acute accent

Character	Code	Code Name	Description
â	&#226;	&acirc;	Small a, circumflex accent
ã	&#227;	&atilde;	Small a, tilde
ä	&#228;	&auml;	Small a, umlaut
å	&#229;	&aring;	Small a, ring
æ	&#230;	&aelig;	Small ae ligature
ç	&#231;	&ccedil;	Small c, cedilla
è	&#232;	&egrave;	Small e, grave accent
é	&#233;	&eacute;	Small e, acute accent
ê	&#234;	&ecirc;	Small e, circumflex accent
ë	&#235;	&euml;	Small e, umlaut
ì	&#236;	&igrave;	Small i, grave accent
í	&#237;	&iacute;	Small i, acute accent
î	&#238;	&icirc;	Small i, circumflex accent
ï	&#239;	&iuml;	Small i, umlaut
ð	&#240;	&eth;	Small eth, Icelandic
ñ	&#241;	&ntilde;	Small n, tilde
ò	&#242;	&ograve;	Small o, grave accent
ó	&#243;	&oacute;	Small o, acute accent
ô	&#244;	&ocirc;	Small o, circumflex accent
õ	&#245;	&otilde;	Small o, tilde
ö	&#246;	&ouml;	Small o, umlaut
÷	&#247;	÷*	Division sign
ø	&#248;	&oslash;	Small o slash
ù	&#249;	&ugrave;	Small u, grave accent
ú	&#250;	&uacute;	Small u, acute accent
û	&#251;	&ucirc;	Small u, circumflex accent
ü	&#252;	&uuml;	Small u, umlaut
ý	&#253;	&yacute;	Small y, acute accent
þ	&#254;	&thorn;	Small thorn, Icelandic
ÿ	&#255;	&yuml;	Small y, umlaut

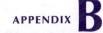

Making the Web More Accessible

Studies indicate that about 20% of the population has some type of disability. Many of these disabilities do not affect an individual's ability to interact with the Web. However, other disabilities can severely affect an individual's ability to participate in the Web community. For example, on a news Web site, a blind user could not see the latest headlines. A deaf user would not be able to hear a news clip embedded in the site's main page. A user with motor disabilities might not be able to move a mouse pointer to activate important links featured on the site's home page.

Disabilities that inhibit an individual's ability to use the Web fall into four main categories:

- **Visual disability:** A visual disability can include complete blindness, color-blindness, or an untreatable visual impairment.
- **Hearing disability:** A hearing disability can include complete deafness or the inability to distinguish sounds of certain frequencies.
- **Motor disability:** A motor disability can include the inability to use a mouse, to exhibit fine motor control, or to respond in a timely manner to computer prompts and queries.
- **Cognitive disability:** A cognitive disability can include a learning disability, attention deficit disorder, or the inability to focus on large amounts of information.

While the Web includes some significant obstacles to full use by disabled people, it also offers the potential for contact with a great amount of information that is not otherwise cheaply or easily accessible. For example, before the Web, in order to read a newspaper, a blind person was constrained by the expense of Braille printouts and audio tapes, as well as the limited availability of sighted people willing to read the news out loud. As a result, blind people would often only be able to read newspapers after the news was no longer new. The Web, however, makes news available in an electronic format and in real-time. A blind user can use a browser that converts electronic text into speech, known as a **screen reader**, to read a newspaper Web site. Combined with the Web, screen readers provide access to a broader array of information than was possible through Braille publications alone.

> "The power of the Web is in its universality. Access by everyone regardless of disability is an essential aspect."
>
> — Tim Berners-Lee, W3C Director and inventor of the World Wide Web

STARTING DATA FILES

There are no starting Data Files needed for this appendix.

In addition to screen readers, many other programs and devices—known collectively as **assistive technology** or **adaptive technology**—are available to enable people with different disabilities to use the Web. The challenge for the Web designer, then, is to create Web pages that are accessible to everyone, including (and perhaps especially) to people with disabilities. In addition to being a design challenge, for some designers, Web accessibility is the law.

Working with Section 508 Guidelines

In 1973, Congress passed the Rehabilitation Act, which aimed to foster economic independence for people with disabilities. Congress amended the act in 1998 to reflect the latest changes in information technology. Part of the amendment, **Section 508**, requires that any electronic information developed, procured, maintained, or used by the federal government be accessible to people with disabilities. Because the Web is one of the main sources of electronic information, Section 508 has had a profound impact on how Web pages are designed and how Web code is written. Note that the standards apply to federal Web sites, but not to private sector Web sites; however, if a site is provided under contract to a federal agency, the Web site or portion covered by the contract has to comply. Required or not, though, you should follow the Section 508 guidelines not only to make your Web site more accessible, but also to make your HTML code more consistent and reliable. The Section 508 guidelines are of interest not just to Web designers who work for the federal government, but to all Web designers.

The Section 508 guidelines encompass a wide range of topics, covering several types of disabilities. The part of Section 508 that impacts Web design is sub-section 1194.22, titled

§ 1194.22   **Web-based intranet and internet information and applications.**

Within this section are 15 paragraphs, numbered (a) through (p), which describe how each facet of a Web site should be designed so as to maximize accessibility. Let's examine each of these paragraphs in detail.

Graphics and Images

The first paragraph in sub-section 1194.22 deals with graphic images. The standard for the use of graphic images is that

§1194.22 (a)   **A text equivalent for every nontext element shall be provided (e.g., via "alt", "longdesc", or in element content).**

In other words, any graphic image that contains page content needs to include a text alternative to make the page accessible to visually impaired people. One of the simplest ways to do this is to use the `alt` attribute with every inline image that displays page content. For example, in Figure B-1, the `alt` attribute provides the text of a graphical logo for users who can't see the graphic.

Figure B-1   **Using the alt attribute**

`<img src="jkson.jpg" alt="Jackson Electronics" />`

Not every graphic image requires a text alternative. For example, a decorative image such as a bullet does not need a text equivalent. In those cases, you should include the `alt` attribute, but set its value to an empty text string. You should never neglect to include the `alt` attribute. If you are writing XHTML-compliant code, the `alt` attribute is required. In other cases, screen readers and other nonvisual browsers will recite the filename of a graphic image file if no value is specified for the `alt` attribute. Since the filename is usually of no interest to the end-user, this results in needless irritation.

The `alt` attribute is best used for short descriptions that involve five words or less. It is less effective for images that require long descriptive text. You can instead link these images to a document containing a more detailed description. One way to do this is with the `longdesc` attribute, which uses the syntax

```
<img src="url" longdesc="url" />
```

where *url* for the `longdesc` attribute points to a document containing a detailed description of the image. Figure B-2 shows an example that uses the `longdesc` attribute to point to a Web page containing a detailed description of a sales chart.

Figure B-2   **Using the alt attribute**

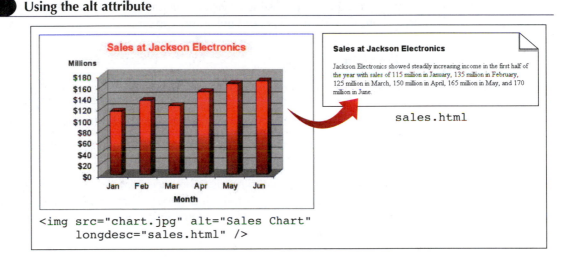

```
<img src="chart.jpg" alt="Sales Chart"
     longdesc="sales.html" />
```

In browsers that support the `longdesc` attribute, the attribute's value is presented as a link to the specified document. However, since many browsers do not yet support this attribute, many Web designers currently use a D-link. A **D-link** is an unobtrusive "D" placed next to the image on the page, which is linked to an external document containing a fuller description of the image. Figure B-3 shows how the sales chart data can be presented using a D-link.

Figure B-3	Using a D-link

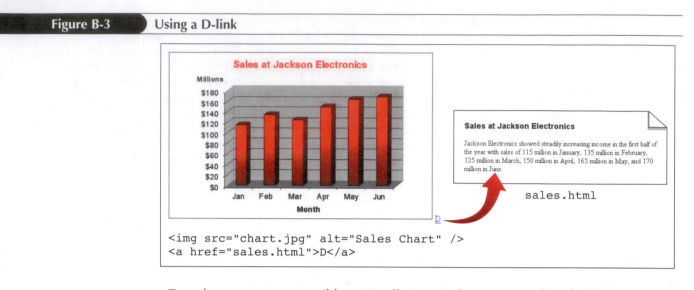

```
<img src="chart.jpg" alt="Sales Chart" />
<a href="sales.html">D</a>
```

To make your pages accessible to visually-impaired users, you will probably use a combination of alternative text and linked documents.

Multimedia

Audio and video have become important ways of conveying information on the Web. However, creators of multimedia presentations should also consider the needs of deaf users and users who are hard of hearing. The standard for multimedia accessibility is

§1194.22 (b) **Equivalent alternatives for any multimedia presentation shall be synchronized with the presentation.**

This means that any audio clip needs to be accompanied by a transcript of the audio's content, and any video clip needs to include closed captioning. Refer to your multimedia software's documentation on creating closed captioning and transcripts for your video and audio clips.

Color

Color is useful for emphasis and conveying information, but when color becomes an essential part of the site's content, you run the risk of shutting out people who are color blind. For this reason the third Section 508 standard states that

§1194.22 (c) **Web pages shall be designed so that all information conveyed with color is also available without color, for example from context or markup.**

About 8% of men and 0.5% of women are afflicted with some type of color blindness. The most serious forms of color blindness are:

- **deuteranopia**: an absence of green sensitivity; deuteranopia is one example of red-green color blindness, in which the colors red and green cannot be easily distinguished.
- **protanopia**: an absence of red sensitivity; protanopia is another example of red-green color blindness.
- **tritanopia**: an absence of blue sensitivity. People with tritanopia have much less loss of color sensitivity than other types of color blindness.
- **achromatopsia**: absence of any color sensitivity.

The most common form of serious color blindness is red-green color blindness. Figure B-4 shows how each type of serious color blindness would affect a person's view of a basic color wheel.

| Figure B-4 | Types of color blindness |

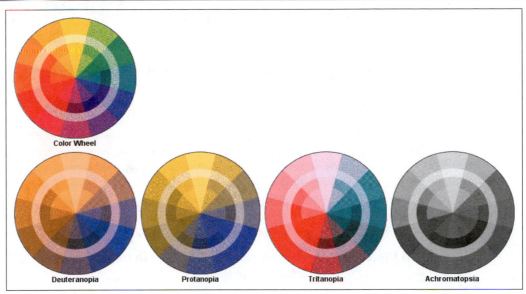

Color combinations that are easily readable for most people may be totally unreadable for users with certain types of color blindness. Figure B-5 demonstrates the accessibility problems that can occur with a graphical logo that contains green text on a red background. For people who have deuteranopia, protanopia, or achromatopsia, the logo is much more difficult to read.

| Figure B-5 | The effect of color blindness on graphical content |

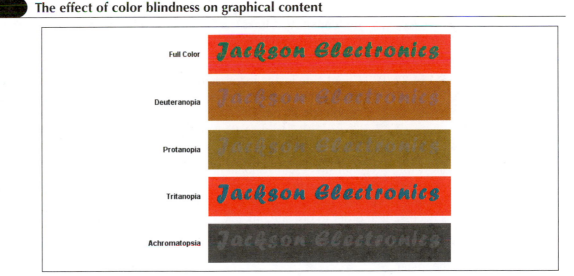

To make your page more accessible to people with color blindness, you can do the following:

- Provide noncolor clues to access your page's content. For example, some Web forms indicate required entry fields by displaying the field names in a red font. You can supplement this for color blind users by marking required fields with a red font *and* with an asterisk or other special symbol.
- Avoid explicit references to color. Don't instruct your users to click a red button in a Web form when some users are unable to distinguish red from other colors.
- Avoid known areas of color difficulty. Since most color blindness involves red-green color blindness, you should avoid red and green text combinations.

- Use bright colors, which are the easiest for color blind users to distinguish.
- Provide a grayscale or black and white alternative for your color blind users, and be sure that your link to that page is easily viewable.

Several sites on the Web include tools you can use to test your Web site for color blind accessibility. You can also load color palettes into your graphics software to see how your images will appear to users with different types of color blindness.

Style Sheets

By controlling how a page is rendered in a browser, style sheets play an important role in making the Web accessible to users with disabilities. Many browsers, such as Internet Explorer, allow a user to apply their own customized style sheet in place of the style sheet specified by a Web page's designer. This is particularly useful for visually impaired users who need to display text in extra large fonts with a high contrast between the text and the background color (yellow text on a black background is a common color scheme for such users). In order to make your pages accessible to those users, Section 508 guidelines state that

§1194.22 (d)   Documents shall be organized so they are readable without requiring an associated style sheet.

To test whether your site fulfills this guideline, you should view the site without the style sheet. Some browsers allow you to turn off style sheets; alternately, you can redirect a page to an empty style sheet. You should modify any page that is unreadable without its style sheet to conform with this guideline.

Image Maps

Section 508 provides two standards that pertain to image maps:

§1194.22 (e)   Redundant text links shall be provided for each active region of a server-side image map.

and

§1194.22 (f)   Client-side image maps shall be provided instead of server-side image maps except where the regions cannot be defined with an available geometric shape.

In other words, the *preferred* image map is a client-side image map, unless the map uses a shape that cannot be defined on the client side. Since client-side image maps allow for polygonal shapes, this should not be an issue; however if you must use a server-side image map, you need to provide a text alternative for each of the map's links. Because server-side image maps provide only map coordinates to the server, this text is necessary in order to provide link information that is accessible to blind or visually impaired users. Figure B-6 shows a server-side image map that satisfies the Section 508 guidelines by repeating the graphical links in the image map with text links placed below the image.

Figure B-6   **Making a server-side image map accessible**

Client-side image maps do not have the same limitations as server-side maps because they allow you to specify alternate text for each hotspot within the map. For example, if the image map shown in Figure B-6 were a client-side map, you could make it accessible using the following HTML code:

```
<img src="servermap.jpg" alt="Jackson Electronics"
 usemap="#links" />
<map name="links">
   <area shape="rect" href="home.html" alt="home"
    coords="21,69,123,117" />
   <area shape="rect" href="products.html" alt="products"
    coords="156,69,258,117" />
   <area shape="rect" href="stores.html" alt="stores"
    coords="302,69,404,117" />
   <area shape="rect" href="support.html" alt="support"
    coords="445,69,547,117" />
</map>
```

Screen readers or other nonvisual browsers use the value of the `alt` attribute within each `<area />` tag to give users access to each area. However, because some older browsers cannot work with the `alt` attribute in this way, you should also include the text alternative used for server-side image maps.

Tables

Tables can present a challenge for disabled users, particularly for those who employ screen readers or other nonvisual browsers. To render a Web page, these browsers employ a technique called **linearizing**, which processes Web page content using a few general rules:

1. Convert all images to their alternative text.
2. Present the contents of each table one cell at a time, working from left to right across each row before moving down to the next row.
3. If a cell contains a nested table, that table is linearized before proceeding to the next cell.

Figure B-7 shows how a nonvisual browser might linearize a sample table.

	Model	Processor	Memory	DVD Burner	Modem	Network Adapter
Desktop PCs	Paragon 2.4	Intel 2.4GHz	256MB	No	Yes	No
	Paragon 3.7	Intel 3.7GHz	512MB	Yes	Yes	No
	Paragon 5.9	Intel 5.9GHz	1024MB	Yes	Yes	Yes

linearized content

Desktop PCs
Model
Processor
Memory
DVD Burner
Modem
Network Adapter
Paragon 2.4
Intel 2.4 GHz
256MB
No
Yes
No
Paragon 3.7
Intel 3.7GHz
512MB
Yes
Yes
No
Paragon 5.9
Intel 5.9GHz
1024MB
Yes
Yes
Yes

One way of dealing with the challenge of linearizing is to structure your tables so that they are easily interpreted even when linearized. However, this is not always possible, especially for tables that have several rows and columns or may contain several levels of nested tables. The Section 508 guidelines for table creation state that

§1194.22 (g)   Row and column headers shall be identified for data tables.

and

§1194.22 (h)   Markup shall be used to associate data cells and header cells for data tables that have two or more logical levels of row or column headers.

To fulfill the 1194.22 (g) guideline, you should use the `<th>` tag for any table cell that contains a row or column header. By default, header text appears in a bold centered font; however, you can override this format using a style sheet. Many nonvisual browsers can search for header cells. Also, as a user moves from cell to cell in a table, these browsers can announce the row and column headers associated with each cell. In this way, using the `<th>` tag can significantly reduce some of the problems associated with linearizing.

You can also use the `scope` attribute to explicitly associate a header with a row, column, row group, or column group. The syntax of the `scope` attribute is

```
<th scope="type"> … </th>
```

where `type` is either `row`, `column`, `rowgroup`, or `colgroup`. Figure B-8 shows how to use the `scope` attribute to associate the headers with the rows and columns of a table.

Figure B-8   **Using the scope attribute**

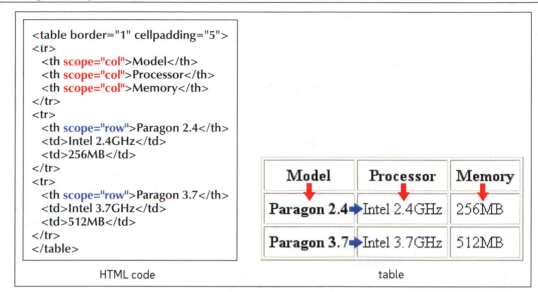

```
<table border="1" cellpadding="5">
<tr>
  <th scope="col">Model</th>
  <th scope="col">Processor</th>
  <th scope="col">Memory</th>
</tr>
<tr>
  <th scope="row">Paragon 2.4</th>
  <td>Intel 2.4GHz</td>
  <td>256MB</td>
</tr>
<tr>
  <th scope="row">Paragon 3.7</th>
  <td>Intel 3.7GHz</td>
  <td>512MB</td>
</tr>
</table>
```

HTML code   table

A nonvisual browser that encounters the table in Figure B-8 can indicate to users which rows and columns are associated with each data cell. For example, the browser could indicate that the cell value "512MB" is associated with the Memory column and the Paragon 3.7 row.

For more explicit references, HTML also supports the `headers` attribute, which specifies the cell or cells that contain header information for a particular cell. The syntax of the `headers` attribute is

```
<td headers="ids"> … </td>
```

where `ids` is a list of id values associated with header cells in the table. Figure B-9 demonstrates how to use the headers attribute.

Figure B-9   **Using the headers attribute**

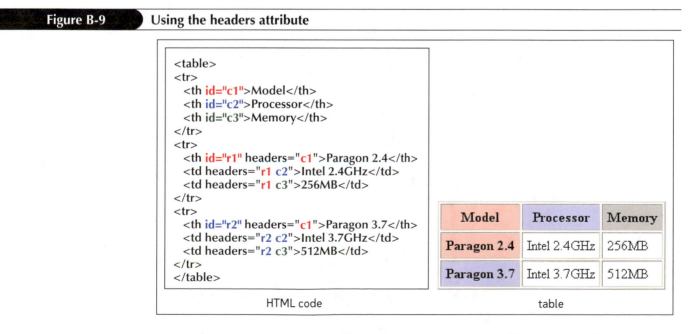

```
<table>
<tr>
  <th id="c1">Model</th>
  <th id="c2">Processor</th>
  <th id="c3">Memory</th>
</tr>
<tr>
  <th id="r1" headers="c1">Paragon 2.4</th>
  <td headers="r1 c2">Intel 2.4GHz</td>
  <td headers="r1 c3">256MB</td>
</tr>
<tr>
  <th id="r2" headers="c1">Paragon 3.7</th>
  <td headers="r2 c2">Intel 3.7GHz</td>
  <td headers="r2 c3">512MB</td>
</tr>
</table>
```

HTML code   table

Note that some older browsers do not support the `scope` and `headers` attributes. For this reason, it can be useful to supplement your tables with `caption` and `summary` attributes in order to provide even more information to blind and visually impaired users. See Tutorial 5 for a more detailed discussion of these elements and attributes.

Frame Sites

When a nonvisual browser opens a frame site, it can render the contents of only one frame at a time. Users are given a choice of which frame to open. So, it's important that the name given to a frame indicate the frame's content. For this reason, the Section 508 guideline for frames states that

§1194.22 (i)   Frames shall be titled with text that facilitates frame identification and navigation.

Frames can be identified using either the title attribute or the name attribute, and different nonvisual browsers use different attributes. For example, the Lynx browser uses the `name` attribute, while the IBM Home Page Reader uses the `title` attribute. For this reason, you should use both attributes in your framed sites. If you don't include a `title` or `name` attribute in the frame element, some nonvisual browsers retrieve the document specified as the frame's source and then use that page's title as the name for the frame.

The following code demonstrates how to make a frame site accessible to users with disabilities.

```
<frameset cols="25%, *">
   <frame src="title.htm" title="banner" name="banner" />
   <frameset rows="100, *">
      <frame src="links.htm" title="links" name="links" />
      <frame src="home.htm" title="documents" name="documents" />
   </frameset>
</frameset>
```

Naturally, you should make sure that any document displayed in a frame follows the Section 508 guidelines.

Animation and Scrolling Text

Animated GIFs, scrolling marquees, and other special features can be sources of irritation for any Web user; however, they can cause serious problems for certain users. For example, people with photosensitive epilepsy can experience seizures when exposed to a screen or portion of a screen that flickers or flashes within the range of 2 to 55 flashes per second (2 to 55 Hertz). For this reason, the Section 508 guidelines state that

§1194.22 (j)   Pages shall be designed to avoid causing the screen to flicker with a frequency greater than 2 Hz and lower than 55 Hz.

In addition to problems associated with photosensitive epilepsy, users with cognitive or visual disabilities may find it difficult to read moving text, and most screen readers are unable to read moving text. Therefore, if you decide to use animated elements, you must ensure that each element's flickering and flashing is outside of the prohibited range, and you should not place essential page content within these elements.

Scripts, Applets and Plug-ins

Scripts, applets, and plug-ins are widely used to make Web pages more dynamic and interesting. The Section 508 guidelines for scripts state that

§1194.22 (l)   When pages utilize scripting languages to display content, or to create interface elements, the information provided by the script shall be identified with functional text that can be read by adaptive technology.

Scripts are used for a wide variety of purposes. The following list describes some of the more popular uses of scripts and how to modify them for accessibility:

- **Pull-down menus**: Many Web designers use scripts to save screen space by inserting pull-down menus containing links to other pages in the site. Pull-down menus are usually accessed with a mouse. To assist users who cannot manipulate a mouse, include keyboard shortcuts to all pull-down menus. In addition, the links in a pull-down menu should be repeated elsewhere on the page or on the site in a text format.
- **Image rollovers**: Image rollovers are used to highlight linked elements. However, since image rollovers rely on the ability to use a mouse, pages should be designed so that roll-over effects are not essential for navigating a site or for understanding a page's content.
- **Dynamic content**: Scripts can be used to insert new text and page content. Because some browsers designed for users with disabilities have scripting turned off by default, you should either not include any crucial content in dynamic text, or you should provide an alternate method for users with disabilities to access that information.

Applets and plug-ins are programs external to a Web page or browser that add special features to a Web site. The Section 508 guideline for applets and plug-ins is

§1194.22 (m) **When a Web page requires that an applet, plug-in or other application be present on the client system to interpret page content, the page must provide a link to a plug-in or applet that complies with §1994.21(a) through (i).**

This guideline means that any applet or plug-in used with your Web site must be compliant with sections §1994.21(a) through (i) of the Section 508 accessibility law, which deal with accessibility issues for software applications and operating systems. If the default applet or plug-in does not comply with Section 508, you need to provide a link to a version of that applet or plug-in which does. For example, a Web page containing a Real Audio clip should have a link to a source for the necessary player. This places the responsibility on the Web page designer to know that a compliant application is available before requiring the clip to work with the page.

Web Forms

The Section 508 standard for Web page forms states that

§1194.22 (n) **When electronic forms are designed to be completed on-line, the form shall allow people using assistive technology to access the information, field elements, and functionality required for completion and submission of the form, including all directions and cues.**

This is a general statement that instructs designers to make forms accessible, but it doesn't supply any specific instructions. The following techniques can help you make Web forms that comply with Section 508:

- **Push buttons** should always include value attributes. The value attribute contains the text displayed on a button, and is rendered by different types of assistive technology.
- **Image buttons** should always include alternate text that can be rendered by nonvisual browsers.
- **Labels** should be associated with any input box, text area box, option button, checkbox, or selection list. The labels should be placed in close proximity to the input field and should be linked to the field using the label element.
- **Input boxes** and **text area boxes** should, when appropriate, include either default text or a prompt that indicates to the user what text to enter into the input box.
- **Interactive form elements** should be triggered by either the mouse or the keyboard.

The other parts of a Web form should comply with other Section 508 standards. For example, if you use a table to lay out the elements of a form, make sure that the form still makes sense when the table is linearized.

Links

It is common for Web designers to place links at the top, bottom, and sides of every page in their Web sites. This is generally a good idea, because those links enable users to move quickly and easily through a site. However, this technique can make it difficult to navigate a page using a screen reader, because screen readers move through a page from the top to bottom, reading each line of text. Users of screen readers may have to wait several minutes before they even get to the main body of a page, and the use of repetitive links forces such users to reread the same links on each page as they move through a site. To address this problem, the Section 508 guidelines state that

§1194.22 (o)   A method shall be provided that permits users to skip repetitive navigation links.

One way of complying with this rule is to place a link at the very top of each page that allows users to jump to the page's main content. In order to make the link unobtrusive, it can be attached to a transparent image that is one pixel wide by one pixel high. For example, the following code lets users of screen readers jump to the main content of the page without needing to go through the content navigation links on the page; however, the image itself is invisible to other users and so does not affect the page's layout or appearance.

```
<a href="#main">
   <img src="spacer.gif" height="1" width="1" alt="Skip to main
content" />
</a>

...

<a name="main"> </a>
page content goes here …
```

One advantage to this approach is that a template can be easily written to add this code to each page of the Web site.

Timed Responses

For security reasons, the login pages of some Web sites automatically log users out after a period of inactivity, or if users are unable to log in quickly. Because disabilities may prevent some users from being able to complete a login procedure within the prescribed time limit, the Section 508 guidelines state that

§1194.22 (p)   When a timed response is required, the user shall be alerted and given sufficient time to indicate that more time is required.

The guideline does not suggest a time interval. To satisfy Section 508, your page should notify users when a process is about to time out and prompt users whether additional time is needed before proceeding.

Providing a Text-Only Equivalent

If you cannot modify a page to match the previous accessibility guidelines, as a last resort you can create a text-only page:

§1194.22 (k)   **A text-only page, with equivalent information or functionality, shall be provided to make a Web site comply with the provisions of this part, when compliance cannot be accomplished in any other way. The content of the text-only pages shall be updated whenever the primary page changes.**

To satisfy this requirement, you should:

- Provide an easily accessible link to the text-only page.
- Make sure that the text-only page satisfies the Section 508 guidelines.
- Duplicate the essential content of the original page.
- Update the alternate page when you update the original page.

By using the Section 508 guidelines, you can work towards making your Web site accessible to everyone, regardless of disabilities.

Understanding the Web Accessibility Initiative

In 1999, the World Wide Web Consortium (W3C) developed its own set of guidelines for Web accessibility called the **Web Accessibility Initiative (WAI)**. The WAI covers many of the same points as the Section 508 rules, and expands on them to cover basic Web site design issues. The overall goal of the WAI is to facilitate the creation of Web sites that are accessible to all, and to encourage designers to implement HTML in a consistent way.

The WAI sets forth 14 guidelines for Web designers. Within each guideline is a collection of checkpoints indicating how to apply the guideline to specific features of a Web site. Each checkpoint is also given a priority score that indicates how important the guideline is for proper Web design:

- **Priority 1:** A Web content developer **must** satisfy this checkpoint. Otherwise, one or more groups will find it impossible to access information in the document. Satisfying this checkpoint is a basic requirement for some groups to be able to use Web documents.
- **Priority 2:** A Web content developer **should** satisfy this checkpoint. Otherwise, one or more groups will find it difficult to access information in the document. Satisfying this checkpoint will remove significant barriers to accessing Web documents.
- **Priority 3:** A Web content developer **may** address this checkpoint. Otherwise, one or more groups will find it somewhat difficult to access information in the document. Satisfying this checkpoint will improve access to Web documents**.**

The following table lists WAI guidelines with each checkpoint and its corresponding priority value. You can learn more about the WAI guidelines and how to implement them by going to the World Wide Web Consortium Web site at *www.w3.org*.

WAI Guidelines	Priority
1. Provide equivalent alternatives to auditory and visual content	
1.1 Provide a text equivalent for every nontext element (e.g., via `alt`, `longdesc`, or in element content). *This includes:* images, graphical representations of text (including symbols), image map regions, animations (e.g., animated GIFs), applets and programmatic objects, ascii art, frames, scripts, images used as list bullets, spacers, graphical buttons, sounds (played with or without user interaction), stand-alone audio files, audio tracks of video, and video.	1
1.2 Provide redundant text links for each active region of a server-side image map.	1
1.3 Until user agents can automatically read aloud the text equivalent of a visual track, provide an auditory description of the important information of the visual track of a multimedia presentation.	1
1.4 For any time-based multimedia presentation (e.g., a movie or animation), synchronize equivalent alternatives (e.g., captions or auditory descriptions of the visual track) with the presentation.	1
1.5 Until user agents render text equivalents for client-side image map links, provide redundant text links for each active region of a client-side image map.	3
2. Don't rely on color alone	
2.1 Ensure that all information conveyed with color is also available without color, for example from context or markup.	1
2.2 Ensure that foreground and background color combinations provide sufficient contrast when viewed by someone having color deficits or when viewed on a black and white screen. [Priority 2 for images, Priority 3 for text].	2
3. Use markup and style sheets and do so properly	
3.1 When an appropriate markup language exists, use markup rather than images to convey information.	2
3.2 Create documents that validate to published formal grammars.	2
3.3 Use style sheets to control layout and presentation.	2
3.4 Use relative rather than absolute units in markup language attribute values and style sheet property values.	2
3.5 Use header elements to convey document structure and use them according to specification.	2
3.6 Mark up lists and list items properly.	2
3.7 Mark up quotations. Do not use quotation markup for formatting effects such as indentation.	2
4. Clarify natural language usage	
4.1 Clearly identify changes in the natural language of a document's text and any text equivalents (e.g., captions).	1
4.2 Specify the expansion of each abbreviation or acronym in a document where it first occurs.	3
4.3 Identify the primary natural language of a document.	3
5. Create tables that transform gracefully	
5.1 For data tables, identify row and column headers.	1
5.2 For data tables that have two or more logical levels of row or column headers, use markup to associate data cells and header cells.	1
5.3 Do not use a table for layout unless the table makes sense when linearized. If a table does not make sense, provide an alternative equivalent (which may be a linearized version).	2
5.4 If a table is used for layout, do not use any structural markup for the purpose of visual formatting.	2

WAI Guidelines	Priority
5.5 Provide summaries for tables.	3
5.6 Provide abbreviations for header labels.	3
6. Ensure that pages featuring new technologies transform gracefully	
6.1 Organize documents so they may be read without style sheets. For example, when an HTML document is rendered without associated style sheets, it must still be possible to read the document.	1
6.2 Ensure that equivalents for dynamic content are updated when the dynamic content changes.	1
6.3 Ensure that pages are usable when scripts, applets, or other programmatic objects are turned off or not supported. If this is not possible, then provide equivalent information on an alternative accessible page.	1
6.4 For scripts and applets, ensure that event handlers are input device-independent.	2
6.5 Ensure that dynamic content is accessible or provide an alternative presentation or page.	2
7. Ensure user control of time-sensitive content changes	
7.1 Until user agents allow users to control flickering, avoid causing the screen to flicker.	1
7.2 Until user agents allow users to control blinking, avoid causing content to blink (i.e., change presentation at a regular rate, such as turning on and off).	2
7.3 Until user agents allow users to freeze moving content, avoid movement in pages.	2
7.4 Until user agents provide the ability to stop the refresh, do not create periodically auto-refreshing pages.	2
7.5 Until user agents provide the ability to stop auto-redirect, do not use markup to redirect pages automatically. Instead, configure the server to perform redirects.	2
8. Ensure direct accessibility of embedded user interfaces	
8.1 Make programmatic elements such as scripts and applets directly accessible or compatible with assistive technologies [Priority 1 if functionality is important and not presented elsewhere, otherwise Priority 2.]	2
9. Design for device-independence	
9.1 Provide client-side image maps instead of server-side image maps except where the regions cannot be defined with an available geometric shape.	1
9.2 Ensure that any element with its own interface can be operated in a device-independent manner.	2
9.3 For scripts, specify logical event handlers rather than device-dependent event handlers.	2
9.4 Create a logical tab order through links, form controls, and objects.	3
9.5 Provide keyboard shortcuts to important links (including those in client-side image maps), form controls, and groups of form controls.	3
10. Use interim solutions	
10.1 Until user agents allow users to turn off spawned windows, do not cause pop-ups or other windows to appear and do not change the current window without informing the user.	2
10.2 Until user agents support explicit associations between labels and form controls, ensure that labels are properly positioned for all form controls with implicitly associated labels.	2
10.3 Until user agents (including assistive technologies) render side-by-side text correctly, provide a linear text alternative (on the current page or some other) for *all* tables that lay out text in parallel, word-wrapped columns.	3
10.4 Until user agents handle empty controls correctly, include default, place-holding characters in edit boxes and text areas.	3
10.5 Until user agents (including assistive technologies) render adjacent links distinctly, include nonlink, printable characters (surrounded by spaces) between adjacent links.	3

WAI Guidelines	Priority
11. Use W3C technologies and guidelines	
11.1 Use W3C technologies when they are available and appropriate for a task and use the latest versions when supported.	2
11.2 Avoid deprecated features of W3C technologies.	2
11.3 Provide information so that users may receive documents according to their preferences (e.g., language, content type, etc.)	3
11.4 If, after best efforts, you cannot create an accessible page, provide a link to an alternative page that uses W3C technologies, is accessible, has equivalent information (or functionality), and is updated as often as the inaccessible (original) page.	1
12. Provide context and orientation information	
12.1 Title each frame to facilitate frame identification and navigation.	1
12.2 Describe the purpose of frames and how frames relate to each other if this is not obvious from frame titles alone.	2
12.3 Divide large blocks of information into more manageable groups where natural and appropriate.	2
12.4 Associate labels explicitly with their controls.	2
13. Provide clear navigation mechanisms	
13.1 Clearly identify the target of each link.	2
13.2 Provide metadata to add semantic information to pages and sites.	2
13.3 Provide information about the general layout of a site (e.g., a site map or table of contents).	2
13.4 Use navigation mechanisms in a consistent manner.	2
13.5 Provide navigation bars to highlight and give access to the navigation mechanism.	3
13.6 Group related links, identify the group (for user agents), and, until user agents do so, provide a way to bypass the group.	3
13.7 If search functions are provided, enable different types of searches for different skill levels and preferences.	3
13.8 Place distinguishing information at the beginning of headings, paragraphs, lists, etc.	3
13.9 Provide information about document collections (i.e., documents comprising multiple pages).	3
13.10 Provide a means to skip over multiline ASCII art.	3
14. Ensure that documents are clear and simple	
14.1 Use the clearest and simplest language appropriate for a site's content.	1
14.2 Supplement text with graphic or auditory presentations where they will facilitate comprehension of the page.	3
14.3 Create a style of presentation that is consistent across pages.	3

Checking Your Web Site for Accessibility

As you develop your Web site, you should periodically check it for accessibility. In addition to reviewing the Section 508 and WAI guidelines, you can do several things to verify that your site is accessible to everyone:

- Set up your browser to suppress the display of images. Does each page still convey all of the necessary information?
- Set your browser to display pages in extra large fonts and with a different color scheme. Are your pages still readable under these conditions?
- Try to navigate your pages using only your keyboard. Can you access all of the links and form elements?
- View your page in a text-only browser. (You can use the Lynx browser for this task, located at *www.lynx.browser.org*.)
- Open your page in a screen reader or other nonvisual browser. (The W3C Web site contains links to several alternative browsers that you can download as freeware or on a short-term trial basis in order to evaluate your site.)
- Use tools that test your site for accessibility. (The WAI pages at the W3C Web site contains links to a wide variety of tools that report on how well your site complies with the WAI and Section 508 guidelines.)

Following the accessibility guidelines laid out by Section 508 and the WAI will result in a Web site that is not only more accessible to a wider audience, but whose design is also cleaner, easier to work with, and easier to maintain.

HTML Elements and Attributes

This appendix provides descriptions of the major elements and attributes of HTML. The elements and attributes represent the specifications of the W3C; therefore, they might not all be supported by the major browsers. Also, in some cases, an element or attribute is not part of the W3C specifications, but instead is an extension offered by a particular browser. Where this is the case, the element or attribute is listed with the supporting browser indicated in parentheses.

Many elements and attributes have been deprecated by the W3C. Deprecated elements and attributes are supported by most browsers, but their use is discouraged. In addition, some elements and attributes have been marked as *obsolete*. The use of both deprecated and obsolete items is not recommended. However, while deprecated items are in danger of no longer being supported by the browser market, obsolete items will probably still be supported by the browser market for the foreseeable future.

Finally, elements and attributes that are new with HTML5 are indicated in the text. Note that some of these elements and attributes are not supported by all browsers and browser versions.

The following data types are used throughout this appendix:

- *char*   A single text character
- *char code*   A character encoding
- *color*   An HTML color name or hexadecimal color value
- *date*   A date and time in the format: *yyyy-mm-dd*T*hh: mm:ss*TIMEZONE
- *id*   An id value
- *lang*   A language type
- *media*   A media type equal to all, aural, braille, handheld, print, projection, screen, tty, or tv
- *integer*   An integer value
- *mime-type*   A MIME data type, such as "text/css"
- *mime-type list* A comma-separated list of mime-types
- **option1**|*option2*| … The value is limited to the specified list of *options*, with the default in **bold**
- *script*   A script or a reference to a script
- *styles*   A list of style declarations
- *text*   A text string
- *text list*   A comma-separated list of text strings
- *url*   The URL for a Web page or file
- *value*   A numeric value
- *value list*   A comma-separated list of numeric values

STARTING DATA FILES

There are no starting Data Files needed for this appendix.

General Attributes

Several attributes are common to many page elements. Rather than repeating this information each time it occurs, the following tables summarize these attributes.

Core Attributes

The following attributes apply to all page elements and are supported by most browser versions.

Attribute	Description
class="*text*"	Specifies the class or group to which an element belongs
contenteditable="*text list*"	Specifies whether the contents of the element are editable (HTML5)
contextmenu="*id*"	Specifies the value of the id attribute on the menu with which to associate the element as a context menu
draggable="true|false"	Specifies whether the element is draggable (HTML5)
dropzone="copy|move|link"	Specifies what types of content can be dropped on the element and which actions to take with content when it is dropped (HTML5)
hidden="hidden"	Specifies that the element is not yet, or is no longer, relevant and that the element should not be rendered (HTML5)
id="*text*"	Specifies a unique identifier to be associated with the element
spellcheck="true|false"	Specifies whether the element represents an element whose contents are subject to spell checking and grammar checking (HTML5)
style="*styles*"	Defines an inline style for the element
title="*text*"	Provides an advisory title for the element

Language Attributes

The Web is designed to be universal and has to be adaptable to languages other than English. Thus, another set of attributes provides language support. This set of attributes is not as widely supported by browsers as the core attributes are. As with the core attributes, they can be applied to most page elements.

Attribute	Description
dir="**ltr**|rtl"	Indicates the text direction as related to the lang attribute; a value of ltr displays text from left to right; a value of rtl displays text from right to left
lang="*lang*"	Identifies the language used in the page content where *lang* is language code name

Form Attributes

The following attributes can be applied to most form elements or to a Web form itself, but not to other page elements.

Attribute	Description
accesskey="*char*"	Indicates the keyboard character that can be pressed along with the accelerator key to access a form element
disabled="disabled"	Disables a form field for input
tabindex="*integer*"	Specifies a form element's position in a document's tabbing order

Event Attributes

To make Web pages more dynamic, HTML supports event attributes that identify scripts to be run in response to an event occurring within an element. For example, clicking a main heading with a mouse can cause a browser to run a program that hides or expands a table of contents. Each event attribute has the form

```
onevent = "script"
```

where *event* is the name of the event attribute and *script* is the name of the script or command to be run by the browser in response to the occurrence of the event within the element.

Core Events

The general event attributes are part of the specifications for HTML. They apply to almost all page elements.

Attribute	Description
onabort	Loading of the element is aborted by the user (HTML5)
onclick	The mouse button is clicked.
oncontextmenu	The user requested the context menu for the element (HTML5)
ondblclick	The mouse button is double-clicked.
onerror	The element failed to load properly (HTML5)
onkeydown	A key is pressed down.
onkeypress	A key is initially pressed.
onkeyup	A key is released.
onload	The element finishes loading (HTML5)
onmousedown	The mouse button is pressed down.
onmousemove	The mouse pointer is moved within the element's boundaries.
onmouseout	The mouse pointer is moved out of the element's boundaries.
onmouseover	The mouse pointer hovers over the element.
onmouseup	The mouse button is released.
onmousewheel	The user rotates the mouse wheel
onreadystatechange	The element and its resources finish loading (HTML5)
onscroll	The element or document window is being scrolled (HTML5)
onshow	The user requests that the element be shown as a context menu (HTML5)
onsuspend	The browser suspends retrieving data (HTML5)

Document Events

The following list of event attributes applies not to individual elements within the page, but to the entire document as it is displayed within the browser window or frame.

Attribute	Description
onafterprint	The document has finished printing (IE only).
onbeforeprint	The document is about to be printed (IE only).
onload	The page is finished being loaded.
onunload	The page is finished unloading.

Form Events

The following list of event attributes applies to either an entire Web form or fields within a form.

Attribute	Description
onblur	The form field has lost the focus.
onchange	The value of the form field has been changed.
onfocus	The form field has received the focus.
onformchange	The user made a change in the value of a form field in the form (HTML5)
onforminput	The value of a control in the form changes (HTML5)
oninput	The value of an element changes (HTML5)
oninvalid	The form field fails to meet validity constraints (HTML5)
onreset	The form has been reset.
onselect	Text content has been selected in the form field.
onsubmit	The form has been submitted for processing.

Drag and Drop Events

The following list of event attributes applies to all page elements and can be used to respond to the user action of dragging and dropping objects in the Web page.

Attribute	Description
ondrag	The user continues to drag the element (HTML5)
ondragenter	The user ends dragging the element, entering the element into a valid drop target (HTML5)
ondragleave	The user's drag operation leaves the element (HTML5)
ondragover	The user continues a drag operation over the element (HTML5)
ondragstart	The user starts dragging the element (HTML5)
ondrop	The user completes a drop operation over the element (HTML5)

Multimedia Events

The following list of event attributes applies to embedded multimedia elements such as audio and video clips and is used to respond to events initiated during the loading or playback of those elements.

Attribute	Description
oncanplay	The browser can resume playback of the video or audio, but determines the playback will have to stop for further buffering
oncanplaythrough	The browser can resume playback of the video or audio, and determines the playback can play through without further buffering (HTML5)
ondurationchange	The DOM duration of the video or audio element changes (HTML5)
onemptied	The video or audio element returns to the uninitialized state (HTML5)
onended	The end of the video or audio is reached (HTML5)
onloadeddata	The video or audio is at the current playback position for the first time (HTML5)

Attribute	Description
onloadedmetadata	The duration and dimensions of the video or audio element are determined (HTML5)
onloadstart	The browser begins looking for media data in the video or audio element (HTML5)
onpause	The video or audio is paused (HTML5)
onplay	The video or audio playback is initiated (HTML5)
onplaying	The video or audio playback starts (HTML5)
onprogress	The browser fetches data for the video or audio (HTML5)
onratechange	The video or audio data changes (HTML5)
onseeked	A seek operation on the audio or video element ends (HTML5)
onseeking	Seeking is initiated on the audio or video (HTML5)
onstalled	An attempt to retrieve data for the video or audio is not forthcoming (HTML5)
ontimeupdate	The current playback position of the video or audio element changes (HTML5)
onvolumechange	The volume of the video or audio element changes (HTML5)
onwaiting	Playback of the video or audio stops because the next frame is unavailable (HTML5)

HTML Elements and Attributes

The following table contains an alphabetic listing of the elements and attributes supported by HTML. Some attributes are not listed in this table, but are described instead in the general attributes tables presented in the previous section of this appendix.

Element/Attribute	Description
`<!-- text -->`	Inserts a comment into the document (comments are not displayed in the rendered page)
`<!doctype>`	Specifies the Document Type Definition for a document
`<a> </a>`	Marks the beginning and end of a link
`charset="text"`	Specifies the character encoding of the linked document (obsolete)
`coords="value list"`	Specifies the coordinates of a hotspot in a client-side image map; the value list depends on the shape of the hotspot: shape="rect" "left, right, top, bottom"shape="circle" "x_center, y_center, radius"shape="poly" "x1, y1, x2, y2, x3, y3, ..." (obsolete)
`href="url"`	Specifies the URL of the link
`hreflang="text"`	Specifies the language of the linked document
`name="text"`	Specifies a name for the enclosed text, allowing it to be a link target (obsolete)
`rel="text"`	Specifies the relationship between the current page and the link specified by the href attribute
`rev="text"`	Specifies the reverse relationship between the current page and the link specified by the href attribute (obsolete)
`shape="rect|circle|polygon"`	Specifies the shape of the hotspot (obsolete)
`title="text"`	Specifies the pop-up text for the link
`target="text"`	Specifies the target window or frame for the link
`type="mime-type"`	Specifies the data type of the linked document
`<abbr> </abbr>`	Marks abbreviated text

Element/Attribute	Description
`<acronym> </acronym>`	Marks acronym text (deprecated)
`<address> </address>`	Marks address text
`<applet> </applet>`	Embeds an applet into the browser (deprecated)
`align="align"`	Specifies the alignment of the applet with the surrounding text where *align* is absmiddle, absbottom, baseline, bottom, center, left, middle, right, texttop, or top.
`alt="text"`	Specifies alternate text for the applet (deprecated)
`archive="url"`	Specifies the URL of an archive containing classes and other resources to be used with the applet (deprecated)
`code="url"`	Specifies the URL of the applet's code/class (deprecated)
`codebase="url"`	Specifies the URL of all class files for the applet (deprecated)
`datafld="text"`	Specifies the data source that supplies bound data for use with
`datasrc="text"`	Specifies the ID or URL of the applet's data source
`height="integer"`	Specifies the height of the applet in pixels
`hspace="integer"`	Specifies the horizontal space around the applet in pixels (deprecated)
`mayscript="mayscript"`	Permits access to the applet by programs embedded in the document
`name="text"`	Specifies the name assigned to the applet (deprecated)
`object="text"`	Specifies the name of the resource that contains a serialized representation of the applet (deprecated)
`src="url"`	Specifies an external URL reference to the applet
`vspace="integer"`	Specifies the vertical space around the applet in pixels (deprecated)
`width="integer"`	Specifies the width of the applet in pixels (deprecated)
`<area />`	Marks an image map hotspot
`alt="text"`	Specifies alternate text for the hotspot
`coords="value list"`	Specifies the coordinates of the hotspot; the value list depends on the shape of the hotspot: shape="rect" *"left, right, top, bottom"* shape="circle" *"x_center, y_center, radius"* shape="poly" *"x1, y1, x2, y2, x3, y3, ..."*
`href="url"`	Specifies the URL of the document to which the hotspot points
`hreflang="lang"`	Language of the hyperlink destination
`media="media"`	The media for which the destination of the hyperlink was designed
`rel="text"`	Specifies the relationship between the current page and the destination of the link
`nohref="nohref"`	Specifies that the hotspot does not point to a link
`shape="rect|circle|polygon"`	Specifies the shape of the hotspot
`target="text"`	Specifies the target window or frame for the link
`<article> </article>`	Structural element marking a page article (HTML5)
`<aside> </aside>`	Structural element marking a sidebar that is tangentially related to the main page content (HTML5)
`<audio> </audio>`	Marks embedded audio content (HTML5)
`autoplay="autoplay"`	Automatically begins playback of the audio stream
`preload="none|metadata|auto"`	Specifies whether to preload data to the browser
`controls="controls"`	Specifies whether to display audio controls

Element/Attribute	Description
`loop="loop"`	Specifies whether to automatically loop back to the beginning of the audio clip
`src="url"`	Provides the source of the audio clip
`<b> </b>`	Mark text offset from its surrounding content without conveying any extra emphasis or importance
`<base />`	Specifies global reference information for the document
`href="url"`	Specifies the URL from which all relative links in the document are based
`target="text"`	Specifies the target window or frame for links in the document
`<basefont />`	Specifies the font setting for the document text (deprecated)
`color="color"`	Specifies the text color (deprecated)
`face="text list"`	Specifies a list of fonts to be applied to the text (deprecated)
`size="integer"`	Specifies the size of the font range from 1 (smallest) to 7 (largest) (deprecated)
`<bdi> </bdi>`	Marks text that is isolated from its surroundings for the purposes of bidirectional text formatting (HTML5)
`<bdo> </bdo>`	Indicates that the enclosed text should be rendered with the direction specified by the dir attribute
`<big> </big>`	Increases the size of the enclosed text relative to the default font size (deprecated)
`<blockquote> </blockquote>`	Marks content as quoted from another source
`cite="url"`	Provides the source URL of the quoted content
`<body> </body>`	Marks the page content to be rendered by the browser
`alink="color"`	Specifies the color of activated links in the document (obsolete)
`background="url"`	Specifies the background image file used for the page (obsolete)
`bgcolor="color"`	Specifies the background color of the page (obsolete)
`link="color"`	Specifies the color of unvisited links (obsolete)
`marginheight="integer"`	Specifies the size of the margin above and below the page (obsolete)
`marginwidth="integer"`	Specifies the size of the margin to the left and right of the page (obsolete)
`text="color"`	Specifies the color of page text (obsolete)
`vlink="color"`	Specifies the color of previously visited links (obsolete)
` `	Inserts a line break into the page
`clear="none|left|right|all"`	Displays the line break only when the specified margin is clear (obsolete)
`<button> </button>`	Creates a form button
`autofocus="autofocus"`	Gives the button the focus when the page is loaded (HTML5)
`disabled="disabled"`	Disables the button
`form="text"`	Specifies the form to which the button belongs (HTML5)
`formaction="url"`	Specifies the URL to which the form data is sent (HTML5)
`formenctype="mime-type"`	Specifies the encoding of the form data before it is sent (HTML5)
`formmethod="get|post"`	Specifies the HTTP method with which the form data is submitted
`formnovalidate="formnovalidate"`	Specifies that the form should not be validated during submission (HTML5)
`formtarget="text"`	Provides a name for the target of the button (HTML5)
`name="text"`	Provides the name assigned to the form button
`type="submit|reset|button"`	Specifies the type of form button
`value="text"`	Provides the value associated with the form button

Element/Attribute	Description
`<canvas> </canvas>`	Marks a resolution-dependent bitmapped region that can be used for dynamic rendering of images, graphs, and games (HTML5)
`height="integer"`	Height of canvas in pixels
`width="integer"`	Width of canvas in pixels
`<caption> </caption>`	Creates a table caption
`align="align"`	Specifies the alignment of the caption where *align* is bottom, center, left, right, or top (deprecated)
`valign="top|bottom"`	Specifies the vertical alignment of the caption
`<center> </center>`	Centers content horizontally on the page (obsolete)
`<cite> </cite>`	Marks citation text
`<code> </code>`	Marks text used for code samples
`<col> </col>`	Defines the settings for a column or group of columns (obsolete)
`align="align"`	Specifies the alignment of the content of the column(s) where *align* is left, right, or center
`char="char"`	Specifies a character in the column used to align column values (obsolete)
`charoff="integer"`	Specifies the offset in pixels from the alignment character specified in the char attribute (obsolete)
`span="integer"`	Specifies the number of columns in the group
`valign="align"`	Specifies the vertical alignment of the content in the column(s) where *align* is top, middle, bottom, or baseline
`width="integer"`	Specifies the width of the column(s) in pixels (obsolete)
`<colgroup> </colgroup>`	Creates a container for a group of columns
`align="align"`	Specifies the alignment of the content of the column group where *align* is left, right, or center (obsolete)
`char="char"`	Specifies a character in the column used to align column group values (obsolete)
`charoff="integer"`	Specifies the offset in pixels from the alignment character specified in the char attribute (obsolete)
`span="integer"`	Specifies the number of columns in the group
`valign="align"`	Specifies the vertical alignment of the content in the column group where *align* is top, middle, bottom, or baseline (obsolete)
`width="integer"`	Specifies the width of the columns in the group in pixels (obsolete)
`<command> </command>`	Defines a command button (HTML5)
`checked="checked"`	Selects the command
`disabled="disabled"`	Disables the command
`icon="url"`	Provides the URL for the image that represents the command
`label="text"`	Specifies the text of the command button
`radiogroup="text"`	Specifies the name of the group of commands toggled when the command itself is toggled
`type="command|radio|checkbox"`	Specifies the type of command button
`<datalist> </datalist>`	Encloses a set of option elements that can act as a dropdown list (HTML5)
`<dd> </dd>`	Marks text as a definition within a definition list

Element/Attribute	Description
`<del> </del>`	Marks text as deleted from the document
`cite="url"`	Provides the URL for the document that has additional information about the deleted text
`datetime="date"`	Specifies the date and time of the text deletion
`<details> </details>`	Represents a form control from which the user can obtain additional information or controls (HTML5)
`open="open"`	Specifies that the contents of the details element should be shown to the user
`<dfn> </dfn>`	Marks the defining instance of a term
`<dir> </dir>`	Contains a directory listing (deprecated)
`compact="compact"`	Permits use of compact rendering, if available (deprecated)
`<div> </div>`	Creates a generic block-level element
`align="left|center right|justify"`	Specifies the horizontal alignment of the content (obsolete)
`datafld="text"`	Indicates the column from a data source that supplies bound data for the block (IE only)
`dataformatas="html |plaintext|text"`	Specifies the format of the data in the data source bound with the the button (IE only)
`datasrc="url"`	Provides the URL or ID of the data source bound with the block (IE only)
`<dl> </dl>`	Encloses a definition list using the dd and dt elements
`compact="compact"`	Permits use of compact rendering, if available (obsolete)
`<dt> </dt>`	Marks a definition term in a definition list
`nowrap="nowrap"`	Specifies whether the content wraps using normal HTML line-wrapping conventions
`<em> </em>`	Marks emphasized text
`<embed> </embed>`	Defines external multimedia content or a plugin (HTML5)
`align="align"`	Specifies the alignment of the object with the surrounding content where *align* is bottom, left, right, or top (obsolete)
`height="integer"`	Specifies the height of the object in pixels
`hspace="integer"`	Specifies the horizontal space around the object in pixels (obsolete)
`name="text"`	Provides the name of the embedded object (obsolete)
`src="url"`	Provides the location of the file containing the object
`type="mime-type"`	Specifies the mime-type of the embedded object
`vspace="integer"`	Specifies the vertical space around the object in pixels (obsolete)
`width="integer"`	Specifies the width of the object in pixels
`<fieldset> </fieldset>`	Places form fields in a common group
`disabled="disabled"`	Disables the fieldset
`form="id"`	The id of the form associated with the fieldset
`name="text"`	The name part of the name/value pair associated with this element
`<figcaption> </figcaption>`	Represents the caption of a figure (HTML5)
`<figure> </figure>`	A structural element that represents a group of media content that is self-contained along with a caption (HTML5)
`<font> </font>`	Formats the enclosed text (deprecated)
`color="color"`	Specifies the color of the enclosed text (deprecated)
`face="text list"`	Specifies the font face(s) of the enclosed text (deprecated)
`size="integer"`	Specifies the size of the enclosed text, with values ranging from 1 (smallest) to 7 (largest); a value of +integer increases the font size relative to the font size specified in the basefont element (deprecated)

Element/Attribute	Description
`<footer> </footer>`	A structural element that represents the footer of a section or page (HTML5)
`<form> </form>`	Encloses the contents of a Web form
`accept="mime-type list"`	Lists mime-types that the server processing the form will handle (deprecated)
`accept-charset="char code"`	Specifies the character encoding that the server processing the form will handle
`action="url"`	Provides the URL to which the form values are to be sent
`autocomplete="on|off"`	Enables automatic insertion of information in fields in which the user has previously entered data (HTML5)
`enctype="mime-type"`	Specifies the mime-type of the data to be sent to the server for processing; the default is "application/x-www-form-urlencoded"
`method="get|post"`	Specifies the method of accessing the URL specified in the action attribute
`name="text"`	Specifies the name of the form
`novalidate="novalidate"`	Specifies that the form is not meant to be validated during submission (HTML5)
`target="text"`	Specifies the frame or window in which output from the form should appear
`<frame> </frame>`	Marks a single frame within a set of frames (deprecated)
`bordercolor="color"`	Specifies the color of the frame border
`frameborder="1|0"`	Determines whether the frame border is visible (1) or invisible (0); Netscape also supports values of yes or no
`longdesc="url"`	Provides the URL of a document containing a long description of the frame's contents
`marginheight="integer"`	Specifies the space above and below the frame object and the frame's borders, in pixels
`marginwidth="integer"`	Specifies the space to the left and right of the frame object and the frame's borders, in pixels
`name="text"`	Specifies the name of the frame
`noresize="noresize"`	Prevents users from resizing the frame
`scrolling="auto|yes|no"`	Specifies whether the browser will display a scroll bar with the frame
`src="url"`	Provides the URL of the document to be displayed in the frame
`<frameset> </frameset>`	Creates a collection of frames (deprecated)
`border="integer"`	Specifies the thickness of the frame borders in the frameset in pixels (not part of the W3C specifications, but supported by most browsers)
`bordercolor="color"`	Specifies the color of the frame borders
`cols="value list"`	Arranges the frames in columns with the width of each column expressed either in pixels, as a percentage, or using an asterisk (to allow the browser to choose the width)
`frameborder="1|0"`	Determines whether frame borders are visible (1) or invisible (0); (not part of the W3C specifications, but supported by most browsers)
`framespacing="integer"`	Specifies the amount of space between frames in pixels (IE only)
`rows="value list"`	Arranges the frames in rows with the height of each column expressed either in pixels, as a percentage, or using an asterisk (to allow the browser to choose the height)

Element/Attribute	Description
`<hi> </hi>`	Marks the enclosed text as a heading, where *i* is an integer from 1 (the largest heading) to 6 (the smallest heading)
`align="align"`	Specifies the alignment of the heading text where *align* is left, center, right, or justify (obsolete)
`<head> </head>`	Encloses the document head, containing information about the document
`profile="url"`	Provides the location of metadata about the document
`<header> </header>`	Structural element that represents the header of a section or the page (HTML5)
`<hgroup> </hgroup>`	Structural element that groups content headings (HTML5)
`<hr />`	Draws a horizontal line (rule) in the rendered page
`align="align"`	Specifies the horizontal alignment of the line where *align* left, center, or right (obsolete)
`color="color"`	Specifies the color of the line (obsolete)
`noshade="noshade"`	Removes 3-D shading from the line (obsolete)
`size="integer"`	Specifies the height of the line in pixels or as a percentage of the enclosing element's height (obsolete)
`width="integer"`	Specifies the width of the line in pixels or as a percentage of the enclosing element's width (obsolete)
`<html> </html>`	Encloses the entire content of the HTML document
`manifest="url"`	Provides the address of the document's application cache manifest (HTML5)
`xmlns="text"`	Specifies the namespace prefix for the document
`<i> </i>`	Represents a span of text offset from its surrounding content without conveying any extra importance or emphasis
`<iframe> </iframe>`	Creates an inline frame in the document
`align="align"`	Specifies the horizontal alignment of the frame with the surrounding content where *align* is bottom, left, middle, top, or right (obsolete)
`datafld="text"`	Indicates the column from a data source that supplies bound data for the inline frame (IE only)
`dataformatas="html|` `plaintext|text"`	Specifies the format of the data in the data source bound with the inline frame (IE only)
`datasrc="url"`	Provides the URL or ID of the data source bound with the inline frame (IE only)
`frameborder="1|0"`	Specifies whether to display a frame border (1) or not (0) (obsolete)
`height="integer"`	Specifies the height of the frame in pixels
`longdesc="url"`	Indicates the document containing a long description of the frame's content (obsolete)
`marginheight="integer"`	Specifies the space above and below the frame object and the frame's borders, in pixels (obsolete)
`marginwidth="integer"`	Specifies the space to the left and right of the frame object and the frame's borders, in pixels (obsolete)
`name="text"`	Specifies the name of the frame

`sandbox="allow-forms|`
`allow-scripts|`
`allow-top-navigation|`
`allow-same-origin"`
	Defines restrictions to the frame content (HTML5)

`seamless="seamless"`	Displays the inline frame as part of the document (HTML5)
`scrolling="auto|` `yes|no"`	Determines whether the browser displays a scroll bar with the frame (obsolete)

Element/Attribute	Description
`src="url"`	Indicates the document displayed within the frame
`srcdoc="text"`	Provides the HTML code shown in the inline frame (HTML5)
`width="integer"`	Specifies the width of the frame in pixels
`<img> </img>`	Inserts an inline image into the document
`align="align"`	Specifies the alignment of the image with the surrounding content where *align* is left, right, top, text textop, middle, absmiddle, baseline, bottom, absbottom (obsolete)
`alt="text"`	Specifies alternate text to be displayed in place of the image
`border="integer"`	Specifies the width of the image border (obsolete)
`datafld="text"`	Names the column from a data source that supplies bound data for the image (IE only)
`dataformatas="html|` `plaintext|text"`	Specifies the format of the data in the data source bound with the image (IE only)
`datasrc="url"`	Provides the URL or ID of the data source bound with the image (IE only)
`dynsrc="url"`	Provides the URL of a video or VRML file (IE and Opera only)
`height="integer"`	Specifies the height of the image in pixels
`hspace="integer"`	Specifies the horizontal space around the image in pixels (deprecated)
`ismap="ismap"`	Indicates that the image can be used as a server-side image map
`longdesc="url"`	Provides the URL of a document containing a long description of the image (obsolete)
`name="text"`	Specifies the image name (obsolete)
`src="url"`	Specifies the image source file
`usemap="url"`	Provides the location of a client-side image associated with the image (not well-supported when the URL points to an external file)
`vspace="integer"`	Specifies the vertical space around the image in pixels (obsolete)
`width="integer"`	Specifies the width of the image in pixels
`<input> </input>`	Marks an input field in a Web form
`align="align"`	Specifies the alignment of the input field with the surrounding content where *align* is left, right, top, texttop, middle, absmiddle, baseline, bottom, or absbottom (obsolete)
`alt="text"`	Specifies alternate text for image buttons and image input fields
`checked="checked"`	Specifies that the input check box or input radio button is selected
`datafld="text"`	Indicates the column from a data source that supplies bound data for the input field (IE only)
`dataformatas="html|` `plaintext|text"`	Specifies the format of the data in the data source bound with the input field (IE only)
`datasrc="url"`	Provides the URL or ID of the data source bound with the input field (IE only)
`disabled="disabled"`	Disables the input control
`form="text"`	Specifies the form to which the button belongs (HTML5)
`formaction="url"`	Specifies the URL to which the form data is sent (HTML5)
`formenctype="mime-type"`	Specifies the encoding of the form data before it is sent (HTML5)
`formmethod="get|post"`	Specifies the HTTP method with which the form data is submitted
`formnovalidate=` `"formnovalidate"`	Specifies that the form should not be validated during submission (HTML5)

Element/Attribute	Description
formtarget="*text*"	Provides a name for the target of the button (HTML5)
height="*integer*"	Specifies the height of the image input field in pixels (HTML5)
list="*id*"	Specifies the id of a data list associated with the input field (HTML5)
max="*value*"	Specifies the maximum value of the field (HTML5)
maxlength="*integer*"	Specifies the maximum number of characters that can be inserted into a text input field
min="*value*"	Specifies the minimum value of the field (HTML5)
multiple="multiple"	Specifies that the user is allowed to specify more than one input value (HTML5)
name="text"	Specifies the name of the input field
pattern="*text*"	Specifies the required regular expression pattern of the input field value (HTML5)
placeholder="*text*"	Specifies placeholder text for the input field (HTML5)
readonly="readonly"	Prevents the value of the input field from being modified
size="*integer*"	Specifies the number of characters that can be displayed at one time in an input text field
src="*url*"	Indicates the source file of an input image field
step="any|*value*"	Specifies the value granularity of the field value (HTML5)
type="*text*"	Specifies the input type where *text* is button, checkbox, color, date, datetime, datetime-local, email, file, hidden, image, month, number, password, radio, range, reset, search, submit, tel, text, time, url, or week (HTML5)
value="*text*"	Specifies the default value of the input field
width="*integer*"	Specifies the width of an image input field in pixels (HTML5)
<ins> </ins>	Marks inserted text
cite="*url*"	Provides the URL for the document that has additional information about the inserted text
datetime="*date*"	Specifies the date and time of the text insertion
<kbd> </kbd>	Marks keyboard-style text
<keygen> </keygen>	Defines a generate key within a form (HTML5)
autofocus="autofocus"	Specifies that the element is to be given the focus when the form is loaded
challenge="*text*"	Provides the challenge string that is submitted along with the key
disabled="disabled"	Disables the element
form="*id*"	Specifies the id of the form associated with the element
keytype="rsa"	Specifies the type of key generated
name="*text*"	Specifies the name part of the name/value pair associated with the element
<label> </label>	Associates the enclosed content with a form field
datafld="text"	Indicates the column from a data source that supplies bound data for the label (IE only)
dataformatas="html|plaintext|text"	Specifies the format of the data in the data source bound with the label (IE only)
datasrc="*url*"	Provides the URL or ID of the data source bound with the label (IE only)
for="text"	Provides the ID of the field associated with the label
form="*id*"	Specifies the id of the form associated with the label (HTML5)

Element/Attribute	Description
`<legend> </legend>`	Marks the enclosed text as a caption for a field set
`align="bottom|left` `|top|right"`	Specifies the alignment of the legend with the field set; Internet Explorer also supports the center option (deprecated)
`<li> </li>`	Marks an item in an ordered (ol), unordered (ul), menu (menu), or directory (dir) list
`value="integer"`	Sets the value for the current list item in an ordered list; subsequent list items are numbered from that value
`<link />`	Creates an element in the document head that establishes the relationship between the current document and external documents or objects
`charset="char code"`	Specifies the character encoding of the external document (obsolete)
`href="url"`	Provides the URL of the external document
`hreflang="text"`	Indicates the language of the external document
`media="media"`	Indicates the media in which the external document is presented
`rel="text"`	Specifies the relationship between the current page and the link specified by the href attribute
`rev="text"`	Specifies the reverse relationship between the current page and the link specified by the href attribute (obsolete)
`sizes="any|value"`	Specifies the sizes of icons used for visual media (HTML5)
`target="text"`	Specifies the target window or frame for the link (obsolete)
`type="mime-type"`	Specifies the mime-type of the external document
`<map> </map>`	Creates an element that contains client-side image map hotspots
`name="text"`	Specifies the name of the image map
`<mark> </mark>`	Defines marked text (HTML5)
`<menu> </menu>`	Represents a list of commands
`compact="compact"`	Reduces the space between menu items (obsolete)
`label="text"`	Defines a visible label for the menu (HTML5)
`type="context|list|` `toolbar"`	Defines which type of list to display
`<meta />`	Creates an element in the document's head section that contains information and special instructions for processing the document
`charset="char code"`	Defines the character encoding for the document (HTML5)
`content="text"`	Provides information associated with the name or http-equiv attributes
`http-equiv="text"`	Provides instructions to the browser to request the server to perform different http operations
`name="text"`	Specifies the type of information specified in the content attribute
`scheme="text"`	Supplies additional information about the scheme used to interpret the content attribute (obsolete)
`<meter> </meter>`	Defines a measurement within a predefined range (HTML5)
`high="value"`	Defines the high value of the range
`low="value"`	Defines the low value of the range
`max="value"`	Defines the maximum value
`min="value"`	Defines the minimum value
`optimum="value"`	Defines the optimum value from the range
`value="value"`	Defines the meter's value
`<nav> </nav>`	Structural element defining a navigation list (HTML5)

Element/Attribute	Description
`<nobr> </nobr>`	Disables line wrapping for the enclosed content (not part of the W3C specifications, but supported by most browsers)
`<noembed> </noembed>`	Encloses alternate content for browsers that do not support the embed element (not part of the W3C specifications, but supported by most browsers)
`<noframe> </noframe>`	Encloses alternate content for browsers that do not support frames (obsolete)
`<noscript> </noscript>`	Encloses alternate content for browsers that do not support client-side scripts
`<object> </object>`	Places an embedded object (image, applet, sound clip, video clip, etc.) into the page
`archive="url"`	Specifies the URL of an archive containing classes and other resources pre-loaded for use with the object (obsolete)
`align="align"`	Aligns the object with the surrounding content where *align* is absbottom, absmiddle, baseline, bottom, left, middle, right, texttop, or top (obsolete)
`border="integer"`	Specifies the width of the border around the object (obsolete)
`classid="url"`	Provides the URL of the object (obsolete)
`codebase="url"`	Specifies the base path used to resolve relative references within the embedded object (obsolete)
`codetype="mime-type"`	Indicates the mime-type of the embedded object's code (obsolete)
`data="url"`	Provides the URL of the object's data file
`datafld="text"`	Identifies the column from a data source that supplies bound data for the embedded object (IE only)
`dataformatas="html| plaintext|text"`	Specifies the format of the data in the data source bound with the embedded object (IE only)
`datasrc="url"`	Provides the URL or ID of the data source bound with the embedded object (IE only)
`declare="declare"`	Declares the object without embedding it on the page (obsolete)
`form="id"`	Specifies the id of the form associated with the object (HTML5)
`height="integer"`	Specifies the height of the object in pixels
`hspace="integer"`	Specifies the horizontal space around the image in pixels (obsolete)
`name="text"`	Specifies the name of the embedded object
`standby="text"`	Specifies the message displayed by the browser while loading the embedded object (obsolete)
`type="mime-type"`	Indicates the mime-type of the embedded object
`vspace="integer"`	Specifies the vertical space around the embedded object (obsolete)
`width="integer"`	Specifies the width of the object in pixels
`<ol> </ol>`	Contains an ordered list of items
`reversed="reversed"`	Specifies that the list markers are to be displayed in descending order (HTML5)
`start="integer"`	Specifies the starting value in the list
`type="A|a|I|i|1"`	Specifies the bullet type associated with the list items (deprecated)
`<optgroup> </optgroup>`	Contains a group of option elements in a selection field
`disabled="disabled"`	Disables the option group control
`label="text"`	Specifies the label for the option group
`<option> </option>`	Formats an option within a selection field
`disabled="disabled"`	Disables the option control
`label="text"`	Supplies the text label associated with the option
`selected="selected"`	Selects the option by default
`value="text"`	Specifies the value associated with the option

Element/Attribute	Description
`<output> </output>`	Form control representing the result of a calculation (HTML5)
`name="text"`	Specifies the name part of the name/value pair associated with the field
`form="id"`	Specifies the id of the form associated with the field
`for="text list"`	Lists the id references associated with the calculation
`<p> </p>`	Marks the enclosed content as a paragraph
`align="align"`	Horizontally aligns the contents of the paragraph where *align* is left, center, right, or justify (obsolete)
`<param> </param>`	Marks parameter values sent to an object element or an applet element
`name="text"`	Specifies the parameter name
`type="mime-type"`	Specifies the mime-type of the resource indicated by the value attribute (obsolete)
`value="text"`	Specifies the parameter value
`valuetype="data|ref|object"`	Specifies the data type of the value attribute (obsolete)
`<pre> </pre>`	Marks the enclosed text as preformatted text, retaining white space from the document
`<progress> </progress>`	Represents the progress of completion of a task (HTML5)
`value="value"`	Specifies how much of the task has been completed
`max="value"`	Specifies how much work the task requires in total
`<q> </q>`	Marks the enclosed text as a quotation
`cite="url"`	Provides the source URL of the quoted content
`<rp> </rp>`	Used in ruby annotations to define what to show browsers that do not support the ruby element (HTML5)
`<rt> </rt>`	Defines explanation to ruby annotations (HTML5)
`<ruby> </ruby>`	Defines ruby annotations (HTML5)
`<s> </s>`	Marks the enclosed text as strikethrough text
`<samp> </samp>`	Marks the enclosed text as a sequence of literal characters
`<script> </script>`	Encloses client-side scripts within the document; this element can be placed within the head or the body element or it can refer to an external script file
`async="async"`	Specifies that the script should be executed asynchronously as soon as it becomes available (HTML5)
`charset="char code"`	Specifies the character encoding of the script
`defer="defer"`	Defers execution of the script
`language="text"`	Specifies the language of the script (obsolete)
`src="url"`	Provides the URL of an external script file
`type="mime-type"`	Specifies the mime-type of the script
`<section> </section>`	Structural element representing a section of the document (HTML5)
`<select> </select>`	Creates a selection field (drop-down list box) in a Web form
`autofocus="autofocus"`	Specifies that the browser should give focus to the selection field as soon as the page loads (HTML5)
`datafld="text"`	Identifies the column from a data source that supplies bound data for the selection field (IE only)

Element/Attribute	Description
`dataformatas="html|plaintext|text"`	Specifies the format of the data in the data source bound with the selection field (IE only)
`datasrc="url"`	Provides the URL or ID of the data source bound with the selection field (IE only)
`disabled="disabled"`	Disables the selection field
`form="id"`	Provides the id of the form associated with the selection field (HTML5)
`multiple="multiple"`	Allows multiple sections from the field
`name="text"`	Specifies the selection field name
`size="integer"`	Specifies the number of visible items in the selection list
`<small> </small>`	Represents "final print" or "small print" in legal disclaimers and caveats
`<source />`	Enables multiple media sources to be specified for audio and video elements (HTML5)
`media="media"`	Specifies the intended media type of the media source
`src="url"`	Specifies the location of the media source
`type="mime-type"`	Specifies the MIME type of the media source
`<span> </span>`	Creates a generic inline element
`datafld="text"`	Identifies the column from a data source that supplies bound data for the inline element (IE only)
`dataformatas="html|plaintext|text"`	Specifies the format of the data in the data source bound with the inline element (IE only)
`datasrc="url"`	Provides the URL or ID of the data source bound with the inline element (IE only)
`<strong> </strong>`	Marks the enclosed text as strongly emphasized text
`<style> </style>`	Encloses global style declarations for the document
`media="media"`	Indicates the media of the enclosed style definitions
`scoped="scoped"`	Indicates that the specified style information is meant to apply only to the style element's parent element (HTML5)
`type="mime-type"`	Specifies the mime-type of the style definitions
`<sub> </sub>`	Marks the enclosed text as subscript text
`<summary> </summary>`	Defines the header of a detail element (HTML5)
`<sup> </sup>`	Marks the enclosed text as superscript text
`<table> </table>`	Encloses the contents of a Web table
`align="align"`	Aligns the table with the surrounding content where *align* is left, center, or right (obsolete)
`bgcolor="color"`	Specifies the background color of the table (obsolete)
`border="integer"`	Specifies the width of the table border in pixels (obsolete)
`cellpadding="integer"`	Specifies the space between the table data and the cell borders in pixels (obsolete)
`cellspacing="integer"`	Specifies the space between table cells in pixels (obsolete)
`datafld="text"`	Indicates the column from a data source that supplies bound data for the table (IE only)
`dataformatas="html|plaintext|text"`	Specifies the format of the data in the data source bound with the table (IE only)

Element/Attribute	Description
datapagesize="integer"	Sets the number of records displayed within the table (IE only)
datasrc="url"	Provides the URL or ID of the data source bound with the table (IE only)
frame="frame"	Specifies the format of the borders around the table where frame is above, below, border, box, hsides, lhs, rhs, void, or vside (obsolete)
rules="rules"	Specifies the format of the table's internal borders or gridlines where rules is all, cols, groups, none, or rows (obsolete)
summary="text"	Supplies a text summary of the table's content
width="integer"	Specifies the width of the table in pixels (obsolete)
<tbody> </tbody>	Encloses the content of the Web table body
align="align"	Specifies the alignment of the contents in the cells of the table body where align is left, center, right, justify, or char (obsolete)
char="char"	Specifies the character used for aligning the table body contents when the align attribute is set to "char" (obsolete)
charoff="integer"	Specifies the offset in pixels from the alignment character specified in the char attribute (obsolete)
valign="align"	Specifies the vertical alignment of the contents in the cells of the table body where align is baseline, bottom, middle, or top (obsolete)
<td> </td>	Encloses the data of a table cell
abbr="text"	Supplies an abbreviated version of the contents of the table cell (obsolete)
align="align"	Specifies the horizontal alignment of the table cell data where align is left, center, or right (obsolete)
bgcolor="color"	Specifies the background color of the table cell (obsolete)
char="char"	Specifies the character used for aligning the table cell contents when the align attribute is set to "char" (obsolete)
charoff="integer"	Specifies the offset in pixels from the alignment character specified in the char attribute (obsolete)
colspan="integer"	Specifies the number of columns the table cell spans
headers="text"	Supplies a space-separated list of table headers associated with the table cell
height="integer"	Specifies the height of the table cell in pixels (obsolete)
nowrap="nowrap"	Disables line-wrapping within the table cell (obsolete)
rowspan="integer"	Specifies the number of rows the table cell spans
scope="col|colgroup|row|rowgroup"	Specifies the scope of the table for which the cell provides data (obsolete)
valign="align"	Specifies the vertical alignment of the contents of the table cell where align is top, middle, or bottom (obsolete)
width="integer"	Specifies the width of the cell in pixels (obsolete)
<textarea> </textarea>	Marks the enclosed text as a text area input box in a Web form
autofocus="autofocus"	Specifies that the text area is to receive the focus when the page is loaded (HTML5)
datafld="text"	Specifies the column from a data source that supplies bound data for the text area box (IE only)
dataformatas="html|plaintext|text"	Specifies the format of the data in the data source bound with the text area box (IE only)

Element/Attribute	Description
datasrc="*url*"	Provides the URL or ID of the data source bound with the text area box (IE only)
cols="*integer*"	Specifies the width of the text area box in characters
disable="disable"	Disables the text area field
form="*id*"	Associates the text area with the form identified by *id* (HTML5)
maxlength="*integer*"	Specifies the maximum allowed value length for the text area
name="*text*"	Specifies the name of the text area box
placeholder="*text*"	Provides a short hint intended to aid the user when entering data (HTML5)
readonly="readonly"	Specifies the value of the text area box, cannot be modified
required="required"	Indicates whether the text area is required for validation (HTML5)
rows="*integer*"	Specifies the number of visible rows in the text area box
wrap="**soft**|hard"	Specifies how text is wrapped within the text area box and how that text-wrapping information is sent to the server-side program
<tfoot> </tfoot>	Encloses the content of the Web table footer
align="*align*"	Specifies the alignment of the contents in the cells of the table footer where *align* is left, center, right, justify, or char (obsolete)
char="*char*"	Specifies the character used for aligning the table footer contents when the align attribute is set to "char" (obsolete)
charoff="*integer*"	Specifies the offset in pixels from the alignment character specified in the char attribute (obsolete)
valign="*align*"	Specifies the vertical alignment of the contents in the cells of the table footer where *align* is baseline, bottom, middle, or top (obsolete)
<th> </th>	Encloses the data of a table header cell
abbr="*text*"	Supplies an abbreviated version of the contents of the table cell (obsolete)
align="*align*"	Specifies the horizontal alignment of the table cell data where *align* is left, center, or right (obsolete)
axis="*text list*"	Provides a list of table categories that can be mapped to a table hierarchy (obsolete)
bgcolor="*color*"	Specifies the background color of the table cell (obsolete)
char="*char*"	Specifies the character used for aligning the table cell contents when the align attribute is set to "char" (obsolete)
charoff="*integer*"	Specifies the offset in pixels from the alignment character specified in the char attribute (obsolete)
colspan="*integer*"	Specifies the number of columns the table cell spans
headers="*text*"	A space-separated list of table headers associated with the table cell
height="*integer*"	Specifies the height of the table cell in pixels (obsolete)
nowrap="nowrap"	Disables line-wrapping within the table cell (obsolete)
rowspan="*integer*"	Specifies the number of rows the table cell spans
scope="col|colgroup| row|rowgroup"	Specifies the scope of the table for which the cell provides data
valign="*align*"	Specifies the vertical alignment of the contents of the table cell where *align* is top, middle, or bottom (obsolete)
width="*integer*"	Specifies the width of the cell in pixels (obsolete)

Element/Attribute	Description
`<thead> </thead>`	Encloses the content of the Web table header
`align="align"`	Specifies the alignment of the contents in the cells of the table header where *align* is left, center, right, justify, or char (obsolete)
`char="char"`	Specifies the character used for aligning the table header contents when the align attribute is set to "char" (obsolete)
`charoff="integer"`	Specifies the offset in pixels from the alignment character specified in the char attribute (obsolete)
`valign="align"`	Specifies the vertical alignment of the contents in the cells of the table header where *align* is baseline, bottom, middle, or top (obsolete)
`<time> </time>`	Represents a date and/or time (HTML5)
`<title> </title>`	Specifies the title of the document, placed in the head section of the document
`<tr> </tr>`	Encloses the content of a row within a Web table
`align="align"`	Specifies the horizontal alignment of the data in the row's cells where *align* is left, center, or right (obsolete)
`char="char"`	Specifies the character used for aligning the table row contents when the align attribute is set to "char" (obsolete)
`charoff="integer"`	Specifies the offset in pixels from the alignment character specified in the char attribute (obsolete)
`valign="align"`	Specifies the vertical alignment of the contents of the table row where *align* is baseline, bottom, middle, or top (obsolete)
`<track> </track>`	Enables supplementary media tracks such as subtitles and captions (HTML5)
`default="default"`	Enables the track if the user's preferences do not indicate that another track would be more appropriate
`kind="kind"`	Specifies the kind of track, where *kind* is subtitles, captions, descriptions, chapters, or metadata
`label="text"`	Provides a user-readable title for the track
`src="url"`	Provides the address of the track
`srclang="lang"`	Provides the language of the track
`<tt> </tt>`	Marks the enclosed text as teletype or monospaced text (deprecated)
`<u> </u>`	Marks the enclosed text as underlined text (deprecated)
`<ul> </ul>`	Contains an unordered list of items
`compact="compact"`	Reduces the space between unordered list items (obsolete)
`type="disc|square|circle"`	Specifies the bullet type associated with the list items (obsolete)
`<var> </var>`	Marks the enclosed text as containing a variable name
`<video> </video>`	Defines an embedded video clip (HTML5)
`audio="text"`	Defines the default audio state; currently only "muted" is supported
`autoplay="autoplay"`	Specifies that the video should begin playing automatically when the page is loaded
`controls="controls"`	Instructs the browser to display the video controls
`height="value"`	Provides the height of the video clip in pixels
`loop="loop"`	Instructs the browser to loop the clip back to the beginning
`preload="auto|metadata|none"`	Indicates whether to preload the video clip data
`poster="url"`	Specifies the location of an image file to act as a poster for the video clip
`width="value"`	Provides the width of the video clip in pixels

Element/Attribute	Description
`<wbr />`	Indicates a line-break opportunity (HTML5)
`<xml> </xml>`	Encloses XML content (also referred to as a "data island") or references an external XML document (IE only)
`ns="url"`	Provides the URL of the XML data island (IE only)
`prefix="text"`	Specifies the namespace prefix of the XML content (IE only)
`src="url"`	Provides the URL of an external XML document (IE only)
`<xmp> </xmp>`	Marks the enclosed text as preformatted text, preserving the white space of the source document; replaced by the pre element (deprecated)

Cascading Styles and Selectors

This appendix describes the selectors, units, and attributes supported by Cascading Style Sheets (CSS). Features from CSS3 are indicated in parenthesis. Note that not all CSS3 features are supported by all browsers and all browser versions, so you should always check your code against different browsers and browser versions to ensure that your page is being rendered correctly. Also many CSS3 styles are still in the draft stage and will undergo continuing revisions and additions. Additional information about CSS can be found at the World Wide Web Consortium Web site at *www.w3.org*.

STARTING DATA FILES

There are no starting Data Files needed for this appendix.

Selectors

The general form of a style declaration is:

```
selector {attribute1:value1; attribute2:value2; ...}
```

where *selector* is the selection of elements within the document to which the style will be applied; *attribute1*, *attribute2*, etc. are the different style attributes; and *value1*, *value2*, etc. are values associated with those styles. The following table shows some of the different forms that a selector can take.

Selector	Matches
`*`	All elements in the document
`e`	An element, *e*, in the document
`e1, e2, e3, …`	A group of elements, *e1*, *e2*, *e3*, in the document
`e1 e2`	An element *e2* nested within the parent element, *e1*
`e1 > e2`	An element *e2* that is a child of the parent element, *e1*
`e1+e2`	An element, *e2*, that is adjacent to element *e1*
`e1.class`	An element, *e1*, belonging to the *class* class
`.class`	Any element belonging to the *class* class
`#id`	An element with the id value *id*
`[att]`	The element contains the *att* attribute
`[att="val"]`	The element's *att* attribute equals "*val*"
`[att~="val"]`	The element's *att* attribute value is a space-separated list of "words," one of which is exactly "*val*"
`[att|="val"]`	The element's *att* attribute value is a hyphen-separated list of "words" beginning with "val"
`[att^="val"]`	The element's *att* attribute begins with "*val*" (CSS3)
`[att$="val"]`	The element's *att* attribute ends with "*val*" (CSS3)
`[att*="val"]`	The element's *att* attribute contains the value "*val*" (CSS3)
`[ns|att]`	References all *att* attributes in the *ns* namespace (CSS3)

Pseudo-Elements and Pseudo-Classes

Pseudo-elements are elements that do not exist in HTML code but whose attributes can be set with CSS. Many pseudo-elements were introduced in CSS2.

Pseudo-Element	Matches
`e:after {content: "text"}`	Text content, *text*, that is inserted at the end of an element, *e*
`e:before {content: "text"}`	Text content, *text*, that is inserted at the beginning of an element, *e*
`e:first-letter`	The first letter in the element *e*
`e:first-line`	The first line in the element *e*
`::selection`	A part of the document that has been highlighted by the user (CSS3)

Pseudo-classes are classes of HTML elements that define the condition or state of the element in the Web page. Many pseudo-classes were introduced in CSS2.

Pseudo-Class	Matches
:canvas	The rendering canvas of the document
:first	The first printed page of the document (used only with print styles created with the @print rule)
:last	The last printed page of the document (used only with print styles created with the @print rule)
:left	The left side of a two-sided printout (used only with print styles created with the @print rule)
:right	The right side of a two-sided printout (used only with print styles created with the @print rule)
:root	The root element of the document
e:active	The element, *e*, that is being activated by the user (usually applies only to hyperlinks)
e:checked	The checkbox or radio button, *e*, that has been checked (CSS3)
e:disabled	The element, *e*, that has been disabled in the document (CSS3)
e:empty	The element, *e*, that has no children
e:enabled	The element, *e*, that has been enabled in the document (CSS3)
e:first-child	The element, *e*, which is the first child of its parent element
e:first-node	The first occurrence of the element, *e*, in the document tree
e:first-of-type	The first element of type *e* (CSS3)
e:focus	The element, *e*, that has received the focus of the cursor
e:hover	The mouse pointer is hovering over the element, *e*
e:lang(*text*)	Sets the language, *text*, associated with the element, *e*
e:last-child	The element, *e*, that is the last child of its parent element (CSS3)
e:last-of-type	The last element of type *e* (CSS3)
e:link	The element, *e*, has not been visited yet by the user (applies only to hyperlinks)
e:not	Negate the selector rule for the element, *e*, applying the style to all *e* elements that do not match the selector rules
e:nth-child(*n*)	Matches n^{th} child of the element, *e*; *n* can also be the keywords odd or even (CSS3)
e:nth-last-child(*n*)	Matches n^{th} child of the element, *e*, counting up from the last child; *n* can also be the keywords odd or even (CSS3)
e:nth-of-type(*n*)	Matches n^{th} element of type *e*; *n* can also be the keywords odd or even (CSS3)
e:nth-last-of-type(*n*)	Matches n^{th} element of type *e*, counting up from the last child; *n* can also be the keywords odd or even (CSS3)
e:only-child	Matches element *e* only if it is the only child of its parent (CSS3)
e:only-of-type	Matches element *e* only if it is the only element of its type nested within its parent (CSS3)
e:target	Matches an element, *e*, that's the target of the identifier in the document's URL (CSS3)
e:visited	The element, *e*, has been already visited by the user (to only the hyperlinks)

@ Rules

CSS supports different "@ rules" designed to run commands within a style sheet. These commands can be used to import other styles, download font definitions, or define the format of printed output.

@ Rule	Description
`@charset "encoding"`	Defines the character set encoding used in the style sheet (this must be the very first line in the style sheet document)
`@font-face {font descriptors}`	Defines custom fonts that are available for automatic download when needed (CSS3)
`@import url(url) media`	Imports an external style sheet document into the current style sheet, where *url* is the location of the external stylesheet and *media* is a comma-separated list of media types (optional)
`@media media {style declaration}`	Defines the media for the styles in the *style declaration* block, where *media* is a comma-separated list of media types
`@namespace prefix url(url)`	Defines the namespace used by selectors in the style sheet, where *prefix* is the local namespace prefix (optional) and *url* is the unique namespace identifier; the @namespace rule must come before all CSS selectors (CSS3)
`@page label pseudo-class {styles}`	Defines the properties of a printed page, where *label* is a label given to the page (optional), *pseudo-class* is one of the CSS pseudo-classes designed for printed pages, and *styles* are the styles associated with the page

Miscellaneous Syntax

The following syntax elements do not fit into the previous categories but are useful in constructing CSS style sheets.

Item	Description
`style !important`	Places high importance on the preceding *style*, overriding the usual rules for inheritance and cascading
`/* comment */`	Attaches a *comment* to the style sheet

Units

Many style attribute values use units of measurement to indicate color, length, angles, time, and frequencies. The following table describes the measuring units used in CSS.

Units	Description
Color	**Units of color**
currentColor	The computed value of the color property (CSS3)
flavor	An accent color chosen by the user to customize the user interface of the browser (CSS3)
name	A color name; all browsers recognize 16 base color names: aqua, black, blue, fuchsia, gray, green, lime, maroon, navy, olive, purple, red, silver, teal, white, and yellow
#rrggbb	A hexadecimal color value, where rr is the red value, gg is the green value, and bb is the blue value
#rgb	A compressed hexadecimal value, where the r, g, and b values are doubled so that, for example, #A2F = #AA22FF
hsl(hue, sat, light)	Color value based on hue, saturation, and lightness, where hue is the degree measure on the color wheel ranging from 0° (red) up to 360°, sat is the saturation range from 0% to 100%, and light is the lightness range from 0% to 100% (CSS3)
hsla(hue, sat, light, alpha)	Semi-transparent color based on the HSL model with alpha representing the opacity of the color ranging from 0 (transparent) up to 1 (completely opaque) (CSS3)
rgb(red, green, blue)	The decimal color value, where red is the red value, green is the green value, and blue is the blue value
rgb(red%, green%, blue%)	The color value percentage, where red% is the percent of maximum red, green% is the percent of maximum green, and blue% is the percent of maximum blue
rgba(red, green, blue, alpha)	Semi-transparent color based on the RGB model with alpha representing the opacity of the color ranging from 0 (transparent) up to 1 (completely opaque) (CSS3)
Length	**Units of length**
auto	Keyword which allows the browser to automatically determine the size of the length
ch	Width of the "0" glyph found in the font (CSS3)
em	A relative unit indicating the width and the height of the capital "M" character for the browser's default font
ex	A relative unit indicating the height of the small "x" character for the browser's default font
px	A pixel, representing the smallest unit of length on the output device
in	An inch
cm	A centimeter
mm	A millimeter
pt	A point, approximately 1/72 inch
pc	A pica, approximately 1/12 inch
%	A percent of the width or height of the parent element
xx-small	Keyword representing an extremely small font size
x-small	Keyword representing a very small font size
small	Keyword representing a small font size

Units	Description
medium	Keyword representing a medium-sized font
large	Keyword representing a large font
x-large	Keyword representing a very large font
xx-large	Keyword representing an extremely large font
Angle	**Units of angles**
deg	The angle in degrees
grad	The angle in gradients
rad	The angle in radians
turns	Number of complete turns (CSS3)
Time	**Units of time**
ms	Time in milliseconds
s	Time in seconds
Frequency	**Units of frequency**
hz	The frequency in hertz
khz	The frequency in kilohertz

Attributes and Values

The following table describes the attributes and values for different types of elements. The attributes are grouped into categories to help you locate the features relevant to your particular design task.

Attribute	Description
Aural	**Styles for Aural Browsers**
cue: url(*url1*) url(*url2*)	Adds a sound to an element: if a single value is present, the sound is played before and after the element; if two values are present, the first is played before and the second is played after
cue-after: url(*url*)	Specifies a sound to be played immediately after an element
cue-before: url(*url*)	Specifies a sound to be played immediately before an element
elevation: *location*	Defines the vertical location of the sound, where *location* is below, level, above, lower, higher, or an angle value
mark: *before after*	Adds a marker to an audio stream (CSS3)
mark-before: *text*	Marks an audio stream with the text *string* (CSS3)
mark-after: *text*	Marks an audio stream afterwards with the text *string* (CSS3)
pause: *time1 time2*	Adds a pause to an element: if a single value is present, the pause occurs before and after the element; if two values are present, the first pause occurs before and the second occurs after
pause-after: *time*	Adds a pause after an element
pause-before: *time*	Adds a pause before an element
phonemes: *text*	Specifies the phonetic pronunciation for the audio stream (CSS3)
pitch: *value*	Defines the pitch of a speaking voice, where *value* is x-low, low, medium, high, x-high, or a frequency value
pitch-range: *value*	Defines the pitch range for a speaking voice, where *value* ranges from 0 to 100; a low pitch range results in a monotone voice, whereas a high pitch range sounds very animated

Attribute	Description
`play-during: url(url) mix repeat type`	Defines a sound to be played behind an element, where *url* is the URL of the sound file; mix overlays the sound file with the sound of the parent element; repeat causes the sound to be repeated, filling up the available time; and *type* is auto to play the sound only once, none to play nothing but the sound file, or inherit
`rest: before after`	Specifies the rest-before and rest-after values for the audio (CSS3)
`rest-before: type`	Specifies a rest to be observed before speaking the content, where *type* is none, x-weak, weak, medium, strong, x-strong, or inherit (CSS3)
`rest-after: type`	Specifies a rest to be observed after speaking the content, where *type* is none, x-weak, weak, medium, strong, x-strong, or inherit (CSS3)
`richness: value`	Specifies the richness of the speaking voice, where *value* ranges from 0 to 100; a low value indicates a softer voice, whereas a high value indicates a brighter voice
`speak: type`	Defines how element content is to be spoken, where *type* is normal (for normal punctuation rules), spell-out (to pronounce one character at a time), none (to suppress the aural rendering), or inherit
`voice-balance: type`	Specifies the voice balance, where *type* is left, center, right, leftwards, rightwards, inherit, or a *number* (CSS3)
`voice-duration: time`	Specifies the duration of the voice (CSS3)
`voice-family: text`	Defines the name of the speaking voice, where *text* is male, female, child, or a text string indicating a specific speaking voice
`voice-rate: type`	Specifies the voice rate, where *type* is x-slow, slow, medium, fast, x-fast, inherit, or a *percentage* (CSS3)
`voice-pitch: type`	Specifies the voice pitch, where *type* is x-low, low, medium, high, x-high, inherit, a *number*, or a *percentage* (CSS3)
`voice-pitch-range: type`	Specifies the voice pitch range, where *type* is x-low, low, medium, high, x-high, inherit, or a *number* (CSS3)
`voice-stress: type`	Specifies the voice stress, where *type* is strong, moderate, none, reduced, or inherit (CSS3)
`voice-volume: type`	Specifies the voice volume, where *type* is silent, x-soft, soft, medium, loud, x-loud, inherit, a *number*, or a *percentage* (CSS3)
Backgrounds	**Styles applied to an element's background**
`background: color url(url) repeat attachment position`	Defines the background of the element, where *color* is a CSS color name or value, *url* is the location of an image file, *repeat* defines how the background image should be repeated, *attachment* defines how the background image should be attached, and *position* defines the position of the background image
`background: url(url) position size repeat attachment origin clip color`	Defines the background of the element, where *url* is the location of the image file, *position* is the position of the image, *size* is the size of the image, *repeat* defines how the image should be repeated, *attachment* defines how the image should be attached, *origin* defines the origin of the image, *clip* defines the location of the clipping box, and *color* defines the background color (CSS3)
`background-attachment: type`	Specifies how the background image is attached, where *type* is inherit, scroll (move the image with the page content), or fixed (fix the image and not scroll)
`background-clip: location`	Specifies the location of the background box, where *location* is border-box, padding-box, content-box, no-clip, a unit of *length*, or a *percentage* (CSS3)

Attribute	Description
background-color: *color*	Defines the color of the background, where *color* is a CSS color name or value; the keyword "inherit" can be used to inherit the background color of the parent element, or "transparent" can be used to allow the parent element background image to show through
background-image: url(*url*)	Specifies the image file used for the element's background, where *url* is the URL of the image file
background-origin: *box*	Specifies the origin of the background image, where *box* is border-box, padding-box, or content-box (CSS3)
background-position: *x y*	Sets the position of a background image, where *x* is the horizontal location in pixels, as a percentage of the width of the parent element, or the keyword "left", "center", or "right", *y* is the vertical location in pixels, as a percentage of the height and of the parent element, or the keyword, "top", "center", or "bottom"
background-repeat: *type*	Defines the method for repeating the background image, where *type* is no-repeat, repeat (to tile the image in both directions), repeat-x (to tile the image in the horizontal direction only), or repeat-y (to tile the image in the vertical direction only)
background-size: *size*	Sets the size of the background image, where *size* is auto, cover, contain, a *length*, or a *percentage* (CSS3)
Block-Level Styles	**Styles applied to block-level elements**
border: *length style color*	Defines the border style of the element, where *length* is the border width, *style* is the border design, and *color* is the border color
border-bottom: *length style color*	Defines the border style of the bottom edge of the element
border-left: *length style color*	Defines the border style of the left edge of the element
border-right: *length style color*	Defines the border style of the right edge of the element
border-top: *length style color*	Defines the border style of the top edge of the element
border-color: *color*	Defines the color applied to the element's border using a CSS color unit
border-bottom-color: *color*	Defines the color applied to the bottom edge of the element
border-left-color: *color*	Defines the color applied to the left edge of the element
border-right-color: *color*	Defines the color applied to the right edge of the element
border-top-color: *color*	Defines the color applied to the top edge of the element
border-image: url(*url*) *size*	Sets an image file for the border, where *url* is the location of the image file and *size* is stretch, repeat, round, none, a *length*, or a *percentage* (CSS3)
border-style: *style*	Specifies the design of the element's border (dashed, dotted double, groove, inset, none, outset, ridge, or solid)
border-style-bottom: *style*	Specifies the design of the element's bottom edge
border-style-left: *style*	Specifies the design of the element's left edge
border-style-right: *style*	Specifies the design of the element's right edge
border-style-top: *style*	Specifies the design of the element's top edge
border-radius: *tr br bl tl*	Specifies the radius of the border corners in pixels, where *tr* is the top-right corner, *br* is the bottom-right corner, *bl* is the bottom-left corner, and *tl* is the top-left corner (CSS3)

Attribute	Description
`border-top-right-radius: horiz vert`	Specifies the horizontal and vertical radius for the top-right corner (CSS3)
`border-bottom-right-radius: horiz vert`	Specifies the horizontal and vertical radius for the bottom-right corner (CSS3)
`border-bottom-left-radius: horiz vert`	Specifies the horizontal and vertical radius for the bottom-left corner (CSS3)
`border-top-left-radius: horiz vert`	Specifies the horizontal and vertical radius for the top-left corner (CSS3)
`border-width: length`	Defines the width of the element's border, in a unit of measure or using the keyword "thick", "medium", or "thin"
`border-width-bottom: length`	Defines the width of the element's bottom edge
`border-width-left: length`	Defines the width of the element's left edge
`border-width-right: length`	Defines the width of the element's right edge
`border-width-top: length`	Defines the width of the element's top edge
`box-shadow: top right bottom left color`	Adds a box shadow, where *top*, *right*, *bottom*, and *left* set the width of the shadow and *color* sets the shadow color (CSS3)
`margin: top right bottom left`	Defines the size of the margins around the top, right, bottom, and left edges of the element, in one of the CSS units of length
`margin-bottom: length`	Defines the size of the element's bottom margin
`margin-left: length`	Defines the size of the element's left margin
`margin-right: length`	Defines the size of the element's right margin
`margin-top: length`	Defines the size of the element's top margin
`padding: top right bottom left`	Defines the size of the padding space within the top, right, bottom, and left edges of the element, in one of the CSS units of length
`padding-bottom: length`	Defines the size of the element's bottom padding
`padding-left: length`	Defines the size of the element's left padding
`padding-right: length`	Defines the size of the element's right padding
`padding-top: length`	Defines the size of the element's top padding
Browser	**Styles to affect the appearance of the browser**
`appearance: type`	Specifies that an element should be displayed like a standard browser object, where *type* is normal, button, push-button, hyperlink, radio-button, checkbox, pop-up-menu, list-menu, radio-group, checkbox-group, field, or password (CSS3)
`cursor: type`	Defines the cursor image used, where *type* is n-resize, ne-resize, e-resize, se-resize, s-resize, sw-resize, w-resize, nw-resize, crosshair, pointer, move, text, wait, help, auto, default, inherit, or a URL pointing to an image file
`icon: value`	Specifies that an element should be styled with with an iconic equivalent, where *value* is auto, a *url*, or inherit (CSS3)
`nav-down: position`	Specifies where to navigate using the arrow-down and arrow-up navigation keys, where *position* is auto, a *target-name*, or an element *id* (CSS3)
`nav-index: value`	Specifies the tabbing order, where *value* is auto, inherit, or a *number* (CSS3)
`nav-left: position`	Specifies where to navigate using the arrow-left and arrow-right navigation keys, where *position* is auto, a *target-name*, or an element *id* (CSS3)

Attribute	Description
nav-right: *position*	Specifies where to navigate using the arrow-left and arrow-right navigation keys, where *position* is auto, a *target-name*, or an element *id* (CSS3)
nav-up: *position*	Specifies where to navigate using the arrow-down and arrow-up navigation keys, where *position* is auto, a *target-name*, or an element *id* (CSS3)
resize: *type*	Specifies whether an element is resizable and in what direction, where *type* is none, both, horizontal, vertical, or inherit (CSS3)
Column	**Styles for Multi-column Layouts**
column-count: *value*	Specifies the number of columns, where *value* is the column number or auto (CSS3)
column-fill: *type*	Specifies whether to balance the content of the columns, where *type* is auto or balance (CSS3)
column-gap: *value*	Sets the size of the gap between the columns, where *value* is the width of the gap or auto (CSS3)
column-rule: *width style color*	Adds a dividing line between the columns, where *width*, *style*, and *color* define the style of the line (CSS3)
column-rule-color: *color*	Defines the color of the dividing line (CSS3)
column-rule-style: *style*	Defines the border style of the dividing line (CSS3)
column-rule-width: *width*	Sets the width of the dividing line (CSS3)
columns: *width count*	Sets the width and number of columns in the multi-column layout (CSS3)
column-span: *value*	Sets the element to span across the columns, where *span* is 1 or all (CSS3)
column-width: *value*	Sets the width of the columns (CSS3)
Content	**Styles to generate content**
bookmark-label: *value*	Specifies the label of a bookmark, where *value* is content, an *attribute*, or a text *string* (CSS3)
bookmark-level: *value*	Specifies the bookmark level, where *value* is an *integer* or none (CSS3)
bookmark-target: *value*	Specifies the target of a bookmark link, where *value* is self, a *url*, or an *attribute* (CSS3)
border-length: *value*	Describes a way of separating footnotes from other content, where *value* is a *length* or auto (CSS3)
content: *text*	Generates a text string to attach to the content of the element
content: attr(*attr*)	Returns the value of the *attr* attribute from the element
content: close-quote	Attaches a close quote using the characters specified in the quotes style
content: counter(*text*)	Generates a counter using the text string *text* attached to the content (most often used with list items)
content: counters(*text*)	Generates a string of counters using the comma-separated text string *text* attached to the content (most often used with list items)
content: no-close-quote	Prevents the attachment of a close quote to an element
content: no-open-quote	Prevents the attachment of an open quote to an element
content: open-quote	Attaches an open quote using the characters specified in the quotes style

Attribute	Description
`content: url(url)`	Attaches the content of an external file indicated in the *url* to the element
`counter-increment: id integer`	Defines the element to be automatically incremented and the amount by which it is to be incremented, where *id* is an identifier of the element and *integer* defines by how much
`counter-reset: id integer`	Defines the element whose counter is to be reset and the amount by which it is to be reset, where *id* is an identifier of the element and *integer* defines by how much
`crop: value`	Allows a replaced element to be a rectangular area of an object instead of the whole object, where *value* is a shape or auto (CSS3)
`hyphenate-after: value`	Specifies the minimum number of characters after the hyphenation character, where *value* is an *integer* or auto (CSS3)
`hyphenate-before: value`	Specifies the minimum number of characters before the hyphenation character, where *value* is an *integer* or auto (CSS3)
`hyphenate-character: string`	Specifies the hyphenation character, *string* (CSS3)
`hyphenate-line: value`	Specifies the maximum number of hyphenated lines, where *value* is an *integer* or no-limit (CSS3)
`hyphenate-resource: url(url)`	Provides an external resource at *url* that defines hyphenation points (CSS3)
`hyphens: type`	Defines the hyphenation property, where *type* is none, manual, or auto (CSS3)
`image-resolution: value`	Defines the image resolution, where *value* is normal, auto, or the dpi of the image (CSS3)
`marks: type`	Defines an editor's mark, where *type* is crop, cross, or none (CSS3)
`quotes: text1 text2`	Defines the text strings for the open quotes (*text1*) and the close quotes (*text2*)
`string-set: values`	Accepts a comma-separated list of named strings, where *values* is the list of text strings (CSS3)
`text-replace: string1 string2`	Replaces *string1* with *string2* in the element content (CSS3)
Display Styles	**Styles that control the display of the element's content**
`clip: rect(top, right, bottom, left)`	Defines what portion of the content is displayed, where *top*, *right*, *bottom*, and *left* are distances of the top, right, bottom, and left edges from the element's top-left corner; use a value of auto to allow the browser to determine the clipping region
`display: type`	Specifies the display type of the element, where *type* is one of the following: block, inline, inline-block, inherit, list-item, none, run-in, table, inline-table, table-caption, table-column, table-cell, table-column-group, table-header-group, table-footer-group, table-row, or table-row-group
`height: length`	Specifies the height of the element in one of the CSS units of length
`min-height: length`	Specifies the minimum height of the element
`min-width: length`	Specifies the minimum width of the element
`max-height: length`	Specifies the maximum height of the element
`max-width: length`	Specifies the maximum width of the element
`overflow: type`	Instructs the browser how to handle content that overflows the dimensions of the element, where *type* is auto, inherit, visible, hidden, or scroll

Attribute	Description
overflow-style: *type*	Specifies the preferred scrolling method for overflow content, where *type* is auto, marquee-line, or marquee-block (CSS3)
overflow-x: *type*	Instructs the browser how to handle content that overflows the element's width, where *type* is auto, inherit, visible, hidden, or scroll (IE only)
overflow-y: *type*	Instructs the browser on how to handle content that overflows the element's height, where *type* is auto, inherit, visible, hidden, or scroll (IE only)
text-overflow: *type*	Instructs the browser on how to handle text overflow, where *type* is clip (to hide the overflow text) or ellipsis (to display the … text string) (IE only)
visibility: *type*	Defines the element's visibility, where *type* is hidden, visible, or inherit
width: *length*	Specifies the width of the element in one of the CSS units of length
Fonts and Text	**Styles that format the appearance of fonts and text**
color: *color*	Specifies the color of the element's foreground (usually the font color)
direction: *type*	Specifies the direction of the text flow, where *type* equals ltr, rtl, or inherit (CSS3)
font: *style variant weight size/line-height family*	Defines the appearance of the font, where *style* is the font's style, *variant* is the font variant, *weight* is the weight of the font, *size* is the size of the font, *line-height* is the height of the lines, and *family* is the font face; the only required attributes are *size* and *family*
font-effect: *type*	Controls the special effect applied to glyphs where *type* is none, emboss, engrave, or outline (CSS3)
font-emphasize: *emphasize position*	Sets the style of the font emphasis and decoration (CSS3)
font-emphasize-position: *position*	Sets the font emphasis position, where *position* is before or after (CSS3)
font-emphasize-style: *style*	Sets the emphasis style, where *style* is none, accent, dot, circle, or disc (CSS3)
font-family: *family*	Specifies the font face used to display text, where *family* is sans-serif, serif, fantasy, monospace, cursive, or the name of an installed font
font-size: *value*	Specifies the size of the font in one of the CSS units of length
font-size-adjust: *value*	Specifies the aspect *value* (which is the ratio of the font size to the font's ex unit height) (CSS3)
font-smooth: *type*	Specifies the type of font smoothing, where *type* is auto, never, always, or a specified size (CSS3)
font-stretch: *type*	Expands or contracts the font, where *type* is narrower, wider, ultra-condensed, extra-condensed, condensed, semi-condensed, normal, semi-expanded, extra-expanded, or ultra-expanded (CSS3)
font-style: *type*	Specifies a style applied to the font, where *type* is normal, italic, or oblique
font-variant: *type*	Specifies a variant of the font, where *type* is inherit, normal, or small-caps
font-weight: *value*	Defines the weight of the font, where *value* is 100, 200, 300, 400, 500, 600, 700, 800, 900, normal, lighter, bolder, or bold

Attribute	Description
hanging-punctuation: *type*	Determines whether a punctuation mark may be placed outside the text box, where *type* is none, start, end, or end-edge (CSS3)
letter-spacing: *value*	Specifies the space between letters, where *value* is a unit of length or the keyword "normal"
line-height: *value*	Specifies the height of the lines, where *value* is a unit of length or the keyword, "normal"
punctuation-trim: *type*	Determines whether or not a full-width punctuation character should be trimmed if it appears at the start or end of a line, where *type* is none, start, end, or adjacent (CSS3)
text-align: *type*	Specifies the horizontal alignment of text within the element, where *type* is inherit, left, right, center, or justify
text-align-last: *type*	Specifies how the last line of a block is aligned for fully justified text, where *type* is start, end, left, right, center, or justify (CSS3)
text-decoration: *type*	Specifies the decoration applied to the text, where *type* is blink, line-through, none, overline, or underline
text-emphasis: *type* *location*	Specifies the emphasis applied to the text, where *type* is none, accent, dot, circle, or disk and *location* is before or after (CSS3)
text-indent: *length*	Specifies the amount of indentation in the first line of the text, where *length* is a CSS unit of length
text-justify: *type*	Specifies the justification method applied to the text, where *type* is auto, inter-word, inter-ideograph, inter-cluster, distribute, kashida, or tibetan (CSS3)
text-outline: *value1* *value2*	Specifies a text outline, where *value1* represents the outline thickness and *value2* represents the optional blur radius (CSS3)
text-shadow: *color x y blur*	Applies a shadow effect to the text, where *color* is the color of the shadow, *x* is the horizontal offset in pixels, *y* is the vertical offset in pixels, and *blur* is the size of the blur radius (optional); multiple shadows can be added with shadow effects separated by commas (CSS3)
text-transform: *type*	Defines a transformation applied to the text, where *type* is capitalize, lowercase, none, or uppercase
text-wrap: *type*	Specifies the type of text wrapping, where *type* is normal, unrestricted, none, or suppress (CSS3)
unicode-bibi: *type*	Allows text that flows left-to-right to be mixed with text that flows right-to-left, where *type* is normal, embed, bibi-override, or inherit (CSS3)
vertical-align: *type*	Specifies how to vertically align the text with the surrounding content, where *type* is baseline, middle, top, bottom, text-top, text-bottom, super, sub, or one of the CSS units of length
white-space: *type*	Specifies the handling of white space (blank spaces, tabs, and new lines), where *type* is inherit, normal, pre (to treat the text as pre-formatted text), or nowrap (to prevent line-wrapping)
white-space-collapse: *type*	Defines how white space inside the element is collapsed, where *type* is preserve, collapse, preserve-breaks, or discard (CSS3)
word-break: *type*	Controls line-breaks within words, where *type* is normal, keep-all, loose, break-strict, or break-all (CSS3)
word-spacing: *length*	Specifies the amount of space between words in the text, where *length* is either a CSS unit of length or the keyword "normal" to use normal word spacing

Attribute	Description
Layout	**Styles that define the layout of elements**
bottom: *y*	Defines the vertical offset of the element's bottom edge, where *y* is either a CSS unit of length or the keyword "auto" or "inherit"
clear: *type*	Places the element only after the specified margin is clear of floating elements, where *type* is inherit, none, left, right, or both
float: *type*	Floats the element on the specified margin with subsequent content wrapping around the element, where *type* is inherit, none, left, right, or both
float-offset: *horiz vert*	Pushes floated elements in the opposite direction of where they would have been, where *horiz* is the horizontal displacement and *vertical* is the vertical displacement (CSS3)
left: *x*	Defines the horizontal offset of the element's left edge, where *x* is either a CSS unit of length or the keyword "auto" or "inherit"
move-to: *type*	Causes the element to be removed from the page flow and reinserted at later point in the document, where *type* is normal, here, or an *id* value (CSS3)
position: *type*	Defines how the element is positioned on the page, where *type* is absolute, relative, fixed, static, and inherit
right: *x*	Defines the horizontal offset of the element's right edge, where *x* is either a CSS unit of length or the keyword "auto" or "inherit"
top: *y*	Defines the vertical offset of the element's top edge, where *y* is a CSS unit of length or the keyword "auto" or "inherit"
z-index: *value*	Defines how overlapping elements are stacked, where *value* is either the stacking number (elements with higher stacking numbers are placed on top) or the keyword "auto" to allow the browser to determine the stacking order
Lists	**Styles that format lists**
list-style: *type image position*	Defines the appearance of a list item, where *type* is the marker type, *image* is the URL of the location of an image file used for the marker, and *position* is the position of the marker
list-style-image: url(*url*)	Defines image used for the list marker, where *url* is the location of the image file
list-style-type: *type*	Defines the marker type used in the list, where *type* is disc, circle, square, decimal, decimal-leading-zero, lower-roman, upper-roman, lower-alpha, upper-alpha, or none
list-style-position: *type*	Defines the location of the list marker, where *type* is inside or outside
marker-offset: *length*	Defines the distance between the marker and the enclosing list box, where *length* is either a CSS unit of length or the keyword "auto" or "inherit" (CSS3)
Outlines	**Styles to create and format outlines**
outline: *color style width*	Creates an outline around the element content, where *color* is the color of the outline, *style* is the outline style, and *width* is the width of the outline
outline-color: *color*	Defines the color of the outline
outline-offset: *value*	Offsets the outline from the element border, where *value* is the length of the offset (CSS3)
outline-style: *type*	Defines the style of the outline, where *type* is dashed, dotted, double, groove, inset, none, outset, ridge, solid, or inherit

Attribute	Description
outline-width: *length*	Defines the width of the outline, where *length* is expressed in a CSS unit of length
Printing	**Styles for printed output**
fit: *type*	Indicates how to scale an element to fit on the page, where *type* is fill, hidden, meet, or slice (CSS3)
fit-position: *vertical horizontal*	Sets the position of the element in the page, where *vertical* is top, center, or bottom; *horizontal* is left or right; or either or both positions are auto, a *value*, or a *percentage* (CSS3)
page: *label*	Specifies the page design to apply, where *label* is a page design created with the @page rule
page-break-after: *type*	Defines how to control page breaks after the element, where *type* is avoid (to avoid page breaks), left (to insert a page break until a left page is displayed), right (to insert a page break until a right page is displayed), always (to always insert a page break), auto, or inherit
page-break-before: *type*	Defines how to control page breaks before the element, where *type* is avoid left, always, auto, or inherit
page-break-inside: *type*	Defines how to control page breaks within the element, where *type* is avoid, auto, or inherit
marks: *type*	Defines how to display crop marks, where *type* is crop, cross, none, or inherit
size: *width height orientation*	Defines the size of the page, where *width* and *height* are the width and the height of the page and *orientation* is the orientation of the page (portrait or landscape)
orphans: *value*	Defines how to handle orphaned text, where *value* is the number of lines that must appear within the element before a page break is inserted
widows: *value*	Defines how to handle widowed text, where *value* is the number of lines that must appear within the element after a page break is inserted
Special Effects	**Styles to create special visual effects**
animation: *name duration timing delay iteration direction*	Applies an animation with the specified *duration*, *timing*, *delay*, *iteration*, and *direction* (CSS3)
animation-delay: *time*	Specifies the animation delay *time* in milliseconds (CSS3)
animation-direction: *direction*	Specifies the animation direction, where *direction* is normal or alternate (CSS3)
animation-duration: *time*	Specifies the duration of the animation *time* in milliseconds (CSS3)
animation-iteration-count: *value*	Specifies the number of iterations in the animation (CSS3)
animation-name: *text*	Provides a name for the animation (CSS3)
animation-play-state: *type*	Specifies the playing state of the animation, where *type* is running or paused
animation-timing-function: *function*	Provides the timing function of the animation, where *function* is ease, linear, ease-in, ease-out, ease-in-out, cubic-Bezier, or a *number* (CSS3)
backface-visibility: *visible*	Specifies whether the back side of an element is visible during a transformation, where *visible* is hidden or visible (CSS3)

Attribute	Description
filter: *type parameters*	Applies transition and filter effects to elements, where *type* is the type of filter and *parameters* are parameter values specific to the filter (IE only)
image-orientation: *angle*	Rotates the image by the specified *angle* (CSS3)
marquee-direction: *direction*	Specifies the direction of a marquee, where *direction* is forward or reverse (CSS3)
marquee-play-count: *value*	Specifies how often to loop through the marquee (CSS3)
marquee-speed: *speed*	Specifies the speed of the marquee, where *speed* is slow, normal, or fast (CSS3)
marquee-style: *type*	Specifies the marquee style, where *type* scroll, slide, or alternate (CSS3)
opacity: *alpha*	Sets opacity of the element, ranging from 0 (transparent) to 1 (opaque) (CSS3)
perspective: *value*	Applies a perspective transformation to the element, where *value* is the perspective length (CSS3)
perspective-origin: *origin*	Establishes the origin of the perspective property, where *origin* is left, center, right, top, bottom, or a *position* value (CSS3)
rotation: *angle*	Rotates the element by *angle* (CSS3)
rotation-point: *position*	Sets the location of the rotation point for the element (CSS3)
transform: *function*	Applies a 2-D or a 3-D transformation, where *function* provides the transformation parameters (CSS3)
transform-origin: *position*	Establishes the origin of the transformation of an element, where *position* is the position within the element (CSS3)
transform-style: *type*	Defines how nested elements are rendered in 3-D space, where *type* is flat or preserve-3d (CSS3)
transition: *property duration timing delay*	Defines a timed transition of an element, where *property*, *duration*, *timing*, and *delay* define the appearance and timing of the transition (CSS3)
transition-delay: *time*	Sets the delay time of the transition in milliseconds (CSS3)
transition-duration: *time*	Sets the duration time of the transition in milliseconds (CSS3)
transition-property: *type*	Defines the name of the CSS property modified by the transition, where *type* is all or none (CSS3)
transition-timing-function: *type*	Sets the timing function of the transition, where *type* is ease, linear, ease-in, ease-out, ease-in-out, cubic-Bezier, or a *number* (CSS3)
Tables	**Styles to format the appearance of tables**
border-collapse: *type*	Determines whether table cell borders are separate or collapsed into a single border, where *type* is separate, collapse, or inherit
border-spacing: *length*	If separate borders are used for table cells, defines the distance between borders, where *length* is a CSS unit of length or inherit
caption-side: *type*	Defines the position of the caption element, where *type* is bottom, left, right, top, or inherit
empty-cells: *type*	If separate borders are used for table cells, defines whether to display borders for empty cells, where *type* is hide, show, or inherit
table-layout: *type*	Defines the algorithm used for the table layout, where *type* is auto (to define the layout once all table cells have been read), fixed (to define the layout after the first table row has been read), or inherit

GLOSSARY/INDEX